Welcoming the alien and stranger is not only a biblical imperative but also a major modern missiological challenge. My colleagues and I have been recently compelled to reflect contextually and practice concretely Christian love while encountering floods of refugees. Over half-a-million Middle-Eastern migrants passed through our neighborhood within a couple of months and continue to come by thousands daily. We have closely observed the refugee trauma as we watched the breakdown of border controls, erection of barbed wire fences and expressed solidarity with desperate peoples fleeing war and searching for places of safety and well-being. As a wholistic missiologist and original Lausanner (active participant since 1974), I warmly welcome and highly recommend this comprehensive study on a globally relevant topic as both foundational and directional. This timely volume is a *missio Dei viatorum* at its best, focused on diaspora from a full-fledged biblical perspective while taking into account the migrant phenomena in their global diversity.

Peter Kuzmic, PhD, Dr. Theol., Distinguished Professor of World Mission and European Studies, Gordon-Conwell TS, USA, Founding Director of Evangelical Theological Seminary, Osijek, Croatia

It has been a rare privilege to support and walk alongside the visionary and Kingdom-minded efforts birthing this timely Diaspora compendium aptly titled "Scattered and Gathered." We are living in an unprecedented Kairos era, when God is uniquely shaping the movements of people that He is committed to revealing His glorious love to. This compendium is a clarion call to the global church to discern the times and to participate with fresh enthusiasm and strategic planning in completing the great commission. The disciplines of applied Missiology and church growth have just received an enormous treasure that with God's anointing will marvelously shape our efforts moving forward.

Bremwell Frentz, Vice President of Global Ministries for the Christian and Missionary Alliance in Canada

After being born as the son of immigrants who left Asia to pursue the "American Dream," I later returned to Asia to share the gospel of Jesus Christ in the land of my father's former enemies, the Japanese. It is my joy to wholeheartedly commend to you this Global Diaspora Missiology Compendium that so powerfully describes the East to West and West to East dynamics of my own family history. This volume puts out a clarion call to the global church about a critically important mission need and strategy. In the most simple and direct fashion I can say to you that you cannot understand the full picture of global mission without understanding Diaspora Missiology.

Michael Y. Oh, Ph.D.
Lausanne Movement Executive Director/CEO

For the past four and a half decades, both my wife and I have lived outside our native countries and moved homes and ministries to several countries in three different continents around the globe. Living in the diaspora and ministering to those living outside their homes has been the story of our lives. In fact this is the story of God dealing with people from the days of Abraham till the latest war in Syria. God calls people to leave their homes and their people and journey to other unknown places, countries and cultures. Through this journey and through difficult and challenging circumstances, God softens the heart of people and direct their attention to Himself. The day of Pentecost became the solid foundation of global mission when Jews from all over the world were present and witnessed the apostles receiving the Holy Spirit spectacularly and starting to speak out the gospel of Truth.

The call to intensify mission work through the Global Diaspora Network led by Drs. Sadiri Joy Tira and Tetsunao Yamamori is a holy, biblical and timely call for our generation and the fulfillment of the Great Commission. The March 2015 GDN Forum in Manila brought together leaders who have labored hard to research and write articles of related subjects to bring the knowledge and information needed to focus on this great need in today's mission. Your eyes will be opened as you read these articles and your heart will burn for the salvation of the millions living outside their homes, many of them in challenging circumstances.

Henri Aoun, Team leader for North Africa, Middle East and the Gulf region
LifeAgape International

This compendium couldn't come at a more compelling time in history, when peoples are being scattered in unprecedented numbers. How is the church to understand and respond to the accelerating global diaspora? A much needed and timely pioneer work, assembling a multitude of authoritative voices, academically rigorous, but brought alive by practical field case studies. Most importantly, it demonstrates the importance of diaspora missiology in God's Mission in the 21st century.

Cindy Perry, South Asia Regional Director Development Associates International, Author: Nepali around the World

This collection of essays presents diaspora realities as a prominent scenario for the *Missio Dei* in our days. The exploration the present day global diaspora experience with the missiological opportunities and challenges it poses for the church, is informative, challenging and encouraging.

Elizabeth Sendek
President, Fundacion Universitaria Seminario Bîblico de Colombia

The publication of *Scattered and Gathered: A Global Compendium of Diaspora Missiology* is a significant milestone. The high quality of the international conversation captured in the book makes it a veritable *tour de force*. A great resource for students and researchers of Christian mission and world Christianity.

Tite Tiénou, Research Professor, Theology of Mission
Tite Tiénou Chair of Global Theology and World Christianity and Dean Emeritus, Trinity Evangelical Divinity School, Deerfield, Illinois

Global diaspora is shaping World Christianity, local churches, denominations, missions, theological trajectories, church planting movements, and more. *Scattered and Gathered: A Global Compendium of Diaspora Missiology* is essential reading on the realities and trends of global diaspora. It provides biblical and theological foundations for diaspora missiology. And it explores strategic possibilities for the church and mission. Case studies and resources support theology and analysis. In brief, it is an invaluable addition to any library of research into diaspora, mission, and World Christianity.

Graham Hill
Vice Principal, Morling Theological College, Sydney, Australia
Author: GlobalChurch: Reshaping Our Conversations, Renewing Our Mission, Revitalizing Our Churches

Scattered and Gathered is very comprehensive and thought provoking as it teaches and informs us about global diaspora movement and mission. The general editors, section editors, and writers are qualified experts in their own respective field of missions. The topics are not only relevant, but facilitate churches and mission organizations to strategic plan for involvement in the needed field of diaspora in Asia and the global village. It provides readers with a timely vision into mission, with passion, for such a time like ours.

Joseph Shao, General Secretary, Asia Theological Association
President, Biblical Seminary of the Philippines

The current movement of people groups around the world has challenged the Church worldwide to carefully contemplate this reality from various perspectives and take into consideration necessary holistic actions required to meet these very real and vast needs with the Gospel of Jesus Christ. This book provides a panoramic picture of Christian approaches to the current issues of the global diaspora from a missiological perspective. It opens our eyes to the kairos of God's redemptive activities among the diaspora and compels the Church to stand by those in need with the love of God in an age of globalization.

Masanori Kurasawa, Former President of Tokyo Christian University and Executive Director of the Faith and Culture Center

This book entails rich analysis of diaspora and migration phenomena from multiple dimensions including biblical, missiological, historical, social, political and economic perspectives. This book challenges the reader to rethink the meaning of identity and belonging in Christ in the context of the contemporary diaspora world and reach out to the people on the move beyond our comfort zone with the love of Christ. This is a book most relevant in our understanding and practice of global mission today, and is definitely worth reading.

Patrick Fung, General Director, OMF International

This compendium comprises a kaleidoscope of rich biblical and theological insights; perspectives from business, technology, demography and international law; and diverse illustrations from local churches as well as ministries to academics, seafarers, refugees, trekkers, children at risk, and victims of sex trafficking. The contributors are reflective practitioners providing examples from every region of the world. Where else in one volume can one find such a breadth of global voices speaking to the critical challenges and opportunities of ministry to, through and beyond the diasporas?

David Bennett, Global Associate Director for Collaboration and Content, Lausanne Movement

When I look back to the first Lausanne publication on the subject of Diaspora following the Lausanne Forum in Pattaya in 2004, I am truly humbled, blessed and excited to see the leadership provided by Dr. Sadiri Joy Tira and Dr. Tetsunao Yamamori that has resulted in the publication of this Compendium entitled: *Scattered and Gathered: A Global Compendium of Diaspora Missiology* following the Lausanne Movement's Global Diaspora Forum that took place in Manila, Philippines in March 2015.

This is a timely, useful and relevant publication given, for example, the events that we are witnessing today of an increasingly violent situation in the Middle East, resulting in accelerated migration and a refugee crisis of untold proportions across the globe. A theologically grounded biblical response to the 'diaspora phenomenon' is provided in this one comprehensive resource by leading experts, both theologians and practitioners' from across the world. It is a resource that every Bible College. Mission Agency and student of the Diaspora should invest in.

Ram Gidoomal, Convener, Diaspora Working Group Lausanne Pattaya Forum 2004, Chairman, Tradecraft PLC

REGNUM STUDIES IN MISSION

Scattered and Gathered

A Global Compendium of Diaspora Missiology

Series Preface

Regnum Studies in Mission are born from the lived experience of Christians and Christian communities in mission, especially but not solely in the fast growing churches among the poor of the world. These churches have more to tell than stories of growth. They are making significant impacts on their cultures in the cause of Christ. They are producing 'cultural products' which express the reality of Christian faith, hope and love in their societies.

Regnum Studies in Mission are the fruit often of rigorous research to the highest international standards and always of authentic Christian engagement in the transformation of people and societies. And these are for the world. The formation of Christian theology, missiology and practice in the twenty-first century will depend to a great extent on the active participation of growing churches contributing biblical and culturally appropriate expressions of Christian practice to inform World Christianity.

Series Editors

A full listing of titles in this series appears at the end of this book

REGNUM STUDIES IN MISSION

Scattered and Gathered
A Global Compendium of Diaspora Missiology

Edited by

Sadiri Joy Tira and Tetsunao Yamamori

First published 2016 by Regnum Books International

Regnum is an imprint of the Oxford Centre for Mission Studies
St. Philip and St. James Church
Woodstock Road
Oxford OX2 6HR, UK
www.ocms.ac.uk/regnum

09 08 07 06 05 04 03 7 6 5 4 3 2 1

British Library Cataloguing in Publication Data
A catalogue record for this book is available from the British Library

ISBN: 978-1-908355-96-6

Typeset by Words by Design
Printed and bound in Great Britain
for Regnum Books International
by TJ International Ltd, Padstow, Cornwall

This book was made possible through the generous financial support of the Korean Diaspora Network and others.

CONTENTS

SECTION 6

ISSUES IN GLOBAL DIASPORA MISSIOLOGY

Paul Sydnor and Larry Caldwell, Section Editors

SECTION 7

GLOSSARY, APPENDICES AND MINISTRY RESOURCES

Tereso Casiño And Charles Cook, Section Editors

FOREWORD

Christopher J.H. Wright

We live in a world on the move – quite literally. There are more migrants in the world today than probably at any time in human history. Certainly more people have been forced to flee from their homes than at any time since the Second World War. And the majority of refugees (some estimate about 80%) are in poorer countries of the so-called developing world. Often, it seems, it is the poor who care for the poorest.

The reasons why people migrate are very varied – and many are explored in this book. There are those who choose to emigrate for social, economic or family reasons, and some do so with relative ease, others with a high level of cultural and personal loss and stress. There are those whose emigration is a response to poverty at home and a desire to support their loved ones through earnings abroad. There are the vast numbers who flee from situations in which they cannot survive, because of war, famine, natural disasters, persecution or destitution. And of course there are those who are forced or tricked into slavery in the vast evil empire of human trafficking.

The Bible knows about all these reasons. In fact, the reality of individuals and whole peoples being on the move permeates the biblical narrative from the day Adam and Eve were driven from the garden in Eden to the scattering of believers in the book of Acts. And when people move around (for whatever reason), that seems to be when God is at work in many significant ways. This is a theme that has been under explored in most books on biblical theology. This book helps to redress that imbalance.

Not surprisingly, the multi-faceted reality of world mission in such contexts has brought to the surface the importance of this theme in the Bible itself, and in missional theology and practice. For of course the Christian church has challenges and opportunities in both directions – in relation to mission both by and among migrant peoples. Many migrants are themselves Christian believers, often with unique opportunities for sensitive witness to the gospel of the Lord Jesus Christ in countries where traditional mission outreach is otherwise impossible. And Christians in some countries have unprecedented opportunities to reach out with the love of Christ in word and deed to migrant or refugee peoples of other faiths arriving in their own homeland, people who may never have met a Christian in their previous life and culture.

Not surprisingly either, the Lausanne Movement has been at the forefront of addressing the issue. For this book is a superb example of Lausanne doing what it does best as the catalytic force that it is in world mission: identifying a major missional challenge and opportunity; convening a global team of people with multiple areas of relevant expertise and experience; researching the issue with rigorous attention to its macro and micro dimensions; examining the phenomena from many angles with rich information and statistical evidence; searching the Scriptures to build a strong biblical and theological understanding and to formulate a robust evangelical response; and providing both challenge and hope through practical examples, potential strategies and inspiring case-studies.

May the God whose Son was a refugee bless and prosper this splendid resource book and the ministries of all who share its vision.

Christopher J. H. Wright
International Ministries Director
Langham Partnership

PREFACE

Sadiri Joy Tira

I will stand my watch
And set myself on the rampart,
And watch to see what He will say to me,
And what I will answer when I am corrected.
The Just Live by Faith
Then the Lord answered me and said:
"Write the vision
And make it plain on tablets,
That he may run who reads it."

Habakkuk 2:1-2 NKJV 1982

Diaspora is not a new phenomenon, nor missiology a novel field of study. In fact, human migration and missions and evangelism discussions are age-old. Thus, it is naive to propose that diaspora missiology was recently conceived in an academic "think tank," or in a coffee shop conversation between missiologists. Diaspora missiology is a contemporary name given to the interdisciplinary field of study that means to comprehensively gather up the multiple strands of migration and missions in order to concisely train kingdom workers to "run" with the vision; a vision that was born in the very heart of God.

As I deliberate over the preface that will frame the missiological undertaking that will take place in this large volume, I am compelled to tell you a story that has spanned nearly two decades. While this volume will discuss statistics, frameworks, and present case studies, readers must recognise the development of a collective vision that took root in the individual hearts of men and women across the globe at a unique time in history, and then was recognised and gathered by the Lausanne Movement[1].

This compendium has in fact been in the making for more than a decade. On every page the vision is being made plain "on tablets." This is a story of God's work from Pattaya, Thailand in 2004, to Cape Town, South Africa in 2010, and then to Manila, Philippines in 2015. Before we launch into the academics, allow me to tell you a story that sees God gathering scattered people.

---

1 The Lausanne Committee for World Evangelization (LCWE) now known as the Lausanne Movement aims "to facilitate global collaboration in making Christ known to all people." Read "About the Movement" at https://www.lausanne.org/about-the-movement. Accessed 24 December 2015.

"A New Vision, A New Heart, A Renewed Call" was the theme of the Lausanne 2004 Forum for World Evangelization held from 29 September-5 October, 2004 in Pattaya, Thailand. There, over 1500 registered participants gathered in a working consultation to deliberate on the task of global evangelism. Through comprehensive research, 31 specific issues were identified as "roadblocks to evangelism."[2] Championed by early proponents of migration and missions studies,[3] primarily, Tom Houston, the former Lausanne Committee for World Evangelization (LCWE) International Director and Ram Gidoomal,[4] a London-based businessman and East Indian migrant from Kenya, one of the roadblocks identified was "Reaching and Mobilizing the Diaspora present in our own lands."

Ram Gidoomal was appointed convener for the Diaspora Issue Group. His co-convener was Patrick Tsang of Chinese Coordinating Committee on World Evangelism (CCCOWE). Tom Houston was the facilitator.[5] Leiton Chinn of the International Student Ministries, T.V. Thomas of the Centre for Evangelism and World Mission, and I, representing the Filipino International Network (FIN),[6] assisted these three leaders. This assemblage became the core group for the Diaspora and International Students Issue Group. The 2005 Lausanne publication – *The Lausanne Occasional Paper No. 55*, also referred to as *The New People Next Door* was a result of their deliberation.

Lausanne Forum 2004 became a pinnacle for Evangelical missions, synthesizing the Evangelical Church "to develop specific action plans to combat the challenges facing the Church."[7] Providentially for the diaspora people, Tetsunao "Ted" Yamamori and Doug Birdsall emerged and were commissioned to become the International Director and Chairman of the Lausanne Committee for World Evangelization (LCWE) respectively. It must be noted that it was under Yamamori's and Birdsall's leadership that the Evangelical vision for migration missions, soon to be dubbed "Diaspora Missiology," would flourish and take the shape that we see today. It must also be noted that though I [Sadiri Joy Tira], then a missiology student of

---

2 "2004 Forum Issue Groups" at https://www.lausanne.org/gatherings/related/2004-forum-issue-groups. Accessed December 25, 2015.

3 This is described further in Chapter 5 of this compendium, "Responding to the phenomenon of migration: Early proponents of Diaspora Missiology and the Lausanne Movement" by Sadiri Joy Tira and Darrell Jackson.

4 In 2011 Ram Gidoomal was appointed Chairman of Traidcraft and the Lausanne Movement Board of Directors.

5 Due to unforeseen circumstances however, Tom Houston was unable to participate at the forum in Thailand, thus T.V. Thomas was tasked to facilitate the Issue Group. During the forum more than 50 missions strategists and practitioners joined them.

6 During the Pattaya Forum 2004, FIN distributed the book *Scattered: The Filipino Global Presence* (Philippines, Life Change, 2004) to all the forum participants.

7 "The 2004 Forum for World Evangelization" at https://www.lausanne.org/gatherings/issue-gathering/2004-forum. Accessed December 25, 2015.

Enoch Wan[8] researching diasporas and migration, participated in Lausanne Forum 2004, it would not be until 2006 when I would meet Yamamori and Birdsall.

In the summer of 2006, Ted Yamamori and I met during a doctor of missiology course he taught on Church Growth Movements at Western Seminary (Portland, Oregon). It became apparent that Dr. Yamamori, my academic mentor, Dr. Wan, and I had an intense mutual interest in diaspora missions. We arrived at the shared vision that God had placed on our hearts over a breakfast of bacon and eggs, and considered how diaspora missions should fit within the Lausanne agenda and strategies. Over the course of the week, the first concerted effort to gather diasporologists was planned for the fall of 2006. The Intercultural Studies department of Taylor Seminary in Edmonton, and Taylor Seminary's Allan Effa[9] volunteered to host the Global Diaspora Missiology Consultation from November 16-18, 2006.[10]

In the following months, we would see the vision of a collaborative diaspora missions effort congeal and a movement assemble within the harbour of the Lausanne Movement, and advocated for by not a few individuals, but of a growing missions movement.

Almost 200 years after one of the greatest missionary-statesmen, Robert Morrison, the first Protestant missionary to the Chinese landed in Macau, Doug Birdsall, by that time Chairman of the Lausanne Committee for World Evangelization (LCWE), and I providentially met in Macau during the seventh conference of the CCCOWE.[11] Looking for a reprieve from the conference proceedings, Doug and I decided to visit Robert Morrison's grave. It was during our cab ride and our subsequent discussion over Robert Morrison's tombstone that we discovered a mutual interest in global missions, in particular, a passion to seeing the diaspora people reached with the gospel and mobilised for the Great Commission. A kindred spirit was

8 Enoch Wan (Ph.D., State University of New York) is Professor of Intercultural Studies and Program Director of Doctor of Intercultural Studies at Western Seminary (Portland). He is Tira's academic mentor and an early advocate of "Diaspora Missiology."

9 The support of Allan Effa (Ph.D., Fuller Theological Seminary) and his institution was pivotal in the early development of Diaspora Missiology.

10 Invited participants to the consultation discussed the impact of global migration on the future of global missions, as well as new missions strategies to be utilized by diaspora Christians. Participants represented major diaspora groups (i.e. Chinese, Japanese, Vietnamese, Jewish, South Asian, Korean, Brazilian, Hispanic, Nepalese, West African, East African, Russian, Arab, Filipino) including missiologists and missions strategists, diaspora leaders and theologians. The Filipino International Network (FIN)-sponsored and Lausanne endorsed consultation was convened by Enoch Wan and Sadiri Joy Tira. Tetsunao Yamamori, then International Director of the Lausannane Committee for World Evangelization, was in attendance.

11 The 7th Chinese Congress on World Evangelization took place in Macau from July 17-21, 2006. More information is available at http://www.cccowe.org/content_pub.php?id=catw200607-3. Accessed December 25, 2015.

formed on this visit, as we thanked God for Morrison's life and ministry among the Chinese scattered all over the globe. This providential meeting is reflective of God's gathering and sowing of his vision.

A few months later, I was tasked to serve as Senior Associate for Diasporas; and was officially installed during the Bi-Annual Leadership Meeting on June 18, 2007 in Budapest, Hungary. There, I was immediately introduced to two Korean leaders, Wonsuk Ma, who at that time was the newly appointed Executive Director of the Oxford Centre for Mission Studies (OCMS) in Oxford, U.K. and Hun Kim, a Bible translator and Korean missionary with Wycliffe. Also with a similar vision for diaspora missions, Wonsuk Ma invited me to give a public lecture on Diaspora Missiology at OCMS,[12] while Hun Kim introduced me to the Korean Diaspora Network in Kuala Lumpur, Malaysia. That was another providential meeting of like-minds and hearts. Almost nine years have passed and these relationships have grown stronger. As you read this book, you may notice the heaven-sent nature of this friendship and ministry partnership with the Koreans and the Lausanne leaders.

Many movements begin with friendships of like-minded individuals. Upon appointment in Budapest, I was tasked to form a committee of complementary individuals to become part of a fledgling Lausanne diasporas committee. With Ted (Yamamori) as my Lausanne adviser, and with careful deliberation, it became clear who should be asked to join the Lausanne Committee for Diaspora.[13] Thank God for Enoch Wan, Elias Medeiros, T.V. Thomas, Greg Paek, and Vergil Schmidt who agreed to the great task of developing the initial stages of Lausanne's diasporas initiative.

No single person can take credit for the birth of diaspora missiology. Evidently, during the LCWE Forum in 2004 and the succeeding years, many more diaspora missions advocates became connected, and the unseen hands of God formed a wider global diaspora network. Innumerable individuals have sacrificially supported the diaspora missiology initiative through Lausanne. Time, resources, and funds have been donated to and by organisations to nurture diaspora missiology at seminaries and churches. All publications published by Lausanne Diasporas have been made possible by donors and are not for profit (to the authors). Diaspora missions is the vision of God for the scattered people to be gathered, and it has been the unseen hands of God through time and through the deliberations and actions of missiologists and practitioners that have brought diaspora missiology to a wider forum and to the global arena of missions.

---

12 The "Diaspora Missiology" lecture took place as scheduled at OCMS on April 7, 2008.

13 This date-specific initiative would officially be called the Lausanne Diasporas Leadership Team (LDLT) and would work together towards the presentation of "Diasporas" at The Third Lausanne (III) Congress at Cape Town, South Africa, October 16-25, 2010.

I like to tell the story of how the late great Dr. Ralph Winter expressed to me in person his thought that during the First Lausanne (I) Congress (1974) in Switzerland and the Second Lausanne (II) Congress (1989) in the Philippines, "the world was different. Those years were marked by dictatorship and the Cold War. The borders of China and Russia were 'closed doors' then."[14] He described a world at the dawn of the digital revolution, before the global marketplace, internet, and social media had rendered the world virtually borderless.[15] "The world has changed. The Unreached People Groups are now scattered all over the world." His admonition to me on taking up the task to advocate for the diasporas with Lausanne, "your generation will have to deal with mass migration and globalization." My generation and my children's and grandchildren's generations! At the time of this writing (December 2015), William Lacy Swing, Director General for the International Organization for Migration (IOM) has named 2015 "The Year of the Migrant."[16]

In this compendium, we delimit our considerations to the umbrella of the Lausanne Movement. Clearly, God is at work around the world, sharing his vision for the world to individuals and organisations who choose to watch the times and listen, but in this particular volume, we, a global diaspora network of friends and colleagues he has brought together, write down the vision to pass on to the generations of the church to come.

> For the vision is yet for an appointed time,
> But at the end it will speak, and it will not lie.
> Though it tarries, wait for it;
> Because it will surely come,
> It will not tarry.
>
> Habakkuk 2:3 NKJV 1982

---

14 I paraphrase some words as this is in my personal memory of Dr. Winter.

15 The economic terms associated with Canadian communication theorist, Marshall McLuhan (incidentally a fellow Edmontonian) in the 1960s. Read more about McLuhan at http://www.marshallmcluhan.com. Accessed December 24, 2015.

16 "The Year of the Migrant" is associated with the November 24, 2015 Report of Director-General, Ambassador William Lacy Swing, presented at IOM's 106th Session of Council, Geneva, Switzerland. https://www.youtube.com/watch?v=7gdYKe4_Fbo. Accessed on December 24, 2015.

ACKNOWLEDGEMENTS

Contributors to this volume gathered from four corners of the globe. Over 50 writers and editors collaborated to bring this volume together. Like migrants the globe over, the writers gathered in distant locations, sometimes through the help of technology such as Skype and various e-mail services, other times at airport cafes between flights – and meeting in person once, over the course of a week, to deliberate and critique each paper. They laboured together from different time zones and continents to produce a volume that would describe the juncture of diaspora and missiology. Though each section was developed independently, the authors shared the focus of diaspora and missions.

The task of assembling this book was too great for just two people, thus the role of the section editors was vital in gathering and assisting the groups of authors. We would like to thank our distinguished colleagues Amador Remigio, Jr. and Darrell Jackson, Thomas Harvey and Miyon Chung, T.V. Thomas and Elias Medeiros, Grant McClung and Cody Lorance, Miriam Adeney and Tuvya Zaretsky, Larry Caldwell and Paul Sydnor, and Tereso Casiño and Charles Cook, who served as section editors to the seven sections, aviating the project into completion. The research and strategies presented in this volume would not have been possible without the scholars and practitioners who took on the responsibility of describing their research and recounting their missions strategies. Furthermore, this volume would be without form if not for the dedication of supporting staff and volunteers.

We deeply appreciate Greenhills Christian Fellowship for hosting the Global Diaspora Network Lausanne Global Diaspora Forum 2015, and the Korean Diaspora Forum and Korean Diaspora Network for specially funding the publication and distribution of this compendium to seminaries world-wide.

In developing this compendium, we had the benefit of generous donations from organizational, institutional, and individual funding partners who are too many to mention here. Their abundant gifts have been beyond measure and are far-reaching.

Finally, our gratitude also goes to academic institutions and missiological associations that have intentionally served as incubators, providing a platform for idea exchange, and are the pioneers of diaspora missiology leading to this project.

In alphabetical order, we list these friends and forerunners of the "scattered and gathered" peoples.

- American Society of Missiology
- Advancing Indigenous Missions (Winnipeg)
- Alliance Graduate School (Manila)

- Asian Theological Seminary (Manila)
- Asbury Theological Seminary (Kentucky)
- Cebu Theological College and Cebu Graduate School of Theology (Cebu City)
- Centre for Evangelism and World Missions (Regina)
- Evangelical Missiological Society
- Filipino International Network
- Filipino Language Christian Congregation (FLCC) at National Evangelical Church (Kuwait)
- Finishing the Task
- First Filipino Alliance Church (Edmonton)
- Freedom in Christ Church (Toronto)
- Greenhills Christian Fellowship (Pasig City)
- Global Diaspora Network: Philippine Board of Trustees and International Board of Advisers
- Jaffray Centre for Global Initiatives at Ambrose University and Seminary (Calgary)
- Kingman Baptist Church (Kingman)
- Koinonia Theological Seminary (Davao City)
- Korean Diaspora Forum
- Korean Diaspora Network
- Life Agape International (Paris)
- Mars Hill Urban Missions Society
- Ontario Filipino Ministerial Fellowship
- Operation Mobilization
- Oxford Centre for Mission Studies (Oxford)
- Pundakit Christian Church (Barangay Pundakit)
- The Christian and Missionary Alliance in Canada
- The Great Commission Global Ministry (Doha)
- The Light House Church (Kuwait)
- The Klemke Foundation
- The Lausanne Movement
- Taylor College and Seminary (Edmonton)
- TIM Centre at Tyndale University and Seminary (Toronto)
- Torch Trinity Graduate School of Theology (Seoul)
- Trans World Radio Canada
- Ukrainian Evangelical Theological Seminary (Kiev)
- Western Seminary (Portland)
- Withee International

Dei gratia,
Sadiri Joy Tira and Tetsunao Yamamori
Edmonton, AB, December 26, 2015

INTRODUCTION

Sadiri Joy Tira and Tetsunao Yamamori

Christian mission "fields" are being redefined. The massive population movements of the last century have radically challenged our study and practice of "mission fields." Where the church once rallied to go out into "the regions beyond," now at the end of the dawn of the 21st Century, Christian missions is required to respond and adapt to the "missions around."[1]

The 21st Century is marked by globalization, technological advancement, and mass migration. In particular international migration, driven by various voluntary and involuntary factors, is increasingly changing demographics, economics, and affecting societies and cultures.

International, continental, and regional migration "is part of a transnational revolution that is reshaping societies, politics around the globe."[2] Castles and Miller observe that: "the old dichotomy between migrant-sending and migrant-receiving states is being eroded. Most countries experience both emigration and immigration... while some countries have taken on an important role as transit zones for migrants."[3] Tira calls this phenomenon "the Human Tidal Wave."[4]

The decades of the 1990s and 2000s have witnessed an influx of internal and international migration. In the aftermath of globalization, regional conflicts, and natural disasters, intergovernmental agencies state that "the overall number of international migrants has increased in the last few years from the estimated 154 million in 1990, to 175 million in 2000, and to 232 million in the present."[5]

---

1 Atul Aghamkar coined the phrase "regions around" in his response to Sadiri Joy Tira's blog post "Redefining Regions Beyond" written for The Lausanne Movement's The Global Conversation. "Regions Beyond: A Response" posted by Atul Aghamkar on May 2, 2012 is available at http://conversation.lausanne.org/en/resources/detail/12258#.VoVRyzag-T8. Accessed September 25, 2015.

2 Stephen Castles and Mark J. Miller, "Introduction," in The Age of Migration: International Population Movements in the Modern World, 4th Edition (Guildford Press, 2009). 7.

3 Castles and Miller, The Age of Migration, 7-8.

4 Sadiri Joy Tira, ed., The Human Tidal Wave: Global Migration, Megacities, Multiculturalism, Pluralism, Diaspora Missiology (LifeChange Publishing, 2013).

5 International Organization for Migration from United Nations Department of Economic and Social Affairs (UN DESA) – "Trends in International Migrants Stock: The 2013 Revision" from United Nations database, POP/DB/MIG/Stock/

Furthermore, the number of internally displaced persons in the world reached 38.2 million in 2014, reflecting an increase from 21 million in 2000 to 38.2 million at the end of 2014.[6] Undoubtedly, all nations have been affected by mass migration internally and internationally, and the Christian church is confronted with the challenges and opportunities presented by this new missiological reality.

The title of this book suggests the overall theme that is developed in it. Readers will recognize that agricultural metaphors are used for the title of this volume. The planet Earth or the whole world is portrayed by the editors and writers of this compendium as a vast farm or field where seeds are scattered during the planting season and the fruits of these plants are gathered during the harvest. The nations are the peoples or ethnic groups while countries are geographical locations. These nations are like scattered seeds planted in many countries of the earth; ultimately being gathered in one city, the City of God or Heaven – the eschatological dwelling place of God's people. Briefly put, the editors and contributors of this compendium believe that God's people all over the globe are seen to be the gatherers, and are mandated by the Lord of the Harvest into the field to gather the nations. This thesis will be developed over the course of six sections, with a resource section available at the end.

The purpose of this compendium is to analyse the development of missions to the "missions around" from a variety of perspectives, and to develop an understanding of the contemporary church's opportunities and responsibility vis-à-vis "Diaspora Missiology," defined by the Lausanne Diaspora Educators Consultation in the Seoul Declaration[7] as: "a missiological framework for understanding and participating in God's redemptive mission among peoples living outside their places of origin." It is the editors and writers hope that this compendium will serve as a comprehensive resource on diaspora missiology for both theological institutions and local ministries that are seeking understanding and intentional action in the current milieu.

The focus of the compendium will be the church in contemporary global situations.[8] The initial section examines (1) the phenomenological realities and trends of global diaspora with the second section (2) providing the

---

Rev.2013, Table 3. http://esa.un.org/unmigration/TIMSA2013/Data/UN_Migrant Stock_2013.xls. Accessed on September 25, 2015.

6 "Internal Displacement Monitoring Centre (IDMC) – Global IDP Figures" http://www.internal-displacement.org/global-figures. Accessed on September 25, 2015.

7 "The Seoul Declaration on Diaspora Missiology" is found at https://www.lausanne.org/content/statement/the-seoul-declaration-on-diaspora-missiology.

8 Global Diaspora Compendium is modelled in title and in format to the conceptual volume of diaspora missions, Scattered: the Filipino Global Presence edited by Pantoja, Tira, and Wan (LifeChange Publishing, 2004) that was distributed to the participants of Lausanne Forum 2004 held in Pattaya, Thailand.

biblical and theological foundations for Diaspora Missiology as a response to the global realities. Section three (3) will propose strategic directions taking the phenomenological, biblical, and theological sections into consideration, and section four (4) will develop the mission of the church in global diaspora. It was the intention of the contributors to present a fair representation of instances from the global church, so section five (5) includes effective regional and national case studies in diaspora missions presenting various ministry models. Finally, a variety of specific diaspora issues in case studies are presented in section six (6) to address specific considerations. While chapters contain their own bibliographies, a resource section seven (7) includes a glossary and appendices for the readers' consideration.

The compendium sections were written and edited by a global representation of contributors and section editors. They were then presented at the Lausanne Movement's Global Diaspora Network Global Diaspora Forum that took place in Manila, Philippines, in March 2015. This compendium follows two previous publications sanctioned by the Lausanne Committee for World Evangelization, now referred to as the Lausanne Movement – a movement of evangelical Christians committed to the vision of "the Whole Church taking the Whole Gospel to the Whole World."[9] In consideration of the international diversity of the authors of this compendium, contributors were given significant latitude in their style of writing, including referencing.

The first of these forerunning publications resulted from the October 2004, Lausanne Forum in Pattaya, Thailand, where the issue of "Diaspora, and International Students" was discussed. The *Lausanne Occasional Paper No. 55*, titled *The People Next Door: Diasporas and International Students* served as a germinal document for the Lausanne Movement's launch of a diasporas focus. Six years later, at the Third Lausanne Congress on World Evangelization held on October 16-24, 2010, in Cape Town, South Africa, the Lausanne Diasporas Leadership Team (LDLT) circulated a paper titled, *Scattered to Gather: Embracing the Global Trend of Diaspora,* to the Congress participants.

---

9 The "three-fold Lausanne slogan" is discussed in detail on the Lausanne Movement website. Available at https://www.lausanne.org/content/twg-three-wholes. Accessed on September 25, 2015.

SECTION 1: PHENOMENOLOGICAL REALITIES AND TRENDS OF GLOBAL DIASPORA

Amador Remigio, Jr. and Darrell Jackson, Section Editors

TRENDS AND REALITIES OF GLOBAL MIGRATION AND DIASPORAS: AN INTRODUCTION

Section Editors: Darrell Jackson and Amador Remigio, Jr.

If diaspora missiology has been defined by *The Seoul Declaration on Diaspora Missiology* (2009) as 'a missiological framework for understanding and participating in God's redemptive mission among peoples living outside their places of origin,' the historical development of diaspora missiology illustrates that these are not missiologies that have arisen from the theoretical speculations of study-bound theologians. Rather, it represents instead the fruit and outcome of personal struggle, experience, testimony, and long-term engagement of its stakeholders with the phenomenological realities of diaspora faith and human migration.

The history of mankind has shown the pervasive and profound influence of migration and diasporas as a critical demographic determinant of globalization, urbanization and the development of a pluralistic polity, economy, society, culture and religion. Thus, the study of migration and diasporas, involving the attempt to understand its significance, its origins, and its substantive implications, has become an increasingly important area of inquiry and study in modern and post-modern history.

From a historical perspective, the study of migration and diasporas encompasses dual aspects: the collection and assembly of relevant demographic information and the systematic interpretation of these in order to discover and elucidate on its meaning, the concomitant implications and the differential impacts these have on human polity, economy, society, culture and religion. Moreover, adopting a phenomenological approach to the study of migration and diaspora will necessarily involve both theoretical and practical considerations as well as initiatives for understanding the various aspects of migration and diasporas, especially through the use of other intellectual disciplines as well as fields of study.

Section one of this compendium, Phenomenological Realities and Trends of Global Diaspora, presents the phenomenological realities relating to migration and diaspora beginning with Chapter 1 (A. Remigio), as it analyzes and evaluates historically derived phenomenological data on globalization, diasporas, urbanization and pluralism in terms of trends and prospects. In this respect, demographic movements (focusing on migration and diasporas) over space and time are viewed from both diachronic and synchronic perspectives as the independent variable that can yield insights in terms of how it has been a major "driving" factor in accelerating globalization, urbanization and the emergence of megacities as well as a pluralistic polity, economy, society, and culture. In this context, globalization is viewed as not just as the development of an increasingly integrated global economy marked especially by free trade, free flow of capital, and the tapping of cheaper foreign labor markets, but as a process that facilitates substantial demographic movements among and between peoples across national boundaries. Missiologically significant insights and implications for the *Missio Dei* are then drawn from these developing trends and prospects on migration and diaspora as these pertain to these dependent variables (viz., globalization, urbanization and the development of a pluralistic polity, economy, society and culture) and what these signify for the Body of Christ at the global, national and local levels.

As for Chapter Two (G. Zurlo), a quantitative study of religious diasporas and religious diversity, based on a taxonomy of the world's peoples, a taxonomy of the world's religions, and a data collection mechanism for assessing both taxonomies, was attempted. Utilizing the taxonomies of religions and peoples from both the *World Christian Database* (*WCD*) and *World Religion Database* (*WRD*), a preliminary examination of religious diasporas shows 316 million people (4.3% of the world's population) from 485 peoples in diasporas around the world. Such quantitative analysis of migration in the context of demographic factors – such as births, deaths, conversions in, conversions out, immigration, and emigration – then provided a synoptic and substantive view of various changes in religious diasporas.

Chapter Three (D. Jackson) sketches a global picture of emerging patterns of the global control and management of migrants. It uses a broad framework that outlines the complexities of rapidly changing national, regional, and global policies pertaining to migration and diasporas, especially when viewed in the current historico-political context of Western nations struggling to respond to Syrian and other migrants from the Middle East. In this respect, it addresses Christians who are concerned and involved in advocating changes to current regulatory frameworks and migration policies. This chapter provides a valuable vantage point for understanding how these current regulatory frameworks on migration and diasporas can be a vital first step to lobbying for the amending and replacing of such frameworks.

Chapter Four (S. J. Tira and D. Jackson) is a 'bridging' chapter between the first three phenomenological chapters and the corresponding discourse in the subsequent chapters of the Compendium (as it responds to and interacts with these phenomenological realities). Tracing the efforts of a group of missiologists who took seriously the indisputable phenomenon of migration at the end of the twentieth century, their efforts to reshape traditional missiology by looking at these demographic trends and realities more intentionally for the purpose of developing diaspora missiology further has indeed gained more traction in terms of the development of kinetic models for operationalizing diaspora missiology even as it makes possible the delineation of its future prospects. Consequently, these efforts have affirmed what is already writ large in this Compendium: there can be no missiology of diaspora or no theology of migration without the God-ordained phenomena of both diaspora and migration becoming and being an integral part of His redemptive story in world history.

1. Globalization, Diasporas, Urbanization and Pluralism in the 21st Century: A Compelling Narrative for the Missio Dei?

Amador Remigio, Jr.

> "Perhaps no force in modern life is as omnipresent yet overlooked as global migration, that vehicle of creative destruction that is reordering ever more of the world as we know it." Jason DeParle in the New York Times, June 26, 2010

> "[Diaspora] may well be the most important undigested reality in missions thinking today is that we simply have not caught up with the fact that most of the world's peoples can no longer be defined geographically." Ralph Winter, endorsement of Scattered: The Filipino Global Presence

Introduction

> "Therefore those who were scattered went everywhere preaching the Word." Acts 8:24

Having ministered to peoples in diaspora for the last twenty two years in the Asia-Pacific, the Middle Eastern, and North American regions leaves me with the profound realization that the divinely orchestrated movement of peoples across geographic boundaries over time continues to figure prominently in the global proclamation and the propagation of the Gospel, the proliferation and development of Christian churches and communities worldwide and the increasing fulfillment of the *Missio Dei*, as God's redemptive plan for mankind moves inexorably towards the eschatological climax of world history. In the churches where I have served, the narratives I have listened to and continue to hear about the experiences of both economic and non-economic migrants (e.g., refugees) are just too compelling and sometimes heartbreaking to be ignored while being conveniently tucked and forgotten in our own private worlds and "comfort zones," especially for those of us who call the First World our home.

The main thrust of this paper will be based on historically derived phenomenological data on migration, diasporas, globalization, urbanization and pluralism that will be analyzed and evaluated in terms of trends and prospects. Specifically, migration and diasporas as the scattering and dispersal of peoples across geographic boundaries have been a running thread and theme that has been woven into the fabric of world history, society, and culture. In this respect, such demographic movements (focusing on migration and diasporas) over space and time are viewed from both diachronic and synchronic perspectives as the independent variable that can yield insights in terms of how it has been a major "driving" factor in accelerating globalization, urbanization and the emergence of megacities as well as the fostering of a pluralistic polity, economy, society, culture, and religion. The anthropogenic impacts and implications of such demographic changes and shifts will then be explored relative to the crucial impact areas of urbanization, multicultural diversity and dynamics and its nexus with competing faiths and worldviews vying for dominance in a pluralistic and post-modern context.

In this context, globalization will be viewed as not just the development of an increasingly integrated global economy marked especially by free trade, free flow of capital, and the tapping of cheaper foreign labor markets.[1] Rather, it will be taken to mean as encompassing also the multifarious impacts that the relentless process of globalization entails. Missiologically significant insights and implications for the *Missio Dei* will then be drawn from these developing trends and prospects pertaining to these dependent variables (viz., globalization, urbanization and the development of a pluralistic polity, economy, society and culture) and what these may signify for the Body of Christ at the global, national, and local levels. Adopting a phenomenological approach to the study of migration and diaspora will necessarily involve both theoretical and practical considerations as well as initiatives for understanding the various aspects of migration and diasporas, especially through the use of other intellectual disciplines.

The history of mankind has shown the pervasive and profound influence of migration and diasporas as a critical demographic determinant of globalization, urbanization, and the development of a pluralistic polity, economy, society, culture, and religion. Thus, the study of migration and diasporas, involving the attempt to understand its significance, its origins, and its substantive implications, has become an increasingly important area of inquiry and study in modern and post-modern history.

From a historical perspective, the study of migration and diasporas encompasses dual aspects: the collection and assembly of relevant demographic information and the systematic interpretation of these in order to discover and elucidate on its significance and meaning as well as the implications these have on globalization, urbanization and the development of a pluralistic polity, economy, society, culture, and religion. The first aspect involves the historical and demographic study of migration and diasporas and must be supplemented by such auxiliary disciplines as geography, economics, political science, anthropology, sociology, ethnography, and other ancillary disciplines. The study of the multifaceted phenomena of migration and diasporas can then yield insight into how it

1 Merriam-Webster, I. (2003). Merriam-Webster's collegiate dictionary. (Eleventh ed.). Springfield, MA: Merriam-Webster, Inc.

influences the growth and development of globalization, urbanization and the formation as well as the dynamics of how a pluralistic polity, economy, society, culture and religion develop. Migration and diasporas therefore, when viewed from a unified or systematic perspective, can lead to the gaining of insights into how such demographic phenomena can substantially impact current and future configurations of globalization, urbanization and the development of a pluralistic polity, economy, society, culture and religion in modern and postmodern history. An adequate understanding of migration and diasporas (as an independent variable that influences globalization, urbanization and pluralism) is therefore necessary into delving into how it significantly shapes polity, economy, society, culture and religion at scale–specific levels in modern and postmodern history.

The use of the phenomenological approach in this paper does not necessarily hew to the concept of *epochē* as indicated in the philosophy of the German thinker Edmund Husserl (1859–1938), the father of Phenomenology. Insofar as the *epochē* concept requires a rigorous adherence to being descriptive about migration and diasporas (particularly in terms of how it impacts religious beliefs and practices, without judging them as to their worth or value), this paper is written from an unabashedly Christian evangelical standpoint whereby historical phenomena and processes are viewed as significantly occurring under the overarching and sovereign plan, purpose and design of Divine Providence or the Judeo-Christian God of both nature and history, with the universe being the tableau where such history unfolds. As Enoch Wan (2004, 4) pleads, evangelical research and discussion (whether these are historical, strategic, experiential, and expositional) on the phenomena of migration and diasporas must be grounded and rooted on the supreme authority of the Word of God. From a Scriptural perspective, the phenomenological emphasis need not necessarily vitiate nor undermine the integrity of this study. Rather, it should lead to a more robust empirical grounding of such phenomena in its historical matrix that can further enhance what may be later seen as theologically normative (Wright 2011), especially in terms of the spiritual meaning and significance of migration and diasporas from the perspective of God's imminent Kingdom. Such an empirical approach should nonetheless go beyond just the mere outlining of demographic statistics and should instead encompass a more human and humane perspective that embraces the positive as well as the negative effects of migration and diasporas.

The German philosopher Edmund Husserl (1859–1938) has had, as the main exponent of phenomenology, a defining influence on the study of religion (Bovell 2007). His program of describing experience and "bracketing" the objects of experience, in the pursuit of essences of types of experience, was contributory to the development of the phenomenology of religion. Nonetheless, Husserl differentiated phenomenology from psychology as he correspondingly viewed psychology as involving itself with facts arising from a spatial-temporal setting, while phenomenology itself deals with timeless essences.

Migration can therefore be viewed as a useful and powerful explanatory variable behind the unfolding of human history and as a motive force in inexorably molding the contours, configurations and terrain of the entirety and totality of human society, polity, economy and culture. The currents and eddies of human history as impacted by migration and diasporas in the last two hundred years have shown the indelible and unmistakable mark, imprints as well as significant bearing of demographic movements in shaping and determining the historical outcomes of anthropogenic interventions, activities and processes at the global, regional, national and local levels.

Global migration and diasporas: some diachronic and synchronic aspects

For the purpose of this paper, there is a need therefore to survey the definitional field in terms of the following demographic phenomena: migration, immigration, emigration and the diaspora.

Human movement across space and time, before the establishment of state boundaries or within one state, is considered as migration. In this sense, migration (as inclusive of diaspora) can involve an increase in internal migration as "a move within a particular country or region" (Knox and Marston 2001, 127) or international migrant flows or flows of people from their country of birth or citizenship to another country, irrespective of whether this is temporary or permanent. Emigration is the act of departing one's own country to live in another, as "a move from a particular location" (Knox and Marston 2001, 127). Immigration is synonymous to emigration as a "move to another location" (Knox and Marston 2002, 127) but the departure from a particular area to another is considered from the standpoint of where the migrant originally came from. Although internal migration is sometimes referred to in this paper, its focal point will be on international migration and their associated diasporas as well as its implications.

Generally, migration can be viewed conceptually as involving the demographic movement from rural to urban areas in developing countries, the demographic movement from poorer to more affluent developing countries and the demographic movement from developing countries to developed countries or as demographic movement between migrant sending nations and host nations in this era of globalization. As Kapur and McHale (2005, 1) notes, "the bulk of migration will take place within developing countries themselves, specifically regarding the movement from rural to urban settings in the giants-China and India;" they also note that "the second largest migration flows will occur internationally, among developing countries (from the poorer to the more affluent developing countries) while a third body of migrants will travel from developing to developed countries."[2] Historically, migration as diasporic movements have increased in scale and scope in spatial-temporal terms, but informal and formal/official definitions of diaspora must be borne in mind in order to ensure their appropriate use and understanding as well as the proper application of the scope and extent of these various diasporas in their historical contexts.

For purposes of consistency, a leveling of the definitional field for this paper will be desirable in insofar as demographic terminology is concerned. Migration in this paper will encompass both the permanent and temporary change of residence by an individual or group within and across national borders. In this sense therefore, it is inclusive of demographic phenomena such as the movement of nomads, migrant labor, human trafficking, commuting, and tourism, even if these are considered transient or transitory events.

Such migrations need to be further analyzed in terms of what are their defining characteristics. Internal and international migration can thus be differentiated. Within any country there are movements of individuals and families from one area to another (for example, from rural areas to the cities), and this is quite different from movements from one country to another. Also, migration may be voluntary or forced. Most voluntary migration, whether internal or external, is undertaken in search of better economic opportunities or housing as well as other social amenities. Forced migrations usually involve people who have been expelled by governments during war or other political upheavals or who have been forcibly transported as slaves or prisoners. Somewhat overlapping these two categories are the voluntary or forced migrations of refugees fleeing war, famine, or natural disasters.

In various instances, the term *diaspora* denotes a sense of displacement for a group of people, whereby this segment of the population that has been dispersed finds itself as separated from its national territory, while retaining some residual hope or desire to return to their homeland at some future time. In this respect, Sheffer (2003) argues that ethno-national diasporas are not recent phenomena but have historic roots that can be traced back to ancient times. The African slave trade from 1500 to 1870 is a fairly recent historical example of an ethnic diaspora where Africans were commercially transferred from the African continent to North and South America (with slaves from the western part of Africa being transported to different areas

---

2 Kapur, Devesh and John Mchale (2005) The Global Migration of Talent: What does it mean for Developing Countries? A CGD Brief. Center for Global Development (CGD) (Washington, D.C., October 2005), 1. Available at www.cgdev.org/sites/default/files/4473_file_Global_Hunt_for_Talent_Brief.pdf

of British, Portuguese, French, Spanish and Dutch domination in North and South America).[3]

For purposes of this paper, diaspora is defined as "the fact of leaving one's homeland and being on the move (voluntary or involuntary migration/immigration) of an individual or a people-group" (Lausanne Diaspora Leadership Team, 2010) or as "peoples on the move."

While a synchronic approach to analyzing migration and diaspora is useful, it will be heuristically desirable and practical to complement these with an intentionally diachronic approach that can usefully illuminate various anthropogenic aspects that are germane in illuminating various aspects of migrations and diasporas, as "peoples on the move."

Demographic movements (focusing on migration and diasporas) over space and time viewed from both diachronic (or over time) and synchronic (at a given point in time) perspectives

Modern geneticists have recently tracked the route of previous migrations through the use of genetic markers in the DNA of various ethnic groups. Using global DNA data to track the historical-geographical spread of humankind out of East Africa from 200,000 years ago onwards, genographic and other scientists plotted the movement of human beings as they began their spread from East Africa to West Africa in terms of generalized routes from East Africa to West Africa and then to the Middle East, South Asia, Southeast Asia and Australia. Later on, humans made their way to Central Asia, East Asia and Siberia as well as to Southern and Northern Europe and then into North America and South America.[4]

Human migrations within recorded history have transformed the physical and human geography (e.g., the racial, ethnic, and linguistic composition of their populations) of both the origin and destination countries. The map of Europe, for example, is the product of several major early migrations involving the Roman and Germanic peoples, the Slavs, and the Turks, among others. And in the course of 400 years – from the late 16th through the 20th century – the Americas, Australia, Oceania, the northern half of Asia, and parts of Africa were colonized by European migrants in the European Age of Expansion. Such overseas migration of Europeans during this period has been estimated to number in the tens of millions of people. Their encounters with the indigenous populations have undeniably transformed physical, human, and cultural geographies.

---

3 http://ad4change.org/african-diaspora-maps/

4 The Genographic Project led by geneticist and anthropologist, Spencer Wells, utilises advanced genetic and computational technologies to gather and analyze research data to understand the interplay of human migration and genetics. National Geographic: The Genographic Project, https://genographic.nationalgeographic.com.

The largest human migration in history was the so-called Great Migration that occurred in two distinct major migrations from Europe to North America in the 19th and early 20th centuries. The first began in the 1840s with mass movements of predominantly family groups from the United Kingdom, Ireland, Germany, and Scandinavia seeking permanent settlement. In the 1880s a second and larger wave developed from eastern and southern Europe, including Poland, Austria-Hungary, Italy, and the Balkan states, and constituted primarily of a movement of single male temporary workers. More than 50 million migrants crossed the Atlantic during the Great Migration of the 19th and 20th centuries, driving major population migrations within the United States.[5]

Slave migrations and mass expulsions also have been considered a recurring thread in human history for millennia.

The largest slave migrations were probably those compelled by European slave traders operating in Africa from the 16th to the 19th century. Over 9 million slaves arrived in the West and were consigned to the Americas,[6] though substantial numbers died in the appalling conditions of the Atlantic passage.

Wars and regional conflicts resulted in mass expulsions of millions of people in the first half of the 1900s. Examples include the 14.5 million people who fled in one direction or another during the 1947 Partition of British India into India and Pakistan, "one of the largest and most rapid migrations in human history".[7] Then at the end of World War II, from 1945-1947, the Allies administered the largest forced expulsion in history, expelling 12 million ethnic Germans from their homes in Czechoslovakia, Poland, and Hungary (and Bulgaria, Romania, and Yugoslavia) and resettling them in defeated Germany.[8]

What would propel the great migrations of the later half of the 20th century is increasing geographical inequality between industrialized regions and non or under-industrialized regions. Since World War II the largest voluntary migrations have involved groups from developing countries moving to the industrialized nations. With the acceleration of the industrial world, a steady stream of workers was recruited from non-industrialized

---

5 Baines, Dudley. Emigration from Europe 1815-1930. London: Macmillan; 1991.

6 Based on analysis of shipping contracts and data from ports, historian on Africa and the Atlantic slave trade, PD Curtin, estimates the number of African slaves arriving in the Americas to be 9.566 million by 1870, with a margin of error of 20% in his book (Curtin, P.D. The Atlantic Slave Trade: A Census. Madison: University of Wisconsin Press; 1969, 268).

7 Prashant Bharadwaj, Asim Khwaja, Atif Mian. "The Big March: Migratory flows after the partition of India." Economic and Political Weekly. August 30, 2008. At http://www.hks.harvard.edu/fs/akhwaja/papers/Big%20March%20EPW%20Publish08.pdf. Accessed December 29, 2015.

8 See R. M. Douglas. Orderly and Humane: The Expulsion of the Germans after the Second World War. Yale University Press, 2012.

countries to perform routine manual labour, often managed by bilateral international agreements[9]. These bilateral agreements between the sending and receiving countries employed a selection process that ensured that migrant workers were well-suited to their work contracts.

Intermarriages of "guest workers" and locals was a direct by-product of post-war migration. Often times, migrants would remain in the host countries, marry, raise families, and become citizens of their receiving country.[10] This further gave way to family reunification programmes.

From the sixties onwards, the number of international migrants has increased almost threefold from 77 million in 1960 to 214 million in 2010 (Pew Research Center 2010). As of 2013, the number of international migrants has increased to 232 million compared to 154 million in 1990 (Pew Research Center 2013). In the US, the number of international migrants has doubled from 23 million in 1990 to 46 million in 2013.

Migration and diaspora: some underlying causes

What Marshall McLuhan observed and predicted in the early sixties in his book "The Gutenberg Galaxy" has come to pass in terms of economic transformation being the main driver in creating a global village. The process of globalization has been marked by a profound and inexorable movement towards increasing socio-cultural and economic cross-border linkages (as well as positive and negative impacts) in the areas of trade, travel, fashion, entertainment, politics, society, and culture (Friedman 2005). Moreover, globalization as theory and praxis poses a challenge to theology as the *leitmotiv* of globalization is a recurrent theme in the transformation of world views, philosophies, ideologies, religious thought systems, faith traditions and the cultural matrix in which both modernizing as well as postmodern societies operate (Carroll and Daniel 2006).

Contributory to the accelerated development of transport and communication networks and its signal role in facilitating globalization has been the dizzying pace of technological change (especially in the areas of computerized information and telecommunications technologies) in both the high and middle income countries as well as in the low income countries.

Intrastate and interstate conflicts has been also one of the determinants in the continuing dispersion and scattering of ethnic groups across national borders and around the world in modern and postmodern history (Passell et al Nov 2012; Friedman 2003).

---

9 World Bank. 1948. Postwar international migration agreements. Washington, DC: World Bank. http://documents.worldbank.org/curated/en/1948/04/2872049/ postwar-international-migration-agreements. Accessed December 29, 2015.

10 Zig Layton-Henry, "Great Britain" in Hammar, Tomas. Editor, European Immigration Policy: A Comparative Study. Cambridge: Cambridge University Press; 1985.

Countries that currently or prospectively face a high risk of state failure are also viewed as countries of "origin" for current and future migrants (as political and economic destabilization tends to be a "push" factor that propels migrants to leave for more politically and economically stable countries) in their search for peace, a more secure "well-being" and economic security (Passell, H et al Nov. 2012, 9). A preliminary list of countries that recently face a high risk of state failure are some Middle East, European, and African countries (e.g., Afghanistan, Iraq, Libya, Ukraine, Syria, Egypt, Jordan, etc.) that have been destabilized in the wake of American and Russian interventionism (among others), civil war, the continuing conflict between the Israelis and the Palestinians and the so-called "Arab Spring," even as these nations have recently become politically, economically, and socially dysfunctional. It is not surprising therefore that political dysfunction in these aforesaid states have had serious repercussions in generating a substantial flow of refugees (in the millions) that have sought more peaceful areas in neighboring countries while impacting the countries that surround (as well as constitute) the European, Mediterranean, Middle Eastern, and African regions (as well as profoundly shaping past and current European and Middle Eastern migration policy, including the handling of illegal and extralegal migrants fleeing such political conflicts and strife by heading towards countries such as Spain, Italy, Greece, Macedonia, Malta, Hungary, Austria, Denmark, Germany, the various Scandinavian countries, and some of the relatively more peaceful countries in the Gulf region of the Middle East).

Recent climate change (specifically global warming) and the concomitant disruption of weather patterns on a worldwide basis have likewise affected a significant proportion of the global population in terms of amplifying current water insecurity in global croplands. Within two decades, more areas (especially in Asia, the Middle East, and Africa) will be subjected to more stress as measured in terms of their forecasted environmental water scarcity index (National Intelligence Council 2012).

Push and Pull factors

Inquiring into the probable factors behind these demographic shifts can therefore be useful in gaining some understanding and insight into the dynamics of what causes such demographic shifts and changes.

Migration is sometimes argued as a response to substantive differences, and there are two major types of these differences that prompt people to move: economic and non-economic (Martin 2005). The factors that encourage a migrant to cross borders, in turn, can be grouped into three categories: demand-pull in destination areas, supply-push in areas of origin, and network factors that link destination and origin.

As Martin (2005) explains:

> For example, a Guatemalan may be recruited to work in Mexican agriculture, a demand-pull factor, and failing crops may encourage him to go, a supply-push factor, in part because friends and relatives went the year before and can tell him about wages and conditions abroad, a network factor. Demand-pull, supply-push, and network factors rarely have equal weights in the migration decisions of individuals or families, and the importance of each factor can change over time. Generally, demand-pull factors combine with supply-push factors to set migration flows in motion, and network factors become more important as migration streams age or mature.

Various schools of thought vie for explanatory power in terms of ascertaining and elaborating what the determinants or driving factors behind migration and diasporas are. Neoclassical economic theory emphasizes that the primary factor for labor migration is the wage difference between two locations. The dual labor market theory posits that migration is caused mainly by the existence of pull factors in the secondary labor market of more developed countries that require low-skilled workers. The new economics of labor migration argues that international migration is a risk aversion strategy employed by low-income households in developing countries. Relative deprivation theory underlines the importance of the consciousness and awareness of the income difference between neighbors or between households in the migrant-originating community as a driving factor for people to migrate. Lastly, there is world systems theory that views migration from a global perspective and identifies that the interaction between different countries (e.g., in terms of trade flows and comparative economic advantages) is a crucial factor in effecting migration and social change within societies.

From these theories, it can be inferred that a combination of "push factors" (e.g., absence of job opportunity at home, persecution, poor medical care, substandard housing, racial or ethnic discrimination, lack of political or religious freedom) and/or "pull factors" (e.g., more jobs in other countries, better living conditions, more educational and health care opportunities, family ties) makes migration an attractive alternative for many. Also, the number of people seeking to migrate by crossing national boundaries will see increased growth in the future, due to demographic and developmental differences, as well as pronounced disparities in the quality of political leadership and governance (Global Commission on International Migration October 2005). The survey of driving factors behind migration and diasporas also highlights the role of both economic and non-economic factors as well as voluntary and involuntary choices faced by migrants especially when they reckon with the calculus of cost and benefits arising from migration in determining their choice to move from one geographic area to another.

From a missiologist's viewpoint, Wan (2007) posits that the dispersion and scattering of peoples are undertaken on the basis of two kinds of forces (i.e., voluntary or involuntary), three classes of choices (more, less, least) and five types of orientations (i.e., outward, inward, return, onward, and stay-put).

A net assessment of the benefits and costs of migration and diasporas will entail taking a hard look at these benefits and costs that have already been documented on a seminal basis (Ember, M., C. Ember, and I. Skoggard, eds. 2005). For example, economic benefits arising from migration and diasporas have been widely documented, especially the billions of dollars in workers' remittances that are sent back annually to the migrants' countries of origin and are a significant source of foreign exchange earnings for these countries.

Affluence in destination countries as a "pull" factor and the migrants' desire for "havens of security, stability and well-being" as a "push" factor

Most of the middle and high income countries in the twenty-first century (with economies where the GDP is relatively denser and therefore generate more wealth) are found as being located north of the equator. Although GDP dense (and more affluent) economies create a bigger ecological footprint (defined here as a measure of the resources used per person over time in each country) compared to low income economies, the prospect of earning higher wages lures potential migrants to these GDP dense economies. Notwithstanding the reality that North America, Western Europe and the Asia- Pacific economies of China, Japan, South Korea as well as Australia and New Zealand exert a disproportionately bigger ecological footprint compared to many low income economies in Africa and South America, GDP dense (and wealthier) countries in the Northern Hemisphere (e.g., OECD) countries are also perceived by prospective migrants to have better infrastructure (e.g., transport and communication networks) as well as health and social welfare systems that significantly improve life expectancy in positive ways. The "greying" of the population in many OECD countries has likewise increased the demand for educated and trained professionals in their healthcare sectors, with the supply of these professionals being sourced from developing countries in the Southern Hemisphere.

Also, high-income countries (especially those that serve as growth engines of the world economy during times of economic boom) in the Northern Hemisphere (e.g., US, Japan, Germany, China) tend to have lower unemployment rates compared to countries from which prospective workers and migrants come from. In countries that have been plagued by poor political and economic governance, political and economic instability, these further reinforce workers and migrants to seek "greener" pastures where prospects of employment are brighter and where political and economic turbulence are viewed as not significant enough to threaten the overall political and economic climate and the prospects for better-paying jobs and employment opportunities. Moreover, significant wage disparities/income gaps between developing and affluent countries also precipitate the move from lower wage to higher wage labor markets (Global Commission on International Migration 2005). It is not surprising therefore that where the levels of economic activity are highest and where there are significant concentrations of wealth and affluence in the Northern Hemisphere is where you find too the preferred countries of destination for legal as well as illegal migrants from many countries in the Southern Hemisphere.

Family reunification as a "pull" factor

Family reunification is probably the most important non-economic factor encouraging migration. In many cases, one member of a family is the initial person who goes abroad and obtains a job and/or residence rights, which explains why the migration literature often uses nautical metaphors, discussing anchor migrants and follow-on chain migration.

Conflict, violence and war as a "push" factor

Conflict, violence and war in areas that have become both political and economic flashpoints have also been a significant "push" factor in migration and diasporas around the world. The two world wars in the twentieth century have caused substantial demographic shifts not just amongst the warring countries but also in those countries where people have chosen to resettle. Recent genocides in Rwanda and Bosnia underline how ethnic cleansing and political persecution prompted citizens who are caught in political conflict between armed stakeholders to flee the areas where they have resided to safer havens. The ongoing Palestinian- Israeli conflict, the invasion of Kuwait by Iraq in the 1990s, the turmoil in Afghanistan and Iraq, the 2011 Arab Spring in the Middle East and North Africa and the resulting political ferment in countries such as Tunisia, Egypt, Libya and Syria have caused sizeable segments of their population to shift geographically to nearby countries (Lebanon, Jordan, and Turkey) where these displaced peoples have sought refuge. What were incipient political conflicts around the world have occasionally escalated into civil war or anarchy, as well as political conquest or turmoil, that were often historical triggers for large-scale demographic movements. Authoritarian regimes (e.g., the Pol Pot regime in Cambodia and military rule in Myanmar) have oftentimes employed forced migration as a tool for social and political control in areas where its perceived security interests are threatened.

Both internal and interstate conflicts have also significantly contributed to the scattering and dispersion of peoples across national boundaries and within nations. This proliferation in the number of active conflicts generally shows what the global trends in violent conflict have been from 1946 to 2009 (Hewitt, Joseph, Jonathan Wikenfield and Ted Robert Gurr, eds. 2009). The locus of both intergroup conflicts as well as religion-linked terrorist attacks (from entities such as governments and insurgent groups like Boko Haram, Al Qaeda, and ISIS in France, the United Kingdom, Ukraine, Afghanistan, Iraq, Lebanon, Libya, Egypt, Nigeria, the United States, and Syria) confirms that such conflicts are indeed widespread from a geographic standpoint. Such conflicts and attacks have generated political turmoil and have caused significant refugee inflows (in the millions) that have spilled over into countries that surround these conflict-torn areas around the world.

Urban areas in affluent countries as a "pull" factor because cities are viewed as the centers of economic opportunity that can provide an improved quality of life

In response to global economic transformation and integration, cities with populations of less than 8 million to more than 10 million have become more ubiquitous around the world in modern and postmodern history. Global population in urban areas has also been forecasted to rise from 50 percent in 2010 to 60 per cent in 2030. More than half of humanity now lives in a city, and the United Nations has predicted that 70 percent of the world's population will reside in urban areas by 2050 (Norton 2013; World Bank 2012).

Climate change, natural disasters, environmental constraints, and the adverse environmental impacts of anthropogenic activity as a "push" factor

Another underlying cause for migration and diasporas is a chain of factors that includes climate change, natural disasters, environmental constraints, and the adverse environmental impacts of anthropogenic activity as a "push" factor (Black, 1998). The continuing degradation of natural resource and ecosystem resources in ecologically vulnerable areas by anthropogenic agents (e.g., resulting in desertification in sub-Saharan Africa) and the drastic changes arising from climate change (e.g., weather pattern shifts that have resulted in droughts and flooding in agriculturally productive areas in Asia and Africa) have likewise been contributory to demographic movements (e.g., by tribal or ethnic groups) to areas which are perceived to offer relatively more food security and/ or higher quality of life levels. Accompanying this development, however, is the attractiveness of the relative accessibility and availability of other areas (especially in the Northern Hemisphere) that are perceived by migrants as having fewer environmental constraints, less drastic climate change, fewer natural disasters, and better environmental quality. Such attractiveness can therefore be viewed as a not insignificant "pull" factor for migration and diasporas.

Past and current indicators that ambient global temperatures are progressively warming up due to increasing greenhouse gas emissions will surely have implications on ecosystems as well as the movements of people within and across national boundaries (Reuveny, R. 2007, 656-673). Significant climate change occasioned by global warming will probably disrupt ecosystems and propel people to migrate and be scattered across political and economic borders. Resource monitoring institutions and governments have already mapped the global cropland areas and water basins that are experiencing water scarcity and insecurity in Central America, South America, Africa, Central Asia, the Middle East, Northeast Asia as well as parts of Southeast Asia (National Intelligence Council 2012). All these environmentally constrained areas have negatively affected economic productivity, as well as human welfare and well-being, and could very well induce demographic movements to areas experiencing lower levels of environmental stress.

As these identified push and pull factors as underlying causes of migrations and diasporas become more compelling (in terms of their rates of growth, intensity, and magnitude) over the short to medium term future, it may be increasingly likely that migrations and diasporas as demographic phenomena will continue to impact both the migrants' countries of origin as well as their countries of destination in terms of accelerating globalization, facilitating pluralism, and heightening sociological pressures that may lead to further ethnic and religious ferment, and sociological as well as political polarization (e.g., an anti-immigrant backlash in some Western European countries).

Global and regional migration and diasporas: recent historical developments and trends

In addition to population growth (due to births) and decline (due to deaths), changes in the dynamics of the demographic composition and structure of human populations further help in the understanding of how populations are transformed and what the role that migration and diasporas play in such demographic change. Youthful and intermediate populations that form part of the significant pool of international migrants are currently concentrated in the Southern Hemisphere (particularly in Asia, Africa, and South America) while mature and post-mature populations are concentrated in the Northern Hemisphere, with the exception of countries such as Australia (National Intelligence Council 2012).

From 1960 to 2010, the number of international migrants (as a cumulative tally of all living people who have migrated across borders) increased from an estimated 77 million people in 1960 to 214 million people in 2010 (Pew Research Center 2010).

More recently, it was reported that globally, there were 232 million migrants in 2013. According to the International Migration Report (United Nations 2013) that the Pew Research Center study used:

> Of these, nearly 59 per cent lived in the developed regions, while the developing regions hosted 41 per cent of the world's total. Of the 136 million international migrants living in the North in 2013, 82 million, or 60 per cent, originated from a developing country, while 54 million, or 40 per cent, were born in the North. Further, 82 million or 86 per cent of the 96 million international migrants residing in the developing world in 2013 originated from the South, while 14 million or 14 per cent were born in the North. (United Nations, International Migration Report 2013, 1)

Furthermore:

> Between 1990 and 2013, the number of international migrants worldwide rose by over 77 million or by 50 per cent. Much of this growth occurred between 2000 and 2010. The developed regions gained 53 million or 69 per cent of the 77 million international migrants added worldwide between 1990 and 2013, whereas the developing regions added 24 million or 31 per cent. While the North gained the largest absolute number of migrants between 1990 and 2013, since 2000 the average annual growth rate in international migrant stock in the South outpaced the growth rate in the North: 2.3 per cent per annum versus 2.1 per cent per annum, respectively. Since 2010, the annual growth rate slowed in both the North and the South: to 1.5 per cent in the developed regions and 1.8 per cent in the developing regions. Of the 53 million international migrants added in the North between 1990 and 2013, 42 million or 78 per cent were born in the South. The remaining 12 million international migrants, or 22 per cent, originated from a country in the North. In the North, international migrants constituted 10.8 per cent of the total population in 2013 compared to 1.6 per cent in developing regions. Between 1990 and 2013, international migrants as a share of total population grew in the North but remained unchanged in the South. (United Nations, International Migration Report 2013, 1)

Statistics from various research organizations, indicate the following ten trends in global migration:

Trend No. 1 The share of international migrants relative to total population (from 1990 to 2013) has grown in the high income countries in the Northern Hemisphere but has remained unchanged in the Southern Hemisphere.

According to the United Nations Population Division, net migration flows show that the net emigration countries (meaning those from where emigrants come from or originating countries) are found in the Southern Hemisphere. In this respect, it is worthwhile noting that the official definition of international migrants, as adopted by the United Nations Population Division (United Nations 2013), refers to these migrants as people outside their country of birth or citizenship for 12 months or more.

Thus, whenever UN Population Division datasets are used in this paper, it is useful to bear in mind that such definition of international migrants will be inclusive of foreign workers, international students, and refugees as well as their descendants. Tourists, foreign aid workers, temporary workers employed abroad for less than a year, and overseas military personnel are typically not included in this UN definition.

On the other hand, many of the net immigration countries (meaning those that are the destination of emigrants or receiving countries) are generally found in the Northern Hemisphere (with the exception of countries such as Australia). The direction of migration shows that the preferred direction has been from the Southern Hemisphere to the Northern Hemisphere from the 1960s onwards.[11] It is evident that the share of the flow of migrants from the Southern Hemisphere to the Northern Hemisphere has been progressively increasing and has more than doubled since the 1960s. Migrants to high-income countries have increasingly outnumbered the migrants to developing countries (excluding Europe and Central Asia) from 1975 to 2005.

Also, the percentage of international migrants moving to high-income nations has increased from 57% in 1990 to 69% in 2013. Likewise an increasing proportion of international migrants have been born in middle-income nations, rising from 48% in 1990 to 58% in 2013. (Pew Research Center 2010)

International immigration in the last fifty years (from 1960 to 2010) has been characterized by a demographic movement from the South America, African, and Asian regions to the preferred migration havens of North America, Western Europe, Middle East, and Australia (Pew Research Center 2010). As for the destination regions of international migrants, the Pew Research Center provides some estimates, as of 2010. Of the world migrant total of 214 million people: 33% (69,990,000) are in Europe; 23% (50,040,000) are in North America; 19% (41,050,000) are in the Asia Pacific region. 13% (28,540,000) are in the Middle East and North Africa. 8% (17,250,000) are in Sub-Saharan Africa. The remaining 3% (7,480,000) are in Latin America and the Caribbean.

As for the regional destinations of international migrants, the migrants that chose the South American and Caribbean regions, as well as the Asia Pacific region, as their destinations constituted 32% of the total number of international immigrants in 1990 while accounting for 25% of the total number of immigrants in 2013. In the period that spans more than two decades from 1990 to 2013, the destination regions of international migrants has been changing (Pew Research Center 2013). Migrants that chose North America and Europe as their destinations increased from 50% of the total number of international immigrants in 1990 to 54% in 2013.

---

11 See "Global Trends" in Net International Migration discussing the period 1950-2010 in United Nations International Migration Report, 11.

Trend No. 2 The share of international migrants as a percentage of the world's population has also increased from 2.6% in 1960 to 2.9% in 1990 and 3.2% in 2013.

In 2013, the United Nations reported:

> Worldwide, international migrants accounted for… about 3.2 per cent of the world population in 2013, compared to 2.9 per cent in 1990. In the North, international migrants constituted 10.8 per cent of the total population in 2013 compared to 1.6 per cent in developing regions. (United Nations 2013, 2)

Moreover:

> …in 2013, international migrants accounted for at least one in every four people in 42 countries or areas. These included small island states in the Caribbean, Melanesia, Micronesia or Polynesia as well as countries in Western Asia. In contrast, in many countries of Africa, Eastern Asia, South America and Southern Asia, migrants accounted for less than 5 per cent of the total population. (United Nations 2013, 7)

Trend No. 3 Europe and Asia combined hosted nearly two thirds of all international migrants worldwide in 2013 but between 1990 and 2013, Northern America recorded the largest gain in the absolute number of international migrants, adding 25 million migrants, equal to 1.1 million additional migrants per year.

In 2013, the United Nations reported that Europe hosted 72 million international migrants, and Asia received 71 million, hosting "nearly two thirds of all international migrants worldwide." This was followed by:

> Northern America host[ing] the third largest number of international migrants in 2013 (53 million), followed by Africa (19 million), Latin America and the Caribbean (9 million), and Oceania (8 million). (United Nations 2013, 2)

It is necessary to highlight that "between 1990 and 2013, Northern America recorded the largest gain in the absolute number of international migrants, adding 25 million migrants, equal to 1.1 million additional migrants per year." (United Nations 2013, 2) [12]

Trend No. 4 The regional origins of international immigrants have changed significantly over more than two decades (from 1990 to 2013).

As for the provenance of international migrants, the Pew Research Center provides some estimates as of 2010. Out of the world migrant total of 214

---

12 "Of the 25 million international migrants added in Northern America during this period, 14 million or 57 per cent were born in the Latin America and the Caribbean, 9 million or 35 per cent originated from Asia, while 1 million or 6 per cent were born in Africa." (United Nations 2013, 2)

million people, 33% (71,510,000) comes from the Asia Pacific region. 28% (60,900,000) comes from Europe. 16% (34,320,000) comes from Latin America and the Caribbean. 10% (27,460,000) is from the Middle East and North Africa. Another 10% (21,390,000) is from Sub-Saharan Africa while 2% (3,760,000) comes from North America.

As for the regional origins of international migrants, the migrants from the South American and Caribbean as well as the Asia Pacific regions constituted 45% of the total number of international immigrants in 1990 while accounting for 52% of the total number of immigrants in 2013. Migrants from North America and Europe decreased from 35% of the total number of international immigrants in 1990 to 28% in 2013. (Pew Research Center 2013)

Trend No. 5 The countries of origin for international immigrants have also changed significantly over more than two decades (from 1990 to 2013).

Pew Research Center notes in 2013 that the origin countries of international migrants have significantly changed (in terms of the number of people living in a country in which they were not born) over more than two decades, from 1990 to 2013. In 1990, the top 10 origin countries of international migrants (progressively numbered in millions) were the following: Russia, Afghanistan, India, Bangladesh, Ukraine, Mexico, China, United Kingdom, Pakistan, and Italy. In 1990, the European countries of Russia, Ukraine, United Kingdom, and Italy dominated the list (accounting for 25.9 million migrants). Next were the migrants from the Indian subcontinent (India, Bangladesh, Pakistan) with 16 million migrants. From the Middle East, Afghanistan had 7.3 million. Mexico had 5 million migrants while China had 4.1 million migrants.

The top 10 countries of origin for all migrants in 2010 were Mexico (12,930,000), India (11,810,000), Russia (11,260,000), China (8,440,000), Bangladesh (6,480,000), Ukraine (6,450,000), Palestinian Territories (5,740,000), United Kingdom (5,010,000), Philippines (4,630,000) and Pakistan (4,480,000) (Pew Research Center 2010).

In 2013, these had changed to the following listing: India, Mexico, Russia, China, Bangladesh, Pakistan, Ukraine, Philippines, Afghanistan, and the United Kingdom. In 2013, the Indian subcontinent (with India, Bangladesh, and Pakistan) had 27.7 million international migrants. Russia, Ukraine, and the United Kingdom (from Europe) had 21.4 million migrants. In 2013, Saudi Arabia and the United Arab Emirates had 16.9 million international migrants. China and the Philippines (in East Asia) had 14.8 million international migrants, while Mexico had 13.2 million international migrants. Australia had 6.5 million migrants in 2013. Rounding up the 2013 list is Afghanistan with 5.1 million international migrants.

The top 10 sending countries, ranked by the size of the diaspora outside of the country (as of 2014) are Mexico, China, United States, India, Turkey, Pakistan, South Korea, Spain, France, and Poland (Todd Johnson Sept. 2014).

Major developing country diasporas that have occurred in developed countries such as the United States, Germany, France are diasporas that have involved immigrants from developing countries such as Mexico, Cuba, El Salvador, the Philippines, India, China, Vietnam, Romania, Morocco, and Algeria (Widmaier, S. and J. C. Dumont 2005/2006).

Furthermore:

> Among the group of countries experiencing net emigration were traditional countries of emigration, such as Bangladesh, China, India, Mexico, Pakistan, and the Philippines. Many of these countries had long-standing ties with traditional countries of immigration, such as Australia, Canada, and the United States, while others had newly established ties with countries in South-Eastern and Western Asia which were recruiting foreign workers (United Nations 2013, 12).

Trend No. 6 In the last 25 years from 1990 to 2015, the listing of the top 10 destination countries of international migrants show significant changes.

In 1990, the top 10 destination countries of international migrants were the United States, Russia, India, Ukraine, Pakistan, Germany, France, Saudi Arabia, Canada and Iran (Pew Research Center 2010).

Then in 2010, the top 10 destination countries for all migrants in 2010 were the United States (42,810,000), Russia (12,270,000), Germany (10,760,000), Saudi Arabia (7,290,000), Canada (7,200,000), France (6,680,000), United Kingdom (6,450,000), Spain (6,380,000), India (11,810,000) and Ukraine (5,260,000) (Pew Research Center 2010).

By 2013, over 51 per cent of all international migrants in the world were living in ten countries (USA, Russia, Germany, Saudi Arabia, UAE, UK, France, Canada, Australia, and Spain). The largest number of international migrants resided in the United States of America: 46 million in 2013, equal to nearly 20 per cent of the world's total. The Russian Federation hosted the second largest number of migrants worldwide (11 million), followed by Germany (10 million), Saudi Arabia (9 million), and the United Arab Emirates and the United Kingdom (8 million each). (United Nations 2013, 5)[13]

---

13 Furthermore, "Between 1990 and 2013, the size of the international migrant stock grew in nearly three quarters of all countries or areas. The United States of America gained the largest number of international migrants between 1990 and 2013: nearly 23 million, equal to 1 million additional migrants per annum. Records show the United Arab Emirates recorded the second largest gain during this period (7 million), followed by Spain (6 million). (United Nations 2013, 5).

In mid-2015, the top 10 host countries of diasporas (ranked by diaspora population), as shown in Table 2 of Gina Zurlo's paper in this section, were the United States, India, France, UK, Germany, China, Russia, Canada, Brazil and Iran (Johnson, T., ed., Sept 2014).

Comparing the top 10 destination countries of international migrants in 1990 and 2013(Pew Research Center 2013), two North American countries (US and Canada) had 27.8 million migrants in 1990 and 53.1 million migrants in 2013.

Traditional countries of immigration, such as Australia, Canada, New Zealand, and the United States gained in population in both 1990-2000 and 2000-2010 periods. In the same period, Italy and Spain started to see an increase in their levels of immigration. Furthermore, countries in the developing regions recruiting labor migrants, such as Qatar, Singapore, and the United Arab Emirates were among the countries experiencing net immigration in both periods." (United Nations 2013, 12).

It is also worth noting that in 2013, the top 10 destination countries (in terms of the percentage of that country's population being foreign born as of 2013) were the United Arab Emirates (84%), Qatar (74%), Kuwait (60%), Bahrain (55%), Singapore (43%), Jordan (40%), Hong Kong (39%), Saudi Arabia (31%), Oman (31%) and Switzerland (29%) (Pew Research Center 2013). As for the United States, its foreign born population (as a percentage of total US population) had risen significantly from less than 5% in 1860 to nearly 14% in 2009.

Trend No. 7 There was also a significant shift in bilateral migration corridors between 1990 and 2013.

The United Nations' reports:

> During the period 1990-2000, seven of the top ten bilateral migration corridors had as destination a country in the North. The United States was the destination of five of the top ten bilateral migration corridors in the world, with large numbers of international migrants originating from China, India, Mexico, Puerto Rico and Viet Nam. Mexico-United States was the largest bilateral migration corridor in the world, with nearly 500,000 international migrants born in Mexico added to the population of the United States each year. (United Nations 2013, 5)

In the following period, 200-2010:

> ...the top ten bilateral migration corridors were equally split, with five corridors having as destination a country in the South and five corridors a destination in the North. Mexico-United Sates continued to be the largest bilateral migration corridor in the world but with much smaller numbers than during the period 1990-2000: an average of 260,000 additional international migrants per year. Countries in Southern Europe, namely Italy and Spain, also became major destinations of international migrants from countries in Eastern Europe. In addition, three of the top ten corridors were between a country in Southern Asia and an oil-producing country in Western Asia,

namely, Bangladesh-Saudi Arabia, Bangladesh-United Arab Emirates and India-United Arab Emirates. Refugees displaced by the war in Iraq as well as refugees falling under the mandate of the United Nations Relief and Works Agency for Palestine Refugees in the Near East (UNRWA) accounted for large numbers of migrants during the period 2000-2010 in Western Asia. (United Nations 2013, 7).

Most recently,

> In the last period, 2010-2013, migration patterns had changed significantly and all but three of the largest migration corridors in the world had as a destination a country in the South. Of the three bilateral migration corridors that had as a destination a country in the North, two were between counties in Europe: Romania-Italy and Poland-United Kingdom. Only one of the ten largest bilateral migration corridors during the period 2010-2013 was between a country in the South and a country in the North, namely Mexico-United States. Of the seven largest migration corridors which had as a destination a country in the South, five were between countries in Asia, including the corridors China-Republic of Korea and Cambodia-Thailand, while two were between countries in Africa, namely Sudan-South Sudan and Somalia-Kenya. Both the corridor Sudan- South Sudan and the corridor Somalia-Kenya involved large numbers of refugees. (United Nations 2013, 7).

From the foregoing datasets, the international pervasiveness of migrant labor has been affirmed and is quite pronounced for Africa, Asia, Western Europe, and Central America as the regions where the emigrants originate. Such migrant labor subsequently heads for the top destination countries in the Northern Hemisphere and the Middle East. For Asia:

> …the oscillation of migrant workers from mainland China to Malaysia, from the Philippines to the US, and even within countries such as India (from rural areas to metropolises such as New Delhi), confirm its pervasiveness. Likewise, the perpetual oscillation of casual Mexican migrant workers (the "wet-backs") to and from the US, as well as the ongoing influx of Turks into W. Germany ("Gasterbeiters"), has elicited attention. (Palmer, P.N. in Atkinson, D.J. and David H. Field 1995, 592)

Critical appraisal of these available migration and diaspora data sets from 1990 to 2013 indicates that these figures provide a synchronic (or "snapshot") view tenable only during specific years when these data were available (e.g., 1990, 2007, 2009, 2010, 2013, 2014). The data gap between 1990 and 2007 illustrates the need to regularly collect and assemble these migration and data sets in order to understand more fully these changes in demographics over time as it occurs in these various geographic contexts.

Trend No. 8 Approximately half of these international migrants are women in 2013.

The United Nations attributes the larger proportion of females in migration due to the:

> ...aging of migrants who had arrived decades earlier and the [to] fact that females, including female migrants, tend[ed] to have a longer life expectancy compared to males. In contrast, male migrants significantly outnumbered female migrants in Asia (58 per cent) and Africa (54 per cent). (United Nations 2013, 7-8).

Trend No. 9 As of 2013, three quarters of all international migrants were between the ages of 20 and 64.

The United Nations reports:

> In 2013, three-quarters of all international migrants were between the ages of 20 and 64. Of the 171 million international migrants of working age, the majority (61 per cent) resided in the developed regions. This distribution had changed little since the year 2000, when 62 per cent of working-age migrants resided in the North (United Nations 2013, 8).

Trend No. 10 In another United Nations (2013) report based on certain projection assumptions, the population of the developed regions will still be growing by 2040-2050, but at a declining rate with net migration being the only source of the projected population growth and natural increase having become negative.

The United Nations has projected the population of the developed regions will still be growing by 2040-2050 using projection assumptions defined in the 2013 United Nations report. However, projections for developing regions show that though the population is projected to continue to grow, it will "at lower rates, due to natural increase while net emigration will have a negligible effect on population size" (United Nations 2013, 14).

Migration and diaspora routes, refugee flows and human trafficking: its dark underbelly

Notwithstanding the utility that this listing of significant diasporas in the previous section may preliminarily have, such listing must not be allowed to mask the phenomena of irregular or illegal migration and those who are viewed as refugees/asylum-seekers and victims of human trafficking that accompany such diasporas.

Refugees

As for refugees as a diaspora category, "there were an estimated 8.8 million registered refugees and as many as 24.5 million internally displaced persons (IDPs) in more than 50 countries in December 2006" according to the United Nations High Commissioner for Refugees (UNHCR); however, the global refugee population could approximate 10 million, if 1.5 million

Iraqi refugees dispersed in the Middle East were taken into account (CIA 2009).

The 1951 UN Convention relating to the Status of Refugees defines 'refugee' as someone who has fled his or her country "owing to well-founded fear of being persecuted for reasons of race, religion, nationality, membership of a particular social group or political opinion." The UN acknowledges that there were 13 million refugees "of concern" worldwide and 38.2 million internally displaced people in mid-2014.[14]

Refugees and asylum seekers move primarily for non-economic reasons: refugees are persons outside their country of citizenship who are prevented or not willing to go back to their home countries because of possible threat or persecution. Most refugees stay in camps near their countries of origin until the situation in their home countries changes or until they are resettled in another country, but asylum seekers arrive in a country and ask to be recognized as refugees. If they are recognized as refugees, they are usually allowed to resettle and make a new life in that country (Martin 2005).

Countries with largest refugee populations (in thousands), 2009 (Economist, 2012) are: 1. Pakistan (1740.7); 2. Iran (1070.5); 3. Syria (1054.5); 4. Germany (593.8); 5. Jordan (450.8); 6. Kenya (358.9); 7. Chad (338.5); 8. China (301); 9. United States (275.5); 10. United Kingdom (269.4); 11. Bangladesh (228.6); 12. Venezuela (201.3); 13. France (196.4); 14. Sudan (186.3); 15. Congo-Kinshasa (185.8); 16. India (185.3); 17. Yemen (170.9); 18. Canada (169.4); 19. Uganda (127.3); and 20. Ethiopia (121.9).

In 2015, the International Association for Refugees (IAFR) provided estimates (in millions) of persons affected by forcible displacement (including refugees, asylum seekers and internally displaced people) who were residents and/or citizens of the following countries:[15] 1. Syria (11.6m); 2. Colombia (6.4m); 3. Iraq (4.1m); 4. Democratic Republic of Congo (4 m); 5. Afghanistan (3.7m); 6. Sudan (2.9m); 7. South Sudan (2.5m); 8. Somalia (2.3m); 9. Pakistan (1.8m); and 10. Central African Republic (1.5m).

Furthermore, as of 2015, the top refugee hosting nations (with the corresponding estimates), according to the IAFR, are: Turkey (1.6m); Pakistan (1.5m); Lebanon (1.2m); Iran (982,000); Ethiopia (659,500); Jordan (654,100); Kenya (551,400); Chad (452,900); Uganda (385,500); and China (301,000).

---

14 The United Nations High Commissioner for Refugees, "Figures at a Glance" at http://www.unhcr.org/pages/49c3646c11.html. Accessed December 29, 2015.

15 International Association for Refugees, "Map of the Refugee Highway" at http://www.iafr.org/toolbox/map-of-the-highway. Accessed December 29, 2015.

Human trafficking

The primary modes of human trafficking include bonded labor, forced labor, debt bondage, and involuntary servitude among migrant laborers, forced child labor, child soldiers, sex trafficking and prostitution, children exploited for commercial sex and child sex tourism. Approximately 800,000 people, mostly women and children, are trafficked annually across national borders, not including millions that are trafficked within their own countries. At least 80% of the victims are female and up to 50% are minors. 75% of all victims are trafficked into commercial sexual exploitation, with almost two-thirds of the global victims trafficked intra-regionally within East Asia and the Pacific, estimated from 260,000 to 280,000 people, and Europe and Eurasia, estimated from 170,000 to 210,000 people (Central Intelligence Agency 2009).

Migration and diaspora routes

How do migrants then reach their countries of destination? Migrants, both legal and illegal, use a variety of modes to reach their destinations from their countries of origin. Various studies have documented the travel routes by air, land and sea in various means of transport. In these studies, these routes have been mapped relative to illegal migration from Central America and South America to the North American countries of the U.S. and Canada, from South Asia, Africa, and the Middle East to several European countries (such as Spain, Italy, and Greece), from South Asia to some countries (Saudi Arabia, Kuwait, Bahrain, Qatar, the United Arab Emirates, and Oman) in the Middle East and from South Asia and Asia to Australia.

Frontline governments have also monitored (and detected) illegal border crossings (by nationality) along the external land borders. Nonetheless, illegal migration oftentimes entails risks that sometimes end in migrant border-related deaths. Regional estimates of migrant border-related deaths have been provided for the years between 1996 and 2014, as compiled by various sources (Frontex 2014). The predominant regions of origin of these illegal migrants that died in 2014 have been specified, with 53% of these migrants coming from the Sub-Saharan Africa, North Africa, and the Middle East. An estimated 75% of these migrant deaths occurred in the Mediterranean region.[16]

Parenthetically, it should be noted that the varying estimates of border deaths in the Mediterranean (from 1993 to 2011) by United and Fortress Europe (as organizations monitoring the migration situation in this region) underlines the degree of statistical uncertainty that surrounds these estimates arising from methodological differences and data constraints.

---

16 Frontex, "Annual Risk Analysis 2014," at http://frontex.europa.eu/assets/Publications/Risk_Analysis/Annual_Risk_Analysis_2014.pdf. Accessed December 29, 2015.

Migration, diasporas and demographic change: its key role as a major "driving factor" in accelerating globalization, urbanization and the emergence of megacities and a pluralistic polity, economy, society, culture and religion

The phenomenon of migration across national borders can also be viewed against the backdrop of what the median age of country-level populations (2010-2030) has been and what it is projected to be by 2030 (National Intelligence Council 2012). What this signifies is that as the "greying" of the populations of many of the countries in the Northern Hemisphere (with mature and post-mature populations) proceeds apace (with the implication that these countries will have to devote more of their healthcare resources to their citizens who are getting advanced in years), a substantial proportion of healthcare workers in these Northern Hemisphere countries will probably be sourced from Southern Hemisphere countries with youthful or intermediate populations.

The continuing migration across national borders in terms of migrant labor in diasporas, as a significant component of global demographic change, can therefore be seen as being contributory to further globalization, secularization, urbanization, and the emergence of societies that are becoming more pluralistic and multicultural (Harvey, T. 2013; Ybarrola, S. 2013).

Accompanied by the relentless advances in information and telecommunications technologies, this has further strengthened the "global village" thesis propounded by Marshall McLuhan in Gutenberg Galaxy (1962, 2011 edition). According to this thesis, instantaneous communication would result in the destruction of geographically based power imbalances and henceforth create a global village.

Also, the geographer David Harvey (1990, 284-307) observed that the postmodern condition is and will be characterized by a "time-space compression" brought about by affordable air travel and the increasingly intensive and extensive use of telephones, fax, e-mail, and other internet-based technologies.

As for urbanization (defined in this paper as the process by which large numbers of people become permanently concentrated in relatively small areas, forming cities), this historical phenomenon has been likewise driven by global demographic change. While the definition of what a city is varies in accordance with who is doing the defining, it has been recommended by the United Nations that countries should qualify that all places with more than 20,000 inhabitants living close together are to be considered as urban.

Seim (2015, 75, 95) argues that the theory and reality of urban migration is built on the observation that the overwhelming number of international migrants move to cities where these migrants are acculturated to engage a pluralistic milieu that "levels the playing field so that diversity can work together in the complex system of materialism."

Given the actual and projected increases in the number of international migrants and other peoples on the move and how these impact globalization, urbanization, and rapid economic changes, what do these signify (in demographic, political, economic, social, and cultural terms) to the countries that send or receive them?

The actual and projected increases in the number of international migrants and other peoples on the move have been contributory to globalization even while such increases have been affected by the processes of globalization, urbanization, and rapid economic change. The movement of migrant labor (Atkinson and Field eds. 1995) across national borders has meant that global economic integration has been assisted by the dispersion and scattering of peoples (the main bulk of which has been economic migrants). In demographic terms, it has been seen earlier that the main trend has been the migration from economically and politically marginalized countries to those countries that are perceived to be more stable politically, more dynamic economically, and are viewed as offering a better future for their children and their families. In political terms though, the migration by international migrants has elicited a wide range of responses, with some of these countries being more welcoming to migrants during economic "boom" times (e.g., Germany and Great Britain) while becoming also anti-immigrant when their economies are experiencing economic downturns (e.g., France, Italy, Spain, Greece, and Australia). In economic terms, international migrants have been seen as augmenting the labor supply markets of "destination" countries even as their remittances have likewise helped boost the economy of the countries that they originally came from in terms of "multiplier" effects that reverberate through the economy. In social and cultural terms, the entry and assimilation of migrants into their destination countries (especially in countries in the Northern Hemisphere) have enriched cultural diversity and have made these countries more pluralistic and multicultural societies. In the countries from which migrants migrate from, migration has been viewed as a political "safety valve" that has seen people who cannot find jobs in their own countries being given an opportunity to migrate to countries where their skills enable them to readily find employment opportunities. From the perspective though of some policy makers in these countries where these migrants originate, migration has entailed some negative consequences with migration being viewed as entailing a "brain drain" of a country's pool of qualified labor and manpower that has served to throttle down the economy as a "growth limiter" (Remigio 2013).

Of the top 10 destination countries for international migrants (with a total number of 119M) in 2013, it is clear that the majority of the top destination areas are all in the Northern Hemisphere with: North America (US and Canada) receiving 53.1M (45%) migrants, Europe (Russia, Germany, UK, France, Spain) with 42.5M (36%) migrants, the Middle East (Saudi Arabia and the UAE) with 16.9M (14%) migrants and Australia with 6.5M (5%) migrants. What does all this imply for the global Christian church and local Christian churches?

Migration, diaspora and the historical-geographical spread of religious beliefs and faith traditions[17]

Previous missionary strategies that exclusively focused on reaching UPGs in Asia, Africa, and Latin America will now have to be re-evaluated, rethought, accordingly reoriented, and redirected in the light of the new demographic realities posed by the scattering of ethnic groups and peoples from the originating countries of international migrants towards the First World and the other countries that are their destinations. Such re-evaluation, rethinking, and reorientation of missionary paradigms, plans, and strategies by evangelical missiologists and practitioners can therefore facilitate the immense task of ensuring that the Great Commission gets to be operationalized in realistic terms for this current generation.

In the proceeding chapter [2] of this section, Gina Zurlo will present the percentages of migrants who have come from each region that identify with each religious group (as of 2010). These statistics indicate that of the religious affiliation of 316 million people living in diasporas (485 people groups), representing 4.3% of the global population, over half of these (50.2%) are Christians, but Chinese folk-religionists have the greatest proportion of adherents in diaspora (56.2%) of all the world's religions. The second most widespread are Zoroastrians (17.4% in diaspora), due to movement from their historic homeland (Iran) to places abroad (such as India and the United States). One interesting observation is that Christians and Muslims together make up 59.6% of the world's population, and represent 74.8% of all people in diaspora, according to the 2015 World Christian Database.

The missiological priorities of the Christian church will have to be realigned to take into account these new demographic realities. The proclamation of the Gospel in both the origin and destination countries will

---

17 The original data subsets presented under this heading, were presented in March 2015 at the Lausanne Movement/Global Diaspora Network Global Diaspora Forum 2015 held in Manila, Philippines. Under this heading, global migration was viewed from the cultural prism of religious affiliation. By disaggregating international migrants in terms of their religious affiliation and faith tradition, what was detailed here were religionists in terms of their estimated number vis-à-vis migrant population, their percentage of the world population and the percentages of the religious groups that have migrated relative to the total number of migrants. However, for this volume, those subsets will be presented in chapter 2, with Zurlo providing a detailed analysis of data collected on religion and diversity in diasporas. This chapter will instead proceed to "unpack" the significance of migration and diasporas for the Missio Dei, and on how the diaspora phenomenon interfaces with ecclesiological, missiological, eschatological, and pastoral perspectives.

definitely take place against the backdrop of pluralism. The challenge of cultural and religious pluralism (where different religions and world views compete in the marketplace (where all these religions affirm that theirs is the way of truth) necessitates sharpening the distinctiveness and the absoluteness of the truth claims of Scripture vis-a-vis the competing truth claims of other faith traditions.

It should be noted that the apparent differences in statistical estimates from the United Nations (2013), the Pew Research Center (2010; 2012 and 2013) and the World Christian and Religion Databases (Johnson Sept 2014) pertaining to global migration, diaspora, and religious affiliation mentioned in Chapter 2 (Zurlo's paper) need not be viewed as necessarily contradictory. Rather, it would be but proper to be circumspect in using the statistical estimates by exercising due diligence in terms of querying and then validating the methodological and data collection as well as analytical assumptions that underlie such estimates.

Unpacking the significance of migrations and diasporas for the *Missio Dei,* the "end of history" and the ushering of God's Kingdom

Ever since God created the world up to today, migration and diasporas have been an indispensable means by which God has accomplished his redemptive purposes through both general revelation and the special revelation (embodied in the Word and Jesus Christ). Even the history of the expansion of the Christian church in all its temporal dimensions (past, present and future) cannot be explained apart from the historical reality of God's sovereignty, ruling over the nations and the moving of His people everywhere (Lausanne Diaspora Leadership Team 2010, 17).

Because global human migration and associated diasporas over space and time profoundly influence peoples, cultures, societies, and nations, it has shaped and continues to be formative and influential in affecting the explosive growth in cities and megacities around the world, the evolution and development of ethno-cultural diversity and the incessant growth of pluralistic and multicultural outlooks and perspectives in the midst of accelerating globalization. Given the actual and projected increases in the number of international migrants and other peoples on the move and how this impacts globalization, urbanization, and rapid economic changes, what does this signify to the global Christian church (in soteriological, missiological, ecclesiological, and eschatological terms) as well as to the local Christian churches in the originating as well as in the receiving or destination countries?

In soteriological and missiological terms, concomitant with the overall increase in global population and the rapid increase in international migration, this implies that more of these migrants will have to be reached with the Gospel message of salvation, especially in their countries of destination. From the ecclesiological perspective, Christian churches in both the origin and destination countries will have to be mobilized and trained so that they can be equipped to serve the spiritual needs of both the emigrants and the immigrants. In eschatological terms, it is more than probable that the dispersion or scattering of peoples across the face of the earth will coincide with the proclamation of the Gospel (Mark 13:10) to all nations and that this is but a prelude to the gathering of the elect (Mark 13:27) before Jesus comes again.

As global migration/diasporas continue to proceed apace while generating ecclesiological and missional challenges and opportunities to the *Missio Dei* and the global church of Christ, how have we responded as evangelical Christians to these challenges and how should we respond given the imperatives laid down by God in His Word? Considering therefore the global migration and diaspora trends (as crucial phenomena driving globalization, pluralism and the propagation of religious faith systems and traditions) mentioned earlier in this paper, what does all these signify and imply for the *Missio Dei*?

If diasporas are neither morally right nor ethically wrong per se, but are seen as the ineluctable outcome of historical events and processes occurring under God' sovereignty, how should we view then all this from a Scriptural and God's Kingdom perspective ? Biblically, the response to migration and diasporas harks back to who God is: His love, righteousness, justice, and his abhorrence of any form of oppression or exploitation. It may also be useful to view the Incarnation as God loving us so much that He took the step of migrating and coming back to humanity so that all of us can in turn migrate back to God (John 1:14; 3:16). As Daniel Groody (2013) observes: "Through Jesus, God enters into the broken and sinful territory of the human condition in order to help men and women, lost in their earthly sojourn, find their way back home to God (Jn 13:1, 3)."[18] As Karl Barth notes, the Incarnation was Jesus' "way into the far country" as a sojourner and refugee (Matt.2:13-17) crossing borders as a result of persecution in order to enter into a place of "otherness." It also recognizes that the acceptance and welcoming of the stranger, alien, and migrant in our midst is synonymous to our acceptance of Christ (Matt 25:34-45) and that the affirmation of the Imago Dei as well as "the presence of God in the foreigner is the enduring foundation for the duty of Christian hospitality" (Baggio, F. and A. Brazal 2009, xii)[19].

Historically, notwithstanding the plight of Hebrew migrant laborers exiled in Egypt as a result of God's judgment for Israel's unmitigated idolatry (Exod. 2:11-5:21) and God's opposition to Pharaoh's oppression of

---

18 Daniel G. Groody, "Catholic Social Teaching and Migration: 1 Perspectives from the US-Mexico Border," http://ordosocialis.de/pdf/Groody/Catholic_Social_Teaching_and_Migration.pdf, 7. Accessed January 10, 2016. Originally in *Review: Pensamiento Social,* Instituto de Estudios Social Cristianos Lima, 1:2013, 41-50.

19 Baggio, F. and A. Brazal (2009) available at http://www.academia.edu/17726200/Faith_on_the_Move, xii.

these laborers, the prevention of injustices in accordance with Mosaic law (Deut. 6:20-25) and the treatment of the poor, alienated and the marginalized, is a litmus test of where a person is in relation to the God before whom we all are accountable (Lev.25; James 2:1-7). As victims of poverty, exploitation, and human trafficking (Prov. 22:22-23), the tragic stories of migrant laborers highlights the moral response to be stirred up and to be outraged at the dehumanizing way in which they have oftentimes been treated even as it reminds us too of our Christian responsibility to protect them (Ps. 82:3-4) and to care for their needs, both materially and spiritually (Exod. 22:21; 23:9; Deut. 10:19; 14:28-29; 15:4; 23:7; 26:12; Luke 12:13-34; 16:19-31).

Corollary to these must be an interrogation of the moral defensibility of forced conjugal separation (as an odious requirement for migrant labor) and its deleterious effects on individuals, families, and cultural values. For it is clear that the biblical norms pertaining to marriage and family life do not condone nor tolerate this practice (Gen. 2:15, 18; Song of Sol. 1:5-6; 4:1-7; Matt.19:4-5). Although the plight of the migrant laborer is oftentimes heart-rending, it does call for an informed and compassionate response, together with a practical, evangelistic concern for the well-being of those who, on account of their disenfranchised and marginalized location in our society, often escape our attention and care (Palmer, P.N. in Atkinson, D.J. and David H. Field 1995, 591-3).

Considering the stark phenomenological realities posed by migration and diasporas in the context of globalization, urbanization, and pluralism, is there a compelling narrative for the *Missio Dei* and the Gospel of Christ as we move inexorably towards the end of history? In the ebb and flow of history, can we detect God's redemptive purpose in the diaspora and migration of peoples across national borders? The answer from His Story in Scripture is certainly affirmative! From the anthropological, hamartiological, and eschatological perspectives, to the extent that the sinfulness of man finds concrete expression through political conflicts and conflagrations that have resulted in wars within, between, and among nations (Mark 13:6-8), the migration of people and the diasporas that follow in its wake can be viewed therefore, as an inexorable part and parcel of the eschatological fabric, as it evokes the signs of the end times. Interestingly, migration and diasporas could lend support to Huntington's (2007) hypothesis that "the fundamental source of conflict in this new world will not be primarily ideological or primarily economic. The great divisions among human kind and the dominating source of conflict will be cultural" (Huntington 1993, 22). He then claims that "the principal conflicts of global politics will occur between nations and groups of different civilizations. The clash of civilizations will dominate global politics. The fault lines between civilizations will be the battle lines of the future" (Huntington op.cit.). The continuing saga of the migration of peoples across the globe and their associated diasporas as a "driving factor" behind globalization, urbanization, and pluralism does play a major role in the ensuing global social, political, and economic ferment and changes (e.g., migration crises and Islamophobia in western Europe and around the world, the furious debate over the orientation and direction of migration and immigration policy in the US and the European Union) that color the prevailing *Weltanschauung* of our time.

Ecclesiological, missiological, eschatological and pastoral perspectives on the diaspora phenomenon as it interfaces with globalization, urbanization and pluralism

In propounding the following questions, my intention is to explore, however tentative and preliminary it may be, some issues that future evangelical researchers may want to further pursue:

SOME PRACTICAL ECCLESIOLOGICAL QUESTIONS:

What should be the response of the Body of Christ (as it considers the gargantuan ecclesiological task posed by Christ's Great Commission in Matt. 28:18-20) at the international, regional, national, and local levels to the phenomena of diasporas and migration as it interfaces with urbanization, pluralism, and religious extremism in a postmodern and globalized world? If the church of Christ has been found wanting and unprepared to meet these challenges posed by global migration and diasporas, how then can we better mobilize and equip God's people in our local churches so that these churches can meaningfully relate and respond wisely to the far reaching implications of diasporas and migration occurring in the context of relentless urbanization, relativizing pluralism, and violent religious extremism in a postmodern, secularized, and globalized world?

A CRUCIAL MISSIOLOGICAL QUESTION:

What does the phenomenon of diaspora (as it interfaces with urbanization, pluralism, and religious extremism in a globalized world) imply for the *Missio Dei* and the Great Commission? De Young, K. and G. Gilbert (2011) argues that the mission of the Church can only be addressed when it grapples with social justice concerns, even as Shalom can never be fully achieved and realized without the Church ensuring that the Great Commission is likewise pursued in obedience to God's mandate. Considering the missiological reality that "those who were scattered went everywhere preaching the Word" (Acts 8:4), could it be that God has, in His sovereignty, allowed the extensive scattering (and sometimes the unspeakable suffering) of His migrant people to enable them to be bearers of the Gospel message to the furthest corners of the earth? Acts 17:16-29 unequivocally implies that He not only "uses" the "diasporas," but also designs, conducts, and employs these for His own glory, the edification of His people, and the salvation of the lost (Lausanne Diaspora Leadership Team 2010, 12). Diasporas then are a missional means sovereignly decreed and blessed by God (Gen. 1:28; 9:1; 12:3; 28:14) under His supreme rule in order to promote the furtherance of His Kingdom and the fulfillment of God's global plan for worldwide missions, otherwise known as the Great Commission (Matt. 24:14; 28:17-20).

Missiologically, the factual realities posed by the migration and diaspora related data and information sets in this paper will hopefully prompt a more rigorous rethinking and prayerful consideration of whether the missiological and missions resources currently deployed by the worldwide Body of Christ are being used wisely and optimally in reaching those who have yet to hear the glorious Gospel of the Lord Jesus. Strategies, policies, plans, programs, projects, and activities for addressing where these migration and diaspora groups and communities are throughout the world will hinge on ascertaining which of these groups and communities have not yet been reached with the Gospel or have had very little exposure to the dissemination of the Good News.

Given resource constraints in terms of Gospel outreach to these communities, there may be a significant need to prioritize which of these regions, countries, groups, and communities have to be ministered to over time. Or, if these groups and communities are in countries that have local Christian churches, encouraging such churches to begin considering creative and Spirit-led ways and initiatives to effectively witness and minister to these groups and communities (especially marginalized ethnic diaspora groups that desperately need help, e.g., refugees, genuine asylum seekers fleeing persecution or political conflicts) in partnership with other stakeholders (such as concerned parachurch organizations) may be a viable option worth exploring. At a more personal and soteriological level, viewing migrants as liminal persons (whose migrant experiences are characterized by ambiguity and uncertainty) could result in a critical rethinking of old, sinful behavioral attitudes and patterns that have been exposed by the Holy Spirit. Through the unique migrant diaspora experience of being removed from the security and comfort of their original homeland, migrants oftentimes experience a spiritual crisis that lowers their resistance to the proclamation of the Gospel into their life and increases their receptivity to the Spirit-led conviction and radical life-changing transformation that God desires.

Should we then attach (or should we read) some missiological or divine significance to the fact that the Judeo-Christian percentage of the people alive today who have migrated is higher than that of any religious group on the face of the earth? God in His sovereignty has allowed or has made it possible that the Judeo-Christian percentage of the people alive today who have migrated is certainly higher than that of any religious group. This represents a strategic missiological opportunity that cannot be missed in terms of how this interfaces with the fulfilment of the Great Commission so that the overarching interests of God's kingdom can be better served. It is therefore incumbent upon the worldwide church of Christ as to wisely ascertain, discern, and determine how it will seize this opportunity to then work out how the church can mobilize these migrant believers in reaching out to migrants of other faith groups and to serve as Christ's witnesses in the increasingly secular, postmodern, and pluralistic destination countries that God has brought them to. What this means at a more practical and operational level, especially where the local churches get to interact with these migrant believers, will have to be prayerfully worked out as the local church discerns what the Holy Spirit would have them do to fulfill God's purpose and design in reaching out to the multitudes of scattered peoples living in the midst of the communities and neighborhoods that the Lord has placed them in.

SOME CRITICAL ESCHATOLOGICAL QUESTIONS:

Are the multifaceted phenomena of diaspora, globalization, urbanization, pluralism, and religious extremism in our time a reflection of the cosmic struggle between good and evil, not just in the seen world but in the heavenlies during these end times? How should we view then the phenomena of diasporas and migration as it interfaces with urbanization, pluralism, and religious extremism in a globalized world given the imminence of Christ's Second Coming (Matt. 24:3-14) and the eventual triumph of good over evil (referencing the eschatological clarion call echoed in Rev. 12:7-17)? Do war and violence with diasporas, urbanization, and pluralism occurring altogether in the context of a globalized world to be seen as signs of the imminence of Christ's Second Coming and the end of this age? If evil seems to currently triumph when we look at sporadic and unpredictable elements of global migration and diasporas as it interfaces with globalization, urbanization, pluralism, and religious extremism...God's assurance is that His coming judgment will eventually vanquish evil for good and that His righteousness will be supremely triumphant.

INTERROGATING OUR PASTORAL IMPERATIVE:

How can we better shepherd (and minister to) God's people at the local church level in the face of both the negative and positive aspects of the diasporas as it interfaces with urbanization, pluralism, and religious extremism in a postmodern and globalized world? There is then a great need for ensuring that the normative mandate for the Body of Christ for undertaking the Great Commission in our generation is truly attuned and responsive to the profound realities and far-reaching consequences and impacts posed by the migration of people and their dispersion into diasporas on the national and global polity, economy, society, and culture. If the facts, figures and information sets presented here in this paper and compendium can be considered as a modest contribution to the process of rethinking, reconsidering, and recalibrating missiological, missions and evangelistic priorities and resources, it is hoped that this initiative can be a meaningful contribution to the careful and wise planning, strategizing and implementing of plans, programs, projects, and activities geared towards reaching these significant migration and diaspora groups and communities with the Good News of Jesus Christ while operationalizing what Christ would have us do to fulfil His Great Commission.

A concluding note

A prime implication of the creative integration of migration and diaspora research with missiological study is the rethinking, reconsideration, and reformulation of "traditional missions theory" (Smith, C. in Moreau 2000, 642-3) into "diaspora missions" as a new providential strategy for traditional missions to be reoriented into diaspora missions and missiology (Tira and Wan 2009). Such diaspora missions and missiology can then be instrumental in ushering us into a transformed, Spirit–led ministry to these "peoples on the move" scattered by God amongst the nations, as we move inexorably towards the end of His redemptive Story when He gathers His people back to Himself.

It is hoped that these modest efforts will help lay the groundwork for the effective cooperation, coordination, and the focusing of those who are at the forefront in working for the Gospel amongst the "peoples on the move." These will also include those who are in the urbanizing areas and megacities, as well as those who are in multicultural ministries tasked with communicating the Gospel in a pluralistic, globalized, and post-modern world. As the wide-ranging implications of global migrations and diasporas become clearer, it should help pave the way for facilitating the planning and implementation of integrated and unified mission, and evangelistic strategies for effectively reaching out to the various "peoples on the move" with the Gospel as God's dynamic power for total human salvation.

May the Church of Christ at this crucial juncture in human history be emphatically prophetic in delineating the profound implications of diasporas in global migration and applying the insights and lessons that the Lord would have us here! May the Spirit truly galvanize the global Body of Christ in taking concrete action on the whole suite of issues, concerns, and challenges that flow from the migration of peoples and their diaspora into the various nations even as we remember that God accompanies us in all our migrant journeys while awaiting Jesus' Second Coming!

May the Triune God grant us His divine wisdom, His insightful discernment, leading guidance, and unerring direction as we ponder over and reflect upon the Kingdom meaning and significance of these phenomenological realities involved in the global migration and diasporas! As we prayerfully study, meditate, and reflect upon His Word, may He imbue us with His zeal, His mercy, His compassion, and a fresh determination to then carry out and accomplish His good, pleasing, acceptable, and perfect will for such a Time as this!

Diaspora

Wheat among the Weeds
Diaspora out in the world
From the tabernacle to synagogues
from the sanctuary to the end of time
the believers, the chosen
living side by side
the lost and the last
those who will be gathered up
and those for the flames
the unquenchable fire
at the end of the age
before the rise
the full flowering
of the kingdom

Raymond A. Foss

For Discussion

1. Define the terms migration, emigration, immigration, and diaspora and discuss their phenomenological significance in shaping world history, society, culture, and religion.
2. What are some of the underlying causes of migration and diasporas in terms of "push" and "pull" factors?
3. As crucial phenomena that drive globalization, pluralism, and the propagation of religious faith systems and traditions, what do migration and diasporas signify and imply for the *Missio Dei*?

Bibliography

African Diaspora for Change [Website]. Accessed at http://ad4change.org/african-diaspora-maps/

Atkinson, D. and D. Field, eds. (1995) "Migrant Labor" in *New Dictionary of Christian Ethics and Pastoral Theology*. Downers Grove, Illinois: Intervarsity Press.

Baggio, F. and A. Brazal, eds. (2009) *Faith on the Move: Toward A Theology of Migration in Asia*. Manila: Ateneo De Manila University Press.

Baines, Dudley. *Emigration from Europe 1815-1930*. London: Macmillan; 1991.

Bharadwaj, Prashant and Asim Khwaja, Atif Mian. "The Big March: Migratory flows after the partition of India." *Economic and Political Weekly*. August 30, 2008. At http://www.hks.harvard.edu/fs/akhwaja/papers/Big%20March%20EPW%20Publish08.pdf. Accessed December 29, 2015.

Black, R. (1998) "Forced Migration and Environmental Change: The Evidence," Chapter 2 in *Refugees, Environment and Development*. New York: Addison Wesley Longman.

Bovell, Carlos R. (Spring 2007) "Husserl's Phenomenological Reduction and the Exclusion of God" in *Westminster Theological Journal* WTJ 69:1.

Carroll, R. and M. Daniel, "The Challenge of Economic Globalization for Theology: From Latin America to a Hermeneutics of Responsibility" in *Globalizing Theology: Belief and Practice in an Era of World Christianity*, ed. C. Ott and H. Netland (Grand Rapids: Baker, 2006), 199–212.

Central Intelligence Agency (2009) *The World Factbook 2008*. https://www.cia.gov/library/ publications/the-world-factbook/.

Conn, Harvie M. (2002) *The Urban Face of Mission: Ministering The Gospel in a Diverse and Changing World*. Phillipsburg: Presbyterian and Reformed Publishing

Curtin, P.D. (1969) *The Atlantic Slave Trade: A Census*. Madison: University of Wisconsin Press; 268.

DeParle, Jason (26 June 2010). "Global Migration: A World Ever More on the Move." *The New York Times*. Accessed at http://www.nytimes.com/2010/06/27/weekinreview/27deparle.html?_r=0/

De Young, K. and G. Gilbert (2011) *What is the Mission of the Church? Making Sense of Social Justice, Shalom and the Great Commission*. Wheaton: Crossway.

Douglas, R. M. (2012) Orderly and Humane: The Expulsion of the Germans after the Second World War. New Haven: Yale University Press.

Ember, M., C. Ember and I. Skoggard, eds. (2005) *Encyclopedia of Diasporas: Immigrant and Refugee Cultures around the World*. Volume 1: Overviews and Topics; Volume 2: Diaspora Communities. Springer.

Economist, 2012, *World in Figures*, London. The Economist Intelligence Unit.

Economist (19 April 2014) "The abuse of migrants: balancing the interests of migrant workers and the countries they live in" *Encyclopedia Britannica* (2009) Digital Edition.

Friedman, Thomas (2003) *Longitudes and Attitudes: The World in the Age of Terrorism*. New York: Anchor.

Friedman, Thomas (2012) *The Lexus and the Olive Tree: Understanding Globalization, 2nd ed.* London: Picador.

Friedman, Thomas L. (2005) *The World is Flat: A Brief History of the Twenty-First Century*. New York: Farrar, Straus and Giroux.

Frontex (2014) *Annual Risk Analysis 2014*. Warsaw: Risk Analysis Unit. frontex.ruropa.eu/ assets/Publications/Risk_Analysis/Annual_Risk_Analysis_2014.pdf

Global Commission on International Migration.2005. "Migration in an interconnected world: new directions for action". *A Report of the Global Commission on International Migration*. October 2005.

Groody, Daniel G. "Catholic Social Teaching and Migration: 1 Perspectives from the US-Mexico Border" in *Review: Pensamiento Social*, Instituto de Estudios Social Cristianos, Lima, 1:2013, 41-50. http://ordosocialis.de/pdf/Groody/ Catholic_Social_Teaching _and_Migration.pdf, 7. Accessed January 10, 2016.

Harvey, David (1990) *The Condition of Postmodernity*. Oxford: Blackwell.

Harvey, T. (2013) "Pluralism, Multiculturalism and Diaspora Mission: Discovering the Relevance of Apostolic Mission Today" (115-134) in Tira, S. *The Human Tidal Wave: Global Migration, Megacities, Multiculturalism, Diaspora Missiology*. Manila: Lifechange Publishing.

Hewitt, Joseph, Jonathan Wikenfield and Ted Robert Gurr, eds. (2009) *Peace and Conflict* 2010. Paradigm Publishers.

Huntington, S. P. (1996) *The Clash of Civilizations and the Remaking of the World Order*. New York: Simon and Schuster.

International Association for Refugees, "Map of the Refugee Highway" at http://www.iafr.org/toolbox/map-of-the-highway. Accessed December 29, 2015.

Jenkins, Philip (2002) *The Next Christendom: The Coming of Global Christianity*. New York: Oxford University Press.

Jenkins, Philip (2008) *God's Continent: Christianity, Islam, and Europe's Religious Crisis*. Oxford: Oxford University Press.

Johnson, Todd M., ed. (Sept 2014) *World Christian Database*. Leiden, Netherlands: Brill.

Johnstone, Patrick (2011). *The Future of the Global Church: History, Trends and Possibilities*. Colorado Springs, CO: Biblica.

Kerr, Amber (2010) "Displaced Persons and Refugees", 316-318 in *Encyclopedia of Global Warming* (Dutch, S., ed.). Pasadena: Salem Press.

Kapur, Devesh and John Mchale (2005) *The Global Migration of Talent: What does it mean for Developing Countries? A CGD Brief*. Center for Global Development (CGD), Washington, D.C., October 2005. Available at www.cgdeve.org/sites/default/files/4473_file_Global_Hunt_for_Talent_Brief.pdf

Knox, Paul and Salle A. Marston (2001). *Places and Regions in Global Context: Human Geography*. New Jersey: Prentice Hall.

Lausanne Diaspora Leadership Team (2010). *Scattered to Gather: Embracing the Global Trend of Diaspora*. Manila: Lifechange Publishing.

Layton-Henry, Zig. "Great Britain" in Hammar, Tomas, Editor. *European Immigration Policy: A Comparative Study*. Cambridge: Cambridge University Press; 1985.

Martin, Philip.2005. "Migrants in the global labor market", a paper prepared for the Policy Analysis and Research Programme of the Global Commission on International Migration. September 2005.

McLuhan, Marshall. (2011 edition) *The Gutenberg Galaxy*. Toronto: University of Toronto Press.

Merriam-Webster, I. (2003) *Merriam-Webster's Collegiate Dictionary*. (11th ed.). Springfield, MA: Merriam-Webster, Inc.

Moreau, Scott, ed. (2000) *Evangelical Dictionary of World Missions*. Grand Rapids: Baker Books.

Muck, T. and F. Adeney (2009) *Christianity Encountering World Religions: The Practice of Mission in the Twenty First Century*. Grand Rapids: Baker Academic.

National Geographic: "The Genographic Project." https://genographic.nationalgeographic.com

National Intelligence Council (2012) *Global Trends 2030: Alternative Worlds*. Washington, DC.

New York Times (June 27, 2010)

Norton, William (2013). *Human Geography*. Oxford: Oxford University Press.

Palmer, P.N. in Atkinson, D.J. and David H. Field (1995). "Migrant Labor" in *New Dictionary of Christian Ethics and Pastoral Theology* (591-593). Leicester, England and Downers Grove, Illinois: Intervarsity Press.

Passell, Henley, Len Malczynski, Marissa Reno and Daniel Villa (November 2012). *Human Ecology, Resilience and Security in 2030*. New Mexico: Sandia National Laboratories.

Pew Research Center (2010) *Global Religion and Migration Database*.

Pew Research Center (March 8, 2012) *Faith on the Move-The Religious Affiliation of International Migrants*. www.pewforum.org/2012/03/08/religious-migration-exec/

Pew Research Center (December 17, 2013) *Changing Patterns of Global Migration and Remittances: More Migrants in US and Other Wealthy Countries; More Money to Middle Income Countries*. www.pewsocial trends.org/2013/12/17/changing-patterns-of-global-migration-and-remittances/.

Remigio, A. (2013) "Global Migrations and Diasporas: A Geographical Perspective" (1-65) in Tira, S., ed. *The Human Tidal Wave: Global Migration, Megacities, Multiculturalism, Diaspora Missiology*. Manila: Lifechange Publishing.

Reuveny, Rafael "Climate Change-Induced Migration and Violent Conflict", *Political Geography 26* (2007):656-73.

Sheffer, Gabriel.2003. *Diaspora Politics (At Home Abroad)*. Cambridge: Cambridge University Press.

Seim, B. (2013) "Diaspora and the Megacities" (67- 114) in Tira, S.,ed. *The Human Tidal Wave: Global Migration, Megacities, Multiculturalism, Diaspora Missiology*. Manila: Lifechange Publishing.

Smith, C. (2000) "Missions Theory" (642-3), in Moreau, S. ed. *Evangelical Dictionary of World Missions*. Grand Rapids: Baker Books.

Stark, R. (2011) *The Triumph of Christianity: How the Jesus Movement became the World's Largest Religion*. New York: Harper One.

Strauss, Stephen (October 2012) "The Purpose of Acts and the Mission of God" in *Bibliotheca Sacra BSAC* 169:676.

Terry, John M (Summer 2011) "The Growth of Christianity in East Asia" in *Southern Baptist Journal of Theology* SBJT 15:2.

Tennent, Timothy C. (2010) *Invitation to World Missions: A Trinitarian Missiology for the Twenty- First Century*. Grand Rapids: Kregel.

Tira, S. and E. Wan (June 12-13, 2009) "Filipino experience in diaspora missions: a case study of Christian communities in contemporary contexts," Commission VII: Christian Communities in Contemporary Contexts, Edinburgh.

Tira, S. and E. Wan (2013) "Diaspora Missiology and Missions in the Context of the 21st Century" (151-164) in Tira, S., ed. *The Human Tidal wave: Global Migration, Megacities, Multiculturalism, Diaspora Missiology*. Manila: Lifechange Publishing.

United Nations, Department of Economic and Social Affairs, Population Division (2013). International Migration Report 2013.

United Nations, Department of Economic and Social Affairs, Population Division (2013). World Population Prospects: The 2012 Revision, DVD Edition.

United Nations High Commission for Refugees (2008) *Climate Change, Natural Disasters and Human Displacement: A UNHCR Perspective.* Geneva: UNHCR.

United Nations High Commissioner for Refugees, "Figures at a Glance" at http://www.unhcr.org/pages/49c3646c11.html. Accessed December 29, 2015.

United Nations International Migration Report, 11, "Global Trends" in *Net International Migration* 1950-2010.

Walters, Jeff K. (Summer 2011) "Looking to a City: Current Themes in Urban Missions" in *Southern Baptist Journal of Theology* SBJT 15:2.

Wan, Enoch (2007). "Diaspora Missiology," in *Occasional Bulletin* (Spring 2007); 3-4, www.emsweb.org.

Wan, Enoch, ed. (2014) *Diaspora Missiology: Theory, Methodology and Practice, 2nd ed.* Portland: Institute of Diaspora Studies, Western Seminary.

Widmaier, S. and J. C. Dumont (2006). *Are Recent Immigrants Different? A New Profile of Immigrants in the OECD based on the Database on Immigrants in OECD Countries 2005/06*. Brussels: OECD.

Winter, Bruce W. (NA 1990) "Theological and Ethical Responses to Religious Pluralism-1 Corinthians 8-10" in *Tyndale Bulletin* TYNBUL 41:2.

Winters, Ralph D. (2004) "Endorsements" in Pantoja Jr., Luis, Tira, S., and Wan, E., eds. *Scattered: The Filipino Global Presence.* Manila: LifeChange Publishing.

World Bank. (1948) *Postwar international migration agreements*. Washington, DC: World Bank. http://documents.worldbank.org/curated/en/1948/04/2872049/postwar-international-migration-agreements . Accessed December 29, 2015.

Wright, Christopher J. H. (Summer 2011) "Truth with A Mission: Reading All Scripture Missiologically" in *Southern Baptist Journal of Theology* SBJT 15:2.

Ybarrola, S. (2013) "Diasporas and Multiculturalism: Social Ideologies, Liminality and Cultural Identity" (135-149) in Tira, S., ed. *The Human Tidal Wave: Global Migration, Megacities, Multiculturalism, Diaspora Missiology*. Manila: Lifechange Publishing.

2. MIGRATION, DIASPORAS AND DIVERSITY: A DEMOGRAPHIC APPROACH

Gina A. Zurlo

Movement of peoples worldwide was a distinguishing characteristic of the twentieth century, and continues to be prominent in the twenty-first.[1] Migrants significantly impact the lands in which they settle in a variety of ways, including local economics, politics, social structures, and even religion. In some cases, migrants bring an entirely new religion into a country or region; in other cases, they import a new form of an existing religion. Such movement creates what is called here "religionists in diaspora" or "religious diasporas."[2] Although some religious diasporas have had a lengthy history, many have expanded around the world in recent decades, such as the growing Muslim populations in Western Europe. Diasporas also have an impact on religious diversity by introducing variety into the religious demographics of countries and regions.

---

1 A preliminary version of this chapter was first published as Todd M. Johnson and Gina A. Bellofatto, "Immigration, Religious Diasporas, and Religious Diversity: A Global Survey," *Mission Studies* 29 (2012): 1–20. Its findings were also presented as a case study in Todd M. Johnson and Brian J. Grim, *The World's Religions in Figures: An Introduction to International Religious Demography* (Oxford: Wiley-Blackwell, 2013). The United Nations estimates that the number of international migrants is now over 200 million, having doubled in the past 25 years, with 25 million added in the first five years of the twenty-first century. See United Nations, "Report to the Secretary-General, International Migration and Development, UN General Assembly, 60th Session," *UN* Doc. A/60/871, May 18, 2006 (New York: United Nations, 2006).

2 Robin Cohen, *Global Diasporas: An Introduction* (Seattle: University of Washington Press, 1997), 26. Cohen identifies nine common features of a diaspora which have particular relevance to this study on religious diasporas: (1) Dispersal from an original homeland, often traumatically, to two or more foreign regions; (2) alternatively, the expansion from a homeland in search of work, in pursuit of trade or to further colonial ambitions; (3) a collective memory and myth about the homeland, including its location, history, and achievements; (4) an idealization of the putative ancestral home and a collective commitment to its maintenance, restoration, safety, and prosperity, even to its creation; (5) the development of a return movement that gains collective approbation; (6) a strong ethnic group consciousness sustained over a long time and based on a sense of distinctiveness, a common history, and the belief in a common fate; (7) a troubled relationship with host societies, suggesting a lack of acceptance at the least or the possibility that another calamity might befall the group; (8) a sense of empathy and solidarity with co-ethnic members in other countries of settlement; and (9) the possibility of a distinctive creative, enriching life in host countries with a tolerance for pluralism.

In order to attempt a quantitative study of religious diasporas and religious diversity, three things need to be in place: (1) a taxonomy of the world's peoples; (2) a taxonomy of the world's religions; and (3) a data collection mechanism by which information related to peoples and religions can be assessed. Taxonomies of the world's peoples and religions exist, and vast efforts are put into the collection of statistics relating to religions, languages, and peoples in today's world.[3] Utilizing the taxonomies of religions and peoples from the World Christian Database (WCD) and World Religion Database (WRD), a preliminary examination of religious diasporas shows 316 million people (4.3% of the world's population) from 485 peoples in diasporas around the world. Quantitative analysis of migration in the context of demography – births, deaths, conversions in, conversions out, immigration, and emigration – provides a comprehensive view of changes in religious diasporas.

Religious freedom

The starting point in any analysis of religious adherence is the United Nations' 1948 Universal Declaration of Human Rights, Article 18: "Everyone has the right to freedom of thought, conscience and religion; this right includes freedom to change his religion or belief, and freedom, either alone or in community with others and in public or private, to manifest his religion or belief in teaching, practice, worship and observance."[4] Since its promulgation, this statement has been incorporated into the state constitutions of many countries, with some even instructing their census personnel to observe this principle. If a person claims to be a Christian, Muslim, Hindu, Buddhist, Sikh, Jew, or affiliated with any other religious group, then no one has a right to say that he or she is not.[5] The Declaration

---

3 The Center for the Study of Global Christianity at Gordon-Conwell Theological Seminary (South Hamilton, Massachusetts) collates and analyzes data on church membership and evangelistic activities collected around the world by Christian denominations, as well as demographics on all the world's religions and their various traditions. Combining these with other relevant data, the Center provides information on global Christianity and religion available to various constituents (religious and otherwise) for research and strategic planning. These data are updated quarterly in Todd M. Johnson, ed. World Christian Database (Leiden, Netherlands: Brill, 2007) and Todd M. Johnson and Brian J. Grim, eds., *World Religion Database* (Leiden, Netherlands: Brill, 2008).

4 The full text of the UN resolution can be found in Paul M. Taylor, *Freedom of Religion: UN and European Human Rights Law and Practice* (Cambridge: Cambridge University Press, 2005), 368–72.

5 An interesting development in a postmodern context is the need to introduce the category "doubly-counted" or "doubly-professing," becoming popularly known as "multiple religious belonging." See Peter Phan, *Being Religious Interreligiously: Asian Perspectives on Interreligious Dialogue* (Maryknoll, NY: Orbis Books, 2004); Catherine Cornille, *Many Mansions? Multiple Religious Belonging and*

has since been distributed in more than 330 languages and serves as the basis for numerous other international human rights declarations, including the 1981 Declaration on the Elimination of All Forms of Intolerance and of Discrimination Based on Religion or Belief.[6] Such public declaration or profession must be taken seriously to ensure a proper functioning of society on multiple levels, not simply in the sphere of religion. Despite the critical importance of religious freedom, however, until 2009 there was no quantitative study that extensively reviewed the sources reporting on how governmental and other actors infringe on the practice of religion worldwide.[7]

Data sources

The collection of data on religion is largely uncoordinated between scholars and uneven across religious traditions, although a wealth of information is available for religious statistical analysis. Starting from the third essential item listed above (a data collection mechanism allowing for the updating of information related to peoples and religions), there are two major sources of information on religious diasporas: data collected by religious communities and censuses taken by governments.

Data collected by religious communities

Most religious communities keep some type of record of their members, ranging from simple lists to elaborate membership reports. The most detailed data collection and analysis are undertaken each year by some 41,000 Christian denominations and their 3.6 million constituent churches and congregations of believers. The latter invest over 1.1 billion USD annually for a massive, decentralized, and largely uncoordinated global census of Christians.[8] This dispersed collection of data provides a year-by-

---

Christian Identity (Maryknoll, NY: Orbis Books, 2002); and Paul F. Knitter, *Without Buddha I Could not be a Christian* (Oxford: OneWorld Publications, 2009).

6 For more information, see Brian J. Grim and Roger Finke, "Religious Persecution in Cross-National Context: Clashing Civilizations or Regulated Economies?" *American Sociological Review* 72:4 (2007): 633–58; Brian J. Grim and Roger Finke, *The Price of Freedom Denied: Religious Persecution and Violence in the 21st Century* (New York: Cambridge University Press, 2011).

7 See the Pew Research Center's Pew Forum on Religion & Public Life, *Global Restrictions on Religion*, December 16, 2009, http://pewresearch.org/pubs/1443/global-restrictions-on-religion; and Rising Restrictions on Religion, August 9, 2011, http://www.pewforum.org/Government/Rising-Restrictions-on-Religion.aspx.

8 In sum, they send out around 10 million questionnaires in 3,000 different languages, covering 180 major religious subjects and reporting on 2,000 socio-religious variables.

year snapshot of the progress or decline of Christianity's diverse movements, offering an enormous body of data from which researchers can track trends and make projections.[9] In a similar way, other religious communities also record members or adherents.

Government censuses

At the same time, many of the world's governments collect information on religious populations. In the twentieth century, approximately half of the world's countries asked a question related to religion in their official national population censuses.[10] In addition, most censuses include data on languages spoken in the home, country of origin, and ethnic background, providing further clues on the religious profile in a given country. National censuses are the best starting point for the identification of religious adherents because they generally cover the entire population. Governments typically take major population censuses around the end of every decade, and then take three to five years to publish the complete data. Obtaining these data every ten years enables the calculation of relatively accurate growth rates, which includes targeting the large-scale movement of religious and ethnic communities.

Resolving apparently contradictory data

Sometimes, the results from these two methods (government censuses and data collection by religious entities) can be strikingly different. In Egypt, for example, where the vast majority of the population is Muslim, elaborate government censuses taken every 10 years for the last 100 years indicate that some 6% of the population declare themselves as or profess to be Christians. However, church censuses reveal the number of individuals

---

9 The Roman Catholic Church performs the most extensive of these inquiries, wherein each year all Roman Catholic bishops are required to answer a 21-page schedule in Latin and one other culturally relevant language asking 140 statistical questions concerning their work in the previous 12 months. The results are published every January in *Annuario Pontificio* (Citta del Vaticano: Tipografia Poliglotta Vaticana).

10 This number gradually declined during the second half of the twentieth century, as developed countries increasingly dropped questions on religion as either too controverisal or expensive (in many countries each census costs over 1 million USD per question). As a result, some countries that historically included a religion question have not included the question in their censuses since 1990. This trend appears to be reversing, however. For example, Britain, which produced the world's first national census of religious affiliation (the Compton Census in 1676) – and later a religion question in the national census of 1851 (though none thereafter) – reintroduced the question in their 2000 census as the best way to receive reliable data on non-Christian minorities.

affiliated to churches to be as high as 15% of the population. The reason for the discrepancy appears to be that due to Muslim pressure on the Christian minority, many Christians are recorded in government censuses by enumerators, or record themselves, as Muslims. Both of these sources – religious bodies and governments – must be considered together to understand fully the entire context of religious diasporas.[11]

Taxonomies of religions and peoples

To enumerate religious diasporas, one must first build two taxonomies, one for religions and one for peoples. The World Christian Database and World Religion Database include 18 standard categories for religion.[12] These categories can be applied directly to any people in the world. For example, Mandarin-speaking Han Chinese in China, numbering 878 million in 2015, are estimated to be 46% nonreligious (agnostic and atheist), 22% Chinese folk-religionist, 19% Buddhist, and 12% Christian.

A "peoples" taxonomy must take into account both ethnicity and language. The approach taken in "Ethnosphere" in Part 8 of the World Christian Encyclopedia was to match ethnic codes with language codes, which produced over 13,700 distinct ethnolinguistic peoples.[13] Not all combinations of ethnicity and language are possible, but nevertheless every person in the world can be categorized as belonging to an (mutually exclusive) ethnolinguistic people. For example, there are ethnic Kazaks who speak Kazak as their mother tongue and ethnic Kazaks who speak Russian as their mother tongue. These are two separate ethnolinguistic peoples.

---

11 In practice, another major source of data is scholarly literature that includes surveys conducted by polling organizations, anthropological studies, and studies on a particular religion within a country.

12 These 18 categories are agnostics, atheists, Baha'is, Buddhists, Chinese folk-religionists, Christians, Confucianists, Daoists, Ethnoreligionists, Hindus, Jains, Jews, Muslims, New religionists, Shintoists, Sikhs, Spiritists, and Zoroastrians.

13 The construction of the taxonomy is explained in more detail in David B. Barrett, Todd M. Johnson, Christopher Guidry, and Peter Crossing, *World Christian Trends, AD 30–AD 2200: Interpreting the Annual Christian Megacensus* (Pasadena, CA: William Carey Library Publication, 2003), part 18, "Ethnolinguistics." The ethnic or culture codes are outlined in David B. Barrett, George T. Kurian, and Todd M. Johnson, eds., *World Christian Encyclopedia: A Comparative Survey of Churches and Religions in the Modern World, vol 2: Religions, Peoples, Languages, Cities, Topics* (New York: Oxford University Press, 2001), table 8-1. The languages are listed in WCE, Part 9 "Linguametrics" and are derived from David Dalby, David Barrett, and Michael Mann, *The Linguasphere Register of the World's Languages and Speech Communities*, 2 vols. (Carmarthenshire, Wales: Linguasphere Press, 1999). All are available online at www. worldchristiandatabase.org.

The next step was to determine the religious breakdown of these ethnolinguistic peoples. This work was begun in the 1970s in Africa, where many Christian churches reported the ethnic breakdown of their congregations. Utilizing data gathered by religions and in government censuses, estimates of religious affiliation for all peoples was completed in the mid-1990s and published in World Christian Encyclopedia, 2nd edition. These data continue to be updated and published in the WCD and WRD. The 2009 Atlas of Global Christianity also examined the more populous world religions in terms of their peoples and languages.[14]

Religious diasporas

In order to locate religious diasporas three steps were taken. First, the WCD and WRD taxonomy of peoples was sorted by ethnic and linguistic codes in sequence. Second, a filter was added so that only unique codes that were present in more than two countries were counted. Third, the largest population was designated as being in the home country and all others as diasporas.[15] The results of this method produced the summary statistics found below in Table 1, the religious affiliation of 316 million people living in diasporas (485 peoples), representing 4.3% of the global population. Over half of these (50.2%) of these are Christians, but Chinese folk-religionists have the greatest proportion of adherents in diaspora (56.2%) of all the world's religions. The second most widespread are Zoroastrians (17.4% in diaspora), due to movement from their historic homeland (Iran) abroad (to mostly India and the United States). One interesting observation is that Christians and Muslims together make up 59.6% of the world's population, and represent 74.8% of all people in diaspora.

---

14 See Todd M. Johnson and Kenneth R. Ross, eds., *Atlas of Global Christianity* (Edinburgh: Edinburgh University Press, 2009), part IV.

15 The methodology was updated from the original version of this article. Initially, the largest people was considered the hub country, and all others diaspora. However, there were limitations to this method, evidenced by the Mestizos in Latin America, which were treated as one people even though they are clearly distinct from country to country. Because Mexico has the largest number of Mestizos, it was treated as the home country and all other Mestizos are considered diasporas. Several exceptions were made in the methodology to avoid this limitation. If a people met any of the following three criteria, they were considered in their hub country, not diaspora: (1) Any people over 20% of a country's population; (2) if the people is the first, second, third, or fourth largest in any country and is over 10% of the country's population; and (3) if any group is over 50,000. The earlier method considered peoples living in more than three countries as diaspora; the updated method cut that number down to two. Another exception is Jewish peoples, which, regardless of language, now have only Israel and Palestine as hub, all else diaspora. The results were checked manually and particular adjustments were made either individually or by a series of rules.

Table 1: Religionists in diaspora, mid-2015

Religion	***Global total***	***% of global pop***	***# in diaspora***	***% in diaspora***	***% of all diasporas***
Christians	2,419,221,000	35.0	158,580,000	6.6	50.2
Muslims	1,703,146,000	24.6	77,737,000	4.6	24.6
Hindus	694,823,000	10.0	19,247,000	2.8	6.1
Agnostics	984,532,000	14.2	15,328,000	1.6	4.8
Buddhists	520,002,000	7.5	14,061,000	2.7	4.4
Ethnoreligion ists	260,240,000	3.8	10,619,000	4.1	3.4
Chinese folk-religionists	14,237,000	0.2	7,999,000	56.2	2.5
Atheists	453,868,000	6.6	4,941,000	1.1	1.6
Jews	65,057,000	0.9	2,156,000	3.3	0.7
New religionists	136,444,000	2.0	1,928,000	1.4	0.6
Sikhs	25,208,000	0.4	1,744,000	6.9	0.6
Baha'is	7,920,000	0.1	580,000	7.3	0.2
Confucianists	14,266,000	0.2	464,000	3.3	0.1
Spiritists	8,468,000	0.1	385,000	4.5	0.1
Jains	5,631,000	0.1	241,000	4.3	0.1
Shintoists	2,827,000	0.0	75,900	2.7	0.0
Zoroastrians	196,000	0.0	34,100	17.4	0.0
Taoists	8,696,000	0.1	13,300	0.2	0.0
Global total	**7,324,782,000**	**105.9**	**316,133,300**	**4.3**	**100.0**

Source: Todd M. Johnson, ed. *World Christian Database* (Leiden/Boston: Brill, accessed September 2014).

In 2012 the Pew Research Center's Religion and Public Life Project released a report for the religious makeup of migrants around the world.[16] The report states that about 214 million people (3% of the world's

---

16 *Pew Forum on Religion & Public Life, Faith on the Move: The Religious Affiliation of International Migrants*, March 8, 2012, http://pewresearch.org/pubs/2214/religion-religious-migrants-christians-muslims-jews. This report measures international migrants, which is different than measuring religious diasporas. International migrants are people who have moved from their homeland within that year (that is, more recent migrants). This article takes a longer, historical view in measuring people who have settled out of their homeland (diaspora).

population) migrated across international borders in 2010. Of these migrants, 49% were Christian and 27% Muslim (different from the percentages above, 27.9% for Christians and 13.7% for Muslims). The most significant discrepency between the two reports is Russia. Pew reported that Russia was home to 12 million immigrants, but the method here produces only 6 million. The discrepency is explained by ethnic Russians who were born in Kazakstan and Ukraine who returned to Russia after the breakup of the Soviet Union. These people went home from being in diaspora by the millions, not people who left their homeland to settle elsewhere. This example illustrates how migration also includes a multi-directional phenomena of movement from homelands and back again.

Host and sending countries

Table 2 examines religious diasporas by the country in which they reside. The United States tops the list, hosting over a third of all religious diasporas worldwide (34.2%); many of these are immigrants from Latin American countries, which explains the enormous number of Christians in diaspora there (86.3 million). Likewise, the Pew study cited the United States as the top destination for all migrants, though especially Christians, Buddhists, agnostics, and atheists. Table 2 ranks India second, with 12.7 million people living there in diaspora, but this only represents 1% of the country's population. Most religionists in diaspora in India are Hindus and Muslims, a result of the 1949 partition between India and Pakistan.

Table 2: Top 10 host countries of diasporas ranked by diaspora population, mid-2015

	Country	*Pop 2010*	*Diaspora #*	*Diaspora %*	*Christians*	*Muslims*	*Hindus*	*Buddhists*
1	United States	325,128,000	111,042,000	34.2%	86,317,000	2,129,000	1,513,000	3,968,000
2	India	1,282,390,000	12,731,000	1.0%	405,000	4,151,000	6,029,000	1,044,000
3	France	64,983,000	12,112,000	18.6%	4,810,000	5,256,000	49,100	493,000
4	UK	63,844,000	8,875,000	13.9%	4,112,000	2,599,000	598,000	157,000
5	Germany	82,562,000	6,968,000	8.4%	4,435,000	1,494,000	93,700	40,400
6	China	1,401,587,000	6,935,000	0.5%	1,069,000	1,571,000	15,800	1,696,000
7	Russia	142,098,000	6,679,000	4.7%	2,089,000	3,049,000	31,400	209,000
8	Canada	35,871,000	6,239,000	17.4%	3,174,000	946,000	411,000	412,000
9	Brazil	203,657,000	5,930,000	2.9%	4,210,000	202,000	10,200	510,000
10	Iran	79,476,000	5,746,000	7.2%	142,000	5,422,000	36,400	480

Source: Todd M. Johnson, ed. *World Christian Database* (Leiden/Boston: Brill, accessed September 2014).

Table 3 examines the countries that send out the largest diaspora communities. Mexico tops the list (as it also does in the Pew report), with 40 million people sent abroad; most have ended up across the border in the United States. China is a significant sending country as well, for both Christians (5.6 million) and Buddhists (5.4 million). The largest concentration of Chinese in diaspora is in the United States and Canada. Four countries on the "sending" list also appear on the "host" list: the United States, India, France, and China.

Table 3: Top 10 "sending" countries, ranked by size of diaspora outside of host country, mid-2015

Rank	*Source country*	*Diaspora*	*Christians*	*Muslims*	*Hindus*	*Buddhists*
1	Mexico	40,341,000	39,223,000	0	0	0
2	China	23,968,000	5,651,000	2,508,000	203,000	5,471,000
3	United States	18,637,000	10,582,000	45,200	0	0
4	India	17,541,000	1,174,000	6,008,000	8,150,000	27,900
5	Turkey	7,532,000	209,000	7,151,000	25,600	0
6	Pakistan	7,240,000	53,500	4,038,000	3,076,000	0
7	South Korea	6,618,000	2,997,000	340	0	1,563,000
8	Spain	6,355,000	5,702,000	0	0	0
9	France	6,008,000	3,964,000	200	0	0
10	Poland	5,863,000	5,116,000	0	0	0

Source: Todd M. Johnson, ed. *World Christian Database* (Leiden/Boston: Brill, accessed September 2014).

Peoples in diaspora

Table 4 ranks the ethnolinguistic peoples in diaspora by the number of countries in which they are found. The top four peoples include several that reflect colonial and economic realities: English, French, and USA White (Anglo-Americans). Han Chinese (Mandarin) and Syrian-Arabian Arab (ranked 4 and 6, respectively), are largely spread out as foreign workers and refugees.

Table 4: Top 10 peoples, ranked by number of countries in diaspora, mid-2015

Rank	People name	Total population 2010	# of countries	Diaspora	% in Diaspora	Majority religionists
1	English	53,909,000	173	2,204,000	4.1%	Christians
2	French	33,662,000	139	4,570,000	13.6%	Christians
3	USA White	126,456,000	120	2,444,000	1.9%	Christians
4	Han Chinese (Mandarin)	894,937,000	116	4,481,000	0.5%	Agnostics
5	German	65,543,000	90	3,313,000	5.1%	Christians
6	Syrian-Arabian Arab	35,436,000	86	1,986,000	5.6%	Muslims
7	Greek	13,693,000	85	3,504,000	25.6%	Christians
8	Russian	131,694,000	75	1,664,000	1.3%	Christians
9	Hindi	145,884,000	75	4,864,000	3.3%	Hindus
10	Italian	33,714,000	64	1,815,000	5.4%	Christians

Source: Todd M. Johnson, ed. *World Christian Database* (Leiden/Boston: Brill, accessed September 2014).

Table 5 ranks ethnolinguistic peoples in diaspora by the percentage in diaspora. This ranking reveals a different phenomenon, with many Jewish groups in diaspora, including millions of English-speaking Jews. The Pew study highlighted Jews as having the highest level of international migration, with 25% of all Jews worldwide as migrants (currently living in another country than their birth country). This is significant for a religion that, on a global scale, is rather small (14 million adherents). Not surprisingly, the majority of Jewish migrants originate from Europe (56%, most notably Russia), and migrate primarily to the Middle East (76%, almost entirely to Israel).

Table 5: Top 10 peoples, ranked by percentage in diaspora, mid-2015

Rank	People name	Total pop 2010	# of countries	Diaspora #	% in Diaspora	Majority religion
1	Jewish (English)	5,657,000	32	5,614,000	99.2%	Jews
2	Marrano (Crypto-Jew)	218,000	6	216,000	98.9%	Christians

3	Dutch Jewish	31,500	5	28,400	90.0%	Jews
4	Circassian	909,000	11	783,000	86.2%	Muslims
5	Jewish	552,000	12	457,000	82.8%	Jews
6	Low German	568,000	11	446,000	78.5%	Christians
7	Coloured (Eurasian)	538,000	9	410,000	76.3%	Christians
8	Jewish (Yiddish)	1,642,000	23	1,246,000	75.9%	Jews
9	Sinti Gypsy (Manush)	220,000	14	140,000	63.6%	Christians
10	Hungarian Gypsy	1,691,000	16	1,064,000	62.9%	Christians

Source: Todd M. Johnson, ed. *World Christian Database* (Leiden/Boston: Brill, accessed September 2014).

Religionists in diaspora

Table 6 presents the largest ethnolinguistic diasporas for each of the four largest religious communities: Christians, Muslims, Hindus, and Buddhists. One can quickly see the origins of peoples representing the largest religious diasporas – Christians (Latin Americans and Europeans; though, significantly, also Filipinos and Koreans); Muslims (Asians and Africans); Hindus (South Asians) and Buddhists (East Asians). This is not surprising; the largest diaspora peoples come from the "traditional homelands" of each religion.

Migration as one component of religious change

The dynamics of change in religious communities over time can be limited to three sets of empirical population data: (1) births minus deaths; (2) converts in minus converts out; and (3) immigrants minus emigrants.

Births minus deaths

The primary mechanism of religious change globally is births minus deaths. Children are normally considered to have the religion of their parents (this is the law in Norway, for example, and many other countries). This means that a religious population has a close statistical relationship to the number of births into the community and the number of deaths out of it. Many religious communities around the world, in fact, experience little else in the dynamics of their growth or decline.

Table 6: Top 10 diaspora peoples by religions, mid-2015

Christians		**Muslims**		**Hindus**		**Buddhists**	
People name	*# in diaspora*	*People name*	*# in diaspora*	*People name*	*# in diaspora*	*People name*	*# in diaspora*
Latin American Mestizo	39,223,000	Sylhetti	3,701,000	Hindi	3,486,000	Vietnamese	1,787,000
Polish	5,116,000	Eastern Pathan	2,674,000	Nepalese (Eastern Pahari)	3,314,000	Han Chinese (Yue)	1,591,000
Norwegian	4,814,000	Moroccan Arab	2,544,000	Sindhi	3,076,000	Korean	1,563,000
Portuguese	4,368,000	Urdu	2,542,000	Gujarati	1,731,000	Japanese	1,559,000
Filipino	3,930,000	Persian	2,315,000	Tamil	866,000	Han Chinese (Mandarin)	1,328,000
Spanish	3,702,000	Kazakh	2,181,000	Telugu	672,000	Sinhalese	733,000
French	3,437,000	Northern Kurd	2,079,000	Eastern Punjabi	460,000	Burmese	688,000
Greek	3,316,000	Algerian Arab	1,950,000	Bengali	285,000	Central Thai	659,000
Korean	2,997,000	Turkish Gypsy (Cingane)	1,855,000	Malayali	230,000	Han Chinese (Min Nan)	563,000
Swedish	2,981,000	Tajik	1,713,000	Orisi (Utkali, Vadiya)	159,000	Central Khmer	374,000

Source: Todd M. Johnson, ed. *World Christian Database* (Leiden/Boston: Brill, accessed September 2014).

Converts in minus converts out

Nonetheless, individuals (or even whole villages or communities) often change allegiance from one religion to another (or to no religion at all). In the twentieth century, this change has been most pronounced in two general areas: (1) Ethnoreligionists (tribal religionists) have converted in large numbers to Christianity, Islam, Hinduism, and Buddhism; and (2) Christians in the Western world have become nonreligious (agnostics or atheists) in large numbers. Both of these trends, however, had slowed considerably by the dawn of the twenty-first century. In fact, today's trends point to religious resurgence, with noticeable decreases in the percentages of nonreligious globally.

Immigrants minus emigrants

It is equally important to consider the movement of people across national borders. During the colonial era in the nineteenth century, small groups of Europeans settled in Africa, Asia, and the Americas. In the late twentieth century, natives from these regions immigrated to the Western world. As a result, in the United States religions such as Islam, Hinduism, and Buddhism grew faster than either Christianity or the unaffiliated. This growth has been almost entirely due to the immigration of non-Christian Asians.[17] In Europe, massive immigration of Muslims has not only been transforming the spiritual landscape but has now become a major political issue, notably in France, Germany, Austria, and Italy, as well as in plans for European Union expansion.[18] In the Central Asian countries of the former Soviet Union, Christianity has declined significantly every year since 1990 due to the emigration of Russians, Germans, and Ukrainians.

The reasons underlying immigration and emigration include economic factors (such as seeking employment), social factors (desire for a better quality of life or family considerations), refugee status (escaping political or religious persecution), and environmental factors (such as natural disasters). These may be described in terms of push and pull factors: push factors are the reasons individuals or groups leave (are pushed out of) their home countries, including denial of needs or rights, while pull factors are the reasons people settle in (are pulled to) particular areas. Pull factors may include better economic opportunities, a preferred climate, lower crime rates, or general stability.[19] Thus, diasporas comprise both individuals who have chosen to leave and those who were forced to migrate. Such delineations, however, are not always clear-cut. A Syrian Orthodox Christian in the Middle East who loses his job, cannot find work in his Muslim-majority community, and feels there is no hope at home might migrate elsewhere in search of employment. Depending on the perspective, he could be considered either a political or economic migrant.[20]

In the twenty-first century, migration trends are already altering the religious compositions of individual countries. By 2100 it might be difficult to find a country in which 90% or more of the population belong to any single world religion.

---

17 In the case of Islam, conversions among African-Americans to Islam also caused increased presence.

18 Turkey's desire for European Union membership has brought out the interesting contrast of a Union that is mainly "Christian" with one that could extend to countries not predominantly Christian.

19 Darrell Jackson and Alessia Passarelli, *Mapping Migration: Mapping Churches' Responses: Europe Study* (Brussels: Churches' Commission for Migrants in Europe, 2008), 5–6.

20 Ibid., 9.

Religious diversity

Underlying the reality of a changing global religious landscape is increasing religious diversity. "Religious diversity" actually includes two levels: intra- and inter-religious diversity. Intra-religious diversity encompasses the diversity found within a given world religion (for example, traditions such as Roman Catholicism, Orthodoxy, and Protestantism within Christianity), whereas inter-religious diversity describes the degree of over-all diversity of distinct religions (Islam, Hinduism, Judaism, and so on) in a given population or area. This article focuses primarily on levels of inter-religious diversity.[21] It is important to note when tracking inter-religious diversity that it can vary greatly from one locale to another, even within a particular country, because religious adherents often cluster in local communities. Such is especially the case for nearly any country receiving significant numbers of immigrants and refugees into major metropolitan areas.[22]

Changes in religious diversity from 1910 to 2010

The twentieth century was a transformative time for religion. In general, the world in 2010 was less religious than it was in 1910. In 1910, nearly the entire world claimed adherence to some form of religious belief. By 2010, however, 11.8% of the world's population was either atheist or agnostic. The reasons for this are twofold: the rise of Communism worldwide, and the phenomenon of secularization, particularly in the global North.[23]

---

21 For a complete survey of intra-religious diversity of Christianity, see Johnson and Ross, *Atlas of Global Christianity*, parts II and III.

22 Ibid., 32.

23 Ibid., 6. But note that the percentage of atheists and agnostics has declined since the collapse of Communism in the former Soviet Union. Here, "global North" is defined in geopolitical terms by five current United Nations regions (comprising 53 countries): Eastern Europe (including Russia), Northern Europe, Southern Europe, Western Europe, and Northern America. The United Nations definition also includes Australia and New Zealand, part of the "global South" in this survey.

Table 7. Religious diversity Index (RDI), 1910 and 2010

Continent/region	Population 1910	RDI 1910	Majority religion 1910	Population 2010	RDI 2010	Majority religion 2010
Africa	**124,541,000**	**0.28**	**Ethnoreligionists**	**1,031,084,000**	**0.38**	**Christians**
Eastern Africa	34,658,000	0.31	Ethnoreligionists	342,595,000	0.45	Christians
Middle Africa	19,445,000	0.09	Ethnoreligionists	124,978,000	0.26	Christians
Northern Africa	30,322,000	0.24	Muslims	199,620,000	0.12	Muslims
Southern Africa	6,819,000	0.50	Ethnoreligionists	58,803,000	0.33	Christians
Western Africa	33,296,000	0.37	Ethnoreligionists	305,088,000	0.53	Muslims
Asia	**1,026,693,000**	**0.37**	**Chinese folk**	**4,165,440,000**	**0.53**	**Muslims**
Central Asia	7,550,000	0.07	Muslims	61,694,000	0.23	Muslims
Eastern Asia	554,135,000	0.37	Chinese folk	1,593,571,000	0.79	Agnostics
South Asia	338,168,000	0.36	Hindus	1,681,407,000	0.38	Hindus
South-eastern Asia	93,859,000	0.50	Buddhists	597,097,000	0.41	Muslims
Western Asia	32,982,000	0.26	Muslims	231,671,000	0.13	Muslims
Europe	**427,044,000**	**0.10**	**Christians**	**740,308,000**	**0.36**	**Christians**
Eastern Europe	178,184,000	0.20	Christians	296,183,000	0.29	Christians
Northern Europe	61,473,000	0.04	Christians	98,795,000	0.42	Christians
Southern Europe	76,828,000	0.04	Christians	154,712,000	0.28	Christians
Western Europe	110,558,000	0.03	Christians	190,618,000	0.50	Christians
Latin America	**78,254,000**	**0.09**	**Christians**	**596,191,000**	**0.15**	**Christians**
Caribbean	8,173,000	0.04	Christians	41,625,000	0.27	Christians
Central America	20,806,000	0.02	Christians	160,546,000	0.08	Christians
South America	49,276,000	0.12	Christians	394,021,000	0.16	Christians
Northern America	94,689,000	0.07	Christians	346,501,000	0.38	Christians
Oceania	**7,192,000**	**0.08**	**Christians**	**36,659,000**	**0.41**	**Christians**
Australia/NZ	5,375,000	0.06	Christians	26,773,000	0.51	Christians
Melanesia	1,596,000	0.13	Ethnoreligionists	8,729,000	0.15	Christians
Micronesia	89,400	0.30	Christians	498,000	0.14	Christians
Polynesia	131,000	0.01	Christians	660,000	0.08	Christians
Globe	**1,758,412,000**	**0.27**	**Christians**	**6,916,183,000**	**0.45**	**Christians**

Source: Todd M. Johnson, ed. *World Christian Database* (Leiden/Boston: Brill, accessed September 2014).

Religious Diversity Index (RDI)

The Religious Diversity Index, based upon the Herfindahl Index (used by economists studying market competition), describes the inter-religious diversity of a particular country's or region's population using a scale from 0.0 (no diversity) to 1.0 (most diverse). Calculating measurements on both the country and regional levels provides a "local" perspective of diversity (country-level) as well as a cross-national view of diversity (regional-level). Table 7 shows that between 1910 and 2010, all but six regions in the world experienced increases in both country and regional RDI levels.[24] Some of the greatest regional increases, primarily due to migration, were found in Western Europe (+0.27 points), Australia/New Zealand (+0.42 points), Eastern Asia (+0.34 points), and Northern America (+0.31 points).[25]

Despite significant changes, since 1910 Asia has remained the most religiously diverse continent in the world. In 1910 over 50% of Asia's population was Chinese folk-religionist or Buddhist; today, these two religions together total only 22%. Ethnoreligions declined from 5.6% of the population in 1910 to 3.7% in 2010. These declines were the result of gains by Muslims (from 16.6% to 26.0%) and Christians (2.4% to 8.5%). However, greater gains were made by agnostics (0.0% to 11.8%) and atheists (0.0% to 2.8%), especially in China.

These religious changes in Asia are not entirely surprising considering the inherently pluralistic nature of Asian culture; in a sense to be Asian is to be interreligious.[26] It is also common for Asians to cross national boundaries in search of work, such as the large Indian and Filipino migrant worker communities in various Persian Gulf countries. The World Bank estimates that three million Indonesian women work abroad, primarily in Malaysia and Saudi Arabia, and mostly in domestic work.[27] Increases in religious diversity are particularly apparent in the global North, however, where secularization and immigration continue to transform the religious landscape (see below).

Another way of viewing religious diversity is examining the number of religions representing greater than a given percentage (for example, 0.5%, 5%, or 10%) of the population of a country. Eastern and South-eastern Asia in particular, claim the most diversity. Only Vietnam has six religions over

---

24 The six regions not experiencing an increase in religious diversity in this time period were Northern Africa, Southern Africa, South-eastern Asia, Western Asia, Melanesia, and Micronesia. For more on measuring religious pluralism, see Pippa Norris and Ronald Inglehart, *Sacred and Secular: Religion and Politics Worldwide* (Cambridge: Cambridge University Press, 2004), 100.

25 Johnson and Ross, *Atlas of Global Christianity*, 33.

26 Phan, *Being Religious Interreligiously*, 117, 127.

27 Nisha Varia, "Asia's Migrant Workers Need Better Protection," *Human Rights Watch*, September 2, 2004, http://www.hrw.org/news/2004/08/31/asias-migrant-workers-need-better-protection.

5%,[28] while only South Korea has five different religions numbering over 10% of the population (Buddhism, Christianity, Confucianism, ethnoreligions, and New Religions).[29]

Implications

The movement of peoples, ideas, and cultures across new boundaries has for many societies become the new normal. The implications of increasing religious diasporas and religious diversity are clearly profound. One salient feature of pluralistic societies is the benefit of religious choice: an individual is no longer tied to the religion of his parents or country of birth if adherents of the world's religions are in one's own backyard. The data also support the idea that allowing people to choose faith or no faith does not kill religion. The world has become more religious since 1970, not less: throughout the twentieth century, and continuing today, the vast majority of the world's population, never less than 75%, have been religious. The high point for the world's nonreligious was around 1970 with 23.5% of the global population; today the figure is about 11.8%.

The world faces a monumental task in both obtaining knowledge of and practicing civility toward other religionists. The increase of religious diversity via migration means Christians in the West are increasingly likely to have friends, and even family members, who are members of the world's religions. This calls for a new, deeper level of engagement with these world faiths. However, the reality is that most Christians in the world are out of contact with Muslims, Buddhists, and Hindus (the world's largest religions). In fact, recent research has shown that 86% of these religionists do not personally know a Christian.[30] In the twenty-first century it is important to realize that the responsibility for engaging these religionists is enormous; Muslims, Hindus, and Buddhists are increasingly found living in traditionally "Christian countries."

An important step for cultivating societies of civility[31] is more thorough education in a variety of areas. The first is world religions, including their histories, texts, theologies, and practices. It is difficult to live compassionately toward one's neighbors if little is known about their worldviews, traditions, and beliefs. A 2010 survey by the Pew Research Center's Religion & Public Life Project found that American evangelicals are less knowledgeable about world religions than are atheists, Jews, or Mormons. Evangelicals answered an average of 18 out of 32 questions

28 Viet Nam's six religions over 5% of the population are agnostics, atheists, Buddhists, Christians, ethnoreligionists, and New Religionists.

29 Johnson and Ross, Atlas of Global Christianity, 32.

30 Ibid., 316–17.

31 For more on Christian civility, see Richard J. Mouw, *Uncommon Decency: Christian Civility in an Uncivil World* (Downers Grove, IL: InterVarsity Press, 2010).

about world religions accurately while on average atheists/agnostics, Jews, and Mormons answered more than 20 of 32 correctly.[32] Another important area requiring more education is the situation of the world outside of one's own context. Many of the world's most pressing problems are out of sight from western Christianity in particular – urban poverty, slum settlements, addiction, slavery – and often issues such as these are a stark reality for those in religious diasporas worldwide. A final area requiring new focus is a renewed spirit for hospitality and friendship with adherents of other religions. Knowing and loving one's neighbor is part and parcel to the Christian message, as well as integral to creating a global society welcoming to people and their religions on the move.

For discussion

1. What are some of the problems relating to the accurate collection of religious demographics and what is the likely impact of this for evangelical mission agencies?
2. Christians and Muslims make up 74.8% of all people in diaspora and Christianity and Islam are missionary faiths. What opportunities and challenges might this pose for evangelical Christians in diaspora?
3. If the world is a more religious place today than it was in 1970, accompanied by increasing global religious diversity, what does this mean for evangelicals living in increasingly religious neighbourhoods? Is being a good neighbour incompatible with being an effective witness for Christ?

Bibliography

Annuario Pontificio. Citta del Vaticano: Tipografia Poliglotta Vaticana.

Barrett, David B., Todd M. Johnson, Christopher Guidry, and Peter Crossing. *World Christian Trends, AD 30–AD 2200: Interpreting the Annual Christian Megacensus.* Pasadena, CA: William Carey Library Publication, 2003.

Barrett, David B., George T. Kurian, and Todd M. Johnson, eds. *World Christian Encyclopedia: A Comparative Survey of Churches and Religions in the Modern World.* Vol 2: *Religions, Peoples, Languages, Cities, Topics.* New York: Oxford University Press, 2001.

Cohen, Robin. Global Diasporas: An Introduction. Seattle: University of Washington Press, 1997.

Cornille, Catherine. *Many Mansions? Multiple Religious Belonging and Christian Identity.* Maryknoll, NY: Orbis Books, 2002.

Cox, Harvey G. The Secular City: Secularization and Urbanization in Theological Perspective. New York: Macmillan, 1965.

32 Pew Forum on Religion & Public Life, "U.S. Religious Knowledge Survey."

Dalby, David, David Barrett, and Michael Mann. *The Linguasphere Register of the World's Languages and Speech Communities*. 2 vols. Carmarthenshire, Wales: Linguasphere Press, 1999.

Grim, Brian J., and Roger Finke. *The Price of Freedom Denied: Religious Persecution and Violence in the 21st Century*. New York: Cambridge University Press, 2011.

———. "Religious Persecution in Cross-National Context: Clashing Civilizations or Regulated Economies?" *American Sociological Review 72:*4 (2007): *633–58.*

Jackson, Darrell, and Alessia Passarelli. Mapping Migration: Mapping Churches' Responses: Europe Study. Brussels: Churches' Commission for Migrants in Europe, 2008.

Johnson, Todd M., ed. *World Christian Database.* Leiden, Netherlands: Brill, 2007.

Johnson, Todd M., and Gina A. Bellofatto. "Immigration, Religious Diasporas, and Religious Diversity: A Global Survey." Mission Studies 29 (2012): 1–20.

Johnson, Todd M., and Brian J. Grim. The World's Religions in Figures: An Introduction to International Religious Demography. *Oxford: Wiley-Blackwell, forthcoming.*

Johnson, Todd M., and Brian J. Grim, eds. *World Religion Database.* Leiden, Netherlands: Brill, 2008.

Johnson, Todd M., and Kenneth R. Ross, eds. Atlas of Global Christianity. Edinburgh: Edinburgh University Press, 2009.

Kaufmann, Eric. *Shall the Religious Inherit the Earth? Demography and Politics in the Twenty-First Century*. London: Profile Books Ltd, 2010.

Knitter, Paul F. Without Buddha I Could not be a Christian. Oxford. OneWorld Publications, 2009.

Mouw, Richard J. Uncommon Decency: Christian Civility in an Uncivil World. Downers Grove, IL: InterVarsity Press, 2010.

Norris, Pippa, and Ronald Inglehart. Sacred and Secular: Religion and Politics Worldwide. Cambridge: Cambridge University Press, 2004.

Pew Forum on Religion & Public Life. Faith on the Move: The Religious Affiliation of International Migrants. March 8, 2012. http://pewresearch.org/pubs/2214/religion-religious-migrants-christians-muslims-jews.

———. Global Restrictions on Religion. December 16, 2009. http://pewresearch.org/pubs/1443/global-restrictions-on-religion.

———. Rising Restrictions on Religion. August 9, 2011. http://www.pewforum.org/Government/Rising-Restrictions-on-Religion.aspx.

Phan, Peter. *Being Religious Interreligiously: Asian Perspectives on Interreligious Dialogue.* Maryknoll, NY: Orbis Books, 2004.

Starke, Rodney, and Roger Finke. Acts of Faith: Explaining the Human Side of Religion. Berkeley: University of California Press, 2000.

Taylor, Paul M. *Freedom of Religion: UN and European Human Rights Law and Practice.* Cambridge: Cambridge University Press, 2005.

United Nations, "Report to the Secretary-General, International Migration and Development, UN General Assembly, 60th Session." UN Doc. A/60/871, May 18, 2006. New York: United Nations, 2006.

Varia, Nisha. "Asia's Migrant Workers Need Better Protection." Human Rights Watch, September 2, 2004. http://www.hrw.org/news/2004/08/31/asias-migrant-workers-need-better-protection.

3. Global Agenda – Global Theology? The Regulation of Migration and Global Diasporas

Darrell Jackson

A personal testimony

With my wife and two children, I emigrated from the UK on the 15th February 2012. As we cleared the security gates and entered the departure lounge at Heathrow airport we were approached by a researcher with an *International Passenger Survey* (IPS). We were two of about 750,000 passengers approached for these surveys in 2012, conducted on behalf of the UK's Office for National Statistics. I was mildly excited as I had been directing a Research Centre in the UK for the previous five years and had used IPS data in a number of our research reports.

We arrived in Sydney, Australia, on the 17th February and approached the immigration desk with our Class 457 Temporary Residents' Visas electronically attached to our British passports. The official inspected them carefully, stamped them and announced cheerily 'Welcome to Australia!' He then leant closer and in a quieter voice, whispered 'You're the kind of immigrants we need here.'

It took a short moment for me to realise the implication of what he had said and as I turned to my wife, I noticed the perplexed look on her face mirroring my own feelings at having just experienced positive ethnic discrimination from a Caucasian immigration official. In that moment I was to learn an unforgettable personal lesson concerning several aspects of migration that had been occupying my interest as a missiologist over the previous five to eight years. Taken together, migration, officialdom, bureaucracy, monitoring, and human agency have always provided fertile soil for nurturing prejudice, control, and the exclusion of other human beings considered undesirable; '*Not* the kind of immigrants we want here.'

William Carey and the East India Company

William Carey was probably not the first missionary to have to deal with officialdom, government regulation, and the power of vested interests in trying to migrate, but he certainly felt their combined force. By the time he set sail for India in 1793, Carey was an outspoken critic of the use of slave labour on the sugar plantations of British-owned Jamaica.[1] His declared boycott of sugar, indicative of a campaigning concern for economic and human justice, doubtless attracted the concerned attention of the British East India Company (the '*Company*') whose commercial interests in the Indian colonies were protected by charters awarded them by the British Crown. The *Company* prevented Carey finding passage to India on a British vessel and it was only several months later that he was able to find passage for India on board a Danish ship, the *Kron Princessa Maria*. Carey's successes doubtless rested upon his willingness to research and navigate the regulatory, legal restrictions, and commercial interests of the late eighteenth century. When Carey left for the Bay of Bengal he did so under the protection of the Danish Crown.

Carey's tenacity in the face of the *Company's* stubborn refusal to allow him passage to a new land has been replicated in countless instances since as many tens of thousands of cross-cultural workers engaged in Christian ministry have criss-crossed the globe. A working knowledge of visa regimes, border controls, employment rights, and residency rights continues to be a vital asset in the effective deployment and continuing service of cross-cultural missionaries.

What this chapter seeks to do

The officialdom that Carey faced will be familiar to many individuals living and working in diaspora situations (including those doing so for the sake of Christian mission) and painfully familiar to migration advocates and lawyers located around the globe. Many of these are well informed about the regulations in force in their own country or region of the world. This section of the Compendium cannot hope to exceed their existing expertise or to keep abreast of ongoing and constantly changing legal and regulatory developments. Instead the intention of this contribution is to sketch a global picture of emerging patterns of the global control and management of migrants. Our hope is to outline the broader framework as a way of complementing existing national expertise. It cannot possibly do justice to the complexities of rapidly changing national, regional, and global regulations, but we hope to outline some of the more significant areas of regulatory policy. This has never been truer than at a time when the Western nations struggle to respond to Syrian and other migrants from the Middle East.

This chapter, therefore, is particularly aimed at Christians concerned to advocate for changes to regulatory frameworks and migration policies. Understanding the current frameworks is a vital first step to lobbying for amendments and replacements to those frameworks.

---

1 Carey, William, *An Enquiry into the Obligation of Christians to use Means for the Conversion of the Heathens*, Leicester: Ann Ireland. 1792, 86.

Global organizations tasked with the responsibility to regulate and manage the movement of migrants

At the global level, organizations such as the UN, especially the UN High Commissioner for Refugees (UNHCR), the International Labour Organization (ILO), the International Organization for Migration (IOM),[2] the World Health Organization (WHO), and the International Red Cross (IRC), are each responsible for contributing to the drafting of regulatory mechanisms and advisory policies that attempt to manage and/or control migration. In their turn, these influence the degree to which migrants are free to migrate from one place to another, the extent to which their rights to employment, education, housing, and welfare are ensured and protected, and determine conditions and requirements applied to asylum, *non-refoulement*,[3] residency, and citizenship. Regulatory frameworks and policies of this nature may be addressed to individual migrants and migration services, but they are usually intended as regulatory frameworks for nation states and their respective agencies or departments.

At the global level, the UNHCR carries significant responsibility for the monitoring and review of refugee, asylum, and migration policies and practices at national and regional level. To monitor a social phenomenon requires a widely understood definition of what it is that is being measured and assessed. Consequently, 'migrant', 'refugee,'[4] 'asylum seeker', and 'internally displaced person'[5] are each defined within the terms of various UN Conventions and Treaties. Doing so helps to establish these definitions within a framework of internationally agreed regulation and policy. Of

---

2 The question of the integration of the work of the IOM with that of the UNHCR remains an ongoing point of discussion. See, for example, Elie, Jerome 'The Historical Roots of Cooperation Between the UN High Commissioner for Refugees and the International Organization for Migration' in *Global Governance*, 16, 2010, 345-360. Also Newland, Kathleen 'The Governance of International Migration: Mechanisms, Processes, and Institutions' in *Global Governance*, 16, 2010, 331-343.

3 Non-refoulement is an important principle in the processing of applications for refugee status and in dealing with asylum seekers. The principle determines that the asylum seeker or refugee cannot be returned or relocated to a country in which the risk of further harm or injury is likely. Available at http://www.unhcr.org/3ae68ccd10.html.

4 The UN defines a refugee as a person who, 'owing to a well-founded fear of being persecuted for reasons of race, religion, nationality, membership of a particular social group or political opinion, is outside the country of his nationality and is unable or, owing to such fear, is unwilling to avail himself of the protection of that country.' UN Refugee Convention (1951), Article 1A(2), 1967 Protocol.

5 The UNHCR defines internally displaced persons as 'persons or groups of persons who have been forced or obliged to flee or to leave their homes or places of habitual residence, in particular as a result of or in order to avoid the effects of armed conflict, situations of generalised violence, violations of human rights or natural or human-made disasters, and who have not crossed an internationally recognised State border.' UNHCR Guiding Principle, 'Introduction,' para. 2.

course, these do not satisfy everybody and they remain a focus for ongoing debate and dialogue, but they do provide a necessary benchmark for comparing practices and policies across the member states of the UN. In addition to the ongoing debate about definition and practices, there is also the extent to which cultural worldview predetermines the ways in which the contractual nature of international regulation are understood differently. Some cultures understand contracts as formal indications of a desire to work together in a flexible and developing relationship. In this view, contracts are readily renegotiated within the context of a healthy working relationship. This has implications for the nature of the consensus surrounding international Protocols and Treaties.

Following the lead of the UNHCR, the most widely used definition of a migrant is that of a person who stays outside their usual place or country of residence for a period of at least one year. The category of asylum seeker is frequently misunderstood and misrepresented in the media, and should strictly only be applied to individuals who have lodged an application with a nation state for the protection afforded them by the grant of refugee status.

Often overlooked in the popular discussion of migration is the phenomenon of those individuals whose movement is internal to the borders of a country. Such individuals might have relocated to another state or province in the country of their citizenship, but do so with a keen awareness of the linguistic and cultural differences. In such instances, the internal migrant is likely to feel they are part of an ethnic minority and might also experience discrimination to varying degrees. A significant factor in this type of internal migration might involve the role of the city in issuing residency or other permits that foster and facilitate the movement of skilled workers in search of employment. Of course, in such instances, there is also the likelihood that international migration will be facilitated.

Other aspects of the migrant experience fall within the sphere of interest of one or more of the global organisations listed above. In addition to the four types of migrant already introduced here, others include, but may not be limited to, the categories of internally displaced persons, irregular migrants, persons seeking re-settlement, migrant workers, economic migrants, trafficked human beings, international students, migrants applying for family reunification, migrant applications for nationality and citizenship, and families involved in cross-border adoption cases.[6] Not yet widely recognised by international Protocols or Conventions is the likely impact of climate change on international migration. The impending likelihood of the need to relocate entire Pacific Island populations is one

6 See Jackson, D. and Passarelli, A. Mapping Migration, Mapping Churches' responses; Europe Study, Geneva: World Council of Churches, 2008, 6-9, and Jackson, D. and Passarelli, A. Mapping Migration, Mapping Churches' Responses in Europe, 2nd ed., Geneva: World Council of Churches, 2016, 26-27 for a brief glossary of terms, definitions, and their sources.

that will require concerted international agreement and action if another humanitarian disaster is to be averted.

Global Conventions and Protocols include, for example, the 1951 UN *Convention on the Status of Refugees* (and its 1967 Protocol), the 1984 UN *Convention against Torture*, the 1990 UN *International Convention on the Protection of the Rights of all Migrant Workers and Members of their Families*, and the 2000 UN *Palermo Protocols* which addresses the smuggling of migrants and the prevention of the trafficking of human beings, especially women and children. ILO Conventions concerning migrants include the 1949 *Convention: Migration for Employment*, the 1958 *Convention: Discrimination [Employment and Occupation]*, the 1962 *Convention: Equality of treatment [Social Security]*, and the 1975 *Convention: Migrant Workers [supplementary provisions]*.

It should be obvious from this wide range of references to Conventions and Protocols that the global control and management of migrants has to take into consideration a complex and multi-layered range of motivations for the global movement of people. Not least among these is the motivation located within the call to Christian, cross-cultural mission.

Equally important is the observation that the majority of international Conventions and Protocols are rights-based (many of which make reference to the UN's 1948 *Universal Declaration of Human Rights*). The same holds for many regional Conventions. In contrast, the majority of national measures are security-based (the US fortification of its border with Mexico or the current Australian policy of turning back boats carrying refugees, for example) and this is increasingly true of regional measures (the creation in 2007 of the EU's external border control agency *FRONTEX*, for example).

Also significant is the fact that the movement of migrants and refugees necessarily requires international agreement, co-operation, and collective action. This has become particularly pressing since the mid-1980s when large numbers of refugees began arriving in the 'developed countries' from regions of conflict (Vietnam, Lebanon, Afghanistan, Angola, Iraq, Somalia, and more recently, Syria). The phenomenon of refugees fleeing such conflict was not foreseen by the architects of the UN *Convention* in 1951, conceived around the reality of relatively small numbers of refugees fleeing communist states in Central and Eastern Europe. The much larger numbers of refugees since the 1980s were as much a product as a contributor to the accelerating pace of globalisation and highlighted many inadequacies of global refugee and migrant organizations. As a result, a number of regional organizations began to play a more proactive role in the regulation and management of migrants and refugees within their own regions of influence.[7]

---

7 See Appleyard, Reginald, 'International Migration Policies: 1950-200' in *International Migration*, 39, 6, 2001, 8-20.

Regional organizations tasked with the responsibility to regulate and manage the movement of migrants

Regional structures add a further layer of protocols and regulations addressing the migration of people within, into, or out from the region. These regional structures include the European Union (EU), the African Union (AU),[8] the Arab Maghreb Union (AMU), the League of Arab States (LAS), the Economic Community of West African States (ECOWAS),[9] the Asian-African Legal Consultative Organisation (AALCO),[10] and the Community of Sahel-Saharan Countries (CSSC).

Illustrative of the manner in which these regional structures function is the example of the European Union. The EU is given legal and political identity through a succession of treaties established and signed by the member states that form the EU. Within those treaties and protocols are the various provisions for the framing of regulations addressing migration policy within the EU. A detailed knowledge of the internal legal and treaty arrangements of the EU is not necessary to appreciate the important point that the legal and political nature and authority of the EU allows it to formulate co-ordinated and coherent policies and protocols that regulate and manage the migration of people across the territories of nearly 30 nation states with a combined population of just over half a billion people. The reach of EU law is hugely significant for the lives of several million refugees, asylum seekers and the many more millions of migrants who ordinarily reside, work, or minister in an EU country that is not their country of origin.

Diaspora missiology and international law

In his 2011 Charles Test Lecture at Princeton, Jeremy Waldron noted that international law had been given inadequate attention by 'the tradition of Christian theology and that the neglect of international law has left Christian theologians fairly tongue-tied [in] responding to the jurisprudential crisis of international law.'[11] Few evangelical expositions of

---

8 In 2009, for example, the AU adopted the Kampala Convention, governing provisions for the protection and assistance of internally displaced persons.

9 In 1979 ECOWAS adopted a Protocol relating to Free Movement of Persons, the right of Residence and Establishment and has supplemented this with three amending Protocols (1985, 1986, and 1990).

10 In 2009, the 48th annual session of AALCO discussed transnational migration, human trafficking, and the smuggling of people, highlighting the organizations coordinated efforts in this area since 2001. See AALCO, 'Report on the Forty-eighth Annual Session of the Asian-African Legal Consultative Organization' in Chinese Journal of International Law, 2010, 179-191.

11 Waldron, Jeremy, A Religious View of the Foundations of International Law, Charles E. Test Lectures, Princeton, NJ, March 2011, 10. Cited in Reed, Esther Theology for International Law, London: Bloomsbury, 2013, 1.

the Pauline injunctions in Romans 13:1-7 to 'submit to the authorities' make any reference to authority beyond the level of the nation state. For the purposes of our current discussion, this leaves totally unaddressed the issue of the authority of either the UN or of the various regional bodies, and the extent to which the authority of these bodies might have been considered by Paul to lie within the scope of his exhortation. Similarly, there remains the extent to which the warnings of Revelation 13 underscore the capacity for all authorities to exercise unwarranted, exploitative, or a corrupting influence upon those from whom they claim varying degrees of loyalty.

This is a significant issue for any theologian attempting to navigate their way through the treacherous waters of international regulations impacting on the rights of human beings, the protection of refugees, the management of asylum resettlement, processes of international adoption, the plight of internally displaced peoples, or the miseries of human trafficking. Christian theology understands itself to have universal scope. Every human being who is caught up in this diverse net of migratory and diaspora situations is considered by Christian theology to bear the *imago Dei*. For this reason alone, every human being is properly at the centre of the church's pastoral and missionary concern and the claim of the Gospel extends over everybody, irrespective of their previous history, their present situation, or their future intentions. The Gospel addresses every refugee and every person living in diaspora. Quite simply, the scope of the Gospel is universal. Theologians, pastors, and missionaries may unintentionally limit the universal impulse of the Gospel where they fail to grapple with the universal character and significance of regulatory frameworks for migration. In short, if we do not have any understanding of, or appreciation for, international migration policy and law, we fail in our pastoral and missionary responsibility. More especially we fail the oppressed and unjustly treated refugee, the trafficked human being, and the 'alien and strangers' who have migrated with relative ease yet who find themselves in a 'strange and foreign land'.[12]

Philip Kasinitz, writing in 2013, notes the way that the migration of people has emerged as a core concern for sociology. In particular, he suggests that societies are now faced with questions that are forced upon them by these new realities. A diaspora missiologist with a truly global vision has to take seriously Kasinitz's concern to address 'questions of how societies negotiate membership and boundaries in the face of globalization, technological innovation, and demographic change.'[13] In addressing these

---

12 Migration policy concerns are addressed by O'Neill, William and Spohn, William, 'Rights of Passage: The Ethics of Immigration and Refugee Policy' in Theological Studies 59, 1, Mar 1998, 84-106.

13 Kasinitz, Philip 'The Sociology of International Migration: Where We Have Been; Where Do We Go From Here?' in Sociological Forum, 27, 1, September 2012, 583.

questions, a number of themes occur frequently: integration, human rights, economics, corruption, security, family, and irregular migration.

The integration of migrant workers in diaspora situations

Statistics reported elsewhere in this Compendium demonstrate that the larger number of migrants relocate for reasons of employment. The degree to which migration is subsequently seen as a net benefit or a net cost to the economy of the country of immigration is rarely settled with reference to increased levels of taxable income or economics. The 'cost' in any particular country is typically filtered through prior convictions about the desirability of integrating migrants that are significantly different to the majority population of the country in question. At heart this is a debate around acceptable levels of diversity set against the broader issue of what constitutes national and ethnic identity.

Popular responses reflect existing political, ideological, ethical, philosophical, and sometimes religious convictions. Diaspora missiology has an important theological contribution to make to this ongoing and vital conversation. The widely quoted words of Swiss author, Max Frisch (1911-1991) 'We asked for workers. We got people instead',[14] sums up the dilemma at the heart of the debate.

The rights of migrant workers are addressed by various Conventions of the ILO (outlined above), regional organizations such as the EU,[15] ECOWAS,[16] and a raft of national regulations from the highly restrictive to the openly encouraging. Falling into this category is a range of mechanisms that facilitate employment and residency. For example, the USA's 'green card' and the EU's 'blue card' contribute to easing the entry of favoured

14 Max Frisch, cited in Kasinitz, Philip 'The Sociology of International Migration: Where We Have Been; Where Do We Go From Here?' in Sociological Forum, 27, 1, September 2012, 582.

15 EU regulations address migrant workers of two main types; firstly, citizens of an EU country with the legal right to employment and residency in any other EU member state and, secondly, non-EU migrant workers. The rights of the first are permanently enshrined within the EU's self-understanding of the unrestricted movement of people. The rights of the second group are determined and governed from time to time according to the prevailing political and industrial or financial situations across the EU. The relevant EU documents are the 1974 Action Plan in Favour of Migrant workers, the 2004 Harmonisation of Labour Markets, and the more recent 2011 Agenda for the Integration of non-EU migrants.

16 The 1990 Supplementary Protocol to the ECOWAS Protocol on Free Movement of Persons, right of Residence and Establishment defines 'migrant worker', 'seasonal worker' and introduces the concepts of 'border area worker' and 'itinerant worker', each of which falls within the broader focus of interest of this paper.

migrants, typically skilled professionals, for the purposes of employment and permanent residency.[17]

Following the grant of residency to a migrant, whether migrant worker, international student, or refugee, a range of further policies may be encountered that are intended to encourage a migrant and any accompanying family members to acquire local language skills and thus gain access to education and employment. These are generally considered central components of national policies fostering migrant integration which, in many cases, have replaced more intentionally multicultural policies.[18] Further regulation is likely to be encountered if the migrant later applies to become a citizen of the host country; language and cultural knowledge tests may be required.[19]

One of the more relevant practices of the Christian community connected with this aspect of migrant integration is the practice of assisting with language acquisition. Many local congregations have discovered that language classes are a practical way of engaging with their new migrant neighbours. In addition to encouraging the journey towards closer integration within the local community, this has the additional potential of fostering a migrant's journey towards Christian faith. It's probably important to note, however, that in some instances, diaspora communities with a strong sense of collective identity may resist the acquisition of local language skills for fear that this will have the result of diluting their sense of being a distinct people in diaspora.

The human rights of the migrant

The origins of international Conventions and Treaties relating to refugee protection and migration emerge as an application of the early UN human rights discourse, a point already noted above. There are alternative ways of framing the contemporary debates and discourse of contemporary migration and diaspora, including economics and strictly historical approaches, but a focus on human rights remains central to refugee, asylum, and anti-trafficking policies. The 1994 San José *Declaration on*

---

17 In 2014, there were 130,000 'green card' places available to migrant workers in four categories (Visa categories EB-1 to EB-4). This compares with 70,000 refugee visas and an unlimited number available for immediate relatives (Visa category IR is typically granted to between 300,000 and 500,000 annually).

18 See Jackson, Darrell 'Europe and the Migrant Experience: Transforming Integration' in Transformation, 28, 1, 2011, 14-28, for a fuller discussion of the political use of integrationism, in preference to multiculturalism, as a way of framing national and regional migrant policy.

19 In Australia, for example, the Department for Immigration and Customs (DIAC) requires applicants for citizenship to have passed a test based on knowledge of Australian Citizenship: Our Common Bond which is available as a written text in 37 languages or is available as a YouTube video or DVD.

Refugees and Displaced Persons recognises the violation of human rights as one of the *causes* of forced displacement, even before it becomes an *integral element* of the experience of displacement or of being a refugee.[20]

Those human rights most commonly referenced in the various Protocols and Conventions include, but are not limited to, humanitarian aid and protection, welfare and healthcare, employment, the rights of minors, religious liberty, and rights that are located in the issues of gender and human sexuality. Frequently cited in this context is the *Convention on the Rights of the Child (UN-CRC)*, adopted by the UN in 1989. The *UN-CRC* contains provisions against the trafficking of children, insists on their right to legal nationality, outlines their right to visit families who may live in more than one country, affirms their right to the use of their own language in a country with a majority language different to that of the migrant child, and requires that the adoptive parents of a child from a culture that is not theirs, should do so in a way that respects the child's religion, culture and language.

In 2012, the *Canadian Medical Association's Journal* reported on recent and sudden policy changes in the Interim Federal Health Program which had guaranteed healthcare for refugees prior to June 30th, 2012. The previous policy had been seen to fulfil Canada's international obligations under the terms of the 1951 *UN Convention on Refugees*, the *Constitution* of the WHO, and the 1948 *UN Declaration of Human Rights*. From June 2012, the Canadian government has only provided healthcare services to refugees whose conditions were deemed to pose a risk to public health or safety. The *CMAJ* article concludes,

> Providing vision care to Bhutanese refugee children facilitates educational success; providing prostheses to Afghan land mine amputees improves employability. Withdrawing such support increases social isolation and compromises physical and mental health.[21]

At times, the human rights of one group of individuals to migrate may come at the expense of the human rights of others. This is at the heart of the current dilemma about how best to respond to migrant health-care workers and to ensure the provision of adequate healthcare services to citizens in the countries from which they have migrated. The former UN High Commissioner for Human Rights, Mary Robinson, acknowledged in 2008 that,

---

20 See Trindade, Antônio A.C. 'Uprootedness and the Protection of Migrants in the International Law of Human Rights' in Revista Brasileira de Política International 51, 1, 2008, 137-168.

21 Arya, N. et al, 'Enter at your own risk: government changes to comprehensive care for newly arrived Canadian refugees' in Canadian Medical Association Journal, 184, 17, Nov 2012, 1875-76.

> Health workers have a clear human right to emigrate in search of a better life. Yet people in source countries hard hit by an exodus of health workers also have the right to health in their own countries.[22]

The Advisory Council mentioned in Robinson's article is one of a number of global bodies (others include WHO[23]) that provides best-practice guidelines in a generally under-regulated area of migration policy. Healthcare professionals represent a valuable global commodity and employment options in the wealthier countries of the world offer opportunities not necessarily available in the migrant health-worker's country of origin. The relative freedom to migrate enjoyed by qualified health-care professionals means it is also an attractive option for Christians seeking an avenue to relocate overseas as a route to missionary service and witness. However, the shadow side of this needs careful and sensitive exploration within the global Christian community. Robinson is surely right to note that it is a matter of global justice that countries of origin have inadequate healthcare provision due to their own health-care workers having migrated to other places. It is strangely ironic to imagine members of a US congregation being tended by nurses from Malawi working within the local US healthcare system, whilst at the same time the congregation is supporting medical missionaries working in Malawi to provide much-needed medical care to Malawian patients in the absence of local healthcare workers.

Economic considerations and regulations

Our discussion of migrant health-care workers leads naturally onto a discussion of the economic factors involved in the phenomenon of migration. In addition to the 'south-to-north brain-drain' there are other important issues involved in the remittances of migrants to their countries of origin, frequently intended to support relatives and families who remain in the country of origin. There are few regulatory mechanisms dealing with remittances and these may, in fact, be actively discouraged by processes of globalization that owe more to the philosophy of free-market capitalism than to notions of global fraternity and common cause. Early attempts by some countries to impose taxation or impose percentages on migrant-earned and remitted income were largely unsuccessful whilst some were found to contravene the ILO's 1949 *Convention: Migration for Employment*.

---

22 Robinson, Mary and Clark, Peggy, 'Forging solutions to health worker migration' in The Lancet, 371, February 2008, 691-693.

23 The 193 member states of the WHO adopted a Global Code of Practice on the International Recruitment of Health Personnel in 2010, outlining 10 Principles and established on the values articulated clearly in the reference from Mary Robinson quoted immediately above.

In the early 1990s, the Cuban Government began allowing the remittance of US dollars into Cuba from diaspora Cubans located in the US. This was a radical re-orientation on the part of the Cuban Government, mirrored in the relaxations permitting diaspora Cubans to visit Cuba. The example of the Philippines' government is also noteworthy. It has, according to the authors of a 2003 report for the World Bank,

> gone much further than other countries in terms of promoting labour migration as a deliberate strategy while at the same time reaching out to its diaspora and including them in national development strategies and economic policy.[24]

The government of the Philippines' *Department of Labour and Employment* oversees the work of the *Philippine Overseas Employment Administration* (POEA) and its *Government Placement Branch*; agencies tasked with the recruitment, training, and preparation of citizens planning to work overseas (officially described as OFWs or Overseas Foreign Workers).

Economic reforms in the area of migrant remittances are inevitably oriented towards a more open market approach. The World Bank, the International Migration Policy Programme, and others have continued to give close attention to patterns of migrant remittances. They cooperate in highlighting reforms to the global financial sector that ensure greater transparency and the integrity of the global transfer of monies from one country to another. Where national authorities have moved to impose regulatory frameworks, these have also primarily been put in place to ensure transparency and efficiency.

Anti-corruption regulation and control

National governments have a tendency to advance cautiously when ratifying regulations dealing with migration and refugees. Naturally, there are many national interests to be considered, not the least of which are the economic interests of the nation. Perhaps surprisingly, legislation and regulation concerning the trafficking of human beings has generally been rapidly adopted and ratified by national governments. Human trafficking is defined by the UN as,

> The recruitment, transportation, transfer, harbouring, or receipt of persons, by means of threat, or use of force or other forms of coercion, of abduction, of fraud, of deception, of the abuse of power or of a position of vulnerability or

24 Addy, D.N. et al, 'Migrant remittances – Country of origin experiences: Strategies, policies, challenges, and concerns', IMP Conference Paper prepared for the World Bank's International Conference on Migrant Remittances, London, October 2003, 18. Available at www.digaai.org/wp/pdfs/remitpaper.doc/.

> of the giving or receiving of payments or benefits to achieve the consent of a person having control over another person, for the purpose of exploitation.[25]

The Council of Europe's *Convention on Action Against Trafficking* was adopted by the Council in 2005 and within the relatively short space of ten years was being enforced in forty European member states. The US *Trafficking Victims Protection Act, 2000* assumes the need for interagency cooperation at multiple levels to control trafficking, prosecute traffickers, and care for the vulnerable victims of trafficking.[26] This insight about multiple levels of co-operation is vital. Research suggests that national and international regulations to combat trafficking are only as effective as the extent that local measures are in place to provide safe housing and various levels of support to enable victims of trafficking to reintegrate back into a life of freedom. The North American Association of Christians in Social Work, in highlighting instances of churches prepared to help meet physical and spiritual needs, indicates that much more could be done by congregations to co-operate with anti-trafficking agencies. The report does not dismiss national and international regulation but it points to the need for collective action at local level to ensure the provisions of these regulations are achieved.

As a footnote to this short section, it's worth noting that people smuggling and human trafficking are not directly equivalent terms. The UN (noted above) defines human trafficking using terms including, 'threat,' 'force,' 'coercion,' 'abduction,' 'fraud,' 'deception,' 'abuse of power,' and 'exploitation.' In particular, Article 3(a) of the UN's *Trafficking Protocol* notes that the definition of 'Exploitation shall include, at a minimum, the exploitation of the prostitution of others or other forms of sexual exploitation, forced labour or services, slavery or practices similar to slavery, servitude or the removal of organs.'[27] People smuggling is distinct from human trafficking in that people smuggling involves merely a payment to a third party for services intended to gain the 'illegal entry of a person into a State Party of which the person is not a national or a permanent resident.'[28] In an act of human trafficking, the individual may be viewed as a commodity, in an act of people smuggling, the individual may be viewed as a client.

---

25 The 2000 UN Protocol to Prohibit, Suppress and Punish Trafficking in Persons cited in Koser, Khalid *International Migration: A very short introduction*, Oxford, UK: Oxford University Press, 2007, 64.

26 Baker, Debra, and Grover, Elizabeth, 'Responding to Victims of Human Trafficking: Interagency Awareness, Housing Service, and Spiritual Care' in *Social Work & Christianity*, 40, 3, 2013, 310.

27 United Nations, UN Protocol to Prohibit, Suppress and Punish Trafficking in Persons, Especially Women and Children. New York: United Nations, 2000. Available at http://www.osce.org/odihr/19223?download=true.

28 United Nations, *Protocol against the Smuggling of Migrants by Land, Sea and Air*, New York: United Nations, 2000, Article 3(a).

The securitisation of migration policy and border control

Border protection remains an enduring aspect of national sovereignty and any diminishing of sovereignty in this area is never surrendered easily by a national government. This was central to the EU's discussions surrounding the real and perceived threats to the national security of its member states and which resulted in the adoption of a common European border policy.

With the accelerating pace of global migration, nation states have adopted policy approaches that assume the need for more stringent mechanisms to manage security risk. This is associated with the strengthening of international governance in these areas. Closely related to this concern has been the adoption of anti-terrorist legislation in those countries where migrants and refugees with permanent residency or citizenship are believed to have offered implicit or explicit support to acts of terror or, indeed, to have been complicit in such acts.

Writing for the IOM in 2009, John Casey notes that,

> In the current climate of concern with security, the general trend is towards a hardening or 'securitisation' of attitudes towards immigration. The movement of people across borders – be it for settlement or tourism – is becoming more restrictive, bureaucratic, and burdened by security concerns.[29]

Casey goes on to comment that the 1948 *UN Universal Declaration of Human Rights* only guarantees freedom of movement *within* the country of residence, recognises the right to leave one's own country, but does not recognise the right to settle in another country. The freedom of refugees or migrants to settle in another country is thereby left to the co-operation and agreement of the various countries into which a migrant or refugee intends to enter.

The regulation of family reunion, adoption, and cross-border marriage

National and international regulations exist to regulate migration policy that relates to cross-border marriage, the adoption of third-country nationals or citizens, and family reunion. As mentioned earlier, countries such as the USA impose no annual limits on the right to residency for certain categories of relatives of US citizens (including spouses, children, and parents of over 18-year old citizens). However, at the time of writing the UK government was coming under increasing pressure to redress a disparity in its handling of citizens of other EU countries and its own citizens. The UK introduced legislation in June 2012 which required the British spouse of a non-EU migrant to prove a minimum annual income of £18,600 in order to demonstrate his or her capacity to support their spouse.

---

29 Casey, John, 'Open Borders: Absurd Chimera or Inevitable Future Policy?' in International Migration, 48, 5, 2010, 14-62.

The UK Court of Appeal decided in favour of the Government policy, finding it lawful, thus clearing the way for 3,600 UK citizens to be denied any right to sponsor their spouse's visa application.[30] A more recent judgement in the European Court of Justice in December of 2014 ruled that other aspects of the legislation touching on family members were in breach of EU law. Complaints have also highlighted the fact that EU citizens resident in the UK are not required to demonstrate the same level of financial income in order to apply for their non-EU spouses to reside in the UK. Regulation and legislation governing family reunion will remain vulnerable to political concerns and motivations, largely driven by concerns for security and social coherence, yet it is equally likely to have to face ongoing challenges from advocates relying upon the framework of human rights legislation.

Whilst the freedom of a citizen to sponsor his or her spouse in the acquisition of residency cannot always be guaranteed, the cross-border adoption of children, on the other hand, rarely attracts the attention of individuals or groups opposed to immigration. The rights of a couple to adopt and raise a child born overseas are rarely queried and it may be true that adopted cross-border children are only infrequently described as 'immigrants,' as claimed by Collinson; 'Children are hardly ever imagined in media images as immigrants, highlighting the special position that foreign-born adoptive children occupy in… cultural imagination.'[31]

It may be that for this reason, the issue of cross-border adoption is only reluctantly ratified by first-world countries. Internationally, the 1993 *Hague Adoption Convention* has been ratified by ninety countries to date. However, adoption measures outlined in the Council of Europe's 1967 *European Convention on the Adoption of Children* have only been ratified by eighteen of the forty-six member states. During the 1970s, for example, Canadian and US Federal authorities were reluctant to regulate the adoption of Canadian babies by US parents.[32] Adoptive parents in the US are most likely to adopt children from China and South Korea. Korea is yet to ratify the *Hague Adoptive Convention* and both Korea and China have developed policies to ensure their adoption procedures are as efficient and streamlined as possible. In contrast, many African countries require adoptive parents to fulfil residency requirements, thus effectively ruling out international adoptions. Other majority world countries restrict or forbid it.

---

30 Travis, Alan, 'Appeal Court: if you earn 18,600 a year your foreign spouse can live in the UK' in The Guardian [Online], 12th July 2014. Available at http://www.theguardian.com/law/2014/jul/11/appeal-court-18600-foreign-spouse-uk.

31 Cited in Leinaweaver, Jessica, 'The Quiet Migration Redux: International Adoption, Race, and Difference' in Human Organizations,73, 1, Spring 2014, 63.

32 See Balcom, Karen, The Traffic in Babies: Cross-Border Adoption and Baby-Selling between the United States and Canada, 1930-1972. Toronto: University of Toronto Press, 2011.

The UN-CRC makes reference to cross-border adoption and its 1986 Declaration on Social and Legal Principles relating to the Protection and Welfare of Children, with Special Reference to Foster Placement and Adoption Nationally and Internationally calls member States to establish policy, legislation and effective supervision for the protection of children involved in cross-border adoption. Concerns common to international and regional regulations are that cross-border adoption should only occur when adoptive parents cannot be identified in the country of origin; that the interests of the child are paramount; that competent authorities or agencies should operate similar safeguards and standards as in-country adoptions; and adoption should not result in improper financial gains.

What is a diaspora missiology to make of the regulation of migrants and Christians in diaspora?

Esther Reed's theological account of international law concludes with several important theologically-framed insights. She argues that it is a point of biblical revelation that all things, including international law, find their *telos* (their goal and conclusion) in God's final wrapping up of human history in judgement and restoration. She adds that the person of Jesus is the source of all legal truth and insists that

> Thinking about international law in Christian theological perspective cannot be separated from questions of the identity and purposes for creation of the self-manifesting God revealed in Jesus.[33]

Reed continues that, for the believer, any hope that people of disparate and diverse political, cultural, and religious backgrounds will ever manage to 'engage constructively together around issues of international law or politics'[34] has to be a hope that finds its origin in the gracious sovereignty of a loving God. It is only the action of this kind of God throughout his Creation that makes it possible for his will to be known, even if only partially and imperfectly, by every society and authority. This includes, of course, knowledge about God's will concerning international law.

Reed's theological convictions require international law to serve the requirements of international justice and peace, concretely and deeply concerned for the particular (personal?) and common (national, regional, international?) good.[35] She argues that these must also be the measures by

---

33 Reed, Esther, Theology for International Law, London: Bloomsbury T&T Clark, 2013, 299.

34 Reed, Esther, Theology for International Law, London: Bloomsbury T&T Clark, 2013, 301.

35 Reed's use of particular and common good can be understood as a way of talking about what forms of international law best address the needs of the individual person (or 'particular') as well as of the needs at national, regional, or international level (hence 'common').

which international Conventions and Treaties are evaluated, irrespective of the degree to which they are criticised for not reflecting truly democratic processes. She suggests that 'something higher (or deeper) than the agreement of states or individuals... has given rise to these norms that continue to attract widespread accord.'[36] In doing so she outlines a rationale for diaspora missiologists to contribute to debating and shaping those norms from within a theologically-shaped worldview.

Her rigour in applying a theological critique, informed by careful attention to the biblical texts, leads her simultaneously to recognise the virtue of a world without borders, acknowledge the biblical reality of separate and distinctive nations, yet critique what she terms 'unrealistic cosmopolitan' views. The relevance of her work for diaspora missiology certainly bears further exploration. It has relevance for those of us working to investigate the concept of a global theology of domicile as well as those who argue that theologically there is a case to be made for the 'good fences make good neighbours' argument.

She concludes her eleven theses by stating three moral priorities for the politics of international law, namely a concern for the poor, oppressed, and marginalised and that these must take priority over the wants of the rich and powerful and those who exclude.

In sum, Reed offers a robustly theological way of engaging with each of the regulatory categories for migration and refugee policy that we have sketched above. Her theology highlights the ways in which we can respond to and evaluate international Conventions and Protocols, particularly their use of human rights discourse. She suggests new ways of talking about, for example, the manner in which the integration of migrant workers into a host society can, collectively, be taken as a more adequate reflection of what it means for *peoples* and *nations* to reflect the *imago Dei*, particularly where the nations in question have significant migrant or diaspora populations. Her emphasis here might furnish diaspora missiologists with new ways of talking about the way in which encouraging migrant and refugee access to education and employment is one way of recognising the biblical narratives relating to the fruitfulness and creativity that reveals, in part, the reality of people created in the *imago Dei*.

In prioritising the moral and ethical claims of the poor, oppressed and marginalised, Reed justifies the enduring Christian concern for regulations ensuring justice and *shalom* for migrants and refugees, irrespective of their circumstances. This would include, for example, migrant workers exploited to the extent that their employers are in breach of employment regulations or who are required to work in a way that treats them merely as employees and denies the biblical revelation that they are primarily people created for work *and* Sabbath-rest. Similarly, advocating for stronger anti-trafficking

---

36 Reed, Esther, Theology for International Law, London: Bloomsbury T&T Clark, 2013, 304.

regulations can be understood as a way of advocating for the liberty of individuals who are exploited and held captive against their will by pimps and others involved in human trafficking (Luke 4:18).

Her attention to the marginalized and vulnerable highlights the plight of children who suffer relational, emotional and psychological damage when raised by distant relatives in the absence of both parents working in another country. It also offers a theologically informed way of discussing the impact of the large-scale migration of healthcare workers upon the healthcare provision for sick and vulnerable citizens in the countries from which the healthcare works have migrated. Her focus on international legislation is a further reminder that any solutions in such situations require global and national organizations to share their responsibility for redressing the imbalances created by the constant demand of the wealthier nations of the world for qualified healthcare workers.[37]

Our final reflection on Reed's relevance to the discussion at hand concerns the issue of border control. She cautiously addresses the desirability of open borders in her conclusions, although she does not address the important distinction made by others between a 'no border' policy and an 'open border' policy.[38] An evaluation of the securitisation of border control policies and practices requires reflection on her discussion of the distinctive nature of peoples and nations and an uncritical 'reduction of humanity to an abstract principle'[39] as well as upon her warning against the 'law of force' trumping the moral priority of the 'force of law.'[40] The discourse of security and risk require a theological critique given the propensity of refugee and migration border controls towards levels of both legitimate and illegitimate force and, occasionally, undue violence.

---

37 The Australian Nursing Journal noted in 2010 an estimated shortage of 25,000 qualified healthcare works in Australia, with attempts made to plug the shortfall through encouraging immigration of skilled healthcare professionals. It notes, with a certain degree of irony, that at the same time there were 27,500 registered but non-working local nurses in Australia. A more comprehensive solution in such situations would require careful exploration of the range of reasons for the non-working status of the locally registered nurses. Blake, Nicholas, 'Nursing Migration: issues of equity and balance' in Australian Nursing Journal, 18, 3, Sep 2010, 24-27.

38 See Casey, John, 'Open Borders: Absurd Chimera or Inevitable Future Policy?' in *International Migration*, 48, 5, 2010, 53.

39 Reed, Esther, *Theology for International Law*, London: Bloomsbury T&T Clark, 2013, 305.

40 Reed, Esther, *Theology for International Law*, London: Bloomsbury T&T Clark, 2013, 306.

Concluding comments

The impulse of missiology is always towards the transformation of concrete Christian practices in response to the mission of God in the world he has created. Christian advocacy *by* migrants or *on behalf of* refugees and victims of trafficking, for example, has a rich tradition of Christian theology upon which to draw. The move from theological worldview to Christian practices suggests that diaspora missiologists have a contribution to make in the formulation of international migrant and refugee policies, conventions and protocols. This is especially important in attempting to ensure that humanitarian and economic regulatory frameworks dignify people created in the image of God and take equally seriously the fallen nature of all human activity in this context. Any global politic that claims to be a *realpolitik* must adequately reflect these realities of the human condition.

For Discussion

1. Identify two or three of the more important international Conventions and Treaties and outline how they most directly impact evangelicals in diaspora situations.
2. How helpful and appropriate do you think it is to develop a theological framework for international law? To what extent does such a theology need to reflect the apparent tension between Romans 13:1-7 and Revelations 13:1-10?
3. Where evangelicals have an opportunity to contribute to the debates surrounding the regulation of migration policy, which aspects of regulatory activity ought evangelicals to prioritise and give greatest attention to, and why?

4. Responding to the Phenomenon of Migration: Early Proponents of Diaspora Missiology and the Lausanne Movement

Sadiri Joy Tira and Darrell Jackson

In including this adapted chapter from Dr Sadiri Joy Tira,[1] the Section Editors understand this as a 'bridging' chapter between the first three phenomenological chapters and what follows in the rest of this Compendium. The origins of this chapter attest to the genesis of a group of missiologists who took seriously the phenomenon of migration at the end of the twentieth century and attempted to shape missiology in a way that took these trends and realities more intentionally into account. We believe that the same intent lies behind the compilation of the current volume.

Consequently, we insist that there can be no missiology of diaspora or no theology of migration without the phenomenon of either diaspora or of migration. These are not missiologies that have arisen from the theoretical speculations of study-bound theologians, but represent the fruit of personal struggle, experience, testimony, and long-term engagement with the realities of diaspora faith and human migration.

However, and more importantly, there remains the fact that diaspora missiology is the activity of individuals who are as committed to the theological enterprise as they are to the human experience underlying migration and diaspora. Sociology and anthropology have been, and remain, essential elements of the interdisciplinary nature of missiology yet they alone are not adequate for interpreting and transforming the shared and individual experiences of migration and diaspora. The account of diaspora offered by the human sciences remains partial and incomplete without the vital contribution of rigorous biblical and theological interpretation. We are confident that the Compendium achieves a unique integration of empirical description, phenomenological analysis, and theological interpretation. The account that follows explains why this had become such an urgent task in the view of these early diasporan missiologists.

As Christian individuals and mission organizations came to appreciate the challenges and *kairos* opportunities of the twenty-first century diaspora, missiologists, mission practitioners, and theologians

1 Originally published as Tira, Sadiri J., "Diaspora Missiology and the Lausanne Movement at the Dawn of the Twenty-First Century" in Chandler H. Im and Yong, Amos, eds., *Global Diasporas and Mission* (Oxford: Regnum Press, 2012) 214-227.

grappled to record the missiological implications. Their academic deliberations were collected in collaborative volumes and these, in their turn, were key contributions to the early documentation of diaspora missions. This would later provide a framework for diaspora missions initiatives.

Early proponents of diaspora missions in the Lausanne Movement included Tom Houston, former International Director of the Lausanne Committee for World Evangelization (LCWE), who wrote about a 'Global Gospel' in 2004, and Samuel Escobar who proposed a 'Migration Model' in 2003.[2] Evangelical missiologists Enoch Wan of Western Seminary and Sadiri Joy Tira of the Filipino International Network developed the insights of Houston and Escobar and introduced definitions of 'diaspora in missions' and 'diaspora missiology.'[3] Diaspora in missions was defined by them as 'dispersed ethnic groups who are actively engaged or actively involved in fulfilling the Great Commission; regardless of vocation and denominational affiliations of individuals involved.' Diaspora missiology was consequently defined as 'a missiological study of the phenomena of diaspora groups being scattered geographically and the strategy of gathering for the kingdom.'[4]

In June 2002, the annual gathering of the American Society of Missiology addressed the topic 'Migration Challenge and Avenue for Christian Mission' and the journal *Missiology* published the proceedings.[5] Increasingly, missiologists are now beginning to recognize the immense potential of Christians in diaspora as already-deployed 'kingdom workers,' and are joining the growing body of academics tracking international migration.

---

2 See Tom Houston, 'Postscript: The Challenge of Diaspora Leaders for World Evangelism,' in Pantoja, Tira, and Wan (eds), Scattered, 363-68, and Samuel Escobar, 'Migration: Avenue and Challenge to Mission,' Missiology 31.1 (2003), 17-28.

3 Enoch Wan and Sadiri Joy Tira have written extensively on diaspora missiology. See their edited volume, Missions Practice in the 21st Century (Pasadena: William Carey International University Press, 2009). A case study discussion appears in Wan and Tira, 'The Filipino Experience in Diaspora Missions: A Case Study of Christian Communities in Contemporary Contexts,' in Enoch Wan and Michael Pocock (eds), Missions from the Majority World: Progress, Challenges, and Case Studies (Pasadena: William Carey Library, 2009), 387-411.

4 See Tira, 'Scattered with a Divine Purpose', and Enoch Wan, 'Diaspora Missiology,' Occasional Bulletin of Evangelical Missiological Society 20.2 (2007), 3-7. Notably, two other prominent scholars outside of the Lausanne Movement, Andrew Walls of Edinburgh Seminary and Philip Jenkins of Pennsylvania State University, contributed heavily to the study of migration and mission.

5 See Missiology: An International Review 31.1 (2003), a special issue devoted to 'Mission and Migration,' edited by Terry C. Muck.

The Lausanne 2004 Forum for World Evangelization held in Pattaya, Thailand, launched the Diaspora Issue Group. This group produced the Lausanne Occasional Paper No.55 *Diasporas and International Students: The New People Next Door.*[6] Furthermore, the book *Scattered: The Filipino Global Presence*, showcasing the Filipino diaspora as an example of diaspora missions, was distributed to all forum participants. The book called for scattered peoples, particularly diaspora Filipinos, to be motivated, equipped, and mobilized for active participation in global missions. It draws together historical demography, biblical theology, missiological methodology, and global strategy and discusses the implications of the Filipino diaspora for global missiology. The editors have been credited for formulating the initial theological treatments of diaspora missiology in this initial volume.[7]

In 2007, under the leadership of Douglas Birdsall and Tetsunao Yamamori, Executive Chairman and International Director of the Lausanne Movement respectively, the LCWE appointed a Senior Associate for Diasporas (Dr Sadiri Joy Tira) and in 2008 he assembled a *Lausanne Diasporas Leadership Team* (LDLT). The LDLT committed itself to catalyzing collaborations between the blossoming diaspora movements (including at that point, Filipino, Chinese, Korean, and Latino). Furthermore, the Lausanne leadership tasked the LDLT to formulate an evangelical diaspora theology and strategy to present at Lausanne III. The strategy that was to be proposed would be officially called 'diaspora missiology.'

In 2009, the *Lausanne Diasporas Leadership Team* convened two consultations that were intended to synchronise evangelical strategies to reach diaspora peoples and to ground the strategies in a deep biblical and theological foundation, established within a robust missiological framework. These were the *Lausanne Diaspora Strategy Consultation*, held in Manila, Philippines, during May 2009, hosted by Greenhills Christian Fellowship, a fast-growing metropolitan congregation in

6 Lausanne Committee for World Evangelization Issue Group No. 26 A and B: Diasporas and International Students, 'Lausanne Occasional Paper 55: The New People Next Door,' in David Claydon (ed), A New Vision, a New Heart, a Renewed Call: Lausanne Occasional Papers from the 2004 Forum of World Evangelization Hosted by the Lausanne Committee for World Evangelization – Pataya, Thailand September 29 – October 5, 2004 (Pasadena: William Carey Library, and Delhi: Horizon Printers and Publishers, 2005), 75-137. Material from the next few paragraphs has been adapted from the Lausanne Committee for World Evangelization booklet, Scattered to Gather: Embracing the Global Trend of Diaspora (Manila: LifeChange, 2010), 6-8, of which Sadiri Joy Tira was one of the principal authors.

7 Luis Pantoja, Jr, Sadiri Joy Tira, and Enoch Wan, eds., Scattered: The Filipino Global Presence (Manila: LifeChange Publishing Inc., 2004).

Metro Manila with a passion to motivate their members for diaspora missions.

The *Consultation* participants came from governmental and non-governmental agencies, seminaries, and denominational and para-church organizations. The result of the consultation included the identification of diaspora peoples, the identification of a range of issues affecting diaspora peoples, and the identification of organizations, groups, and individuals ministering specifically with and to diaspora peoples. Furthermore, a group of participants from academic institutions were tasked to form a committee to plan a *Lausanne Diaspora Educators' Consultation* to respond to the many questions raised regarding the future of diaspora missiology after Lausanne III.

At the *Lausanne Diaspora Educators' Consultation* hosted by Torch Trinity Graduate School of Theology, Seoul, South Korea, in November 2009, participants produced *The Seoul Declaration on Diaspora Missiology*, which redefined diaspora missiology as 'a missiological framework for understanding and participating in God's redemptive mission among people living outside their place of origin.'[8] The *Declaration* also summoned the church, including its mission agencies and academies, to motivate, equip, and mobilize diaspora kingdom workers. Another significant development initiated by the Consultation was the establishment of *Regional Diaspora Educators' Teams*.

With the new insights of diaspora missiology gained through these two consultations it was intended that the evangelical church would use existing resources to train diaspora Christians already *in situ*, offering both formal and non-formal levels to mobilize a mission force requiring no 'missionary visa' and no mission agency-sponsored international travel. Moreover, it was argued that diaspora kingdom workers need face no political restrictions and fewer 'closed doors.' Finally, diaspora kingdom workers need not be self-sufficient, but would be sustained by collaborative networks and partnerships.

Taking forward the Lausanne diaspora agenda, the *European Diaspora Educators' Team*, led by Thomas Harvey of the Oxford Centre for Mission Studies, convened the *LCWE Diaspora Educators' Consultation (Europe)* on the 16th April 2010, in Oxford. The *North American Diaspora Educators' Team*, led by Grant McClung, gathered on 22-23rd September 2010, in Charlotte, North Carolina.

When the Lausanne Congress for World Evangelisation (Lausanne III) met in Cape Town, 2010, diaspora and mission were featured during one of the plenary sessions and presented twice during separate

8 See 'The Seoul Declaration on Diaspora Missiology,' available at https://www.lausanne.org/content/statement/the-seoul-declaration-on-diaspora-missiology. November 14, 2009, accessed December 29, 2015. See also the end of this chapter. 'Diaspora Missiology' was initially defined by Enoch Wan, and was redefined at the 2009 Seoul Consultation.

multiplex sessions due to high demand from the participants. The LDLT presented a position paper on the theology of diaspora entitled *Diasporas and God's Mission*. This paper was published as one of a wide and rich collection in *Scattered to Gather: Embracing the Global Trend of Diaspora* and distributed to participants in Cape Town. More strategically, diaspora missions was affirmed in section IIC.5 of the *Cape Town Commitment Call to Action*, the official declaration of the Lausanne Congress.[9]

Towards the conclusion of Lausanne III, the Global Diaspora Network was conceived in order to broaden the diaspora network and project the diaspora agenda beyond the Cape Town event. It would officially replace the former LDLT, which was a specific initiative devoted to preparation for Lausanne III. With the support of the Lausanne Leadership, an International Board of Advisors, composed of respected diaspora scholars and practitioners, was formed in 2011. The GDN headquarters/secretariat office was established in Manila and officially registered under the Securities and Exchange Commission of the Philippines, providing the GDN with a legal identity. Its Advisory Board inaugural session took place in France in February 2011. Through the Global Diaspora Network, Sadiri Joy Tira began in 2012 to build a wider and stronger organization dedicated to the agenda of diaspora and mission from within the Lausanne Movement.[10] In June 2011, the Lausanne Leadership Biennial Meeting in Boston, Massachusetts, officially announced that a *Global Diaspora Forum* would take place in March 2015 in Manila.

Under the umbrella of the Lausanne Movement, the GDN is committed 'to bear[ing] witness to Jesus Christ and all his teachings,' in 'every sphere of society' and 'in the realm of ideas.'[11] The GDN gathered Asian regional educators for the *Far East Asia Diaspora Educators' Consultation* held in Manila in August 2011 to continue the work of LDLT in nurturing networks of kingdom collaborations.

By 2011, diaspora missiology was gaining ground in academic and training institutions. In the summer of 2011, Alliance Graduate School in Manila unveiled its *Institute of Diaspora Missiology*. In the winter of 2011, the *Jaffray Centre for Global Initiatives* at Ambrose University

9 The Cape Town Commitment Call to Action can be accessed at https://www.lausanne.org/content/ctc/ctcommitment#p2-3, accessed December 29, 2015.

10 The GDN operates under the Lausanne Movement and embraces its philosophy of ministry: 'Together we seek to bear witness to Jesus Christ and all his teachings, in every part of the world – not only geographically, but in every sphere of society and in the realm of ideas.' Its formation was announced on Lausanne Global Conversation at http://conversation.lausanne.org/en/conversations/detail/11347#.VobibyinxQc, accessed December 29, 2015.

11 From the Lausanne Movement, cited on the GDN's official website, http://www.global-diaspora.com/, accessed December 29, 2015.

College (Calgary, Canada) introduced its diaspora missiology specialization and a series of diaspora courses offered at college and seminary levels. Finally, in the spring of 2012, the *Ukrainian Evangelical Theological Seminary* launched the Eurasian Diaspora Study Centre. Finally, it's worth recognizing that there are an increasing number of evangelical students in doctoral programs of seminaries, universities, and colleges around the world who are writing diaspora-related dissertations. Their research and writing will provide important contributions to the growing body of diaspora missiology literature.

The GDN Advisory Board convened again in Toronto on 2-5 July 2012. Deliberations included shaping the Lausanne diasporas' agenda for the next three years, including the planning of more regional educators consultations, as well as preparing for the *Global Diaspora Forum* in Manila in March 2015.

'Kinetic' mission theologies and practices: missiological implications from Cape Town to 'Beyond'

The current trends and realities of migration and diaspora require missiologists and mission practitioners to re-evaluate cherished theories and practices of mission that remain territory-specific and geographically focused. The world is increasingly 'borderless' and new transnational, non-spatial, and moving or 'kinetic' missiologies become more urgent in the face of the gospel challenge to reach the millions of scattered peoples wherever they are.

In his paper, *Diaspora Missiology*, Enoch Wan discusses the four elements of 'traditional missiology vis-à-vis diaspora missiology,' including perspectives and paradigms. Wan claims that the perspective of traditional missiology is:

> ...geographically divided, and its current paradigm is still based on Ralph Winter's ethnic blocks and accessibility to the Gospel [while] the perspective of diaspora missiology is non-spatial, 'borderless' or transnational and global, and its paradigm involves the twenty-first century reality of 'viewing and following God's way of providentially moving people spatially and spiritually.'[12]

Ralph Winter's 2004 endorsement of the book *Scattered* suggests that '[Diaspora missiology] may well be the most important undigested reality in missions thinking today. We simply have not caught up with the fact that most of the world's people can no longer be defined geographically.'

Understandably, it has been a challenge for contemporary missiology to adjust its orientation around the traditional mission paradigm of 'going from here to there,', and differentiated between 'foreign' versus

---

12 Enoch Wan, Diaspora Missiology, 6.

'local' mission. However, the GDN has invested in the promotion of kinetic mission models that target people in diaspora, wherever they are, and which complements traditional mission by employing resources already on the ground. This has involved training diaspora Christians already on location or in preparation for deployment, both at formal and non-formal levels (and not just career missionaries).

Some have asked what diaspora missiology looks like in practice. There are many examples of diaspora missions as evidenced by the growing body of literature, including many personal accounts of the effects of migrant Christian workers. This *Compendium*, through its case study Chapters, adds to that body of work.

While there are growing initiatives in diaspora missiology, there is currently no synchronized effort in the evangelical academic community to train kingdom workers for diaspora missions. As the phenomenon of diaspora is increasingly recognised as a major issue in the twenty-first century, the GDN has continued to insist that it is becoming ever more urgent to include diaspora missiology in the curricula of evangelical academic institutions. Moreover, it has committed itself to a concerted effort to teach diaspora missions and diaspora missiology both at formal and non- formal levels. The stated goal is to train future pastors, international workers, missionaries, and lay leaders. Intentional diaspora training would prepare workers for *kinetic mission* in the 'borderless world.'

Future prospects

Diaspora missions can be expected to accelerate as academics and practitioners implement diaspora missiology, particularly in the light of the work on the *Global Diaspora Forum 2015* and the subsequent preparation of this current *Compendium*. Both the *Forum* and *Compendium* have created a space for Dr Tira and other members of the GDN to derive diaspora missions models and motifs that were present in the *Cape Town Commitment Call to Action.*[13]

a) 'Church and mission leaders' should be encouraged to embrace *kairos* opportunities by 'recogniz[ing] and respond[ing] to the missional opportunities presented by global migration and diaspora communities, in strategic planning, and in focused training and resourcing of those called to work among them' (*Cape Town Commitment*, IIC.5.A).

b) 'Christians who are themselves part of diaspora communities' should be encouraged to 'discern the hand of God, even in circumstances they may not have chosen, and to seek whatever

13 See appendix E for complete text of the Cape Town Commitment Call to Action IIC.5.

opportunities God provides for bearing witness to Christ in their host community and seeking its welfare. Where that host country includes Christian churches, immigrant and indigenous churches together,' must be urged 'to listen and learn from one another, and to initiate co-operative efforts to reach all sections of their nation with the gospel' (*Cape Town Commitment*, IIC.5.C).

c) 'Christians in host nations which have immigrant communities of other religious backgrounds' must be encouraged to 'bear counter-cultural witness to the love of Christ in deed and word, by obeying the extensive biblical commands to love the stranger, defend the cause of the foreigner, visit the prisoner, practise hospitality, build friendships, invite into our homes, and provide help and services' (*Cape Town Commitment*, IIC.5.B).

These models and motifs represent core values and concepts lying at the heart of *kinetic mission models*. Crucially, they lie at the centre of the Lausanne Movement's vision of 'the Whole Church taking the Whole Gospel to the Whole World.'[14][15]

For Discussion

1. What do you think are likely to be some of the distinctions between a programme in Diaspora Studies and a programme in Diaspora Missiology? Why is this important for the evangelical student of diaspora and migration?
2. What theological and missiological support might the first half of the Lausanne Movement's Cape Town Commitment ('A Confession of Faith') provide for the wide-ranging activities of the Global Diaspora Network? Do you think Appendix E, found in Section 7 (excerpted from the CTC's 'Call to Action') is consistent with the CTC's first half ('A Confession of Faith')?
3. What does the new terminology of 'kinetic' mission imply? What are potential benefits and/or weaknesses of the use of this new terminology?

---

14 See Appendix B for the Seoul Declaration on Diaspora Missiology.
15 See Appendix E for the Cape Town Commitment.

SECTION 2: BIBLICAL AND THEOLOGICAL FOUNDATION FOR DIASPORA MISSIOLOGY

Thomas Harvey and Miyon Chung,
Section Editors

Bible, Theology and Diaspora: An Introduction

Section Editors: Thomas Allan Harvey and Miyon Chung

Being on the move has been and will continue to be a significant aspect modern life and ministry. Indeed, around the globe, the pressure of increased migration is in the news as officials, religious leaders, academics, and the average person attempts to cope with the steady flood of immigrants. All in their own way seek resources by which to respond. Some turn to legal structures, others to informed research, yet as Christians we have a remarkable source in Scripture that can serve to orient and inform sound spiritual and practical mission and ministry today.

The Bible gives a unique perspective given that migrants and migration loom large when it comes to the fulfillment of God's purposes for creation and its redemption. It reminds us that God not only chooses people who are on the move to fulfill his plans and purposes for creation and its redemption, God is seen as the one who at various times has called his chosen people to leave their homes and travel to new lands. This divine vocation informs the chapters that follow. Here we will examine the role of migration and migrants in the Old and New Testaments of the Bible. We will also consider some of the theological and ethical implications Biblical revelation has for mission and ministry today to, through, and beyond the people on the move.

This section of the Compendium begins with chapters that consider Old and New Testament perspectives on migration and will conclude with chapters that look at migration theologically and ethically. The chapters are arranged to provide the reader with a biblical understanding of migration and some tools to engage theologically and ethically with migration and migrant peoples.

M. Daniel Carroll R. (Rodas), in his chapter *Diaspora and Mission in the Old Testament*, considers the contribution of the Old Testament to understanding mission. First the Old Testament provides a *description* of migration and the crucial challenges that face those on the move in terms of survival, as sense of identity, and crises of belief at times when they feel abandoned by God. This material can serve to remind Christians in all situations of the difficult realities migrants encounter. It also serves as a rich resource for people on the move. In reading and engagement with the Old Testament, people on the move see people in similar circumstances who have experienced liberation and empowerment through faith in God and his intervention in their lives. They can see in the Old Testament narratives that God is concerned about migrants like themselves. Secondly, the Old Testament provides a crucial *theological orientation* for reflection on diaspora missions. The mission of the people of God to bless the "clans of the earth" is a mandate that requires movement and dispersion among the peoples of the earth. Finally Carroll notes the *ethical dimension* of the Old Testament that holds his people accountable to their concern and compassion towards people on the move, which includes the expectation that they will minister to those facing the traumas of migration through real intervention on their behalf.

Steven S. H. Chang, in his chapter *From Opportunity to Mission: Scattering for the Gospel in the New Testament Story*, looks at how diaspora people in the New Testament were prepared and used for mission. He begins with the way the New Testament takes into consideration the Jewish diaspora, cultural tensions in the Greco-Roman world, and the role of Roman rule upon the Jewish diaspora. This then provides the background for the role diaspora Jews play in the New Testament story that rests in the place of diaspora in the plan of God. Finally, Chang looks at the tension between Jews and Gentiles in the New Testament in light of their diaspora setting and how those conflicts shaped Christian identity and core beliefs.

In emphasising mission that is to, through and beyond people on the move, Harvey argues that it is important to note that this encompasses not only the object of mission, but its means. Accordingly mission studies need to go beyond history and description and address the attitude and orientation of mission in light of its roots in diaspora. He notes that God's chosen people are called from creation onwards to be "on the move" and this should inform our understanding of, attitude toward, activity in, and character of, mission.

Paul Woods, in his chapter *God, Israel, the Church and the Other: Otherness as a Theological Motif in Diaspora Missions*, considers the impact of globalisation and related trends in communications and how these have enhanced transportation making it easier for some people to move substantial distances. He brings out the individual and communal identity of the migrant who comes into a neighbourhood or community as both an individual and a perceived representative of a group. These arrivals are often very different from locals in their physical appearance, socio-economic status, language and culture, family structures, social mores, and expectations. As such they are often identified as the "Other." This "Otherness" that exists between host and migrant is a key aspect of the relationship between local Christian communities and incoming migrants. The presence of migrants requires Christians in the host community, and indeed migrants themselves, to ask why a person should go out of his or her comfort zone and interact with someone very different: "Why bother with someone so dissimilar to oneself? How should Christians deal with otherness and how does this speak into ministry to diaspora peoples?"

Thomas Harvey, in his chapter *Pilgrims on a Journey: Diaspora and Mission*, offers a bridge between biblical and theological/ethical reflection. Harvey begins by looking at two covenants central to a biblical understanding of mission: creation and redemption. These two covenants orient mission to, through and beyond diaspora communities. In briefly recounting the story of creation, fall and redemption, Harvey brings out the dynamic character of biblical Christian mission. Accordingly, Creation, Fall, and Redemption should not be approached as static theological categories, but as ideas caught up in an intricate theological dance of initiative and response to, through and beyond people on the move.

Terry McGrath, Victoria Sibley-Bentley, Andrew Butcher, and George Wieland, in their chapter *Mission to & from Diaspora: Influencing the Context for Mission,* explore the Biblical and theological basis needed to influence thinking in policy-making and decision-making of national leaders, especially in relation to migrants and diaspora, on both a governmental level and within church leadership. Using the New Zealand context (the context of the paper's authors) as a case study, the authors examine the application of principles to influence church and state.

5. Diaspora and Mission in the Old Testament

M. Daniel Carroll R. (Rodas)

Introduction

Purpose and orientation of the essay

The history of humanity is defined in part by the migration of individuals, families, and entire communities. Since time immemorial, natural disasters, economic need, armed conflict, political and religious persecution, racial and cultural marginalization – among other factors – have generated relocation within national or ethnic boundaries or across borders.[1] It should not be surprising that the Old Testament contains accounts of migration, since such movements also characterized the ancient world. On the one hand, the Old Testament portrays many of these experiences, especially of the people of God, and locates them within the sovereign plan of God. The displacements of Israel (and other nations) are not haphazard accidents of history. On the other hand, the Old Testament connects the life of his people outside of the land to God's mission to redeem the world. The Lord directs the unfolding of his purposes through their diasporas.

There are at least three ways that the Old Testament contributes to diaspora missiology and mission, and these provide the outline of this chapter. The first contribution is *descriptive*. Migration is central in many ways to the biblical story from the very first chapter of Genesis. The Old Testament depicts the multiple challenges to the survival, identity, and faith of the people of God as they live in other lands. This material can sensitize non-diasporic people to the difficult realities that migrants face. At the same time, the Old Testament represents a wonderful fund of texts for those in diaspora. They can recognize that their lives find parallels in biblical Israel and that today, as then, God is concerned about migrants. Some minority scholars have proposed a diasporic hermeneutics in order to better appreciate these accounts.[2]

---

1 For recent migration data and bibliography, see Amador A. Remigio, "Global Migration and Diasporas: A Geographical Perspective," in Human Tidal Wave: Global Migration, Megacities, Multiculturalism, Pluralism, Diaspora Missiology, ed. S. J. Tira (Manila: LifeChange, 2013), 1-65.

2 E.g., from an Hispanic diaspora perspective in North America, see Luis R. Rivera-Rodríguez, "Toward a Diaspora Hermeneutics (Hispanic North America)," in Character Ethics and the Old Testament: Moral Dimensions of Scripture, ed. M. D. Carroll R. and J. E. Lapsley (Louisville, KY: Westminster John Knox, 2007), 169-

Second, the Old Testament offers a *key theological orientation* for diasporic missiological reflection. In Old Testament terms, the essence of the mission of the people of God is to be a blessing and a channel of blessing to "all the clans of the earth" (Gen. 12:3, my translation). Later in the essay, this mandate will be defined and then illustrated by how several individuals in the biblical narratives fleshed out this mandate in their dispersions. Therein lie lessons for modern appropriation of that calling.

Third, the Old Testament makes clear that diaspora missions carries an *ethical dimension*. To engage migration with sober realism and genuine compassion requires dealing with news reports and testimonial literature that tell of drownings at sea and fatalities from heat and dehydration in the desert. This also means learning to deal with the traumas of those on the move, which for some includes physical abuse, sexual violation, and cruel exploitation by human traffickers. The most heart-wrenching victims often are women and children, the most vulnerable of migrants. Many displaced persons also face difficult legal issues related to their legal status as refugees, as asylum seekers, or as authorized or undocumented immigrants. In addition, diaspora communities often endure sociocultural, economic, and political marginalization and persecution in their new land. These difficulties cannot be ignored. The Old Testament, more specifically the measures in the Law designed to alleviate the plight of outsiders, can serve as a guide for incorporating moral concerns into diaspora missiology, the formulation of mission strategies, and wider contextual participation in migration issues. There is an inescapable connection between missiological discussions and human rights concerns.

Limitations of space require that what follows be a selective presentation of the relevant biblical material.[3] Before dealing in turn with the three aforementioned dimensions of diaspora and mission in the Old Testament, the second part of this Introduction cites the treatment of Old Testament material that appears in a recent significant publication and then remarks on the growing conviction beyond missiological circles that the biblical diasporas are relevant for the Christian church as a whole.

89; Jean-Pierre Ruiz, Readings from the Edges: The Bible and People on the Move (Studies in Latino/a Catholicism; Maryknoll, NY: Orbis, 2011); M. Daniel Carroll R., "Reading the Bible through Other Lenses: New Vistas from a Hispanic Diaspora Perspective," in Global Voices: Reading the Bible in the Majority World, ed. C. S. Keener and M. D. Carroll R. (Peabody: Hendrickson, 2012), 3-26.

3 I have written extensively on the Bible and migration elsewhere. See my Christians at the Border: Immigration, the Church, and the Bible (2d ed.; Grand Rapids, MI: Brazos, 2013); "Biblical Perspectives on Migration and Mission: Contributions from the Old Testament," Mission Studies 30, no. 1 (2013): 7-25; "Immigration: Looking at the Challenges through a Missional Lens," in Living Witness: Explorations in Missional Ethics, ed. J. Rowe and A. Draycott (Downers Grove, IL: InterVarsity, 2012), 258-77.

Scholarly missiological work on Diaspora in the Old Testament

The number of publications that relate diaspora realities to the biblical text is increasing. Some argue in a general way that migration is an essential biblical theme as the foundation for a broader discussion of mission issues; others try to correlate specific passages or biblical characters to the experiences of particular local diaspora communities.[4] Two examples of sustained studies of the Old Testament appear in *Diaspora Missiology*, a volume edited by Enoch Wan.[5] One chapter helpfully surveys the lexicon of scattering in both testaments. The variety in vocabulary suggests the importance of the topic in the Bible. The second explores in some detail the diaspora experiences of the patriarchs and of Israel in Egypt and during the Babylonian exile. What is particularly useful in this second chapter is the weaving of the biblical material with observations pertaining to contemporary diaspora communities. These issues include the nature of group identity, the reasons for migration, the roles of leaders and advocates, the complex interface between outsiders and host cultures, the significance of a collective memory of diaspora experiences for faith, and the ongoing links that migrants have to their homeland.

Interestingly, in the last few decades the concept of the people of God as aliens in the world is finding traction as a fundamental metaphor for what it means to be a Christian and for how the church should evaluate its engagement within increasingly secular and hostile environments. In addition to the diasporic orientation from specific minority communities mentioned earlier, three outstanding examples of this orientation for the church as a whole are the late ethicist John Howard Yoder[6] and Old

---

4 For appeals to the Bible as the basis for a broader discussion of diaspora, see, e.g., Jehu J. Hanciles, Beyond Christendom: Globalization, African Migration, and the Transformation of the West (Maryknoll, NY: Orbis, 2008), 140-48; Fleur Houston, You Shall Love the Stranger as Yourself: The Bible, Refugees and Asylum (New York, NY: Routledge, 2015). For the connection between biblical texts and contemporary case studies, see, e.g., Mission Studies 30 (2013), nos. 1 and 2; Van Thanh Nguyen and John M. Prior, eds., God's People on the Move: Biblical and Global Perspectives on Migration and Mission (Eugene, OR: Wipf & Stock, 2014).

5 Narry Santos, "Exploring the Major Dispersion Terms and Realities in the Bible," and Ted Rubesh, "Diaspora Distinctives: The Jewish Diaspora Experience in the Old Testament," in Diaspora Missiology: Theory, Methodology, and Practice, ed. Enoch Wan (Portland: Institute of Diaspora Studies, 2011), 21-38 and 39-72, respectively.

6 Although the exile is an important image for Yoder in general, note especially his "See How They Go with Their Face to the Sun," in For the Nations: Essays Evangelical and Public (Grand Rapids, MI: Eerdmans, 1997), 51-78; cf. John C. Nugent, The Politics of Yahweh: John Howard Yoder, the Old Testament, and the People of God (Eugene, OR: Cascade, 2011), 74-87, 149-71. The work of ethicist Stanley Hauerwas also deserves mention in this regard.

Testament scholars Walter Brueggemann and Daniel Smith Christopher.[7] We will return briefly to their work later in this chapter. What these scholars demonstrate – and this is of great importance – is that the burgeoning focus on diaspora in missiology resonates with its centrality for Christian faith. This wider appreciation confirms the timeliness and relevance of this growing missiological interest.

Migration: Central to the Biblical Narrative

Genesis opens with the creation account, which climaxes on the sixth day with the creation of humanity in the image of God (1:26-30). After six declarations that what God had spoken into existence was "good" (1:4, 10, 12, 18, 21, 25), the text now states that he regards this completion of the created order as "very good" (1:31). One aspect of the mandate given to humans in 1:28 is that they are to fill the earth (cf. 1:22). Said another way, from the very beginning, geographic movement is part of what it means to be human. This does not mean that every human being must continually be on the go, but rather that migration will characterize humanity's life on earth. Motivations and numbers vary by context and era, but this impulse is embedded in our very being. This call is linked to the charge to "subdue" and "rule" the earth and its creatures (1:26, 28) and to "work" and "take care" of the garden (2:15) as God's vice-regents.[8] This connection suggests that humanity will accomplish its divine calling and multiple responsibilities as it moves across the face of the earth. In the divine economy, migrations are to be purposeful in relationship to God, the created order, and other human beings.

The setting of the garden is irreparably changed with the disobedience and sin of chapter three. Here starts the journey of humanity, driven to wander not by submission to the tasks set out by God, but by judgment. Adam and Eve are banished from the garden (3:23-24), and later Cain is cursed and sent away from the presence of God (4:13-16). The mandate to fill the earth is repeated after the Flood (9:1), and the geographical breadth of the Table of Nations in chapter 10 is testament to its fulfillment.

---

7 Walter Brueggemann, Cadences of Home: Preaching among Exiles (Louisville, KY: Westminster John Knox, 1997); idem, Out of Babylon (Nashville, TN: Abingdon, 2010); Daniel L. Smith-Christopher, A Biblical Theology of Exile (Overtures to Biblical Theology; Minneapolis, MN: Fortress, 2002), 189-203.

8 Christopher J. H. Wright, The Mission of God: Unlocking the Bible's Grand Narrative (Downers Grove, IL: InterVarsity, 2006), 421-28; idem, The Mission of God's People: A Biblical Theology of the Church's Mission (Biblical Theology for Life; Grand Rapids, MI: Zondervan, 2010), 49-52. The creation of humanity in the image of God reveals the worth and potential of all human beings. This foundational truth bears communicating in many diaspora situations, where migrants and their communities often are seen as inferior to the native born population.

The construction of the Tower of Babel is a project grounded explicitly in humanity's refusal to follow God's design to fill the earth (11:4). Once again, scattering is forced by divine punishment, even as it is a gracious intervention to limit the frightening potential for unrestrained evil (11:5-7). From this dispersion arose humanity's languages, cultures, and bounded territories (10:5, 20, 31).[9] Some deny or minimize the condemnatory tone of this narrative by emphasizing the wonderful creativity and variety of human cultures and the fact that these rich differences are maintained into the glorious visions in Revelation (5:9-14; 7:9-17); they are, it is claimed, an expression of the incredible capacities of those made in God's image! To play one emphasis against the other, however, is to misread *this* text. The tower truly was an amazing technological feat, but at its core it was a defiant act against God. Cultural diversity and achievement – of settled and migrant communities – were born, as it were, at Babel. Consequently, from a biblical perspective, every human social construct is imbued with both incredible beauty and deep sin.

From the expansive canvas of humanity's dispersion in Genesis 10-11, the narrative narrows its attention to the movements of one man – Abram – and his family. Their trek begins in Ur in southeastern Mesopotamia, continues to Haran to the northwest, and finally turns south into Canaan (11:27–12:5). The life of Abram and the other patriarchs will be marked in large measure by landlessness as pastoral nomads, or roaming Bedouin-like sheepherders, among the more established populations of the land (23:4; cf. Deut. 26:5). Beyond this largely unsettled way of life, there are several short-term migrations to other places to find food in time of famine.

One scene is acutely alarming (Gen. 12:10-20). Readers can appreciate the flight to Egypt to survive hunger, but Abram's plea for his wife Sarai to put her person in jeopardy by saying she is his sister in order to ensure his own safety is shocking. Abram and Sarai indeed are related (20:12), but how could he entertain such a dangerous ploy, and why was she willing to go along? Studies of strategies employed by migrants can illumine the passage. Desperate people go to extreme measures to survive, and women regularly have taken the greatest risks for the sake of their families. A willingness to lie to get across a border and to gamble with one's physical integrity are not uncommon features of immigrant stories. The decision of Abram and Sarai is not different from the actions of many who today flee natural disasters, war, and deprivation.

The Joseph narrative demonstrates some of the dynamics of assimilation in diaspora (Gen. 37-50). Joseph is sold into slavery and taken into Egypt. He is hardworking and honest and eventually becomes head of Potiphar's

---

9 The order of chapters 9-11 is literary, not sequential. Chapter 10 is an extended interruption that informs the reader of the spread of the descendants of Noah's sons (9:24-27). Chapter 11 returns to the narrative flow after the death of Noah (9:28-29) and explains the impetus behind the dispersion and the proliferation of languages of chapter 10.

household, but then he is unfairly put in prison after refusing to be seduced by his master's wife. Whom do the authorities believe: the foreigner or the native-born woman of status? Once he is released into Pharaoh's court, Joseph acculturates into Egyptian society. He shaves according to Egyptian customs for his position (41:14) and is introduced with much pomp to his new political role (41:41–43). He is given an Egyptian name and marries an Egyptian woman (41:45). Joseph dresses and puts on the facial make-up appropriate to his position in that cultural context, so that even his brothers do not recognize him (43:8; 45:1–15). Joseph follows Egyptian social mores by not permitting them to eat with him (43:32). He speaks the Egyptian language and pretends to need an interpreter when he speaks with his brothers (42:23-24). In all of this, though, this immigrant does not forget his roots. Joseph gives his two sons Israelite names related to his faith in God (41:50–52), and he communicates with his family in his mother tongue. Joseph presents his father Jacob without embarrassment to Pharaoh, even though Egyptians despised shepherds (46:31–47:12). Upon his death, Joseph is embalmed according to Egyptian practice (50:26; cf. 50:3), but he already had made provision to return his remains to his homeland (50:24-25; cf. Exod. 13:19; Josh. 24:32). Joseph is a fascinating example of an immigrant, who learns to live competently and with integrity in multiple sociocultural and linguistic worlds.

Other biblical characters display varying levels of integration into their foreign contexts. Daniel and his friends have to serve Babylon, the empire that had destroyed their country. They are given new names and reeducated to be functionaries for Nebuchadnezzar, but they hold on to their culture (note that they ask for their own food) and stake their lives on their belief in God (Dan. 1-6). In the same time frame, but not in a royal setting, Ezekiel lives in diaspora along the Kebar River with other displaced Judahites. Reluctantly, he rehearses the reasons for their plight, exhorts his people to be faithful in that new setting, and offers them the hope of the restoration of their homeland and of a new, glorious temple. Jeremiah deals with the unfounded expectation of those in exile that the time away would be short (Jer. 25:11-12; 29:10; cf. Dan. 9:2). The people were overwhelmed, confused, and expectant of divine succor. Jeremiah must redirect their energies to adapting to life in Babylon.[10] The anonymous author of Psalm 137 expresses the anger and humiliation of those who had witnessed first-hand the horrors of war and had been forcefully removed. Brueggemann describes the emotions of those recent arrivals as those of despair, rootlessness, a sense of God's absence, moral incongruity, and an unhealthy

---

10 A few years later, Jeremiah is taken against his wishes to Egypt after the assassination of Gedeliah, the Babylonian governor (2 Kings. 25:22-24; Jer. 30). In contrast to his encouraging words to those in Babylon, the prophet condemns the fight to Egypt (Jer. 41-45).

self-focus, as they tried to make sense of the defeat of their armies and, seemingly, of their God and the loss of all that they knew and cherished.[11]

Several decades later, Ezra leads a group back to the land to establish a Torah-observant community. He has little desire to assimilate to Persia, yet nonetheless he appreciates his need to take advantage of imperial support to accomplish his project. The case of Nehemiah is sharply different. He is cupbearer to Artaxerxes, the Persian king, a job that demanded absolute loyalty to the monarch and the empire. Still, Nehemiah is attentive to news from Jerusalem, an interest that modern studies label a characteristic of transnationalism.[12] With royal backing, he leaves to rebuild the city walls but returns to his post when finished. Though these two men reflect diverse points on the assimilation spectrum, they stand together to read the Law to the people and are uncompromising in their call to preserve a pure Jewish identity (Ezra 9-10; Neh. 5, 8-10, 13). In contrast, Esther (a Persian name; Hadassah is her Jewish name, 2:7), winner of a beauty pageant and then queen, shows no interest in returning. Esther grows in her commitment to her people through the guidance of her kinsman Mordechai, as she navigates how to foil Haman's plan for ethnic cleansing. These exiles – Daniel, Ezekiel, Ezra, Nehemiah, and Esther – process the diaspora in distinct ways due to their chronological distance from the dispersion, their particular situations, and their personalities. Recent diaspora research has begun to investigate the generational and socioeconomic differences among migrant populations, issues that are evident in the Old Testament narratives.

These various biblical texts remind us that all peoples and groups at one time in their history were wanderers (ultimately, starting from Babel) and rebellious against God. These narratives illustrate, too, various strategies diaspora peoples employ to navigate their new surrounding and ways they sustain a level of cultural identity and ties to their land of origin. There is much here that matches experiences of modern diaspora peoples and that can provide valuable insights – whether cultural, pragmatic, or theological – for diaspora missiology.

Mission for and in Diaspora

Defining the mission of the people of God

Discussion of the mission of the people of God in the Old Testament inevitably is wide-ranging, because of the amount of material, diverse

---

11 Brueggemann, Cadences of Home, 3-11.

12 Sociologist Peggy Levitt is a leading voice in this research. Note, e.g., her "Roots and Routes: Understanding the Lives of the Second Generation Transnationally," Journal of Ethnic and Migration Studies 35, no. 7 (2009): 1225-42.

genres, and the large span of time represented in its content and production. At the same time, a constant theme throughout is the mission to be a blessing (Gen. 12:1-3).[13]

The terminology and concepts of this passage are connected self-consciously to the preceding narratives. To begin with, in stark contrast to humanity that aspires to make a name for itself in independence from God (11:4), Yahweh promises to make the name of his people great as they fulfill their calling (12:2). Their reputation will be rooted in service to him and all peoples. Second, the term "clans" (*mišpᵉhōt*)[14] in 12:3 is the same word used in 10:5, 20, 31-32. Literarily, this wordplay conveys the point that all those groups in chapter 10, whose origins go back to the dispersion from Babel, are the targets of the divine plan. The mission of the people of God, who begin as an extended family on the move, is set *within* and *for* a world of diaspora, among those nations whose heart defies God. Such is his grace! Third, the structure of 12:1-3 is informative. Because Abram and his descendants will be blessed by Yahweh (12:2a, b), they are to be a blessing to others (12:2c-3). Mission flows naturally from an obedient and bountiful relationship with the covenant God to the rest of the world.

How does the book of Genesis define "bless" and "blessing"? The concept is introduced in chapters one and two. It is related to material abundance and procreation (1:21-22, 28), but also has a spiritual dimension. God blesses the seventh day (2:2-3). It will be day of rest, and later in the Pentateuch instructions are given to set aside the Sabbath for human rest and worship of the LORD. Blessing in the Genesis narratives, therefore, is comprehensive. Blessing is both physical and spiritual; it is holistic. The following chapters bear this out.

God's hand in material blessing is evident in the birth of children (21:1-2; 25:1-4; 29:31–30:24; 46:8-27; 47:27), and in the accumulation of harvests, flocks, servants, and wealth (13:2; 24:35; 26:12-14; 29:20, 27-30; 30:43; 47:27); he helps the patriarchs find water (26:17-22). Others enjoy material blessings through the patriarchs in fulfillment of the divine mission to be a channel of blessing. Abram rescues his nephew Lot (14:1-16); Jacob cares for Laban's herds and oversees their increase (30:29-30; 31:6, 28-42); Joseph serves Potiphar (39:2-5) and Pharaoh with integrity and saves Egypt from famine (47:13-26).

On the spiritual side, the commission to be a blessing is manifest through testimony, prayer, and sacrifice. The patriarchs demonstrate their faith in Yahweh by building altars and openly calling upon his name (12:7-

---

13 M. Daniel Carroll R., "Blessing the Nations: Toward a Biblical Theology of Mission from Genesis," Bulletin of Biblical Research 10, no. 1 (2000): 17-34; Wright, The Mission of God, 189-221; idem, The Mission of God's People, 63-81; cf. T. Desmond Alexander, From Paradise to the Promised Land (3rd ed.; Grand Rapids, MI: Baker Academic, 2012), 146-60.

14 English versions also have translated the term as "families" (NRSV, NASB, NKJV, ESV, CEB) or "peoples" (NIV).

8; 13:18; 26:25; 32:20; 35:1-7). They speak of Yahweh with those they engage (30:30; 31:5-13, 42; 33:5, 10-11; 40:8, 12-16, 25-33, 50-52), bless others in his name (14:18-24; 47:7, 10), and intercede so that God might withhold judgment (18:16-32; 20:7, 17-18). Those with whom the patriarchs come into contact witness these marvels and confess that they have seen Yahweh bless the lives of his people (14:18-24; 21:22-24; 24:31, 50; 26:29; 30:27; 31:27-30, 50, 53; 41:37).

The lives of the patriarchs are fraught with challenges of all kinds. Their responses affect the fulfillment of their mission to be a blessing. Theirs is a physical pilgrimage, but also one of faith. While in their best moments they profess the name of Yahweh, at other junctures they exhibit cowardice, lie, betray one another, and question their fate. One of the most egregious failures of the Genesis narratives is the vengeance wrought on the people of Shechem for the violation of Dinah (Gen. 34). The sons of Jacob attack the men of that area after they had become incapacitated after submitting to circumcision. The very sign of the covenant gave them occasion to kill and dispossess one of the clans of the earth! The highlights of the Genesis narratives are found in chapters fifteen and twenty-two. In Genesis 15:6 Abram is commended for believing the impossible promise of an heir. More weighty are the words of the angel of the LORD in 22:15-18. The call of 12:3 is repeated, and the condition for fulfilling the mission is clearly stated: obedience to the will of Yahweh (22:18; cf. 18:19).

These passages of Genesis teach that the people of God were created for mission, the mission to be a blessing to a rebellious world that seeks to displace him. This mission is both material and spiritual, extending the redemptive purposes of God into every area of human existence. From the beginning, God's people have been on the move; while some will settle, others scatter. To accomplish that mission of blessing, they are to be faithful to God, whatever the circumstances. There will be failures and setbacks but, as they grow in faith and display lives of integrity, they become God's vessels of blessing.

Living out the mission in Diaspora

The Old Testament depicts a number of examples of authentic belief in diaspora, some of which were touched on earlier. This section highlights Jeremiah 29. The book of Jeremiah has received recent attention in missiology from biblical scholars in a general sense, because it testifies to God's concern for the nations and Israel's universal mission; Israel's history was a means by which the nations of the earth eventually would come to know him (e.g., 1:5; 3:17; 4:1-2; 6:18; 33:8-9).[15] I want to focus,

---

15 See, e.g., Christopher J. H. Wright, "'Prophet to the Nations': Missional Reflections on the Book of Jeremiah," in A God of Faithfulness: Essays in Honour of J. Gordon McConville on His 60th Birthday, ed. J. A. Grant, A. Lo, and G. J.

however, on that specific chapter. This passage has garnered much interest in diaspora missions circles, so it merits particular attention.

Jeremiah 29 contains the prophet's correspondence to those who had been taken from Judah into exile in 598-597 B.C.E.[16] King Jehoiakim's rebellion against the Babylonian empire had spurred Nebuchadnezzar to march west with his armies to punish this insubordinate vassal. Before their arrival Jehoiakim died, and his son Jehoiachin took his place. His reign was short-lived, as he, the royal court, and many others were removed to Babylon as the empire's initial penalty and warning against further defiance. Jehoiachin's uncle, Mattaniah, whose name was changed to Zedekiah, was then put on the throne (2 Kings. 24:1-17). The exiles, who received the prophet's letter, were displaced before the horrific siege of Jerusalem and the subsequent deportation that would occur about a decade later (586 B.C.E.). There would be yet another Babylonian attack on the region in 582 after the assassination of the governor Gedaliah. On these three occasions, many thousands were led away from Judah.[17]

What were the living conditions of that first wave of Judahites in exile? The books of Daniel and Ezekiel and this chapter in Jeremiah can give the impression that life was relatively peaceful and prosperous. Recent archaeological findings are providing a more comprehensive and nuanced picture beyond what might be gleaned from this Old Testament material. According to these data, experiences were quite varied.[18] Some would have worked as servants, others in agriculture or as corvée (or forced) labor on construction projects such as irrigation canals. Apparently, a number eventually did achieve a modicum of economic stability and social

---

Wenham (LHB/OTS 538; London: T. & T. Clark, 2011), 112-29; Jerry Hwang, "The Missio Dei as an Integrative Motif in the Book of Jeremiah." Bulletin for Biblical Research 23, no. 4 (2013): 481-508; cf. Michael W. Goheen, A Light to the Nations: The Missional Church and the Biblical Story (Grand Rapids, MI: Baker Academic, 2011), 49-74.

16 Scholars debate how many letters are reflected in the chapter: e.g., do vv. 24-32 attest to additional letters beyond the one sent by Jeremiah with the envoys of King Zedekiah (v. 3)?

17 Note the numbers in 2 Kings 24:14; 25:11-12; Jer. 52:28-30. The size of the diasporic community is a topic of discussion. The broader diaspora population included those who fled to Moab, Ammon, and Edom (Jer. 40:11-12), as well as others who fled to Egypt after the assassination of Gedeliah, the governor appointed by the Babylonians (2 Kings 25:25-26; Jer. 41-44).

18 For this paragraph see Smith-Christopher, A Biblical Theology of Exile, and the relevant essays in Brad E. Kelle, Frank Ritchel Ames, and Jacob L. Wright, eds., Interpreting Exile: Displacement and Deportation in Biblical and Modern Contexts (Ancient Israel and Its Literature 10; Atlanta: Society of Biblical Literature, 2011) and in John J. Ahn and Jill Middlemas, eds., By the Irrigation Canals of Babylon: Approaches to the Study of the Exile (Library of Hebrew Bible/Old Testament Studies 526; London: T. & T. Clark, 2012). Not all agree on the extent of the exiles' fortunes.

standing.[19] Babylon also had a policy of settling some displaced groups together and allowing them to live somewhat independently. There now is evidence of Judean villages in the region of Nippur. The fact that Ezekiel is able to gather elders might reflect the existence of this sort of community (Ezek. 8:1; 14:1; 20:1; cf. 1:1; 3:15). In addition, biblical scholars are beginning to appropriate refugee research, forced migration and diaspora studies, and trauma theory to reconstruct what life away from the land may have been like. These new perspectives alert us to distinguish the potentially different experiences of that first generation in Babylon from those of later exiles and to be on the lookout for other nuances in the biblical material.

Those who heard Jeremiah's message probably were still smarting from being carted away against their will by imperial decree. Beyond the emotional and physical effects of a forced migration, was the impact on the exiles' view of the world. According to the theological mindset shared across the ancient Near East, military defeat meant defeat of one's chief god by the god of the victorious army. In other words, life in exile not only required dealing with the pragmatics of life and the tragedies of human loss, it also meant having categories to comprehend somehow the negation of a belief system centered on Yahweh – with the attendant impression on the people's understanding of the meaning and direction of existence itself. What the exiles took as the very nature of things, along with all of its legitimating rituals (personal, familial, and communal), had been turned on its head. These cultural and religious challenges would be much more disturbing, when Judah would be devastated by the massive destruction of 586. The book of Lamentations depicts the frightening aftermath of the Babylonian onslaught. What can the prophet tell his people, who had suffered loss (note that the letter is to the "surviving elders," v. 1)?

The purpose of the letter is to move those in exile away from the anger, bitterness, and despair about their fate and to reorient their appreciation of Yahweh their God vis-à-vis the deities of the empire. These are not simply words of consolation and encouragement from Jeremiah's heart; this letter delivers the very oracles of Yahweh (vv. 4, 10, 16, 20). They must hear what *He*, the one true God, speaks into their new circumstances and rethink what they must now do and be. The fact that the letter is sent with royal envoys added to its credence (v. 3).

What complicated the situation both in exile and back at home in Judah was that other voices were claiming to speak for God and were offering a very different message. These prophets and leaders were declaring that the time away from the land would be short and that the Babylonian juggernaut would not take the capital city. All was not what it seemed; Yahweh would

19 Of course, the life of Daniel and his friends and of Judah's king and family (cf. 2 Kings 25:27-30) in the Babylonian royal precincts would not be characteristic of the broader exilic population.

win, and they could go home soon! This reassuring word was being proclaimed among the exiles and surely had gotten a positive reaction from some (note 29:8-9, 21-22, 24-32). There also was unrest in the empire in 595-594 B.C.E., and perhaps there were those who may have been tempted to participate in that conspiracy because of these unfounded hopes.[20] Jeremiah had confronted these false prophets directly in Jerusalem (Hananiah, Jer. 28; cf. 27:9, 14). His contrary message was perceived as treason and had generated vehement opposition (11:18-23; 18:18; 20:1-2, 7-8; chpts. 26, 36-38) and personal anguish (12:1-6; 15:10-21; 16:1-9; 17:14-18; 18:19-23; 20:14-18). The words given to Jeremiah at his call had warned him of that coming storm of rejection (1:17-19).

There are at least two key interrelated and inseparable points to Jeremiah's letter. First, he must change their view of God. Against all appearances, the prophet proclaims that Yahweh is sovereign. In the midst of all the sociocultural and religious contradictions of their displacement and the chaos of their current political situation, Yahweh is in control. Their diaspora was not a mistake, nor was he absent. He was the one who had sent them to Babylon (v. 4), and who would return them to the land in his timing and in accordance with his good plans for their future (vv. 10-14). Later chapters in the book, beyond this letter, contribute to that vision of restoration (chpts. 30-33). Moreover, Yahweh was moving history beyond the present: another judgment lay ahead for Judah after the sending of the letter (vv. 15-23), and Babylon one day would fall (chpts. 25, 50–51). He was behind the rise and fall and the movements of all peoples (cf. Am. 9:7). In new and surprising ways the exiles were seeing that Yahweh was the one, truly global, omniscient, omnipotent, and omnipresent deity, who, as he had always been, was committed to them. In other words, the diaspora was the locus for fresh, *significant theological reflection.*

Second, the circumstances also led to *reflection about the mission of the people of God* (vv. 5-7). Thinking about their missional role went hand in hand with a reconfiguration of their understanding of how life in exile was to be construed and carried forward. The center of their community no longer could be the Temple, with all that it signified for their worldview and lifestyle, or the land that they and their ancestors cherished. On the one hand, this reconstitution meant there had to be a greater focus on how to appropriate their scripture within this Gentile context (eventually this would lead to the development of the synagogue and the elaboration of oral law and *halakah*).[21] These efforts were internally directed. On the other hand, there also had to be a different formulation of their engagement outward, with that foreign context.

---

20 J. A. Thompson, The Book of Jeremiah (New International Commentary on the Old Testament; Grand Rapids, MI: Eerdmans, 1980), 544-46.

21 Mesopotamia would grow into and remain a thriving center of Judaism until the mid-twentieth century. Some of the Jewish sages there produced the Babylonian Talmud in the fourth and fifth centuries C.E.

Yoder speaks of the "*Galuth* [i.e., exile] as Vocation." As a transplanted marginal and defeated community, the exiles had no civil influence and were markedly different in multiple ways from their surroundings.[22] This arrangement would characterize how they were to incarnate their faith; diaspora now was both a way of life within and a calling to their context. Wright has a set of beautiful turns of phrase to describe what had to happen in the mindset of the exiles for this shift to bear fruit: refugees had to recalibrate themselves as residents, mourners would need to become missionaries, and they had to no longer define themselves as victims but instead embrace the challenge of being visionaries.[23]

More specifically, Jeremiah tells the exiles that Babylon must become home. They are to settle down, plant their crops, marry[24] and have families (vv. 5-6). These actions clearly communicate that their stay would be multigenerational; they were to dig roots in their diaspora. For some, this would mean the stipulated seventy years; for others, that region would be their residence for centuries. Crucially, the language of these lines has significant links to other passages.[25] For instance, the command to increase echoes the words of Genesis 1:28, which would find special expression in the divine promise to make Abram's descendants into a great nation and to multiply his offspring. That is, the Babylonian diaspora was the place that they had been placed to fulfill their human mandate and their mission as the people of God.

The exiles also are to seek the *shalom* of their new dwelling (v. 7). This, of course, is a rich Old Testament term that carries the sense of well-being, prosperity, and the absence of violence. In the Hebrew, it is repeated three times in this verse, underscoring its importance. What is not specified in any detail, however, is *how* they are to seek the *shalom* of this place to

---

22 Yoder, "See How They Go with Their Face to the Sun."

23 Christopher J. H. Wright, The Message of Jeremiah: Against Wind and Tide (The Bible Speaks Today; Downers Grove, IL: IVP Academic, 2014), 289-99; cf. the practical aspects that Wright mentions based on this passage in idem, The Mission of God's People, 222-43.

24 At this point, it is unlikely that the prophet contemplated intermarrying with those outside the exilic community. Issues of intermarriage were very much a concern to the returnees (see Ezra 9-10; Neh. 13). The epigraphic evidence suggests that over time this endogamy would give way to intermarriage.

25 Some scholars connect these words to Deut. 20:5-9 and the stipulations for exemption from war. This lexical link is said to suggest that Jeremiah is saying that there should be no involvement in the violent conspiracies of the day. Their presence is to be positive, not subversive. See, e.g., Louis Stuhlman, Jeremiah (Abingdon Old Testament Commentaries; Nashville, TN: Abingdon, 2005), 251. Also, the command to build and plant repeats terms from Jeremiah's call, which is repeated a number of times throughout the book (1:10; 12:14-17; 18:7-9; 24:6; 31:28, 40; 42:10; 45:4).

which God had taken them. At the very least, they are to pray for it.[26] That would have been hard. Certainly they knew to pray for *Jerusalem* and *its* peace (122:6), but to pray for their conquerors must have gone against the very core of their being, especially as they were not to pray for God's vengeance upon Babylon but for his hand of favor. How long did such a change in conviction take? How long did the conflicted emotions produced by this command linger? How many never could bring themselves to do this? How might the horror of Judah's end a few years later have affected their reception of these words (cf. Ps. 137)?

The vagueness of the command to seek the *shalom* would have allowed for freedom for its personal, and communal working out in that context. To be committed to the *shalom* of that foreign land is another expression of that mandate to be a blessing to the peoples of the earth. As explained in the previous section of this essay, their greatness would come as they served as God's channels of blessing to others.

In diaspora, the people of God would see him in a new light and ideally understand their existence as missional. The last two occurrences of *shalom* in verse 7 relay the benefit of investing in their new land. In its *shalom* there would be *shalom* for the exiles. Their mission in diaspora would be for the good of those around them and for their own good as well. So it is today. Communities of faith in diaspora need to appreciate the greatness of their sovereign God and embrace the open call to advance the *shalom* of their new setting. In being obedient to the mission of being a blessing they affirm the very reason for their life before God and the world. Recent publications and conferences are demonstrating that now, as then, contexts of diaspora are opportunities for new thinking about God and mission.

Law, diaspora missions, and immigrant advocacy

In addition to the descriptive and theological dimensions of diaspora missions is the ethical. This third component arises from Old Testament legislation regarding the sojourner, or foreigner. We begin our discussion by looking briefly at the nature of law. From a sociology of knowledge perspective, law is a foundational component of what is called the "social construction of reality." Legislation organizes a social world and through its legal stipulations, sanctions, institutions, and personnel maintains the framework for what is deemed to be fundamental to the proper functioning of any given society. As such, law plays a key role in shaping the worldview, attitudes, behavior, and identity of a people. A society's laws

26 There are ironic contrasts with other passages in Jeremiah. The false prophets had assured Jerusalem that shalom lay in their future, when what was coming was an invasion (6:14; 8:11). The prophet Jeremiah was commanded not to pray for his own people, because their judgment was irrevocable (7:16; 11:14; 14:11). In both cases, what was impossible for Judah would be true for Babylon.

offer a glimpse into what (and whom) it cherishes or eschews; into what are its ideals, fears, and the substance of its moral fabric.

Legislation regarding outsiders is part of that social cosmology. Are they welcome? If so, are all to be shown hospitality, or just certain groups? How is entry into that society controlled? How is acceptance, suspicion, or rejection of the outsider made manifest (and perpetuated) through specific laws? What formal (and colloquial) labels are given to foreigners? What is permitted and prohibited to them? What are the criteria that underpin migrant legislation: ethnicity or skin color, country or region of origin, religious background, economic station? In the introduction to this chapter mention was made of the harrowing experiences that many migrants endure in their journeys. Is there any awareness of or concern for these trials and tribulations in a society's laws? If not, why not?

Those who have entered in an unauthorized manner face additional pressures connected to their illegal status before the law. These include the fear of detention and deportation, the inability to claim minimal worker rights and fair compensation, not being qualified to apply for basic social services or medical coverage, and social rejection by the native born or even by other outsiders who have a longer history in that society. The severity of economic and political exclusion and of social marginalization depends on the particular context.

Much more could be said about the connections between legislation and migration, and consequently between law and a diaspora missiology. Old Testament Law can provide guidance in such matters. It is helpful to recognize, as Christopher J. H. Wright has explained, that Old Testament Law was designed for God's redeemed people to incarnate its priestly role as a beacon *to* and *among* the nations *for that time and place* (Deut. 4:5-8). At the same time, though, the law codes of Exodus, Leviticus, and Deuteronomy are not bound to that world of long ago. Wright's paradigm approach demonstrates the ongoing contribution of that ancient Law for social ethics and mission today.[27] His idea, which I find convincing, is that Israel's legislation reflects transcendent divine values and commitments and thus is able to continue to function as a model – not as something to be imitated in its details, but as containing laws whose particulars offer important orientation for the contemporary appropriation of those same values and commitments. The concrete contextualization found in Israel's laws and sociopolitical structures, in other words, will look very different in contemporary societies.

This paradigm approach can be applied to the topic of migration. Migration occurred in the world of the Old Testament, and that reality

---

27 For ethics, see Christopher J. H. Wright, Old Testament Ethics for the People of God (Downers Grove, IL: InterVarsity, 2004), 62–74, 182–211, 314–25. For mission, see idem, The Mission of God, 289-23, 329-44, 357-96; and The Mission of God's People, 96-147.

surfaces within its laws.[28] No other ancient law code contains anywhere near the amount of legislation dealing with outsiders. The openness toward the immigrant, in other words, is one of the unique features of the people of God.[29] To begin with, Old Testament Law appreciated the vulnerability of the outsider. In those days, because of the lack of the governmental safety nets that many societies enjoy today, help during times of sickness, hunger, childbirth, death, and natural disasters had to come through the extended family. These extended families often lived together in multigenerational households or in the same village or town. As a foreigner, the immigrant did not have that close support system. What is more, because ancient Israel was predominantly an agrarian peasant society, livelihood was tied to ownership of property. According to the Law, property was to be passed down through the male line. Accordingly, foreigners would have found it difficult to own land. So, immigrants were vulnerable in multiple ways. They were dependent on the Israelites for charity in times of need, protection, and work. In not a few cases, the sojourner is grouped in the Law along with the poor, widows, and orphans as those most defenseless before the harsh vicissitudes of life (e.g., Deut. 10:18; 16:11; 14:29).

Old Testament Law contains provisions designed to meet the needs of the immigrant. For example, foreign workers were not to be exploited. They were to be granted the Sabbath rest (Exod. 20:10; 23:12; Deut. 5:14) and be paid a fair wage in a timely manner (24:14-15). Outsiders and their families were allotted a portion of the harvest to gather food and would benefit from a triennial tithe (Lev. 19:9-10; Deut. 14:28-29; 24:19-22).[30] Their treatment in legal matters was to be equal to that of the native born; unfair intimidation and biased judgments were forbidden (Deut. 1:16-17; 24:17-18; 27:19). Foreigners even could be included in Israel's worship, that most precious center of its cultural life and identity (e.g., Exod. 12:45-49; Lev. 16:29; Deut. 16:11, 14; 26:11). Finally, the command to "love your neighbor as yourself" (Lev. 19:18), which referred to dealings with

---

28 For a fuller discussion, in addition to the relevant sections in the sources cited fn. 3, see my "Welcoming the Stranger: Toward a Theology of Immigration In Deuteronomy," in For Our Good Always: Studies on the Message and Influence of Deuteronomy in Honor of Daniel I. Block, ed. J. S. DeRouchie, J. Gile, and K. J. Turner (Winona Lake: Eisenbrauns, 2013), 441-62. I work with the final canonical form of the text. Some have tried to coordinate an evolving engagement with outsiders with a hypothetical reconstruction the history of the composition of the legal material. For summaries of various approaches, along with his own proposal, see Mark A, Awabdy, Immigrants and Innovative Law: Deuteronomy's Theological and Social Vision for the GR (FAT 2/67; Tübingen: Mohr Siebeck, 2014).

29 In The Immigration Crisis: Immigrants, Aliens, and the Bible (Wheaton, IL: Crossway, 2009) James K. Hoffmeier argues that these laws applied only to legal immigrants. I find this neither persuasive nor provable.

30 Ruth is an example of an immigrant (and widow), who takes advantage of the gleaning laws.

fellow Israelites, was extended to "love the foreigner" (Lev. 19:33-34). Loving the "Other," in other words, was the true test of love of neighbor.

At the same time, Israel would have had expectations of immigrants. They surely would have had to learn the language to work and take part in the various dimensions of that society. Foreign residents also were mandated to listen to the periodic reading of the Law (Deut. 31:9-13), an exercise that would serve to inculturate them into the ways of Israel. Participation in religious life also implies conversion to Israel's faith. In sum, the immigrants' integration into ancient Israel required adaptation and adjustments on the part of immigrant and native born alike.

Old Testament Law does not sanction disobedience to these legal measures. Instead, it appeals to two deeper, internal motivations. First, Israel was constantly reminded that they were to treat the immigrant well because of their own painful experience as foreigners in Egypt (Exod. 22:21; 23:9; Lev. 19:18, 34; Deut. 24:17-18). To remember that painful past was to welcome the foreigner in the present. That national historical memory was to engender an ethos of sensitive hospitality. They were not to do to the newcomers in their midst what had been done to them years earlier. They were not to become, as it were, the Egyptians.

The second motivation arose from the person and commitment of God (Deut. 10:17-19; cf. 24:14-15). Israel was to love the sojourner, simply because the LORD does. He does this, the text says, in tangible ways by providing food and clothing (Deut. 17:18); so must his people love the stranger. They were the means by which his mercy would come to the immigrants in their midst. Their care for the outsider was a yardstick for how well they knew and obeyed God!

The fact that the Law incorporates the outsider reveals a key dimension of diaspora missiology. At the very least, Christian communities should teach their members to reach out to the foreigners who live among them. To provide for them in tangible ways in the name of our God is proof of our relationship with him. Second, this divine concern for the stranger was given expression in Old Testament Law. Therefore, *as part of their vision for diaspora missions*, it behooves believers today to think about how they might influence contemporary legislation to better reflect God's commitment to the immigrant.

It has been well documented that, for diverse reasons and in different parts of the world, some evangelical Christians have misgivings about participation in social and political affairs. The Old Testament Law teaches that involvement on behalf of the immigrant (as well as for the poor, widows, and orphans) is part and parcel of God's demands on his people. The theological and hermeneutical challenge is to ask what legislation for the care of the sojourner that somehow echoes divine concerns might look like today. The pragmatic challenge is how to affect constructive legal reform in the broader society that would reflect, at least in some measure, those divine ideals. Engaging the messy and hard business of formulating just and compassionate laws vis-à-vis the immigrant is an inescapable dimension of living and working with diaspora populations.

Conclusion

There is much in the Old Testament that can inform diaspora missiology. This essay has argued, howbeit in summary fashion, that these contributions are in the three areas of description, theology, and ethics. First, the depictions of life in diaspora that are found in Old Testament narratives correlate with what many migrants and diaspora peoples experience today. These texts can sensitize the non-diasporic to the plight of the immigrant. At the same time, they can encourage the immigrant that the Old Testament is a wonderful resource for their life and faith.

Second, the Old Testament teaches that the mission of the people of God is to be a blessing to others. This mission mandate was given originally to the wandering patriarchs, who lived, according to the biblical presentation of Genesis 10-12, among the dispersed "clans" of the earth. That mission holds true throughout the Old Testament and finds particular expression in Jeremiah's letter to the exiles in Babylon as seeking the *shalom* of Judah's conquerors.

Third, and last, involvement with diaspora peoples and matters inevitably means engaging immigrant legislation. Although Old Testament law was designed for another context, its values rise above that era and geography and can suggest directions for implanting God's designs in contemporary laws. In sum, the Old Testament offers a wide-ranging, relevant, and constructive theological framework for diaspora missions.

For discussion

1. What are the three principle ways that the Old Testament can contribute to diaspora missiology and mission?
2. How do the opening eleven chapters in the book of Genesis connect the nature of humanity with migration?
3. What are some new insights into the narratives of the biblical text that a diaspora approach offers?
4. How does the book of Genesis define the mission of the people of God?
5. What were the motivations in Old Testament Law to be hospitable to the outsider? What lessons could be drawn for the people of God today?

6. From Opportunity to Mission: Scattering for the Gospel in the New Testament Story

Steven S. H. Chang

Introduction

The New Testament story begins with the birth and expansion of the church, a phenomenon that begs much explanation. The Gospels focus on the foundational figure of Jesus Christ, but even he is understood in light of the phenomenon of the church (Luke 1:1-4). How did the church, first established by Jews, grow to include Gentiles? Why were Christian assemblies, distinct from both Jewish and Gentile assemblies, appearing throughout the known world of the first century? How did Christianity become so mission oriented? These were the questions on the minds of those witnessing this first-century phenomenon. And the answers were found in the Jewish diaspora.[1]

The birth and expansion of the church would not have been possible without the Jewish diaspora, because most of the first Christian converts and missionaries were diaspora Jews. The world was prepared for the coming of Christ in the scattering of the Jews centuries before, but particularly so during the Hellenistic and Roman periods. Reeling from Jewish conflicts with Hellenism, the diaspora setting of the first-century world formed the seedbed of Christian mission and its core beliefs. Rife with issues and ideas that only make sense in light of its diaspora setting, the New Testament story reveals how God used the diaspora communities to establish and grow the church.

This essay investigates in three parts how diasporas were prepared and used for mission in the New Testament story. First, a cursory sketch of the diaspora setting of the New Testament story explores the scope of the Jewish diaspora, the clash of cultures in the Greco-Roman world, and the effect of Roman rule on the Jewish diaspora. Second, a closer look at the role diaspora Jews play in the New Testament story suggests their importance in the plan of God. Third, a consideration of the struggles between Jews and Gentiles in the diaspora setting of the New Testament church highlights how those conflicts shaped Christian identity and core beliefs.

---

1 "The Diaspora" with a capital "D" is used today to refer to the Jewish dispersion. However, to avoid confusion and awkwardness, I will prefer "Jewish diaspora" in this paper without meaning any disrespect to the Diaspora.

The Diaspora setting of the New Testament story

The diaspora setting of the New Testament story was complex and any attempt to describe it will fall short. Nevertheless, it is important to sketch out the Jewish diaspora in the Greco-Roman world in order to appreciate how it shaped the early Christian community and expansion.

Jews in the Diaspora

By the first century, the Jewish people were scattered in large numbers throughout the Roman Empire and beyond. For example, some 180,000 Jews lived in Alexandria in Egypt,[2] another 180,000 lived in the cities of Asia Minor, and up to 60,000 lived in Rome.[3] Although it is difficult to pin down, the population of the Jewish diaspora far exceeded the number at home. Depending on the population size of Palestine (1 to 2.5 million), possibly up to six million Jews lived in the diaspora.[4] Overpopulation at home was probably a major cause of Jewish migration in the first century.

The total geographical scope of the Jewish diaspora is uncertain, but there is evidence that Jews were dispersed over a vast territory. Philo of Alexandria gives a snapshot as he pleads favor for Jerusalem from emperor Gaius: "[I]t is not one city only that would then be benefited by you, but ten thousand of them in every region of the habitable world, in Europe, in Asia, and in Africa, on the continent, in the islands, on the coasts, and in the inland parts."[5] The list of locations is extensive, including regions surrounding Palestine (Egypt, Phoenicia, and Syria), provinces toward Asia Minor (Pamphylia, Cilicia, Bithynia, and Pontus), European regions (Thessaly, Boeotia, Macedonia, Aetolia, Attica, Argos, and Corinth and the Peloponnesus), well-known islands (Euboea – a Greek island, Cyprus, and Crete), and "the countries beyond the Euphrates" (Babylon and beyond). According to Philo, Jews had spread to "every region of the habitable world" in the first century.

---

2 J. J. Collins, Between Athens and Jerusalem: Jewish Identity in the Hellenistic Diaspora (2d ed.; Grand Rapids: Eerdmans, 2000), 114. Philo (Flacc. 43) claims that there was up to 1 million Jews in Alexandria in his time, which is certainly exaggerated since the total population was only about half a million.

3 E. S. Gruen, Diaspora: Jews amidst Greeks and Romans (Cambridge: Harvard University Press, 2002), 15; W. R. Stegner, "Diaspora," DPL 211.

4 E. J. Schnabel, Early Christian Mission, Vol. 1, Jesus and the Twelve (Downers Grove: IVP, 2004), 122-124. Population estimates are notoriously speculative. P. R. Trebilco and C. A. Evans, "Diaspora Judaism," DNTB 286, admit: "Scholars often suggest that five to six million Jews were living in the Diaspora in the first century, but such figures can be only speculative."

5 Philo, On the Embassy to Gaius, 283. Cited from C. D. Yonge, The Works of Philo: Complete and Unabridged (New Updated Edition; Peabody: Hendrickson, 1995), 783.

A comparable catalog is found in Acts 2 where Luke says that there were Jews dwelling in the holy city "from every nation under heaven" (Acts 2:5).[6] He lists some fifteen locations, including the imperial city of Rome, undoubtedly mentioned because of its importance both geopolitically and to the story of Acts. Parthia, Media, Elam, and Mesopotamia (Acts 2:9a) cover the region east of the Euphrates, reaching far into the Parthian Empire (modern-day Iran).[7] The reference to "Judea" is likely used in the broadest sense to include Syria.[8] Cappadocia, Pontus and Asia, Phrygia and Pamphylia (Acts 2:9b) include the region that encompasses nearly all of modern-day Turkey, but curiously missing are major Roman provinces, Galatia and Cilicia. Reference to Egypt and "the parts of Libya near Cyrene" (Acts 2:10) shift the focus to North Africa. From there, attention moves northward to Rome. "Visitors from Rome (both Jews and converts to Judaism)" (Acts 2:10-11a) seems unnecessary since other regions would have had converts to Judaism, but Luke is particularly sensitive to a Roman audience in his writings. The final two, Crete and Arabia, representing an island and a desert, may be included to show how ubiquitous the Jewish people were.

Both Philo and Luke affirm the vast scope of the Jewish diaspora in New Testament times. Like Philo's, Luke's list is certainly not comprehensive and major regions like Macedonia and Greece are overlooked even though thriving Jewish communities existed there. However, his point is that diaspora Jews from as far away as Rome were present at the birth of the church and had a significant role in its expansion.

The clash of civilizations

As much as the New Testament corroborates the Jewish diaspora, it also reverberates with the clash of three civilizations: Jewish, Greek, and Roman. To be sure, other cultures existed in the first century, but no others dominate the New Testament story as much as these three. The old Greek civilization left behind a rich culture of ideas (philosophy and religion) that rivaled that of the Jews and outshined that of the Romans. Accordingly, the clash of ideas in the New Testament is normally between Greeks and Jews (e.g., 1 Cor. 1:22, 24). The Greeks planted colonies and propagated their culture and language far and wide, in many ways setting an example for the Jewish diaspora in the Roman era. Thus, Greek is the language of both the New Testament and the Jewish diaspora. The older Jewish civilization dominates the New Testament in other ways. The influence of Jewish

---

6 All Scripture citations are from the NIV 2011 unless otherwise noted.

7 These diaspora Jews may be descended from the exiles during the Assyrian and Babylonian periods, of whom Josephus says much about. See Josephus, Ant. 11.133; 15.14; 18.310–79; F. F. Bruce, The Book of Acts (NICNT; Grand Rapids: Eerdmans, 1988), 55-56.

8 Bruce, Acts, 56.

monotheism, for example, is unmistakable as is that of the Jewish scriptures, which all of the New Testament writers, to one degree or another, were meditating on, albeit in a Greek translation (LXX). Still, it is the Romans who politically ruled over the everyday lives of New Testament people. After all, Jesus died on a Roman cross (with a sign in Aramaic, Latin, and Greek) and the Romans destroyed the Jewish Temple (A.D. 70). The Romans dominated the political sphere in the first century and relished the height of their imperial ambitions.

Judaism itself was profoundly transformed by its clash with the Greek world and the conflict was most felt in the lives of diaspora Jews.[9] One of the earliest conflicts in the church was between "Hellenistic Jews" and "Hebraic Jews" (Acts 6:1). Although differences between Jews at home and in the diaspora should not be exaggerated since Jerusalem itself was thoroughly Hellenized in the first century,[10] it is also reasonable to suggest that Jews were more likely to be assimilated to Greek culture in the great diasporic centers such as Alexandria, Antioch, and Asia Minor, than at home. The Acts narrative bears this subtle distinction out. This and other conflicts reveal that the clash of Judaism and Hellenism played a significant part in shaping the Christian identity and community.

A new Roman peace

The Romans transformed the diaspora landscape. Augustus ushered in the *pax Romana* that essentially united the former Hellenistic kingdoms and much of the Jewish diaspora under a single political structure. By the first century, the Roman Empire ruled an immense territory stretching as far west as Spain and as far east as Syria and Egypt. The imperial administration aggressively made improvements to infrastructure in order to maintain control. Soldiers and imperial power had to flow into the provinces and frontiers while goods and taxes had to flow back to Rome.[11] For this reason, the Romans built and upgraded roads with superior technology, including stone paving and drainage, and tightly monitored their usage. These roads connected major cities all over the empire, especially to Rome. In addition to roads, the Romans controlled the entire Mediterranean Sea and simply called it *Mare Nostrum* (Our Sea). Their naval superiority not only vanquished foes but also suppressed piracy,

---

9 In John 7:35, the Jewish opponents wonder if Jesus means to go to "the Dispersion (diaspora) among the Greeks" (ESV) to teach Greeks as his word that they cannot follow where he is going.

10 See M. Hengel, Judaism and Hellenism: Studies in their Encounter in Palestine during the Early Hellenistic Period, Vols. 1 & 2 (Philadelphia: Fortress, 1981).

11 S. E. Alcock, Graecia Capta: The Landscapes of Roman Greece (Cambridge: Cambridge University Press, 1993), 221.

making sea travel/transport safer.[12] These improvements to the infrastructure, though motivated by the Roman need for control and supplies, had the positive effect of improving travel, communication, and trade for the whole empire. This resulted in a new era of unprecedented movement across older political and cultural boundaries that were either impossible or at least very difficult to traverse before Roman rule.

Although the *pax Romana* was anything but peaceful,[13] its positive benefits to diaspora movement and later to Christian mission are undeniable. With improved infrastructure, the New Testament world under Roman control was well prepared for the movement of people. With chronic overpopulation at home, more Jews chose to live in the "colonies" of the dispersion.[14] The earlier Jewish and Hellenistic diasporas now moved more freely in search of opportunities and new tastes. The Roman administration often showed favor to the Jewish diaspora, giving them special privileges to practice their religion all over the empire. The collection of the Temple tax and pilgrimages to Jerusalem were greatly aided by these developments.[15]

The extent of the Jewish diaspora, the clash of civilizations, and the Roman peace in the first century prepared the biblical world for the establishment and expansion of the Christian church. The impact of these developments to the Christian movement can hardly be overstated. A closer look at the role of diaspora Jews in the story of the New Testament will consider some of that impact.

The Diaspora Jews in the New Testament story

The diaspora experience is part and parcel of the New Testament story. Jesus himself with his family experienced the diaspora life in Egypt (Matt. 2:13-15).[16] In particular, diaspora Jews are foundational in the initial expansion of the church. Both nameless and well-known diaspora figures

---

12 Merchant ships became more numerous and bigger in size during the Roman era and large Roman grain ships fed the imperial city with Egyptian grain. See A. J. Parker, "Shipwrecks and Ancient Trade in the Mediterranean," ARC 3:2 (1984): 99-113.

13 K. Wengst, The Pax Romana and the Peace of Jesus Christ (London: SCM, 1987).

14 Gruen, Diaspora, 241-242.

15 Josephus (J.W. 2:280) notes some 3 million Jews in Jerusalem during the feast of unleavened bread in the A.D. 60s.

16 For an interesting study of Jesus' migration to Egypt and other "withdrawals" in Matthew's gospel, see P. Hertig, "Jesus' Migrations and Liminal Withdrawals in Matthew," in God's People on the Move: Biblical and Global Perspectives on Migration and Mission (ed. Van Thanh Nguyen and J. M. Prior; Eugene: Wipf and Stock, 2014), 46-61.

play significant roles in the New Testament story, suggesting that God prepares and uses diasporas for mission.

The nameless Diaspora missionaries

The story of the earliest church in Acts is replete with nameless diaspora. As mentioned above, the unidentified diaspora Jews "from every nation under heaven" in Acts 2 play a crucial role in the birth of the church in Jerusalem. But they are also critical to Christian mission. In the sovereign plan of God, these diaspora are gathered in Jerusalem for Pentecost only to hear the gospel message and take that message back into their diaspora setting. They are the first missionaries in Acts. Luke's mention of "visitors from Rome" (Acts 2:10) is the only plausible explanation of how the gospel first reached Rome.[17] If so, the most influential center of western Christianity had its beginning not in apostolic figures such as Peter or Paul, but in anonymous missionaries of the Jewish diaspora.

In Acts, the restoration of the kingdom (Acts 1:6) occurs when witnesses in the diaspora preach the gospel to all nations (Acts 1:8). Accordingly, when persecution broke out after the stoning of Stephen, unnamed diaspora missionaries scattered (*diaspeirō*)[18] "throughout Judea and Samaria" and those who scattered "preached the word wherever they went" (Acts 8:1, 4). Since "all except the apostles" were dispersed, they were presumably either former diaspora Jews who had accepted Peter's preaching of Acts 2-4 or homeland Jews who through persecution were thrust into the diaspora. Philip was one of those scattered (Acts 8:4). The scattering did not stop with "Judea and Samaria." Acts 11:19 indicates that "those who had been scattered (*diaspeirō*) by the persecution that broke out when Stephen was killed traveled as far as Phoenicia, Cyprus and Antioch, spreading the word only among Jews." But some diaspora Jewish Christians began to preach the gospel to Greeks in the city of Antioch (Acts 11:20). The nameless diaspora Jewish Christians make a very important leap for Christian mission. They bridge the immense divide between Jews and Greeks, and initiate a targeted mission to Gentiles, virtually unknown in diaspora Judaism.[19] The countless numbers of nameless diaspora perform perhaps

---

17 D. J. Moo, The Epistle to the Romans (NICNT; Grand Rapids: Eerdmans, 1996), 4.

18 For a study of diaspora terms in Scripture, see N. F. Santos, "Exploring the Major Dispersion Terms and Realities in the Bible," in Diaspora Missiology: Theory, Methodology, and Practice (ed. E. Wan; Portland: Western Seminary, Institute of Diaspora Studies, 2011), 21-37.

19 Scholarly consensus today contends that Judaism was not mission oriented with some qualifications. See the study by M. F. Bird, Crossing Over Sea and Land: Jewish Missionary Activity in the Second Temple Period (Peabody: Hendrickson, 2010), esp. 149-156. See also Schnabel, Early Christian, 1:93-122; Collins, Between Athens and Jerusalem, 262-264; I. Levinskaya, The Book of Acts in Its

the most significant part in the unfolding of God's plan in the New Testament story. They are gathered and scattered for the sake of the gospel.

Paul and his Diaspora associates

The characteristics of these nameless diaspora missionaries may be fleshed out by a closer look at the named diaspora figures amply described in the story of Acts. The most important diaspora Jew in the New Testament is the apostle Paul. He and his many diaspora associates are often the focus of Luke's narrative in Acts.

Paul's diaspora background is intriguing and somewhat anomalous.[20] He is both a Roman citizen and a Pharisee (Acts 16, 22; Phil. 3:5). He impresses people with his Greek and Hebrew abilities (Acts 21:37; 22:2). His family had migrated to Tarsus of Cilicia, and became citizens of this extraordinary Hellenistic city (Acts 21:39). It is uncertain whether his forebears were forcibly displaced or relocated voluntarily. Given his dual citizenship and stellar multicultural education (Greek education in Tarsus and Hebrew Torah education in Jerusalem), it is not unthinkable that his family's move to Cilicia was to seek greater opportunity for descendants. If so, Paul and his family must be viewed as an example of a successful diaspora Jewish household. His suitability for apostolic ministry "to the Gentiles" (Acts 9:15; 13:46; 18:6; Gal. 2:8-9) is remarkable, and only explained by a diaspora upbringing. He is able to proclaim the gospel in such fabled Greek cities as Athens and Corinth. His superb ability to write letters in Greek, learned and honed in the diaspora, might explain his importance in the New Testament canon.[21] He is highly accessible to people of various cultures and backgrounds, betraying the advantages of his multicultural diaspora upbringing (1 Cor. 9:20-22).

Paul is not alone. Barnabas is a diaspora Jew from Cyprus (Acts 4:36) and significantly, a landowner, perhaps another diaspora success story. The field he sells may be in Cyprus, to which he keeps a close connection (Acts 13:4; 15:39).[22] It seems Barnabas is a formidable presence before the Greeks. In Lystra, he is mistakenly worshipped as Zeus, the most

---

Diaspora Setting, BAFCS 5 (Grand Rapids: Eerdmans, 1996), 19-33. Cf. J. J. Scott, Jewish Backgrounds of the New Testament (Grand Rapids: Baker Academic, 1995), 341-342, who is more positive.

20 See J. M. G. Barclay, Jews in the Mediterranean Diaspora: From Alexander to Trajan (323 BCE–117 CE) (Edinburgh: T&T Clark, 1996), 381-395, who argues that Paul was highly assimilated yet not accommodating to Hellenism as a diaspora Jew.

21 Not only are thirteen letters attributed to him, but he also probably influenced Luke who penned more of the New Testament than any other.

22 It is possible that Barnabas and Paul were asked to "remember the poor" (Gal. 2:10) because they were successful diaspora Jews who had both the reputation and resources to help the poor.

prominent of the Greek gods (Acts 14:12, 18), and escapes the stoning fate of Paul. His level of assimilation must have been high since Paul seems surprised that "even Barnabas" (Gal. 2:11) was misled to withdraw from Gentiles. Timothy is a highly assimilated diaspora Jew from Lystra, who had a Jewish mother, but a Greek father. He was assimilated enough that he was uncircumcised when Paul met him (Acts 16:1-3). Timothy travels far and wide, accompanying Paul (e.g., through Asia Minor, Troas, and Macedonia, Acts 16:6-10), carrying his letters (e.g., 1 Thess. 1:1; Phil. 1:1), and running his errands (e.g., 1 Cor. 4:17; 16:10; Phil. 2:19; 1 Thess. 3:6; 2 Tim. 4:13). He is associated with Christians in the cities of Rome, Corinth in Greece, Philippi and Thessalonica in Macedonia, and Ephesus and Colossae in Asia Minor, not to mention the place where the letter to the Hebrews was written (Heb. 13:23). Aquila is a diaspora Jew from Pontus, the coastline north of Galatia, but living in Rome. Claudius's expulsion of the Jews from Rome forced Aquila to move to Corinth (Acts 18:2). He and his wife, Priscilla, had successful ministries in Rome (Rom. 16:3), Corinth (Acts 18), and Ephesus (1 Cor. 16:19; 2 Tim. 4:19).[23] Apollos is a diaspora Jew from Alexandria, "a learned man, with a thorough knowledge of the Scriptures" (Acts 18:24). His ministry in Corinth is noteworthy (Acts 18:27-28; 1 Cor. 1:12; 3:4-5, 22; 4:6). In sum, Paul and his diaspora associates are capable missionaries, well equipped from their diaspora experiences. They form the core of the Christian mission force in Acts that significantly impact the Roman landscape.

Diaspora as God's instrument

In Acts, Luke emphasizes God as the divine orchestrator of the Christian mission, just as he was in the suffering, death, and resurrection of the Messiah. While the disciples were exhorted to be Christ's witnesses "in Jerusalem, and in all Judea and Samaria, and to the ends of the earth" (Acts 1:8), they hardly strategize, nor willingly leap into the mission field. Rather, they are scattered by persecution, as were many of their Jewish predecessors. In addition, Luke's point in Acts 2 is not only that a new age of the Holy Spirit had arrived, but also that God, fully in control, had prepared the Jewish diaspora and the Roman world for the spread of the gospel. By the middle of the Acts story, these nameless diaspora "from every nation under heaven," through persecution, had scattered back to their diaspora homes, becoming essentially Christ's witnesses "to the ends of the earth," thereby fulfilling the prophecy of Isaiah as a light to the

---

23 VanThanh Nguyen, "Migrants as Missionaries: The Case of Priscilla and Aquila," in God's People on the Move: Biblical and Global Perspectives on Migration and Mission (ed. Van Thanh Nguyen and J. M. Prior; Eugene: Wipf and Stock, 2014), 62-75, sees in Priscilla and Aquila how Christians on the move have "become a key factor in the expansion of the church."

Gentiles (Isa. 49:6; Acts 13:47). Examples of diaspora Jewish Christian missionaries in Acts suggest that diaspora experiences equipped them to take the gospel throughout the Roman Empire. Hence, a larger picture emerges. God orchestrated the Jewish diaspora and prepared diaspora Jews to evangelize the Gentiles.[24] The Great Commission is fulfilled through the Jewish diaspora as God's instrument for mission. However, that God prepared and used the Jewish diaspora is only the beginning. Persecution, conflicts, and crises shaped the identity, core beliefs, and life purpose of those who were scattered.

The Diaspora conflicts in the New Testament story

With the birth and expansion of the church, the new Christian community was not immune to struggles arising from the clash of cultures in the diaspora setting. The inclusion of Gentiles, which genuinely surprised many Jewish Christians (Acts 10:45), caused all kinds of cultural, religious, and theological tensions. For centuries, Jews experienced these same conflicts in the diaspora and so it was natural for diaspora Jewish Christians to lead in bridging the gap between Jews and Gentiles in the church.

Identity crises and conflicts in the church

Jewish identity in the first century world was based on both religious and ethnic boundaries.[25] Thus, on the one hand, Roman officials, in enforcing the collection of the Temple tax, determined Jewish identity by religious practice. On the other hand, Timothy was circumcised (Acts 16:3) based on the matrilineal principle, which itself was developed in the diaspora.[26] Religious aspects of diaspora Jewish identity were multifaceted.[27] A collective connection to Jerusalem was important, as the Temple tax and pilgrimages for major festivals show, as well as individual connection to the local diaspora community of synagogues. But as a people of the Book, upholding the Mosaic Law, including its cultic, ritual, and moral obligations, was probably the surest way to demonstrate their identity.[28]

---

24 As suggested by Santos, "Exploring the Major Dispersion Terms," 36-37. See also N. F. Santos, "Diaspora in the New Testament and Its Impact on Christian Mission," Torch Trinity Journal 13.1 (2010): 17-18.

25 Barclay, Jews in the Mediterranean Diaspora, 404.

26 Levinskaya, Diaspora Setting, 2-17.

27 See Barclay, Jews in the Mediterranean Diaspora, 413-442, for a more comprehensive treatment of identity traits of diaspora Jews.

28 E. S. Gruen, "Diaspora and Homeland," in Diasporas and Exiles: Varieties of Jewish Identity (ed. H. Wettstein; Berkeley: University of California Press, 2002), 18-46, argues that diaspora Jewish identity was not simply a matter of text or location, defined either by the Book or by exile and restoration to Jerusalem.

When Jewish Christians first formed the majority in the church, they must have defined Christian identity initially by Jewish ethnicity since every Christian was also a Jew. Jewish ethnic pride continued to be a problem for the church (2 Cor. 11:22; Rom. 2:17). However, when Gentiles were included into the church some strict Jews among the Jewish majority tried to define Christian identity through religious practices associated with Judaism, namely law-keeping and circumcision. Church leaders, themselves Jews, responded and insisted on defining Christian identity with the person of Jesus Christ. A good example of this identity struggle between the old (Jewish) and the new (Christian) is Paul's confession in Philippians 3. In countering his Jewish opponents who put "confidence in the flesh," he says, "I have more" (Phil. 3:4). The catalog of credentials is impressive for a diaspora Jew: "circumcised on the eighth day, of the people of Israel, of the tribe of Benjamin, a Hebrew of Hebrews; in regard to the law, a Pharisee; as for zeal, persecuting the church; as for righteousness based on the law, faultless" (Phil. 3:5-6). But Paul has thrown out these qualifications in order to "gain Christ and be found in him" (Phil. 3:8-9). His new identity, in contrast to the old, is established in relationship to his Lord.

A new community of faith

The gap between Jews and Gentiles was more like a "dividing wall of hostility" (Eph. 2:14). For most Jews, the differences in culture, in ethnicity, and in religious beliefs and practices were irreconcilable. Thus, many Jews in the church struggled to accommodate Gentiles. Battle lines were drawn on issues such as kosher food, idolatry, and immorality, which were all deeply offensive to Jews. In the Jewish worldview, Gentiles were by definition sinful (Gal. 2:15). As a people of the Book, the Jewish Christians turned to the only place they knew for guidance – the Mosaic Law (Torah). Their solution to the Gentile problem was to require them to follow the law and be circumcised. They gave Gentiles an ultimatum: "Unless you are circumcised, according to the custom taught by Moses, you cannot be saved" (Acts 15:1). On the one hand, it is interesting to note that some Gentile converts, following their predecessors who converted to Judaism, probably would have eagerly agreed to the demand. On the other hand, some highly assimilated diaspora Jews, themselves uncircumcised, may have felt the demand to be excessive and sectarian.

The new Christian community had to decide whether or not they would follow the old Jewish custom of circumcision. At the Jerusalem council of A.D. 49, church leaders determined that circumcision and law observance should not be required of Gentiles and informed the diaspora churches of

---

Rather, the Jewish diaspora accommodated an identity based both on the text and the homeland.

their decision. Curiously, they advise Gentiles to abstain from four practices that amount to idolatry, and this, out of sensitivity to Jews in the diaspora (Acts 15:21). Paul's contribution to the discussion is not recorded at length in Acts, but his letters show an unambiguous awareness of the issues at hand. In A.D. 48, Paul was in the thick of things when Jewish Christians from Judea had come to his churches in Galatia and began teaching a "different gospel" (Gal. 1:6; cf. Acts 15:5). Nine years later in A.D. 57, Paul is still setting out the solution to the Jew-Gentile divide, but this time with less emotion.

He and other church leaders pondered the question of what sets members of the new Christian community apart. It could not be the old Jewish identity symbol of circumcision. In Romans, Paul harkens the mixed audience of Jewish and Gentile Christians back to the figure of Abraham (Rom. 4). Like John, Paul believes that while "the law was given through Moses, grace and truth came through Jesus Christ" (John 1:17). Accordingly, both Jews and Gentiles "are not under the law, but under grace" (Rom. 6:14). When grace, and not law, becomes the basis of righteousness, then the example of Abraham demonstrates that circumcision cannot adequately set Christians apart. Paul argues that since Abraham was declared righteous before he was circumcised (Rom. 4:10-12), it was his faith in the promise of God that set him apart, the promise that God would make him "a father of many nations" (Rom. 4:17; Gen. 12:1ff). The notions of grace and faith among the nations resonated deeply with diaspora Jews. They particularly understood grace (or favor) as an admired trait in their Gentile rulers, who could very easily turn on them if not for grace. Simply trusting in the grace of God became a new identity symbol. For Paul, God had always intended that faith should be what sets his community apart. The new Christians must be a community of faith, not a community of circumcised law observers.

The first Jewish Christians were able to maneuver through these tough identity issues and bridge the divide between Jews and Gentiles particularly because they were diaspora Jews, battle worn from centuries of cultural conflict. Similarly, Christians in the diaspora are better prepared to overcome their cultural shackles and proclaim the gospel of grace across cultures. They are enabled to identify themselves by faith alone rather than culturally bound symbols and practices of their homeland. The early church's emphasis on faith sets an example for diaspora Christians today to proclaim and live out a pure gospel of faith rather than the Christian culture of their homeland, and to challenge their homeland counterparts to be free from the temptation to propagate Christian "colonies" and from culturally fettered forms of Christianity.

A new unity in Christ

The first inclusion of Gentiles forced the church and its leaders not only to reconsider the practices of circumcision but also to envision a new corporate identity, united in the person of Jesus Christ. The diversity of the diaspora setting was a mixed blessing for the early church. If the church remained exclusively Jewish, it could not have grown or even survived. Yet, because it was open to all "by faith," unity was particularly challenging. The solution was a new unity "in Christ." Paul writes to the Galatian churches, "There is neither Jew nor Gentile… for you are all one in Christ Jesus" (Gal. 3:28; cf. Col. 3:11; 1 Cor. 12:13). Each believer is justified "in Christ" (Rom. 3:24), and so "in Christ," a person is a new creation, possessing eternal life and finding grace. But all believers are also given a new corporate identity in that "in Christ" they are bonded to one another. Those "in Christ" form the body of Christ. Paul writes in Romans 12:5, "… so in Christ we, though many, form one body, and each member belongs to all the others." The church as the body of Christ cannot be divided because Christ himself is not divided (1 Cor. 1:13).

The Corinthian church was particularly prone to divisiveness. A major reason for 1 Corinthians was division: "Now I mean this, that each of you is saying, 'I am *of Paul*,' and 'I *of Apollos*,' and 'I *of Cephas*,' and 'I am *of Christ*'" (1 Cor. 1:12; NASB; emphasis added). The Greek construction suggests that belonging was socially important for the believers in Corinth, particularly in the multicultural setting of the diaspora. Paul reminds them later in his letter: "and you (pl.) are *of Christ* and Christ is of God" (1 Cor. 3:23; emphasis added). Note the change from singular (I) to plural (you). For Paul, believers not only belong to Christ, but to one another (1 Cor. 12:15). Perhaps Paul learned the importance of belonging from his diaspora experience. He concludes his discourse on unity, striking a balance between the group and the individual: "Now you (pl.) are the body of Christ and individually (*ek merous*) members of it" (1 Cor. 12:27; ESV). That believers together belong to Christ and to one another especially resonates with diaspora people.

The body metaphor highlights both unity and diversity (1 Cor. 12:12), but also the connection and cooperation between the parts. Diaspora people more intensely desire to belong, which is often lost in migration. They search for both individual and corporate identity. The individual identity of being a new creation "in Christ" helps heal the identity struggles of a diaspora existence while the corporate identity as the body of Christ offers connectedness and a chance to be a part of something greater than oneself. Diasporas today who long for identity need the gospel that gives them more than a mere multicultural identity. They can be identified with the Lord of creation and have a sense of belonging both to Christ and to the larger community of his body, the church. They need to hear about diversity and unity in balance, celebrating differences created by grace yet finding common ground in the faith.

A new Christian Diaspora

With a new identity in Christ, the believers have a new purpose and mission. They are sent ones (missionaries) for Christ's sake. Jesus viewed his own identity and purpose as the One who was sent by the Father. His disciples were to take on a similar identity and mission: "As the Father has sent me, I am sending you" (John 20:21). The apostle Paul, looking back on his calling and ministry, recalls his encounter with the risen Lord and the new identity and mission he received: "Go; I will send you far away to the Gentiles" (Acts 22:21; 26:17). Paul, the diaspora Jew, was now to become a diaspora for Christ, sent with a purpose – "to preach the gospel where Christ is not known" (Rom. 15:20).

But Paul is just one of many diaspora Jews turned diaspora for Christ. The New Testament story hints at the rise of a new Christian diaspora from the old Jewish one (1 Pet. 1:1; James 1:1). Like the preceding Jewish diaspora, the Christians scatter because of persecution, in God's sovereign plan. Indeed, the diaspora Christians, perhaps more than diaspora Jews in the first century, thought of their scattering as an exile.[29] The new Christian diaspora are "strangers and exiles on the earth" (Heb. 11:13; 1 Pet. 1:1; 2:11).[30] Christians are longing for a restoration to a spiritual homeland, figuratively represented by Jerusalem. As some diaspora Jews sentimentally (and biblically)[31] longed to be restored to Jerusalem, the Christian exiles also longed for the "new Jerusalem" (Rev. 21), which is nothing short of the return of Christ and the consummate realization of the heavenly kingdom.

In persecution as the initial cause of diaspora, the old Jewish and new Christian diasporas converge. Beyond that, however, an important difference arises. The Jews moved for opportunity and advantage both in the Hellenistic age and especially during the Roman peace. The new Christians moved not only for opportunity and advantage but also for witness and mission. Mission purpose drives Christians to go into the diaspora and to all nations. With the reception of the gospel message, there was a transformation of diaspora motive from opportunity to mission. For diasporas today, the same gospel message may transform the very purpose for which they find themselves in the diaspora setting. In the larger picture

---

29 The Jewish people may not have believed that the exile was over, even though many had returned to Jerusalem. See N. T. Wright, The New Testament and the People of God (Minneapolis: Fortress, 1992), ch. 10. But diaspora existence is not portrayed negatively by diaspora Jews (Gruen, Diaspora, 232ff).

30 I. M. Duguid, "Exile," NDBT 475, defines exile as "the experience of pain and suffering that results from the knowledge that there is a home where one belongs, yet for the present one is unable to return there."

31 Gruen, Diaspora, 232-239, suggests that diaspora Jews generally did not think of themselves as being in exile, but diaspora Jews often referred back the biblical history of exile as a paradigm for their own diaspora experience in deference to Jerusalem.

of today's globalized, multicultural world, God may be preparing the numerous diasporas in order to raise from among them a Christian diaspora who labor and move with the grander purpose of bearing witness to Christ rather than merely to realize a better life.

Conclusion

The New Testament story began with the scattering of the Jews centuries before Christ. God had prepared the world with the Jewish diaspora for the coming of the Messiah. In the fertile soil of diaspora Jews gathered in Jerusalem, the gospel was planted and the church was born. These same diaspora Jews, transformed by the gospel with a new identity, unity, and purpose, became the first missionaries, taking the gospel back into the diaspora setting and bearing witness to Gentiles. Their scattering, both voluntary and involuntary, became the basis for the mission of the earliest church. Thus, in the New Testament story, God was raising up a new diaspora for Christ out of the old Jewish diaspora, who move not merely for opportunity but for mission.

The rise of a Christian diaspora becomes a model for diaspora missions today and shows that the sovereign God ministers to and through the diaspora communities to grow the church. Equipped with this biblical picture, diasporas today may comprehend the divine strategy that prepares them to receive the gospel, transforms their identity and purpose, and disperses them into the nations to become a new diaspora for Christ.

For discussion

1. How did God prepare the world in and through the Jewish diaspora for the coming of Jesus Christ?
2. In what ways were the Jewish diaspora used to spread the gospel of Jesus Christ?
3. Name some of the diaspora Jews turned Christian missionaries in the New Testament story. What were their contributions to the mission of the church?
4. What would be the main tenets of a New Testament theology of diaspora missions?
5. In the light of how God worked in and through diaspora Jews in the New Testament story, what is the significance of that biblical story for global diasporas today?

Bibliography

Alcock, Susan E. *Graecia Capta: The Landscapes of Roman Greece*. Cambridge: Cambridge University Press, 1993.

Barclay, John M. G. *Jews in the Mediterranean Diaspora from Alexander to Trajan (323 BCE – 117 CE)*. Edinburgh: T&T Clark, 1996.

Bird, Michael F. *Crossing Over Sea and Land: Jewish Missionary Activity in the Second Temple Period.* Peabody: Hendrickson, 2010.

Bruce, F. F. *The Book of Acts*. New International Commentary on the New Testament. Grand Rapids: Eerdmans, 1988.

Collins, John J. *Between Athens and Jerusalem: Jewish Identity in the Hellenistic Diaspora*. 2d ed. Grand Rapids: Eerdmans, 2000.

Duguid, I. M. "Exile." Pages 475-479 in *New Dictionary of Biblical Theology*. Edited by T. D. Alexander and B. S. Rosner. Dowers Grove: IVP, 2000.

Gruen, Erich. S. *Diaspora: Jews amidst Greeks and Romans*. Cambridge: Harvard University Press, 2002.

___. "Diaspora and Homeland," In *Diasporas and Exiles: Varieties of Jewish Identity*, edited by H. Wettstein,18-46. Berkeley: University of California Press, 2002.

Hengel, Martin. *Judaism and Hellenism: Studies in their Encounter in Palestine during the Early Hellenistic Period.* Vols. 1 & 2. Philadelphia: Fortress, 1981.

Hertig, Paul. "Jesus' Migrations and Liminal Withdrawals in Matthew," in *God's People on the Move: Biblical and Global Perspectives on Migration and Missions*, edited by Van Thanh Nguyen and J. M. Prior, 46-61. Eugene: Wipf and Stock, 2014.

Levinskaya, Irina. *The Book of Acts in Its Diaspora Setting*. BAFCS 5. Grand Rapids: Eerdmans, 1995.

Moo, Douglas J. *The Epistle to the Romans*. NICNT. Grand Rapids: Eerdmans, 1996.

Nguyen, Van Thanh. "Migrants as Missionaries: The Case of Priscilla and Aquila," in *God's People on the Move: Biblical and Global Perspectives on Migration and Mission*, edited by Van Thanh Nguyen and J. M. Prior, 62-75 Eugene: Wipf and Stock, 2014.

Parker, A. J. "Shipwrecks and Ancient Trade in the Mediterranean." *Archaelogical Review from Cambridge* 3:2 (1984): 99-113.

Santos, Narry F. "*Diaspora* in the New Testament and Its Impact on Christian Mission." *Torch Trinity Journal* 13 (2010): 3-18.

___. "Exploring the Major Dispersion Terms and Realities in the Bible," in *Diaspora Missiology: Theory, Methodology, and Practice,* edited by Enoch Wan, 20-37. Portland: Institute of Diaspora Studies, 2011.

Scott Jr., Julius J. *Jewish Backgrounds of the New Testament.* Grand Rapids: Baker Academic, 1995.

Schnabel, Eckhard J. *Early Christian Mission*, Vol. 1, *Jesus and the Twelve*. Downers Grove: IVP, 2004.

Stegner, W.R. "Diaspora" in *Dictionary of Paul and His Letters*, edited by G. F. Hawthorne and R. P. Martin, 211-213. Downers Grove: IVP, 1993.

Trebilco, P.R., and C. A. Evans. "Diaspora Judaism," in *Dictionary of New Testament Background*, edited by C. A. Evans and S. E. Porter, 282-296. Downers Grove: IVP, 2000.

Wengst, Klaus. *The Pax Romana and the Peace of Jesus Christ*. London: SCM, 1987.

Wright, N. T. *The New Testament and the People of God*. Minneapolis: Fortress, 1992.

Yonge, Charles Duke. *The Works of Philo: Complete and Unabridged.* New Updated Edition; Peabody: Hendrickson, 1995.

7. God, Israel, the Church and the Other: Otherness as a Theological Motif in Diaspora Mission

Paul Woods

Introduction

By its very nature migration involves otherness. Migrants move from one part of a region, or even of the world, to another, in search of freedom, employment, or opportunity. Some seek to escape difficult situations in their place of origin. Others move unwillingly, as a result of poverty, danger, or even trafficking. Generally, people move from a place where they 'fit in' to a greater or lesser extent, to one where they are perceived as outsiders or foreigners. In addition, depending on the reasons for their migration, the nature of the receiving community, and subjective perceptions on both sides, migrants can be seen as a resource to be exploited or a threat to be controlled.

Globalisation and related trends in communications and transportation have made it easier for some people to move substantial distances. When a migrant comes into a neighbourhood or community, he or she comes as both individual and perceived representative of a group. Newcomers may be very different from the locals in physical appearance, socio-economic status, language and culture, family structures, social mores, and expectations. Inasmuch as these factors show difference from the majority they identify a person as Other (NB: *Other* with a capital 'O' is used as a technical term). Otherness between host and migrant, on individual and group basis, is an essential element in missional encounters between Christian communities and incoming migrants.

The otherness of migrants forces Christians in the host community, and indeed migrants themselves, to ask why a person should go out of his or her comfort zone and interact with someone very different. Why bother with someone so dissimilar to oneself? How should Christians deal with otherness and how does this speak into ministry to diaspora peoples?

Background

It may be instructive to look briefly at migration issues as these relate to otherness. Although migrants and host community are often mutually Other, otherness is not symmetric, because those entering a community from outside often lack resources and knowledge, and are vulnerable in terms of employment, opportunity, and even basic human rights. Even expat professionals have their own subjective vulnerabilities and struggles. In addition, migrants are always a minority, latecomers compared with those who 'were there first.'

Concerning attitudes, otherness is not a binary issue and a host majority can ascribe degrees of otherness and acceptance to different migrant groups. In Western Europe there is less fear of Polish immigrants than people obviously 'foreign' in appearance or religion. The Caucasian expat is more welcome in Singapore than the contract labourer from Tamil Nadhu. At the same time, migrants have their own attitudes to and perceptions of the host community.

In many parts of the world migration is bifurcated (Yeoh 2003); governments make clear distinctions between people entering a country based on ethnicity, social or employment status, and gender. Immigration and labour laws often reflect a kind of utilitarian perspective, such that highly skilled expats might interact relatively easily with the locals while migrant labour is removed to dorms or substandard housing after a hard day's work.

Migration systems theory (Castles & Miller 2003) argues that people rarely move as individuals or simply to achieve the greatest benefit. Migrants form chains, linking with those who have gone ahead of them, and making use of relationships and shared knowledge – family and friendship connections are especially important for those of lower status.

Existing relationships and historical linkages create communities in the host nations. Small ethnic provision shops and larger presences such as Chinatowns are part of an extended space linking migrant communities with their homelands, reinforcing identity and otherness in the mind of both host and migrant. Migrants may be labelled and categorised simplistically – the people who 'always do this' or 'always dress like that.' People, in groups, appear seemingly from nowhere and retain their own sense of identity and clannishness. Modern migration produces instant otherness within our communities.

Acknowledging that someone is different from ourselves is not inherently wrong or harmful; indeed it is part of our self-definition. Otherness is the corollary to our own sense of self, as we interact with others. We ascribe different degrees of otherness to the people we meet. Otherness which is positive and accepting can help us embrace the diversity around us, while negative and discriminating otherness entails unhealthy value judgments which may boost our self-esteem. There is thus a distinction between healthy and toxic otherness.

Zizioulas states the problem of the Other in the locus of western culture, but his words are relevant to all cultures and are worth quoting at length:

> In our culture protection from the other is a fundamental necessity. We feel more and more threatened by the presence of the other. We are forced and even encouraged to consider the other as our enemy before we can treat him

> or her as our friend. Communion with the other is not spontaneous; it is built upon fences which protect us from the dangers implicit in the other's presence. We accept the other only in so far as he or she does not threaten our privacy or in so far as he or she is useful for our individual happiness (Zizioulas 2007, 1).

Following this, Zizioulas introduces St Maximus' *difference* and *division*. Difference is the healthy acknowledgement of otherness while division is negative and isolating. Difference accepts the Other without requiring him or her to come over to our side, but division defaults to an impoverished form of 'peaceful co-existence' (2).

Going further, we can identify two theoretical extremes in how we relate to Others. One response is total separation and indifference, zero engagement. The other is total domination and control, often associated with a strong power dynamic between host and migrant, and one person forcing their own aims or prescriptions onto another who has no means of resisting. These two extremes can be characterised as total division and total identity respectively. For Christians, the unity and diversity of the Trinity is the antidote to these two flawed positions.

Because our (sinful) self-affirmation comes through rejection of the Other, the basis of our outreaching to the Other is a healthy affirmation of our personhood flowing from a correct relationship with our Creator. Fear of the Other is in reality fear of otherness; we can only accept other people in so far as they are willing or able to be like us.

Two 20th century Jewish philosophers, Martin Buber and Emmanuel Levinas, are helpful here. Buber's (1958) classic *I and Thou* classifies relationships into the *I-thou* and the *I-it*. In the first we speak *to* a person, while in the second we speak *about* someone. If the thumb and first two fingers form three orthogonal axes, *I-thou* points *to* someone (along the first finger), while *I-it* points *at* someone or something obliquely (along the second finger). For good measure, using *it* for the third person pronoun (rather than *he* or *she*) devalues the Other still further.

In addition, each interaction we have with an Other ultimately connects with the God who created and stands behind all people; thus 'in each *thou* we address the *eternal Thou*' (Buber 1958, 6) in whom 'the extended lines of relations meet' (75). Seeing through and beyond *thou* to the *eternal Thou* is a transformational, ethical experience, which joins the two great commandments of scripture, to love God with our whole being and love one's neighbour as oneself. All *I-thou* relationships should ultimately point to and reflect *I-eternal Thou.*

The ethical demand of the Other is important to Levinas. Although 'the Other is what I am not' (1987, 83), rather than see this *non-I* as a threat, Levinas chooses to view him or her as 'kin or someone who could be' (Morgan 2007, 33). 'To recognise the other is to recognise a hunger. To recognise the other is to give' (Levinas 1969, 73).

The responsibility inherent in our relationship with the Other is communicated powerfully through Levinas' metaphor of the *face*, a 'plea of the weak to the powerful or the poor to the rich' (Morgan 2007, 66). Like Buber, Levinas believes that we commune with God through our relationship with the Other.

Both scholars require us to be present and available, and even responsible, for the Other. For Christians this outward facing orientation of God's people derives primarily from the nature and practice of the Triune God, His interactions with His people in both Testaments, and the character of the community which places its faith in Him.

In the rest of this article will be unpacked the concept of otherness as it relates to God Himself, the nation of Israel in scripture, the Lord Jesus Christ, and the church. We shall look at otherness within an entity (internal) and explore how that entity relates to the external other.

God and otherness

The ability and responsibility of the church to relate to the Other is based in faith in a God who relates to the Other, within and without Himself. Indeed, Muncada (2008, 42) comments that 'a theology of migration must start with the blessed Trinity.' The creator God is distinct from and other to His people. Yet His nature and actions provide models for us, within the constraints of the ontological and moral difference between perfect infinite deity and fallen finite humanity.

God is in Himself a complexity, a triune community in which each member relates to two Others. Within the very being of God there is perfect positive otherness (St Maximus' *difference*), as the three persons relate and function in perfect love and respect, with none of the tainting caused by the sin and insecurity resulting from the rupture of relationship between Creator and created. God's absolute freedom 'to be completely for and in the Other' (Rowan Williams in the introduction to Zizioulas 2007, xi) entails the provision of space by and for each member of the Trinity (Moltmann 2008), in which takes place the divine perichoresis of love and devotion.

For Moltmann (2008, 374), understanding the Trinity as spaces as well as persons means that there is giving and receiving of otherness, complementary notions of *ek-stasis* (lit. *outward standing*) and *kenosis* within the Godhead. The divine persons manifest unity in diversity, echoing Muncada's (2008) Trinitarian love within and beyond the persons and Japanese theologian Nozomu Miyahira's (1997) conceptualisation of the Trinity as 'three betweennesses, one concord.'

Turning to the church, Zizioulas claims that the only model for communion and otherness is the Trinity. If those within the church are to relate properly to each other and the outside world they must reflect the inner relationships of the triune God, whence comes a Christian ethics which respects and rejoices in the Other.

Not only does God display a perfect instantiation of healthy otherness within Himself; His interaction with His human creatures and the creation is also a model for us. The Bible presents God as creator of a natural world of plants, animals, and human beings that are Other to Him, yet which He loves and sustains. At the Fall we became doubly Other to God because of our rebellion against Him, as well as our ontological difference from and inferiority to Him. Humanity's rejection of God makes Him into a negative Other (St Maximus' *division*), yet He chooses mercy, protecting the first people as He exercises judgment upon them. Later He calls Abram and establishes a people through whom He will model relationships and reveal Himself to the world. God takes the sovereign decision not to see otherness as toxic and negative, and makes space for and comes to us, in Eden, through the tabernacle, in the temple, in the incarnation of His Son, and in the kingdom through the Spirit. In this, we see God's sovereign decision not to see otherness as negative and toxic.

Moltmann's idea of space goes beyond the Godhead and out into the creation, because God is a 'threefold divine Space for the indwelling of all creatures' (375). The space is created by and creates otherness, welcoming the created Other with perfect love. What I call the *space of acceptance* is dependent on God, our entry into it the aim of God's the redemptive plan through the death and resurrection of Jesus Christ. It is faith in Christ which brings access to the 'glory sphere' (Gruenler 1986, 130).

As people move into the *space of acceptance* it grows and extends towards those still outside. We join a derivative perichoretic community of human beings interacting with God and each other. Note that space and acceptance are precious notions for migrant people constrained by law, race, status, time, and location.

We turn now to the first cultural community to which God related as Other, and through whom He extended the space of acceptance. Today's church is separated from ancient Israel by space, time, and culture, yet their ancient ethos of how to relate to the Other feels remarkably appropriate for us today.

Israel and otherness

The covenant people were instructed about how to manage otherness within the community, including those without faith in YHWH, and to use their moral and religious otherness as witness for God to the surrounding nations.

The Pentateuch requires Israel to treat migrants within the community fairly, particularly the sojourner, a kind of resident alien. There is a tension between proclaiming the goodness and openness of YHWH by welcoming and treating the foreigner with a civil status equivalent to that of an Israelite and also marking him out as a religious Other. The result is what I call the *attractive vector*; the high ethical and moral standards of a faith in God which marks a person as a religious other also draw him or her towards Israel's God.

The combination of fair treatment and faith witness by Israel to the ethnic and religious Other is based on a few interconnected factors. The first is the nation's responsibility as a missional community, which served God by being rather than going (Wright 2000). Related to this is the requirement that Israel remain different from the peoples around it, to be holy, as God is holy. Added to this is Israel's formative experience in Egypt, the memory of which God uses to urge appropriate treatment of migrant others.

The missional responsibility of Israel has been discussed in terms of centrifugal and centripetal mission, and the ethical commission of God to His people. Blauw (1962, 34) coins the terms *centripetal* and *centrifugal* because for him there is no Great Commission in the OT (see also Bosch 1991). These same categories are affirmed by Peters (1972, 2), for whom 'Israel and the temple…draw people to themselves and the Lord.' The nation and its religious centre attract people not only to the Lord in religious faith and allegiance but also to His people. There is thus potential assimilation (Timmer 2011) and belonging, a reduction in otherness.

It is noteworthy that as God instructs Israel to be distinct, He instructs them to treat outsiders ethically and mercifully, commands fundamentally missionary in nature. Election, ethics, and mission form a 'missional logic' (Wright 2010, 93).

The scripture links fair treatment of aliens with Israel's suffering at the hand of the Egyptians. By the time of Deuteronomy, Egypt had become a national memory with an ethical demand rather than a personal experience of deprivation and pain. There are several statements requiring fair treatment and inclusion of the Other which include a reminder of Israel's troubled time in Egypt (Exod. 22:21, 23:9; Lev. 19:34; Deut. 10:19, 16:11, 24:17-18, and 24:21-22).

For Alexander (2008, 86), the exodus represented an 'ongoing activity' for Israel and not just something from the past, and surely the same applies for the suffering in Egypt, recorded in graphic terms. Slavery is the most common motif, found in Exodus 6:2-7, 20:2; Deuteronomy 5:6, 5:15, 6:12, 6:21, 7:8, 8:14, 13:5, 13:10, 15:15, 16:12, 24:18, 24:22; Leviticus 26:13. There are also abuse and unreasonable demands (Exod. 2:11-12, 5:10-18), suffering and misery (Exod. 2:23, Exod. 3:17, Neh. 9:9), and the lifting of a club against Israel (Isa. 10:24). Egypt is an iron-smelting furnace (Deut. 4:20, 1 Kings 8:51, Jer. 11:4) and the forced labour endured by the Israelites (Exod. 1:11-14, Deut. 26:5-6) is racial hatred or attempted genocide in Exodus 1:8-10, 1:15-22. The intense suffering, racism, and even potential national extinction commodified Israel as the ultimate distant

Other, and the powerful imagery warns Israel never to treat aliens as they had been treated.

From the Israelites' suffering in Egypt, the mercy of God in the exodus, and the prohibition of maltreatment of resident aliens, I derive two paradigms. One is the negative *Egypt paradigm* of Pharaoh > Israel > Alien, and the other is the positive *Exodus paradigm*, God > Israel > Alien. Israel is required to extend the same *Exodus* to the alien as God extended to them – which resonates with Pleins' 'theology of obligation' (2001, 52). In fact, not only is Israel not to do the negative things that Egypt did, she must act positively towards the undeserving. The *Exodus paradigm* is congruent with Bernat's (2009, 47) observation that as a vulnerable party 'the foreigner is to the Israelite as the Israelite is to God'. God relates to Israel as healthy or positive Other, and Israel must do the same to the alien. What I call *cascading otherness* (God to Israel, Israel to the alien) is to be redemptive and just. Furthermore, as Buber (1958) tells us, in any *I-thou* interaction, behind the human thou stands the *eternal Thou* of the Exodus.

The instructions on how to manage otherness within the community and between it and the surrounding unbelieving nations form two parts of a whole for Israel and the church, as we shall see. These dual aspects of otherness are also seen in the person and work of Christ.

Christ and otherness

Jesus' life and experience on earth are marked by otherness, with regard to Israel and the Gentiles, and even as a human being. His status and experiences are consistent with those of Israel and in many ways normative for His church. The internal otherness and relating to external Others we see in the life of Christ are echoes of the situation of the Trinity and inform the church.

For Christ, otherness occurs at the incarnation. For a God who is spirit and infinite to appear in finite flesh and dwell among His creatures involves otherness. In a way which we cannot fully understand there is otherness within the body and mind of Christ because of the presence of humanity in His earthly person.

In his genealogy of Christ, Matthew lists Joseph (a racial and social Other in Egypt) and Abraham the wandering alien. The inclusion of three Gentile women (Rahab, Ruth, Bathsheba) represents the bridging of racial and social otherness, as the first was a prostitute, the second a poor migrant, and the third an adulteress.

Jesus' rejection because of His teaching and ministry moved Him from near to distant Other. In His final week the acclamation of the triumphal entry turns to the shrieks of 'Crucify Him' and Jesus suffers the 'hard betrayal' of Judas' treachery (John 18:5) and the 'soft betrayal' of Peter's denial (Luke 22). At His death, Jesus' cries of '*My God, why have You forsaken me?'* (Mark 15:34, Psalm 22:1) speak of toxic otherness, 'full alienation from God' (Witherington 2001, 399).

The church and otherness

In the NT there are various descriptions of and prescriptions for otherness concerning the church. Fundamental to our understanding of this are the idea that Jesus is an exemplar for His people and that no servant is greater than his master.

Jesus' washing of the disciples' feet, demonstrates that bringing the gospel to people involves meeting and serving them (John 13:1-17). Newbigin (1987) understands Peter's objection to having his feet washed as a desire to keep social norms intact, while for Carson (1991) the race factor is implicitly present, because some Jews saw this as a task for Gentile slaves. Gruenler (1986, 90) connects Jesus' concern for the Other with the 'characteristic motif' of the Trinity and the church that is to be formed in its image.

In John 14:10-12, Jesus reveals that His ministry derives from the Father and that He and the Father are mutually indwelling (14:10). However, the Father's acceptance and empowerment of the Son extend beyond the Trinity to include Christians (14:12). Believers in Jesus will do the divine work of accepting and loving the Other, subject to the limitations of our fallen human nature. The cascading from Father to Son to church means that the 'emerging community ...is...to image the divine Community in its plurality and oneness' (Gruenler 1986, 126).

The connection between finite man and infinite God means that Father and Son will make their home with those who love and obey Jesus (John 14:23). Christians now share in the divine life to some extent through 'the adoption into God of his own human handiwork' (Steenberg 2009, 129). The unity of believers is a reflection of the unity of the Godhead and of our participation in it (Newbigin 1987, 234).

Jesus' prayer for unity among the disciples, including those yet to believe (John 17:20-21) anticipates a unity similar to that between Father and Son (17:22), embrace and acceptance of the Other without discrimination. But the end of Jesus' prayer is not just two distinct levels of unity, one divine and the other human; Christians are also united with the Trinity as a witness to the world (17:21 and 23). Unity cannot exist if there is negative otherness, and a healthy attitude to otherness commends the gospel to the world.

The Corinthian church is infamous for its division, toxic otherness based primarily on social status (Blue 1991). There were a number of binary divisions or in- and out-groups in Corinth (Blue 1991), and Paul juxtaposes the foolish and the wise, the weak and the strong, and the lowly and the boastful in order to show the foolishness of human categories and undermine the negative otherness associated with them.

Paul deals with abuse of the Lord's Supper in 1 Corinthians 11. It is ironic that in an event designed to look away from self and toward the church and the *eternal Thou* who deconstructs our human divisions, the Corinthians also demonstrate factionalism. The same flaw governs attitudes towards the spiritual gifts. Paul's body metaphor removes all exclusion based on human categories (Hansen 2010), and 1 Corinthians 12:12-13 expresses his passion for unity in diversity, the functioning of otherness within the body of Christ. Lossky (1976, 167) encapsulates this neatly: the unity of redeemed humanity is based on the resurrection of Christ while its diversity is the work of the Holy Spirit. Paul's reasoning flows logically into 1 Corinthians 13, vv.4-5 of which shows us how to relate to the Other.

The second letter to the Corinthians contains the one binary distinction which Paul accepts and indeed insists upon, believer versus unbeliever (6:14ff). Paul the evangelist has demonstrated his indifference to human categories in the light of the gospel, yet here, as in the OT, the language seems almost aggressively exclusivist. However, the thrust of Paul's thought is that this boundary is porous and crossed by faith in Christ.

In Galatians, Paul is frank about his background, his enthusiasm for Judaism, and earlier opposition to the church. Paul is a man for whom everything has changed, because the gospel defuses negative or distant forms of otherness and brings reconciliation. All who belong to Christ are descendants and heirs of Abraham (3:29); they are his seed and look forward eschatologically to what Christ has for them. Galations 3:28 is Paul's classic statement of otherness bridged and reduced by the gospel. His apparent refutation of the binary categories of Jew/Gentile, slave/free, and male/female denies not basic human differences but their relevance for the church, in which 'bodily inscribed differences are brought together, not removed' (Volf 1996, 48). Paul's avoidance of the two extremes of complete indifference and suffocating control creates a dynamic middle ground for the church's response to migration.

In vv.26-29 we see through the eyes the *eternal Thou*. Each Levinasian *face* of the Other, brother or sister in Christ, represents one behind whom stands that *eternal Thou*. We can never commodify the (migrant) other as *it*. Loving your neighbour as yourself (5:14) and serving one another, reject any utilitarian view of the Other. Paul contrasts the acts of the flesh (5:19ff) and the fruit of the Spirit (5:22ff), the flesh centring on the self at the expense of Others while the fruit of the Spirit goes beyond the self, embracing and loving the Other. Colossians 3:8-14 says something similar about relationships between individuals and groups, combining unity and forgiveness. Christian identity means granting *Exodus* to the Other, including those who are very different.

In 1 Peter Christians are exiles, scattered people (1:1), Other vis-à-vis the world, like the Israelites after the Exodus. Peter summarises how Christians should live among non-Christians (Volf 1994). The first four verses remind us of Hebrews 11, although Volf (1994) prefers to draw our alien-ness less from the history of Israel and more from Christ. However, there is continuity between Israel and the church and the moral obligations given to God's people in both Testaments.

Again, the boundary between member and non-member of the faith community is clear yet porous. Peter's readers previously had neither been a people nor received mercy, and in 2:10 there is a connection with Hosea, one of whose children was named *Not my people* and another *Not loved.* Through His mercy and sovereign action God reduces negative otherness, and His church is to partner with Him in this.

Because they are other to mainstream society Christians are to bear witness to it (2:11-12), and thus correct behaviour towards the Other goes beyond the faith community. Slaves are to obey unpleasant as well as decent masters, as part of their witness for Christ. Finally, Peter advocates love, hospitality, and mutual service (4:8-10), a degree of inclusiveness and acceptance within the Christian community that speaks to those outside. Gamble's (2007) summary of Christian service for the unbelieving community contrasts Christian *caritas*, which expected nothing in return, with Roman *liberalis*, which was based on reciprocity. Host communities often relate to migrants on a transactional basis and *caritas* should inform Christian attitudes. Unity and healthy otherness within the body of Christ are derived primarily from the divine life, yet embrace of the Other must also operate from believer to nonbeliever.

Here, Christ's *kenosis* at the incarnation is a model for us as we relate to God, to other Christians, and to those outside the church. In this 'kenotic approach to the other' (Zizioulas 2007, 6) communion depends on a person's otherness and not on any other attributes. We relate to Others not based on our perception of their worthiness, but because they are there – a *face*.

Ministry and otherness

This article concludes with a glance at practical ministry. Both Testaments have shown that God's people must have mercy on the Other, the outsider, because of their own experience. Believers are Other to the established, mainstream order of the world. They may have undergone persecution because of their allegiance to God, who urges them: *be merciful to outsiders because you know how it feels*. As we encounter people outside the community of faith, we must be mindful of our own status as outsiders and attract them by our relationship to God, community life, and moral standards.

As the church remains distinct from, while engaging with, the Other, the result is an *attractive vector*, which is consistent with the thought of Zizioulas. He looks upon Others not in terms of past or present, but of future; an eschatological, missional perspective means that "every 'other' is in the Spirit a potential saint" (6). For Christians, the church is the primary arena for healthy relationships, yet we should treat non-Christian Others as well as we treat brothers and sisters in the Lord. Non-Christians are human Others to us and this is more fundamental than the *difference* (or more often *division*) between believer and non-believer. Also, our appropriate behaviour toward them may be part of their journey to faith.

Moltmann (2008) takes the eschatological view that being 'in Christ' means that we are in a 'moving room', going towards perfection, restoration, and consummation. This obliges us to accept Others in the name of Christ, from gratitude at what He has done *for* us and in expectation of what He will do *with* us.

Thinking about the Other by combining what is and what might be can liberate and empower churches struggling with diversity. When migrant Others appear in our communities and churches, differences in ethnicity, culture, and social status can be very obvious. Furthermore, modern migration brings otherness into settled host communities very quickly. Churches may feel confused or even threatened at the prospect of dealing with migrants, whether they are Christian or not. A church which embraces migrants may never be the same again. One response in countries with large numbers of migrants is the employment of pastoral staff to look after autonomous ethnic fellowships within the larger church. But one weakness of this keyhole or remote approach may be that true intercultural fellowship is missing even though established churches are serving the Lord and His people.

Yet the Scripture says a lot about diversity. The body metaphor of First Corinthians is surely not limited to the use of spiritual gifts, and the reconciliation between Jew and Gentile in Galatians points to a broader rainbow of colour and culture within the church. Revelation 7 shows us a marvellous picture of unity and diversity within the kingdom of God, now and into the future. Something similar is portrayed in Revelation 21; the glory of the nations being brought into the holy city shows that all cultures are purified by the gospel and woven into the kingdom by God.

To be Christian is to expect diversity and live in fellowship with the Other. Our God, the one and three, is our example of His own nature and actions, mediated through the experience and ethics of His people. He asks us to view otherness and Others positively and as a blessing. This is a clear theological thread running through scripture.

For discussion

1. When we come across a migrant or outsider to our community what can be done to go beyond seeing him or her simply as a representative of a larger group? What hints for action and challenges to our prejudices can we gain by reading the New Testament?

2. Modern migration often works through chains. How can people in migrant sending and receiving countries make use of chains and migrants going backwards and forwards in the transnational space to spread the gospel and advance discipleship? Where and how could we identify and place gospel workers along migration chains?
3. How much of our fear of the Other is actually a reflection of our own inadequacy and insecurity? How can our identity in Christ remove the need for self-affirmation which is often sought by denigrating the Other?
4. The divine Trinity forms spaces into which He invites humanity. What about our churches and other Christian groupings? Does our communal spiritual life also create spaces for the Other? How do we react when our often mono-cultural, established life and worship spaces are invaded by newcomers? At the end of the day, to whom do these spaces belong?
5. A Christian space established on the basis of God's love and grace should be one of holy communitas, where cultural and social norms of acceptability based on ethnicity, status, gender, and origin are undermined or even removed. How can we educate and liberate our church members to see themselves as liminal people while still in their own towns, churches, and denominations?

Bibliography

Alexander, T. Desmond. (2008). *From Eden to the New Jerusalem.* Nottingham. IVP.

Bernat, D. (2009) *Sign of the Covenant: Circumcision in the Priestly Tradition.* Atlanta: Society of Biblical Literature.

Blauw, J. (1962). *The Missionary Nature of the Church.* London: McGraw Pub.

Blue, B. (1991). The House Church at Corinth and the Lord's Supper: Famine, Food Supply, and the Present Distress. *Criswell Theological Review* 5(2), 221-239.

Bosch, D. (1991). *Transforming Mission: Paradigm Shifts in Theology of Mission.* New York: Orbis Books.

Buber, M. *I and Thou.* Edinburgh: T & T Clark, 1958.

Carson, D. (1991). *The Gospel According to John.* Leicester: IVP.

Castles, S., and Miller, M. (2003). *The Age of Migration: International Population Movements in the Modern World.* Basingstoke: Palgrave Macmillan.

Gamble, R. (2007). "Christianity from the Early Fathers to Charlemagne," in A. Hoffecker (Ed.), *Revolutions in worldview: Understanding the flow of western thought* (100-138). Phillipsburg: P&R Publishing.

Gruenler, R. (1986). *The Trinity in the Gospel of John: A Thematic Commentary on the Fourth Gospel.* Grand Rapids: Baker Book House.

Hansen, B. (2010). *All of You are One: The Social Vision of Gal 3:28, 1 Cor 12:13 and Col 3:11.* London: T&T Clark.

Levinas, E. (1969). *Totality and Infinity: An Essay on Exteriority.* Pittsburgh: Duquesne University Press.

Levinas, E. (1987). *Time and the Other.* Pittsburgh: Duquesne University Press.

Lossky, V. (1976). *The Mystical Theology of the Eastern Church*. Crestwood: St Vladimir's Seminary Press.
Miyahira, N. (1997). "A Japanese perspective on the Trinity," *Themelios 22*(2), 39-51.
Moltmann, J. (2008). "God in the world – the world in God," in R. Bauckham and C. Mosser (Eds.), *The Gospel of John and Christian Theology* (369-381). Grand Rapids: Eerdmans.
Morgan, M. (2007). *Discovering Levinas*. Cambridge: Cambridge University Press.
Muncado, Felipe (2008). *Faith on the Move: Towards a Theology of Migration in Asia.* Manila: Ateneo de Manila Press.
Newbigin, L. (1987). *The Light Has Come: An Exposition of the Fourth Gospel.* Edinburgh: The Handsel Press.
Peters, George W. (1972). *A Biblical Theology of Missions.* Chicago, IL: Moody.
Pleins, J. (2001). *The Social Visions of the Hebrew Bible: A Theological Introduction.* Louisville: Westminster John Knox Press.
Steenberg, M. (2009). "The church," in M. Cunningham and E. Theokritoff (Eds.), *The Cambridge Companion to Orthodox Christian Theology* (121-135). Cambridge: Cambridge University Press.
Timmer, D. (2011). *A Gracious and Compassionate God: Mission, Salvation and Spirituality in the Book of Jonah.* Nottingham: Apollos.
Volf, M. (1994). *Soft difference: Theological Reflections on the Relation between Church and Culture in 1 Peter.* Ex auditu, 10 August, 1994. Yale Center for Faith and Culture.
Volf, M. (1996). *Exclusion and Embrace: A Theological Exploration of Identity, Otherness, and Reconciliation*. Nashville: Abingdon Press.
Witherington, B. (2001). *The Gospel of Mark: A Socio-Rhetorical Commentary.* Cambridge: Eerdmans.
Wright, C. (2000). *Christian Mission and the Old Testament: Matrix or Mismatch?* Henry Martyn Seminar at Westminster College, Cambridge, 9 November 2000.
Wright, C. (2010). *The Mission of God's People: A Biblical Theology of the Church's Mission*. Grand Rapids: Zondervan.
Yeoh, B. (2003). *Migration, International Labour and Multicultural Policies in Singapore*. Unpublished paper, Department of Geography, National University of Singapore.
Zizioulas, J. (2007). *Communion and Otherness: Further Studies in Personhood and the Church*. London: T & T Clark International.

8. Pilgrims on a Journey: Diaspora and Mission

Thomas Harvey

> Peter, an apostle of Jesus Christ, to the chosen migrants dispersed throughout Pontus, Galatia, Cappadocia, Asia, and Bithynia; chosen according to the plan of God the Father in the sanctification of the Spirit for obedience to Jesus Christ: May grace and peace be multiplied to you.1 Peter 1:1, 2[1]

Introduction

In an insecure world, humans tend to seek refuge in grounded and stable communities. In contrast, God turns to the sojourner, the alien, and the stranger to announce the blessing and shalom of his security. Thus, Peter's salutation addresses "strangers," "aliens," and "migrants" scattered across Asia Minor as divinely "chosen," empowered by God to fulfill his purposes.

That divine election, its biblical and early church roots, and its open-ended relevance to mission and ministry today are the subject of this chapter; i.e. in what ways do the Scriptures inform and orient effective integral mission…

- ***to*** diaspora people whether they are economic migrants, forcefully displaced refugees or simply people on the move.
- ***through*** individuals and communities on the move to spread the Good News of Jesus Christ and be a blessing to the all the nations of the earth.
- ***beyond*** ethnic, cultural and national barriers to fulfill his purposes and work for the establishment of his Kingdom of peace and righteousness.

In emphasising mission that is to, through and beyond people on the move, it is important to note that this encompasses not only the object of mission, but its means. Accordingly mission studies need to go beyond history and description and address the attitude and orientation of mission in light of its roots in diaspora. As we shall note, God's chosen people are called from creation onwards to be "on the move" and this should inform our understanding of, attitude toward, activity in, and character of mission.

This chapter begins by looking at two covenants central to a biblical understanding of mission: creation and redemption. These two covenants orient mission to, through and beyond diaspora communities. In briefly

---

1 My translation.

recounting the story of creation, fall and redemption, my intent is to bring out the dynamic character of biblical Christian mission. Accordingly, Creation, Fall, and Redemption should not be approached as static theological categories, but as ideas caught up in an intricate theological dance of initiative and response to, through and beyond people on the move.

A tale of three journeys: creation, fall and redemption

To understand the relationship between mission and migration, three journeys should be kept in mind. The journey of creation, the journey of the fall of humankind, and the journey of redemption initiated by God and fulfilled in Christ. The first began with the covenant at creation between God and humankind. According to the Genesis account, humankind were ordained by God to exercise stewardship over creation. Though that divine service began in the Garden of Eden, it was intended to encompass the entire earth (Gen. 1:28); fruition of the earth and the multiplication of humanity required it.[2] Thus, for humankind to fulfill the creation covenant required migration; a physical journey from the Garden to the ends of the earth and in so doing to fulfill their obligation to God and for creation to come to full fruition.

As the biblical scholar William Dumbrell has pointed out, the narrative of Genesis 2 places before humankind a physical, intellectual, and spiritual journey if they are to attain maturation and perfection. Ancient Near Eastern gardens were walled off to afford a secure environment. In Genesis 2, Adam and Eve abided in the security of the garden that afforded peaceful communion with each other and with God even as it allowed for their maturation in competency and character through personal communion with God. As humans gained wisdom and understanding the garden would bear fruit accordingly and gradually be extended to encompass the whole earth. [3] This was then a physical, intellectual, and spiritual pilgrimage whose progress and ultimate fulfilment rested upon communion and collaboration with God.

Disobedience, however, diverted humankind. In Genesis 3, Adam and Eve are banished from the garden. They and their progeny are compelled to embark on a harsh and hostile exile marked by disorientation and ultimately death. Without God's personal nurture and tutelage communion with God

---

2 As William Dumbrell has noted, it is the orientation and movement of the divine command that not only orders the Genesis accounts, but the whole of Scripture as well. A good biblical introduction to the orientation of Scripture can be seen in Dumbrell's Search for Order: Biblical Eschatology in Focus. In terms of Christian self-understanding and mission, this orientation is addressed in Christopher J. H. Wright's The Mission of God's People: A Biblical Theology of the Church's Mission.

3 Dumbrell, 16-23

afforded, ignorance, ineptitude and over-reach ensue. Communion gives way to contention, as individuals, tribes and nations conflict over land and bounty, and the temporary wealth, security, and power they afford (Gen. 3:17). Greed's bitter harvest is insecurity, exploitation, hording, distrust, violence, dissolution and despair, as evidenced in Genesis 3-11. Without communion, no pathway leads to progress towards the promise and fulfillment set before humankind at creation.

Redeeming Diaspora

So God chose a sojourner to begin a third journey. In Genesis 12:1, God summons Abram to leave home and family and to trust him as his guide. God gives him the new name Abraham, "father of many nations," and bestows upon him and his seed the gift and vocation of redemption. From Genesis chapter 12 onward, Scripture unveils the unfolding election of Abraham, Israel, and Jesus Christ to fulfill the redemptive purposes of God.

These three journeys, creation, the fall, and redemption, are the covenantal backdrop to mission and ministry ***to, through*** and ***beyond*** people on the move. They encompass human potential, plight, and promise: the potential of creation, the plight of the fall, and the promise of redemption, through an elect people who sojourn through the world. Each is only understood in light of the other two and all involve people on the move.

1. To _ The Object of Mission

This background is critical to understanding mission and ministry ***to*** people on the move. It reminds us that to one degree or another all human beings are on a physical and spiritual journey that is at once ordained, tragic, and hopeful. Ordained, in that human-beings are divinely called to be on the move to bring about God's will, tragic in that apart from the grace of God the goal of this journey is unattainable, and hopeful in that through Christ, God has provided a way to restore diaspora peoples to communion with God.

To whom then is mission directed? Clearly it is ***to*** people on the move. Though Biblically that is well grounded, over the past two centuries mission and missiology have tended to assume stasis. In the 19th and early 20th century, the study of mission focused on regions and nations. More recently missiology has emphasized cross-cultural or intercultural mission. Though more cognizant of people on the move, they also lean toward permanency rather than movement and transition. Emphasis on "people groups," tends to analyze culture, ethnicity and language in terms of an originating culture often in a given geographical region.

The recognition that mission is ***to*** people on the move, doesn't lessen the value of the study of language, cultural and intercultural studies. What it does encourage is consideration of these in light of the movement of people globally. Hence, sharing the Gospel with Ethiopians living in Paris will be very different from the same work in Addis Ababa or in more rural areas of the Ethiopia. Certainly, knowing the language, being familiar with traditional values and cultural patterns will be extremely helpful in each context, yet effective mission will also need to pay considerable attention to how those frameworks change as groups of people move from rural to urban or to radically different social settings overseas.

Given the fall, catalysts for movement include war, scarcity, economic necessity or political or religious persecution just to name a few. These physical and spiritual distortions are multi-layered, overlapping and often inter-related. For example, migrants often face:

1. The physical vulnerability of being on the move.
2. Psychological trauma associated with their forced migration.
3. Lack of local identity or recognition in the places they reside.
4. Lack of protection of the law especially for those who are considered illegal immigrants by the host nation. As a result, such immigrants live under the threat of arrest, imprisonment and deportation.
5. Given the traumatic circumstances that often accompany persons on the move, many experience shame or guilt especially if they were involved in conflict or fled from family or communal disorder.
6. Many suffer as a result of separation from their family or loss of loved ones.
7. Often migrants dwell in urban areas populated with other migrants struggling for survival, which can lead to tension and violence between competing groups.

The above is only a tentative list and by no means comprehensive. Nonetheless, it brings to the fore the complexity of ministry and mission to people on the move. Holistic mission and ministry, by definition, will attempt to address the physical, psychological and spiritual needs these conditions produce.

Accordingly ***to*** people there is a need to address:

1. Physical and psychological care.
2. The need for security and safety.
3. Working to understand and address issues of legal immigration or illegal status.
4. Questions of personal and communal identity.
5. Spiritual care for those grappling with guilt and shame.
6. The need for grace, forgiveness, redemption and renewal.
7. Building peaceful coexistence with neighbors especially in multi-cultural contexts.
8. Restoration of relationship with God and neighbors in areas marked by crime and violence.

Exclusive emphasis on any one of the above to the exclusion of the others is redemptively insufficient for it fails to fully appreciate how the covenants of creation and redemption are entwined.

Emphasis upon the covenant to humankind at creation reminds us that movement and migration are fundamental to flourishing and fulfillment. Thus, ministry and mission to diaspora peoples should address the relationship between redemption, vocation and fulfillment. Due to the Fall, migration is now traumatic and tragic and produces wounded bodies and souls that need physical and spiritual healing. Being "lost" is no mere Christian metaphor; apart from Christ, human beings lack the communion and compass needed for guidance and direction. This is why people on the move are often more open to the Gospel than when they are settled. On the move, they recognize their need for mercy, grace, renewal and meaning. The Bible reveals not only God's story but their own. Through faith in Christ and baptism many recover their identity in Christ as they find in the church security, solace, compassion, care, redemption and renewal in the calling of Christ.

2. Through _ *The Means of Mission*

That God chose the migrant Abraham to work out his plan of redemption shouldn't strike us as strange given that much of the Old Testament canon was collected, inscribed, written and read during and after the Babylonian captivity. The paradox of Israel's unique election in exile served as the crucible of God's revelation and redemption revealed through the account of the wanderer, the migrant, the captive, and the exile. Through the stories of Abraham, Isaac, Jacob, Joseph, Moses, and Elijah, Israel articulated how a displaced people dispossessed of their land and scattered amongst the nations remained the chosen vessel of the one true God to bless the nations. We see this in the command of Moses in the wilderness:

> See, I have taught you decrees and laws as the LORD my God commanded me, so that you may follow them… Observe them carefully, for this will show your wisdom and understanding to the nations, who will hear about all these decrees and say, "Surely this great nation is a wise and understanding people." What other nation is so great as to have their gods near them the way the LORD our God is near us whenever we pray to him?" (Deut. 4 5-7)

The Exodus, the giving of the law, the presence of God in the tabernacle that moves with Israel are not only witnesses to Israel's redemption but inform the nations what restored relationship with God entails. "Wisdom and understanding" afford blessings and fruition, hearkening back to the covenant made with humankind at creation now manifest in the redemption of Israel.

Jeremiah's prophecy resonates with this divine vocation when he tells the people to "seek the peace and prosperity of the city." Jeremiah reminds the exiles that as strangers in a strange land they were not to view their captivity as a dead end, but part of God's unfolding divine will; exile is not the demise of Israel's sacred vocation, but its paradoxical fulfilment. Accordingly, exile suggests a distinct status and not total absorption into the foreign cultural milieu. Israel's witness required its distinct covenantal status and identity. Their identity as God's chosen diaspora was critical to their own welfare as well as to the surrounding city, for in their relationship to Yahweh, they bear witness to his redemptive activity through Israel to the nations. Hence, the faithfulness of God to Israel offered blessing within and without.

Diaspora and the New Testament

The blessing of witness on the move can be seen in the ministry of Jesus and his disciples and the missionary journeys of Paul and others in the Early Church.

The earliest writings of the New Testament were penned by Paul. As a Diaspora Jew, Paul was fluent in Greek, Aramaic and Hebrew and at home in the multi-cultural reality of Late Antiquity. His missionary journeys traced Jewish diaspora communities along the Roman highways of Asia Minor. There he would preach the Gospel first to the Jew and then to the Gentile as his path led him from Jerusalem to Caesarea, to Philippi to Rome to Illyricum. Paul's missionary band was also made up of Diaspora Jews or Gentile converts. As fellow travelers, they learned their craft and their understanding of the Gospel and its significance on the road and amongst diaspora peoples.

Indeed, the Gospels of Mark and Luke bear the marks of that influence. Emphases on Jesus' itinerant ministry from Galilee to Syria, the Decapolis to Samaria, and Samaria to Jerusalem are not accidental. Jesus, the Messiah, summed up the promises and blessings of Abraham. He broke political, cultural, ethnic, and spiritual borders to announce his Good News to all who had ears to hear. In his encounters with Jew and non-Jew alike he revealed the Kingdom of God for those who had eyes to see and ears to hear through his display of divine power, and message of mercy and forgiveness. Thus, the Gospels record Jesus' mission and ministry on the move.

Diaspora and the Early Church

By 70 CE the early churches were largely just as Peter describes them as "chosen migrants dispersed throughout Pontus, Galatia, Cappadocia, Asia, and Bithynia." They had become the sacred vessel of the Gospel carrying the Gospel to the ends of the empire.

By the 2nd century CE, Tertullian viewed the dispersed communities as essential to the spread of the "rule of faith." Unlike pagan texts and nostrums, Tertullian observed that the "rule of faith" was the order of life and Godly discipline establishing the rule of Christ now made manifest through the diaspora communities. As he notes, "Any group of things must be classified according to its origin." The origin of true religion was the "primitive church of the Apostles." From this Apostolic trunk ***through*** true branches of the diaspora, the Gospel was spreading out over the known world. It was the diaspora that bore the Apostles' "rule of faith": i.e. the coherence, unity, and truth of Christ and the Apostles. As the plumb line of the Gospel, they offered an authentic spiritual unity within the spiritual, intellectual, and cultural cacophony of the Roman Empire.[4]

To some, this emphasis upon a "distinct community" might appear culturally conservative and a mission that displaces cultural difference. In fact, the Apostolic Rule of Faith provided a unity that embraced the cultural diversity of the early church. This paradox is evident in the Jerusalem Council of Acts. To include Gentiles through recognition of a spiritual circumcision of faith and not circumcision of the flesh allowed election and mission to be shared by the Gentiles as well without having to become Jewish.[5]

Thus, the rule of faith led to discernment in mission by providing an identifiable set of truths whose implications went beyond doctrine. This can be seen in subsequent councils that would address a host of ecclesial, social, ethical, and political matters. They grappled with matters as diverse as whether Christians could serve in the military or whether priests who had denied the faith under the compulsion of torture could be forgiven. Codified in the Old and New Testaments, Apostolic teaching and authority provide continuity in terms of identity and vocation in ever new situations and cultures as the church journeys outward in mission.

The continuity that runs through Scripture and through the early church provides insight into how God uses diaspora communities to bring about his redemptive and transformative work today. When it comes to mission ***through*** people on the move, diaspora is neither arbitrary nor accidental. By their very experience, diaspora communities are able to draw from and apply Scripture, tradition, and reason to bring meaning to their own situation and through witness and testimony to fellow travellers whom they bump up against in our multicultural world. Diaspora fellowships and churches are significant in mission as resident aliens. They offer a sense of identity and a stable community. They can be good friends and neighbours who understand the physical, psychological, legal, and spiritual struggles of fellow migrants. They offer understanding, acceptance, experience, assistance and spiritual balm that open aliens and strangers up to the grace

---

4 This adds the mission dimension to what Pelikan noted in terms of the social implications of apostolicity. Ibid 25.

5 Note that this does not suggest in any way the supersession of Gentile Christians but rather recognition that the election of Abraham is now shared by faith and that diaspora Gentile churches find their root and identity in Israel.

of Christ and an open invitation to join this body of *chosen migrants dispersed* throughout the world by faith.

As we have seen, the Gospel offered ***through*** migrant communities resonates deeply with both the covenants of creation and redemption. In terms of redemption, they witness to the virtues of the migrant whether that is the faith of Abraham, the wisdom of the captive Joseph, the leadership of Moses, the prophetic insight and resistance of Elijah, the itinerant ministry of Jesus or the missionary zeal of Paul and the Early Church. In terms of fruition, migrant communities are able to offer assistance, guidance, and experience that can help displaced people to be fruitful in their new home. Further as noted in Deuteronomy and in Jeremiah, the presence of the Godly alien can be a source of wisdom and knowledge to their neighbours. They are called to bless the nations and societies they inhabit. Thus, rather than being a drag on society, they have unique gifts that bless, inform, and transform the societies they inhabit.

3. Ministry and Mission beyond People on the move.

The mission of God revealed in Scripture is ***to*** and ***through*** persons on the move. This section looks ***beyond*** diaspora communities to examine the significance and impact upon wider society of diaspora mission. Certainly the size and impact of diaspora are directly tied to growth in the size and speed of globalisation today. The pressures these create on urban centers that are struggling to absorb a dizzying array of ethnic and cultural groups are enormous. Nonetheless, historically, Christianity has not only thrived in multi-cultural settings, it has had an enormous impact on societies facing social and political upheaval.

This was certainly true in the Roman Empire where Christianity found root and proved a key catalyst in the transformation of the empire. In large measure, this significant impact had to do with the character of the diaspora Christian churches at the time:

> Urban society in the early Roman Empire was scarcely less complicated than our own… It's complexity—its untidiness—may well have been felt with special acuteness by people who were marginal or transient, either physically or socially or both, as so many of the identifiable members of the Pauline churches seem to have been. In any case, Paul and the founders and leaders of those groups engaged aggressively in the business of creating a new social reality. [6]

Establishing a "new social reality" faced stiff spiritual and political resistance for it challenged the tenuous ethnic and religious harmony the empire rested on. Urban settings in Late Antiquity afforded a cornucopia of exotic cults, mystery religions, and variegated deities. Each was allowed to

---

6 Wayne Meeks, The First Urban Christians: The Social World of the Apostle Paul (New Haven:Yale University Press, 2003), 105.

pedal their spiritual wares so long as they didn't disturb public order. Yet Paul's polemic against the patroness deity of Ephesus in Acts 19 did precisely that. Servicing the worship of the mother goddess Artemis lined the purses of merchants, provided government revenues and fed deference to imperial cult as well. Thus, Paul's challenge caused civil uproar and nearly cost him his life.

Paradoxically, even as Paul's diaspora missionary preaching threatened the religious and political status quo, it offered a more compelling and compassionate unity. In urban centers Gentile, Jew, barbarian, Scythian, slave, and free dwelt cheek to jowl. Within these gritty environs the "new social reality" of Christian *koinonia* beckoned. Marginalized aliens, in conversion faith and baptism, put on fresh garments of identity in Christ. These proffered a fraternal dignity and spiritual mission; as migrants among migrants, the Great Commission to "disciple the nations" was now their calling as the Gospel moved beyond their own culture and people to their neighbors from other cultures.

This Christian counterculture not only provided a new communal sense, the virtues and values of the community exposed and challenged the pomp, decadence and violence of imperial Rome. This inversion is captured in the Epistle to Diognetus:

> Christians are not distinguished by country, language, or custom. They live in their countries, but only as aliens. They busy themselves on earth, but their citizenship is in heaven. They obey the laws, but in their own lives they go far beyond what the law requires. They love all, but by all are persecuted. They are quiet and peaceable, but they are condemned. They are put to death, and yet they are brought to life. They are defamed, but are vindicated. Reviled yet they bless, when slighted they show due respect. They do good, yet are punished as evildoers; and punished they rejoice because they are brought to life. [7]

The Pax Romana (Peace of Rome) was founded upon dominating violence but the Kingdom of Christ was built on the peace of service and suffering. The divine inversion founded in the crucified Lord challenged the pigeonholes of the Imperium. The church offered a peace for slave, plebeian, and patrician that the State could not. While Romans owed their allegiance to the powerful but arbitrary Caesar, Christians bowed down to the Prince of Peace whose peaceable kingdom encompassed heaven and earth. Thus even while Christians were hounded in the empire as subversive, their very suffering commended itself to the vast swaths of the population who suffered.

Here lay the secret of the Church Militant. Its weapons were suffering and martyrdom that exposed the true character of Roman rule even as it affirmed the ultimate authority of the church in Christ. This inversion can

---

7 The So-Called Epistle to Diogenetus. Ethereal Christian Classics: Early Church Fathers online at: http://www.ccel.org/ccel/richardson/fathers.x.i.ii.html.

be seen in the letter of the presbyters Moses, Maximus, and their companions during the Decian persecution of the church:

> For what more glorious or more felicitous could happen to any man from the divine condescension than, undaunted before the very executioners, to confess the Lord God; than to confess Christ, the Son of God, among the various refined tortures of the cruel secular power and even with the body twisted and racked and butchered and even dying yet with a free spirit… than to receive the heavenly kingdom without any delay; than to have been made a colleague in the Passion of Christ; than to have been made a judge of one's judge by the divine condescension… than not to have obeyed human and sacrilegious laws against faith… than by dying, to have overcome death itself which is feared by all… than to have struggled against all of the pains of a mutilated body with strength of spirit… than to account it life that one has lost one's own? And we have conquered the enemies of God already by this very fact that we have not yielded. And we have overcome nefarious laws against truth.[8]

Thus one of the most powerful impacts of the church beyond the diaspora was the countercultural narrative of the early church that produced an identity, unity, virtue and values that offered a far better society than pagan Rome.

Given the surprising continuities between Late Antiquity and our own, forging a "new social reality" today through Christian diaspora has profound missiological implications for our modern world. Much like the early church, diaspora churches offer a social alternative in our modern mega-cities. As urban centers grow in size and diversity, Christian churches made up of diaspora groups represent compelling witness to other marginalised and transient people.

Diaspora and mission in our modern pluralistic multicultural world

This transformative impact of the early church upon society is often missed by those averse to emphases upon a "Social Gospel." To rediscover the impact of diaspora mission on society today requires that churches move beyond the pigeon-holes offered by sanctioned secular pluralism and multiculturalism. Though modern cities are pluralistic and multicultural, what is often not recognized is that pluralism and multiculturalism are ideologies and not mere descriptions. As ideologies, they eschew religious emphases upon conversion from one religion to another. To justify this stance, they point to the poisonous tie between imperialism and global missions and their legacy of forced conversions. They argue that historically mission has denigrated and displaced indigenous religions and cultures. Given that legacy they argue that conversion has no place in

---

8 As quoted in Ivo Lesbaupin, Blessed are the Persecuted (Hachette UK: Hodder & Stoughton Religious, 1988), 50-51.

modern society and should give way to dialogue and establishment of harmony between cultures and religions. Further that a multi-cultural peace requires religious beliefs to be treated as simply matters of private opinion and thus kept within the religious boundaries of the physical churches and not beyond.

Certainly, Christian missions should begin with repentance for insensitivity and failure to treat others with dignity. Indeed where Christian mission fell into league with imperial power that embraced dominion, coercion, and manipulation it embodied more often the Lordship of Caesar rather than the crucified Lord Jesus Christ. Nonetheless, precisely here missionary alliance with despotic power distorted the evangelism of the early church that reached beyond its cultural boundaries through the very power of the powerless revealed in Christ. In today's multicultural and pluralistic milieu, the diaspora church has the opportunity to shed its imperial garments for the vestments of the Crucified Lord. Nonetheless, like the early church, diaspora mission should recognize that it is Christ's inversion of the powers that leads to the church's critique of idolatry, superstition, polytheism, the glorification of violence and the defiling enslavement to cults of hedonism, fertility and de-personalised sexual license. The ideology of multiculturalism may seek to silence the church, but here the church cannot be silent but must witness to the personal and social transformation of diaspora mission

In terms of the common good, diaspora mission in a multicultural and pluralistic milieu has opportunity rediscover the early church's insistence upon the unity of truth revealed in Christ. Members of many diaspora churches come from non-Western cultures where sacred and secular, spirit and matter, faith and knowledge are not rigidly separated. They represent a rich resource for mission engagement spiritually, socially, economically and politically. As with the early church, diaspora churches can give witness to a common good that is at once holistic and extends beyond the church in its manifold cultural diversity yet unity in Christ. This will require a willingness to challenge regnant secular reason that would consign faith and revelation to the realm of the private and inconsequential.

Perhaps the greatest challenge will be to rediscover the catholic nature of mission. The term "catholic" is often misunderstood by evangelicals to refer to the Roman Catholic Church. Nonetheless, "catholic" should be a term that is true of all churches. By "catholic" we affirm that all churches are at once unique and at the same time one in Jesus Christ regardless of their geographical, cultural, social, or ethnic background. The particularity of the churches is represented in the cultural diversity of diaspora churches, yet their unity is discovered in the one Lord and one faith of their one baptism in Christ.

This unity and vitality of the Global churches can inspire courage in their Western brethren. It is a reminder that mission begins with the marginal and the displaced who know what it means to speak truth to secular power. In diaspora movement and mission we are reminded that Jesus journeyed from Galilee to confront the religious leaders in Jerusalem, and Paul ventured from Jerusalem to preach the Gospel in Rome. In diaspora the church reflects its mission roots as the church from the margins now engages the great urban centers of the world with the Gospel.

The diaspora churches represent the unity of the universal church through their ties to persecuted believers around the globe. These ties allow diaspora churches to support and nurture the Gospel in the lands from which they've sojourned. As expatriate citizens of other nations, they give voice to the suffering of their people. Through their gifts and witness they provide economic assistance and give voice to those imprisoned and silenced in their homelands. In this way, they bear public witness to the lordship of Christ and his universal rule in a hostile world.

In contrast to the growing sense of anomie beguiling Western understandings of pluralism and multiculturalism, diaspora churches and diaspora mission can offer the sense of identity, meaning and vocation in Christ that account for yet transcend culture or tribe. The early church discovered that identity, continuity and discernment flowed from the apostolic deposit of the rule of faith. In Word, sacrament, shared ministry and mission, the church through diverse diaspora congregations can do the same in urban centers today. Nonetheless, the ecclesia's apostolic identity remains frayed and forgotten in modernity as divisions that have haunted the church now multiply exponentially in our postmodern age.

Nonetheless, there are powerful forces at work to bring churches together through diaspora churches and mission. Paradoxically it is often pressure placed upon churches by secular governments that encourage ecumenical identity, common cause, and mission engagement. In Singapore, churches joined together to present a united front to the government to protect church property, raise ethical concerns regarding life sciences, and preserve the right to witness to Christ with persons of other religions or no religion at all.[9] Large gatherings of evangelicals at Cape Town 2010, or more Mainline Protestant church conferences such as Edinburgh 2010, have brought together diverse church and mission leaders from around the globe in common cause and mission. Global Conference leaders and delegates were a catalyst towards greater unity. Indeed, their voices held sway as can be seen in the subsequent statements of both conventions which questioned the false dichotomy between evangelism and social action that has dominated Western missions over the past century.

As Christians join in mission with others beyond the walls of their own cultures and denominational frameworks they are able to reveal a solidarity seriously lacking in modern urban society. In so doing they have the

---

9 Thomas Harvey, "Engagement Reconsidered: The Fall and Rise of a National Church Council in Singapore," Trinity Theological Journal, Vol 14. (Singapore: Trinity Theological College, 2006).

opportunity rediscover the continuity and identity of the ecclesia's apostolic roots.

Conclusion

We live in an age of rapidly expanding migration. Urban centers sprawl outward filled with enclaves of people from around the globe. It is not uncommon to walk along and hear several languages in a single block or sense tension between rival ethnic communities living on the same city block. In terms of mission and ministry the proximity of different cultures, beliefs, economic classes and moral persuasions present both challenges and opportunity.

In terms of evangelism, this diversity represents great opportunity. Diaspora allows Christians to share the Good News with people and communities who come from countries closed to the Gospel. Refugees, overseas students, economic migrants, and tourists are often in search of the comfort and reconciliation that comes through Christ. They are looking to know more about their surroundings and can be quite open to joining in new and different welcoming communities who can help them to cope with challenges they face. Nonetheless this opportunity can easily be squandered. Rather than seeing the great opportunities for witness and ministry, too often diaspora groups turn inward or are looked down upon by native Christians. Rather than appreciating the differences of culture and identity of migrants, too often Christians adopt a superior attitude or rejection and anger toward those different than themselves. Indeed it is distressing to find so many who self-identify as "evangelicals" who see Christians as those who share their race, culture, or ethnicity.

Part of what is required if Christians of all stripes are to be effective in evangelism is to recognize God's election of the wanderer, the migrant, and the refugee. As we saw in the Epistle of Diogenetus and Peter's salutation, the elect are the "resident aliens." The profound recognition that Christians are first and foremost pilgrims on the move should be cultivated in churches. As we have noted, human beings are called to be on the move whether that be fulfilling the command to establish the reign and fruition of God or in being part of the spiritual seed of Abraham, the migrant, who by faith was the means by which God redeems humankind. Indeed, when this attitude and understanding take root, mission ***to, through and beyond*** diaspora people becomes all the more effective.

Some argue that this missional embrace of an attitude of the "resident alien" represents an unwarranted withdrawal from wider society. They argue that our primary identity and responsibilities should be first to clan and nation. Certainly, ties of blood and soil appeal to our deepest held values and rightly so because we are deeply indebted to family, culture, people and nation. They are the brick and mortar of our very selves and without them we are nothing. Nonetheless, as important as they are, the

Gospel reaches beyond these walls to people and cultures very different from our own. Diaspora requires us to seek a more fundamental unity than our natural family, cultural or ethnic ties. In the stranger we encounter a potential brother or sister in Christ. When we embrace the alien, the refugee, or the immigrant we embrace Christ.

In Christ, we as resident diaspora find our redemption and fulfillment. We now share in the great work of establishing the reign of God and reaching out to fellow travelers on the road to introduce them to our redeemer, friend, and guide who leads us homeward in good company.

For discussion

1. What do we mean by mission being ***to***, ***through*** and ***beyond*** people on the move?
2. Can you provide an example of mission ***to*** diaspora people: for example economic or political migrants, those suffering religious persecution, persons travelling with members of family especially the young and elderly?
3. In what ways can ministry ***through*** diaspora people address the aspects of Creation and Redemption as discussed in the chapter?
4. List some of the physiological (health), physical (material condition) and spiritual distortions that people on the move often face and what are ways that the church and your engagement can help to address the issues that arise because of them?
5. Why might migrant people be struggling with guilt and shame? How does Scripture address such guilt and shame and how might you effectively minister to those struggling with guilt or shame?
6. Do you feel that evangelism is appropriate when ministering to the displaced people due to economic, political, or spiritual hardship? How would you justify your view on this biblically, theologically, and spiritually?

9. Mission to and from Diaspora: Influencing the Context for Mission

Terry McGrath, Victoria Sibley-Bentley, Andrew Butcher and George Wieland

Introduction

The Biblical and theological basis behind mission is long standing and is well documented. Since God's command to Abraham to 'go' and be a blessing to all nations (Genesis 12:1-3), there has been a succession of examples in Scripture and history of individuals being influential and catalysts to God's purposes amongst the nations. What has not been explored to the same extent is the Biblical and theological basis for the need to influence thinking in policy making and decisions of national leaders, especially in relation to migrants and Diaspora, on both a governmental level and within church leadership. This paper will look more in depth at this topic and the applications from these principles, using the New Zealand context (the context of the paper's authors) as a case study.

In today's world, marked by war, extremism, poverty, instability and natural disaster, the number of displaced peoples and refugees is ever increasing. In addition, desires for a better life, education, work opportunities, health care or greater experiences has led to a rise in movement of people throughout the world and the formation of Diaspora communities globally, including 50 million refugees. According to the 2013 New Zealand Census,[1] 25.2% of New Zealand's population were born overseas. This is a staggering number which adds to the complexity of contexts within New Zealand. Many of the values that underpin much of New Zealand society come from the Treaty of Waitangi: a founding document between the original people of the land (the *Tangata Whenua* – Maori) and the later European settlers (the *Pakeha*). In particular, the principle of partnership is fundamental to the biculturalism that underlies New Zealand society. Maori values are hence central to the way society functions, the identity of New Zealand, and heavily influence government policy. One primary example of this is the Maori proverb *He aha te mea nui o te ao? He tangata! He tangata! He tangata!* – What is the most important thing in the world? It is the people, the people, the people. As a small country with a small population of just over four million, people in

---

1 http://www.stats.govt.nz/Census/2013-census/profile-and-summary-reports/quickstats-culture-identity/birthplace.aspx

New Zealand have more opportunities to speak directly into government and government policy, this includes the Church, and some of these stories will be shared later on in this paper, particularly the contribution being made by credible and appropriately skilled people who are able to positively influence national policy. The aim of this paper is to present and illustrate opportunities for influencing community involvement, Church leadership and government policy with regard to supporting, caring, ministering to and encouraging ministry from Diasporas in our communities and nations.

Background

On entering a host country and culture, every refugee, temporary migrant and permanent migrant comes with his/her own individual needs that require to be met. These needs can range from assistance with language, and understanding host country cultural and religious practices, to helping find accommodation and work, and enrolling in study programmes, to providing hospitality and friendship, to name a few. Many of these needs will be able to be met by the community, education providers, employers, social agencies/groups and faith communities. However, there are some needs which are best met in conjunction with the implementation of changes to governing policies. For example, the support and right status of refugees and provision for them under government schemes and through social services is aided by Church and community initiatives.

In the sphere of social psychology and human development, Jensen's (1998) ideas on Social Cohesion explain the stages necessary for an individual to feel grounded in society. These stages are: belonging, participation, inclusion, recognition and legitimacy, and are particularly important for migrants, refugees and international students to feel 'at home' in their host country. Government policy, in conjunction with church and community involvement can substantially assist each international to belong, participate, be included, be recognised and have legitimacy in New Zealand. This fundamental bias now underscores immigration support policy, and seeks to assist in meeting practical and social needs for internationals, to enable them to settle well in the country that will become their home.

In many countries, the socio-cultural context presents opportunities for the Church to engage in wider society, beyond the grassroots level, to meet observed needs and to highlight areas of need for advocacy and speaking into government policy-setting. In this paper, New Zealand will be used as a case study illustrating missions aspects related to opportunity for speaking into and supporting government policy initiatives for migrants, and the transitions of Diaspora communities both into and within the country.

Within the New Zealand context, Harold Turner (1992) influenced the idea of three levels of mission: individual, social and cultural. The individual level includes "loving service of the Gospel to individuals in personal need." This is the grassroots level of mission and encompasses community involvement. The second level of mission is aimed at the wider social, political and economic systems that enable communities and society to function. The third level of mission aims to transform the culture of society and the values and norms that underlie it.

These three levels overlap and can have a domino-like effect on each other, with the much further reaching aim of assisting and enabling people through supporting and influencing government policy. A global historical example of this would be the influence of William Wilberforce and the Clapham Sect in the abolition of the slave trade, brought about through speaking into the consciousness of the British public, and directly into government and policy. In New Zealand, the size of the population and the country, and its democratic nature and relative informality in regards to access to decision makers enable greater and easier participation in highlighting societal concerns to government, without the need for extensive lobbying resources. Worldwide, the journey of highlighting awareness and transforming social conscience is a challenge for thinking and caring Christian people. Contextual challenges also exist for the church and its people appropriately positioned to be influencers. Size and complexity must appear daunting in countries like the USA, yet God calls us to speak from a position of faith and humility into the areas of our expertise as our part in serving Him within our nation.

As a multi-cultural nation built largely on migrant populations and Diaspora communities, the Church in New Zealand has a unique window of opportunity to be working in, with and through Diaspora in New Zealand. This opportunity for involvement occurs in both the settlement and engagement aspects of migration, and can be used to bring issues of need to the attention of government policy-setters. In light of this, two different challenges for Christians in New Zealand today arise, which play a significant part in thinking strategically about missions, to, from and within the Diaspora:

1. How can Christians and the wider Church speak into government policy and practice regarding migrants and Diasporas?
2. How can Christian Diasporas be salt and light in influencing government policy and Church leadership in their host country?

At a basic level, these challenges include both mission for and within Diaspora. The challenges and their Biblical and theological underpinnings will be looked at in further detail following. However, in addition to this, within these challenges are two further strands which also need exploring:

1. The role Christians have in highlighting the needs that affect Diaspora communities. This is largely a reactive response to current situations and comes loosely under the umbrella of advocacy.

2. The role of supporting policies, policy-setters and leadership to enable refugees, temporary migrants and permanent migrants to settle well and feel a sense of belonging within the host community, country and culture. This can be both reactive (in terms of the previous experiences of other Diaspora) and also pro-active in bringing about change and transformation in society through legislation and provision of appropriate support structures.

Biblical underpinnings

The Biblical and theological foundations of these challenges and strands are highly significant. In looking at Biblical examples of people speaking into nation policies, several main themes emerge, which are applicable today: advocacy, the fulfilment of God's purposes and God's heart/intention for people, the need for credibility among people seeking to influence change with policy makers, and recognising and supporting good policy, which works for the well-being of people.

The Old Testament significantly points to the concept of migration, demonstrated particularly in God's command to Adam to "fill the earth" (Gen. 1:28). God never intended His people to be static. Furthermore, the Old Testament frequently refers to a *"sojourner," "stranger," "alien" or "foreigner"*...The word used means *"to dwell for a time in another land which is not one's own."*[2] Accordingly, the Old Testament provides instructions for migrants and foreigners in the community (e.g. provision for foreigners during the Passover in Exodus 12:43-49). In fact, God commands His people to care for foreigners in their midst (for example in Leviticus 19:9 and 19:33-34). Throughout the Old Testament, one common theme of mission occurs repeatedly: that God's people are blessed in order to be a blessing to others. God not only desires that all people would come to know Him, but that the care provided by God's people to those yet to know Him would be the avenue of witness.

Parts of the New Testament build on this understanding of migrants/Diaspora and the unique Gospel opportunities afforded to and by them. This is exemplified, particularly in Acts, and in the great commission, given by Jesus to the disciples in Matthew 28:19 to "*go and make disciples of every nation*" and Matthew 22:39 "*Love your neighbour as yourself.*" Central to this is, understanding God's heart for all people.

The Bible contains numerous exhortations to advocate on behalf of those who have no ability to speak out or be heard. For example, Proverbs 31:8-9 – *"Speak up for those who cannot speak for themselves, for the rights of all*

2 Athena O. Gorospe, "What Does the Bible Say about Migration? Three Approaches to the Biblical Text," in God at the Borders: Globalization, Migration and Diaspora eds. C. Ringma, K. Hollenbeck-Wuest, and A. Gorospe (Manila: OMF Literature, 2015), 126.

who are destitute. Speak up and judge fairly; defend the rights of the poor and needy." Also, Jeremiah 22:3 states – "*this is what the* Lord *says: Do what is just and right. Rescue from the hand of the oppressor the one who has been robbed. Do no wrong or violence to the foreigner, the fatherless or the widow, and do not shed innocent blood in this place.*" Several Biblical stories demonstrate examples of migrants speaking out and influencing host country/global policy. Examples include:

1. **Moses**, Exodus 5, goes to Pharaoh to ask for God's people to be set free from slavery and oppression. Moses visited Pharaoh on several occasions delivering God's messages to him. Pharaoh's rejections and the associated consequences meant Moses had to persist until Pharaoh eventually allowed the Hebrew people to leave Egypt. Moses, a Hebrew migrant by descent, had fled Egypt for Midian, where he made his home and remained for a number of years before returning to Egypt in obedience to God. His story is uniquely typical of the migrant stories included in the Bible.
2. **Joseph,** a son of Israel, was able to save Egypt from famine and ultimately provide for the preservation of Abraham's progeny – the children of Israel, by his standing and credibility with Pharaoh.
3. **Nehemiah,** whose request to King Artaxerxes, Nehemiah 2, that he be allowed to go to Jerusalem to rebuild the city, was granted because of the standing and reputation that Nehemiah had within the King's court.
4. **Daniel,** taken into captivity in Babylon, experienced the value of Nebuchadnezzar's policy of providing paths of opportunity for young forced migrants. In that context of positive opportunity for engagement in the new culture and context, Daniel takes his primary bearing from within his relationship with God. Throughout the years, this remained firm and steady and led to opportunities for God's purposes to be manifest (Dan. 6:16, 20-22)
5. **Esther and Mordecai's** story illustrates God's purposes being worked out through people whose characters were conditioned by their experiences of forced migration, their Jewish identity and their consciousness of God's sovereignty and purposes being used for the benefit of His people.

Examples of Diaspora stories are significant as they show God at work in and through migrants affecting national and even international policy to work out His purposes. The context into which the early church came into being was one of significant people movement across borders for a diversity of reasons. Many of these movements reveal God's purposes to bless the early church and those who they come into contact with (Caldwell, 2015). For example:

1. In the book of Philemon, Paul pleads with Philemon to receive **Onesimus,** his escaped slave, as a brother in Christ on his return, a

unique concept of the Gospel crossing social and class divides within a diasporic context.

2. In Acts 24, 25 and 26 Paul stands before **Felix and Festus**, respectively. Both were influential Roman officials, who were temporary migrants due to work and heard the Gospel from Paul in their line of duty.
3. **Priscilla and Aquila** (Acts 18), itinerant business people, had experienced circular migration, forced to move from Rome to Greece when the emperor Claudius expelled the Jews from the capital functioning as agents of the Gospel and supporters of mission (through Paul).
4. **Apollos** (also mentioned in Acts 18) is an example of an academic on the move who comes to fully understand the Gospel and goes on to fulfil God's purposes for him as an enlightened teacher.
5. The Apostle **Paul**, born in Tarsus, the capital of Cilicia and a Roman province comes into a context to hear the Gospel through being sent as an international student for higher education to Jerusalem to study.
6. **Lydia**, a migrant business woman comes to Philippi from Thyatira. There she hears the Gospel and spreads it amongst her household and village many of whom it could be assumed were also migrants.
7. The **Antioch church**, described in Acts 11:19 was essentially a church comprised of refugees. The church became one of the most significant and influential mission sending churches in early Christianity possibly due in part to the experience, migrant mind set and awareness of its leaders.

From Pentecost at the beginning of Acts and throughout Acts, Diaspora have been significant in establishing the church and initiating mission. According to Wieland (2015), reading Acts missionally leads to the realisation that the examples of scriptures can influence and motivate people to leadership and action. Being aware of such biblical examples can be encouraging to individuals whom God has sovereignly placed or allowed to be in a position to influence policy outcomes for the Gospel, in particular, the Gospel in and through Diaspora. For those finding themselves in such positions, there is a need to be encouraged, and to recognise, like Esther, the challenge of position and context. For the Church in New Zealand, this recognition needs to come from the encouragement and input of Christian leaders aware of the opportunities for influencing policy and advocating for transforming policies that enhance the fulfilment of God's purposes. A useful application of Romans 13 in the area of being subject to governing authorities is the move from passive acquiescence to governing authorities to being involved in contributing and supporting the development of good policy and processes of governance.

Before moving on to talk of this it would be useful for us to comment on, for example, the church groups and community groups in Auckland who are reading Acts missionally under the influence of George Wieland, who coincidentally also offers a similar course through Carey Baptist College, as prompting mission related action among developing leaders. In effect those involved are reflecting on Auckland as a city of migrants and its parallels for New Zealand as a country of migrants. Reflecting on the scriptures within a context may influence action within the context and lead to a desire for relevant mission within that context. Being aware of the Holy Spirit's leading within the contexts of Acts (many of which are diasporic contexts) invokes parallel actions within the city of migrants, Auckland and the country of migrants, New Zealand.

Illustrations from New Zealand experience

New Zealand has a young history, dating back to the 13th Century, when the first inhabitants are said to have come to New Zealand from Polynesia, an extension of the migrant flows from Babel into Central and East Asia. These first people to arrive in New Zealand were called Maori. 400 or so years later, various Europeans migrated to the islands of Aotearoa (Māori name for New Zealand). Whalers, sealers and missionaries amongst the Maori people were earliest European arrivals and later settlers in search of land and agricultural economic advantage. The Church came to New Zealand in two distinct models 1) mission to reach Maori, and 2) a plural range of churches to serve the immigrant European community. Conflict naturally arose between European settler mission and mission among the Maori.[3]

As a young nation built predominantly on migration, consciousness of diaspora lineages have always been a part of the New Zealander's psyche and New Zealand's present reality is that 25.2% of population are born overseas[4] (Census 2013). In the challenges encountered due to current immigration and emigration, New Zealand's short history and collective diasporic consciousness may make meeting the challenges easier than for an older, larger more established country. However, with the pace of societal change due to migration influences accelerating over the last 20-30 years, New Zealand has had its own unique challenges and opportunities for providing support and developing policy to assist positive settlement outcomes for the increased numbers and diversity of migrants, refugees and international students entering the country. Accordingly, there has been a need to review New Zealand policy and openness to change in conjunction with migration increases to New Zealand rather than sit back and passively allow things to work out.

---

3 For more information, see Michael King, History of New Zealand (Auckland: Penguin, 2003).
4 http://www.stats.govt.nz/Census/2013-census/profile-and-summary-reports/quickstats-culture-identity/birthplace.aspx.

New Zealand has a culture where policy and practice are reviewed frequently. A robust example of this can be found in "International Students in New Zealand: The Making of Policy Since 1950" (2004), by Nicholas Tarling. In the 1950s, New Zealand's policy on international students centred on those who came to study under the Colombo aid plan. In terms of mission opportunity, in this aid era the Church (and the wider community too) were happy to be naturally supportive of the relatively small number of international students from a few countries. Over time, the economic advantages afforded in providing international education became more apparent and New Zealand's policy changed, enabling international student education to become a market commodity for New Zealand. International students brought in significant financial benefit to New Zealand for education providers, associated industries, local economies and the government through taxes.

New Zealand's policy on international students had changed from aid to trade. These policy shifts as identified by Tarling, are further discussed in Andrew Butcher's *"A sin of omission: New Zealand's export industry and foreign policy (with Terry McGrath)."* The title of which is indicative of researchers, who are also Christian, speaking into the policy environment. However, during the shift to the trade era, community consciousness also shifted to the economic advantages of the many international students, who contributed significantly to the percentage of disposable income spent in New Zealand. A significant role church leadership has had to play is awakening the church to the missions opportunities afforded by the presence of large numbers of international students, who may become carriers of the Gospel to their families, friends and communities on return to their countries of origin. Further comment on this point is made subsequently.

The aspect of community perceptions of international students offering economic advantage led to increased numbers of incidents of economic exploitation in international student consumption areas, such as, accommodation, entertainment and available low cost (often under minimum wage) labour. The need for protection and advocacy on behalf of international students arose, as did the need to offer appropriate care for the increased numbers and diversity of international students as they settled in to life and study in New Zealand. The Ministry of Education, International Unit, developed policy to support international education in keeping with normative New Zealand educational standards and due to its consultative approach to policy development, it was realised that the living and support aspects for international students also needed some minimum standards. Accordingly, the Code of Practice for the Pastoral Care of International Students[5] came into being as a regulatory amendment to the Education Act.

---

5 Code of Practice for Pastoral Care of International Students www.nzqa.govt.nz/providers-partners/caring-for-international-students/.

Pastoral care aspects for international students became mandatory by regulation, and as it would happen, in New Zealand, professional development support for education provider staff tasked with responsibilities was sought from amongst members of the community skilled in pastoral care (Pickering 2006) including John Pickering, and other persons with acknowledged Christian commitments and roles, one of the authors of this paper, Terry McGrath. Many of these people owed their recognised expertise to their involvements within the New Zealand Christian community. The role the wider community (the church included) could play in pastoral care for international students became recognised and importantly, associated with the development of good policy, and from supporting good policy with associated good practice came opportunity. International Student Ministries (ISMNZ), a missions group focused on reaching and discipling international students, developed in this context as did Operation Friendship, a local church based ministry movement. These, and other church and Christian ministries identified as caring for international students, were included as community participants able to be involved with education providers in meeting their Code responsibilities.

Missional thinking into the migrant context of New Zealand has been catalysed by rapid growth in numbers of international students in New Zealand through the decade from the mid-1990s to the mid-2000s. Opportunities to stay after education are limited, so most international students return to their countries of origin or go to other countries. In so doing some have become carriers or agents for the Gospel. The increased number of international students coupled with increases in migration from the distinctly different cultures of Asia (as compared to the earlier European and Pasifika migrant flows) has focused greater attention on mission to and from the Diaspora. Accordingly, some insightful Christian leaders have intentionally sought to create ways to influence the church to be involved in such mission. External expert visitors, presentations at church leadership gatherings, student testimonies, Bible and theological school training courses as well as inviting and publishing carefully considered written submissions all contributed to the concept of churches engaging in mission this way. Some examples of this intentionality to awaken the church to aspects of mission to and from the Diaspora include:

1. The visit of Gordon Showell-Rogers, ex Friends International director, to NZ in the late 1990s was effective in promoting mission amongst international students and catalysing ministry developments within Operation Friendship, ISMNZ and building awareness amongst churches and student ministries.
2. George Wieland's Carey Baptist College course in Acts and its practical Reading Acts Missionally for students and also for Christians in the Auckland community is a past and present influencer of developing ministry workers.

3. Written testimonies provided in Pete Cossey's (2009) "Changing Lives" in the chapter on International Student Ministries illustrate the powerful effect of international student testimonies. Frequently students presenting their own testimony in churches and conferences have provided powerful influence.
4. An invited chapter by Terry McGrath and Victoria Sibley (2011) "Opportunities with Overseas Students", in vol. IV of *New Visions New Zealand* illustrates publication of strategic information for NZ Christian Leadership reading and consideration.

Putting the international students and policy shifts aside, it is important to realise on one hand, the age of New Zealand's history enables the country to be less confined and more accepting and flexible in the mix of cultural values and identities that underpin much of its society today. But on the other hand, New Zealand is still working out its identity, and hence any issues/policies around caring for the diversity of needs and cultures must also be read in conjunction with the bi-cultural underpinning of New Zealand. Having struggled with adopting an identity of bi-culturalism in terms of the *Tangata Whenua* (the first settlers, Maori) in partnership with *Pakeha* (European settlers), New Zealand is now facing the challenge of going into a significantly diverse multi-cultural society as successive waves of settlement from the Pacific, Europe and Asia in particular are altering the population make up. (Trilin et al 2005) The opportunity for the Church to speak into the debates related to this challenge are significant, and that it has a clear voice of input to the character of New Zealand, and to the part influential Christians can play in shaping this.

The changes in the cultural identity and make up of New Zealand society means that the face of Christianity in New Zealand is also changing from mainly "Anglo-Celtic" (Butcher and Wieland 2014) with a significantly high proportion of Christians in New Zealand originally from Asian and Pacific countries and cultures. In a paper "Not a Western Story: the Christian faith and migrant communities in New Zealand," Andrew Butcher (2007) writes that "80% of Pacific peoples in New Zealand are Christian, according to the 2006 Census, and the church plays a central role in Pacific culture and life" (1). This change inter-culturally within the Church is also a challenge for the Church, related to its own engagement with the rich resources of leadership and ability coming into its ranks through migration.

The changes in New Zealand society related to this rapidly increasing diversity have stretched the thinking of researchers and policy developers. As New Zealand is a small place, there has been opportunity for input from all quarters. Research and writing has become part of that open context for input, including contributions from committed Christians. One author's story stands out in terms of this opportunity and the sovereignty of God's purposes. Terry McGrath, who had been involved with Andrew Butcher and John Pickering in a range of inputs by means of writing articles, conference presentations and small research projects related to international students and their pastoral needs, was invited to write a proposal on migrant research related to the engagement of Asian communities. Hilary Smith joined these three and they constituted a research team that was successful in being awarded the project, and in due course produced "*Engaging Asian Communities in New Zealand,*" (McGrath et al 2004). This research investigated Asian migrant communities' challenges in moving from the liminal space of initial settlement to fully legitimised New Zealanders engaging fully and freely in all that is New Zealand. As a back story, just prior to this, Terry (the research team coordinator) was involved in the Lausanne 2004 forum in the working group that produced "*The New People Next Door – A Call to Seize Opportunities*" (Lausanne Issues group 2005), a book produced by the Issue Group of Diasporas and international students. The interaction with other practitioners and researchers and learning from others involved in speaking into the policy environment in their countries was invaluable. The associated stimulus in this experience influenced the approach to the research, in particular, the importance of listening to migrant voices. This experience is further reflected on in an invited chapter in a book on researching in communities (McGrath et al 2007) and includes comment on a Christian organisation, ISMNZ, engaging in leading research and how the Christian ethos assisted the research process and allowed respect for peoples, which in turn enabled migrant voices to emerge in contextually relevant ways.

Several spin-offs from this research project occurred, including it being used to influence thinking about government policy in respect of migrants and refugees. Its adoption of the Jensen (1998) paradigm in relation to social cohesion supported the associated ideas influencing policy and programme design in the wider national context for refugee and migrant settlement Ministry of Social Development (2008). Andrew Butcher, one of the research team, went on to become director of research and policy at ASIANZ, the government foundation that had commissioned the research. Andrew's role at ASIANZ involved influencing policy development and commissioning research, some of which is highly relevant for the Asian Diaspora in New Zealand. Several attributes combine in leading to good outcomes for Diaspora communities, as well as paving the way for mission to and from Diasporas. These include, thinking missionally, working in the Diaspora context, and functioning with integrity and credibility. While this is no different from the call of all Christians in the workplace, being in a role of influence has allowed Andrew[6] to contribute to policy development, in much the same way as the biblical figures referenced earlier.

The smallness of New Zealand provides a unique context and opportunity to speak into government policy. In larger countries, such as,

---

6 At the time of writing Andrew Butcher has concluded his time at ASIANZ foundation and taken up the role of Research Director for the Ministry of Justice.

for example, the U.S.A, a great deal more resources are needed to lobby the government. However, the smallness of New Zealand enables easier access to communicate concerns to government, as generally there is no plethora of voices all speaking on the same issue at the same time from different perspectives. For an individual or a group of like-minded people, being the critic of conscience is easier in New Zealand due in part to:

1. A focus on issues rather than politics.
2. The role that articulated values play in policy setting e.g. respect for life, the rule of law, freedom of sea navigation.
3. The role that non-articulated, but commonly felt and understood values have. For example, the importance placed on people above other considerations undergirded the Code of Pastoral Care for International students and New Zealand's policies and practices on migrants, refugees and temporary workers.
4. New Zealand's sense as an immigrant nation with a diversity of religions, and founded on biculturalism. This identity allows voices from, and on behalf of, migrants to emerge.

In our next section we tie together the above point related to Diaspora voice emergence and mission from the Diaspora. The church very often mirrors the attitudes, norms and mores of the community in which it is set. Acting biblically can be a challenge when it is contrary to what is normative in the context of setting. Policies and practices conducive to giving new migrants a voice and legitimacy in the wider society also aid their participation in mission.

Emergence of voices and mission from the Diaspora

In New Zealand, as in many other countries, churches are seen as safe havens and places of hospitality and care for all, regardless of ethnicity, cultural background, gender or social standing. In alignment with the research of Tom Harvey (in press), there are various difficulties and issues which migrants, especially refugees, may experience. These include the vulnerability of being in a new country surrounded by a new culture, where often there is a new or different language to learn, and where there is often no immediate and close support base. For some migrants there may be associated trauma with needing to leave their home country, and potentially their family members also, particularly where forced migration is involved, or when family members are left behind in unsafe situations and places. While these issues are potentially medium to long-term in nature, there are also other issues which arise for many migrants and which need to be responded to, for example loneliness and isolation, childcare services, language assistance, transport needs, financial hardship, accommodation requirements, and normal everyday activities and situations. As a result of these issues, finding individual identity, acceptance and belonging can be incredibly challenging.

A further challenge associated with the rapid increase in numbers of internationals, is that often (and through no fault of their own), migrants, refugees and international students find themselves in the liminal spaces of society, often forming groups of people from the same culture (or country) which sit on the outskirts of, or overlap to a certain degree, with the local community without necessarily becoming integrated into the community. The problem with this, is that it can be very isolating and minimising of friendships, which can lead to a sense of feeling that there is no one place or community of belonging. In his paper "Finding Communities in Liminality: Invitations from the Margins in the New Testament and in Contemporary Mission," George Wieland (2015) discusses further the difficulties associated with the liminality of migrant communities. In referencing a Chinese Church in Auckland, Wieland also notes that liminality also occurs when people from the host nation participate in events held by migrants and migrant communities. The main problem with liminality is that it prevents people from feeling that they belong and from feeling settled. The Church here has an opportunity to connect with these people on the margins and limits of society, and assist them in feeling that they belong, as well as help provide paths to a full sense of legitimacy as New Zealanders.

It is within this overall context that migrants often find a place to belong, friendship, and a community to be part of and participate in, in local churches, church groups and community groups. From the relationships that are formed in these communities, ministry to migrants occurs and over time increasingly ministry from migrants, particularly if the culture of the church encourages it. The emergence of the migrant voice in the context of the church is best seen in and through the migrant believers as they are encouraged in fully emerging and using the gifts God has given to them for building up the body and for mission in the community. Church and community leadership are avenues for the migrant voice to be effective. It is incumbent on the church to lead in this way and if the context of society is also conducive, then ministry from the Diaspora rapidly becomes a reality.

It would take a long time to describe the many avenues in which mission from the Diaspora may occur. The paths for it can be somewhat convoluted but frequently the gifts and abilities of particular migrants along with their individual sense of vision and call contribute greatly to the emergence of mission from the margins of the liminal migrant space to within the mainstream. Where a countries policy settings and practices reduce barriers, ministry from the diaspora moves from a liminal context to being more likely to affect the mainstream. The following are some illustrative examples of this happening in the New Zealand context:

1. The Race Relations Commissioner in New Zealand is a pivotal government role for enhancing successful diversity engagement. During the last twenty years three of the four Race Relations

Commissioners have been first generation Diaspora: Dr Rajen Prasad (Fiji) 1995-2000, Gregory Fortuin (South Africa) 2001-2002 and Joris de Bres (The Netherlands) 20012-2013. Gregory Fortuin serves as an example of an adult migrant moving from the liminal space of the migration context into the mainstream but with a sense of Christian missional identity and ethos. In taking up his current role with the Salvation Army, Lt-Colonel Rod Carey said of him *'He is an excellent motivator, an enthusiastic facilitator with a very strong Christian faith, and is excited to have this opportunity to work with vulnerable people in the mission of The Salvation Army.'*[7] Fortuin's open identification with Christian faith and involvement with Christian mission have been hallmarks of his public service. No doubt he is a person of ability and talent but the church and community attitudes have been significant in facilitating passage for his talents.

2. Creating pathways to leadership in mission and the church for the Diaspora is important and whilst many churches and missions have no theoretical barriers to progressing opportunities for migrants to serve in leadership, it is often attitudes at the coalface that keep them in liminal spaces. Reaction to the enactment of policies in the wider social context of New Zealand related to human rights and social cohesion has affected church members in the attitudinal domain as they have come to share worship and break bread, so to speak, with people of many other cultures. Ethno-centrism within churches has diminished and increasingly gift and call are being recognised first and foremost. Where migrants themselves progress into key church and mission leadership roles, they are very often able to assist in reducing attitudinal barriers for others. Local churches in their leadership composition are increasingly reflecting similar cultural mixes to the communities they are set in. This change has been progressive and incremental rather than abrupt.
3. The Elim Church in Botany, Auckland exemplifies an approach to diversity in an area of high migration settlement. Its leadership team is multicultural and draws from Pastors and leaders of several different language and cultural ministries within. There are pathways to leadership development that may start off in a language/cultural ministry subset or in a multicultural ministry setting. Significantly similar patterns are happening in local churches as they seek to reflect their communities of setting in their mission outcomes.

7 "Employment Plus Welcomes New Director," accessed July 13, 2015, http://www.salvationarmy.org.nz/research-media/media-centre/local-news/EPlus-new-director.

4. Archbishop Winston Halapua, born and raised in Tonga, now serves as Tikanga Pasifika within the Anglican Church of Aotearoa, New Zealand and Polynesia and in so doing contributes influence from the Diaspora to the Diaspora and the wider church and the community. Nationally organised expressions of church and mission are increasingly reflecting the Diaspora contribution. The Christian Network of New Zealand, the overarching peak body for evangelical Christianity in New Zealand reflects this in the composition of its advisers and governance. New Zealand based Missions agencies have a growing proportion of mission candidates and members drawn from amongst the Diaspora. Mission from the Diaspora is an increasing feature of Christianity in New Zealand.
5. Korean migrants, at one stage both the largest Asian migrant group to New Zealand and heavily Christianised and conservative and which have become a feature of Presbyterian churches here, have caused changes in the dynamic that the church operates in, changes in the identity of the church, its missional focus and the way its leadership works Butcher (2014). Like their Polynesian predecessors effect on the Methodist church and the current Filipino migrations on the Catholic Church, these migration waves exemplify the renewing influence the arrival of a Diaspora church can have.

Often migrant churches establish their own forms and engage in mission to those they identify closest with. Many of the new Chinese churches stand out in that regard and they have become significant in reaching other Chinese migrants and Chinese international students in particular, thus exhibiting a clear example of Mission to the Diaspora from the Diaspora.

In fact, "Diaspora fellowships and churches are significant in mission as resident aliens. They offer a sense of identity and a stable community. They can be good friends and neighbours who understand the physical, psychological, legal, and spiritual struggles of fellow migrants. They offer understanding, acceptance, experience, assistance and spiritual balm that open aliens and strangers up to the grace of Christ and an open invitation to join this body of *chosen migrants dispersed* throughout the world by faith" (Harvey in press, 6-7). Largely, the New Zealand church has embraced the concept of Diaspora fellowships and there are many examples of existing churches opening up their facilities to welcome such fellowships. One outcome of doing so is the further development in partnership that results in multicultural fellowships to meet the needs that arise naturally from settlement and engagement.

The Church has a role to play in creating safe havens for the newly arrived and mission to them. Of even greater significance is Churches nurturing and equipping Diaspora for mission and encouraging and supporting them in realising their call within the context that God has sovereignly placed them in. Mission to the Diaspora enhances all aspects of mission from the Diaspora and mission to the Diaspora has to align with the fullest potential of ministry from the Diaspora. In the few examples we have given we have sought to illustrate this. We note also that where the context in which mission takes place, mission is enhanced when the policy and practice settings for migrants, refugees and international students encourages belonging and participation and there is a means by which they are included, recognised and legitimised in their interactions with the wider society. This starts with the church and it should be the practice of the church to lead the way, as to do so is to ensure the Diaspora in the ambit of the church are part of multiplying in mission.

Conclusive remarks

While New Zealand is a young country underpinned by a bi-cultural identity and values, the current multi-cultural nature of New Zealand presents additional dilemmas for New Zealand society, government policies and the Church in New Zealand. For example, with the rapid increase of Diasporas, the question arises as to whether churches should remain mono-lingual and mono-cultural or whether there is a need for them to become multi-lingual as well as multi-cultural. This paradigm shift is not easy to conceptualise or facilitate, particularly given the rich history behind the establishing of many of the traditional 'settler' churches in New Zealand and the cultural identities that they grew out from.

Despite these challenges and dilemmas, the presence of Diasporas in New Zealand presents unique opportunities for the Church in ministry to and through Diasporas. Meeting practical needs is one example whereby churches and communities can support and engage with migrants, refugees and international students. However, there are also opportunities at a more national level to support and influence policy that directly affects Diasporas in New Zealand. In particular, the placing of people with credibility, who have genuine concern for the care and welfare of Diasporas, in places of influence is particularly important for a small country like New Zealand, where even just a few people can have significant influence, particularly on the development of good policy. The Church has a role in enabling Diasporas to be voices of influence in their communities, in church leadership and in national leadership, by which they can significantly shift the thinking of a nation and transform society. The importance of what God is doing in and through Diasporas needs to be supported by the Church, and enabled to flourish.

Conclusion

The Biblical and theological basis behind mission is long standing and well documented. God's purposes are being worked out in many contexts and ways in our modern world. God's command to Abraham to 'go' and be a blessing to all nations is coming to fruition in many ways, not least, in and through the Diaspora moving amongst the nations. Immigrants, refugees, and international students are increasingly recognised for their significance to the nations and church contexts in which they find themselves. Government policies are being framed around the needs and opportunities occasioned by the movement of people into and out of the nation. The Church has both responsibility and opportunity to be participants in various ways amongst these Diaspora movements. At national and even international arenas, the Church can, and should, have a voice in policy formation, as the Church has a role to play in both assisting at practical community and national levels in providing support, as well as recognising the significant part and roles Diasporic communities and individuals can play in furthering God's purposes. To take such action, we in the Church need to release and affirm people who are well placed for such missions influence. As a Church, we need to be open to recognising the importance of mission to, mission with, and mission from the Disapora, and to work to bring them from the margins of Church and society to be mainstream participators in the outworking of God's purposes. This is both our responsibility and our opportunity.

Let us be reminded of Harold Turner's view and, like the church in Antioch, become agencies for the spread of the Gospel to, with and from the diasporic communities resident within our parishes and the country as a whole, doing whatever is required to enable the spread of the Gospel at grassroots, community and national level so that all may hear and respond.

For discussion

1. This paper is set in a New Zealand context and reflects on the ideas of Harold Turner (1992) regarding three levels of mission, individual, social, and cultural. As you reflect on the context you are most familiar with discuss the relevance of these ideas to the passage of the Gospel in your context.
2. The Biblical underpinnings for the ideas explored in this paper are examined. Discuss the significance to ministry amongst, with and from diaspora communities of these Biblical underpinnings. Include reflections of relevant to your own context.
3. In illustrating from their New Zealand experience the authors comment, "[a] significant role church leadership has had to play is awakening the church to the missions opportunities afforded by the presence of large numbers of international students…" (a significant group for mission amongst, with, and from the diasporic community). Drawing from the illustrations and knowledge of your own context, discuss the role church leadership plays in ensuring mission at the three levels Turner espouses occurs and how church leadership can be influenced for such a role.

4. Mission from the diaspora to the wider society may or may not be a significant product of mission within the diaspora. Using the concept of liminality, George Wieland, one of the authors notes the difficulties faced by diasporic communities and individuals in their normal experience of engagement and their experience of the church in particular. Discuss the importance of and the ways the church may be an agency to reduce liminality within its ranks as a starting point to ensuring mission within, with and from the diaspora occurs. Feel free to draw off the illustrations given in the paper and from your knowledge and experience.
5. The authors conclude with some of the challenges before the church and society in their context regarding growing diasporic community impacts. As you think about the challenges illustrated, and those that might be pertinent in your context, discuss the importance of mission with the Turner paradigm in mind and especially how the church can act to identify, encourage, release and affirm people well placed to enable mission to occur at all levels (especially levels that might influence the transformation of the culture of society around the of engagement of diasporic communities and enhance the passage of the Gospel amongst through and from).

Bibliography

Buchanan, Paul G. "Lilliputian in Fluid Times: New Zealand Foreign Policy after the Cold War," *Political Science Quarterly* 125:2 (2010): 255–279.

Butcher, Andrew."The Cross in Cross Cultural, Three encounters and the struggle for national identity." Paper presented at the Migrant cross-cultural encounters conference, at University of Otago, Dunedin November 24-26, 2014.

______. "Friends, Foreign and Domestic: (Re) converging New Zealand's Export Education and ForeignPolicies," *Policy Quarterly*,5:4 (2009): Wellington: Institute of Policy Studies, Victoria University of Wellington.

______. "Not a Western Story: the Christian Faith and Migrant Communities in New Zealand," *Aotearoa Ethnic Network Journal.* 2:2 (August 2007): http://www.aen.org.nz/journal/2/2/AENJ.2.2.Butcher.pdf.

Butcher, Andrew and Terry McGrath, A sin of omission: New Zealand's export industry and foreign policy," in *Social Policy Review 23: Analysis and Debate in Social Policy, 2011,* ed. C. Holden, M. Kelly, and G. Ramia. Bristol: The Policy Press, 2011.

______. "God and Golf: Koreans in New Zealand." New Zealand Journal of Asian Studies 15:2 (December 2013) 57.

______. "Go from your country": Missiological reflections on Asian Christians in New Zealand" *Stimulus: The New Zealand Journal of Christian Thought and Practice* 02/2010; 18(1):2-8 or online at: http://www.academia.edu/8855504/_Go_from_your_country_Missiological_reflections_on_Asian_Christians_in_New_Zealand_with_George_Wieland/.

Caldwell, Larry W. "Diaspora Ministry in the Book of Acts." In *God at the Borders: Globalization, Migration and Diaspora* (Manila: OMF Literature and Asian Theologica, 2015).

Census 2013, QuickStats about Culture and Identity: Birthplace and People Born Overseas http://www.stats.govt.nz/Census/2013-census/profile-and-summary-reports/quickstats-culture-identity/birthplace.aspx

Cossey, Pete. "International Student Ministries" *Changing Lives: Mission Agencies and their Stories* (Strategic Missions Charitable Trust, 2009).

Gorospe, Athena O. "What Does the Bible Say about Migration? Three Approaches to the Biblical Text." In *God at the Borders: Globalization, Migration and Diaspora* (Manila: Asian Theological Seminary & OMF Literature Inc, 2015)

Harvey, Thomas. "*Pilgrims on a Journey*: Diaspora and Mission Part II: Biblical and Theological Foundations for Diaspora Missiology" section eds. Thomas Harvey and Miyon Chung In *Scattered and Gathered: A Global Compendium of Diaspora Missiology*. Edited by Sadiri Joy Tira and Tetsunao Yamamori (In press).

Jensen, J. *Mapping Social Cohesion: The State of Canadian Research*. Canadian Policy Research Network (1998).

King, Michael. *History of New Zealand*. Auckland: Penguin, 2003.

Lausanne Issue Group on Diasporas and International Students (2005) The New People Next Door: A Call to Seize the Opportunities Occasional Paper No. 55 Lausanne Committee for World Evangelisation, 2005.

Lewis, N. "Political projects and micro-practices of globalising education: building an international education industry in New Zealand," *Globalisation, Societies and Education*, 9:2 (2011): 225-246

____. "Code of practice for the pastoral care of international students: making a globalising industry in New Zealand," *Globalisation, Societies and Education*, 3: 1 (2005): 5-47.

McGrath, Terry, Paul Stock, and Andrew Butcher. *Friends and Allies: The Impacts of Returning Asian Students on New Zealand Asia Relationships*. Wellington: Asia New Zealand Foundation, 2007.

McGrath, Terry, Andrew Butcher, J. Pickering, and H. Smith. *Engaging Asian Communities in New Zealand*. Wellington: Asia New Zealand Foundation, 2005.

McGrath, Terry, Andrew Butcher, Y. Koo, J. Pickering, and H. Smith, "Engaging Asian communities in Aotearoa New Zealand: An exploration of what works in community research in Williamson." Edited by R. DeSouza *Researching with Communities*' Muddy Creek Auckland, London 2007.

McGrath, Terry and Victoria Sibley. "Opportunities with Overseas Students," in vol. IV of *New Visions New Zealand* (2011).

Ministry of Education, International Unit. *Code of Practice for Pastoral Care of International Students*. Available at http://www.nzqa.govt.nz/providers-partners/caring-for-international-students/.

Ministry of Social Development. *Diverse Communities – Exploring the Migrant and Refugee Experience in New Zealand*. Strategic Social Policy Group, Wellington, NZ, 2008.

Pickering, J. (2006). *Models of Pastoral Care* ie Limited, February 2006.

Tarling, Nicholas. *International Students in New Zealand: The Making of Policy Since 1950*. Auckland: New Zealand Asia Institute, University of Auckland, 2004.

Trilin, Andrew Drago, Paul Spoonley, and Noel Watts, Editors, "New Zealand and International Migration: A Digest and Bibliography. 4." *School of Sociology, Social Policy and Social Work.* Palmerston North: Massey University, 2005.

Turner, Harold. "The Gospels Mission to Culture in New Zealand" http://www.latimer.org.nz/wp-content/uploads/Harold-Turner-The-Gospels-Mission-to-Culture-in-New-Zealand.pdf.

Wieland, George M. "Finding Communities in Liminality: Invitations from the Margins in the New Testament and in Contemporary Mission," in *We Are Pilgrims: Mission From, In and With the Margins of a Diverse World*, edited by Darren Cronshaw and Rosemary Dewerse, 46-52. Melbourne: Urban Neighbours of Hope, 2015.

Wieland, George M. "Reading Acts Missionally in a City of Migrants," in *God's People on the Move: Biblical and Global Perspectives on Migration and Mission*, edited by Van Thanh Nguyen and John Prior, 144-58. Eugene, O.R.: Pickwick, 2015.

SECTION 3: TOWARD STRATEGIC DIRECTIONS FOR DIASPORA MISSIONS

T.V. Thomas and Elias Medeiros, Section Editors

Toward Strategic Directions for Diaspora Missions: An Introduction

Section Editors: T.V. Thomas and Elias Medeiros

Any ministry needs a vision. However, it is not enough to just have a vision. Effective ministry results when vision is stewarded with strategy along right directions coupled with expertise for skilled action. This section considers eight key areas related to Diaspora missions today. Each author deals with the assumptions, issues, and principles regarding their area of proficiency, presenting practical directions for local congregations, mission organizations and theological institutions. These scholars and practitioners represent a variety of cultural, denominational, experiential, and academic contexts.

Elias Medeiros, an ordained minister of the Gospel since 1975, worked in pioneer church planting in the Amazon region and in the rural and urban contexts of Recife, Brazil. He deals with the question: What is the role, the place, and the contribution of the local churches in Diaspora mission (or missional Diasporas)? He addresses key assumptions but emphasizes that local churches are THE means by which God's work through God's workers will be done in God's world, and proposes seven directions for local churches worldwide to pursue.

Warren Reeve, the former Senior Pastor of the Lighthouse Church in Kuwait deals with the role, the place, and the contribution of the International Churches (ICs) and fellowships in Diaspora missions. Realizing the fact that today one can find international churches in almost every major city in the world, Reeve proceeds to describe several characteristics of such churches, and points to three major strategic directions for them in every major city.

Peter Vimalasekaran, originally from Sri Lanka, has lived and worked among refugees in Germany since 1988 and he is currently immersed in meeting the challenges of the massive refugee crisis in Europe. Based on a biblically-derived working definition, he introduces principles and essentials to be considered in order to effectively reach out to refugees anywhere, anytime. Peter offers church leaders strategies to effectively minister to refugees – how to approach refugees; how to equip believers in churches for refugee ministry; and how to launch church planting movements among them.

Martin Otto began an evangelical ministry to seafarers in 1987 in Hamburg, Germany and serves as the Director of the Church on the Oceans Seminary in Manila, Philippines. Wrestling with the reality of thousands of seafarers scattered around the world in "floating prisons" for several months of each year, Martin exposes their cultural, physical, emotional, economic, and above all, their spiritual situations. He concludes by presenting strategic directions for transforming "floating prisons" to "floating churches" where forgotten opportunities can be explored for the sake of making disciples of all nations.

Leiton Edward Chinn, the Lausanne Senior Associate for International Student Ministry (ISM) and member of the World Evangelical Alliance Mission Commission has co-authored with his wife, Lisa, whose ministry career focused on International Students. The Chinns realize that the international academic world represents a critical arena for nurturing "agents of Diaspora missions." They first paint the statistical reality of escalating numbers of international students before highlighting the strategic value of Diaspora missions to, through and beyond internationals from the academic world.

João Mordomo is actively involved in Business As Mission (BAM) and serves as Lausanne's Senior Associate for BAM. After presenting several nuances that describes BAM, Mordomo zooms into the relevance of BAM in the context of to, in, and through Diaspora. He defends the integration of BAM and Diaspora missions with multiple reasons. In view of the Great Commission, he passionately invites readers to strategically implement the use of business through the scattering of His people.

Cecilia J. Casiño, a missionary-educator and catalyst for diaspora missions, highlights the reasons, contexts, relationships, and the crucial needs that affect children on the move with their parents or without them. Within the framework of the Scriptures and the context of present realities, Casiño discusses the key issues, recognizes the challenges but points to the incredible missional opportunities. She concludes by emphasizing that ministry to children on the move is a crucial task and points to strategic directions on how to facilitate it.

Joseph Vijayam is the Senior Associate of Technology for the Lausanne Movement. Doubtless "Information and Communication Technology" (ICT) is one of the most powerful tools in the world today. Vijayam advocates that technology is an effective tool to reach Diaspora peoples, how it can be utilized in context of the Diaspora experience, and the multiple ways by which technology could serve the people in Diaspora. It facilitates migration, communication and connection with the homeland, coalescing homogenous diaspora communities, becomes a forum for exchange of ideas, fosters collective action, and more.

Our prayer is that the Lord of the harvest will continue to ignite many more innovative approaches, unleash all congregations and raise up an army of harvesters to reach the people on the move.

10. LOCAL CHURCHES IN MISSIONAL DIASPORAS

Elias Medeiros

Five convictions or assumptions guide this article. First, Diasporas are, doubtless, a global irreversible phenomenon with significance for every local church in the world. Such migrations are "considered one of the defining global issues of the twenty-first century, as more people are on the move today than at any other point in human history."[1] As a matter of fact, Diasporas have always been vitally important throughout the history of redemption and contemporary history, and it is especially crucial in Christian missions today.

Second, any evangelical local church, denomination or Christian institution that is indifferent towards this theo-graphical[2] historic moment in regards to Diaspora missions is already failing regarding the Great Commission of the Lord Jesus Christ and will regret it later. But my appeal here is directed to local churches everywhere.

Third, the local church is indispensable in reaching out to the people on the move both by moving towards them, by moving with them, by moving through them, and even beyond them (among the still unengaged peoples groups). The church was created to be on the move, to be in diaspora reaching out to the nations; not to be passive, but actively and intentionally engaged across the street and around the *oikomene* (the inhabited world). As the "Seoul Declaration on Diaspora Missiology" clearly and truthfully states: "That the *church*, which is the body of Christ, is the principal means through which God is at work in different ways around the globe."[3]

Fourth, Diaspora Missiology (DM) will not succeed without having the "full" engagement of the local churches. In other words, to be actively involved and committed to the local churches is not optional. It is biblically mandatory. To involve theological institutions is a must, but to have the local churches committed to "Diaspora Missiology" is a *sine a qua non* condition. As a matter of fact, there is not just a correlation but a causal

---

1 Sam George, "Diaspora a Hidden Link to 'From Everywhere to Everywhere' Missiology" in Missiology: An International Review, Vol. XXXIX, no. 1, January 2011, p 46, read the whole article 45-56.

2 I thought to title this article: "The theo-graphy of Diasporas and the Local Churches," based on Acts 17:26, 28 as it is written: "And He…has determined their [every nation of men] their pre-appointed times and the boundaries of their dwellings…for in Him we live and move [journey]…"

3 http://www.lausanne.org/content/statement/the-seoul-declaration-on-diaspora-missiology.

relationship between the active role of the local churches and the success of DM. Otherwise DM runs the risk of becoming just one more academic discipline in our theological institutions, conferences, and forums. Therefore, it is central to consider the place and the role of the local churches in missional diaspora.

The Church as the means

Whatever we teach, discuss, plan, and do, the church will always be THE means by which God's work through God's workers will be done in God's world.[4] Other institutions may contribute towards the work of making disciples of all the nations across the street and around the world, but the mission was explicitly given to the church. And the church will succeed, as Jesus stated: "…on this rock [Jesus Christ, the Son of the Living God] I will build My church, and the gates of Hades [hell] shall not prevail against it."[5]

After asking the question: "Who do men say that I, the Son of Man, am?"[6] Jesus addressed the church, represented by his disciples at that moment. The question was: "But who do you say that I am?" We should know what the nations say and think about Jesus, but the church is the body of Christ, built by Christ, having Christ as the cornerstone and foundation, holding the confession that "Jesus Christ is the Son of the Living God." This is the gospel.

> The beginning of the gospel of [which consists of, of which the content is] **Jesus Christ, the Son of God**.[7]
>
> Therefore those who were **scattered** went **everywhere preaching the word**. Then Philip went down to the city of Samaria and **preached Christ** to them.[8]
>
> Paul, a bondservant of Jesus Christ, called *to be* an apostle, separated **to the gospel of God** which He promised before through His prophets in the Holy Scriptures, **concerning His Son Jesus Christ our Lord**, who was born of **the seed of David** [King] according to the flesh…[9]

The professing of the local church

The local church is, doubtless, as a confessional (professing) community called to be light and salt among the nations by professing Jesus Christ,

---

4 I assume that the readers are members of a local church somewhere and many have been directly supported (prayerfully, financially, logistically, etc.) by local churches and their individual members.

5 Matthew 16:18. All the biblical quotes in this article are taken from the New King James Version (NKJ 1982).

6 Matthew 16:13. Bold added.

7 Mark 1:1. Bold added.

8 Acts 8:4-5. Bold added.

9 Romans 1:1-3. Bold added.

especially among the people on the move and the unengaged peoples groups. Such is the profession of those who are saved as individuals and as a community of believers: Jesus Christ is the Son of the living God, the incarnate Word preached, the gospel of God. This is a very simple confession, but not simplistic. First, because only those who have been transformed and moved by the Spirit of God can make such a profession of faith. As Jesus clearly declared to Peter: "…flesh and blood has not revealed *this* to you, but My Father who is in heaven."[10] Second, because such a profession expresses what we believe in our hearts as individual (not individualistic) members of the body of Christ.

> …if you confess with your mouth the Lord Jesus and believe in your heart that God has raised Him from the dead, you will be saved. For with the heart one believes unto righteousness, and with the mouth confession is made unto salvation.[11]

Third, because such a profession of faith is the theme of our worship, preaching, praising, prayer, and practice. We preach Christ, we sing Christ, we pray in the name of Christ, and we do all things for the glory of Christ. And the perseverance of the saints is conditioned to the communion of the saints:[12] Christ, therefore, is the theme of the worship service, the singing, and the prayers of all the saints from every tribe, tongue, and nation.

> Now when He had taken the scroll, the four living creatures and the twenty-four elders fell down before the Lamb, each having a harp, and golden bowls full of incense, which are the prayers of the saints. And they sang a new song, saying: "You are worthy to take the scroll, and to open its seals; for You were slain, and have redeemed us to God by Your blood Out of every tribe and tongue and people and nation.[13]

The local church and Diaspora mission

Therefore, "diaspora mission" will not succeed without the intentional, intensive, purposeful biblical, theological, and practical participation of the local church. Every church of the Lord Jesus Christ not only looks forward to that day with expectation, but will live and work and minister as a scattered people of God sent to make and to gather disciples of all, in all, and through all the nations across the street and around the world. To

---

10 Matthew 16:17.

11 Romans 10:9-10. Consider also 1 Corinthians 15:1-4: "Moreover, brethren, I declare to you the gospel which I preached to you, which also you received and in which you stand, by which also you are saved, if you hold fast that word which I preached to you unless you believed in vain. For I delivered to you first of all that which I also received: that Christ died for our sins according to the Scriptures, and that He was buried, and that He rose again the third day according to the Scriptures…"

12 Read Hebrews 3:12-14; 10:23-25.

13 Revelation 5:8-9.

gather the scattered, the people on the move, is not an option, nor an alternative, nor even just part of the "program" of the church of the Lord Jesus Christ; it is the mission, the work, the privilege, and the responsibility of every local body of Christ. This is what the "Great Commission" and the empowerment of the Holy Spirit in Acts 1:8 are all about.

The local church and parachurch organizations

The church – locally, regionally, nationally, and universally speaking – is the organized organism instituted by Christ and assured by Christ to succeed. At the end, when everything is said and done, we will have a new heaven and a new earth with God the Father, Son, and Holy Spirit, the Holy Angels, and His people.

> The city had no need of the sun or of the moon to shine in it, for the glory of God illuminated it. The Lamb *is* its light. And the nations of those who are saved shall walk in its light, and the kings of the earth bring their glory and honor into it. Its gates shall not be shut at all by day (there shall be no night there). And they shall bring the glory and the honor of the nations into it. But there shall by no means enter it anything that defiles, or causes an abomination or a lie, but only those who are written in the Lamb's Book of Life.
>
> And he showed me a pure river of water of life, clear as crystal, proceeding from the throne of God and of the Lamb. In the middle of its street, and on either side of the river, *was* the tree of life, which bore twelve fruits, each *tree* yielding its fruit every month. The leaves of the tree *were* for the healing of the nations. And there shall be no more curses, but the throne of God and of the Lamb shall be in it, and His servants shall serve Him. They shall see His face, and His name *shall be* on their foreheads. There shall be no night there: They need no lamp nor light of the sun, for the Lord God gives them light. And they shall reign forever and ever. Then he said to me, "These words *are* faithful and true." And the Lord God of the holy prophets sent His angel to show His servants the things which must shortly take place. "Behold, I am coming quickly! Blessed *is* he who keeps the words of the prophecy of this book."[14]

Para-church organizations cannot and will not finish the task of world evangelization nor even survive without the spiritual, personal, and financial support of the local churches. We praise the Lord for such agents which come forth in the context of the local churches. Such organizations are brought forth and used by the Lord of the Church to work with and to work through the local churches. Mission agencies need to work closer and more accountably to them.

---

14 Revelation 21:23-22:7 KJ21

They should also reconsider their work in light of people on the move.[15] They are important and crucial to consider in the context of the local churches. After all, it is by the church (as it is defined, described, and decreed in the Scriptures) that the "manifold wisdom of God might be made known… to the principalities and powers in the heavenly *places*."[16]

The roles of the local church in Diaspora mission

God seeks worshipers.[17] The role of the local church is to bring glory to the Lord by witnessing, making disciples, and planting churches among, through, with, and within all nations, all peoples (including the peoples on the move), all tribes, all families, and in the entire inhabited world. Such expectations are followed by the promise that this work will be fulfilled by the churches,[18] composed and represented by the Apostles and all the other believers at the time of the resurrection and of the ascension of Christ:

> …Jesus came and spoke to them [the eleven], saying, "All authority has been given to Me in heaven and on earth. Go therefore and make disciples of all the nations, baptizing them in the name of the Father and of the Son and of the Holy Spirit, teaching them to observe all things that I have commanded you; and lo, I am with you always, *even* to the end of the age." Amen.[19]

And,

> "But you [the eleven plus the one hundred and twenty in Jerusalem] shall receive power when the Holy Spirit has come upon you; and you shall be witnesses to Me in Jerusalem, and in all Judea and Samaria, and to the end of the earth."[20]

The role of local churches is to assist the people on the move in the most varied areas and needs, especially in their greatest need. The greatest need of every human being is to be reconciled with God through Jesus Christ. This implies that every member of the local church in their respective callings and giftedness is empowered to minister to the people on the move. The needs of the people on the move are inexhaustible: emotional (they need counselors), social (they need social workers), legal (they need attorneys, judges), physical, financial, clinical (they need health care professionals), and so forth. The local churches can "engage" every professional they have.

---

15 See John Baxter's interview: "Western Agency, Meet the Diaspora: A Conversation with John Baxter," International Journal of Frontier Missiology, 30:3 Fall 2013, 119-121.
16 Ephesians 3:10.
17 John 4:23.
18 Matthew 24:14 NKJ.
19 Matthew 28:18-20 NKJ.
20 Acts 1:8.

Such roles were already played and exemplified throughout redemptive history, starting with the calling of Abraham to live in Diaspora for the sake of blessing all nations and to glorify the Lord. God called Abraham in a context of diaspora and dispersion of the nations (tower of Babel).[21] Abraham was blessed and moved to live in Canaan (a cursed people)[22] to bless them.

When God's people became a nation, the Lord liberated them from Egypt and made them a "moveable treasure" to bless all other nations.

> Now therefore, if you will indeed obey My voice and keep My covenant, then you shall be a special treasure to Me above all people; for all the earth *is* Mine. And you shall be to Me a kingdom of priests and a holy nation. These *are* the words which you shall speak to the children of Israel.[23]

The role of living in unity and communion as the people of God, under His authority and Word, as witness of being sent by the Father in this world – is that the world may believe.[24] The Diaspora of God's people, their obedience to the Lord's command, the covenant made with them, and their election as "a special treasure to" the Lord pointed and led to their role as "a Kingdom of priests" for the sake of God's redemptive plan for the nations. The history of the Christian Church in the book of Acts and throughout the ages is the history of God's people in such roles. Every time the Church neglected their role as God's people, for God's glory, according to God's Word for the blessings of the nations, the Church failed in discipling the nations.

Local churches ministry: seven options in missional Diasporas

How can the local churches serve the Lord in the context of the people on the move? First, if God's work will succeed among all the more than 300 million peoples on the move, we, as the church, ought to research the demographics around and beyond us in order to clearly understand the constituency of our countries, estates, cities, barrios, and immediate neighborhoods. A local church or group of local churches could form a committee in order to carry out such studies.

Start with this question and consider what follows: where do we find people on the move in our neighborhood, city, State, in educational institutions; refugee camps and refugees in residential areas; international workers; some specific and selected parts of your town – people on the

21 Genesis 11:1-9.
22 Genesis 9:25 cf. Genesis 12:5-6.
23 Exodus 19:5-6.
24 "I do not pray for these alone, but also for those who will believe in Me through their word; that they all may be one, as You, Father, are in Me, and I in You; that they also may be one in Us, that the world may believe that You sent Me" (John 17:20-21).

move tend to agglomerate, concentrate in some areas of the city and in specific cities; stores and local businesses – gas stations, hotels, restaurants, family-run stores; sports associations and college teams; religious centers (mosques, Hindu temples, etc.).

Second, the next step could be to recruit, to train, and to provide ways by which the involvement and serious commitment of all local, independent, and denominational churches and their ecclesiastical leaders, internal organizations, and every member of every department (children, youth, single, married, men, and women) will be brought on board. The time is always now to work on the preparation of the previous, present, and next generation – elderly, young-adults, youth, adolescents, and children.

Third, we also need to discover all types of local church models and modus operandi that are biblically sound[25] in the context of the people on the move. It is not enough to discover one way to reach out to them, but we must find all the ways, types, means, approaches that churches and agencies which are successfully engaged in such endeavors are using.[26] All this information is readily available over the web and through other electronic social media. It is not a lack of references, but apathy and lack of initiative that block local church members from accessing such valuable and practical information.

Fourth, churches in metropolitan areas ought to plant not just local homogenous churches, but international, multi-ethnic, multi-racial churches, missional, diaspora congregations.[27] Such "International churches can play a unique role in penetrating into and reaching the unreached people groups of the world without compromising their responsibility to minister to and evangelize the expatriate community." [28] On the other hand the already existent International churches around the world should become more purpose-driven regarding Diaspora missiology.

As Ernest Klassen observed in the particular case of the Capital City Baptist Church in Mexico City, such churches "are uniquely positioned to not only have an impact upon the globalized Diaspora of the expatriate community, but by the grace of God, to be instrumental in reaching English-speaking [groups], indigenous people, especially among the largely

---

25 Consider Paul's principles in 1 Corinthians 9:14-23 and 10:31-11:1.

26 See the Case Studies chapters in this Compendium.

27 See the article in this section by Warren Reeve, "Unleashing Great Commission Potential Through International Churches."

28 Ernest Eugene Klassen, "Exploring The Missional Potential Of International Churches: A Case Study Of Capital City Baptist Church, Mexico City" (DMin diss., Asbury Theological Seminary, 2006), 71. For more concise and practical information regarding international churches, see Warren Reeve, "Unleashing Great Commission Potential through International Churches," in this same section of this compendium.

unreached sectors of the professional class and the aristocracy."[29] Doubtless, the church will have to evaluate pastors and leaders regarding their ministerial missional vision, including a diversity of qualified ethnic background leaders as well. We need more Antioch-church-types.[30]

Fifth, there are numerous resources available today over the web. Local missional churches everywhere should take advantage of such assets. There are no excuses for not being involved in missional diaspora church planting and discipleship movements everywhere. Any local church or church leader can access material and models of local churches projects in the context of the people on the move on practically every continent and in every major city in the world today.[31]

Sixth, just do it. Any size church can start a movement towards reaching and working with the people on the move, both believers and unbelievers. The motivation of every department and small group in the context of a local church ought to start from their local ecclesiastical authorities. They can do it by preaching, training, and taking the initiative to meet people on the move in their immediate neighborhood. If such work has not yet been done, it is not for lack of migrants around them, nor for lack of resources, nor for lack of models, but, many times, negligence, indifference, and accommodation. In other words, organize your local church to be active, not passive. Don't wait for things to happen. Jesus has already commanded things to happen and to be done. Things will not happen by chance.

Seventh, here are some practical biblical ways to start the training of every member of the local church in reaching out to the people on the move across the street and around the world: (1) Each member of your church, even the children, can pray for opportunities to minister to Diaspora people, plan to use such occasions, and be active as a member of the church; (2) Teach them to take the initiative to contact a family in diaspora and invite and encourage them to come to church with you and pick them up; (3)

---

29 Ernest Eugene Klassen, "Exploring The Missional Potential Of International Churches: A Case Study Of Capital City Baptist Church, Mexico City" (DMin diss., Asbury Theological Seminary, 2006).

30 In the church at Antioch the following were prophets and teachers: Barnabas, Simeon called Niger, and Lucius of Cyrene, Manaen, who had been brought up with Herod the tetrarch, and Saul (Acts 13:1).

31 For instance, consider the following resources already available: Tereso C. Casiño, Withee Mission International: A Strategic Model for Diaspora Missions in the 21st Century 30-34; Pioneers (www.pioneers.org) Exponential (www.exponential.org), "model for planting multi-ethnic churches in diaspora for Zimbabwean reverse missionaries in Britain Zimbabwe" (http://place.asburyseminary.edu/cgi/viewcontent.cgi?article=1605&context=ecommonsatsdissertations); a search on "diaspora church planting models" will suffice to convince the reader in this regard. The case studies reports are numerous. Another case in point is the work of the Korean brethren: S. Hun Kim and Wonsuk Ma, eds. The Korean Diaspora and Christian Mission (Oxford: Oxford Centre for Mission Studies, 2011), first published by the "Korean Research Institute for Diaspora."

Invite someone for dinner, brunch, lunch, etc. to your house; (4) Get involved with the diaspora friends of your children at school, sports associations, and so forth; (5) Use the resources the Lord has blessed you with (your house, telephone, car, computer, etc.) to bless diaspora friends; (6) Distribute appropriate Christian literature when the occasion arises – Bibles, proper evangelical books, tracts, and so forth; (7) Take the initiative to talk with people in diaspora whom you already know; (8) Use wisely some special occasions – birthday parties, weddings, anniversaries, trips, graduation times, etc. (9) Always be ready and open to make friends across the street and around the world.

Conclusion

Individual Christians and local churches interacting with those in Diaspora must constantly seek to ground all of their discussions (expositional, historical, strategic, and experiential) in careful scrutiny of the Word of God. This will surely involve consideration of at least one very specific biblical teaching – the Great Commission.

Local church leaders must never make the mistaken assumption that everyone in all of our churches fully understands and lives out Christ's command to make disciples of all the nations. This biblical command should regularly and forcefully be brought before all God's people. The question must constantly be asked if we really are making disciples of all the nations. As Donald McGavran argued, "The purpose of missiology [and I would add 'Diaspora' missiology] is to carry out the Great Commission. Anything other than that may be a good thing to do, but it is not Missiology." [32]

The migration or diasporic trends as described in this compendium means that the missiological opportunities before us are greater than ever before in the history of mankind.[33] Diaspora missions may be understood simply as applying the Great Commission – making disciples of all nations – to the remarkable demographic realities of our twenty-first-century world. This is missions through the local churches to the diasporas, through the diasporas, and even beyond the diasporas, in obedience to Jesus' command in Matthew 28:19-20:

> And Jesus came and spoke to them, saying, "All authority has been given to Me in heaven and on earth. Go therefore and make disciples of all the nations, baptizing them in the name of the Father and of the Son and of the Holy Spirit, teaching them to observe all things that I have commanded you; and lo, I am with you always, *even* to the end of the age." Amen.

---

32 Quoted by David J. Hesselgrave, Paradigms in Conflict: 10 Key Questions in Christian Missions Today (Grand Rapids, MI: Kregel Publications, 2006), 316.
33 Enoch Wan, "Diaspora Missiology," Occasional Bulletin of Evangelical Missiological Society (Spring 2007), 3.

The commander–in-chief commissioned every local church and their leaders to make disciples of all the nations by going, teaching, baptizing those who believe, congregating them to the body of believers, and training them to make disciples across the street and around the world for the glory of God, the edification of His people, and the salvation of the lost from everywhere to everywhere.[34]

For discussion

1. How does the Bible describe, define, and depict the place and the role of the people of God both in the Old and the New Testament? Select some texts, meditate on them, and share your findings.
2. How does the Bible describe, define, and depict the place and the role of the Diasporas throughout the Old and the New Testament? What do such Diasporas have to do with the place and the role of the people of God in the Bible? List three main implications.
3. What are the means, the motives, and the message by and through which your local church, as part of the people of God, will minister to, through and with the Diasporas? List them and share your insights.
4. What are you personally and individually doing as a member of a local church to foster such means, motives, and message? Prayerfully consider this question, make a resolution, commit yourself to it, and do something.

---

34 For a detailed exposition on the migrant churches, see Elias Medeiros, "God Scatters to Gather through His People: A Missional Response to Migrants Churches," in Reformed Means Missional: Following Jesus into the World, ed. Samuel T. Logan, Jr. (Greensboro, NC: New Growth Press, 2013).

11. Unleashing Great Commission Potential through International Churches

Warren Reeve

In almost every major city in the world you can find them. They come in all sorts of flavors with a diversity of demographics and emphases. They come in all sizes – small, medium, large, and extra-large. They are found in developed and developing countries, and they are part of a growing movement, with a largely unrecognized and untapped potential to play a major role in the Great Commission. They are the phenomenon known as *international churches and fellowships (IC)*. International churches and fellowships are congregations that primarily serve expatriates – people of various nationalities and church backgrounds living outside their home or passport countries. They may be denominational or non-denominational, with a variety of visions for their place in God's mission in the world. The IC is the intersection where multiculturalism, pluralism and urbanization simultaneously collide and co-exist. That intersection is where God gathers the scattered to reach the world with the Good News.

Some version of the IC has been around for centuries. Perhaps it can be traced back to the Antioch Church in Acts 13:1-3 which describes the DNA of an IC. It began with Jewish expatriate believers meeting in ancient Syria. They welcomed Greek and Roman Gentiles cross culturally. Then, the Jewish and the Gentile believers sent the gospel to indigenous people all over the world. This is the Great Commission from the outside in. Is it possible to follow the same biblical narrative from the expatriate to indigenous people today? With the turn of the 21st century the world is experiencing the highest levels of international migration in history and migrants are collecting in the IC. Expatriates from every tribe, nation, language and people hear the redemptive message of the sacrificial Lamb through the IC (Rev. 5:9).

Characteristics of international churches

Global Diaspora and nationals

A majority of the attendees are global diaspora expatriates with foreign passports who are in the country for work, education, or a multitude of other reasons. Alternately, in some major cities the majority of IC attendees reflect the growing number of nationals who have been internationalized through substantial overseas experience and are culturally more at home in an IC than in the national or local church. Additionally, there are nationals who desire to hear and learn English. In limited-access countries, however, it is sometimes illegal for local nationals to attend an IC; government regulations may require attendees to present their passports at the door.

Composition diversity and denominational distinctives

ICs express a rich diversity reflecting a mix of nationalities, cultures, and classes with strong global and global-nomad perspectives. They are usually very intentional in preserving a focus on this diversity, with a primary concern to serve and minister to expatriates. Typically, ICs are international, inter-cultural, multi-class, and non-denominational. Understandably, some denominationally based ICs may not always have the same breadth of multi-denominational expression. Denominational driven ICs forfeit the fullest kaleidoscope of potential that can be found in a non-denominational church, because often the healthiest, most holistic, and deepest impacting ICs are not driven by denominational distinctives, but motivated by a more inclusive understanding and practice of the whole counsel of God.

English and foreign language

ICs function in an international language (mostly English) not universally spoken in the host country. Usually, a significant proportion of those attending the church have English as a second or third language. English is the official language in over 60 countries and has the most diverse audience, having penetrated even the most remote regions of the globe through media.[1] Many ICs have planted ethnic congregations that conduct services in languages other than English. Additionally there are national churches that include among their ministries an English-speaking service. In these cases, the English-speaking congregation may grow to a point that it becomes independent of the mother church, and becomes an IC in its own right. One example of this ministry progression is Cornerstone Community Church in Seoul, South Korea, which grew out of the Young Nak Church. There are well over 100 English speaking churches in Korea.[2]

Turnover and demographic

There is rapid turnover in most IC's. One would assume that these highly mobile attendees would be less likely to develop a deep connection to the

---

1 David Pederson, Expatriate Ministry: Inside the Church of the Outsiders (Seoul, Korea: Korean Center for World Mission 1999), 4.
2 Ibid., 38.

IC as they transition in and out of the country. However, these global nomads often learn how to quickly develop deep relationships out of sheer necessity. Many ICs face unusual demographic issues. "There are two important age groups missing in the IC," said John Adams, former Associate of the Quito Ecuador's English Fellowship Church, "College and Career (18-24) and retired-aged grandparents."[3] However, European IC's report that "twenty something" adults make up a significant portion of the IC demography. The IC is an incredible context to mature within towards the next country of destiny.

Churches that are *not* international churches

Some fellowships have the appearance of an IC, but are not accurately described by the term *international church*. These expatriate churches often minister to a single ethnic, national, or language group. They tend to be inwardly focused and are wary of cultural diversity. Such congregations may encourage a ghetto mentality among the specific expatriate population they serve. In addition, some churches include the word "international" in their name, but do not identify with the IC characteristics. Why would a congregation call itself "international" when it lacks a multi-national, multi-cultural focus? Some may do so to reflect their focus and engagement in world missions. For whatever reason, without an emphasis on cultural diversity and an explicit aim to minister to all expatriates with intent to mobilize toward Great Commission impact, such churches fall short of the Acts 13 model.

The missional international church

Historically, ICs tended to be more insular and operated in maintenance mode. In 1987, International Congregations/Christians Abroad Director Art Bauer attempted to capture the evolution of the IC from colonialism in six single descriptive phrase(s): American Union, International, English, Context, Missional, and Evangelical.[4] Bauer said "The English-speaking International Congregation is a multi-cultured, multi-denominational, local fellowship of expatriate people who are united in Christian belief and who share an identity as foreigners with English as a common language."[5] Since then, ICs are intentionally moving toward a more aggressive model of Kingdom expansion as compared to an ecumenical agenda. Now they are becoming *missional*. In the excellent unpublished article entitled "Gateway to the Nations: The Strategic Value of the International Church in a

---

3 Kenneth D. MacHarg, "English-Language Churches Serve Expats in Foreign Lands" Christianity Today, February 25, 1999, 2.
4 Art Bauer, *Being in Mission* (New York: Friendship Press, 1987), 12-13.
5 Ibid.

Globalized Urban World"[6] missiologists Michael Crane and Scott Carter wrote in 2014: "ICs around the world are making an invaluable contribution to the church's mission to make disciples of every nation. Around the world God has used IC's as instrumental in sowing seeds of the gospel of Jesus Christ on the frontiers of lostness." [7] The most encouraging and exciting characteristic trend of the IC is utilizing IC expatriates for outreach. Where local governments and cultural contexts allow for it, ICs are initiating various service ministries. Pastor Jacob Bloemberg of the Hanoi International Fellowship (HIC) in communist Viet Nam has developed and implemented a strategy called *Love Hanoi: Engaging City Leadership through Christ-Centered Civic renewal*. His doctoral dissertation, written for Bakke Graduate University, has received several impacting responses.[8] The Hanoi City Chief of Police invited HIC to the newly built theater at police headquarters to present Love Hanoi. "The official government security website praised the protestant churches campaign to 'Love Hanoi' in their online report of the event." [9]

To foster ICs in their missional journey, the Missional International Church Network (MICN) began in 2000.[10] It is the most comprehensive, non-denominational collection of IC leaders conducting annual conferences in Asia and the Middle East since 2004. IC Leaders from over 30 countries representing multiple denominations, mission agencies and churches participate together with intent to equip leaders to unleash the Great Commission in the diverse and transient contexts in which they live and serve.[11] The Fellowship of European International Churches is a relationally based network that has operated since 2004 with representation from nearly every nation in Europe. The Chinese International Fellowship network is also a highly relational network within China. The Global International Church Network was founded in Jakarta in 2015. These networks, along with world mission leaders, will collapse their annual conferences and meet together for the *Global Church for a Global World* conference in Hong Kong April 11-14 2016. This will be the largest assembly of IC leaders ever gathered together with intent towards signing a covenant declaring that the International Church is uniting to contribute to unleash the Great Commission in their respective nations.

---

6 Michael Crane and Carter Scott, Gateway to the Nations: The Strategic Value of International Churches in a Globalized Urban World (unpublished paper, August 28, 2014) 1.

7 Ibid.

8 Jacob Bloemberg, Love Hanoi: Engaging City Leadership Through Christ-Centered Civic Renewal, July 2014.

9 Police report: www.anninhthudo.vn/thoi-su/chao-nam-moi-2015/586388.antd.

10 Missional International Church Network and it's beginning is recorded in the article entitled "From the Seeds of an Idea to a Community of Envisioned Leaders" 2013 on http://www.micn.org.

11 Ibid.

Strategic expressions of the missional IC unleashing the great commission

An IC with a missional mindset is strategically positioned to have a significant impact for the gospel, both locally and globally. The growing number of expatriates around the world provides a unique Kingdom expansion opportunity. ICs serve as an oasis for virtually all global diaspora people and therefore facilitate the potential for a multitude of ministries.

Evangelism to expatriates

These global nomads can be far more open to the gospel than at home. When expatriates are physically displaced and are experiencing culture shock, they tend to become spiritually displaced as well. Torn from the familiar and comfortable, they experience so much change in their daily, temporal life, that they become more open to change in their spiritual life, and may be ready to seriously consider the claims of the gospel. The local IC becomes a haven of familiarity, with some people who speak their own language and understand their culture. Back in their own country, this family may not have been interested in attending church, but in the host country they are far more likely to accept an invitation to attend a service. First, they may come to socialize with others from their background. As they continue attending services, they hear the gospel, perhaps for the first time, and they come to faith in Christ. In this context, Christmas and Easter, other holidays, special occasions and events, are especially important celebrations in the IC. The IC becomes a home away from home and often a place of refuge where the expat can receive Jesus as Saviour.

Sending and receiving

The IC is the divine intersection of migration, multiculturalism, and pluralism so that people are meeting people, catching the gospel on the ride to the next intersection. New disciples who come to faith in Christ through the ministry of the IC become ambassadors for Christ wherever they are sent. This is God's genius of the diaspora, scattering the gathered to gather the scattered. Mission is no longer from here to there, but from everywhere to here and here to everywhere. Global diaspora disciples are Christ's ambassadors in homes and workplaces. Christian Filipinos who are household servants in Arab homes in the Middle East are able to bring the Good News to those who would otherwise never hear it. Could a mission agency position such a gospel witness in limited access nations? Diaspora positioned disciples follow in the footsteps of the Hebrew servant girl in Naaman's household, who told her master that the prophet in Israel could heal his leprosy (2 Kings 5). These disciples need the fellowship and teaching of missional ICs to recognize the road that God has placed them on and how to travel it by sending and receiving the gospel.

Platform of influence

Well-established international ICs provide a platform for empowering international, trans-denominational Kingdom initiatives. ICs are strategically positioned and poised to host any number of ministries that otherwise would not have a platform in their respective city. In the 1990s, ICs with a regular weekly attendance of 500 were considered large. In 2015, there are ICs that are ten times that size. The larger, more mature and long-term ICs around the globe provide platforms to empower expatriates and local Christians with equipping and training. For example, leadership training initiatives like Willow Creek's Global Leadership Summits using multimedia presentations can offer world-class presentations on various topics hosted by well-resourced and well-equipped ICs. Expatriates in turn can be equipped and empowered for their next international posting. Like a baton, the gospel is passed from one messenger to the next in a continuous diaspora relay.

Influencing influencers

Manaen, who was brought up with Herod the tetrarch, forfeiting his available political opportunity, found Christ and is named in the Church at Antioch. Some influential person somehow communicated Christ to Manaen. The IC today, like Antioch yesterday, contains influencers that are politically connected, positioned in the marketplace and poised to be used by God to bring influencers to faith in Christ. Consequently, these influencers are used to exponentially expand the Kingdom of God through their influence. The Missional IC is a composition of believers that prioritizes influencing the influencers to bring 21st century Manaens to faith in Christ and increase the scope and reach of the gospel.

Discipleship training

David Pederson, in his book *Expatriate Ministry*, refers to the mission, ethical, and social tensions intrinsic in the context of the IC which can produce spiritual maturity in the believer.[12] This is God's accelerated spiritual growth apprenticeship plan where these tensions can produce a refining and purifying of believers into mature influencers. When the challenge to maturity is received and it is time to be commissioned into God's next assignment, there is a deep, wide, understanding and experience of God's work in the nations. It can be said that once believers have

---

12 David Pederson, 46.

matured through the influence of an IC that they are ruined for the ordinary and prepared for the extraordinary. The IC can produce well rounded, wholistic, multi-cultural disciples that reproduce themselves when they move onto their next country or back to their country of origin.

Denominational resourcing

ICs can be a regional resource for mission agencies. For missionaries in limited access countries the presence of a strong, healthy IC can provide emotional and spiritual support as well as ministries to children, youth, and adults enabling the missionary to concentrate more fully on their ministry. In addition, some missionaries receive supplemental financial support from their IC; in some cases they receive more support than from their home base. When missionaries experience the healthy fellowship of an IC, it adds value to the mission agency's ministry agenda, fulfilling on a local scale what the agency is attempting to accomplish globally. The missional IC seeks to ask missionaries, "How can we help you fulfill your mission?" What mission agency wouldn't want a local IC pastor to ask such an empowering question?

Service to society

The local IC is filled with people who are multilingual and multicultural. While they speak English or another international language, some tend to gain some fluency in the local language as well and become familiar with potential cultural barriers that a newcomer may encounter. As a result, the IC often becomes a helpful hub for connection and communication, a bridge from the outside to the inside. In the midst of natural disasters or political upheavals, the IC can help facilitate the work of relief organizations through translation, straddling cultural divides, and providing ground level intelligence as to how to provide their service where most needed. When "outside help" fails to harness the expertise of the local IC, they often run into unnecessary challenges with language, culture, and logistics.

Crisis response

ICs initiate Kingdom influence in ways traditional missionary approaches cannot. ICs have the strategic advantage of being in the right place at the right time. This was dramatically illustrated in one limited-access country when public concern hit a fever pitch over the outbreak of the life-threatening illness severe acute respiratory syndrome (SARS). The IC in that region responded proactively by passing out packets of information about the disease, including methods of prevention and treatment. Government officials, who in the past had been indifferent or even hostile to the church, observed this practical expression of Christian concern for the plight of their people and said they were impressed by the kind of people the church was producing. This compassion further earned the right for the IC to welcome nationals into the church.

Urban church model

A trend has been emerging where the missiological strategies and principles of contextualization within the missional IC church, are being embraced by the leadership in the ever changing urban church in the Western world. This is a fascinating dynamic to observe. The "Great Commission" is more effectively occurring in the Western context of multiculturalism, pluralism, and diaspora because effective IC Pastors provide examples and contexts where missiological principles can be modeled.

Political opportunity

The IC has an open door into limited access and historically closed nations through the United Nations Universal Declaration of Human Rights (UDHR). This document is the world's most translated declaration. Article 18 states: "Everyone has the right to freedom of thought, conscience and religion; this right includes freedom to change his religion or belief, and freedom, either alone or in community with others and in public or private, to manifest his religion or belief in teaching, practice, worship, and observance."[13] The far reaching influence of the UDHR motivated the writing of the Cairo Declaration of Human Rights (CDHR). The net effect of the UDHR and the CDHR is that limited access nations and virtually every country in the world, in diversified degrees, has exchanged economic prosperity through working expatriates for varying degrees of religious freedom. As a result, ICs have been planted all over the world. There is an IC of more than 500 led by an American Pastor in Saudi Arabia because of this strategic political opportunity.

Conclusion

The global diaspora is a worldwide phenomenon. It is estimated that some 240 million people live and work outside of their country of origin. This phenomenon is changing the fabric of communities globally; it challenges our homogeneity and our ethnocentricity. Everywhere one travels in the East and the West, the North and the South, people are saying, "We just aren't the same anymore; we are now a mix of color, class, culture,

---

13 United Nations Universal Declaration of Human Rights: Article 18 4. 1948. Available at http://www.lexmercatoria.org. Accessed September 21, 2010.

language, and food which we once never imagined possible." Among the Diaspora communities there are many believers who are potential ambassadors for the Kingdom. This global spreading of followers of Jesus into the far flung places of the globe is often at their own initiative and expense. The IC has a critical role to play in their spiritual stability and effectiveness. Therefore, the IC is a uniquely placed independent body of internationals with spiritual potency, godly leadership, financial resources, and geographic context poised to initiate and launch workers into the unreached people groups and into the global diasporas by extending the arms of Jesus to them.

Many ICs today do not necessarily fit the traditional paradigm of a religious social club for expatriates who are distant and isolated from their host country and culture. ICs are seriously engaging as functional contributors to the mandate of God's global mission. This makes the IC a viable investment of mission funds and personnel, because they can carry the gospel to places that it would otherwise never go. Significantly more resources from denominations and mission agencies need to be channeled to expedite these efforts. ICs properly planted and nurtured, grow to become viable and self-supporting within a few years.

God is sovereign and He is up to something profound and on a very grand scale. When the Church recognizes God's intentional placement of people in the stream of the global diaspora collected in the IC, we will be one step closer to unleashing the potential of the Great Commission.

For discussion

1. The first recorded International Church described in Acts 13:1-3 practiced the Great Commission from the outside in, and then the inside out. Jews and Gentiles collected and worshipped together. Then they prayed, resourced, and commissioned the first International Workers to indigenous people. How could this narrative be repeated where the global diaspora is collecting in the International Church to unleash the Great Commission?
2. The 21st century International Church is an oasis for spiritually thirsty people and a launching pad for dynamically equipped disciples. The receiving/sending ebb and flow of the International Church is like a seminary on wheels. What could be done to leverage further potential and increase impact to unleash the Great Commission through the International Church?
3. Between 1987 and 2015, the International Church has transitioned from a colonial fellowship of introspective expatriates to a missionally minded force that is boldly embracing the Great Commission mandate. How can denominational organizations empower the International Church toward further expansion and

development so that both denomination and International Church are synergistically fulfilling the Great Commission?

4. Limited access nations in diversified degrees have exchanged economic prosperity through working expatriates for varying degrees of religious freedom. This means that International Churches are planted in places that traditional mission agencies cannot go. How could these agencies assist in the planting and empowering of the International Church in limited access nations?

Bibliography

Bakke, Ray, and Jim Hart, *The Urban Christian: Effective Ministry in Today's Urban World.* Downers Grove IL: InterVarsity Press, 1987.

Bauer, Art *Being in Mission* (New York: Friendship Press, 1987). 12-13.

Blanchard, Ken Phil Hodges, *Lead Like Jesus*. Nashville TN: Thomas Nelson, 2008.

Bloemberg, Jacob, *Love Hanoi: Engaging City Leadership through Christ-Centered Civic Renewal.* Hanoi: Jacob Bloemberg, 2013.

Bloemberg, Jacob, *Love Hanoi: From Exploration to Formation.* Hanoi: Jacob Bloemberg, 2014.

Chipps, Graham, *Learning the Pilgrimage of the Cross: An International Church Vision.* Unpublished paper, January 13, 2015.

Ford, Leighton, *Transforming Leadership: Jesus' Way of Creating Vision, Shaping Values & Empowering Change.* Downers Grove IL: InterVarsity Press, 1991.

MacHarg, Kenneth. *English-Language Churches Serve Expats in Foreign Lands. Christianity Today*, February 25, 1999.

MacHarg, Kenneth, D. *English-Language Churches Serve Expats in Costa Rica, Around the World.* Published Tico Times, March 8, 2005.

Olson, C. Gordon, *What in the World is God Doing? The Essentials of Global Missions.* Lynchburg VA: Global Gospel Publishers, 2013.

Pederson, David. *Expatriate Ministry: Inside the Church of the Outsiders*. Seoul, Korea: Korean Center for World Missions, 1999.

Sanders, J. Oswald, *Spiritual Leadership: Principles of Excellence for Every Believer.* Chicago, IL: Moody Publishers, 2007.

Tira, Sadiri Joy, and Enoch Wan, Enoch, eds., *Missions in Action in the 21st Century*. Ottawa ON: Printbridge, 2011.

Tira, Sadiri Joy, ed. *The Human Tidal Wave.* Manila: LifeChange Publishing, Inc. & Jaffray Center for Global Initiatives, 2013.

United Nations Universal Declaration of Human Rights: Article 18 4. 1948. Available at http://www.lexmercatoria.org. Accessed September 21, 2010.

Unpublished papers and pamphlets which describe the history or ministry of International Congregations.

Albrecht, Wally, International Church Survey 2014. Commissioned by the MICN network.

Crane, Michael and Scott Carter. *Gateway to the Nations: The Strategic Value of International Churches in a Globalized Urban World.* Unpublished paper Aug, 28, 2014.

MacHarg, Kenneth, D. *An Unusual Breed; Expats See Familiar Worship in Foreign Setting*. Unpublished paper, May 12, 2005.

MacHarg, Kenneth, D. *Hymns, Prayers, Sermons: Familiar worship in an unfamiliar setting – International Congregations Serve Expats Worldwide.* August 2000.

Websites used

www.micn.org
www.lexmercatoria.org
www.anninhthudo.vn

Events, conferences, consultations and meetings attended that have influenced most of my thinking. The reality is that there is little published on the International Church.

Asia Pacific International Church Pastor's and Wives Conference
- 2002 Kuala Lumpur, Malaysia
- 2004 Chennay, India
- 2005 Rotorua, New Zealand

Christian and Missionary Alliance International Church Think Tank
- 2000 Budapest, Hungary

Fellowship of European International Churches
- 2015 Bratislava, Slovakia

Global Church Global World: Round Table Talks
- 2014 Atlanta, USA
- 2015 Hong Kong, China
- 2015 Bratislava, Slovakia

Lausanne Global Diaspora Network Consultation
- 2010 Manila, Philippines, 2009

Lausanne Congress
- 2010 Cape Town, South Africa, 2010.

Missional International Church Network Conferences
- 2004 Jakarta, Indonesia
- 2005 Abu Dhabi, UAE
- 2006 Bangkok, Thailand
- 2007 Bali, Indonesia
- 2008 Phnom Penh, Cambodia
- 2009 Kuala Lumpur, Malaysia
- 2010 Bangkok, Thailand

2011 Penang, Malaysia
2012 Hanoi, Viet Nam
2013 Kuwait City, Kuwait
2014 Beijing, China
2015 Bangkok, Thailand

12. Strategies for Reaching Refugees

Peter Vimalasekaran

Introduction

The rising tide of suffering humanity needs Christians, as well as others, to take action and care for these human beings. Recent crises in countries like Syria, Iraq, Libya, Southern Sudan, Palestine, Pakistan, and other nations, have led to waves of refugees fleeing their homelands, for a more secure place. At the same time, many nations have closed their borders to escaping refugees, in order to protect themselves from having to deal with such misery. The question is: How do we, as Christians, respond to the needs of the growing numbers of refugees in our world? Does God care for these needy refugees? How should a church respond to the refugee situation?

There are no shortages of definitions for refugees.[1] However, the author has chosen his own working definition for refugee: "A person created in God's image, who has to leave his/her home country in order to escape from any form of life-threatening situation, to another country in search of protection and provision".[2]

Biblical basis for refugee ministry

In the Bible, we find numerous accounts of God's people, who were sojourners or refugees.[3] Understanding the biblical account of the people of God will provide the biblical basis for refugee ministry.

The Hebrew word '*rwg'* (*gwr*) means, "to dwell as a stranger, become a refugee, or stay or stop as a stranger." However, the nom. 'reG' (ger) is used in the OT mostly in the sense of a "sojourner' or "alien."[4] "In the NT (and in the LXX) the Greek word 'paroikos' is used to translate the Hebrew 'gēr' and to convey the idea of a sojourner or resident alien."[5]

Adam and Eve's plight from the Garden of Eden as outcasts (Gen.1-3), Cain's story as a "wanderer," (Gen. 4: 12-16), and the lives of Abraham,

1 The most accepted definition is by the United Nations High Commissioner for Refugees (UNHCR), which was founded in 1951. UNHCR defines refugee as a person who: "Owing to well-founded fear of being persecuted for reasons of race, religion, nationality, membership of a particular social group or political opinion" (UNHCR Self-study module on Refugee Status Determination 2005, 5).

2 Vimalasekaran, 2008, 6.

3 Mummert 1992.

4 Van Gemeren, NDOTTE 1997, 836-37.

5 The Anchor Bible Dictionary, 104.VI.

Isaac, Jacob, Joseph, Moses, David, Ruth, and others as strangers in the world, helps us understand the nature of refugees' lives in our time.[6]

In the New Testament (NT), we have several examples of refugees. In Matt. 2:13-15, we have the story of the Lord Jesus and his parents, who escaped to Egypt as refugees. In Acts 8:1, 4; 11:19-21, we read that believers were "dispersed" or "scattered"[7] because of persecution. These scattered believers, outside of their homeland, became refugees and strangers. Norwood contends, "All the Early Christians were refugees, either involuntary or voluntary."[8] The Apostle Peter uses the same word *paroikoj* in 1 Peter 2:11 to show that Christians in this world were strangers and aliens. These biblical examples call us to minister to refugees and serve them for the glory of God.

Serving refugees with a right understanding

A holistic approach

Refugee ministry falls under the category of holistic ministry. It seeks to minister to the whole person. That is, body and soul. "...through the transforming power of the gospel."[9] According to Ndumu, "The evangelistic and cultural mandates testify to the personal and social renewal of life." She continues, "...that God wants, to free people from the bondage of sin, oppression, and injustice."[10] Wagner[11] further suggests, "We use the term 'mandate' to indicate that both are mandatory, never optional."[12] Refugees' emotional, physical, and spiritual needs should be taken into consideration.

The Lord Jesus Christ ministered with a holistic approach. He "treated man as a totality, thus challenging the church not to neglect any aspect of human nature."[13] One should avoid two extremes: (1) Ministry to the needy, hungry, and strangers, while avoiding the presentation of the gospel

---

6 (Gen. 4: 12-16; 12:1ff; 20:1; 23:3; 27: 41- 28: 5; 36:6-7; Deut. 26: 5; Isa. 58: 6:7; Jer. 7: 5-7; 22: 3-5; Ezek. 22: 7; Zech. 7: 10).

7 "In the NT, diaspeiro is used for the scattering of Christians that took place after persecution arose in Jerusalem (Acts 8: 1, 4; 11: 19)" (Mounce, 2006, 617).

8 1969, 52.

9 McConnell 2000, 448. See also Bassham, 1979.

10 Ndumu 2003, 62.

11 Wagner gives five views held by scholars: 1. Mission involves cultural mandate only; 2. Cultural mandate is prioritized over evangelistic mandate; 3. Both mandates have equal weight, no priority given to either of them. 4. Evangelistic mandate has priority over the cultural mandate; and 5. Pre-Lausanne view, mission is the evangelistic mandate (1989, 102).

12 1989, 101.

13 Ndumu 2003, 63.

of the Lord Jesus Christ; (2) Presenting the gospel, but overlooking the immediate concern for the refugee's temporal needs.

There is no doubt that refugees are very needy and we must help them in their plight, providing for their physical needs, and caring for their souls. As with anything else, if we are not *intentional* about what we are doing, we may not achieve the things we want to achieve.

Engaging with cultural understanding

Understanding refugees and their backgrounds is essential to know how to help them and share the good news with them. Therefore, one needs to take time to find out details related to their origin, cause of conflict, cultural upbringing, linguistic background, social status of their group, and other anthropological information to effectively reach out to refugees. This will enable one to better relate to the group of refugees, offering them effective help and support in their situation. Cultural knowledge and sociological functioning will provide valuable information to reach them with the gospel of our Lord Jesus Christ and serve refugees with the love of God.

Not just victims but also a capable people

We need to understand that most Refugees are not just looking for handouts and support. Many refugees are smart and bring unique abilities. They are looking for opportunities to exercise their abilities, skills, and attain their dreams. Quite often we look at refugees as victims and forget to see them as people with ability and capacity to reach higher things. We have seen refugees defying all the odds and getting to places where they wanted to go. They are strong-minded people, flexible in adapting to situations, and even defying their enemies to reach their goals. So, it is essential that we empower, enable, and encourage them in reaching their potential by overcoming a victim mentality. We can also learn from them. Refugees bring with them rich cultural values that can help us. Example, eastern Hospitality is something people in the west can learn from them and practice in their homes and churches. The resilient nature of many refugees is a very admirable quality that we can learn from them. There are many other good things we can learn from these refugees. Empower refugees by helping them rise above a victim mentality. Refugees need to be encouraged and supported to help them become independent and stand on their own feet.

Refugee women and children are facing uphill struggles[14]

Refugee women and children are facing untold struggles as refugees. Refugee women are left with their children without their husbands, caring for their children in a hostile environment is not an easy option. Refugee women's concerns include sexual violence, human trafficking, and gender specific discrimination. Many women refugees are sexually abused and treated as if they have no rights. These women lack a voice for their case and for their children. Refugee children are also facing many hardships and uncertain futures, particularly in the area of education. Therefore, it is a paramount need to specifically care for refugee women and children. This should lead us to specifically strategize and creatively minister to refugee women and children.

Advocacy for their rights and long-term solutions

It is important that we must not neglect the rights of refugees as God's image bearers. It is God who asks his people to care and support these needy people. In other words, when we advocate for refugee rights, we are glorifying God. We need to be a voice for the voiceless and ask our politicians to do the right things. We also need to advocate for long-term solutions for refugee struggles in their countries of origin. This should include political solutions to refugee issues and work with appropriate organisations and political institutions to bring about lasting and helpful solutions.

Essentials in reaching out to refugees

a) Prayer – Praying for refugees is not a small matter. It is the most important thing anyone can do in showing love for refugees. This can be done by individuals and groups. It is important to pray with like-minded people for refugees and encourage others to do so as a group.

b) Hospitality – Most of the refugees are in need of good hosts who practice hospitality[15] for the sake of the gospel. This is something the NT teaches and that we, as Christians, should exercise, "Do not neglect to show hospitality to strangers, for thereby some have entertained angels unawares" (Heb. 13:2). Refugees have sometimes faced much trouble and neglect within their countries and therefore, extending our love to those in need by way of an open home has a particular impact on their lives.

c) Practical Support and Help – Practical help for caring and supporting strangers and refugees is well attested to in the Bible. The Israelites were commanded to leave the produce that fell to the ground, so that the

---

14 https://en.wikipedia.org/wiki/Refugee_women_and_children (accessed on 1.10.2015).

15 The Greek word for hospitality is filoxenia which means 'love of strangers.'

sojourners or aliens could glean and live on it.[16] In Leviticus 19:9-10[17]; 23:22, harvesters were to leave the produce intentionally for the poor, whereas Deuteronomy 24:19-22 exhorts the harvester not to go back to collect what was overlooked or forgotten.[18] Commenting on Leviticus 19:9-10, Keil and Delitzsch maintain that "Laws concerning the conduct towards one's neighbor, which should flow from unselfish love, especially with regard to the poor and distressed."[19]

In the book of Ruth (2:1-17), a similar practice helped Ruth and Naomi to survive in their need. "To her are applied passages such as Leviticus 19:19-10; 23:22; Deuteronomy 24:19-22 – the last on the right of gleaning, the first two on the rights of the stranger, widow, and orphan."[20] Yahweh commands that strangers and the needy should be provided with food and clothing. (Deut. 10:18). This is a basic need for all people. Therefore, Yahweh wants strangers, fatherless, and orphans to have this basic need met. Yahweh not only loves the Israelites (Deut. 10:15) he loves the strangers too (Deut. 10:18-19). Brueggemann writes, "What was YHWH's initiatory commitment [love] to Israel is now to become Israel's derivative commitment to the stranger." He further explains, "Israel's attachment to YHWH is to be enacted as an attachment to the vulnerable in society (see 1 John 4:19-20)."[21]

d) Remembering that Time is Short[22] – Many refugees are on the move. Most of the time, they have to move from one place to another. Therefore, time is a crucial factor for those who work among refugees. They have a limited timescale to help, support, and share the Good News of the Lord Jesus Christ. Therefore, one has to be creative and consider engaging with refugees, not forgetting they may move on to another place.

e) Networking with Others – The scale of refugees in the world requires networking together as an essential part of the work. Refugees move from place to place. In some cases, governments move refugees from one camp to another. In other cases, refugees themselves keep moving. It would be a

---

16 Lev. 19:9-10; 23:22; Deut. 24:19-22. Mayes suggests that this was ancient custom to leave something as an offering to pagan gods, "leaving behind a portion of the produce in the field as an offering for the gods or spirits fertility" (1991, 327). However, he sees no such practice in this passage, rather it was a humanitarian act.

17 Harris writes, "These verses are almost identical with 23:22. Chapter 19 has an added phrase referring to vineyards. Deuteronomy 24:22 gives the same law in other words" (1990, 603).

18 Bennett 2002, 104.

19 Keil and Delitzsh 1981, 419.

20 LaCocque 2004, 63.

21 Brueggemann 2001, 131.

22 Of course this time-limit would vary where a refugee is and where he or she ended up. Most of the refugees who move to a safer country may be granted refugee status and thus he or she would live entire live in their adopted country. In that case there is no time limit. However, most refugees are in a place where they may not stay for a long time.

great help, if one could map out the path or the place where they generally move to or are kept. Once one has an understanding of how and where refugees might reside, one can try to create a networking group, involving people in the area, local churches, and organisations that work with refugees. *Networking with other like-minded people, local churches and organisations is imperative in this ministry.*

In particular, local churches play a vital part in reaching out to refugees, since anyone interested in the Christian faith may be encouraged to attend a church to be nurtured and helped to grow in the Christian faith. For example, in Germany, refugees have to come initially to a 'Registration Centre' and then they will be transferred to various camps in that Province. People working with refugees in the Registration Centre; seek to maintain a networking group, in order to connect refugees with others in the area where a refugee might be sent to.

f) Sharing Resources – The magnitude of refugees requires so many resources for their needs. Whether they are for their physical needs or for their spiritual needs, resources are in short supply. Therefore, it is important that those who work among refugees share resources to help and support refugees.

g) Mobilisation of Refugee Workers – Mobilising and motivating Christians to get involved in refugee ministry, is essential in reaching out to refugees. Generally, there is a negative understanding of refugees and why they leave their homes. We need people with the heart of God to care and love those in need. To achieve this, we need to mobilise people in local churches and provide the right information regarding the plight of refugees. We also need to ask mission agencies to see this need and encourage them to develop a strategic ministry plan for refugees.

Approaches in reaching refugees

a) Having a Compassionate Heart and Understanding – Being trustworthy and loving is crucial, since many refugees are treated badly by their fellow citizens and thus have to run away from them. They are hurt, broken and will have difficulties in trusting others. We need to understand what they have gone through in their lives; suffering, betrayal, and horrible treatment by other human beings. Therefore, it is essential that we come near to these refugees with the compassionate heart of God, making sure that we do not manipulate them in their desperate situations; rather coming alongside them, feeling their pain, concern and worry and caring for them in a genuine and honest way.

b) Human Touch – Many refugees long for a loving human touch in their lives. They look for someone who is able to come near to them, sit with them, and show that they care for them. Also the proximity to the person is key to reaching out to their souls. We need to come near to them to share the gospel. We cannot reach someone's (refugees included) heart with the gospel if we don't know how to get close to the person. We can have a wonderful programme, eloquent speeches, and a wonderful presentation, but if we don't come near to the person and win his trust, there will be very little success in reaching out to that person. Therefore, we must come to refugees and meet them where they are at, and be appropriate in their context. Refugees are always in great need and so, touching their lives with care and love is the immediate need for many of them. So, it is essential that we come close to them and win their heart and mind in order to share the Good News.

c) Openly Sharing the Good News – If you come near to a refugee and he is willing to hear you, then you need to talk and share the Good News with him. Quite often, we do all the basic things to reach a person but are not willing to open our mouths to share the Good News. Somehow we think that it will happen. That might be so, but it is essential that we open our mouths and tell them what the Lord Jesus Christ has done for them through His sufferings, death, and resurrection. There is no substitute for openly proclaiming, in an appropriate situation, the wonders of God's grace.

d) The Story of the Suffering Saviour – Most refugees can immediately identify with the Suffering Saviour and Jesus' experiences as a Refugee in Egypt (Matt. 2). This is a powerful story that will resonate with many people who have travelled the same road of despair, hopelessness, and so much hurt. It is our joy to share this particular story and help them to identify their stories with the Saviour who gave His life for them.

e) Providing Resources – Giving resources to help refugees understand and grow in the gospel. This means we need to provide them with Bibles and biblical resources to learn, grow, and become committed to the Gospel-centered life.

f) Be Intentional in Discipleship – Many refugees need support and help in the area of discipleship. Since many of them are always on the move, it is important to think of short-term discipleship training. It should be precise, concise, and culturally adaptable, in encouraging refugees in their situations and challenging them to be "gospel bearers" wherever they go.

g) Training – Training for ministry personnel is an important part of the strategy too. If a person does not get enough training and encouragement in what he or she does, he or she can become less interested, or ambivalent to the work. It does not necessarily have to be formal training, but various encouraging ministries such as conferences, meetings with like-minded workers, and visiting similar refugee ministries to inspire a refugee ministry person are also effective.

Practical ideas of reaching refugees

There are so many ways in which we can reach out to refugees in their situation. The diversity of refugees demands us to be creative in the way we reach out to them. Each situation demands various methods in evangelising refugees. Here are some ways in which we have reached out to refugees. These may not be the way everyone should engage with refugees, but one can learn from these methods and use imagination to create different ideas to communicate the love of God.

Language teaching
JESUS DVDs
Helping with legal issues
Transport
Special events organised for refugees – Christmas meals, Easter celebrations, etc.
Medical needs/Hospital visitation
Facilitating cultural events
Drop-in centre (women issues must be specifically supported and catered for)
Sports camp, football, cricket, etc.
Camp visitation, simply visiting them, and showing interest in their lives
Practical support (Bicycles, clothes, food, etc.)
Using multimedia Technology, Skype, Internet, Mobile phones, etc.
Special worship events for refugees
Support for traumatised refugees
Helping with integration/inclusion
Being there for them as their friends
Advocating for refugees rights and for sustainable solutions for their cause
A spokesperson for refugee needs
Ministry to refugee Children (education, special support events)
Support children educational needs (Homework support, language assistance, etc.)
Providing job training and improve their skills
Assist them to find suitable jobs for their skills and abilities

Equipping and engaging churches and believers

Several years of ministry among refugees have helped me to understand the importance of local churches and their involvement in refugee ministry. All our efforts to reach refugees will not be very fruitful if we don't have a local church being part of the work. One of the Iranian refugees who became a Christian said, "The church is the one thing that comes to us refugees first in the camp and is the last to leave us." This is significant for us to know, that a church plays a vital role in supporting and helping refugees in their situations.

a) Provide Information – It is important to provide information to Christian believers regarding the situation of refugees. Quite often, they were told negative stories of refugees and how refugees take resources from them. Therefore, providing people with the reality of the situation and reminding Christians of their responsibilities to the needy, is vital.

b) Intercultural and Interreligious Training – Equipping believers to engage in refugee ministry in churches is paramount. In areas of intercultural communication, integration, religious diversity, and discipleship, courses should be offered as a way of helping believers to reach out to refugees.

c) Provide Opportunities to Serve – It is important to provide opportunities to as many as possible to be involved in refugee ministry. This should include believers from host-nations as well as refugees themselves. This is important in strategically reaching out to refugees.

Christian Refugees. Recent struggles in some parts of the world have caused many Christians to flee their homelands becoming refugees. Many refugees who are Christians, and those who have become Christians, can relate better to their own as they share a culture and the experience of being refugees. The body of Christ must engage with them and support them in their struggles. We can help and encourage Christian refugees to live out their faith in their refugee context and involve them in refugee ministry. This would be great witness to many who find themselves in a similar situation.

Organise a Group. It would be very helpful, if a group of people came together and organised themselves to minister to refugees. This group could mobilise themselves. A key person is identified and takes up the responsibility to oversee the group. Then establish goals for what to do and who is responsible for what. Meet regularly for prayer and encouragement. Organise events for church-goers and other believers, like information events, Refugee Sunday, etc.

d) Stories of Refugees – Testimonies and stories of refugees will encourage many believers in how the Lord is working among refugees and extending God's kingdom among them today.

e) Church-planting among Refugees – Since there are thousands of refugees moving to new places, there is a great need for them to meet and worship God. There are multiple approaches that can be applied to planting churches among refugees.

i. Integrational Church-planting – Integrational church planting means, refugees who arrive in a host nation being integrated into local churches or start a new ministry with local people and refugees. This requires refugees being able to speak the language of their host nation and being able to adjust to their new culture etc. This can help refugees settle into a new country with ease and help, particularly with refugees' children being assimilated into their new culture. However, there are many challenges too, such as preserving refugees' own identities, their cultural values and etc.

ii. Mono-cultural Church Approach – Many refugees escape their homes because of persecution of their particular ethnic groups. When they are away from their own communities, they are much more aware of their own ethnic or national identity. This is a very sensitive issue for many refugees and therefore, we need to respect their concerns. There is no doubt that we can help many ethnic groups to preserve their identity and still be a part of a church. This model does not mean that a mono-cultural church should avoid other cultures; rather it should seek to have a biblical view of church and be willing to work together with other cultural churches. After all, Christ's priestly prayer, in John 17:2-13 clearly suggests that Christ's church is one and all his children are one people.

iii. Multi-ethnic church Approach – Multi-ethnic churches are a growing trend in many parts of the world. Since many nations are congregating in one place, a multi-ethnic church model will support and help refugee communities in their quest to integrate and live in a new country.

I am in full agreement with De Ymaz, "...pursuit of the multi-ethnic local church is, in my view, not optional. It is biblically mandated for all who would aspire to lead local congregations of faith."[23] A multi-ethnic church will proclaim that salvation is for all peoples, languages and persons (Eph. 3:14-15; Gal. 3: 28; Rev. 5:9). This is vital for refugee ministry and its goal in reaching diverse groups of people. "The purpose and goal of global, multi-ethnic ministry is ultimately doxological: God will be honored by 'all nations' everywhere in His dominion. Nothing less will adequately praise Him." [24]

For practical reasons, multi-ethnic church planting is very appealing to many internationals. Since they are not in their own country, they gravitate towards foreigners who have similar struggles to their own. Here a refugee will find his or her place too.

vi. Multi -congregation Church Planting – This means, we have several groups having their own worship in their own languages separately and then, from time to time, meeting together as one church. They may share the same name of a church and resources. This approach has been very successful and appealing to some refugees.

Conclusion

The biblical mandate to care for refugees is clear and binding. Refugee ministry is not only based on our compassionate feelings, rather God's Word demands us to care for refugees and share the love of God with them. Reaching refugees with the gospel of the Lord Jesus Christ and sharing our lives with refugees is not an optional thing, rather it should be our mission. As the disciples of the Lord Jesus Christ, we are urged by our Master to care for those who are marginalised, persecuted, and have no place of their own. A biblical understanding of refugees should drive us to care for them in the way the Lord has commanded His Church. Christians have made a difference to many lives in this world and they continue to care for them too.

Refugees are not incidental in God's plan, rather God wants them to know Him and He is not far away from them either.[25] According to Acts

---

23 De Ymaz 2007, xxix

24 Larsen 2007, 12

25 26 And he made from one man every nation of mankind to live on all the face of the earth, having determined allotted periods and the boundaries of their dwelling place, 27that they should seek God, and perhaps feel their way toward him and find him. Yet he is actually not far from each one of us, 28for "'In him we live and move and have our being'; as even some of your own poets have said," 'For we are indeed his offspring' (Acts 17:26-28, ESV).

17:26-28, all things happen in this world with God's knowledge. He wants all of His people to come to know Him and also have a relationship with Him.

Of course, refugee ministry is a very need-based service. This means, we need to provide practical help and support in their situations. We need to care for their bodies and their souls. Therefore, a holistic ministry approach is indispensable and vital.

It is also important that local churches remember that it is their role and duty to serve refugees and support them in every way they can. In fact, the church of Christ has the biblical mandate to reach out to refugees in their plight.

Finally, planting churches among refugees should be an important part of refugee ministry, in particular, multi-ethnic churches. There are four models that I have suggested that can help and that we could apply, according to the context. We need to find creative ways to help them express their faith. It is important to realise there is not just one way to do church, and therefore, we should be able to explore new ways to plant churches among refugees for the glory of God.

For discussion

1. Discuss how we can be certain that the God of the Bible loves strangers/refugees and He wants us to care for them.
2. In what ways are local churches in your city/community involved in refugee ministry? If that is not a current reality, what steps can be taken to develop such a ministry?
3. What can be done to empower refugees to help them rise above a victim mentality?
4. Explore avenues of being an advocate ("a voice for the voiceless") for the rights of the refugees and to pursue long-term solutions.

Bibliography

Atkinson, David. 1983. *The Wings of Refuge*. Downers Grove, IL: IVP.

Bassham, Rodger. 1979. *Mission Theology: 1948-1978 Years of Worldwide Creative Tension Ecumenical, Evangelical, and Roman Catholic.* Pasadena, CA: William Carey Library.

Bennett, Harold V. 2002. *Injustice Made Legal: Deuteronomic Law and the Plight of Widows, Strangers, and Orphans in Ancient Israel.* Grand Rapids, MI: William B. Eerdmans Publishing Company.

Bretherton, Luke. 2006. The Duty of Care to Refugees, Christian Cosmopolitanism, and The Hallowing of Bare Life. *Studies in Christian Ethics* 19. 1, 39-61.

Brueggemann, Walter. 2001. *Deuteronomy*. Nashville: Abingdon Press.

Bush, Frederic. 1996. *Word Biblical Commentary: Ruth.* Dallas, TX: Word Books.

Calvin, John. 1979. *The Book of Psalms*. Grand Rapids, MI: Baker.

Craigie, Peter. 1983. *Word Biblical Commentary: Psalms 1-50.* Dallas, TX: Word Books.

Cole, Alan. 1991. *Tyndale New Testament Commentaries: Galatians*. Grand Rapids, MI: Eerdmans.

De Ymaz, Mark. 2007. *Building a Healthy Multi-Ethnic Church.* San Francisco, CA: John Wiley & Sons, Inc.

Flanm, Paul. 1998. *Refugee Ministry: Towards Healing and Reconciliation. Mission Studies*, 15, no. 29: 99-125.

Freedman, Noel. 1992 (Editor in Chief). *The Anchor Bible Dictionary*, New York, NY: Doubleday.

Gaebelein. Frank. 1981. *The Expositor's Bible Commentary: John and Acts.* Grand Rapids, MI: Zondervan.

Gundry, Robert. 1994. *Matthew*. 2nd Edition. Grand Rapids, MI: Eerdmans.

Hamilin, E. John. 1996. *International Theological Commentary: Ruth*. Grand Rapids, MI: Eerdmans.

Hartley, John. 1982. *Word Biblical Commentary: Leviticus.* Dallas, TX: Word Books.

Hagner, Donald. 1993. *Word Biblical Commentary: Matthew 1-13.* General Editors, David A. Hubbard and Glenn W Barker. Dallas, TX: Word Books.

Harris, R. 1990. *The Expositor's Bible Commentary: Leviticus*, Vol. 2. General Editor Frank E. Gaebelein. Grand Rapids, MI: Zondervan.

Hendriksen, William. 1973. *New Testament Commentary: Matthew*. Grand Rapids, MI: Baker.

Hesselgrave, David. 1999. "The Role of Culture in Communication." *Perspectives on the World Christian Movement*, p 392-396. Edited by Ralph D. Winter and Steven C. Hawthorne. Pasadena, CA: William Carey Library.

________. 1983. "Christ and Culture." *Perspectives on the World Christian Movement*, 365-366. Edited by Ralph D. Winter and Steven C. Hawthorne. Pasadena, CA: William Carey Library.

Hiebert, Paul. 1999. "Cultural differences and the communication of the Gospel." *Perspectives on the World Christian Movement*, 373 – 384. Edited by Ralph D. Winter and Steven C. Hawthorne. Pasadena, CA: William Carey Library.

________ . 1999. "Social structure and church growth. *Perspectives on the World Christian Movement*, 422 – 428. Edited by Ralph D. Winter and Steven C. Hawthorne. Pasadena, CA: William Carey Library.

Kaiser, Jr., Walter. 1997. *The New Interpreter's Bible: The Book of Leviticus.* Eds. Leander E. Keck. Nashville, TN: Abingdon Press.

Keil, C, and F. Delitzsch. 1971. *The Pentateuch, Vol. 1.* Reprinted. Grand Rapids, MI: Eerdmans.

LaCocque, Andre. 2004. *A Continental Commentary: Ruth.* Translated by K.C. Hanson. Minneapolis, MN: Fortress Press

Larsen, Samuel. 2007. *The Church: Blender or Symphony? Reformed Quarterly, Fall, 12-13.*

Lausanne Committee for World Evangelization. 2005. *The New People Next Door.* Pattaya, Thailand. (http://www.lausanne.org/documents/2004forum/LOP55_IG14.pdf)

Lenski, R.1964. *The Interpretation of St. Matthew's Gospel.* Minneapolis, MN: Augsburg Publishing House.

Lingefelter, S., and Marvin K. Mayers. 1986. *Ministering Cross Culturally.* Grand Rapids, MI: Baker Books.

Loescher, Gil. 1993. *Beyond Charity: International Cooperation and the Global Refugee Crisis*. New York, NY: Oxford University Press.

Mayes, Andrew. 1991. *New Century Bible Commentary: Deuteronomy*. General Editors, Ronald E. Clements and Matthew Black. Reprinted. Grand Rapids, MI: Eerdmans.

McConnell, Douglas. 2000. "Holistic Missions." In *Evangelical Dictionary of World Missions*. A Scott Moreau, gen. ed. Pp. 448-449. Grand Rapids, MI: Baker Books.

Micklem, Nathaniel. 1953. *The Interpreter's Bible: Leveticus*. Eds. George Arthur Buttrick. Nashville, TN: Abigdon-Cokesbury Press.

Mounce, William (General Editor). 2006. *Mounce's Complete Expository Dictionary: Old & New Testament Words*. Grand Rapids, MI: Zondervan.

Mummert, Ronald and Jeff Bach. 1992. *Refugee Ministry: In the Local Congregation*. Scottsdale, PA: Herald Press.

Ndumu, Winifred. 2003. *Holistic Ministry Among the Somali Refugees in Kenya: Its Evangelistic and Social Challenges to Africa Inland Church Kenya in the 21st Century*. D.Min. diss., Reformed Theological Seminary.

Norwood, Frederick. 1969. *Strangers and Exiles: A History of Religious Refugees. Vol.1*. Nashville, TN: Abingdon Press.

Schreiner, Thomas. 2003. *The New American Commentary: 1, 2 Peter, Jude*. E. Ray Clendenen (General Editor). Nashville, TN: Broadman and Holman Publishers.

Singleton, Burt. "Finding and Ministering to Refugees." *In the Refugee Among Us: Unreached Peoples'83*. Eds. Edward R. Dayton and Samuel Wilson, 61-76. Monrovia, CA: MARC. No date is given.

Singleton, Burt, and Loc Le chau. "Discovering a Plan For Refugee Evangelization." *In the Refugee Among Us: Unreached Peoples '83*. Eds Edward R. Dayton and Samuel Wilson, 151-166. Monrovia, CA: MARC. No date is given.

Todla, Stephanos. 1985. The Refugee Problem in Africa. *African Ecclesial Review* 27: 115-119.

UNHCR. 2005. Refugee Status Determination: Identifying Who is a Refugee, Self-Study Module 2. www.unchr.org.

Van Gemeren, Willem (General editor).1997. *New International Dictionary of Old Testament Theology and Exegesis. Vol. 1*. Grand Rapids, MI: Zondervan.

Vimalasekaran, Peter. 2008. *"A Biblical Model for Refugee Ministry: The Refugee Ministry of European Christian Mission International in Freiburg, Germany 2000-2007."* DMin diss., Reformed Theological Seminary, Jackson, MS.

Wagner, Peter. 1989. *Strategies for Church Growth*. Ventura, CA: Regal Books.

Wenham, Gordon. 1987. *Word Biblical Commentary: Genesis 1-15*. Dallas, TX: Word Books.

Wilson, William. 1987. *New Wilson's Old Testament Word Studies*. Grand Rapids, MI: Kregel Publication.

Westermann,Claus and Ernst Jenni. 1997. *Theological Lexicon of the Old Testament*. Translated by Q Mark E. Biddle. Grand Rapids, MI: Hendrickson.

Wilch, John. 2006. *Concordia Commentary: Ruth*. St. Louis, MO: Concordia Publishing House.

Websites accessed

http://www.unhcr.org/cgi-bin/texis/vtx/home (accessed 1st October, 2015).

http://www.bmi.bund.de/EN/Home/home_node.html (accessed 1st October, 2015).
http://www.unhcr.org/basics/BASICS/3b028097c.html (accessed 5th October 5, 2007).
http://www.bmi.bund.de/cln_012/nn_161630/Internet/Navigation/DE/Themen/Auslaender__Fluechtlinge__Asyl__Zuwanderung/Statistiken/statistiken__node.html__nnn=true (accessed 5th October, 2007).
http://www.bmi.bund.de/cln_012/nn_165228/Internet/Content/Themen/Auslaender__Fluechtlinge__Asyl__Zuwanderung/Statistiken/Heimatlose__Auslaender__Id__51397__de.html (accessed 5th October, 2007).
http://www.statistik-portal.de/Statistik-Portal/de_jb01_jahrtab2.asp (accessed 5th October, 2007).
http://www.lausanne.org/documents/2004forum/LOP55_IG14.pdf
http://www.bmi.bund.de/cln_012/nn_165228/Internet/Content/Themen/Auslaender__Fluechtlinge__Asyl__Zuwanderung/Statistiken/Konventionsfluechtlinge__Id__51399__de.html (accessed 5th October, 2007).
http://www.bmi.bund.de/cln_012/nn_165228/Internet/Content/Common/Lexikon/__Einzelseiten/Asylbewerberzahlen__seit__1999__Id__51354__de.html (accessed 5th October, 2007).
www.zuwanderung.de/english/2_neues-gesetz-a-z/asylverfahren.html (accessed 8th October, 2007).
https://en.wikipedia.org/wiki/Refugee_women_and_children (accessed on 1st October, 2015)

13. Diaspora Missions on the High Seas

Martin Otto

Introduction

Seafarers are scattered throughout the world. It is mind boggling to realize that as much as 90 percent of world trade is hauled by ships. In international trade, over 50,000 merchant ships help to transport every kind of cargo. In 2012, 9.2 billon tons of goods were loaded at the world's ports.[1] The world fleet is registered in over 150 nations and manned by over a million seafarers of virtually every nationality.[2] Seafarers work on cargo ships, super tankers, container ships, reefer ships, car ships, cruise ships, fishing vessels, and every kind of ship imaginable. Without the hard work of seafarers on the vast oceans we could not maintain our standards of living.

Origins of the world's seafarers

According to Sam Dawson of the ITF [3] there are only a few countries in the world that do not supply seafarers. 170 countries identify themselves as having a merchant marine interest and are members of the International Maritime Organization (IMO). The estimated population of seafarers is around 1.5 million. The seafarers serving on internationally trading merchant ships is estimated to be in the order of 466,000 officers and 721,000 ratings (non-officers who work on deck or engine).[4] This does not include fishermen worldwide. Historically, the OECD countries (North America, Western Europe, Japan, etc.) remain an important source for officers, but a growing number of officers now are recruited from the Far East and Eastern Europe. The vast majority of the shipping industry's ratings are recruited from developing countries in the Far East and South East Asia. Also, Eastern Europe has recently become an increasingly great supplier of seafarers especially from the Ukraine, Croatia, and Latvia. The

---

1 http://unctad.org/en/publicationslibrary/rmt2013_en.pdf (accessed 15.9.14).

2 http://www.ics-shipping.org/shipping-facts/shipping-and-world-trade (accessed 5.8.14).

3 The International Transport Workers' Federation (ITF) is a global union federation of transport workers' trade unions.

4 http://www.ics-shipping.org/shipping-facts/shipping-and-world-trade/number-and-nationality-of-world's-seafarers (accessed 15.9.14).

largest supply countries are the Philippines, China, Indonesia, India, Russia, and the Ukraine.

According to the Philippine Overseas Employment Administration (POEA), the Philippines are the world's main supplier of seamen since 1987. In 2010, POEA reports the recorded number of Filipino seafarers to be 347,150. One out of five seafarers abroad on ships is a Filipino. According to the Department of Labor and Employment of the Philippines, around 229,000 Filipino seamen were on-board merchant shipping vessels around the world at any given time. This figure translates to more than 15 percent of the 1.5 million mariners worldwide, making the Filipinos the "single biggest national bloc" in the shipping industry.[5]

Living in floating prisons

Seafarers are a unique occupational group of migrant workers who live "sea-based" lives. This Diaspora people have a special social identity as migrants because they have no host destination while traversing international waters throughout their contracted time. They are truly "suspended migrants." The arena of work for seafarers is the ocean-going vessel. They work on all types of ships from six to twelve months away from home. On cruise ships they work an average of 12 hours a day in a seven-day work week. In such "circulatory" or "transversal" labor migration, the seafarers living and working together on-board ships create a common culture. Yet, they retain their own common language, values, norms, and beliefs.[6]

On huge cruise ships, companies employ more than 1,000 seafarers from many nations. The biggest cruise ship, the Oasis of the Seas, has 2165 seafarers from 65 different countries![7] They are confronted with other cultures and find it hard to communicate freely with each other in solidarity. Therefore, misunderstandings and conflicts commonly arise on-board.

Almost every seafarer feels lonely and isolated. A statement made by many seafarers is this: "We are living in a floating prison." After their contract at sea, seafarers have a vacation of two to three months during which time they need to go through various trainings from their shipping

---

5 http://www.ics-shipping.org/shipping-facts/shipping-and-world-trade/number-and-nationality-of-world's-seafarers (accessed 5.8.14).

6 See Evita L. Jimenez, 'Diaspora of Filipino Seafarers: A Look at the Flag of Convenience (FOC) System', a presentation during the JCJ Maritime Forum Series, Mariners System, Manila, May 2010; this document is available online http://marinerscanaman.edu.ph/Maritime-Affairs-and-Papers/DIASPORA%20of%20Filipino%20Seafarers.PPT%20JCJ%20June%2028%202012.pdf (accessed 22.9.14).

7 http://web.archive.org/web/20120220080037/http://www.oasisoftheseas.com/presskit/Oasis_of_the_Seas.pdf (accessed 15.9.14)

companies in order to keep up to date with today's maritime laws and regulations at sea. If you add all the months of vacation in a seafarer's career of 35 years he would have spent 30 years away from home, from his family and friends. Consequently, many pertinent questions arise: Where is home for the seafarer? How can he be a good husband, father and grandfather, if he is seldom home? What is the impact on his marriage and family? How does it affect his physical, emotional, and spiritual health? Furthermore, being a seafarer is also one of the world's most dangerous occupations. According to IMO in 2012, 1,000 sailors died at sea. The rate of suicide for international seafarers is triple that of shore workers and they are 26 times more likely to be killed at work.[8]

In the last three decades, I have visited more than 20,000 ships and talked to thousands of seafarers. There is a real dilemma for seafarers which they find not easy to overcome. These are some of the problems they are facing while at sea:

- Separated from his family for a long time – an average of nine months away from home and only two months vacation. Although during his vacation the shipping company might call him to do certain courses like first aid, etc, getting his papers in order, and updating his medical paperwork. So that further shortens his time with his family.
- The long absence from home creates difficulties to maintain a loving relationship with his wife and children.
- Long absences from home contribute to the challenge of maintaining his role as father to his children. Shame creeps in as the seafarer feels he may be neglecting his children and cannot do enough for them.
- Severe loneliness during the many days at sea.
- Homesickness is especially a common experience during the first weeks after joining the vessel.
- Struggles with all kinds of temptations that one can imagine.
- Communication problems can be expected if the seafarer is not fluent in the English language.
- Cultural problems arise when working with many people of other ethnicities from various countries.
- Long hours of hard work (between 8-14 hours daily).
- Relatively low pay for the hardship of work the seafarer faces.
- Feels like a stranger at home when he realizes that his family has learned to live without him, therefore he struggles with an identity problem.
- Health problems are prevalent, and acute ones face those who work especially on chemical tankers.

8 http://www.missiontoseafarers.org/media-centre/statistics (accessed 15.9.14).

- Spiritual problems as the seafarer cannot participate in the community of his church and take in Bible studies etc.

Reaching the seafarers with the gospel

Most missiologists, evangelism, and church-planting strategists are "land-locked" in their thinking. They miss the universal fact that there is more water than land on our planet's surface. For as long as there is water, we can expect to have seafarers on-board the ships.

In Mark 16:15, Jesus instructed his disciples to "Go into all the world and preach the good news to all creation." The straight-forward and obvious implication is we are to reach everyone with the good news everywhere. This includes the global population of seafarers who live and work six to nine months abroad on a particular ship. During the contract of a sailor, he can be reached with the gospel at the various ports of the world. Sailors come from diverse religious backgrounds (Buddhist, Christian, Hindu, Muslim, Sikh, etc.). Seafarers being lonely would welcome a friendly visit and the building of an authentic bridge of relationship. The sailor could be introduced to other believers including those who speak his same language. These relational bonds can provide opportunities to sow the seed of the gospel, Bibles, Christian literature, and JESUS DVDs can be provided for their ongoing use in their journeys on the high seas. If seafarers become followers of Christ, then there is the potential of the spread of gospel among fellow sailors on-board the ship and the dispersing of the good news of Jesus to the farthest corners of the world.[9]

Recognizing this opportunity, the Seamen's Christian Friend Society (SCFS) was founded in London in 1846 as a mission to seamen – to evangelize and disciple seafarers on-board the ships. Its goal is "to help seafarers spiritually by telling them about the love of Christ, but also helping them in practical ways." Today, the ministry of SCFS is established in many ports around the world including Rotterdam, Antwerp, Hamburg, Bremerhaven, Cork, Dublin, Belfast, Sydney, Manila, Iloilo, and St. Lucia, SCFS' hope is to "strengthen Christians in their belief and explain the gospel to unbelievers in order to bring them closer to the Lord." SCFS staff members meet with docked seafarers. SCFS' ministry includes services, Bible distribution, Bible Self-Study material distribution, inspirational music, film distribution, and other Christian literature. They also provide physical, emotional, and spiritual care for seafarers. Practical assistance, such as taking seamen to local shops, and providing seamen with a way to make phone calls or to provide SIM cards or top up cards or facilitate internet access for the seafarers are significantly caring gestures. Similar

9 Read of the many examples of effective evangelism given in Martin Otto's Seafarers: A Strategic Missionary Vision (Carlisle, UK: Piquant, 2001).

seamen mission agencies include the Sailor Society, Korea International Maritime Mission, and Port Ministry International, to name but a few.

Planting floating churches on ships

The planting of churches on ships is now a growing reality. One of the pioneers of this innovative ministry was Filipino Christian entrepreneur couple, Rodrigo and Delores Rivera, who launched what is now known as RD Fishing Industry Inc. in 1983, with headquarters in General Santos, Philippines.[10] Their tuna harvesting business in the South Pacific seas has a total of 14 fleets – 11 medium-sized fishing boats and three large purse and seine-type boats and their accompanying tenders.[11] On each of his ships, he assigns a very well-trained pastor who is paid to be on-board to spiritually minister to the ship's crew. Personal counseling, group Bible study, prayer and worship services are conducted by him. Many seafarers have come to faith in Jesus and then been discipled on-board the vessels. Some of them have spiritually matured and gone on to become strong ministry leaders.

The Diaspora Filipinos are not only settled in many lands, but they are also scattered across the oceans of the world. It is estimated that at least seven percent of Overseas Foreign Workers (OFWs) are genuine believers in Christ. With more than a quarter million sea-based OFWs there are conceivably over 32,000 witnesses for Jesus Christ on-board ocean-going vessels.

To expedite the ministry to the seafarers, Filipino International Network (FIN) sponsored a Consultation on-board the Operation Mobilization ship, the *MV Doulous*. The fruit of the consultation was the launching of a four-day course in April 2008 to train Christian Filipino seafarers to become intentional in reaching seafarers and becoming pastors on the ships. Since the launch, this course has been offered four times a year, resulting in hundreds of Christian Filipinos returning to their ships with a missional agenda of evangelizing, discipling, and starting churches on the ships, Today, Filipino seafarers are leading churches on several ships.[12] Other Christian nationals are beginning to lead churches on-board other ships. On the cruise ship *"Prinsendam"* an Indonesian church functions and is led by Christian Indonesian seafarers. On the *"Queen Victoria"* a Sri Lankan Christian leader facilitates weekly Bible studies and they are multicultural/multiethnic in composition. On a cruise ship of Disney Cruise Lines, several Christians from different countries in Central and South America are in the initial stages to launch a church on-board. Keeping track

---

10 Vladimir S. Bunoan, "Fishing for Success: Rodigo Rivera Sr" in NEGOSYO (Quezon City, Manila: ABS – CBN Publishing, 2006), 239-243.

11 Ron Goshulak, "Gone Fishing," Alliance Life (February 26, 1997), 19-20.

12 For testimonies of Filipino seafarers leading such churches on the ocean see Martin Otto's Church on the Oceans: A Missionary Vision for the 21st Century. (Carlisle, UK: Piquant, 2007).

of the number of churches on ships is almost impossible. The strategy of planting churches on the oceans is surely gaining acceptance and popularity.

Maximizing the potential on and beyond the ships

The majority of the global Churches are ignorant of these churches on ships on the oceans. An important role for seamen's mission agencies is to communicate to Christians and churches onshore of the existence and uniqueness of churches on-board the ships.

This calls for the critical need to form an international network of seamen mission agencies that could collaborate, coordinate, and communicate to harness the synergy of the respective ministries. This network could enable the achievement of several critical things.

1. Create a network website which has downloadable resources. It should be a go-to site to seek information about ministry to seafarers.
2. Help create partnerships between churches on the shore with churches on the ocean to ensure mutual prayer and support.
3. Coordinate all the seaport missionaries and volunteers and provide contact details on the website so that seafarers can contact them.
4. Network the leaders of churches on the oceans so that they are able to communicate to each other.
5. Develop teaching and equipping digital resources to help seafarers and their left-behind families in how to handle their respective challenges and how they can strengthen relational ties.
6. Provide resources for church leaders about how to help the seafarers maximize family relationships when they are back home from their work on the seas and how to help the left-behind families to cope during his absence from home.
7. Design a *Bible School At Sea* kit with a curriculum using digital resources. This will include biblical disciple-making, leadership, pastoral, and missiological content. This type of training could be a source for future recruits for full-time vocational ministries at sea or on land.

Conclusion

The Diaspora situation for more than a million seafarers worldwide is an ambivalent one. It is a tragedy to see seafarers working under such difficult circumstances. The seafarers carry every kind of cargo to our countries and thus help us to live a life that lacks nothing. At the same time the western world should not be satisfied with this situation but take up the challenge and reach out to these forgotten people on the seas. We can make friends with seafarers, Help them in their often traumatic situation and find ways to share the love of Christ with them. By doing so, we will be able to follow the command of Jesus in Matthew 28:19-20 "Therefore go and make disciples of all nations, baptizing them in the name of the Father and of the Son and of the Holy Spirit, 20 and teaching them to obey everything I have commanded you. And surely I am with you always, to the very end of the age."

For discussion

1. Why do seafarers commonly say, "We are living in a floating prison?"
2. The negative impact on the seafarer's family is huge. How can a local church practically address the issues?
3. Explore possible ways local churches in port cities engage in the ministry of hospitality to seafarers.
4. What is the unique missionary role of ethnic specific Diaspora congregations in port cities?

14. AGENTS OF DIASPORA MISSIONS IN AND FROM THE ACADEMIC WORLD

Leiton Edward Chinn and Lisa Espineli Chinn

Introduction: definition and historical context

The initial global recognition that authenticated diaspora missions in the academic world occurred at the Lausanne 2004 Forum in Thailand which combined the Diaspora and International Student Ministry Issue Groups as an emerging strategic direction for the Church. It came after nearly a century of intermittent growth of the international student ministry (ISM) movement.[1] It received further recognition with the addition of a Lausanne ISM Special Interest Committee in 2007, multiple sessions on ISM at the Third Lausanne Congress/Cape Town 2010; and the installation of Leiton Chinn as the Lausanne Senior Associate for ISM in 2012.

Internationals in the academic world (foreign passport holders with a student or work visa) represent one of the most strategic people groups in the fulfillment of the Great Commission. While a consensus of dictionaries generally confine "academic" to the higher educational institutions of universities and colleges, the evolving strategic boundaries of the academic world in relation to diaspora missions is expanding to include the increasing numbers of temporary-resident middle and high-school students from abroad.[2]

"Agents" of diaspora missions in the academic environment are all who participate in the "Missio Dei" among internationals at educational institutions, whether on campus or in the community. Traditionally, this includes professionals like ISM or campus ministry staff and employees on campuses such as faculty, administration, and staff, who serve or relate with international students, scholars, researchers, or language students. However, the majority of missional agents engaged in outreach among international students are volunteers, whether as peers on campus or from churches in the community. A recent development is the growing focus to equip Christian internationals in the academy as a potential mission force sent forth from the campus.

Numerous national student ministry movements of the International Fellowship of Evangelical Students (IFES) have outreach among

1 ISM is used as a generic reference for "international student ministry." See Section VII, Glossary.

2 The scope of this chapter does not include the children of immigrants, refugees, or other naturalized citizens who become enrolled as students.

international students and faculty as part of their campus strategy, of which Australia, Canada, the Netherlands, and the United States are well developed. Australia Fellowship of Evangelical Students/FOCUS has about sixty-five ISM staff at twenty-five campuses, and InterVarsity USA has had around about 100 ISM staff and another 100 staff engaged with internationals in over 300 chapters. An indigenous ISM in Korea is International Students Fellowship with outreach in five cities and on twenty campuses. ISM New Zealand (ISMNZ), which initially developed within the New Zealand Navigators ministry, was established in 2000. It has over forty staff on sixteen campuses in six cities and active partnership with over twenty churches and organizations. Bridges International (Cru/USA) has 315 full-time staff and 87 staff ambassadors (part-time) in approximately 200 locations. Probably the oldest sustained and exclusively student-led ISM is Overseas Christian Fellowship (OCF) of Australia, which began in 1959.

Increasingly, mission sending agencies, such as SIM International, are including ministry among international students in their structure. Denominations like the Lutheran Church Missouri Synod, the Assemblies of God, and the Presbyterian Church in America are developing ISMs in the U.S.

The genesis of an intentional, national diaspora mission focusing on the academic world may be traced to the origins of the Committee on Friendly Relations Among Foreign Students (also known as the CFR) in 1911, in New York, by John R. Mott. Mott is highly recognized as a strategic visionary leader of numerous global missionary organizations. Even with his eyes actively scanning the "fields abroad," Mott also noticed the foreign mission field that had come to America.[3] The CFR, which later changed its name to International Student Service, was the primary agency that planted seeds for the incremental development of international student services and ministry during the four decades leading to the 1950s.[4]

Park Street Congregational Church in Boston continues a highly effective ISM spanning more than sixty years. In 1953, Bob Finley, a returned missionary from China founded International Students Inc. (ISI), as a mission agency exclusively focused on foreign students in America, which currently has about 350 staff. Then in the mid-80s, ISI helped to establish ISM Canada (ISMC) and International Students Christian Services (now called Friends International) in the United Kingdom. ISMC has about 110 staff and 500 volunteers collaborating with 100 churches in

---

3 Leiton E. Chinn, "Diaspora Missions on Campuses: John R. Mott and a Centennial Overview of the International Student Ministry Movement in North America," Global Diasporas and Mission, Chandler H. Im and Amos Yong, Eds, Regnum Edinburgh. Centenary Series, vol. 23 (Regnum Book Publishers, 2014).

4 Mary A. Thompson, Unofficial Ambassadors: The Story of International Student Service (1982).

Canada, and Friends International has seventy full-time staff, and over sixty affiliated staff working with 250 churches in the U.K.

In 1975, a former international student gave a message on *"The Great-Blind Spot in Missions Today"* at the World Missions Conference of Boston's Park Street Congregational Church.[5] That challenge was about how the Church often failed to see the tremendous opportunity and potential for world missions to and through foreign scholars. There has been encouraging progress in moving from blindness to vision and action over the last forty years. However, there still remains a great need for the Holy Spirit to replace various shades of blindness with clarity, and to call congregations, agencies, and believers to be involved in ISM globally, and the preparation of Christian international students for their role in God's mission back home or elsewhere.

International student mobility: global trends and strategic implications

The trend of an ever increasing number of international students remains constant. Globally the number of international students grew from 1.3 million in 1990 to 4.3 million in 2011,[6] and to 4.5 million in 2012.[7] The number of foreign tertiary students enrolled worldwide increased by 50% between 2005 and 2012, and the total number is estimated to have surpassed five million in 2015.[8] UNESCO projects 7 million international students by 2020,[9] and the OCED (Organisation for Economic Co-operation and Development) anticipates eight million by 2025 at a projected growth rate of 60% in overall global mobility over the next decade.[10] Statistics of international students in receiving countries are one factor for the Church in the host nation to consider its responsibility to be hospitable, and the missional opportunity to contextually engage in ISM.

Numerical growth (in parenthesis) of international students at some of the top eight receiving countries in relation to 2013 data from *Project Atlas: Trends and Global Data 2014* (Institute of International Education):

5 Leiton E. Chinn, "International Student Ministry: Blind-Spot to Vision," unpublished paper presented at the Lausanne Diasporas Strategy Consultation, Manila, May, 2009.

6 The International Mobility of Students in Asia and the Pacific (UNESCO, 2013).

7 Education at a Glance 2014, Organisation for Economic Cooperation and Development (OECD).

8 Education at a Glance 2015, Organisation for Economic Cooperation and Development (OECD).

9 "International Education Supply & Demand: Forecasting the Future," Trends & Insights for International Education Leaders, June, 2013.

10 "Four Trends That are Shaping the Future of Global Student Mobility," ICEF Monitor, September 2, 2015.

United States 886,052 (966,333 F-1 and M-1 students; *SEVIS By the Numbers*, July, 2014)
United Kingdom 481,050
China 356,499 (almost 380,000 from more than 200 countries, 2014)[11]
France 295,092
Germany 282,201 (301,350 in 2014; *ICEF Monitor*, June 29, 2015)
Australia 247,093 (543,123 in July, 2015)[12]
Canada 237,635 (336,497 in 2014, *ICEF Monitor*, November 25, 2015)
Japan 135,519 (184,155 in May, 2014; *ICEF Monitor*, July 1, 2015)

Europe is the top destination region, hosting 48% of all international students, followed by North America with 21% of the global total, and Asia with 18%.[13]

In 2015, the United States had more than a million international students, including middle and high-school, and English language learners. In 2014/15, the number of international students in the U.S. increased by 10.0% to a record high of 974,926 students. Canada now had 336,497 international students in 2014[14] and is striving for 450,000 by 2022.[15] While the ISM movement in North America has steadily grown for over sixty years, there has not been the opportunity of regular ISM seminary courses to prepare the next generation of ISM workers. As diaspora missiology gains momentum, more Christian graduate schools and seminaries should offer at least an introductory course in ISM, and perhaps a concentration in ISM within a M.A. in Intercultural Studies that could lead to a certification in ISM.[16] Providing ISM related courses will generate much needed research to advance the ISM movement.

Historically the primary flow of international students has been to North America, Europe, Australia, and New Zealand. New Zealand had 110,198 international students in 2014.[17] Since 2000 there has been an increasing number of Asian nations seeking to establish education hubs deliberately recruiting international students. This new trend is elevating the Asia-Pacific region as a primary destination attracting students intra-regionally

11 Rahul Choudaha, "How China Plans to Become a Global Force in Higher Education," The Guardian, October 12, 2015.

12 Monthly Summary of International Student Enrollment Data-Australia-YTD July 2015, Australian Government Department of Education and Training.

13 Karen MacGregor, "The Shifting Sands of International Student Mobility," University World News, September 12, 2014.

14 "Canada Books Another Strong Year of International Enrollment Growth," ICEF Monitor, November 25, 2015.

15 CBCNews.ca (Radio-Canada National Public Broadcasting), January 15, 2014.

16 Leiton E. Chinn, "Academic Training in ISM," unpublished paper presented at GPS'09, Columbia International University, May 2009.

17 "New Zealand's Enrollment Up 13% in 2014," ICEF Monitor, July 31, 2015.

and from outside of the region.[18] China has surpassed France, Germany, and Australia and only trails the U.K. and U.S. as the top receiving nation and will likely meet a goal to have 500,000 foreign students by 2020.[19] Australia had about 527,000 international students in 2013[20] and Malaysia's *Vision 2020* program is aiming for 200,000 international students.[21] While Korea had 85,000 foreign students in 2014, the government has a goal of 200,000 by 2023.[22] But the issue of quality of education remains a challenge for some Asian nations as the proliferation of private higher education institutions often lacks government regulations.[23] Contextualized ISM strategies need to be developed for the Asia-Pacific region and one approach is through occasional Lausanne Asia-Pacific Regional ISM Leadership consultations.[24]

Nearly 300,000 European students received grants to study or train within the European region in 2012-13 under the European Union's student mobility program, *Erasmus*. Germany had over 301,000 international students in the 2014 academic year, and will likely reach its goal for 350,000 foreign-students by 2020.[25] Russia is giving priority to recruiting international students, increasing the number of its scholarship recipients from 15,000 in 2015 to 20,000 in 2016.[26]

Turkey's plan to be a regional education hub attracting 150,000 international students by 2020[27] has been upgraded to recruit 200,000 by

---

18 Leiton E. Chinn, "International Student Ministry: A Most Strategic Yet Least Expensive Opportunity for Global Missions Arises in Asia," Asia Missions Advance, January, 2014.

19 "State of International Student Mobility in 2015," ICEF Monitor, November 5, 2015.

20 "Australia Reverses Three-Year Enrollment Decline in 2013," ICEF Monitor, March 25, 2014.

21 "Malaysia Continues to Build Its Position As a Regional Education Hub," ICEF Monitor, June 23, 2014.

22 "Korea aims for 200,000 foreign students by 2023," ICEF Monitor, October 13, 2015.

23 "Higher Education in Asia and the Search for a New Modernity: An Introduction", Asia: The Next Higher Education Superpower?, Rajika Bhandari and Alessia Lefebure, Eds, AIFS Foundation and Institute of International Education, 2015.

24 The 2009 Lausanne Asia-Pacific Regional ISM Leaders Consultation was convened in Singapore to prepare for Lausanne III/Cape Town 2010; the 2015 Forum in Singapore had 70+ participants from 17 countries.

25 "Foreign Enrollment in German Universities Reach Record High," ICEF Monitor, July 30, 2014.

26 "Russia Moving to Expand International Student Recruitment," ICEF Monitor, September 30, 2015.

27 "Turkey Aims to Build on Recent Gains to Host 150,000 International Students by 2020," ICEF Monitor, June 24, 2014.

2023.[28] South Africa ranked eleventh as a receiving nation, with over 60,000 international students in 2009.[29] Brazil is a leading South American country for international student exchange,[30]and Colombia is planning to attract more international students.[31] Africa, Latin America, and the Middle East are three regions needing further development of ISM. While the UAE sends about 8,500 students abroad for tertiary-level study, it hosts over 54,000 in return; how might International or English-speaking congregations and fellowships integrate this reality into its goals?[32]

Another recent trend is the world-wide growth of post-graduate international students with a projection of 340,000 Chinese and 209,000 Indian post-graduates by 2024.[33] Some campus ministries, like InterVarsity USA, have specialized staff for Graduate and Faculty Ministry that includes ISM, and other national campus ministries might consider similar staffing.

While the data about international students usually pertains to undergraduate and graduate students at colleges and universities, there are other categories of internationals that comprise the diaspora of the academic world. Besides the growing number of special students learning the host nation's language, or non-degree students in vocational and technical schools, there are post-graduate scholars, researchers, faculty, administrators, and staff who come from other countries. There is a new trend of high-school and middle-school international students who arrive for longer than the traditional semester/year abroad program that is gaining momentum. In the U.S. the number of high-school international students, coming mostly from China and Korea, has grown from 6,500 in 2007 to 65,000 in 2012.[34] How might para-church youth agencies and church-based youth ministries engage in the new wave of youthful international students?

Distance learning and on-line courses that are growing in popularity, and which may gather cohorts of international students to a host country for one or two week classroom sessions, offer innovative mission opportunities.

Although the numbers of foreign students have steadily increased globally, the growth of diaspora missions among the students has been minimal until the mid-1980s, and mostly occurring in North America,

---

28 "Turkey: government invests record amount in HE scholarships," The PIE News, August 13, 2014.

29 Project Atlas/South Africa (Institute of International Education, 2014).

30 "Brazil Extends Science Without Borders with 100,00 New Scholarships," ICEF Monitor, July 4, 2014.

31 "Colombia's Efforts to Become an International Education Study Destination," Pie Chat, The PIE News, August 8, 2014.

32 "UAE Education Sector Set for Robust Growth" ICEF Monitor, September 4, 2014.

33 "New Report Forecasts Postgraduate Mobility Trends Through 2024," ICEF Monitor, October 15, 2014.

34 Leiton E. Chinn, International High School Students in the U.S., workshop at the 2014 National Conference of the Association of Christians Ministering among Internationals, Atlanta, Georgia, May 31, 2014.

Europe, and the Asia-Pacific region. International student ministry growth in each of the regions is currently being enhanced by developing networks: the Association of Christians Ministering among Internationals (ACMI) in North America; collaboration between national movements of IFES and Friends International in Europe; and the Lausanne Asia-Pacific Regional ISM Leaders network. South Africa has a few emerging international student ministries, and promising initiatives under consideration in Kenya and Ghana may forge future collaboration in the southern African region. Leaders of national ISMs are associating via the Lausanne ISM Global Leadership Network, which also became linked with the World Evangelical Alliance Mission Commission in 2014.

Traditionally, the focus of ISM is that of welcoming and reaching students from other countries coming to a host nation. But there is another trend of student mobility with untapped missiological implications. That is the accelerating growth of Study Abroad programs which offers a broad and natural highway for expanding diaspora ministry in the academic community. It is an undeveloped but potentially high-yield mission strategy, involving the deliberate mobilization, training, and sending of national Christian students to study abroad as Christ's missional agents, a kind of "reverse ISM." Christian schools could promote Study Abroad as an integrated mission and academic opportunity. Students may strategically select high priority countries and campuses to go to for study, research, culture, and language learning and engage in ministry. National campus ministries may consider establishing a Study Abroad Missions Mobilizer position. Mission agencies could also develop Study Abroad Partnerships in which their field missionaries participate in receiving "international" students, from their homeland, into their work. In a parallel manner, Christian faculty could be encouraged to "teach abroad" or intentionally participate in faculty-exchange for a summer, semester, or year.

Strategic value of diaspora missions *"to"* internationals of the academic environment

1. Reaching unreached/unengaged people groups (UUPGs)

Many internationals on campuses around the world come from Unreached/Unengaged People Groups (UUPGs) or the "10/40 Window" and, may potentially, impact the UUPG's where a church fellowship may not yet exist or only be in an infant stage. Countries and cultures that may close the door to missionary presence and practice ironically open their doors widely in sending or permitting their future leaders to study abroad. Consider the strategic implications of the top four sending nations of students to the U.S. in 2014: China (304,040); India (132,888); South

Korea (63,710); and Saudi Arabia (59,945).[35] Since the US, Australia, Canada, UK, and New Zealand account for over 85% of international students from India,[36] what relevance does that have for ISM strategic planning? Students from Japan have demonstrated more interest in Christianity after departing Japan. There continues to be a significant responsiveness to the gospel among Chinese students and scholars in other countries since the mid-80s. Those from cultures and religions that may be in opposition to or hostile towards Christianity are grateful for the opportunity to freely explore the Christian faith while in another country. Ministries engaged with students from UUPGs and the 10/40 Window should develop relevant strategies, including consideration of security issues for those abroad and for returnees.

2. Influencing the world's future leadership

Among the immense strategic values of diaspora missions in the academic world is the reality that most graduates will eventually assume roles of leadership in whatever spheres of engagement they participate in. The U.S. State Department lists about 300 world leaders who have studied in the U.S.[37] The Church has the exceptional opportunity to affect the future leadership of the world through transformative hospitality towards internationals who reside in and around its campuses.

3. Engaging church members of all ages in global missions at home

Local churches, and some denominations, have been discovering the great value of ministry to internationals on campus. Their members are volunteer missionaries right at home and often using their homes. "Glocal"(global/local) missions is not only for adults, but for whole families, from children to grandparents, who may be equally involved in hospitality, or as host-country language conversation partners, cultural mentors, and often serve as volunteer host-families/friends in collaboration with schools in the neighborhood. Church members appreciate the opportunity to directly participate in global cross-cultural relationships of mutual enrichment without having to relocate overseas or learn another language. It is not uncommon to hear testimonies by volunteers who wanted to serve overseas but could not, that they welcomed the fact that "overseas" has come to their campuses, communities, and sometimes show up in their churches. As a single person, Edith Hayward of Winnipeg,

---

35 Open Doors 2015 Fast Facts, Institute of International Education.
36 Indian Student Mobility Research Report 2015: Latest Trends from India and Globally (M.M Advisory Services, 2015).
37 "Armed with U.S. Education, Many Leaders Take on World," Washington Post, August 19, 2012.

Manitoba, Canada wanted to go to India as a missionary, but she could not. But later, she and her husband hosted and discipled Bakht Singh who lived with them as a newly converted international student from the Sikh religion. Little did they realize that their guest would one day be the greatest evangelist and church-planter in India in the 20th century.[38] Greater emphasis should be given to train volunteers and ISM staff for imparting basic missional understanding and resourcing for Christian international students to be lifelong agents in the Great Commission.

Most church members will not be called to serve in another country as career missionaries, or to relocate as "tent-makers" or engage in "business as mission" abroad, but most members who remain at home can open their hearts and homes to welcome internationals from the campus. What needs to be emphasized is the reality that direct personal involvement in diaspora missions locally could be an added dimension to one's world missions involvement beyond prayer and financial support of missionaries.

4. Pastors and local mission committees recognize the extraordinary value of ISM

Pastors and local mission committees extol the tremendous strategic value of missions to internationals at nearby campuses that are accomplished with relatively minimal or no budget expenditures, because the church members often fully or largely absorb the expenses. Having a growing number of internationals involved in the life of the church also constantly provides a visual reminder of world missions.

5. Mission agencies

Mission agencies are likewise embracing the strategic value of including diaspora missions to internationals on campuses in their strategic plans. The research of a missiology thesis concludes that,

> The most effective way workers can prepare to serve overseas is to invest one or more years ministering with international students. Ministering to international students needs to be given a stronger emphasis in the preparation of mission candidates. Workers who minister to international students before going overseas were shown to be much more effective than their peers.[39]

---

38 T.E. Koshy, Brother Bakht Singh of India (2003) and Jonathan Bonk, "Thinking Small: Global Missions and American Churches," Missiology, April, 2000.

39 Patrick Lai, Tentmaking: Business as Mission (Authentic Media, 2005).

6. Retired and returned overseas workers and residents

Some sending agencies are encouraging their retiring and returned missionaries to serve among international students from the country or language group they served overseas. Similarly, short-term mission participants could befriend international students and be involved in a ministry among internationals after they return. Those who have resided abroad as "tent-makers" or for business, as well as national students that studied abroad should consider engaging in outreach among internationals on a nearby campus after their return.

7. Learning and linkages from internationals on campus

New missionary recruits having pre-field connection with internationals from the academic community could enhance their culture and language learning. Also, students from other nations could possibly open doors of linkage with key people on the mission field. International students may provide critical information and perspective in developing mission strategy. Both John R. Mott and Ralph D. Winter were inspired and informed by international students that contributed to the development of the Student Volunteer Movement and the "Hidden Peoples" concept respectively.[40]

8. Homeland/ethnic, Diaspora churches caring for their own international students

Just as churches are recognizing the need to provide missionary and MK care of their members serving abroad, so might homeland and diaspora or ethnic churches consider caring for students from their homeland. Some diaspora or ethnic churches are being proactive in welcoming their national students in a foreign land. Some students prefer to be part of their cultural or ethnic church rather than venture into the host-country church. Korean churches in America and churches in Korea have demonstrated a significant commitment to minister to Korean students in America and other nations. In 1986, the first KOSTA (Korean Students in America) conference was held, and it spawned a KOSTA convention every year in North America, as well as Europe (including Germany and France), England, Japan, and Russia to provide evangelical leaders and students with the opportunity for fellowship and training.[41] In some situations where there may not be an ethnic church with cultural equivalence to the homeland, some internationals from the academic community have established their own fellowships.

---

40 Leiton E. Chinn, "Reflections on Reaching the International Student Diaspora in North America," Global Missiology, July, 2014.
41 KOSTA website: https://www.facebook.com/kostausa.

Diaspora missions *"through"* and *"beyond"* internationals from the academic world

It is imperative that participants involved in ministry "to" internationals on campus give critical attention to discipleship that builds up and sends forth believers as agents of mission wherever God leads them.

In considering missions *"through"* internationals, how might Christian internationals from the campus minister as Christ's ambassadors *to their own people* while overseas and also back home, when they return for visits or relocate? One campus ministry sends their international disciples back home on "summer mission trips." Churches should proactively explore avenues for internationals to develop and use their gifts for ministry both in the host country and among their own people back home. Internationals in the academic environment who plan to return home should consider joining, or at least visiting, a church of their national or cultural heritage as part of their preparation. Would cell-group and house-church models be more relevant for some internationals? How might discipleship and leadership development be contextualized for those planning to return home?

Christian internationals should be encouraged to reach their own people while studying or living abroad. A student from a highly restrictive country that is increasing its outflow of students abroad now follows Jesus as Savior and Lord because of the initial impact of a Christian host family. He is having a significant ministry among his fellow nationals and training others to do the same. Christian international students could be called upon to help orient and train the host church or campus ministry for ministry among people from their country or culture.

The recognition and need for relevant preparation and contextualized discipleship of student returnees for reentry transition and service back home has been developing since the introduction of *Think Home: A Reentry Guide for Christian International Students* in 1984.[42] *Home Again: Preparing International Students to Serve Christ in Their Home Countries* is rich with perspectives gleaned from multiple visits and interviews with returnees.[43] Japanese Christian Fellowship Network was birthed at the 1990 Intervarsity Urbana Student Missions Conference by Japanese students, and specializes in preparing Japanese Christian students abroad for reentry, and the churches in Japan for the receiving of returnees. Contextualized discipleship for reentry anticipates potential religious and spiritual challenges of returnees, such as indigenous cults, the occult, persecution, traditional and contemporary forms of idolatry, etc.

Examples of returnees contributing to the growth and maturity of the Church back home include John Sung who came to Christ while studying

---

42 Lisa Espineli Chinn, Think Home (InterVarsity ISM Department, revised 2011); Think Home has been translated or adapted into several languages.

43 Nate Mirza, Home Again (Dawson Media, 2005).

in the US in the mid-1920s and returned to China and Southeast Asia like an apostolic missionary, and is described as "the greatest evangelist China has ever known."[44] A significant number of senior denominational and church leaders of Malaysia and Singapore experienced spiritual conversion and discipleship as part of the Overseas Christian Fellowship in Australia since the late 1950s. Two sisters returned to their Middle-Eastern nation after studying abroad and had an outstanding ministry among their people. An international graduate remained abroad for a second degree and helped to prepare fellow students for reentry to their homeland. Now he is back home and mobilizing pastors and campus ministers to help returnees in his "closed" country.

What about those Christian international students who remain abroad and don't return home? They might extend their stay through professional training opportunities, internships, and possible employment in some countries, and some may transit from temporary-resident student status to permanent resident. They can maintain strong connections with family, friends, and colleagues by utilizing various media and electronic means and could receive ministry training from the growing field of internet ministry. A global "skype discipleship" effort is bearing encouraging fruit among returnees.

Another example of remaining abroad but deliberately ministering to the homeland is a former Muslim student from Indonesia who came to Christ while studying in America and lived with the authors for a period. He is successful in the marketplace in the U.S. and is a founding member and leader of a mission agency to Indonesia.

Mission *"beyond"* by the diaspora of the academic world encompasses cross-cultural witnessing in deed and word to both national and international people on campus and in the host-country community. Many Christian international students and graduates who remain in the host country and serve as ISM volunteers or staff workers have been exceptional in effective ministry among their fellow national students as well as students from other countries and cultures. A seminary student from Africa transformed an American church and its priest, who later became a catalytic bishop in a denominational renewal movement.[45] Many alumni of OCF Australia are now missionaries, including Dr. Patrick Fung who is the first non-Caucasian to be the International Director of Overseas Missionary Fellowship. The current Director of International Student Ministries of New Zealand who came to Christ and was discipled as an international student by ISMNZ, returned home to direct a ministry in Malaysia, and then was called to serve in leadership of the ISM that built him up in the faith back in New Zealand. After completing a seminary degree, a student

---

44 From the Foreword by J.R. Stott, Flame for God, Leslie T. Lyall (Overseas Missionary Fellowship, 1954).

45 Phone conversation with Anglican Bishop Alden M. Hathaway, August, 2014.

returned home to a limited-access country and is mobilizing others to reach the growing number of international students in their city. Greater emphasis should be directed to encouraging Christian internationals in the academic world to consider missionary service among international students. ISMs, churches, campus ministries, and mission agencies, where possible, should give attention to recruiting international graduates to serve as ISM staff or for other mission roles.

How might international students be encouraged and given a vision for the Great Commission? Certainly each ministry among internationals on campus should include God's global mission as part of its discipleship curriculum and encourage attendance at mission conferences. There is a special International Students Track at the Urbana Student Missions Conference. Supplementing missions teaching and inspiration would be a cross-cultural missions practicum and engagement provided by the church, campus ministry, or numerous other mission agencies and ministries. For various reasons, such cross-cultural ministry experience may be limited to occur in the host country where the students are.

Response to a strategic reality

Gradually, the Church is recognizing and responding to the reality that diaspora missions of the academic world probably offers the most strategic opportunity for engaging in the Great Commission at home. It not only entails ministry "to" internationals on campus, but equally the training of internationals for God's Missio Dei in their lives and callings, whether they remain abroad or return home.

For discussion

1. Describe your relationship with an international studying or working at a nearby campus. If you do not know any, what may be ways to meet some?
2. List any ISMs you could visit in your area. If there are none, and if you or your church or organization wanted to pioneer an ISM, what would be some initial steps to take?
3. How would you encourage international Christians on campus to be involved in making disciples of all nations in the context of their own campus?
4. Look at two (2) national ISM websites. Briefly share some of its ideas or information that maybe relevant to your context.

Bibliography

Some ISM websites:

ACMI (Association of Christians Ministering among Internationals): www.acmi-ism.org
Australia Fellowship of Evangelical Students/FOCUS: https://www.afes.org.au/page/focus
Bridges International (Cru): www.bridgesinternational.com
China Outreach Ministries: www.chinaoutreach.org
Friends International (UK): www.friendsinternational.org.uk
IFES Netherlands: http://www.ifes-ism.nl
InterFACE: www.iface.org
International Students Inc: www.isionline.org
ISM Canada: www.ismc.ca
ISM Inc (Lutheran Church Missouri Synod): www.isminc.org
ISM New Zealand: www.ismnz.org.nz
InterVarsity (USA): http://ism.intervarsity.org
The Lausanne Movement: http://conversation.lausanne.org/en/resources/detail/10785

For further reading and research, see Part VII: Resources; Supplemental Reading on Diaspora Missions in the Academic World.

15. Business as Mission (BAM) to, in and through Diaspora

João Mordomo

Peoples have been "on the move" since the time of the tower of Babel (Gen. 11). Yet as Enoch Wan has noted, "the movement of people spatially at an unprecedented scale is a global phenomenon of the 21st century" (2011: 3). He goes on to observe that "the changing landscape of the 21st century, namely, the global phenomena of large-scale diaspora and Christendom's shifting center of gravity, requires serious reflections on the missiological conceptualizations and strategies for Christian missions" (Wan 2011: 3).[1] As the leader of a developing-world mission agency focused on catalyzing church planting among unreached and diaspora peoples,[2] I have engaged in serious reflection on, and development of, several such strategies, one of which – business as mission (BAM) – is the subject of this chapter.

Business as Mission (BAM)

BAM is commonly defined as "a for-profit commercial business venture that is run by Christians according to biblical principles and intentionally devoted to being used as an instrument of God's holistic mission (*missio Dei*) to the world, and is operated in a cross-cultural environment, either

---

1 For more on Christendom's shifting center of gravity, see Mordomo 2014a: 144-151.

2 Throughout this chapter I refer to unreached people groups (UPGs), which are defined as ethnic groups "among which there is no indigenous community of believing Christians with adequate numbers and resources to evangelize this people group." (http://joshuaproject.net/help/definitions, accessed on 30 October 2015.) The value of this definition for our purposes is that, in accord with the biblical "all nations" mandate (Matt. 28:19-20), it places emphasis on ethnicity rather than geography, and thus includes and applies to unreached diaspora groups as well. In other words, a diaspora group may be considered unreached if it is part of a larger unreached ethnic group. For example, Somalis as an ethnic group, in their totality, are considered to be a UPG. Therefore, Somalis in, say, America, may be considered to be biblical priorities for evangelism, since they are a (diaspora) subset of a larger UPG. To put it differently, Somalis anywhere outside of their land of origin are an unreached diaspora group (UDG).

domestic or international" (Johnson 2009: 27-28).[3] Alternatively, in order to include BAM's doxological drive, special strategic relevance to unreached peoples in restricted-access contexts, and the "fourfold bottom line" – as well as to *not restrict* BAM to cross-cultural activity only[4] – I define BAM as "the doxologically-motivated strategic development and use of authentic business activities (especially small to medium sized, or SME) to create authentic ministry opportunities leading to the transformation of the world's least-reached people and peoples spiritually, economically, socially, and environmentally" (Mordomo 2014: 235-236).

As can be seen in the two definitions above, the "BAM house" is large and diverse, and BAM methodology is applicable and relevant in almost any missionary/missional arena.[5] In the spirit of accommodation – in the best sense! – I therefore suggest that there are four "rooms" in the "BAM house," as seen in the scale below:

	Monocultural	**Cross-cultural**
Reached	BAM 1	BAM 2
Unreached	BAM 3	BAM 4

Table 1 – BAM Scale

A brief description of each "room" is necessary:[6]

3 This is an adapted version of Johnson's definition. The adaptations were suggested by Johnson in a Skype call with the author in September 2014.
4 Defining BAM as "cross-cultural" unnecessarily excludes the very real need for BAM activities to be undertaken by the small communities of autochthonous believers that often exist among unreached people groups. This is especially true for diaspora communities.
5 The narrower – and, in my mind, appropriate – focus on unreached peoples has in some contexts over the past decade given way to a broader scope that includes monocultural activities and work among relatively reached peoples. As Steve Rundle has pointed out, "the term 'business as mission' (BAM) is now almost ubiquitous in mission circles, and it is hard to find anyone who does not support the idea or claim to be involved in it in some form or fashion" (Johnson 2009: 15). I have taken this into consideration in my definition and my BAM scale.
6 For further explanation of the BAM scale, as well as case studies, see Mordomo, 2014, 236-244 and 266-291. An argument could be made to maintain, for the sake of clarity, the integrity and spirit of the original BAM definitions' focus on unreached peoples, and utilize another nomenclature for my scale, such as "Kingdom business" or "transformational business," both of which are broader by definition. I am equally happy with this, i.e. a KB scale or TB scale.

1. BAM 1 is BAM activity done by a person or people who are operating monoculturally, i.e. in their own cultural context, and among a reached people group. For example, a BAM company operated by Brazilians among the general Brazilian population (and not, for example, the indigenous, Arab, Japanese or Eastern European communities) in the southeast of Brazil – which has an evangelical population of well over 25% – falls into the BAM 1 category.
2. BAM 2 also takes place among a reached people or people group, but in a culture foreign to that of the "BAMers." While the business aspect may be more difficult due to the foreign environment, the ministry aspect likely will not be overly challenging since it is a reached context. This is to say that the challenge to minister cross-culturally will be present and real, but it will not include the need for pioneer ministry, especially church planting, since there are already viable churches present. An example of BAM 2 would be a BAM business run by Brazilians from the largely evangelical southeast of the country but operating in the Amazon region, or the northeast of the country – which are significantly different than the southeast – or operating in many regions of the Western world or sub-Saharan Africa.
3. BAM 3 is more biblically strategic since it takes place among an unreached people group (UPG), and the ministry challenges will be significant. However, due to the fact that the cultural context is native to the BAM operators, they will not have the additional business challenge that they would in a new culture. An example of this would be a BAM company operated by Indian believers *from* the state of Bihar, *in* the state of Bihar, which Luis Bush has called the core of the core of the 10/40 Window. Another example would be of any group within their own historical, cultural, and national context – say Brazilians in Brazil – focusing a BAM business on an unreached diaspora community in their midst.[7]
4. BAM 4 is also a more strategic choice from a biblical perspective, since it is among a UPG. However, this also means that the ministry challenge is likely to be great – since it is among a UPG *and* cross-cultural – and the business challenge also likely will be great, since the business operators are functioning in a cross-cultural business context.

---

7 For more on diaspora missions, see: Enoch Wan, Diaspora Missiology: Theory, Methodology, and Practice (Portland, OR: Institute of Diaspora Studies, Western Seminary, 2011); Sadiri J. Tira, *Human Tidal Wave: Global Migration, Megacities, Multiculturalism, Diaspora Missiology* (Manila, Philippines: LifeChange, 2013); Payne, J. D. Payne, Strangers Next Door: Immigration, Migration, and Mission (Downers Grove, IL: IVP Books, 2012).

To, in and through Diaspora

In order to understand BAM's relevance to diaspora missions, we must first examine several key terms. "Diaspora" refers to mass movements of people, specifically "the phenomenon of dispersion of any ethnic group from their homeland" (Tira 2013: xxi). "Diaspora missions," however, cannot be defined so succinctly. There are three types of diaspora missions (Wan 2011: 5), each with its own dynamics:[8]

1. *Missions TO diaspora* refers to host culture Christians, and Christians sent from elsewhere (i.e. missionaries), reaching members of the unreached diaspora groups in their midst with the transforming message of the Gospel. In other words "non-diaspora" to "diaspora." Examples include American, Brazilian, and European Christians reaching out to recently arrived Syrian Muslim refugees in their midst, or Han Chinese Christians reaching out to Hui and Uyghur Muslims in major Chinese cities. (See Figure 1 below.)

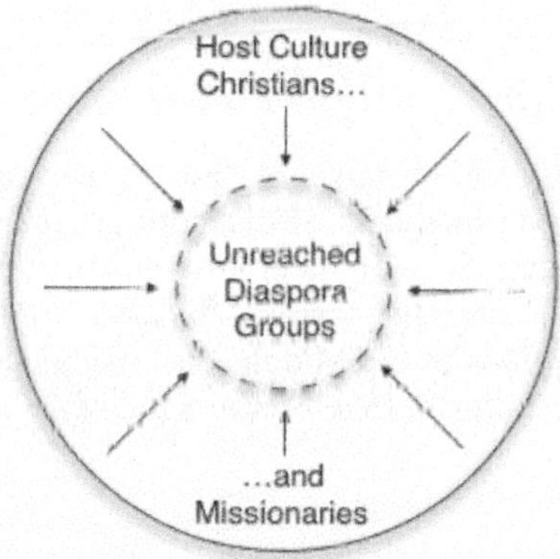

Figure 1 – Missions TO Diaspora

2. *Missions IN diaspora* refers to diaspora Christians ministering to the unreached of their own diaspora group and/or among other (unreached) diaspora groups within the same host culture. In other words, "diaspora" to "diaspora." An example of the former is Indian Christians reaching Indian Hindus or Muslims in England. Examples of the latter are Brazilians in England reaching Kurds and Venezuelans in Spain reaching Moroccans (see Figure 2 below). It is important to note here that in the experience of many organizations, including our own, diaspora Christians from one

---

8 Wan's categories are missions "to," "through," and "by and beyond" the diaspora. Although my definitions are similar, I opt for "to, in and through," in an attempt to achieve further clarity.

group are often more effective at reaching members of other diaspora groups than the host culture is, due to "positive" issues (such as affinity on the part of the diaspora groups), as well as "negative" issues (such as animosity or resentment on the part of the host culture toward immigrants).

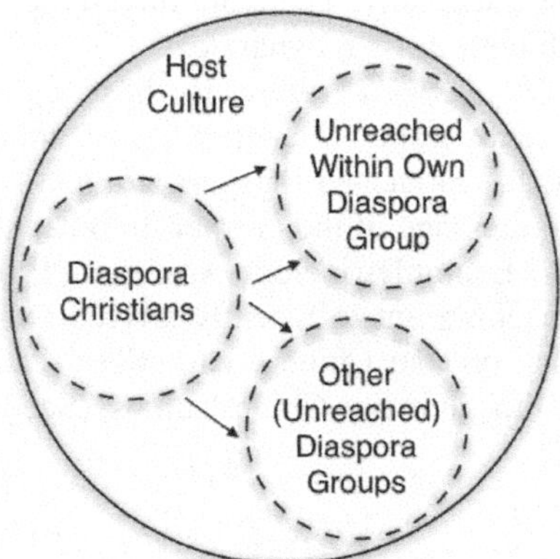

Figure 2 – Missions IN Diaspora

3. *Missions THROUGH diaspora,* i.e. *by way of* diaspora groups, refers to Christian members of diaspora groups reaching out to the non-Christian members of their host cultures, and to the world's remaining UPGs. In other words, "diaspora" to "non-diaspora." An example is Filipinos in the Middle East reaching out to members of their Arab host cultures. (See Figure 3 below.)

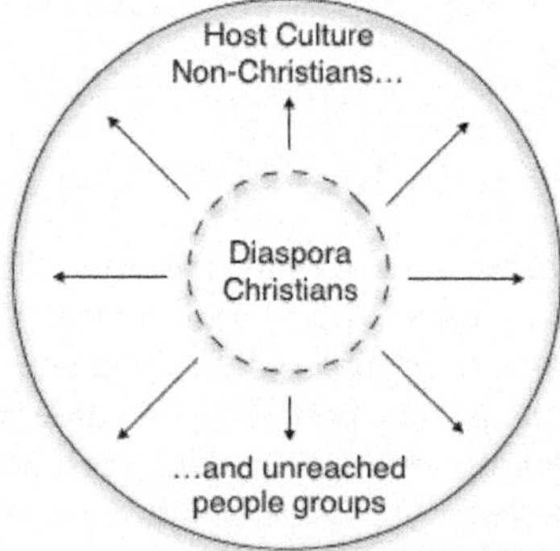

Figure 3 – Missions THROUGH Diaspora

The integration of BAM and Diaspora missions

It is not my intention in this short space to examine the relevance and use of BAM methodology in each of the three dimensions of diaspora missions separately. Rather, we shall consider the relationship of BAM to diaspora missions as a whole and briefly look at implications for BAM to, in, and through diaspora communities. To do so, we must first recognize the relationship of business in general with diasporas. Sam Cho has observed that two of globalization's "children" are the accelerated growth of international business and the diaspora of peoples, and "when these two global phenomena are put together" they cause the "rise of a common culture of humankind" (2011, 264). This common culture, that of the international business world, derives from the intricate and synergistic relationship between international business and the global movement of peoples. Many diaspora members maintain transnational ties, connecting countries, communities and businesses, and the common culture that business creates, provides a unique venue for ministry to, in, and through diaspora peoples. BAM, then, plays an increasingly important strategic role in diaspora missions. As Tetsunao Yamamori has observed, "The use of business in global outreach is a strategy of choice for the context of the 21st century mission" (Tunehag et. al. 2004, 7). We understand this to be equally true for diaspora missions, for multiple reasons:

1. Both BAM and diaspora have always been components of God's mission, with dynamic interplay between them. It is not difficult to discern that Abraham, for example, was highly familiar with both. Abraham was the father of the Jewish nation, a people of diaspora. From their very inception, they were a people sent by God, a people on the move: "The Lord had said to Abram, 'Go from your country, your people and your father's household to the land I will show you.'" (Gen. 12:1) Vocationally, Abraham seems actively to have been involved in business related to livestock, silver, and gold (Gen. 12:16; 13:2), and as he journeyed, so did his business activities. Abraham serves as an example or type of missions through diaspora ("bless the nations") which strategically employs business for the purpose of proclaiming God's glorious message of redemption, reconciliation, and transformation to all peoples, one which seems to have been normative for much of redemptive history. The Apostle Paul is another example. His was not a "conventional" missionary model. He demonstrated in Corinth, in Acts 18:1-4, both his belief in the importance and power of professions in ministry, and his conviction that while God doesn't call all His children to full-time vocational ministry, He does call them all to minister full-time, leveraging their professions as a context for ministry. This is especially true with business and it is easy to conclude that Paul's apostolic church-planting teams among unreached and diaspora peoples were built around business activities. As Roger Yoder has observed, "throughout the history of God's people, the Gospel has been brought to new parts of the world primarily by migration of financially independent Christians...[who] were dispersed..."

(2014, 23). BAM to, in, and through diaspora is not new, but rather a "back to the future" missions model and strategy.

2. BAM generally prioritizes the reaching of those ethnic and national groups who historically have not been reached with the Gospel. The U.N. calculates that there are 232 million international migrants (UNDESA, 2013, 1). Nearly 100 million of them come from countries in which reside the ethnic groups that Joshua Project categorizes as unreached. In other words, 42% of the world's migrants come from historically unreached ethnic groups and/or countries, and BAM is conceived with them in mind.[9]
3. Over half of all international migrants (123 million of the 232 million) reside in Europe and North America (UNDESA, 2013, 1), i.e. in countries that are economically developed, historically Christian, and that afford both religious and economic freedom. There are few, if any, legal restrictions on presenting the Gospel. When the millions of migrants who reside in relatively open societies in Asia, Africa, and Latin America are included, over three-quarters of all diaspora people live in contexts where the Gospel can be freely proclaimed *and* business development is generally – and sometimes strongly – encouraged.[10] What a tremendous opportunity for the Church to present the transforming power of the Gospel freely to the "world next door,"[11] not only through befriending people but by employing them in BAM activities and Kingdom Companies.[12]

---

9 To arrive at this number (97,259,000), I juxtaposed the Joshua Project list of unreached peoples by country (http://joshuaproject.net/global_statistics) with the UNDESA Migrants by Destination and Origin database (http://esa.un.org/unmigration/TIMSO2013/data/subsheets/UN_MigrantStockByOriginAndDestination_2013T10.xls). Interestingly, my conclusion that 42% of the world's migrants (97,259,000 of 232,000,000) are from unreached peoples mirrors the Joshua Project statistic that 42% of the world's people groups (7050 of 16,761) and people (3,001,557,000 of 7,176,827,000) are unreached.

10 I cannot emphasize this point strongly enough. The threads of religious and economic freedom are inextricable. According the Fraser Institute's 2015 Human Freedom Index, which measures 76 distinct indicators of personal (including religious) and economic freedom, 44 of the top 50 countries are historically Christian, and are the primary recipients of diaspora peoples. (See http://object.cato.org/sites/cato.org/files/human-freedom-index-files/human-freedom-index-2015.pdf. Accessed on 30 October 2015.) Diaspora missions and BAM, it would seem, were made for each other.

11 Phrases such as "the world next door" and the like are often used to refer to diaspora people and communities. See, for example, Hopler (1995), Phillips et. al. (1997), Houston et. al. (2004), and Payne (2012).

12 "A for-profit business whose central focus is the advancement of God's Kingdom on earth" (Mordomo 2014, 6).

4. There is a renewed and growing vision in churches around the globe to engage the so-called laity in God's mission to/among the unreached (Mordomo 2014, 208-218). As Cho notes, "Missionary life should be a requirement for all Christians now. Without distinctions between missionary Christians and non-missionary Christians, there is only one distinction, that between missionaries and non-Christians" (2011, 277). Scripture urges all Christians to be "salt and light" for the glory of their Father (Matt. 5:13-16), not merely a select few "religious professionals." The BAM Manifesto, therefore, calls "upon the Church worldwide to identify, affirm, pray for, commission, and release business people and entrepreneurs to exercise their gifts and calling as business people in the world – among all peoples and to the ends of the earth" (Tunehag et. al. 2004, 62). BAM activities can and should be undertaken to, in, and through unreached diaspora communities not only for their sake, but also for the sake of engaging – to borrow from the Lausanne Movement's motto – *the whole church* to take the whole Gospel to the whole world.[13]
5. Entrepreneurship is highly encouraged and valued by BAM, and many diaspora people by nature and/or experience are entrepreneurial. It is not difficult to imagine BAM entrepreneurs in host countries creating businesses to employ members of unreached diaspora communities. What is less obvious and, in the long-run, more important, is to recognize that "Diaspora entrepreneurs are uniquely positioned to recognize opportunities in their countries of origin, to exploit such opportunities as "first movers," and to contribute to job creation and economic growth" (Newland and Tanaka 2010,1). In other words, Christians reaching out to migrant communities, even when done through BAM initiatives, is only half of the equation. There is tremendous and eternal value and blessing, of course, for the migrants who come to know Christ in their host country, for they likely never would have had that opportunity in their home country. The long-term benefit, however, is in equipping these now Christ-following migrants themselves to bless their home country, peoples and people by employ an entrepreneurial spirit in or on behalf of their home context. According to Newland and Tanaka, of the Migration Policy Institute, "Recent research suggests that diaspora entrepreneurship can contribute to development by creating businesses and jobs, stimulating innovation, creating social capital across borders, and channeling political and financial capital toward their countries of origin" (2010: 1). Diaspora community

13 For more on this – "vocation, work and ministry in biblical perspective" – I highly recommend R. Paul Stevens' book entitled The Other Six Days (Grand Rapids, MI: William B. Eerdmans Publishing Company, 1999).

BAMers add an essential third bottom line focus, a third type of profit, in addition to the economic and social, namely, spiritual.

6. The global drift from wealth by ownership of property and land to wealth from intellectual property has direct implications for ministry to diaspora communities through business. Land in nearly every culture is crucial to identity. Diaspora groups lose their connection to their historical land and therefore, in some cases, their access to wealth mechanisms. This can lead to the loss of their very identity. Yet this does not have to be the case. Intellectual capital is increasingly the basis for business startups around the globe. Business development for, in and through diaspora communities provides means for both creating and accessing wealth *and* finding their real identities or discovering new ones.
7. Job creation (and its resultant wealth creation) is a key component of BAM and meets a primary need of diaspora communities. At the risk of oversimplifying, there are two broad socio-economic groups among migrant communities that relate directly to entrepreneurship and job creation:
   a) One group consists of those migrants whose push-pull factors[14] relate to poverty and their desire to escape it. The push motivation is stronger than the pull motivation. They are pushed away from poverty and a context where jobs are scarce, toward opportunity in contexts where jobs are available.[15] The Church has the potential to mold migration patterns for the benefit and blessing of would-be migrants by way of job creation, whether through the work of BAM entrepreneurs (monocultural or cross-cultural) who create jobs in the home country of the would-be migrant (thus mitigating the need for migration), or through job creation – by host country Christians or by members of the same or other diasporas – in the new home/host country of the migrant.
   b) The second group consists of migrants who are motivated less by "push" and more by "pull." In other words, they generally are not considered poor and rather than being *driven by* something, they are *attracted to* something. Research indicates that while the motivations of this group are not financial, per se, they are, as in

14 "Push factors are those that push people to migrate (usually in the country of origin), and pull factors are those that attract them to the destination country" (de Haan and Yaqub 2009, 1).

15 Research suggests that it is rarely the poorest of the poor who attempt migration (de Haan and Yaqub 2009, 5). The mobilization/sending of BAMers to the least of the least will always be a necessary component of God's global mission, both in obedience to the Great Commission and pragmatically because, as Prahalad's research has shown, there are tremendous business opportunities among the poor ("a fortune to be made at the bottom of the pyramid") which lead to dignity and the eradication of poverty (Prahalad 2006).

the case of the first group, job-related. For example, Winchie and Carment's research concerning international migrants' motivations uncovered 17 significant reasons for wanting to emigrate, only two of which were mentioned by over 50% of respondents: "lack of opportunity for advancement in job" (72.7%) and "lack of *suitable* employment" (51.6%) (1989: 99). More than merely creating jobs, BAM "will allow people to retain the dignity, self-esteem, healthy pride, and realistic hope that come from being usefully employed and economically self-sufficient [and] this increased purchasing power ignites the economic multiplier effect and spreads the economic benefit to the entire community" (Johnson 2009, 34-35).

Recommendations

It is clear from Scripture and history that God intends to fulfill the Great Commission both through the scattering of his people[16] and the use of business, and the dynamic interaction between the two. It is clear from church history that He has repeatedly done so. This being the case, several recommendations are in order:

1. Greater interaction (praying, reporting, planning, resource sharing) between diaspora mission leaders and networks and BAM leaders and networks should be encouraged, and venues and mechanisms created. Both groups are well represented within the Lausanne movement and elsewhere. Both already have dozens of functioning networks (built around geography, ethnicity, specific activities, etc.) to draw upon. A Diaspora BAM network could be developed, but perhaps the starting point would be for groups like the Global Diaspora Network to begin to explore the use of BAM, and the Business as Mission Global Think Tank to begin to consider BAM applications within diaspora communities.
2. In the same way that BAM ecosystems are being developed, which include incubators, training programs, investment funds and more, they should be done with diaspora missions in mind. Figure 4 below demonstrates one possible conceptualization of such an ecosystem, and the Shanghai Korean Business Forum seems to be a case in point. Founded in 2007, it is a network of diaspora Christians which seeks to integrate business and missions (Cho 2011, 264). One of the many "secular" examples is the African Diaspora Network,

16 Ralph Winter notes that while the scattering may be voluntary or involuntary, it is nonetheless a biblical mission mechanism that God has repeatedly and effectively used throughout history (2009, 211).

which "aims to encourage sustainable economic growth and employment by supporting African diaspora entrepreneurs."[17]

a) With respect to BAM *to* diaspora communities, host culture Kingdom business (KB) owners and executives should be engaged and equipped to become proactive toward hiring from diaspora communities. In other words, they should be challenged to move their Kingdom business[18] toward becoming a Great Commission Company, which Rundle and Steffen define as "a company founded primarily for the purpose of seeing Christ revealed to least-evangelized peoples" (2003, 40).[19] My research indicates that Christian business owners do not automatically have this vision but rather are in need of having it instilled in them (Mordomo 2014, 289).

b) With regard to BAM *in* and *through* diaspora groups, my comments in point two above are especially relevant. In the same way that the African Diaspora Network "aims to encourage sustainable economic growth and employment by supporting African diaspora entrepreneurs" the global BAM community has the potential to create mechanisms such as BAM incubators and investment funds specifically to awaken and empower diaspora Christians to become BAMers to unreached diaspora communities (their own and others) *and* host cultures.

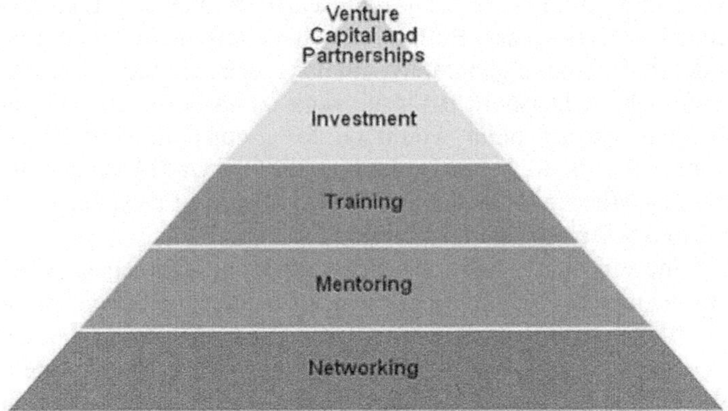

Figure 4 – Levels of Commitment to Diaspora Entrepreneurship[20]

17 http://www.diasporamarketplace.org/about-african-diaspora-marketplace, accessed on February 24, 2015.

18 Nebulously defined as "A for-profit business whose central focus is the advancement of God's Kingdom on earth" (Mordomo 2014, 6) and roughly the equivalent of BAM 1 on my scale above.

19 Roughly equivalent to BAM 3 or BAM 4 on my scale above.

20 Newland, K. and Tanaka, H. (2010, 18).

3. The convergence between BAM and diaspora missions is virtually unexplored in the academic arena. For example, a search of the ProQuest database of thesis and dissertation titles returned no hits for "diaspora AND business," "diaspora AND entrepreneurship," and "diaspora AND poverty."[21] A search of the Evangelical Missions Quarterly archives also points to a dearth of applicable research in this field. While the search uncovered approximately 20 articles directly related to diaspora missions (and a few dozen more indirectly related), there was not a single article related to the use of BAM in diaspora missions. This is a fascinating field for original scholarly research, and it is wide open.

To paraphrase Tunehag's definition of BAM, applying it specifically to the diaspora missions arena, "Business as Mission is about real, viable, sustainable, and profitable businesses *to, in,* and *through* the diaspora; with a Kingdom of God purpose, perspective, and impact; leading to transformation *of, in,* and *through* diaspora peoples spiritually, economically, socially, and environmentally – to the great glory of God" (2008, 5). May the global church *realize* that there are tremendous needs and opportunities among diaspora peoples, *rise up* to the challenge, and *reach out* through BAM!

For discussion

1. Discuss the ministry implications of the four "rooms" in the "BAM house."
2. What are the two "children" of globalization? How do they contribute to BAM playing an increasingly strategic role in Diaspora missions?
3. What are the double blessings of Christians of the host culture reaching out to Diaspora communities through BAM initiatives?
4. List all transformational possibilities of BAM to, and through Diaspora.

Bibliography

Cho, S. (2011). "Business, Diaspora and the Future of Mission: Reflections on Shanghai Korean Business Forum." In Kim, S., and Ma, W. (2011). *Korean Diaspora and Christian Mission*. Eugene, Oregon: Wipf & Stock. 264-280.

---

21 Search conducted on 26 Feb. 2015. This is especially surprising since I did not use words related to missions or ministry, revealing that the academy at large (and not merely those who are spiritually motivated) has not truly begun to treat this domain (the convergence of diaspora and business) with rigor. Also surprisingly, there were only two returns for "diaspora AND missions," both of them related to Korean diaspora missiology.

de Haan A., and Yaqub S. (2009). "Migration and Poverty Linkages, Knowledge Gaps and Policy Implications." Social Policy and Development Programme Paper Number 40, United Nations Research Institute for Social Development. < http://www.unrisd.org/80256B3C005BCCF9/httpNetITFramePDF?ReadForm&parentunid=82DCDCF510459B36C12575F400474040&parentdoctype=paper&netitpath=80256B3C005BCCF9/(httpAuxPages)/82DCDCF510459B36C12575F400474040/$file/deHaanYaqub.pdf>. Accessed on 22 Feb. 2015.

Hopler, T. and M. (1995). *Reaching the World Next Door.* Downers Grove: IVP.

Houston, T., Thomson, R., Gidoomal, R., and Chinn, L. (2004). *Diasporas and International Students: Lausanne Occasional Paper no. 55.* Lausanne Committee for World Evangelization. < http://www.lausanne.org/docs/2004forum/LOP55_IG26.pdf>. Accessed on 21 February 2015.

Johnson, C. Neal. (2009). *Business As Mission: A Comprehensive Guide to Theory and Practice.* Downers Grove, IL: IVP Academic.

Joshua Project. < http://joshuaproject.net/global_statistics>. Accessed on 20 Feb. 2015.

Mordomo, J. (2014a). Dando um Jeito: *An Integrated Theological, Historical, Cultural and Strategic Study of* Missio Dei *to, in and through Brazil* (Ph.D. dissertation). Ramona, CA: Vision International University.

_____. (2014b). *An Integrative Study of Doxological Metanarrative, Mission, Motivation and Mechanism* (Doctor of Intercultural Studies dissertation). Portland, OR: Western Seminary.

Newland, K. and Tanaka, H. (2010). "Mobilizing Diaspora Entrepreneurship for Development." Washington, DC: Migration Policy Institute.

Payne, J. (2012). *Strangers Next Door: Immigration, Migration and Mission.* Downers Grove, IL: InterVarsity Press.

Phillips, T., et al. (1997). *The World at Your Door: Reaching International Students in Your Home, Church, and School.* Minnesota: Bethany House.

Prahalad, C. K. (2006). *The Fortune at the Bottom of the Pyramid.* Upper Saddle River, N.J: Wharton School Pub.

Rundle, S. and Steffen, T. (2003). *Great Commission Companies: The Emerging Role of Business in Missions.* Downers Grove, IL: InterVarsity Press.

Stevens, R. Paul (1999). *The Other Six Days: Vocation, Work, and Ministry in Biblical Perspective.* Grand Rapids, MI: William B. Eerdmans Publishing Company.

Tira, S. E. S. B. (2013). *Human Tidal Wave: Global Migration, Megacities, Multiculturalism, Diaspora Missiology*. Manila, Philippines: LifeChange Pub.

Tunehag, M., McGee, W., and Plummer, J. (2004). *Business as Mission: Lausanne Occasional Paper no. 59.* Lausanne Committee for World Evangelization. <http://www. lausanne.org/docs/2004forum/LOP59_IG30.pdf>. Accessed on 20 February 2015.

Tunehag, M. (2008). "God Means Business! An Introduction to Business as Mission, BAM." Unpublished monograph.

United Nations Department of Economic and Social Affairs, Population Division. (2013). "The number of international migrants worldwide reaches 232 million." *Population Facts,* No. 2013/2, Sept. 2013. <http://esa.un.org/unmigration/documents/The_number_of_ international_migrants.pdf>. Accessed on 20 February 2015.

United Nations, Department of Economic and Social Affairs, Population Division (2013b). "Trends in International Migrant Stock: Migrants by Destination and Origin (United Nations database, POP/DB/MIG/Stock/Rev.2013)." < http://esa.un.org/unmigration/ TIMSO2013/data/subsheets/UN_MigrantStockByOriginAndDestination_2013T10.xls>. Accessed on 20 Feb. 2015.

United Nations Department of Economic and Social Affairs, Population Division. (2014). "International Migration 2013: Migrants by origin and destination." *Population Facts,* No. 2013/3, rev. 1, April 2014. <http://esa.un.org/unmigration/documents/The_number _of_international _migrants.pdf>. Accessed on 20 February 2015.

Wan, Enoch Y. (2011). *Diaspora Missiology: Theory, Methodology, and Practice.* Portland, Or:Institute of Diaspora Studies: Western Seminary. Kindle Edition.

Winchie, D., and Carment, D. (1989). "Migration and Motivation: The Migrant's Perspective." *International Migration Review* Vol. 23, No. 1 (Spring, 1989), 96-104.

Winter, R., & Hawthorne, S. (2009). *Perspectives on the World Christian Movement: A Reader.* 4th Ed. Pasadena, CA: William Carey Library.

Yoder, J. H., & In Koontz, G. G. (2014). *Theology of Mission: A Believers Church Perspective.* Downers Grove, Illinois: InterVarsity Press.

16. Children in Diaspora

Cecilia J. Casiño

Introduction

This chapter intends to present reasons and contexts behind the mobility of children under eighteen years of age. Children from both economically depressed and affluent nations encounter issues, challenges, and discipleship opportunities for being diaspora children. Biblical framework is also included as a reminder that missions to diaspora children is Bible-based and therefore could not and should not be taken for granted. Every section is discussed briefly, yet it provides a window, wide enough for relevant discussion and future expansion.

Contexts and reasons for children mobility

There are various reasons why children move. Whatever the reason behind a child's mobility, there is always a consequential or pre-existing context an individual child needs to contend with. Most positive stories are expressed with excitement, anticipation, and great hope. On the contrary, negative stories are expressed in lament, grunts, disgust, and rebellion. Generally, a diaspora child's performance in society is determined by the attitude and worldview the individual develops and nurtures inwardly based on environmental shifts and transition experiences.

A. Children move when their parents move

Transnational mobility of children due to parents' job placement is not a new phenomenon. It has been happening to children of artists, athletes, church leaders, and missionaries, soldiers, professional and skilled workers, among others, whose service is highly in demand on a global scale. In baseball alone, Kevin Quinn says that American baseball teams are dominated by international players from Latin America and an increasing number from Japan. Many other sports teams worldwide welcome potential international athletes from different corners of the globe, e.g., basketball, soccer, or Olympic-related sports. Most athletes represent their own family. Those who are married may be living with their children who are still in pre-school, primary, middle school, and high school.[1] In the area of

1 Kevin Quinn, 2003.

diplomatic relations, one can imagine several hundreds of children below eighteen who live with their parents overseas.

In addition to the number of children crossing international borders, thousands of long-term missionary families and church leaders are scattered around the world. These families are affiliated with different missions organizations in various parts of the globe. According to the Center for the Study of Global Christianity at Gordon-Conwell Theological Seminary, there are approximately 400,000 Christian missionaries commissioned in 2010. It is also noted that there is an increase in the number of missionaries coming from nations that are unlikely thought of as missionary-senders.[2] Furthermore, the International Labour Organization is cognizant of the increase of migrant workers at international level. The ILO reports an estimated 232 million migrants around the world due to the growing demands and pace of economic globalization.[3]

B. Children move when their parents find new relationships

Children are very likely to move when their parents end up in separation or divorce. Some children find themselves living with single parents due to death of spouse or abandonment of family responsibilities. As a result of these unsuccessful relationships, many single parents along with their children move to distant places to find more promising jobs that could provide for their own and children's needs. They also move to create a fresh environment for themselves and their families. Many of them set their hopes on overseas job placement in order to gain economic and emotional stability.

In the process of moving from one place to another, many single parents experience difficult and desperate situations that could render them vulnerable, thus, seeking protection and security in new relationships. Fortunately, some of these parents find new relationships that seem to be more stable and favorable to themselves and their children. Undeniably, there are those who fall into the wrong hands.[4]

The number of blended families in many parts of the world continues to rise. A study reveals that "60 % of all remarriages in the U.S. eventually end in legal divorce – about 65% of remarriages involve children from

---

2 Steffan, Melissa. "The Surprising Coutnries Most Missionaries Are Sent From And Go To." Christianity Today (7/25/2013): http://www.christianitytoday.com/gleanings/2013/july/missionaries-countries-sent-received-csgc-gordon-conwell.html.

3 http://www.ilo.org/global/topics/labour-migration/lang--en/index.htm.

4 Banschick, Mark. "The High Failure Rate of Second and Third Marriages. Why are second and third marriages more lilely to fail?" *Psychology Today,* February 06, 2012, http://www.psychologytoday.com/blog/the-intelligent-divorce/201202/the-high-failure-rate-second-and-third-marriages/.

prior marriages and form blended families."[5] Another survey reflects that 1,300 families are formed each day, and around 18 million children live in stepfamilies.[6]

A model of blended families that has become more apparent recently includes children of parents in former marriages under eighteen being adopted by a spouse in the remarriage. This process necessitates the moving of children from the custody of grandparents or immediate relatives to a newly built home of a diaspora spouse and a new-found marriage partner. Whether or not the children would change their name to follow the adoptive parent's last name, the task of adjusting to a new family system becomes extremely overwhelming, especially when it involves other children on their adoptive parent's side and much more so when it involves intercultural and intercontinental blend.[7]

C. Children move when their parents are unable to provide for the family

Countless families in developing and "dreamer countries" suffer from lack of resources for their daily needs. Many of them seek for better opportunities far and near in order to sustain basic necessities. Others just give their infants or older children up for adoption.[8] However, families who see adoption as the last remedy would resort to the departure of one or both parents in a family to work away from home. In this regard, children who are not able to take care of themselves are left with a nanny, grandparents, or other trustworthy relatives and friends.[9] They are either uprooted from their original home to stay with their primary caregivers, or they join in their parents' adventure in a foreign land.

There are two scenarios that could come out of this context and reason for mobility. Either the parents leave home to work abroad and the children are left behind, or *vice versa*. The International Labour Organization has released encouraging news regarding the decline in number of children in forced labor from 246 million to 168 million in 2000. Yet, despite the progress reflected in the report, there are still 168 million children out there waiting and longing to be rescued from the difficult and hazardous environments that are choking their growth as persons.[10]

---

5 5 Winning Step Families: Helping Blended Families Succeed. http://www.winningstepfamilies.com/BlendedFamilyPatternofSuccess.html/.

6 http://www.2equal1.com/advice/facts-stats-about-blended-families/.

7 For a list of written materials and professional help that could enable remarried couples and stepfamilies become successful in their practical daily living visit, Ron L. Deal, http://www.smartstepfamilies.com/view/about-smart-stepfamilies.

8 http://travel.state.gov/content/dam/aa/pdfs/fy2014_annual_report.pdf.

9 Gamez 2012, 132-143.

10 http://www.ilo.org/global/topics/child-labour/lang--en/index.htm#a2, based on "Making Progress Against Child Labour – Global Estimates and Trends 2000-2012

D. Children move when there is a need for academic, scholarship, and skills training

Scholarship, academic, and practical skills training are among the most noted reasons for children under eighteen moving away from home. It is considered voluntary if a child chooses or consents to relocate in order to avail of opportunities and scholarship grants for quality education away from home. On the other hand, it is considered involuntary when the relocation is against the child's desire even if it means gaining better education and opportunities that could ensure a better future.

The concept of educating children in boarding schools has become popular among middle class and diaspora families worldwide. Many parents choose to send their young children from the age of five or older to boarding schools due to what they believe as more beneficial round the clock learning even after the last school bell rings.[11] In 2011, the South Korean government reports 16,000 Korean children in boarding schools compared to that of 2001, which was only around 8,000.[12]

The invitation to become global citizens through language and cultural immersion as well as academic/skills training has been a very attractive trend that could continue to flourish. A good number of agencies and institutions in different parts of the world host international student exchange programs or offer courses that could equip children for global roles and tasks.[13]

E. Children move when greed and irresponsibility overcome adults

Children face a great dilemma when they find themselves in the clout of greedy and irresponsible adults. This situation leaves them with limited or no choice at all. This scenario also comes in too many different forms: parents who could not sustain their families use their children as members of the work force to bring in cash for family subsistence; children are sold for quick money; children are forced into sex slavery to the benefit of both parents and brokers; children are forced into labor camps to earn money that they may not even receive; children are trafficked so adults could enjoy luxurious living and power. The UNODC report reveals that almost 20% of

---

(ILO-IPEC, 2013), http://www.ilo.org/ipec/Informationresources/WCMS_221513/lang--en/index.html.

11 http://ismk.org/mk-parents/schooling/boarding-schools.html.

12 Ang and Kwok, "Elite Boarding Schools Spreading through Asia," December 23, 2012, http://www.nytimes.com/2012/12/24/world/asia/elite-boarding-schools-spreading-through-asia.html?pagewanted=all&_r=0.

13 http://childrenofallnations.com/student-ambassador-exchange/?gclid=CKmDmeLI1sgCFdePHwodE6ME6g; http://pax.org/families?gclid=CPm3v5HJ1sgCFVMYHwod5NkDNw.

all trafficking victims worldwide are children.[14] All these situations force children to leave home involuntarily, with some isolated cases, voluntarily. Either way, the process of transporting trafficked children is difficult, dirty, and dangerous.[15]

F. Children move when unsafe environments emerge

Unsafe environments that displace children include natural calamities such as floods/flash floods, drought, tsunamis, earthquakes, hurricanes, among others. These are conditions that are way beyond human control, and children suffer the most. Global aid could make their life safer, but in many cases, help is delayed by challenging circumstances, including human-made disasters like greed and corruption. Human-made calamities render children the most vulnerable. Other forms include abuse, exploitation, oppression, persecution, political and religious conflicts, to mention but a few. Robert Beckhusen reports that children, as young as eleven years of age, are recruited as soldiers trained to carry out murderous acts for drug cartels in Mexico. Many of them are in the mix of school dropouts, street gang members, and unskilled workers.[16] Besides child soldiers, there are also children trafficked in organ trade, slavery, and prostitution.[17]

Based on the above contexts of children mobility, the UN emphasizes the need of some form of protection for people who have become victims of human-made calamities including those victimized by severe socio-economic deprivation, lack of food, water, education, health care, and a livelihood.[18] Other related organizations seeking to protect and ensure the best interests of children worldwide include the UNHCR (The UN Refugee Agency), UNICEF (The UN Children's Fund), ICRC (The International Committee of the Red Cross), International Save the Children Alliance, Terre des Hommes, World Vision International, Action for the Rights of Children, and the Committee on the Rights of a Child.[19]

---

14 http://www.unodc.org/unodc/en/human-trafficking/global-report-on-trafficking-in-persons.html; Tira 2013, 39.

15 Forsyth, 2011.

16 "How Mexico's Drug Cartels Recruit Child Soldiers as Young as 11," 03.28.13, 6:30 AM, http://www.wired.com/2013/03/mexico-child-soldiers/; International Crisis Group: The International Conflict Prevention Organisation, http://crisisgroup.tumblr.com/post/46597828127/how-mexicos-drug-cartels-recruit-child-soldiers.

17 UN.GIFT.HUB "Global Initiative to Fight Human Trafficking." http://www.ungift.org/knowledgehub/en/about/trafficking-for-organ-trade.html/.

18 http://www.kidsdata.org/topic; http://www.un.org/en/globalissues/briefing papers/refugees/nextsteps.html.

19 http://www.unhcr.org/pages/49c3646c1f4.html.

Biblical framework

Biblical models of diaspora children are evident in both Old and New Testaments. 2 Kings 5:2 speaks of Syrians taking away a "little maid" (*AMP*) from Israel who was transported to become a slave to Naaman's wife. Genesis 37:27-28 presents the success story of a "boy" (*AMP*, v. 30) named Joseph who was sold by his brothers to Midianite and Ishmaelite merchants, who then transported him to Egypt where he initially served as a slave and later a master.

In the New Testament the model of Christ coming to earth as a child in order to fulfill God's redemption plan should challenge Great Commission churches and missions organizations to prioritize disciple making among children (Matt. 1:23, 2:11; Luke 2). It is tragic that children are probably the most neglected people group in many churches – an ironic reality to what churches and missions organizations do in foreign lands outside their localities/countries where they assist abused, exploited, oppressed, underprivileged, and victimized children.

A series of interviews conducted by Ministry Today reveals that many pastors prioritize the care of adults more than children. The report also indicates that these pastors consider children's ministry as something to endure rather than a ministry to enjoy.[20] Two notable organizations that focus on developing a biblical framework for outreach and discipleship among children and youth, including those in diaspora, are the 4/14 Window Movement and Child Evangelism Fellowship. The 4/14 Window Movement launched a Global Initiative that would raise up a new generation from the 4/14 Window to transform the world.[21] The Child Evangelism Fellowship presents ministry models that cater to the holistic needs of children worldwide.[22] To put all this in perspective, John Piper emphasizes the inclusive nature of Matthew 28:19, "Make disciples of *panta ta ethne*" includes "all nations/Gentiles."[23] This biblical worldview impacts the scope of disciple making – all ages, all races, all cultures, all humankind.

Ministry to children is not a waste of time and resources. Every diaspora child, rich or poor, is a precious soul that needs guidance through formative stages of life.[24] Transnational children need godly adults who could help them develop wholesome concepts of themselves as they struggle with the question, "Am I a good person, a not so good person, a bad person?"[25]

---

20 Barna, George. "America's Primary Mission Field." *Ministry Today.* (12/31/2007) http://ministrytodaymag.com/life/children/16473-americas-primary-mission-field/.

21 4 to 14 Window Movement. http://www.4to14window.com/#414-eng/.

22 Child Evangelism Fellowship, Good News Clubs, Military Children's Ministries. http://www.cefonline.com/-military-ministries/.

23 http://www.desiringgod.org/articles/unreached-peoples#panta.

24 Dobson 1995, 7-21.

25 Coles 1997, 3.

The formative stage of children is the best season wherein they learn and develop the skill of judging between right and wrong. It is the crucial stage when the positive and negative view of individual significance is established.[26] James Dobson asserts that children go through the heady confidence years wherein they honestly think that they hold the power to become the center of the universe. But those years give way to self-doubt and insecurity.[27] This observation is a strong reminder that shaping perspectives and directing the power and potential in children is the task at hand, diaspora children included.

Issues, challenges, and missional opportunities

Each event of a child uprooted from a valued life foundation poses uncertainty and sense of instability. This experience threatens a child's sense of identity and security just by leaving the familiar behind. Even if the familiar represents less potential than the unknown, a child may experience fear and paralyzing concepts of what will be. Among the prevalent issues and challenges diaspora children wrestle with are identity crisis, culture shock, integration into host culture, integration of cultural heritage into adoptive culture, social graces, and gender roles in family and society.

Joan left her original home for the first time in the middle of her fourth grade due to her father's job relocation. Moving to a foreign country, halfway across the globe was hard enough, but relocating in the middle of the school year made it even worse due to English language deficiency.

Back home her life was comfortable because she was surrounded by nurturing relatives, teachers, and friends. She also lived in a wholesome home environment. To her, there was no reason to move away from it all.

When Joan's family arrived in her new home overseas, everything seemed to fall into place, except the details that were related to her studies. Her first day of school was very exhausting because she felt completely lost compared to her new classmates. Each passing day became longer and longer. It was hard for Joan to figure out why she was even there and who she had become.

On the third week, Joan became ill. Her parents could not figure out the cause of her physical ailment that persisted even after seeing a doctor. Fortunately, someone who understands the plight of diaspora children assisted Joan in connecting the dots between her sickness and its symptoms. This person discovered that the prolonged sickness was due to exhaustion caused by the long distance flight, time difference,

26 Cecilia Casiño, "Children on the Move: Missional Challenges and Opportunities, COMHINA, Miami Florida, Nov. 2-5, 2011.

27 Dobson 1995, 53-54.

homesickness, emotional turmoil due to challenges and threats of the unfamiliar, and nervousness and fear of the unknown.

Many diaspora children share Joan's issues and challenges, whether they come from impoverished or affluent contexts. Each circumstance could be different depending on the place from which a child is uprooted, the destination and its dynamics, and the process of uprooting, but there is a general feeling of displacement and/or misplacement among them all. Joan was fortunate to enroll in a school that taught and exemplified a biblical worldview. It did not take very long before she could overcome her inward and outward issues. She spent a short time surviving but a much longer time thriving.

Diaspora children who come from impoverished situations that are pushed into slavery, prostitution, and forced labor face unimaginable challenges and difficulties that even adult minds could hardly process. Refugee children as the case in point have extremely limited choices. They persistently seek to go to countries that are ready to welcome and protect them. Yet, a very small percentage of refugees around the world is given a chance to leave refugee camps.[28]

Millions of diaspora children are damaged physically, emotionally, mentally, and spiritually. They experience enormous amounts of crisis and pain on a daily basis – most of it could be eased through proper protection, provision, and guidance.[29]

Turning deaf ears and cold hearts to the rapidly growing number of diaspora children within, near, and beyond our geographic borders has come to a point of near impossibility. They now live among us! They are likened to seedlings ready to be transplanted or replanted in new growth environments. The urgent task at hand is what J. D. Payne calls "R.E.P.S. – Reach, Equip, Partner, and Send."[30]

Great Commission churches and missions organizations are currently confronted with the task to take action, not just receive the challenge, in rescuing and equipping diaspora children in our neighborhoods and mission fields. Whatever background, culture, educational level, family structure, gender, race, and religion diaspora children represent, they pose themselves before us in dire need of assistance, guidance, protection, and opportunity to grow and become well-versed in transition and coping skills as well as academic, emotional, practical, and spiritual skills.[31]

Churches and missions groups should not lose sight of the discipleship aspect of their humanitarian effort. Utilizing both aspects of the task could ensure the empowering of diaspora children for future leadership, reduce

---

28 http://globalfrontiermissions.org/refugee-work/.

29 Find strategies in meeting needs of diaspora children in [+] GFM: Until All Have Heard, "Refugee Work," (http://globalfrontiermissions.org/refugee-work/).

30 Payne 2012, 139.

31 Raising Children in the Diaspora: Suggestions. http://www.angelfire.com/ar/arawelo/essays.html.

the likelihood of them becoming liabilities to society by coaching them to become law-abiding citizens of their adoptive countries, and lastly, to enable them to give back to social structures and kingdom building missions.[32] The Network of International Schools (NICS) with twenty-one K-12 schools in seventeen countries, as of 2015, model an effective way of training, equipping, and discipling diaspora children for life.[33]

Upholding a welcoming and wisdom-based spirit and setting aside discrimination, prejudices, personal preferences, legalism, and resistance to change could lead to far-reaching results. Ted Ward testifies to how he developed the "can do" attitude that enabled him to walk, sometimes run, hopefully and victoriously through challenging times. He asserts that through it all, God was ahead of him preparing the way and building bridges – those he sought to find that he might be able to connect with his future. In the same manner, diaspora children need adults to instill the "can do by God's grace" attitude in their young lives that they may be strongly connected with their life on earth now and their life beyond.[34] When diaspora children reach this point, their success stories and testimonies could significantly impact the lives of their parents, relatives, friends, and communities.

Diaspora children have authentic experiences of being away from their original home and loved ones. Most of them have been thrown into the mill of cultural diversity, peculiarity, pluralism, rejection, self-sacrifice, scrutiny, and discrimination, among others. There might have been instances when they ended up objects of personal interests serving as showcases. As such, diaspora children who display tenacity by coming out whole from the rough mill of life could serve as great candidates for leadership and ministry functions that could serve both of their worlds – the one they had to leave behind earlier in life and their adoptive nations respectively – then transcend those borders.

The illustration below shows the potential scope of influence a diaspora child could achieve if provided with a proper environment for growth and equipping in biblical worldview and academic/skills training.[35]

Conclusion

Ministry to children on the move is a crucial task. Considering the number of children that comprise global migration implies potential and

32 Harkavy 2007, 33-49.

33 http://www.nics.org/news/.

34 Elmer and McKinney 1996, 7-26.

35 Visit http://www.nics.org/ for a model of reaching diaspora children in academic contexts; For an example of assisting diaspora children visit the Consulate General of India, Houston at http://www.cgihouston.org/news/display/58; See Coleman, 1977, 15-29; 103-112 for theological principles that children's ministers need to examine in order for them to help kids keep their faith beyond their teens).

power in developing future leadership, cultural and social structures, and a more diverse and transcending work force. This is an unprecedented opportunity the Church must seize and engage in intentional ministry among Diaspora children.

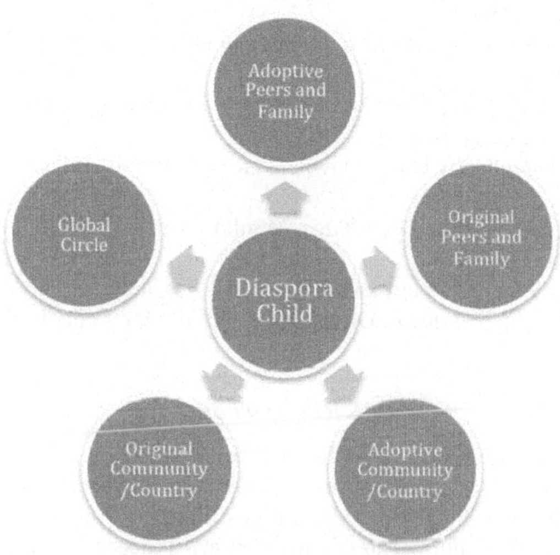

Figure 1: A Diaspora Child's Potential Scope of Influence

For discussion

1. Discuss the positive dimensions that "Children in Diaspora" have in developing into global citizens.
2. What are the involuntary ways children move? Discuss the consequences.
3. Evaluate biblically the implications of the statement, "these pastors consider children's ministry as something to endure rather than a ministry to enjoy."
4. What are the nationalities of Diaspora children within a half-mile radius of your church or home that you can identify and pray for? How can you mobilize agencies, churches, and organizations to practically meet their various needs?

Bibliography

Books

Coleman, Robert E. ed. *Evangelism on the Cutting Edge*. Old Tappan, New Jersey: Fleming H. Revell Company, 1986.

Coles, Robert. *The Moral Intelligence of Children*. New York: Random House, Inc., 1997.

Dobson, James. *Life on the Edge*. Carol Stream, Illinois: Tyndale House Publishers, 2007.

Elmer, Duane and Lois McKinney, eds. *With an Eye on the Future*. Monrovia, California, MARC Publications, 1996. Ward, Ted. "With an Eye on the Future," In Elmer and McKinney.

Gamez, Ana M. *Blessing OFWs to Bless the Nations*. Makati City, Philippines: Church Strengthening Ministry, Inc. 2012.

Harkavy, Daniel with Steve Halliday. *Becoming a Coaching Leader*. Nashville, Tennessee: Thomas Nelson, Inc., 2007.

Payne, J. D. *Strangers Next Door*. Downers Grove, Illinois: InterVarsity Press, 2012.

Tira, Sadiri Joy. *The Human Tidal Wave*. Manila, Philippines: LifeChange Publishing, Inc. 2013.

Walton, John H., Victor H. Matthews, and Mark W. Chavalas. *Bible Background Commentary: Old Testament*. Downers Grove, IL: InterVarsity Press, 2000.

URL Sources

[+] GFM: Until All Have Heard, "Refugee Work," <http://globalfrontiermissions.org/refugee-work/> accessed October 28, 2014.

4/14 Window Movement. "They are the Largest People Group to Reach" <http://www.4to14window.com/about/overview/> accessed July 15, 2014.

Child Evangelism Fellowship. <http://www.cefonline.com/index.php?option =com_content&view=section&id=4&Itemid=100048> accessed July 16, 2014.

Children of All Nations. <http://childrenofallnations.com/student-ambassador-exchange/?gclid=CKmDmeLIlsgCFdePHwodE6ME6g> accessed October 22, 2015.

Consulate General of India, Houston. <http://www.cgihouston.org/news/display/ 58> accessed July 14-15, 2014.

George Barna, "America's Primary Mission Field" <http://ministrytodaymag.com/ index.php/ministry-life/children/16473-americas-primary-mission-field> accessed July 15, 2014.

Intercountry Adoption. Bureau of Consular Affairs, U.S. Department of State. <http://travel.state.gov/content/dam/aa/pdfs/fy2014_annual_report.pdf> accessed October 22, 2015.

International Labour Organization. <http://www.ilo.org/global/standards/subjects-covered-by-international-labour-standards/migrant-workers/lang--en/index.htm> accessed July 14-15, 2014.

International Society of Missionary Kids (ISMK), "Boarding Schools," <http://ismk.org/mk-parents/schooling/boarding-schools.html> accessed October 28, 2014.

John Piper. Unreached Peoples: The Unique and Primary Goal of Missions. <http://www.desiringgod.org/articles/unreached-peoples#panta> accessed July 15, 2014.

Kevin Quinn. "Foreign Invasion: International Athletes Taking Over American Games" in Marist News Watch. <http://www.academic.marist.edu/mwwatch/spring03/articles/Sports/sports4.htm l> accessed October 28, 2014.

KIDSDATA.ORG. A Program of Lucille Packard Foundation for Children's Health. <http://www.kidsdata.org/topic> accessed July 16, 2014.

Kristiano Ang and Yenni Kwok, "Elite Boarding Schools Spreading through Asia," December 23, 2012, <http://www.nytimes.com/2012/12/24/world/asia/elite-boarding-schools-spreading-through-asia.html?pagewanted=all&_r=0> accessed October 28, 2014.

Luc Forsyth. "3D Jobs: Dirty, Demeaning, and Dangerous" <http://lucforsyth.com/2011/12/3d-jobs/> accessed August 13, 2014.

"Making Progress Against Child Labor," <http://www.ilo.org/ipec/Informationresources/WCMS_221513/lang--en/index.htm> accessed October 28, 2014.

Marck Banschick. "The High Failure Rate of Second and Third Marriages" in Psychology Today <http://www.psychologytoday.com/blog/the-intelligent-divorce/201202/the-high-failure-rate-second-and-third-marriages> accessed August 13, 2014.

Melissa Steffan. "The Surprising Countries Most Missionaries Are Sent From and Go To." Posted 7/25/2013 12:36PM <http://www.christianitytoday.com/gleanings/2013/july/missionaries-countries-sent-received-csgc-gordon-conwell.html?paging=off> accessed October 28, 2014.

Network of International Schools. <http://www.nics.org/news/>accessed October 22, 2015.

P.A.P. Blog // Human Rights, etc. <http://filipspagnoli.wordpress.com/stats-on-human-rights/statistics-on-xenophobia-immigration-and asylum/statistics-on-migration/> accessed July 15, 2014.

PAX Academic Exchange. <http://pax.org/families?gclid=CPm3v5HJ1sgCFVMYHwod5NkDNw> accessed October 22, 2015.

Pew Research: Social and Demographic Trends, <http://www.pewsocialtrends.org/2013/12/17/changing-patterns-of-global-migration-and-remittances/> accessed July 15, 2014.

Raising Children in the Diaspora: Suggestions. <http://www.angelfire.com/ar/arawelo/essays.html> accessed October 28, 2014.

Robert Beckhusen, "How Mexico's Drug Cartels Recruit Child Soldiers as Young as 11," 03.28.13, 6:30 AM, http://www.wired.com/2013/03/mexico-child-soldiers/ accessed October 28, 2014.

Ron L. Deal. http://www.smartstepfamilies.com/view/about-smart-stepfamilies accessed July 9-15, 2014.

The Combined Ministries of Nova Shalom Marriage Ministries International and University of the Family and 2=1 Discover the Power. <http://www.2equal1.com/advice/facts-stats-about-blended-families/> accessed July 11-15, 2014.

The International Crisis Group: The International Conflict Prevention Organisation, <http://crisisgroup.tumblr.com/post/46597828127/how-mexicos-drug-cartels-recruit-child-soldiers> accessed October 28, 2014.

The UN Department of Economic and Social Affairs. Population Division: International Migration. <http://esa.un.org/unmigration/wallchart2013.htm> accessed July 15, 2014.

United Nations Office on Drugs and Crime. <http://www.unodc.org/unodc/en/human-trafficking/global-report-on-trafficking-in-persons.html> accessed July 15, 2014.

UN.GIFT.HUB, Global Initiative to Fight Human Trafficking, <http://www.ungift.org/knowledgehub/en/about/trafficking-for-organ-trade.html> accessed October 28, 2014.

UN: Resources for Speakers on Global Issues. <http://www.un.org/en/globalissues/briefingpapers/refugees/nextsteps.html> accessed July 15, 2014.

UNCHR. <http://www.unhcr.org/pages/49c3646c1f4.html> accessed October 22, 2015.

U. S. Department of State. Office of the Historian. <https://history.state.gov/countries/archives> accessed October 28, 2014.

Winning Step Families: Helping Blended Families Succeed. <http://www.winningstepfamilies.com/BlendedFamilyStatistics.html> accessed July 11-15, 2014.

17. Technology and Diaspora

Joseph Vijayam

Introduction

Information and Communications Technology, or ICT, has become one of the most powerful tools responsible for facilitating the experiences, relationships, livelihoods, social engagements and religious affinities of migrant peoples around the globe. New media is the socio-cultural environment which the diaspora everywhere have embraced in their new adopted country. They seem more comfortable within its virtual boundaries than the physical socio-cultural reality of their host country. Ubiquitous, low cost Internet and mobile phone based communication has created a new era in human relationships wherein "connectedness" within a community is no longer measured by physical distance, but by the level of online activity. Immigration (*and the diaspora as its direct consequence*) is deeply transformed by this change according to some scholars, who even speak of the new figure of the "connected"[1] or "interconnected"[2] migrant.

Technology is used by diaspora in far greater proportion than "native" populations. A recent study done in the United States shows that immigrants have greater familiarity and usage of mobile and internet technologies than the average American.[3] A similar study in the United Kingdom showed a higher rate of adoption and use of Internet and communication technologies by immigrants and ethnic minorities compared to the U.K. population as a whole.[4] Technology is used in different ways by diaspora populations in different economic classes, occupations, geographies, and cultural contexts. A deeper understanding of

---

1 Diminescu, Dana "The connected migrant: an epistemological manifesto," *Social Science Information* 47, no. 4 (2008): 565-79.

2 Ros, Adela "Interconnected immigrants in the information society" in *Digital Diasporas*, ed. Andoni Alonso and Pedro Oiarzabal (Reno: University of Nevada Press, 2008), 19-38.

3 Welcoming Center for New Pennsylvanians, Digital Diaspora: How immigrants are capitalizing on today's technology (Philadelphia: 2012). Available from http://www.immigrationresearch-info.org/report/other/digital-diaspora-how-immigrants-are-capitalizing-todays-technology. Accessed February 14, 2015.

4 Kluzer, Stefano and Codagnone, Cristiano, "ICT adoption by immigrants and ethnic minorities in Europe: Overview of quantitative evidence and discussion of drivers," *Migration, Diaspora and Information Technology in Global Societies*, ed. Leopoldina Fortunati, Raul Pertierra and Jane Vincent (New York: Routledge, Taylor and Francis Group, 2012), 191.

the ways in which technology is used and consumed by diaspora peoples helps us to use this tool in ways that extend our friendship and ultimately enable us to introduce them to Jesus.

While new immigrants are found to be receptive to the Gospel, and the Internet is increasingly used for evangelism and discipleship across all populations, bringing the two together the diaspora as a target group and technology as an evangelism tool is an effective combination.

Technology is an indispensable means of interaction for the Diaspora

> Yesterday the motto was: immigrate and cut your roots; today it would be: circulate and keep in touch.[5] Dana Diminescu

Every form of new media, whether it is mass media such as television, radio, and the World Wide Web or personal media, such as mobile phones, email, social networking, and instant messaging all are integral to the daily experience of migrants around the globe. Most of these digital media tools are available at very low cost to no cost. They are available round the clock. They are available on demand. They are available almost everywhere – both in the host land and in most home lands. Even though they are living away from home, migrants are far less separated from those they have left behind in their countries of origin and are in deeper relationships with people belonging to their own ethnic minority in their host country.

This constant use of media has prompted sociologists to refer to the current generation of migrants as "mediatized migrants" who live media-saturated lives.[6] It is no longer a single form of media, but the mishmash of a smorgasbord of mass media and personal communicative media, that is affecting the what, where, why, and how a person lives in his or her host country.

Young people everywhere who are in their twenties are often referred to as the first generation of "digital natives." Those born in 1990s and later have grown up with the Internet being a part and parcel of their communication and information gathering channels. It is therefore, no surprise that younger migrants are able to more easily pick up and move to another country. They are also the most likely to feel less isolated than people of earlier generations when they migrate. According to the United Nations Information Services, there were 232 Million international

---

5 Diminescu, 568.

6 Krotz, Friedrich "Mediatization: A concept with which to grasp media and societal change" in *Mediatization: Concept, changes, consequences*, ed Knut Lundby (New York: Peter Lang, 2009), 19-38.

migrants living abroad worldwide in September 2013. [7]A large number of them are youth. According to the United Nations Department of Economic and Social Affairs and Population Division, 2 out of every 5 newly arriving migrants are aged 18-29, accounting for 26 to 57 percent of international migrants.[8]

The reasons for migration are often related to education, employment, marriage or family reunification and humanitarian. All these factors for migration apply in greater proportion to young adults and explain why younger people are more on the move. At the same time, we cannot deny the fact that new media has played a role in easing the burden and stress of moving to a foreign land thereby facilitating greater levels of migration among that age group. Therefore, starting with the very act of moving from one country to another and culminating in structuring the daily schedule of an immigrant, technology is the game-changer.

Technology serves the Diaspora peoples in multiple ways

There are multiple ways in which technology is used by diaspora peoples. The key thing to remember is that technology is a tool used at the discretion and initiation of the migrant and in that sense it puts him or her in the driver's seat. Hence, it is an empowering tool in the hands of the migrant. The most common ways in which it is used are as follows: (1) to facilitate migration, (2) for communication and connection with the homeland, (3) to coalesce homogenous communities of immigrants in their host country, (4) as a forum for exchange of ideas, beliefs, plans, and dreams, (5) as a bulletin board for jobs, educational opportunities, residential facilities, community events, dating, marriage alliances, etc., (6) to foster collective action, (7) to facilitate financial transactions across borders through online remittances, trading and exchange of goods and services.

To facilitate migration

Migration happens through networks of people. Charles Tilly, described as the founding father of 21st century sociology, states that "the effective units of migration were and are neither individuals nor households but sets of

---

7 United Nations Information Service, "232 Million International Migrants Living Abroad Worldwide – New UN Global Migration Statistics Reveal." (Vienna: UNIS, 2013). Available from http://www.unis.unvienna.org/unis/en/pressrels/2013/unisinf488.html. Last modified on September 11, 2013. Accessed February 14, 2015.

8 United Nations Department of Economic and Social Affairs Population Division, "International Migration in a Globalized World: The Role of Youth" Technical Paper No. 2011/1. (New York: 2011). Available from http://www.un.org/en/development/desa/population/publications/technical/index.shtml.
Accessed February 14, 2015.

people linked by acquaintance, kinship, and work experience."[9] Pioneer migrants make early connections and cause others within their circle of influence in their homeland to follow in their footsteps. People tend to migrate to places where they have contacts, often depending on those contacts for access to the new country. This pattern of chain migration becomes self-sustaining over time leading to the creation of a community of immigrants belonging to the same ethnic minority.

A fundamental assumption of the migration network approach is that a multidirectional flow of information lies at the basis of every migratory process.[10] Social media provides a means to maintain ties with family and friends at home giving a sense of belonging and connectedness to the past, while at the same time an avenue to explore and build new ties in the new country. Social network sites such as Facebook, MySpace, Youtube, Twitter, LinkedIn, etc., are built around interest groups. Hence, they are fertile soil for people to connect with other migrants, explore possibilities and build social capital with past migrants in a way that ultimately facilitates their own migration. Once a decision is reached, communication technologies such as email, VoIP, instant messaging, and mobile phones enable and expedite the process of migration.

Communication and connection with the homeland

There are over 300 million active Skype users around the world. According to a study conducted in Japan in February 2013,[11] 75% of internationally-located families use Skype to communicate with their family members abroad. More than half of these users contact their overseas families more than once a week. The primary purpose to call family members abroad is to know their situation and to make sure they are doing well. 94% of the calls made on Skype by internationally located families were free of cost (they did not use Skype's paid services).

The interesting thing about services such as Skype and Google Hangouts is that they are audio-visual and real-time. Besides these popular communication technologies, social media applications such as Facebook, Instagram, and WhatsApp are being used widely among diaspora peoples to connect with family members in their homeland by sharing experiences, photos, and videos with each other. These technologies give a sense of

---

9 Tilly, Charles "Transplanted Networks" in *Immigration Reconsidered*, ed. Virginia Yans-MacLoughlin (New York: Oxford University Press, 1990), 84.

10 Dekker, Rianne and Engbersen, Godfried "How social media transform migrant networks and facilitate migration" International Migration Institute Working Papers Series 2012, no 64 (Oxford: Oxford University Press: 2012). Available at http://www.imi.ox.ac.uk/publications/ working-papers/wp-64. Accessed February 14, 2015.

11 Available at http://www.slideshare.net/goc1126/skype-marketing-final-28623964. Last modified on November 26, 2013. Accessed February 14, 2015.

"being present" at family occasions and being involved in each other's lives with frequent updates enabling a level of engagement that was unimaginable just a decade ago.

Coalescing homogenous diaspora communities

Immigrants of all countries of origin and destination highly value connectedness with their ethnic community. This is an important factor that affects their well-being. In previous generations new connections and rekindling of weak links happened at community events such as religious, social and cultural events. It required physical presence at a certain place and at a certain time. Those who could not be there due to distance, cost, work schedules, etc. stayed isolated and thus less adjusted to their new environments.

Today, most of these connections happen through the use of technology. The Internet with all its associated technologies has made it possible for people to connect instantly from their homes and at their own pace. Social media has taken migrant networks to a new level of connectedness by creating an opportunity to build one's social capital quickly and selectively with those whom they have more in common. Weak ties can develop into strong ties through better matching of people coupled with altruistic motivations.

A forum for exchange of ideas

Cyberspace is a free for all, open and rich information source. Some would claim that the Internet is responsible for the democratization of knowledge. New immigrants seek information that is unique to their situation as newcomers, distinct from the sorts of information sought by the general population in their adopted country. The search ability of the Internet is one of its most powerful and useful attributes. Hence, the outsized valuation of Google, Yahoo, Baidu, and every other search engine. Since the advent of search engines people with niche requirements such as immigrants have found the Internet to be a treasure trove of information and ideas to share and to consume. For example, Miguel, aged 36, who migrated from Brazil to the Netherlands to work, testifies to the ease of finding needed information: "There [Orkut group – Brasileiros na Holanda] you find an exchange of information on your rights, the consulate, the language. Everything."[12]

---

12 Dekker, 12.

As a Community Bulletin Board

Similar to the previous point, but with increased specialization and focus of the Internet, there are specialized websites and web forums dedicated to educational and employment opportunities, housing, dating and even matchmaking that are targeted to specific groups of immigrants or ethnic communities.

An example of this type of a website is shaadi.com which has a section dedicated to marriage alliances for Indian immigrants living abroad, classified by region of the world even down to specific regions within a country. Such websites form an infrastructure that facilitates arranged marriages for Indians living abroad by acting as a broker between those who are seeking alliances as it is customary in their country of origin. This was an extremely difficult task prior to the launch of such sites.

To foster collective action

When a national leader travels abroad, he or she often looks to the diaspora of his nation to rally behind him or her for political mileage. Countries having sizeable populations living abroad have looked to them for financial and social support. They are seen as an influential vote bank.

Technology, especially social media has enabled diaspora peoples to engage in collective action on issues such as gender equality, education and religious freedom in their home countries. During the Arab Spring, there were thousands of people from among the Arab diaspora living in Western countries who used Facebook and Twitter to raise awareness and enlist support for the cause of the "rebels" fighting dictatorial and oppressive regimes in Arab countries.

To facilitate financial transactions

According to Mahmoud Moheildin of the World Bank, migrants from developing countries sent home around $404 billion through formal channels, with overall global remittances totaling $542 billion.[13] In some poor countries, there are entire hamlets, villages, and small towns whose economy depends solely on the remittances received from their emigrants to wealthier countries. Due to high transfer fees charged by brick and mortar banks, a number of wire transfer dotcom startups on the Internet, and mobile phone money transfer services have emerged in recent years providing competitive rates and expedient transfers. A few successful market entries in this space are TransferWise, Dwolla, TransferGo, Xoom, Azimo, etc.

---

13 Available at http://www.euractiv.com/sections/euro-finance/remittances-and-savings-diaspora-can-finance-development-303838. Last modified on January 8, 2014. Accessed February 14, 2015.

Technology is an effective tool in discipling Diaspora peoples

> "When a revelation is coming, it's like a phone. A message comes to you. The ring is right here, in my heart. Driiinnggg, driiingg. And then, I'll be stuck. Then I hear the voice talking to me. And it tells me "do this, because I want this to be done right now!" God is holy, you know, God is technology. Everything we have right here, it is God's, thanks to God's spiritual existence. When you have a good relationship with God, the frequency is very good, the signal is strong. If you are good with your prayers, the communication is good. IF you are messed up and if you are in a conflict with people, the reception is bad." – Pastor Joshua, Congolese Pentecostal pastor, Atlanta, USA.[14]

Pastor Joshua's use of a telephone connection as a means to hearing God's voice is imaginative and interesting. However, it is not theologically correct to say that God is technology. Technology ought to be explored in a godly manner for the purpose of exalting and glorifying God, i.e. the edification of God's people in Diaspora and the salvation of the lost across the street and around the world.

The ease with which relationships are built online, especially leading to conversations that can be both personal and anonymous at the same time, makes the Internet a powerful tool for one to many and one to one conversations. Whether through messages broadcasted or podcasted through digital mass media, or spiritual formation exercises through mobile applications, or personal counseling through the Internet, or prayer support through social networking, new media is an indispensable tool for evangelism, discipleship, and ministry to the diaspora.

Due to their limited social interaction with people in the host country, diaspora peoples are quick to engage with those who are willing to interact with them through new media on matters related to the soul. This presents an incredible opportunity for the Church in the host country to reach the diaspora who are seeking answers to life's questions in a new and complex situation, to equip diaspora Christians as Gospel workers among their communities in the host country, or among their families and friends when they return to their countries of origin. Internet based communication technologies such as Skype are used for sharing the Gospel and discipling family and friends in their home country. China's leading microblog company, Sina Weibo, has over 400 million users including Chinese overseas students. Some of them are new believers who are using microblogs to share their faith with their online followers, many of them back in China.[15]

---

14 Garbin, David and Vasquez, Manuel, "God is Technology, mediating the sacred in the Congolese diaspora" in *Migration, Diaspora and Information Technology in Global Societies*, ed. Leopoldina Fortunati, Raul Pertierra and Jane Vincent (New York: Routledge, Taylor and Francis Group, 2012) 157.

15 Charisma News: "Chinese Christians use Internet to share faith, discuss persecution." Available from http://www.charismanews.com/world/35109-chinese-

The familiarity and use of Internet and communication technologies among the diaspora has led to many of them becoming pioneers in the use of such technologies to share the Gospel. MahaJesus.com and JesusCentral.com are two examples of websites set up by immigrants to reach and disciple those who are more likely to browse a website than to enter a church building or go to an evangelistic event.

I am astounded by the number of posts on Facebook, Twitter, Instagram, and Pinterest sharing prayer requests, inspirational messages, and praise reports that circulate among those who are within my own extended family and friends who are immigrants in America. These posts often circle back to those who are in the home country and create a virtual support group that is walking together in a faith journey. With today's communication technology being instantaneous and historical, personal and public, words and pictures, audio and video, the quality and quantity of Christian fellowship has taken a new meaning. When I think about it, I cannot help but thank God for placing me on earth at this very moment in time.

Technology should be used in moderation

Although technology has been enthusiastically embraced by diaspora peoples almost universally, it is important to note that there are some serious negatives to this trend. While most of the drawbacks of the widespread use of technology in social interaction are common to society as a whole, there are some which are more noticeable in the case of the diaspora. Studies show that the specific use of the Internet [by the diaspora] alters their senses of love and attachment, family life and other kinds of intimate social relationships.[16] While their sense of belonging is enhanced through the use of technology, especially through social media, there is a significant loss in terms of experiencing the richness of co-present encounters. In an article titled "Diasporic communities online," Myria Georgiou stresses the significance of sharing everyday-life experiences for maintaining a sense of community.[17] This is especially true for diaspora peoples as interpersonal interaction in the physical world is necessary to enable their integration into the society of the host country. As with everything else in life, moderation in the use of technology would be prudent.

---

christians-use-internet-to-share-faith-discuss-persecution. Accessed October 25, 2015.

16 Miller, Daniel and Slater, Don. *The Internet: An Ethnographic Approach.* (Oxford: Berg Publishers, 2000) 56.

17 Georgiou, Myria. "Diasporic communities online: A bottom up experience of transnationalism" in *The Ideology of the Internet: Concepts, Policies, Uses*, ed. K. Sarkasis and D. Thussu (New York: Hampton Press, 2006), 131.

For discussion

1. Why are the diaspora more likely to use the Internet and communication technologies when compared to the native population in their host countries?
2. Give an example of a technology device or service that you have seen used by an immigrant community to increase connectedness with each other. This could be a website, a mobile app or a generic technology tool that is used by a specific immigrant community in a geographic region.
3. What is the main reason for a diaspora person to go online when seeking answers to spiritual questions?
4. How can the local church use technology to engage with the diaspora living among them?

SECTION 4: THE MISSION OF THE CHURCH IN GLOBAL DIASPORA

**Grant McClung and Cody Lorance,
Section Editors**

The Mission of the Church in Global Diaspora: An Introduction

Section Editor: Grant McClung

In our study of diaspora missiology thus far we have considered it phenomenologically, theologically and strategically – essentially examining what is happening in our day in terms of the ever-accelerating movement of peoples from everywhere to everywhere, reflecting upon these realities through the lens of Scripture and then beginning to consider the implications of these things for mission in our day. All this has led us inescapably to the most practical and most spiritual of all missiological questions – "So what?" What do we, the Body of Christ living for and serving the Triune God in the 21st century, do in response to all this? What is the mission of the Church and what is the mission of churches in the context of massive human migration, rapid urbanization and overwhelming forces of globalization? What do we do now?

In this section, we make no claims to exhaustively answer this supremely important question. Indeed we hope that the chapters which follow will provoke and inspire 10,000 new questions, articles, conversations, and books which will join our humble effort to understand and articulate the mission of the Church in the midst of a world in constant motion. We have ventured the beginning of an answer, however, and in doing so have come to believe that two principles must be laid down as essential groundwork for properly understanding all that follows.

First, we must insist that whatever the mission of the Church is in today's diasporic world, it is certainly a mission for both the diaspora churches (churches started by and/or consisting primarily of migrants) and the churches of the host nation (churches started by and/or consisting primarily of non-migrants). Certain of our authors may emphasize one of these categories over the other, but there are implications for both types of church in all of the following chapters.

Secondly, any discussion of the mission of the Church cannot avoid the obvious and imperative ecclesiological questions of the nature, purpose, practice, membership and structures of the Church. We have taken this section to be equally about missiology and ecclesiology and have encouraged our authors to reflect on how diaspora realities impact our understanding of the Church. Migration, urbanization and globalization have changed the face of world, have transformed geo-political boundaries, have turned cities upside-down and have created innumerable new ethno-cultural hybrid identities among people groups. Should we really be surprised if these forces also expand and even begin to break down the borders of our ecclesiology? We proceed from this foundation then with seven chapters which each take their turn dealing with our central question. We will begin at the beginning by rooting any contemplation of the role of churches in diaspora mission in a spirituality modeled after the incarnation and crucifixion of the Lord Jesus – recognizing that the Church on mission in a diaspora age must stay connected to its head, the Migrant Savior (Adhikari, Lorance, Rajendran). From there we must consider the Church on mission from multiple angles. We will see the challenges of the African-American church as a marginalized community playing host to diasporas in their neighborhoods and ponder the unique potential such churches have for mission from the periphery (Mack-Lacey). Two chapters will then present two very different diaspora communities – namely Koreans (Im, Oh) and Africans (Asamoah-Gyadu) – as agents of mission and spiritual renewal in their new places of residence. These diaspora churches indeed have limitations and struggles but nevertheless stand as hopeful signs of how the Lord is now mobilizing majority world peoples to advance the Kingdom of God in all the world. Another chapter will reflect on themes of churches as surrogate families for people on the move recognizing that filial transnationalism is a reality that the people of God must understand and respond to in order to fulfill their mission in a migratory world (George). Taking this to another level, we consider in our sixth chapter that the phenomena of diaspora has presented churches with unprecedented opportunities to pursue, embrace and showcase the beauty of intercultural unity in the family of God (Baker, Im, Thomas). Finally, we close our section by acknowledging and anticipating the rise of global cities and considering the role of the Church as an eschatological community with a mission to shape the souls of these increasingly diverse and rapidly growing urban centers (Ko).

Of course, this will only temporarily satisfy us in our quest to answer the "so what?" question with which we began. So many other considerations come to mind. We have heard stories of transitional, Christ-centered communities established by and for trafficked women who live, work and worship together. Another testimony has come to us from the outskirts of a global city in the Arabian Peninsula where exploited migrant laborers from South Asia come and go to a makeshift building at the base of a mountain to receive prayer and to hear the Gospel. Miraculous signs and wonders have been reported and many Hindus and Muslims have come for a few days, given their lives to Christ, and then moved on to the next stop in their diasporic journeys. Such transient communities of faith surely bear a striking resemblance to "church" but nevertheless stretch the bonds of our typical ecclesiological traditions and force us to reimagine our approach to mission. We can reference many other cases in addition to those mentioned here, but it is enough for now simply to underline the fact that so much more research and reflection must be done. We encourage everyone who studies these pages to diligently work to expand on our efforts.

Having thus acknowledged the limits of our work on this subject, we nevertheless may conclude the following. The mission of the Church in an age of diaspora is a mission that will be played out mostly in the cities and primarily by diaspora and host nation churches who are comfortable operating at or from the margins of society. Diaspora mission will moreover be conducted mainly by the people of God as they embrace intercultural unity and as they understand themselves as family for one another and for non-Christians. Above all, we may conclude that the mission of the Church in global diaspora is a mission that flows out of our communion with and imitation of the Migrant Savior, Jesus Christ. We eagerly commend to you the following chapters and encourage you to prayerfully and carefully reflect on the implications of each for your own church family and mission context.

18. A Cross for the Scattered: Cruciform Spirituality for the Church on Mission among Diasporas

Lachi Adhikari, Cody Lorance and P. Rajendran

Scenes from the scattered[1]

> And he made from one man every nation of mankind to live on all the face of the earth, having determined allotted periods and the boundaries of their dwelling place, that they should seek God, and perhaps feel their way toward him and find him. (Acts 17:26-27a ESV)

Scene 1: from militant to missionary by way of Mae La

Wa Soe[2] was born in *Kawthoolei*, "the land without evil," better known as Burma or Myanmar by non-Karen S'gaw speakers. From a Buddhist monastic background, he found Christ as a youth and grew to be a natural leader in his village. Life took a drastic turn after Wa Soe participated in the pro-democracy protests of 1988. The violent reaction of the Burmese government meant fleeing his home, family, and everything he had ever known. After years of hiding in the jungles, struggling to survive, a gun his constant companion, Wa Soe made his way to the safety of a refugee camp in Thailand.

He wasn't content, however, to idle away life in a makeshift hut living on rations and imbibing hopelessness. Wa Soe's heart went out to his fellow Karen. He knew many still hiding in the jungles, lacking food and medicine and unable to safely cross over into Thailand. Wa Soe began to make risky excursions back across the border to deliver these needed items. By this time, he had become something of a warrior survivalist – a rugged militant who knew how to navigate the sweltering jungles, how to avoid

---

1 The following narratives are drawn from experiences of the authors on the mission field. They depict actual events and persons and form part of the history of one small diaspora-focused, church-based ministry called Trinity International Baptist Mission (Trinity International). The authors are most intimately familiar with this particular ministry due to their direct involvement, but recommend close examination of many other very remarkable ministries around the world which provide excellent models of the church on mission among diasporas. In particular, we would like to mention Withee Mission International (South Korea, http://withee.org), Calvary Charismatic Baptist Church (United Kingdom, http://www.ccbc.org.uk), and MoveIn (Canada, http://movein.to). For more information about Trinity International Baptist Ministry, visit http://tibm.org.

2 A pseudonym.

military patrols, and how to use his gun if he didn't. Soon it seemed that medicine and food wasn't enough to truly satisfy his scattered kinsmen. They were asking him to pray, read Scripture, lead hymns and even preach. Having long prayed for the end of violence in Burma, Wa Soe began to realize that it was peace with God that people most desperately needed. Wa Soe put away his gun and took up the cross, convinced that God had called him to serve the Kingdom of Christ.

Wa Soe began studying in his refugee camp at Kawthoolei Karen Baptist Bible School and College, self-described as "a theological institution displaced" (Brief history 2010), and soon was enjoying a vibrant ministry in the camps. Wa Soe became an evangelist, a chaplain, a pastor, and a Bible school teacher. Strangely, he felt himself settling into a rhythm of life that was joyful, fruitful, peaceful – even, in a sense, comfortable. In 2007, however, the resettlement of refugees from the Mae La camp to Western nations began. Initially unwilling to leave his ministry, Wa Soe became convinced of God's calling when a group of diaspora Korean missionaries teaching at the Bible college laid their hands on him, prayed, and commissioned him to go to the United States to preach the gospel and there to plant churches among his fellow Karen refugees.

The Trinity International Baptist Mission (hereafter: Trinity International) team met Wa Soe and his family on the first day they arrived at their new overpriced and under-maintained apartment in the Chicago suburbs. A small house church made up of diaspora-focused missionaries and lay people, Trinity International's team found themselves that day busy carrying household goods and second-hand furniture into the otherwise empty apartment. Amid improvised lessons on the use of refrigerators, stoves, light switches, and toilets, they began to exchange stories with Wa Soe and his family. Soon came the realization that both groups were in Chicago for the same conscious purpose – to serve Christ by proclaiming and demonstrating His gospel among diasporas. It was long after the resulting home Bible study became a church and the church became multiple churches that Wa Soe told the leader of the Trinity International team what that first meeting had meant to his faith: mere hours after landing in a strange and frightening new land came confirmation from the Holy Spirit that God indeed had brought Wa Soe to the United States for a purpose. Wa Soe, that day, determined in his heart to live in Chicago with missional intentionality among his new neighbors of many nations.

Scene 2: a suburban Lhotshampa and a sanskritized savior

Southern Bhutan has been the homeland for thousands of ethnically Nepali "Lhotshampas" for generations. It was there, in the plains surrounding the tiny city of Galephug that Siva Pithakotey[3] grew up. He managed to finish

3 A pseudonym.

high school and marry before government-sponsored violence and oppression against Nepalis forced his family to leave their prosperous five-acre farm and flee Bhutan. Siva and thousands of other Bhutanese-Nepalis eventually made their way through India and across the Nepalese border where they settled in refugee camps established by the United Nations (Photo Voice; Bhutanese Refugee Support Group 2010).

Once in the camps, Siva's education provided him the opportunity to work as a teacher in one of the schools established for refugee children. For a decade he taught science and mathematics before finally being promoted to headmaster, a position he held until he left the camps in 2008 when the United States granted asylum to Siva, his wife, and their three adult children. Packing up whatever they could fit into a few bags, they bid family, friends, and neighbors a teary farewell and set out on their long and uncertain journey to America.

The Pithakoteys arrived in Chicago and upon moving into their apartment, Siva's three children were quickly befriended by their neighbors, a Karen family active in the church Wa Soe had started. Hungry for friendship in their strange and lonely new land, they were eager, in spite of their Hindu faith, to accept the invitation of their new friends to attend a Bible study.

That night's study was like no other. Cody Lorance, the senior pastor of Trinity International, had been co-leading the new Karen Baptist Church with Wa Soe during its first year of existence and it was Cody's turn to teach the midweek Bible study. Ordinarily, he would do this in English with Wa Soe providing translation into Karen S'gaw. However, the presence of their Bhutanese-Nepali guests required a change in strategy. It seemed that only one of them, Siva's son, could speak any English at all and that he was altogether unfamiliar with English religious terminology. Cody was forced to draw upon his limited vocabulary of Sanskrit religious terms, something he had been picking up from Trinity International's work among Indian immigrants, to "re-explain" what he was talking about to Siva's son while Wa Soe was translating for the Karen speakers. Siva's son, who like most Nepali Hindus was somewhat familiar with Sanskrit religious terminology, then translated it all into Nepali for his sisters. The result, less chaotic than it sounds, served to open the door of the gospel for the new diaspora group.

That night, Cody drove his new Bhutanese-Nepali friends back to their home and met their father. Siva would share much later that in those early days of their resettlement in Chicagoland he and his wife were willing to allow their children to follow Christ because they hoped that Jesus would be able to heal their daughter of the frequent seizures that had plagued her for so long. When she was baptized two months after that first meeting, the seizures left and Siva was encouraged to explore Christ for himself. The contextualized worship gatherings developed in partnership between Trinity International and several diaspora-focused missionaries from India made it easier for him, along with much of the rest of the local Bhutanese-Nepali community, to do just that. Eventually, Siva and his wife gave their lives to Christ. While his diaspora journey has been fraught with great difficulties and setbacks, Siva is recognized both as a diaspora church and community leader.

Scene 3: of first fruits and future harvest

Lachi Adhikari knelt on the floor of a bookstore turned *mandir*[4] in Chicago's "Little India" neighborhood and related her personal story of migration and faith to a roomful of captivated Americans. Herself, a Lhotshampa, Lachi's story had much in common with Siva's. She was born in Bhutan at the peak of the Bhutanese government's systematic persecution of her people and thus was carried away from her homeland by her parents before she was even old enough to walk. Growing up, refugee camp life was all she ever knew, spending the first two decades of her life in eastern Nepal's crowded Beldangi camp. Several years after being resettled with her family in one of the world's most international cities, Lachi now found herself struggling to help host nation Christ-followers understand the critical importance of diaspora mission.

"I am from a Brahmin[5] family and we are strict Hindus," she explained. "Growing up in the refugee camp, I would often see Christians and even foreign missionaries. But the missionaries never spent time with us. They would stay in the Christian homes and minister in the churches. In 18 years, no one ever told me about the Lord Jesus – not even once."

Indeed, Lachi's first exposure to the gospel was days after arriving in the United States. It was actually Siva's children that first invited her and her sisters to attend a contextualized Nepali worship gathering then being led by missionaries from Trinity International. The use of Sanskrit mantras, bells, incense, narrative preaching, and *bhajans*[6] were familiar and welcoming to Lachi as a high-caste Hindu, allowing her to draw near to both the message and the messenger of Christ with her heart and mind. It wasn't long before she devoted her life to the Lord Jesus, ultimately becoming a teacher, spiritual leader and missionary. Lachi's challenge to host nation churches is to cast aside fear of the unknown and discomfort with things that are culturally unfamiliar so as to draw close to the people on the move. She contends that in diaspora missions simply giving

---

4 Sk. "Holy place" or "temple."

5 Brahmins are the highest of the traditional four Hindu castes or classes. It is often described as the "priestly" caste.

6 A bhajan is a particular style of devotional singing especially common in South Asian Hindu communities. For more on this topic, read Chris Hale. "Aradhna: From Comfort to Discomfort, from Church to Temple," in *International Journal of Frontier Missiology* 24:3 (2007): 147-50. http://www.ijfm.org/PDFs_IJFM/24_3_PDFs/147-150Hale.pdf/.

charitably to migrants is not as important as mutual sharing and relational reciprocity. "When Americans are willing to stay in my house, eat my food, and listen to my story, I no longer feel that we are foreigners – we are family."

Contemplating the Lord of this harvest

The above scenes illustrate the dynamics of the Church on mission to, through and beyond diasporas. Wa Soe, Siva, Lachi and their families represent the "people on the move" – the more than 230 million individuals residing outside their country of origin (United Nations: Department of Economic and Social Affairs 2013). Their stories provide a glimpse into a 21st century world in which, like never before, people keep moving, especially to the cities and yet remain globally interconnected. The purpose of this chapter is to contemplate the Lord of *this* harvest and to draw from the example of his own migrations and sufferings implications which will effectively reshape our churches after his image and thus transform the way we engage in mission among diasporas. Above all, engagement in mission is a spiritual matter, flowing out of the corporate devotion of believers to the Triune God. It is, as Paul declared, "the love of Christ" which "urges us on" in mission (2 Cor. 5:14 NRSV) and this is no less true today as God reshuffles the nations of our diasporic world. To begin our reflection we shall introduce an important Biblical motif relevant to diaspora mission:

"The Babel Complex"[7] (Gen 11:1-9)	The centripetal tendency to resist diasporic movement (as either hosts or migrants) is akin to the prevailing attitude of those would-be builders of the "Tower of Babel" who considered their own agenda of "name-making" as primary over and against God's purpose of filling the earth with His image-bearers. God's response to the disobedience of Babel was to forcibly scatter the people – an act of judgment but also of mercy as it set humanity back on the track of obeying God's "fill the earth" command. (LCWE 2010) (Pocock, Van Rheenen and McConnell 2005) (Casiño 2011) (Jung 2010) (George 2011) (Howell 2011) (Wan 2010)

Table 1: The Babel Complex

7 The term "Babel Complex" is taken from the book Scattered to Gather: Embracing the Global Trend of Diaspora where it is simply defined as "the desire to be centripetal; never centrifugal" (LCWE 2010).

Pursuing cruciformity in Diaspora mission

"Then they said, 'Come, let us build ourselves a city and a tower with its top in the heavens, and let us make a name for ourselves, lest we be dispersed over the face of the whole earth.'" (Gen. 11:4 ESV)

Understanding the Babel complex in Diaspora mission

When God created the first humans, He gave them a commission to multiply and "fill the earth" (Gen. 1:28 ESV). His vision was that the planet would teem with the crown of His creation – His image-bearers. Even after the Fall, when sin had seemingly wrecked this vision, God re-commissioned Noah to go and "fill the earth" (Gen. 9:1 ESV). The divine plan had not been thwarted.

From the beginning, God's purpose has been missional. Through the movement of humanity into all the earth, there should be no place in which His image is not manifest. Especially under the New Covenant, this movement is particularly important as it facilitates the intermingling of God's ambassadors – Christ-followers, through whom is spread everywhere the fragrance of the knowledge of the Lord Jesus (2 Cor. 2:14) – with those who are estranged from him. Far from haphazard, this scattering is superintended by a sovereign God who determines the times and places in which people live in order to accomplish His salvific purposes (Acts 17:26-27). "Since the creation of the world, therefore, diasporas have been an indispensable means by which God accomplishes his redemptive purposes through Jesus Christ" (LCWE 2010).

Against this backdrop of diaspora as "a missional means decreed and blessed by God" (LCWE 2010) we attempt to understand the sin of Babel. It is common to view Genesis 11:1-9 as an example of God's disdain for human hubris, the quest to make a name for oneself rather than to glorify God. But this is only part of the story. On the whole, we see exhibited in the builders of Babel a conglomeration of attitudes which oppose God's diasporic missional purposes and lead humanity to rebel against His "fill the earth" command. This "Babel Complex" is marked by at least four interrelated attitudes to which we now turn:

Centripetal tendencies

First, there is displayed in the builders of Babel a marked centripetality – they do not want to "fill the earth." The underlying motivation for the construction of the tower was not to "make a name" for themselves but rather to prevent their being globally dispersed (Gen. 11:4). They fear their scattering as it would certainly bring with it a loss of safety and security, loneliness, and vulnerability (Waltke 2001).

Those who have suffered through the tragic experience of forced displacement understand this fear far better than to those who have always enjoyed freedom of residency and movement. Displacement and migration often strip individuals of their sense of belonging, power and honor. It is little wonder that refugees who are ultimately resettled into Western nations find themselves permanently unsettled in their hearts and minds – moving from apartment to apartment, job to job, and city to city struggling to lay hold of the ever elusive sense of being home.

Competing agendas and contingencies

Secondly, the people in our narrative have exchanged the surpassing value of God's diasporic missional vision for their own agenda. God wants to fill the earth with His image-bearers, but they seek security, prosperity, comfort, and a name that will be remembered for all generations. Having tasted the hardship of migration (Gen. 11:2), the builders cannot conceive of good coming from diaspora. They have seemingly lost touch with the grand metanarrative of God as creator, redeemer, and sovereign and are looking to write their own story with baked bricks.

Missional convenience

A third attitude exhibited by the builders is the nearly universal tendency towards convenience. It is a hallmark of sin to seek one's own pleasure above pleasing God (Gen. 3:6), to take the path of least-resistance instead of the hard road of obedience. For the builders their brief experience of migration was enough to tell them that it would be much easier to settle together in the fertile plain of Shinar than to scatter over all the earth. Once settled, they utilized their collective ingenuity in an attempt to secure a comfortable and prosperous existence through the technological advancements of brick-baking, city-constructing, and tower-building. Any thought of obedience to God's diasporic call was far from their minds.

Cultural clinging

A final attitude in the Babel Complex that must be considered is the urge to cling to one's own culture as superior to all others – to demand absolute assimilation and conformity and to reject diversity. The seed of this attitude is apparent in the Babel narrative among the builders who are described as "one people" with "one language" (Gen. 11:6). This uniformity was so highly prized among the people that when it was removed, they found it impossible to either live or work together. The seed planted at Babel has developed into the full-grown ethnocentrism of today which inspires all manner of fear, racism, discrimination, hatred, and genocide. This attitude dangerously obscures one's view of the multicolored wisdom of God which is manifest in people from every culture who find unity *in* diversity around the person and work of Jesus Christ and causes one to view diasporic phenomena as a threat to the cultural homogeneity that is regarded as so precious.

The Babel complex summarized

The Babel Complex continues to plague humanity today. It is the most significant obstacle to the Church's engagement in diaspora mission. The centripetal church or Christ-follower resists God's outward call to cross national borders and cultural barriers, preferring instead the safety and familiarity of home. Other believers move out diasporically but do so for education, economics, or even as refugees, all the while oblivious to God's greater redemptive purposes for migration. Still others view diaspora as merely a convenient way to engage in mission without having to sacrifice much in the way of the comforts they've grown accustomed to. Finally, there are those churches who in their practice of diaspora mission still manifest the kind of ethnocentrism that should be anathema in the body of Christ. They demand assimilation to the host society, prefer the role of benefactor to partner, and have no patience for contextualization. In the figure below, we have attempted to illustrate the four prevailing attitudes that characterize the Babel Complex:

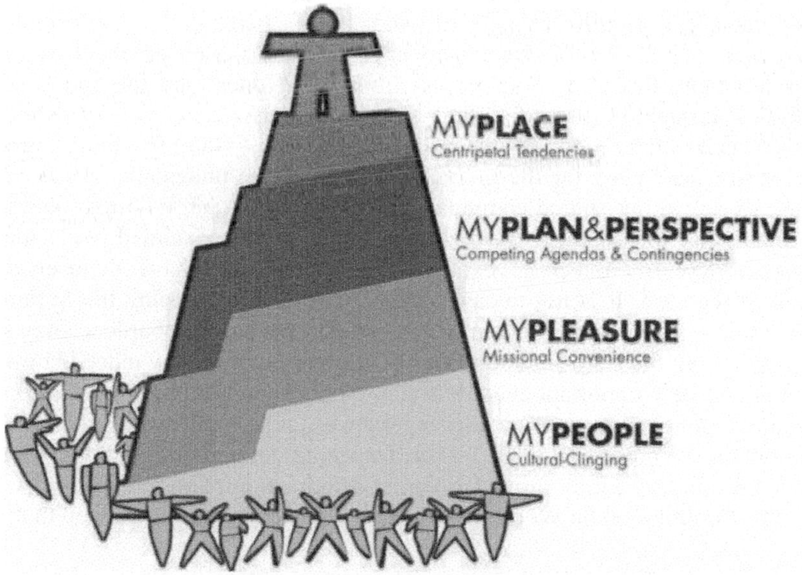

Figure 1: The Babel Complex (design by Vincent Lee)

As the above illustrates, the Babel Complex is inherently self-centered. It creates distance between gospel-bearers (whether diasporic or not) and diaspora peoples (whether Christ-followers or not) through the cultivation of attitudes which, by their nature, foster alienation. If we are to faithfully join in God's redemptive mission among diasporas, we must find a way to descend this tower, climbing down the ladder to draw near to the people on the move. This can only be accomplished as we learn to follow the "migrant God" (Jackson 2011) (Vanier 1992) who left heaven for Calvary modeling for His disciples the very attitudes that we must imitate in diaspora missions.

Understanding cruciformity in Diaspora mission

The antidote to the Babel Complex is the cross. Engagement in diaspora mission that is faithful to the mission of Jesus requires cruciformity – the imitation of Christ's incarnation and crucifixion – and thus a new kind of contemplation upon the Lord Jesus as the Migrant Savior. He is our diasporic forerunner[8] who experienced "exile, social marginalization, and… rootlessness in and through [His] incarnate life" (Jackson 2011). Sadly, this aspect of the Christ-life is almost entirely ignored by mainstream Christian thought which often emphasizes intellectual and emotional adherence to certain accepted theological positions and statements as the way to "know Jesus". We do well to remember that the migrations and sufferings of the Lord Jesus were more than mere historical facts with theological implications. These were lived experiences of Christ and remain a significant part of who he is. Perennially comfortable churches and Christ-followers who have never experienced the loss of displacement, the pain of separation from loved ones, and the agony of physical torment must confess their spiritual poverty in not understanding this crucial dimension of their Lord's identity. Humbly, they must recognize their need for the migrant who brings the undeniable riches of their stories to our shared communion table. The migrant, who may know nothing else of Jesus, nevertheless is intimately acquainted with the Migrant Savior's diasporic experiences because they have themselves walked the road. It is not to say that the Muslim child fleeing the Syrian civil war or the Hindu woman trafficked across national borders knows *enough* about the Lord Jesus but simply to point out that they indeed know something very important about him that others may not. Diaspora mission requires churches to treasure the experiences, stories and wisdom of the people on the move and to seek ever deepening communion with them so as to become more fully formed as Christ's body on mission in the world.

The Commission on World Mission and Evangelism has noted well that:

---

8 We have in mind here not only the Incarnation as ultimate migratory journey, but also the fact of Jesus living life constantly on the move from one city to the next, "having no place to lay his head," and even his experience of forced displacement as refugee in Egypt (cf. Matt 2).

> The migration of Jesus to our world was not simply a journey but a way through which God reconciles humanity with himself.... This event shapes the entire missionary activity of the Church (2010).

Moreover, Christ is the one who moved away from the security of Jerusalem and "suffered outside the gate" (Hebrews 13:12 ESV). Churches are called to acknowledge that like Him "here we have no lasting city" and to "go to him outside the camp and bear the reproach he endured" (Heb. 13:14, 13 ESV). The *Carmen Christi* may be well-applied as a model for diaspora mission:

> Have this mind among yourselves, which is yours in Christ Jesus, who, though he was in the form of God, did not count equality with God a thing to be grasped, but emptied himself by taking the form of a servant, being born in the likeness of men. And being found in human form, he humbled himself by becoming obedient to the point of death, even death on a cross. (Phil. 2:5-8 ESV)

Here is Christ submitting to the centrifugal movement of God the Father by leaving heaven. He enters the world with the Father's plan of redemption his only aim. Forsaking self-gratification and ease, Jesus takes the form of a servant and is obedient to the Father's call even to the point of death. And far from clinging onto his glorified pre-incarnate state, he empties Himself and becomes a man – fully contextualized to those he is called to serve.

As the Babel Complex consists of four interrelated attitudes of self-interest, so cruciformity in diaspora mission requires a departure from each of these. We are to be, as it were, dispersed from Babel with crosses borne pursuing the Migrant Savior that goes before us among the scattered. This cruciform dispersion consists of four movements which we have illustrated below;

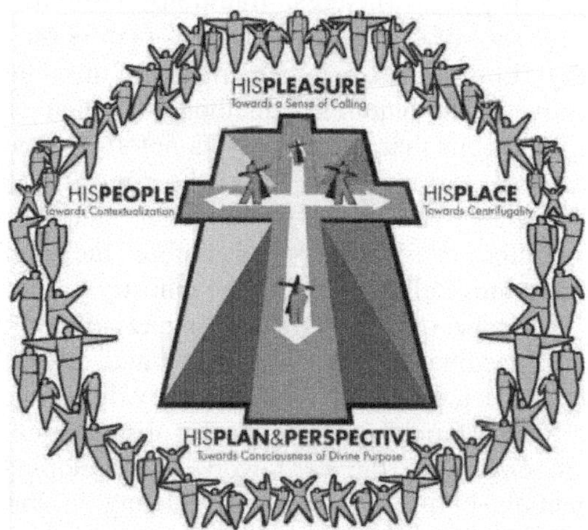

Figure 2: Cruciformity in Diaspora Mission (design by Vincent Lee)

We must turn our attention now to an elaboration upon these four movements. In so doing, we will begin to see how churches may leave Babel for Calvary in our mission among diasporas.

First movement: From my place to his place
Moving from centripetal tendencies to embraced centrifugality

When Wa Soe was offered the opportunity to move his family to the United States, his natural instinct was to stay put in the Mae La refugee camp. There in his adopted home of Thailand he had forged a life that was reasonably comfortable and predictable as well as a fruitful ministry. It took the fervent prayers and wise counsel of diasporic Korean missionaries to overcome his centripetal tendencies and convince Wa Soe to embrace the centrifugal leading of the Holy Spirit.

We have already seen that God is behind the global movement of humanity – orchestrating it for the sake of mission. We are "called to embrace and even to engage" this centrifugal, diasporic movement (Pocock, Van Rheenen and McConnell 2005) and to "move along with God" (Wan 2010). Our natural inclination, however, is centripetal. We see this in Wa Soe's former mindset, as well as in cases of Christ-followers in their homeland who resist in one way or another God's call to engage the diaspora peoples around them. The attitude of centripetality is characterized by such attributes as:

- **Immovability** – Churches or individuals often resist large/small scale geographic movement in favor of the comfort, security, predictability, and/or familiarity of home.
- **Inflexibility** – Churches are too often unwilling to change plans, routines, strategies, structures, traditions, customs, policies, and more for the sake of engagement in diaspora mission.
- **Unhealthy "Long-termism"** – The nature of mission among people on the move often requires a methodology that is also "on the move." This means that permanency is not always possible or even to be preferred. For example, a church or ministry planted among seasonal migrant workers or international students may only last several months or a few years before the members of the congregation move elsewhere, but the ministry must nevertheless be planted. Churches that minister among diasporas may find themselves needing to adjust policies and re-design ministries frequently to keep up with the constantly evolving needs of diaspora peoples. Such churches must not be discouraged from always seeking to engage in the hard work of developing detailed and circumstantial short-term ways of engaging in diaspora mission (Jackson 2011).

Diaspora is central to God's redemptive mission, but embracing diaspora mission demands that churches and Christ-followers surrender to the often centrifugal leadings of the Holy Spirit – a kind of death. In this we are to take up our cross and follow the Migrant Savior who left the splendor of heaven for the dusty roads of Palestine.

Second movement: from my plan to his plan
Moving from competing agendas and contingencies to a prevailing consciousness of God's diasporic purposes

When Siva first moved to the United States from Nepal, his mind was preoccupied with the "American Dream." He envisioned a future of economic prosperity for himself and educational opportunities for his children. Becoming a follower of Christ greatly transformed Siva's perspective on the purpose of diaspora movement. He gradually began to see God using migration to bring many of his family members and friends to faith in Christ and soon began looking for ways to join in the process by encouraging loved ones on the move, helping to facilitate the process, and sharing the message of Jesus with them. While he would be quick to confess that diaspora phenomena involves a tremendous amount of pain and human suffering, Siva has also come to understand that it is a divine means by which God fulfills his redemptive plan among all peoples.

Enoch Wan has explained that people move either voluntarily or involuntarily in response to various factors which may either "push" them out of their place of origin or "pull" them into a new land (2007). Numerous factors may be noted such as economic and educational opportunities, war, human trafficking, family reunification, natural disasters, and more. However, all of these factors denote an essentially *unconscious* participation in diasporic movement that is orchestrated by God.

As Siva's story illustrates, faithful engagement in diaspora mission requires more than mere centrifugal movement. Both diaspora and host nation churches must be awakened to God's missional purposes for diaspora. They must become convinced that no factor of human migration is more significant than that of the Holy Spirit who has decreed all such migration for the sake of mission. When this consciousness develops all competing agendas and contingency plans fade away. Even Biblical examples such as Daniel and Joseph, whose diasporic conditions were the result of the horrors of human trafficking, were able to see the hand of God in their movement and be a positive witness for truth (Gen. 50:20). Tereso Casiño writes:

> "Ministry-sensitive Christians will find migration as a strategic channel for doing their own share of the missionary task. Geographical mobility, whether forced or unforced, voluntary or involuntary, may be interpreted as a God-given opportunity to spread the good news (2011)."

Diaspora churches in particular must be "motivated and mobilized" as they constitute one of the "most strategic missionary forces in the history of missions" (LCWE 2010). In the first place, Miriam Adeney has argued that the inherent liminality of diaspora creates certain cross-cultural strengths in a person that can "blossom into mission" (Adeney 2011). These "liminal, hyphenated, polycentric, multilingual Christians" are the "natural bridge-builders" who can lead cross-cultural mission endeavors to other diaspora communities (Adeney 2011). Hun Kim (2011) has added that diaspora peoples are "more attune to religious plurality than their [non-migrant] counterparts," a trait that "enhances their missionary capacity to maintain effective Christian witness in the face of religious pluralism." Thomas Harvey (2011) has added that diaspora Christ-followers can gain access through their non-religious vocations to nations which block access to traditional missionaries.

In spite of the compelling potential for mission that diasporas represent, churches often struggle to give God's plan for diaspora the attention it deserves. Competing agendas and contingencies will need to be held in check. In particular, churches must guard against:

- **Unawareness** – Churches must provide Biblical education regarding God's purpose behind the scattering of peoples so as to ensure that their members remain connected to the grand Biblical metanarrative of God orchestrating all the movements of humanity for his own missional purposes.
- **A Negative-only Perspective** – The tendency to see human migration only in a negative light must be replaced with a view of diaspora that is hopeful even in the presence of suffering.
- **Self-interest** – Most diaspora people have only personal or earthly interests in mind when they consider their own migration. If they are Christ-followers, they must be exhorted to embrace God's purposes as infinitely superior to their own.

Min-young Jung (2010) has written that diaspora Christ-followers are "where they are not by chance, not by human plan in pursuit of worldly dreams, not by unfortunate random twist of history. They are there for a reason, for a great purpose, for the ultimate cause". But diaspora Christians and their host country counterparts need to be converted from "self-serving" to "missional" in their perspective of diaspora phenomena. This is also a kind of death, a move towards cruciformity in pursuit of the one who could say, "Father, not my will, but yours be done" (Luke 22:42).

Third movement: from my pleasure to his pleasure
Moving from convenient mission to mission as calling

The opening stories of this chapter all found an intersection in the history of a small, diaspora-focused ministry and church called Trinity International Baptist Mission. Trinity International began in 2004 when its founders, who at the time were preparing for traditional "overseas" missions, responded to a clear call from God to "bring the hope and wholeness of Christ to people scattered everywhere" (Trinity International Baptist Mission 2010). They were later joined by team members from around the world who had previously set their eyes on mission fields in Tibet, Indonesia, Ethiopia, Nepal and elsewhere. For each missionary that joined the team, engaging in diaspora mission was a matter of obedience to God's call rather than of geographic, economic, or cross-cultural convenience.

Unfortunately, the "language of convenience" has too often been associated with diaspora missions. It is suggested that diaspora missions can be practiced "easily" as "mission at your doorstep" that doesn't require linguistic or cultural border-crossing (Wan 2011). Churches in Western host countries in particular have been told that they "no longer have to look beyond their own local context;" they don't have to go to the world because "the world has come to us" (Howell 2011). Elsewhere it has been emphasized that migration means that the nations are "easily within reach" and "with relatively small input toward their immediate needs, tangible results can be produced" (Baeq, et al. 2011). Moreover, it is described as safer since there is "no political danger" in engaging in diaspora mission in Western nations (Baeq, et al. 2011).

This kind of language obscures the fact that while there are certain strategic advantages presented by the context of diaspora mission, we do not engage in it *because* it is cheaper, easier, closer, safer, or less time-consuming. In many cases, we find that diaspora mission can be significantly less convenient. For example, it is usually more expensive to live in global cities such as Chicago, Paris, Dubai or Singapore where large diaspora populations reside than in relatively homogenous rural villages. Migrant churches have also found it to be a huge investment of time and finances to bring pastors from their home countries to lead their congregations. When one factors in the unique realities of forced displacement, human trafficking, intergenerational conflict, ethnic tension, and psychological distress there begins to emerge a picture of diaspora missions that is anything but "easy."

Indeed, diaspora mission is something to which churches are *called*. Writes T.V. Thomas (2010), "Whatever the size, wherever they go, we have a responsibility to reach out to them with the gospel… the Great Commission demands that we reach out to people on the move." It is a matter of obedience first. To guard against the attitude of "missional convenience," churches engaged in diaspora mission should be on the lookout for:

- **The pursuit of comfort** – Often Christ-followers involved in outreach to their immigrant neighbors do so on their own terms, when their schedule permits, and so long as it doesn't impede their pursuit of health, wealth, and happiness. Many avoid diaspora mission involvement that would seem too difficult. Homes of immigrants that are overrun by cockroaches or bedbugs or which are located in crime-infested areas are avoided by many host nation churches. This kind of avoidance is noticeable to migrants themselves who understand that those who are unwilling be present with them and to endure what they have no choice but to endure do not actually love them.

- **A preference to get "what I want"** – At least unconsciously, many churches engage in diaspora mission in order to satisfy their own wants and agendas. A youth group may need a good mission trip idea or a Bible study fellowship may need to do a service project. Adopting a refugee or an immigrant family for a short period of time, ignorant of God's larger plans for that family and their community, can often cause more harm than good. The volunteers may feel a sense of gratification as a result of their cross-cultural encounter, but God's purposes in mission are often left unserved.
- **Language of convenience** – We must be wary of such verbiage that suggests that the reason to engage in diaspora missions is that doing so is more convenient than traditional missions. Instead we must use themes of calling and obedience in our conversations about diaspora mission.

A story from the history of Trinity International has emerged as paradigmatic for their understanding of the move from convenience to calling in diaspora missions. Some years ago one of their missionaries, a North American, was spending time in the apartment of a family of Rohingya refugees from Burma. The missionary had spent considerable time cultivating a reciprocal relationship of mutual trust, respect, and love. That day in particular, he had already spent hours with the family – struggling through broken English, downing endless cans of orange *Fanta*, and consuming more than his share of spicy food. After some time, there was a knock at the door. The head of the household, Muhammad,[9] opened the door to find an unknown, American man. The visitor told Muhammad that he was a Christian and that his church was donating free food to needy families. Muhammad was invited to come to the parking lot and take the food he wanted. Muhammad stared blankly at the man for an uncomfortably long time before the American repeated the invitation, more slowly, emphasizing the words "free" and "food." Finally, Muhammad replied with a curt "Okay," and slammed the door. The missionary heard Muhammad mutter something under his breath in Burmese before returning to his place on the sofa and to his can of *Fanta.*

Churches longing to be engaged in diaspora mission after the pattern of the Migrant Savior must ask themselves on which side of the door they wish to do ministry. If on the inside, H.L. Richard (2010) has noted that there is a "cost to [such] ministry… the cross hurts". One must learn not only to extend hospitality but to receive it, to welcome diaspora peoples

---

9 A pseudonym.

and to go to them. To meet with them not only for 15-30 minutes but to learn to stay there with them until your efforts to speak their language and their efforts to speak yours have been completely exhausted. To stay until tea has become lunch and lunch has become dinner. To stay until their bedbugs have become your bedbugs and then to stay longer. Only a deep sense of divine calling will prove powerful enough to carry us so far away from our comfort zones. Here again Christ is our predecessor who gave up the pleasures of heaven and submitted to the call of crucifixion.

Fourth movement: from my people to his people
Moving from cultural clinging to contextualization

When Lachi first encountered the contextualized, Christocentric Nepali *satsang*, later to become the regular worship gathering of TriEak Parmeshwar Mandali,[10] she was greatly surprised. Most Hindus of her caste had long ago written off Christianity as a foreign religion, opposed to Nepali culture. But here was an American devotee of Christ, chanting Bible verses in Sanskrit, singing *bhajans* about the Lord Jesus, and using fascinating stories to teach spiritual truths. Incense and candles burned on an altar, giving Lachi the sense that, even in her displacement as a refugee, this was a sacred time and here was a sacred place. Beyond this liturgical contextualization, Lachi found the missionaries of Trinity International pursuing a kind of relational contextualization as well. They worked hard to learn how to develop relationships that the Bhutanese-Nepalis understood to be close. They entered into life with the refugees. They not only worked to assist the newcomers with their efforts to integrate into American society but engaged in *inverted assimilation* – striving to learn the language and adapt to the culture of Bhutanese-Nepalis. Gradually, long-standing cultural barriers between Lachi and the knowledge of Christ fell away and she surrendered to His Lordship.

It has been suggested that crossing linguistic and cultural barriers isn't necessary in diaspora mission (LCWE 2010). Brian Howell has argued against the pursuit of contextualization in diaspora missions, writing, "I would argue that a better approach to mission work and ministry generally is through biblical virtues practiced by the established [host country church] rather than starting with principles of contextualization to be employed by mission specialists" (Howell 2011). Howell's case against contextualization is built upon four contentions:

1. Strategies of contextualization become "rapidly obsolete as populations respond to the wider context" (Howell 2011).
2. Contextualization limits participation in diaspora mission to a limited number of "mission specialists" (Howell 2011).

10 Trinity International started TriEak Parmeshwar Mandali, a ministry among Nepali-speaking Hindus, in 2009.

3. Contextualization is powerless to "illuminate complex situations of globalization, cultural change, and hybridity" and tends to exclude concerns for power, economics, gender, race, and inequality (Howell 2011).
4. It is better to emphasize biblical virtues such as compassion, hospitality, and justice (Howell 2011).

All of these contentions must be rejected. First, we have addressed the importance of flexible methodology in diaspora mission. Whether second generation immigrants will speak Nepali or not is irrelevant to the fact that newly arriving immigrants speak it now and will more readily understand the gospel in their heart language. Besides this, Howell suggests too strongly the inevitability of cultural assimilation. Sam George (2011) has argued instead that the experience of migration, uprooting, and alienation often contributes to a heightened need for identity and community. Tereso Casiño (2011) has added that diasporas tend towards "strong ethnic group consciousness sustained over a long time". Other missiologists cite specific examples of the Jewish, Korean, and Chinese diasporas which have maintained and even intensified their distinct cultural identities (Oh 2011) (Choi 2011) (Baeq, et al. 2011) (Tan 2011). Darrell Jackson (2011) has explained that while some migrants choose assimilation, others consciously seek to integrate with the host society in ways that allow the preservation of their unique cultural distinctiveness, and still others prefer instead to intentionally organize themselves around specific cultural or religious allegiances.

Secondly, the suggestion that contextualization limits diaspora mission engagement to "missionary specialists" begs the question 'why.' Howell (2011) says that "the goal of missiology should be to empower the local church to engage in mission" but that the use of contextualized strategies in diaspora mission "excludes the [host nation] church from having much of a role". Howell does not explain why this is the case, but perhaps believes that the pursuit of contextualization is simply too difficult for most Christ-followers. It is too difficult to develop cross-cultural competencies and learn a new language, to engage in respectful interreligious dialogue, and to seek to understand one's immigrant neighbor in order to better communicate the love of Christ in a way she can understand. In this case we are reminded that the call to diaspora mission includes the demand to abandon notions of "convenient mission." Howell may be correct in suggesting that empowering host country Christ-followers to pursue contextualization is somewhat impractical, but, as he has said elsewhere, "pragmatics do not make good theology, nor I would argue, do they make good missiology" (Howell 2011).

Howell's third contention is that contextualization is powerless to "illuminate complex situations of globalization, cultural change, and hybridity" and excludes concerns for power, economics, gender, race, and inequality (Howell 2011). However, when contextualization is pursued as incarnation and, particularly among diasporas, as *inverted assimilation*, it lands the cross-cultural worker into the lived experience of migrants. It is not just to be a friend as the missionary might understand friendship but to be a friend *contextually*, "to know and to care about what truly matters to the other person" (Jeong 2010). When contextualization is pursued as incarnation, issues of power, inequality and hybridity are indeed illuminated because the missionary shares these experiences alongside her migrant friends. Her advocacy and works of compassion and hospitality are of greater resonance to the diaspora in which she ministers because they are done by her as an insider, with intimate understanding of the heartbeat of the community, rather than simply as a well-meaning foreigner.

Finally, Howell suggests that it would be better for Christians to emphasize "biblical virtues" such as compassion, hospitality, and justice rather than to pursue contextualization. This contention has two problems. First, Howell himself admits that virtues such as hospitality and compassion must be practiced "with an eye toward how particular actions and attitudes take on meanings in a given context" (Howell 2011). This insight must not be glossed over, as "well-meaning" churches are *not* always understood to be so. Contextualization is essential if we desire to effectively communicate compassion, hospitality, and love to migrants. But beyond this, Howell neglects the fact that the pursuit of contextualization itself is undergirded by clear biblical principles. For example, contextualization values diversity and the unique giftings of each people (Eph 4:7, Rev 21:26). Contextualization promotes integration which preserves cultural distinctiveness, rather than assimilation which obscures them. In so doing, it allows for host churches to be greatly enriched and renewed by their correspondence with Christ-followers from other nations who are encouraged to bring with them their own culturally-contextualized expressions of discipleship and "local theologies" (Jackson 2011). Thus contextualization sees the migrant as a "hallowed person" (Sydnor 2011), who is no mere recipient of charitable acts, but someone with a story, value, gifts and experiences to share. Above all, contextualization uplifts the biblical virtue of gospel proclamation. At its heart, contextualization is about illuminating biblical truth and becoming all things to all people so as to reach as many as possible (John 1:9, 1 Cor. 9:22).

In fact, many missiologists have called for contextualization in diaspora mission (LCWE 2010) (Lorance 2010) (Richard 2010) (Connor 2006) (Casiño 2011) (Song 2010) (Jackson 2011) (Tan 2011). To be sure, pursuing this holistically is difficult and costly, running against our natural urge to cling to our own cultural preferences, biases, and traditions. If churches are to pursue cruciformity in our engagement in diaspora mission, we must guard against the following:

- **Demanding assimilation** – Churches on mission must advocate for integration which promotes unity *and* preserves diversity rather than unbiblical assimilation.

- **Ethnocentrism** – Instead of assuming that our own cultural preferences are the only legitimate ways to do things, we must move towards the radical practice of *inverted assimilation* in which Christ-followers seek to enter into the cultural context of their diaspora neighbors through language and cultural acquisition and holistic, incarnational contextualization.
- **Benefactor mentality** – This is the false assumption that migrants are only to be viewed as objects of charity. Instead we must move towards the cultivation of reciprocal relationships in which even the migrant is seen as a person of great intrinsic value, a teacher of wisdom, and a net contributor to their new communities.

Once again, the costly nature of cruciform diaspora mission is modeled by Christ who did not consider equality with God "a thing to be grasped" but entered into human flesh, taking the form of a servant (Phil. 2:7). If we are to follow Him, we too must be willing to let go of our cultural preferences and walk the difficult road of incarnation.

Conclusion

We have perhaps drifted quite far from the days when impassioned missionaries packed their belongings in their own coffins as they boarded ships bound for some unknown port in a mysterious land. We feel ourselves far removed from the times of Judson and Carey, who buried wives and endured harsh persecution; of Moon and Aylward, who forsook marriage and scorned difficulty, poverty, and mental and physical hardship; and of Ricci and de Nobili, who so thoroughly embraced Christ's incarnational model that their own native cultures became something of a distant memory. But such models must not become mere relics of mission history. We must recapture the cruciformity inherent in all Christ-centered missions – foreign, domestic, and diasporic. Christ's call to ambassadorship is a call to imitation, incarnation, and crucifixion for the sake of the gospel. The Lausanne Covenant has stated well that "the church which preaches the cross must itself be marked by the cross" (The Lausanne Movement 1974). This call to cross-marked mission is of particular importance in the realm of diaspora where temptations toward convenience and self-interest, dabbling and volunteerism are so strong – subtly suggesting that in our modern, technologically-advanced, and globalized society, "taking up the cross" in mission may no longer be necessary. We who are of Christ must reject this notion. Paul's diasporic mission was one of laying down his life every day (1 Cor. 15:31). Should ours be any different?

Perhaps the key to the Church's faithful participation in mission in an age of unprecedented migration, urbanization, and globalization is to make the painful but joyful climb down the ladder from the lofty heights of Babel to commune with the people on the move – to look deeply into the tear-moistened eyes of the world's tempest-tossed sojourners, to live with and listen to them and so to see in them reflections of our Migrant Savior. Beholding him more fully, we will surely be transformed, by degrees of ever-increasing glory, into the image of the one who remains the only hope of the world.

For discussion

1. Take time now to prayerfully reflect upon Scriptural passages related to the migrations or sufferings of the Lord Jesus. Also, find a migrant friend whose story you are unfamiliar with and ask them to share it with you. What do you hear God saying to you?
2. How have you seen the Babel Complex hinder diaspora mission in your context? As you consider the diaspora or host nation churches in your context, what are some of the most important and immediate changes that need to be made?
3. What are the best examples you've seen of churches and ministries imitating the Migrant Savior in their practice of diaspora mission?
4. Many missiologists see the influx of diaspora Christ-followers into Western nations as a providential means by which God may intend to bring revival to post-Christian societies. If this is true, what are the implications for national mission agencies and denominations especially in terms of partnerships, power-sharing, and leadership?

Bibliography

Adeney, Miriam. "Colorful Initiatives: North American Diasporas in Mission." *Missiology: An International Review,* 39 (2011): 5-23.

Baeq, Daniel Shinjong, Myunghee Lee, Sokpyo Hong,, and Jonathan Ro. "Mission from Migrant Church to Ethnic Minorities: A Brief Assessment of the Korean American Church in Mission." *Missiology: An International Review*, 39 (2011): 25-37.

Casiño, Tereso. "Why People Move: A Prolegomenon to Diaspora Missiology." In *Korean Diaspora and Christian Mission,* edited by Hun Kim and Wonsuk Ma. Oxford: Regnum Books, 2011.

Choi, Sungho "Identity Crisis for Diaspora Community." In *Korean Diaspora and Christian Mission*, edited by Hun Kim and Wonsuk Ma. Oxford: Regnum Books, 2011.

Chun, Do Myung. "Kingdom-centered Identity: The Case of Bicultural Korean-Brazilians." In *Korean Diaspora and Christian Mission*, edited by Hun Kim and Wonsuk Ma. Oxford: Regnum Books, 2011.

Commission on World Mission and Evangelism. "Mission Spirituality and Discipleship: Beyond and Through Contemporary Boundaries." *International Review of Mission* (2010): 106-124.

Connor, Phillip. *A Biblical Missiology for North American People Groups.* Alpharetta, GA: North American Mission Board, 2006.

George, Sam. "Diaspora: A Hidden Link to 'From Everywhere to Everywhere' Missiology." *Missiology: An International Review*, 39 (2011): 45-56.

Hale, Chris. "Aradhna: From Comfort to Discomfort, from Church to Temple," in *International Journal of Frontier Missiology* 24:3 (2007): 147-50. http://www.ijfm.org/PDFs_IJFM/24_3_PDFs/147-150Hale.pdf/.

Harvey, Thomas A. "Diaspora: A Passage to Mission." *Transformation: An International Journal of Holistic Mission Studies*, 28 (2011): 42-50.

Howell, Brian M. "Multiculturalism, Immigration and the North American Church: Rethinking Contextualization." *Missiology: An International Review*, 39 (2011): 79-85.

Jackson, Darrell. "Europe and the Migrant Experience: Transforming Integration." *Transformation: An International Journal of Holistic Mission Studies*, 28 (2011): 14-28.

Jeong, Matthew and Chul Jeong. "Korean Evangelicals' Response Toward Muslim Neighbours." In *Korean Diaspora and Christian Mission*, edited by Hun Kim and Wonsuk Ma. Oxford: Regnum Books, 2011.

Jung, Min-young. "Diaspora and Timely Hit: Towards a Diaspora Missiology." In *Korean Diaspora and Christian Mission* edited by Hun Kim and Wonsuk Ma. Oxford: Regnum Books, 2011.

Kawthoolei Karen Baptist Bible School & College. *Brief history.* Mae La Camp, Thailand: Kawthoolei Karen Baptist Bible School & College, 2009. https://sites.google.com/site/kkbbsc/home/brief-history.

Kim, S. Hun. "Receiving Mission: Reflection on Reversed Phenomena in Mission by Migrant Workers from Global Churches to Western Society." *Transformation: An International Journal of Holistic Mission Studies*, 28 (2011): 62-67.

Kim, S. Hun. "Migrant Workers and 'Reverse Mission' in the West." In *Korean Diaspora and Christian Mission*, edited by Hun Kim and Wonsuk Ma. Oxford: Regnum Books, 2011.

Lausanne Committee for World Evangelization. *The Lausanne Covenant.* Lausanne, Switzerland: The Lausanne Movement, 1974. http://www.lausanne.org/covenant.

Lausanne Committee for World Evangelization. *Scattered to Gather: Embracing the Global Trend of Diaspora.* Manila, Philippines: LifeChange Publishing, Inc., 2010.

Lausanne Diaspora Educators Consultation. *The Seoul Declaration on Diaspora Missiology.* Seoul, South Korea: The Lausanne Movement, 2009. http://www.lausanne.org/documents/seoul-declaration-on-diaspora-missiology.html.

Lorance, Cody. "An Introduction to Contextualization Among Hindus." *Lausanne Global Conversation,* June 6, 2010, http://www.conversation.lausanne.org/en/conversations/detail/10373/.

Oh, Doug D. "History of the Korean Diaspora Movement." In *Korean Diaspora and Christian Mission* edited by Hun Kim and Wonsuk Ma. Oxford: Regnum Books, 2011.

Photo Voice; Bhutanese Refugee Support Group. "Introduction." *Bhutanese Refugees: The Story of a Forgotten People*. London: Photo Voice, 2010. http://www.photovoice.org/bhutan/.

Pocock, Michael, Gailyn Van Rheenen, and Douglas McConnell. *The Changing Face of World Missions: Engaging Contemporary Issues and Trends.* Grand Rapids, MI: Baker Academic, 2005.

Richard, H. L. "Good News for Hindus in the Neighborhood." *Rethinking Hindu Ministry II: Papers from the Rethinking Forum*, Pasadena: William Carey Library, 2010: 32-35.

Song, Minho. "The Diaspora Experience for the Korean Church and its Implications for World Missions." In *Korean Diaspora and Christian Mission*, edited by Hun Kim and Wonsuk Ma. Oxford: Regnum Books, 2011.

Sydnor, Paul N. "Understanding the Forced Displacement of Refugees in Terms of the Person." *Transformation: An International Journal of Holistic Mission Studies*, 28 (2011): 51-61.

Tan, Kang-San. "In Search of Contextualized Training Models for Chinese Christian Diaspora in Britain." *Transformation: An International Journal of Holistic Mission Studies*, 28 (2011): 29-41.

Thomas, T.V. "Ministering to Scattered Peoples: Global Phenomenon of Diaspora." *Lausanne Global Conversation*. The Lausanne Movement, 2010. http://conversation.lausanne.org/en/conversations/detail/11660.

Trinity International Baptist Mission. "Our Story." *Trinity International Baptist Mission*, Aurora, IL: Trinity International Baptist Mission, 2010. http://www.tibm.org/our-story.html.

United Nations, Department of Economic and Social Affairs, Population Division. *Trends in International Migrant Stock: The 2013 Revision*. United Nations, 2013.

Vanier, Jean. *From Brokenness to Community*. Mahwah, NJ: Paulist Press, 1992.

Waltke, Bruce. K. *Genesis: A Commentary*. Grand Rapids, MI: Zondervan, 2001.

Wan, Enoch. "Diaspora Missiology." *Occasional Bulletin of Evangelical Missiological Society* (2007): 3-7.

Wan, Enoch. "Diaspora Mission Strategy in the Context of the United Kingdom in the 21st Century." *Transformation: An International Journal of Holistic Mission Studies*, 28 (2011): 3-13.

Wan, Enoch. "Korean Diaspora: From Hermit Kingdom to Kingdom Ministry." In *Korean Diaspora and Christian Mission* edited by Hun Kim and Wonsuk Ma. Oxford: Regnum Books, 2011.

Wan, Enoch. "Ministering to Scattered Peoples – Moving to Reach the People on the Move." *Lausanne Global Conversation*. The Lausanne Movment, 2010. http://conversation.lausanne.org/en/resources/detail/11438.

19. Making Ends Meet: Embracing Opportunities for Diaspora Mission from Churches at the Margins

Carol A. Mack-Lacey

Introduction

In Matt. 28:18-20, Christians are called to the Great Commission, yet doing ministry at the margins comes with many complications – especially if one is among the disenfranchised. Inequality, and the attendant problem of poverty, complicates our desire for ministry. As a child growing up in a large city, I lived in a community characterized by inequality. On one end of the block towering fences stood as sentinels on opposite sides of the street where we played at their thresholds with fear and wonder. On the junk yard side, the guard dog, rusty sheet metal, and barbed wire growled their warning, "Keep Out!" On the middle-class side, a chain-linked, galvanized steel fence; cropped lawn; and well-dressed children mocked the same. Many urban communities around the world are like that short city block where I spent my childhood.

For the powerless, these symbols of disparity prevail as reminders that we are unequal neighbors. Such symbols, at least in our formative years, tell us our place in the world. Members of disenfranchised communities have an entrenched perspective – levied by incessant misfortune – that defies their steps toward social action through missional living, particularly toward diasporas who may be seen as a competitors in the struggle to survive in a context where resources are limited. This chapter explores how disenfranchised community churches might reimagine their place in fulfilling the Great Commission among diasporas moving into their neighborhoods.

After briefly discussing poverty as a dilemma that occurs from natural and human causes and speaking of it in connection with Jewish and first-century Christian perspectives, I will discuss the barriers to sacrificial living among Christians with limited resources. Then I will consider how engaging in diaspora mission from the fringes of society is possible as churches embrace biblically-oriented ways of living in community with others. Finally, I will present illustrations of how marginalized churches and Christians can transform their spaces and minister to their newest neighbors.

Poverty – its unsettling truths

How many times have we evaded compassion the way we avoid a stranger in a crowded marketplace when we could not, or would not, respond to a human need? Who can tackle something as big as poverty anyway? After all, didn't Jesus say, "For you always have the poor with you" (Mark 14:7 NASB)? Of course, this is an unsettling topic to discuss – both for the rich who live at a comfortable distance and the working class who are nearest the slippery slope. This is not a problem that can be solved with social programs, government reforms, and scientific breakthroughs alone.

Poverty permeates the fabric of society like dye bonds with fiber. It is part of the way we are as humans in a complex world. Without delving into an exhaustive historical survey to define poverty, we will suffice to say that poverty thrives where wars and natural disasters leave barren landscapes. The derelict streets of Juba in South Sudan (Verini 2014) ravaged by civil war or New Orleans' Lower Ninth Ward after Hurricane Katrina (Allen 2015) are prime examples. Poverty and inequality strip men of the dignity of caring for their families by systems that reject them for their birth lineage, color, disability, or religion. St. Louis, USA; Soweto, South Africa; and Bogota, Colombia easily come to mind. Poverty is where the powerless have no voice and where the ingenuity, creativity, and vibrancy of one are exploited without regard by another.

Poverty was widespread in biblical history. Consequently, God's disdain for the bolstering of power and privilege is conveyed throughout His commands (Deut. 10:17-19; 15:7-11). In these verses, the Hebrew word, *ebyôn*, refers to the destitute poor; i.e., those who live below subsistence and are without a remedy. Generosity to the poor was at the heart of the new kingdom paradigm that God was establishing through His people. Likewise, the NT distinguishes between those who depend on society for alms, in Greek *ptōchos*, and those poor, *penēs*, who have limited means (Mark 14:7) (New International Dictionary of New Testament Theology 1986, 820).

While facing Calvary, Jesus elevates care for the poor above duty to acts of kindness one performs willingly and expectantly until He returns. Here is the scene from Mark 14:3-7 (NASB):

"While He was in Bethany at the home of Simon the leper, and reclining at the table, there came a woman with an alabaster vial of very costly perfume of pure nard; and she broke the vial and poured it over His head. But some were indignantly remarking to one another, "Why has this perfume been wasted? For this perfume might have been sold for over three hundred denarii, and the money given to the poor." And they were scolding her. But Jesus said, "Let her alone; why do you bother her? She has done a good deed to me. For you always have the poor with you, and whenever you wish you can do good to them; but you do not always have Me."

Barriers to sacrificial living

Marginalized churches who want to answer the Great Commission must find ways to overcome the internal and external forces that compromise their ability to become the blessing and answer to prayer many people in diaspora need. It is easy to resort to inaction when churches that can do – won't, and those that would do – can't. We must ask, however, what ideas or resources are missing as possible interventions, solutions and blessings because *you* are not there for diasporas who are often also materially poor and ethnically marginalized? This all-encompassing "you" includes members of churches in disenfranchised communities who have long braved the turbulent waters of life's uncertainties and thus have much to share with new migrant communities. When Jesus responded to Simon the Leper's guests, He spoke to the least affluent and the rich, leaving the door for social action wide open. He said, "why do you bother her… whenever you wish, you can do good to [the poor]; but you do not always have Me" (Mark 14:3 NASB).

With this retort Jesus extinguished the crossfires of hypocrisy and hatred. Have you ever wondered which one of them would have actually taken the vial of ointment, sold it, and distributed it to the poor? Which poor? Would it be their friends or fellow citizens or ethnic kin? Would it be the ones who were the eyesore of the neighborhood that made them uncomfortable? Would it be the ones who performed the most menial labor to bring them comfort or wealth? Would it be the ones for whom they could receive the greatest commendation for their gift? Commentator G.A. Chadwick wisely notes, "Whenever generous impulses express themselves with lavish hands, some heartless calculator reckons up the value of what is spent, and especially its value to 'the poor' … who would be worse off if the instincts of love were arrested and the human heart frozen" (Chadwick 1893, 362).

If we wish to bring God's kingdom paradigm to our societal spaces, we must become aware of the subtle and not-so-subtle cues that muddle our thinking about how we live among people who depend upon society. Though not the only cause in depressed communities, certain forms of language and norms perpetuate social forces such as racism, sexism, ageism, and classism – to name a few. These keep the powerless from living an abundant life (John 10:10). In *A Framework for Understanding Poverty*, Ruby Payne (2003, 41-51) explains that "distinct cueing systems" are hidden as language and norms in the speech and habits of every economic class. These cues, which are evident in our communication about possessions, money, social access, family structure, and relationships differ between poor, middle, and rich classes; and perpetuate long-held degrees of separation. It is no surprise that these divisive norms are also apparent among marginalized churches and have the effect of isolating them from missional opportunities among diasporas. On one hand, the harsh truths about status and place are as present as the rusty steel fences that remind the disenfranchised of the horror they are trying to escape. On the other, economic stability, just visible through the crisscrossed wires of their neighbors, indicates how far one still must reach. Yet, churches must seize opportunities to do good whenever they can. In order to free one's heart and hands for kingdom-oriented actions, therefore, we must dismantle these towering barriers that stand between notions of "us" and them."

Samuel Roberts (2001, 137-149) notes a tendency among African American Churches to combine literal and liberal frameworks in relating the Bible to their unique ethical life. This tailored reading of Scripture to fit one's own struggle has the power to illuminate truths that are often missed by Christians at the center of society, but can just as often "trivialize" biblical standards thereby creating a "canon within a canon" or interpretation in "its own world". These entrenched beliefs can run counter to biblical teaching for relating to the world around us and thus reinforce the barriers that insulate the disenfranchised from sharing the gifts (wisdom, ingenuity, compassion, etc.) they possess with new diasporas and, in turn, receiving from their migrant neighbors critical resources. The cultural exchange which would enable both communities to flourish is cut off before it has a chance to begin.

The Bible is clear about love for one's neighbor and cultivating communities which protect all the disenfranchised (Mark 12:30-31; Luke 10:30-37; Acts 6:4-8). Henri Nouwen (1979, 94) has noted, "A Christian community is a healing community not because wounds are cured and pains are alleviated, but because wounds and pains become openings or occasions for a new vision." Holding the Scriptures as authoritative means that even disenfranchised Christians are called to "seek the welfare of the city" with all of its ethnic hues and social nuances (Jer. 29:7 NASB). Dismantling the barriers which hinder this missional life calls for new ways of sacrificial living among diasporas.

Biblically-oriented ways of living

The Bible apportions loving action as the unique responsibility for the Church (Wright 2004, 53-54). Does this mean one person's burden should be eased at the cost of another? In God's design, self-giving and burden-bearing brings wholeness (Longnecker 2010, 283-291). Accordingly, self-sacrifice connects us with both the socially vulnerable and ethnically different – and, through them, to Christ – by the grace and power of God (Matt. 25:35). Reflecting upon Paul's collection for the poor saints in Jerusalem, we see a new kind of "Macedonian Call" in which the Corinthian Church is admonished by the example of the comparatively poor Macedonians' collective action (2 Cor. 8:1-15) (Georgi 1992, 41-140). Bruce Longnecker (2010, 283-291) has argued that Paul advocated for equal participation in believing communities in this collection. His campaign for the poor was situated within the larger narrative of Christ's living body reaching every nation. Each "miniature act of generosity" is part of God's grand structural reform and the poor are collaborators in His sovereign plan through which they affect eternal change. In this configuration, the poor have a voice and equal seating with the rich at the Master's banquet table (Luke 14:22-24). Those who are unable to be materially generous are "gifted" in ways other than economic generosity. As contributing members in "corporate generosity," the poor are remembered along with the rich (Longnecker 2010, 285-289).

The Macedonians gave with abundant joy in spite of their deep distress and extreme poverty (2 Cor. 8:1-5). How did abundant joy and extreme poverty unfurl along the wingspan of generosity? How did these hunted, persecuted, and scattered catch a glimpse of greatness in the wreckage around them? From what storehouse do the least likely draw courage to become a blessing? How did despised Gentiles embrace loving kindness for Jews? They first gave themselves to God. Not first as in time, but rather above all. Giving themselves above all, created a kind of holy discontinuity thereby recasting them as co-laborers in the plan of God rather than as an oppressed, incapacitated people. Such surrender was only made possible by God's grace. Paul testified that the Macedonians gave "according to their ability and beyond their ability… of their own accord" (2 Cor. 8:3 NASB). It takes God's grace to step beyond one's own limitations, particularly those imposed by society. It takes walking with God.

In *With: Reimagining the Way We Relate to God*, Skye Jethani (2011, 18-80) has emphasized life with God as treasuring and uniting with God as superior to the self-centered patterns by which people attempt to mitigate fear and suffering. He suggests four patterns, namely: "life from God," which is using God to supply material desires; "life under God," which is obedience to God through rituals and morality to secure blessings and avoid calamity; "life over God," which is using God as a source and applicable instructions for blessings; and finally, "life for God," which is using God and His mission for a sense of direction and purpose.

Certainly, God is our source and the one on whom we must rely; however, these postures seek to use God as a means to an end (Jethani 2011, 101). Conversely, union with God through Christ is an invitation to experience life differently. Jethani (2011, 110-152) writes, "Hope is what allows us to keep our bearing in turbulent seas; it is the assurance that the chaos we experience in this world will not win, but God's purposes will overcome.". Churches in poor and forgotten communities must discover the "treasures of union with God" (Jethani 2011, 123-140) through prayer, renewed minds, and by uniquely experiencing His divine providence in their circumstances and the shining possibilities for doing good among diasporas. Sometimes these come in small gestures and at other times in glaring, inescapable causes. At the intersection of small and great, ends do meet to fill cavernous needs among both the marginalized long-term residents of a city and their new diaspora neighbors.

Portraits of hope

The following examples illustrate how disenfranchised Christians and churches have defied the barriers of class and debilitating self-perceptions by renewing their communities through kingdom-oriented, Christ-centered giving among other vulnerable peoples. All interviews were confidential. Fictitious names were used by request or mutual agreement. Place of employment has also been withheld at the author's discretion.

- *Mobilizing against corruption.* Sarah, a U.S. missionary, visited the Philippines in 1984 where she served people living alongside a garbage dump. Much like the dump in Payatas, Philippines today or in Nairobi, Kenya at Dandora, children and adults salvage trash to sell for survival.[1] In one family, a newborn died; however, they could not bury the infant without paying a bribe for release of their pauper's grave allotment. As a single, multi-ethnic community, they appealed to government authorities, and were awarded the burial allotment.[2]
- *Providing transportation.* Sarah also served in war-torn Yei, a medium-sized city in South Sudan. There orphan teenagers used a wheelbarrow from their orphanage to transport a crippled man to church services in spite of the dangers on the road.
- *Learning the system.* Not long after their arrival to the U.S. from the Republic of Congo, Frantz and Martina's 5-year-old son was placed in a St. Louis hospital's intensive care unit for a sickle cell crisis. With advice from friends from an inner city church, they received financial assistance from the hospital to nurture their son back to strength.[3]
- *Sharing for survival.* Blessing, a Rwandan genocide survivor, witnessed deep poverty during her 15-years in Kenya's Kakuma refugee camp. She also witnessed her neighbors clothing those in need and sharing their best food to nurture the sick back to health.[4]
- *Collective savings.* In Kansas City, Missouri (USA), James saw low-wage factory workers from Mexico, Guatemala, Honduras, El Salvador, Cuba, and Nicaragua create a community savings account for neighbors with extreme needs. Fifty-dollars from each member

---

1 Drawn from Philippines: Real Lives. "Below the Poverty Line: Living on a Garbage Dump." http://www.unicef.org/philippines/reallives_12171.html (accessed June 2, 2014). Media Centre. And "Surviving Against All Odds in Nairobi's Dandora Area." http://www.unicef.org/kenya/media_10454.html (accessed June 7, 2014).

2 Sarah, interviewed by author, May 27, 2014.

3 Frantz and Martina, interviewed by author, May 31, 2014.

4 Blessing, interviewed by author, April 1, 2014.

on a routine pay cycle became a $500 answer to someone's prayer. Rather than a $50 loss for one, this gift made them strong together.[5]

- *Being neighbors*. Migrant families from Bosnia flanked Ruth's apartment. Although she had seen many changes in her 85 years, refugee resettlement in St. Louis, MO rapidly transformed her familiar neighborhood, particularly for this Mississippi born, African American widow. She knew what it was like to be a young mother without help. Through her love for children she crocheted Granny Square blankets for every expectant newborn next door, as she had done for over 20 years for fellow church members. With the babies' grandmother on the other side, she enjoyed the company of a neighbor over a cup of strong Bosnian coffee, although they could not communicate in a common language.[6]

Conclusion

These accounts reflect the kind of sacrificial living to which Paul's Macedonian example calls marginalized churches today who now find themselves with neighbors from many nations. Christians from disenfranchised communities do not have to be missing in action in diaspora mission. Indeed, they are vital collaborators in God's plan. As churches walk with God, showing love to their neighbors, and bearing witness to the gospel through kingdom-oriented living and actions, barriers of class, race, gender, culture, language, and all the rest are overcome. Thus others' needs find a place in our expression of the Christ-life in previously unimaginable ways.

For discussion

1. The influx of migrants to a given city is often viewed as a threat by urban poor communities who may see diasporas as competitors in the struggle to acquire limited resources such as jobs or social welfare. How can churches in marginalized communities overcome these perceptions (whether actual or imagined) and become active participants in diaspora mission?
2. What are the unique gifts of the disenfranchised churches in your city? What gifts do the diasporas (whether Christian or not) bring to the table? What opportunities for interconnectedness (consider potential community or church initiatives) are being missed which could not only lead to furthering the gospel, but also to the flourishing of your city?

---

5 James, interviewed by author, February 15, 2014.
6 Ruth, interviewed by author, June 11, 2014.

3. List practical steps that could be taken to awaken disenfranchised churches in your context to their role in fulfilling the Great Commission among their migrant neighbors.

Bibliography

Allen, Greg. "Ghosts of Katrina Still Haunt New Orleans' Shattered Lower Ninth Ward." *NPR*, August 3, 2015, updated August 18, 2015. Accessed December 23, 2015. http://www.npr.org/2015/08/03/427844l7/ghosts-of-katrina-still-haunt-new-orleans-shattered-lower-ninth-ward.html.

Bennett, Harold V. *Injustice Made Legal: Deuteronomic Law and the Plight of Widows, Strangers, and Orphans in Ancient Israel.* Grand Rapids: William B. Eerdmans Publishing Co., 2002.

Blomberg, Craig L. *Neither Poverty Nor Riches: A Biblical Theology of Material Possessions.* Grand Rapids: William B. Eerdmans Publishing Co. 1999.

New International Dictionary of New Testament Theology. s.v. "Poor." Grand Rapids: 1986.

Chadwick, G. A. "The Gospel According to St. Mark" in *The Expositor's Bible.* Edited by W. Robertson Nicoll, 5th ed. London: Hodder and Stoughton, 1893.

De La Torre, Miguel. *Doing Christian Ethics from the Margins*. Maryknoll: Orbis Books, 2004.

Georgi, Dieter. *Remembering the Poor: The History of Paul's Collection for Jerusalem.* Nashville: Abingdon Press, 1992.

Holman, Susan R. ed. *Wealth and Poverty in Early Church and Society*. Grand Rapids: Baker Academic, 2008.

Jethani, Skye Jethani. *With: Reimagining the Way You Relate to God.* Nashville: Thomas Nelson, Inc. 2011.

Longnecker, Bruce W. *Remembering the Poor: Paul, Poverty, and the Greco Roman World.* Grand Rapids: William. B. Eerdmans Publishing Co., 2010.

Martin, Ralph P. *2 Corinthians*. World Biblical Commentary. vol. 40. Waco: Word Books, 1986. 248-291.

Media Centre. "Surviving Against All Odds in Nairobi's Dandora Area." http://www.unicef.org/kenya/media_10454.html (accessed June 7, 2014).

Nouwen, Henri J. M. *The Wounded Healer: Ministry in Contemporary Society.* New York: Image Gooks, Doubleday, 1979.

Payne, Ruby K. *A Framework for Understanding Poverty.* Highlands, TX: Aha Process, Inc., 2003.

Philippines. *Real Lives.* "Below the Poverty Line: Living on a Garbage Dump." http://www.unicef.org/philippines/reallives_12171.html (accessed June 2, 2014).

Pohl, Christine. *Making Room: Recovering Hospitality as a Christian Tradition.* Grand Rapids: William B. Eerdsmans Publishing Co., 1999.

Roberts, Samuel K. *African American Christian Ethics*. Eugene: Wipf and Stock Publishers, 2001.

Verini, James. "How the World's Youngest Nation Descended into Bloody Civil War." *National Geographic*, September 30, 2014. Accessed December 23, 2015. http://news.nationalgeographic.com/news/special-features/2014/10/141001-south-sudan-dinka-nuer-ethiopia-juba-khartoum.html.

Wright, Christopher J. H. *Old Testament Ethics for the People of God*. Downers Grove: IVP Academic, 2004.

20. TRENDS AND ISSUES OF THE KOREAN DIASPORA CHURCHES IN THE USA

Chandler H. Im and John Jungho Oh

> The new immigrants represent not the de-Christianization of American society but the de-Europeanization of American Christianity.
>
> R. Stephen Warner, 2004, Professor of Sociology at the University of Illinois at Chicago

This chapter[1] focuses on the Korean diaspora communities and churches[2] across the USA. A brief history of the influx of Korean immigration, along with an overview of the Korean diaspora churches, is given. Four areas of concern and challenge, and three areas of strength and opportunity, pertaining to the Korean diaspora churches (hereafter abbreviated as the KDCs) vis-à-vis the Korean diaspora communities in the USA are also elucidated. The final section contains this topic's missiological implications.

The Korean Diaspora churches' growth and expansion

Among the people of the worldwide Korean diaspora, there is a tongue-in-cheek saying: wherever the Chinese go (around the world), they open Chinese restaurants; wherever Koreans go, they plant churches. Although it is said in an overly generalized fashion, almost as a joke, the statement carries a lot of weight in reality. Ever since the first wave of Korean immigrants hit the Hawaiian shore in the 1900s, KDCs have been planted and growing in numbers steadily, especially after the Immigration and Nationality Act of 1965, which opened the floodgate for the major Korean immigration wave in the United States. Consequently, the numbers of the KDCs in North America have increased exponentially over the last five decades: 30 KDCs (1967); 150 (1972); 600 (1980); 1,700 (1989); 3,288 (1994); 2,988 (2000); 4,182 (2006); and 4,709 (2013) (Suh 2014).

---

1 The contents of this paper mostly come from portions of two sources previously published. Chandler H. Im, "The Korean Diaspora Churches: Their Concerns and Strengths" in Chandler H. Im and Amos Yong (eds.) Global Diasporas and Mission (Oxford, UK: Regnum, 2014); John Jungho Oh, "The Mission of God and the Korean Diaspora Churches in the USA" [in Korean], Mission Korea Review vol. 3 (August 2013): 2-6.

2 One limitation of this paper is that only Protestant churches are discussed; Catholic and other non-Protestant churches are not discussed unless specified.

The dynamics of change within the Korean Diaspora Churches in the USA

According to the U.S. Department of Homeland Security (2012), the total number of Koreans who became legal permanent residents (LPRs) of the USA is 83 during fiscal years[3] 1940-1949; 4,845 during 1950-1959; 27,048 during 1960-1969; and 241,192 during 1970-1979 (See Table 1).

Table 1: Legal Permanent Resident Flow of Koreans: Fiscal Years 1940 – 1999

1940 - 1949	1950 - 1959	1960 - 1969	1970 - 1979	1980 - 1989	1990 - 1999	Total
83	4,845	27,048	241,192	322,708	179,770	775,646

Source: U.S. Department of Homeland Security, Office of Immigration Statistics

Through the 1970s and 1980s, the worship services of youth and college groups within the KDCs gradually pivoted from Korean to English. When the English-speaking primary school-aged students graduated and entered youth groups, the language of the youth group worship services eventually switched from Korean to English within a few years. Therefore, towards the end of the 1980s, almost all church education departments had shifted their choice of language for worship services from Korean to English.

Through the 1980s, new Korean immigrants continued to arrive in increasing numbers (See Table 1). The primary school-aged students adjusted well and integrated quickly into the English worship services. However, their older siblings in secondary school and college had a more difficult time adjusting to English worship services, the only language available for worship towards the late 1980s in the KDCs. Therefore, with the newly arrived immigrant families of the late 1980s pleading for a Korean worship service for their older children, a handful of Korean diaspora mega-churches started parallel Korean-speaking youth and college worship services. However, only those churches that had the financial capability to pay salaries for two separate staffs were able to do so. A more accurate scenario is that by the end of the 1980s, the English-speaking generation constituted not all but the majority of the education department, with a small minority speaking Korean in the KDCs.

The first English-speaking ministries (EM)[4] appeared towards the end of the 1980s and early part of the 1990s. Korean immigration had continued to

3 Years for immigration statistics refer to fiscal years (October 1 to September 30).

4 English Ministry (EM) here refers to an English-language worship service provided only for adult members who are beyond college age. Although a church may offer English-speaking worship services, if it includes youth and college students, along with adult members, then for this paper, it is not considered an EM.

grow throughout the 1980s. However, the annual number of Koreans who became LPRs decreased throughout the 1990s (See Table 1). With the decreasing trend in Korean immigration throughout the 1990s, it seemed that the pleading for Korean-language worship service for youth and college students would slowly dissipate. However, this was a miscalculation by the KDC leaders because only the statistics on the LPRs had been considered in the analysis.

A more detailed analysis that includes both the number of Koreans who became LPRs and Korean nonimmigrant visitors[5] – such as pleasure and business travelers, students, temporary workers, and families – reveals a more accurate scenario of the dynamics of the changes within the KDCs in the USA. A foreign national visiting the USA in a nonimmigrant visa status fills out an I-94 Nonimmigrant Arrival/Departure Record at a port of entry upon admission to the USA.[6] The total number of I-94 admissions by Koreans reported in fiscal year 1985 was a mere 91,000, which increased to 235,000 in 1990 (USINS 2002), and to 849,593 in 1996 (USDHS 2006) a whopping 834 percent increase in 11 years, from 1985 to 1996.[7] In summary, the annual number of Koreans who became permanent residents has been decreasing since the early 1990s. However, the total number of Korean nonimmigrant individuals to the USA has increased exponentially.

With the fast declining immigration of permanent residents during the 1990s, the exponential growth of the number of the KDCs in North America quickly plateaued in the 1990s and hit the highest number at 3,334 in 1997. Moreover, in 2000, the total number of the KDCs in North America had decreased by 346, to 2,988 (See Figure 2). It appeared that the KDCs' fear of the church following the declining trend of the immigration of the permanent residents was becoming a reality. However, as the church

---

5 See Randall Monger, Nonimmigrant Admissions to the United States: 2012, Office of Immigration Statistics, Policy Directorate, U.S. Department of Homeland Security, 2012, http://www.dhs.gov/sites/default/files/publications/ois_ni_fr_2012 .pdf, accessed 29 August 2013. The Office of Immigration Statistics divides foreign nationals legally staying in the USA into three major categories: legal permanent residents; refugees and asylees; and nonimmigrant visitors. Monger defines nonimmigrants as "foreign nationals granted temporary entry into the United States. The major purposes for which nonimmigrant admission may be authorized include visits for business or pleasure, academic or vocational study, temporary employment, and to act as a representative of a foreign government or international organization."

6 Randall Monger in Nonimmigrant Admissions to the United States: 2012 defines nonimmigrant admissions as referring to the "number of events (i.e., entries into the U.S.) rather than individuals." According to this definition, in any given fiscal year, the count of admissions will always exceed the number of individuals arriving since an individual might enter the USA multiple times in a year.

7 In the 21st century, the annual number of I-94 admissions by Koreans has averaged above one million.

wrestled with this very concern, the nonimmigrants very quietly mushroomed and filled the void created by the declining LPR immigrants.

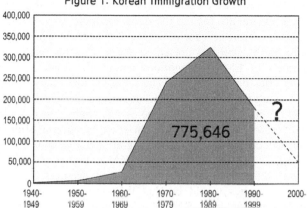

Figure 1: Korean Immigration Growth

Figure 2: Growth of the Korean Diaspora Churches in North America

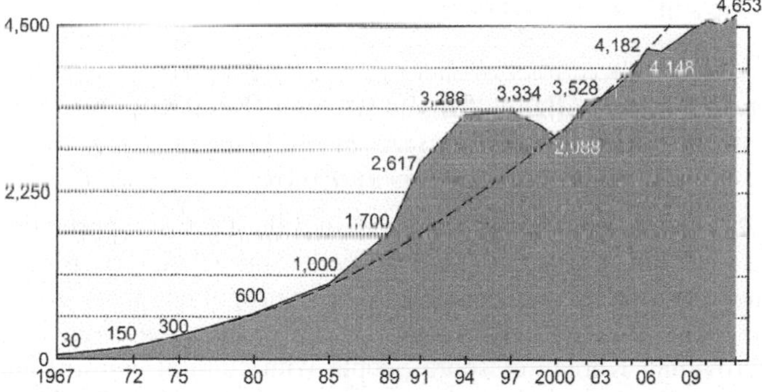

As the total population of Koreans in the USA has increased, especially through nonimmigrant short-term residents, the median age of the Korean-speaking generation has basically continued to remain the same. Therefore, the KDC's projection during the 1990s that in the coming 21st century the median age of the Korean-speaking generation would grow older and near retirement because of the decreasing trend in the immigration of LPRs was falsely based on insufficient data. Moreover, the KM generation's proposal to the EM generation that a transition from KM leadership to EM leadership in the KDCs would occur did not materialize. For the most part, the EM generation continued to remain mostly as a department within the KDCs. However, in the 21st century, a new and different transition is definitely transpiring in the KDCs. The membership of the KDCs is pivoting from LPRs and naturalized citizens to nonimmigrant short-term residents.

The present and future of the Korean Diaspora Churches in the USA

Just as the 1.5 generations[8] of the 1970s and 1980s started the first English-speaking ministries (EM) when they became adults, the 1.5 generations of the 21st century would eventually realize the need for their own worship structure that corresponds with the ever-changing 21st century when they become adults. Based on the statistics presented above, it is reasonable to expect growing numbers of EM congregations among the KDCs in the USA; however, reality cries out differently. The reality is that many of the EM generations are leaving the KDCs. Then what is the underlying reason for this disparate reality? It is beyond the scope of this chapter to provide an adequate explanation for this disparity, but a brief explanation is offered later. As a consequence of the disparity, a generational disconnect has emerged within the KDCs. The weakness of the KM churches would be that they may be too ethnocentric in membership and perspective. The weakness of the EM churches would be that they may be too "peer-centric." It is imperative upon both KM and EM generations to work together to fulfill the image of the Church in the New Testament that is both multi-ethnic and multi-generational.

Areas of concern and challenge for the Korean Diaspora Churches in the USA[9] "islandization" of the Korean diaspora communities and KDCs[10]

The Korean diaspora communities in general, and the KDCs in particular, still look like scattered islands in an ocean called the USA. The biggest "Korean islands" in the USA are located in the metropolitan areas of Los Angeles, New York, Chicago, Washington D.C., Atlanta, San Francisco, and Seattle. Providing Korean diaspora people with cultural comfort and safety zones, these Korean communities have evolved in relative isolation, somewhat distanced from other neighboring ethnic communities and mainstream America. This cultural tendency to stick with "my own people" also seems to be common in other Korean diasporas around the world. In addition, this phenomenon actually can be seen – to some extent – among

8 For the purposes of this section, "1.5 generation," the children in immigrant families, is defined as those who are born in Korea and attended primary school for a minimum of one to two years in Korea before immigrating to the USA and graduated high school in the USA.

9 I (Im) have identified and listed only four items in this section due to space limitation. There are several other issues left un-mentioned. I will leave those to later discussions and to others to explore.

10 Cf. Chandler H. Im, "Beyond the Korean Line: Toward the Multi-Ethnic Ministry in North America," Presentation at Korean Diaspora Forum in Fullerton, California, 5 May 2011.

other ethnic diaspora communities and churches in the USA and around the globe.

In addition, a majority of the KDCs and Korean Christians in the USA do not seem to have meaningful relationships with neighboring churches and non-Korean neighbors, including Christians, in large part due to language (English) barriers and cultural differences. However, coming from a homogeneous culture, certain Korean ethnocentric tendencies might have played a major role in this isolationistic behavior.

Culturally, the KDCs in the USA often identify neither with the Church in Korea nor with the Church in America.[11] They possess a distinct "third culture" milieu as churches in diasporic mode. Biblically and theologically, however, many KDC traits of being aloof and too Korean community-centric – separated from or not interfacing much with other non-Korean communities, denominations, and churches – would be unhealthy, for all the KDCs too, belong to the universal Church as well.

The "silent exodus" of the English-speaking generations from the KDCs

Korean-American, English-speaking generations have been leaving the KDCs by droves, which is commonly referred to as the "silent exodus."[12] In a recent survey of second-generation Korean Americans, 54.2% left KDCs after high school, 26.1% during college years, and 10.7% after college. Of those who left KDCs, 45.7% did not attend any church (Korea Times 2012). The top five reasons for the "silent exodus" of the English-speaking members were: not seeing "vision/hope" in KDCs (40.9%); having language barrier issues (35.8%); lacking a sense of ownership in KDCs (32.7%); becoming atheists (31.9%); and, switching to mainstream ("American") churches (30.7%) (Korea Times 2012).[13] And 55% of the second-generation perceived the silent exodus to be a "dire situation." However, it is also necessary to point out the fact that this phenomenon of the silent exodus from (any) church is not exclusive to U.S.-born Korean Americans; it appears that this church-leaving trend generally applies to all the postmodern young generations in the country, regardless of their ethnic/cultural backgrounds.

---

11 There are some exceptions to this. For instance, certain KDCs in the USA and around the world still belong to and are governed by their mother denominations based in Korea.

12 See also Peter Cha, Paul Kim, and Dihan Lee. "Multigenerational Households," in Viji Nakka-Cammauf and Timothy Tseng (eds.), Asian American Christianity Reader (Castro Valley, CA: The Institute for the Study of Asian American Christianity, 2009), 127-38.

13 For this question/category, researchers allowed multiple answers.

Lack of Korean-American pastors at the KDCs

A contributing factor to the silent exodus explained above is lack of U.S.-born Korean-America pastors at KDCs, or a silent exodus of Korean-American (English-speaking) pastors themselves from KDCs. One Korean-American pioneer pastor in his 60s declared that "This is a national crisis!" within the KDCs in the USA, and that first-generation senior pastors have to pay more attention to this crucial issue.[14] We unreservedly concur with his assessment.

The top six reasons for Korean-American English ministry (EM) pastors' departure from KDCs were: 1) cultural conflict or differences with first-generation Korean senior pastor (59%); 2) leadership conflict with first-generation Korean senior pastors (40%); 3) lack of clear sense of calling to (English) ministry (32%); 4) call from another church (29%); 5) lack of ministry experience (24%); and, 6) low compensation (22%) (Korea Times 2012). On average, Korean-American EM pastors served KDCs for 3-5 years (51%), 1-2 years (25%), and under one year (9%).

In addition, another disturbing reality is that enrollment levels of Korean-American students at mainstream seminaries in the USA have been very low and seemingly in decline, compared with Korean-speaking and international students from Korea. According to a 2007 survey conducted by John Oh, a 1.5-generation mission leader, the difference between Korean-speaking seminarians and English-speaking (or bilingual) Korean-American seminarians at these seminaries were too wide to ignore: Southwestern (370 vs. 20); Golden Gate (100 vs. 20); Trinity in Illinois (100 vs. 25); Gordon-Conwell (140 vs. 60); Talbot (200 vs. 50); and Fuller (1,700 vs. 200) (Oh, 2012). The numbers of U.S-born Korean Americans have been increasing in Korean diaspora communities since 1903. Accordingly, there were, are, and will be dire needs for KDCs to hire and retain more EM pastors. However, low enrollments of Korean-Americans at seminaries, coupled with Korean-American pastors' silent exodus from the KDCs themselves, is a huge issue for the KDCs in the 21st century. Therefore, there are and will likely be vast shortages of Korean-American pastors in the USA.

Generation transition and leadership issues at the KDCs

In the 1990s, several prominent and highly respected Korean senior pastors[15] at KDCs publically proclaimed that in the 21st century, Korean ministries (KMs) would meet in small sanctuaries and (bigger) EMs would

---

14 I. Henry Koh, Korean Ministry Coordinator at Presbyterian Church in America, personal conversation (30 July 2008).

15 Dong Sun Lim of Oriental Mission Church (L.A.); Hee Min Park of Youngrak Presbyterian Church (L.A.); Kwang Shin Kim of Grace Church (Fullerton, CA), et al.

meet in the main sanctuaries. In reality, in part due to the silent exodus, as explained above, this transition from the KM-strong mode to the EM-strong has not happened in the KDCs. Also, the tsunami of nonimmigrant visitors – international students and workers, long-term visitors, etc – since the 1990s, has more than made up for the declining numbers of immigrants from Korea, thereby perpetuating the need for Korean-language worship services at the KDCs. Second, generational leadership transitions from first-generation senior pastors and leaders to 1.5-generation senior pastors and leaders that all expected to take place at large and mid-sized KDCs in the 21st century have happened on a very small scale, partially because of a high supply of capable pastors who came from Korea as international students to pursue advanced degrees at American seminaries. If this trend of no or little leadership transition to the next generation persists, and likely it will, many bilingual and bicultural 1.5-generation pastors and leaders, many in their 30s-40s now, will continue to feel powerless in and disheartened with the KDCs.

Areas of strength and opportunity for the Korean Diaspora Churches[16]

While the KDCs are losing their second-generation membership, much of the optimism discussed in this section pertains to first-generation immigrants, particularly since Korean immigration trends are expected to continue unabated going forward.

High church attendance

According to U.S. Census' data, 1,423,784 Koreans/Korean-Americans lived in the USA in 2010. It is estimated that the number of the Korean population in the USA in 2010 would increase to be about 2 million when the undocumented, international students and workers, et al. who did not participate in the 2010 Census are added. If that's the case, as of 2010, on average, one Korean(-American) Protestant church existed for every 417 Korean(-American) residents in the USA.[17] In that regard, Koreans could possibly be the most evangelized or most church-attending (-affiliated) ethnic/diaspora group in the USA.

---

16 I (Im) have identified and discussed only three items in this section due to space limitation. More can be included here that I will leave to later discussions and to others to explore.

17 As of 2011, the U.S. state for the highest ratio between the KDCs and its Korean population was Arkansas (175: 1 KDC), and the lowest ratio was Minnesota (1,249: 1 KDC). Korean Churches Yellowpages (L.A.: Christian Today, 2012), 93 and 202.

Fervent prayer life

The KDCs in the USA have experienced phenomenal growth and expansion in the past few decades for several reasons. One key component of this success can be contributed to fervent prayer life of KDCs' members. As mission historian Tetsunao Yamamori correctly claims, "Every significant movement begins with prayer, and is sustained by prayer."[18] As in churches in Korea, most KDCs in the USA have an early-morning prayer service that usually begins between 5:30AM and 6:00AM, five or six times a week. This early morning ("dawn prayer" in Korean) service or tradition applies to those KDCs without their own buildings, too; they normally use their host churches' buildings for the morning services. Generally, the KDCs also have a week-night, usually Wednesday or Friday, service, in which corporate prayer time is often included.

Evangelism outreach to non-Christians

Another byproduct of the Korean diaspora in the USA is the non-Christian Korean people's contact with, and openness to the Gospel. An exceedingly high percentage at that time, about 40% of the early immigrants to Hawaii were Christians, and many more were exposed to Christianity before or right after their arrival in Hawaii (Chang 2003). In 2002, it was estimated that up to 70% of the Korean diaspora in the USA attended churches (Kang 2002),[19] and 61% and 10% of Koreans/Korean Americans in the USA are Protestants and Catholics respectively, according to a 2012 survey done by the Pew Forum on Religion & Public Life, whereas the corresponding number in Korea indicated less than one-third of the South Korean population in 2005 were Christians, both Protestants and Catholics combined.[20] Arrival and living in the USA has enticed many non-Christians, often lonely and homesick, to step into KDCs' buildings for various reasons. As a direct result of their church-going activity, either voluntarily or through a friend's invitation, many who had no previous religious affiliation (23%)[21] or followed other religions (5%), such as

18 Tetsunao Yamamori, personal conversation (6 May 2011).

19 Our interpretation from the article is that the 70% figure mentioned is believed to include Protestants and Catholics.

20 2005 South Korea Census: Among the Korean population, 18.3% were Protestants and 10.9% Catholics. The Korean census is taken every 10 years (…1995, 2005, 2015, etc.). http://pewresearch.org/pubs/657/south-koreas-coming-election-highlights-christian-community, accessed 17 July 2012.

21 2005 South Korea Census: Among the Korean population, 46.9% indicated that they had no religious affiliation. http://pewresearch.org/pubs/657/south-koreas-coming-election-highlights-christian-community, accessed 17 July 2012.

Buddhism[22] in Korea, have become Christians for the first time in their new adopted land (Korea Times 2012).

Missiological implications

Over the last few decades, Korean-dominant pockets or enclaves have popped up and been expanding in major cities across the USA. However, it seems the Korean diaspora communities and KDCs have not had significant interaction with other neighboring communities and their churches. This process of growth in cultural isolation is not exclusive to the Korean diaspora communities and churches in the USA.[23]

Against this backdrop of the fast-transforming multi-ethnic/multi-cultural/multi-religious realities of the USA, then, what would be some mission implications for the Korean diaspora churches, leaders, and mission agencies in the USA? [24]

Overlooking Diaspora neighbors

Korean churches, Christian leaders, and mission agencies in the USA have heavily focused on overseas missions. As a result, many of them have overlooked or underemphasized the need to reach out to the nations (ethnolinguistic people groups) within the U.S. borders. It is of monumental importance that the KDCs and Korean Christian leaders in the USA soon recognize the USA as an important and strategic mission field, and then actively engage in cross-cultural ministries and missions here.[25]

In other words, Korean churches, Christian leaders, and mission agencies in North America have overemphasized the Great Commission mandate (Go to the ends of the earth!), and underemphasized the Great Commandment's second mandate (Love your neighbor as yourself!). They

---

22 2005 South Korea Census: Among the Korean population, 23.1% were Buddhists. http://pewresearch.org/pubs/657/south-koreas-coming-election-highlights-christian-community, accessed 17 July 2012.

23 Simply put, it feels safe and comfortable to mingle with people from one's own culture who speak the same language. However, the L.A. Riots of 1992, in which Koreans suffered tremendous losses as an ethnic group, was a historic turning point, which shook up this kind of complacent mentality among Koreans in the USA. After the 1992 riots, L.A.'s Korean leaders, including Christian pastors, saw the need to connect more meaningfully with leaders from African-American and other non-Korean communities.

24 For this section, I (Im) have identified and explained only three such implications due to space limitation. I will leave other mission implications to other scholars to explore and discuss.

25 One positive example of this would be: SEED International, a U.S.-based Korean-American mission agency, at its annual board meeting in November 2010, recognized the USA as a strategic mission field and made intentional efforts to encourage multi-ethnic church planting and cross-cultural missions here.

need to challenge and teach Christians how our unbelieving neighbors – i.e., people from all over the world, which include American-born peoples – need Jesus Christ as well.

Racial reconciliation

Korean churches, Christian leaders, and mission agencies in the USA need to intentionally invest their time, resources, and efforts into racial reconciliation, unity, and collaboration among the diverse people groups – e.g., with Japanese-Americans, African-Americans, Latin Americans, and Caucasian-Americans – in the Body of Christ in the USA.

Multicultural partnerships

In reaching out more to other diaspora churches and leaders (see above), Korean churches, Christian leaders, and mission agencies in the USA need to deliberately and passionately join hands with other non-Korean ministry/mission networks, especially connecting with influential mainstream networks such as the Mission America Coalition (U.S. Lausanne) and Ethnic America Network, to collaborate with and maximize efforts and resources.[26]

By and large, the Korean diaspora churches (and communities) still exist like "islands" on the face of the U.S. church and mission landscape. It is imperative that the KDCs and their leaders make more intentional efforts to reach out to create meaningful "bridges" within their respective communities and with other non-Korean communities. If not, the KDCs' spheres of Christian and mission influence may not extend much beyond their "Koreatown" boundaries.

For discussion

1. Most churches in diaspora eventually face generational challenges such as those described in this chapter. What are these challenges like in your context? Are diaspora churches in your nation experiencing their own "silent exodus" of 1.5 and 2nd generation peoples? To what extent are first generation leaders raising up and empowering younger leaders who are perhaps more assimilated to the host nation?
2. How have you seen a tendency towards ethnic isolationism hinder diaspora churches in your city from engaging fully in God's mission to other diasporas or to non-Christian nationals around them? Do

26 A good example of this kind of joint effort with the mainstream would be the First and Second 4/14 Movement Summits, hosted by The Promise Church (Senior Pastor: Rev. Dr. Nam Soo Kim) in New York in 2009 and 2010.

you see examples of diaspora churches who have abandoned the "island" mentality for the sake of mission?

3. To what extent do national church, denomination and agency leaders in your context involve diaspora churches in the formation and implementation of a corporate vision to reach your nation with the Gospel?

Bibliography

Cha Peter, Paul Kim and Dihan Lee. "Multigenerational Households," in *Asian American Christianity Reader* edited by Viji Nakka-Cammauf and Timothy Tseng. Castro Valley, CA: The Institute for the Study of Asian American Christianity, 2009.

Chang, Roberta W. S. and Wayne Patterson. *The Koreans in Hawaii: A Pictorial History, 1903-2003.* Honolulu: University of Hawai'i Press, 2003.

Im, Chandler H. "Beyond the Korean Line: Toward the Multi-Ethnic Ministry in North America," Presentation at Korean Diaspora Forum in Fullerton, California, 5 May 2011.

Im, Chandler H. "The Korean Diaspora Churches: Their Concerns and Strengths" in *Global Diasporas and Mission* edited by Chandler H. Im and Amos Yong. Oxford: Regnum, 2014.

Kang, Connie K. "Church Takes a Monumental Shape." *Los Angeles Times*, October 26, 2002. http://articles.latimes.com/2002/oct/26/local/me-religkorean26.

"Korean Pastors' Work Period 3-5 Years at the Most," [in Korean] *Korea Times*, June 28, 2012. http://www.koreatimes.com/article/737519/.

Lugo, Luis and Brian J. Grim. "Presidential Election in South Korea Highlights Influence of Christian Community." *Pew Research on Religion and Public Life Project,* December 12, 2007. http://pewresearch.org/pubs/657/south-koreas-coming-election-highlights-christian-community.

Monger, Randall. *Nonimmigrant Admissions to the United States: 2012*, Office of Immigration Statistics, Policy Directorate, U.S. Department of Homeland Security, 2012. http://www.dhs.gov/sites/default/files/publications/ois_ni_fr_2012.pdf.

Oh, John. "Korean Diaspora Churches for the Mission of God," [in Korean] *Mission Insight*, Vol. 2. Incheon, South Korea: The Juan International University Press, 2012.

Oh, John Jungho. "The Mission of God and the Korean Diaspora Churches in the USA" [in Korean], *Mission Korea Review* vol. 3 (August 2013): 2-6.

"The Rise of Asian Americans." *Pew Research Socail and Demographic Trends,* April 4, 2013. http://www.pewsocialtrends.org/2012/06/19/the-rise-of-asian-americans/.

Suh, Insil. "5,929 Korean Churches abroad, 4,323 in the USA" [in Korean], *Christian Today* (29 January 2014), http://christiantoday.us/sub_read.html?uid=21674§ion=sc154§ion2

U.S. Department of Homeland Security. *Yearbook of Immigration Statistics: 2005*, Washington, D.C.: U.S. Department of Homeland Security, Office of Immigration Statistics, 2006. http://www.dhs.gov/xlibrary/assets/statistics/yearbook/2005/OIS_2005_Yearbook.pdf.

U.S. Department of Homeland Security. *Yearbook of Immigration Statistics: 2011*, Washington, D.C. U.S. Department of Homeland Security, Office of Immigration Statistics, 2012. (http://www.dhs.gov/sites/default/files/publications/immigration-statistics/yearbook/2011/ois_yb_2011.pdf).

U.S. Immigration and Naturalization Service. *Statistical Yearbook of the Immigration and Naturalization Service, 2000*, U.S. Government Printing Office: Washington, D.C., 2002. http://www.dhs.gov/xlibrary/assets/statistics/yearbook/2000/Yearbook2000.pdf.

Warner, Stephen R. "Coming to America: Immigrants and the Faith They Bring," *Christian Century* 121 (10 February 2004), 20-23.

21. Prayer and Power from the South: African Diaspora Churches on Mission

J. Kwabena Asamoah-Gyadu

Introduction: the North needs Jesus Christ

African immigrant Christianity is a microcosm of wider developments in which, as David Barrett, Andrew Walls, Lamin Sanneh and Kwame Bediako will have it, the demographic center of gravity of the Faith has shifted massively from the Northern to the Southern continents. "The era of Western Christianity has passed within our lifetimes, and the day of the Southern churches is dawning," is how Philip Jenkins (2011) casts this development. African churches in global North settings, although looked upon as "religious others," are illustrative of this transformation of Christianity into a non-Western religion and thus of mission as primarily an enterprise to be increasingly led by the Southern churches.

The new African immigrant churches have their own mission agenda within secularizing Western societies as far as Christian presence is concerned. Ultimately, the significance of these new diaspora churches lies in their perception that the North needs Jesus Christ, who appears in the testimony of John as "the Way, the Truth and the Life" (John 14:6). Thus unlike Israel that refused to do so within their depressing exilic conditions, African diaspora Christians, driven by feelings of the workability of the Gospel through prayer under difficult circumstances and empowered by the Holy Spirit, seek to sing the songs of the Lord in foreign lands.

In this chapter, we will consider African diaspora churches whose religio-cultural past influences their present mission engagement and uniquely suits them for affirming the supremacy of Jesus Christ in today's Northern contexts of competing religious ideas and secularization.

The "otherness" of African Diaspora Churches

The premise on which we proceed is that the new demographic strengths of mission are emerging from the global South (and East): Asia, Latin America and Africa. However, there is an obstacle for these new mission agents to overcome, namely that the churches from the South are different from those of the North. African diaspora churches, precisely because they represent a Christianity received within entirely different contexts than those from which earlier missionaries came, offer types of Christianity in which certain religio-cultural values remain palpable. In particular, African diaspora churches differ from their "missionary originals" because Africans, against the backdrops of indigenous experiences and interpretations of Scripture, privilege the pneumatic over the cerebral aspects of the faith. In African religious traditions, what is ultimately real is the spiritual. Thus through the pneumatic forms of Christianity expressed by African diaspora churches, we can discern what the ordinary African considers critical to the faith. These would include not simply the fact that Jesus Christ is Lord but that he also, by the power of the Spirit, intervenes in real life situations decimating the power of witches and demons and restoring people to hope and fulfillment within the physically and spiritually precarious diaspora in which faith has to be lived. A colleague living in the UK once asked me: "Why do African Christians living in our country spend so much time praying?" My answer was simple: "When they ask God for their daily bread, they really mean it!"

The result, as Philip Jenkins (2011) argues, is a situation in which it is easy to find religious behaviors and rituals in African church practices that Westerners often interpret as going beyond the bounds of theologically orthodox Christianity. In that sense, African immigrant churches have often been looked upon in the West as "religious others" and placed in the same category as non-Christian religious traditions. This is, in part, because a number of radical writers, as Jenkins argues, still link Christianity with Western imperialism and do not recognize the ways in which Christianity has been transformed through African hands. The otherness of these African immigrant churches in the eyes of their hosts stems from a stubborn resistance to the collapse of European missionary hegemony in the Western imagination.

African diaspora churches have been described as representing the future face of Christianity in Western Europe, but this is not always understood as positive development. In most parts of Europe, the typical African immigrant church is a "religious other" professing an adulterated variant of Christianity that is considered biblically suspicious and theologically deficient by their hosts. In line with this cautious attitude towards African churches German theologian Claudia Währisch-Oblau (2009) notes how the United Evangelical Mission of Germany, for example, had operated under the assumption that migrant churches were formed in search of religious identity suited to the original religio-cultural backgrounds of their members and therefore virtually placed a question mark on the type of Christianity being expressed, seeking to provide them "better" direction. In many cases immigrant congregations with historic links to German missions were expected to function under German church leadership and work within their ecclesial structures. The general attitude towards the new churches, described by Währisch-Oblau, has been dismissive:

> [While] in London and Amsterdam, Cologne and Prague church buildings are being turned into shops, housing space or even pubs, new congregations started by migrant Christians have been setting up worship spaces in disused

> factory halls, car parks, or even converted cinemas. These Christians and congregations represent a Christianity that, if noticed at all, is mostly perceived to be foreign, transient, and diasporal, in short: a minority phenomenon which might need some protection and support, but nothing that would have an impact on majority Christianity. (2009)

Such an attitude, however, can have the effect of blinding us to the work the Holy Spirit is doing today through diaspora churches as agents of mission and spiritual renewal in the North. Thus Wonsuk Ma (2011) has noted that it is now the turn of the churches of the South to revive the Western church. The role of diasporas in the midst of the secular West is therefore critically important. Indeed many immigrant churches and their leaders have come to define themselves as "missionaries" who are "planning to reach out not only to their own nationals, but to [Western] society as a whole" in the bid to bring revival to "dead" churches (Wahrisch-Oblau 2009). Demographic changes, Jenkins notes elsewhere in his book, naturally come with consequences for the religio-cultural landscape. New immigrant churches will follow cultural patterns more akin to their home societies than to host nations (Jenkins 2011). This makes them different, but it also signals their unique suitability for mission today. In spite of the globalization of Islam and the resulting fears, many of today's immigrants are African Christians and in concurrence with Jenkins, I believe that "they raise the prospect of a revitalized Christian presence on [Northern] soil" (2011).

African Christianity encountering western secularization

African Christianity and Christianity in Africa may not necessarily mean the same thing. Christianity in Africa in its real sense would refer to communities defined by their belief in the Lord Jesus Christ and the way these beliefs are expressed as part of the common witness of world Christianity on the continent. African Christianity, on the other hand, refers to expressions of Christianity informed by the primal worldviews embedded in African cultures and available also on the global stage. This would make it seem as if the Christianity of the South has strayed from older orthodoxies but as Jenkins (2011) attests, they have in almost all cases remained firmly within the limits of what may be considered authentic Christian traditions. "Far from inventing some new African or Korean religions that derive from local cultures," he writes, "the rising churches usually preach a strong and even pristine Christian message" (Jenkins 2011). In that respect, the lordship of Jesus Christ could be said to constitute the basis of all Christianity but that faith is not expressed the same way across cultures precisely because cultures and peoples differ.

Many African Christians who migrate keep their faith alive in their new countries. Speaking from the perspective of African Diaspora Christianity and its encounter with secularizing Western countries, I use the expression "secularizing" advisedly knowing that in many such places Christian recession has not necessarily excluded spirituality from private spheres. Not only are there many non-Christian new religious movements emerging within Western communities but there is also the practice of new forms of spirituality facilitated by the media, especially the internet and other social media. It is in the midst of these developments that non-Western forms of Christianity have gained prominence – a development which teaches us that God is still active in history working his purposes out in Jesus Christ as Lord. God may perhaps be doing this by using the foolish things of the world to shame the wise; the weak things to shame the strong; and the lowly things of this world; and the despised things – and the things that are not – to nullify the things that are, so that no one may boast before him (1 Cor. 1:27-29).

The African Diaspora Church as an apostolic body

The presence of African Christians in the diaspora drives home the point that even Christianity, in spite of whatever shared core beliefs it may have, is not a monolithic faith. In terms of their sense of mission, the self-definition of African immigrant Christian communities is very apostolic. African church leaders in the North today, whatever their Christian persuasion, are driven by a divine mandate to bring the Gospel back to those who originally provided it (Haar 1998). The mindset is that by prayer, the manifestations of power and the empowerment of the Spirit lost ground could be reclaimed for Christ.

Hendrik Kraemer argued that the Church is by its nature and calling an "apostolic body" which means, the Church is sent into the world with a specific mission for the whole world (Kraemer 1956). In his words:

> As an apostolic body the Church is commissioned to proclaim – by its kerygma of God's acts of salvation in Christ, by its koinonia as a new community living in bonds of peace and charity – the message of God's dealings with, and purpose for, the world and mankind. This message has to go out to all men, in all lands, in all situations and civilizations, in all conditions and spheres and circumstances of life, so witnessing to God's redemptive order in Jesus Christ, by word and deed. (Kraemer 1956)

The critical expressions in Kraemer's submission above include his reference to the Christian community as an "apostolic body." This is a function of the Church also articulated in the historic creeds. The others include the fact that the message of the redemptive purposes of God in Christ is meant for all humankind, in all lands, in all situations and civilizations and in all conditions, spheres and circumstances of life. Kraemer further makes the point that the "apostolic outreach" of the church implies embracing the "certainty of a given and knowable truth" (Kraemer 1956). This truth is believed to possess preeminence over all others including human philosophies no matter how sublime these may sound. In line with this thinking, African Christians although migrated to find economic opportunities, "consider that God has given them a unique opportunity to spread the good news among those who have gone astray" (Haar 1998).

In the pursuit of this apologetic agenda against other faiths and human philosophies, Kraemer suggests that the Church "has to define also its relation to the various aspects of culture as a whole, and has to indicate the motives and roots of its missionary character" (Kraemer 1956). These issues were raised within the context of how Christianity through the life and theology of the Church engages with non-Christian religious peoples and traditions. In our context however, we seek to apply this understanding of the mission of the Church of the Lord Jesus in diaspora situations of secularism, alienation, rejection of the idea of the Holy and the inability to fit into Northern Christian communities as a result of the cultural gaps and not in a few cases racist attitudes towards minority Christian enclaves.

Retrieving the stolen: African Diaspora Church on mission

There are different reasons for the movement of people. They move in tandem with the movement of capital and resources or as their perceptions of and opportunities for better living conditions become available elsewhere. Migration takes place as transnational economic corporations and organizations of intellectual, social and political life grow in number and require more transnational personnel to operate and serve. There are many others who move because their very survival depends on such movement. For many Africans, migration occurs because fields are dry, crops have failed or simply because of one form of persecution or another. Whatever the reason for migration, for many Africans, the process of moving from beginning to end involves important religious dimensions including rituals of facilitation, breakthroughs and survival. It is thus not uncommon for prayer centers in Ghana and Nigeria for example to receive potential migrants who come with their passports for prayer and anointing as they apply for visas or if already secured, for protection and success on the journey.

These are the people who constitute the African churches in diaspora. Migration has offered them opportunities to see at firsthand what has happened to Christianity in the land of the missionaries and they feel empowered to do something about the situation. Many may even be undocumented but the dynamism of their faith belies the troubles that they often go through as illegal aliens. Their circumstances are such that some amount of ethnic bonding and boundary creation may be inevitable. They have therefore often been seen as practicing the "ghettoization" of religion. Nevertheless it is incorrect to suggest that mission and witness are peripheral to the lives of African diaspora Christian communities. One day as we waited for a German Methodist service to close to enable Ghanaian

Methodists in Hamburg who rent the building to begin the service, one Ghanaian remarked to me that "the hearts of these Germans has been stolen by the devil." It was for him the only explanation for a nation so blessed by God to turn its back on him and question his existence.

Thus there is much prayer in these diaspora churches for personal concerns – particularly proper documentation, employment, health, family and deliverance from witches seeking to thwart endeavors away from home. However, there is also prayer that God will deliver Northern nations from the claws of the devil who according to Peter, prowls around like a lion looking for someone to devour (1Pet. 5:8). In John 10:10, Jesus described the devil as one who comes but to "steal, kill and destroy," activities which in contemporary immigrant Christian thought are actualizing through secularization, homosexual ordinations, and the public promotion of what may be considered morally wrong and detestable in the eyes of African churches. The activities through which the devil has stolen the hearts and minds of Western Europeans are also supposed to include the invocation of evolutionist theories as explanations for the existence of the universe, the barring of prayer in public places, and the treatment of homosexuality as a human right rather than a moral issue condemned by the Bible.

Incarnation as a missionary model for African Diaspora Churches

There may be other reasons for the establishment of immigrant churches by non-Westerners living in the developed West, but the thought that secularization is the devil's way of stealing, killing and destroying Christianity in the North is a strong motivation for the evangelistic activities of diaspora churches. In a sense Christian mission is now being interpreted with African biblical lenses. Thus as scholars such as Währisch-Oblau has pointed out, in the minds of many members of immigrant Christian communities, they are working with God on a rescue mission to Northern nations to return people to the God in whom all are supposed to "live and move and have their being" (Acts 17:28).

Migration and Christian mission have been interwoven with each other since God the Creator first revealed himself to humanity in the First Adam. The mandate of the God of mission to Adam then was clear and empowering:

> God blessed them and said to them, "Be fruitful and increase in number, fill earth and subdue it. Rule over the fish and the sea and the birds of the air and over every living creature that moves on the ground. (Gen. 1:28)

After the Fall, this mandate was renewed through different covenants from Noah and Abraham to Moses and David culminating in the Word, God himself becoming flesh and dwelling with humanity. In the words of the Gospel according to St. John: "We have seen his glory, the glory of the One and only, who came from the Father full of grace and truth" (John

1:14). What cannot be missed in our consideration of diaspora mission is the fact that God revealed himself in Jesus Christ as a mission strategy.

Mission, interpreted through the incarnational model is described in the work of Jehu H. Hanciles. In a poignant argument Hanciles (2003) has noted that the version of the Great Commission recorded in Matthew 28:18-20 is unlikely to retain its primacy in the growing non-Western missionary movement. The fact is that those involved in diaspora mission as immigrants from the South are working from the periphery. This mission, in contrast to their Western forbears, Hanciles (2003) notes, "comes not from the centers of political power and economic wealth but from the periphery". Thus the model of mission that fits the diaspora initiatives is the Johannine version with its implications of humble service and vulnerability on account of the fact that it follows the incarnation principle. Hanciles draws out the implications of the incarnational model of mission in relation to the vulnerabilities associated with diaspora life in the following words:

> Christ's life and ministry included the travail of a refugee, the pain of uprootedness, and the alienation that comes with being a stranger. Even the emptying of status to take on the form of a servant has its parallels in the migrant experience… Non-Western Christian migrants live among new peoples, dwell in the neighborhood, and are pressed into varying degrees of adaptation and assimilation, though often without entirely losing cultural traits. Much about their experience also evokes sharp images of the biblical paradigm of God's people as pilgrims, migrants, and refugees… God's revelation to humanity does not occur from the centers of world power but in the margins of society. (2003)

The aggregate meaning of all this is that it may take "Wise men" following a divine star to discern that the little vulnerable baby in the manger is actually the incarnate God in the midst of his own creation. In relation to diaspora Christianity, the great new fact of our time which has momentous consequences for mission is that the great migration that took colonialism and Christianity to the non-Western world has now gone into reverse. Immigrants are now beginning to have a significant place in Western Christian history, for it may be that in some areas of the West at least, "Christianity will be associated increasingly with immigrants" (Walls 2002). It must not surprise us, talking about mission to the ends of the earth therefore, that a high level of internationalism has crept into the missionary agenda of the contemporary African Pentecostal/charismatic movement.

Power from Nigeria to Ukraine: a case of African Diaspora Church on mission

To illustrate the ways in which immigrant Christianity is engaging with secular Europe, consider the life and work of Sunday Adelaja, a Nigerian charismatic pastor who has been working in Europe for twenty years. His story has been of particular interest to me in the last decade because the difference that a single immigrant Christian has made in Eastern Europe generally and in the Ukraine in particular is phenomenal. By most accounts one of the largest megachurches in Europe, Embassy of the Blessed Kingdom of God for All Nations has long been drawing huge crowds away from the state-related Eastern Orthodox Churches. Adelaja's church has attracted large numbers of former alcoholics, drug addicts and prostitutes who now openly testify about their salvation and transformation in Christ.

Apart from the African origins of its founder there is little that is specifically African or Nigerian about Embassy. I concede that the African identity of the founder is very significant but this must be placed within its proper context. With its 25,000 strong membership being almost entirely white Eastern European, Embassy does not belong to the same category as the many African immigrant churches that have burgeoned within the African Diaspora in Western Europe and North America since the 1990s. Indeed from its logo to the use and display of banners in worship and the international agenda of its founder, there are three main identities that seem critical to the self-understanding of Embassy. The first is the immigrant status of its founder; the second is the church's Pentecostal/charismatic status characterized by a strong theology of power and spiritual warfare; and third, the deliberate pursuit of a transnational agenda in mission.

Catherine Wanner, who has also studied Embassy, speaks to its transnational focus when she notes that unlike early evangelical communities that either sought to retreat from the world because of its corrupting elements or strove to prove that they are *in* the world but not *of* it, Embassy "aims to remake the world in its own image, radically altering, once again, evangelical sensibilities and responses to worldly, profane matters" (Wanner 2007). This transnational agenda is evident in both the name of the church and its logo. She captures succinctly the meaning of the logo as follows:

> The symbol of [Embassy] is a globe with Africa forthrightly positioned in the center. The globe is capped by a golden crown with a cross. Just below the crown is a light emanating from Ukraine, which remains otherwise unmarked. The light from Ukraine shines throughout Europe and the Middle East. Africa figures prominently, but the light and energy of the church emanate from Ukraine around the world. (Wanner 2007)

The name of the church was also chosen to reflect the transnational understanding of Christian mission: The Church is the representative of God on the earth, His "embassy." Therefore we, children of God, are the citizens of His Divine Kingdom and not citizens of this world! The Blessed Kingdom of God is a place for the destruction of curses. At the head of every kingdom is a king. Our King is Jesus Christ! He is the Lord of all nations; Jesus Christ is the Savior for everyone, irrespective of his age, color or skin, nationality and social status.[1] The witness of Adelaja in Eastern Europe has been strong and stands as a powerful example of what African diaspora churches on mission can accomplish.

Conclusion: singing the songs of the Lord in a foreign land

Scripture has much to say about issues of immigration, dealing with "the other", the marginalized, stranger and vulnerable. The point of Peter's vision (Acts 10) was to prepare him to embrace Gentile converts among whom the Holy Spirit was also active. The Spirit of God is a Spirit of inclusion so it is by the experience of the Spirit that Gentiles come to inherit the blessing of Abraham (Gal. 3:14-15). The incarnation was about redemption through identification. When through the incarnation, divinity was translated into humanity, God in Christ as the Second Adam fully and completely identified with fallen human nature in order to redeem it. God disempowered himself that he might empower his people in the course of mission.

Further, the bearer of redemption not only started life in a context of deprivation because "there was no room for them in the inn" but also became a refugee shortly thereafter. M. Daniel Carroll Rodas reminds us that the joy of the nativity scene and the wonder of the visit of the Magi were soon overtaken by scenes of the senseless death of innocent children and the flight of refuges. The migration of Joseph, Mary and the baby Jesus, he notes, "locates the Jesus story within a movement that spans history, of people desiring a better life or escaping the threat of death" (Rodas 2008). Throughout the New Testament, it is within such diaspora conditions that the Gospel takes root and the hope is that as Christianity moves from the South to the North, we shall discern in it the move of God empowering the weak to fulfill his purposes within the strong. These are truths evident in the life of the head of the Church, Jesus Christ, which challenges Northern Christians to respond positively to the diaspora churches as agents of mission who spread the Gospel in the midst of similar alienating conditions which many African immigrants must endure.

The question of diaspora Israel, "how shall we sing the song of the Lord in a foreign land" (Ps. 137:4) has been reinvented in the lives of contemporary African immigrant Christians who are seeing possibilities rather than impossibilities. The words from this cry of Israel in exile have become an important running theme in the discourse on immigrant Christianity. In the original story, the depression of exilic life led God's people to abandon worship because they felt forsaken by the God of promise. In contrast, through their dynamic worshipping presence and intentional efforts to both reverse the traditional notions of mission going

---

1 Stated in Church of the Embassy of the Blessed Kingdom of God for all Nations: 8th Anniversary Brochure (Kiev, 2002), 5.

only from North to South and also to stand against the secularization processes underway in the North, African diaspora churches have chosen a different path from their historic forbears. We may say that they are increasingly heading the admonition of Peter who urged, "As aliens and strangers in the world ... live such good lives among the pagans that, though they accuse you of doing wrong, they may see your good deeds and glorify God on the day he visits us" (1Pet. 2:11-12).

For discussion

1. The religio-cultural "otherness" of African diaspora churches has been presented here as both an obstacle and an opportunity for mission. Consider the perspectives and responsibilities of both the diaspora and host nation churches in your context. How can they work together to overcome these obstacles and embrace the opportunities for mission?
2. The author argues that diaspora churches represent a great hope for spiritual revitalization in the global North. Do you agree with the notion that "the North needs Jesus" and that God is choosing to use diaspora Christians as agents of renewal?
3. This chapter again returns to themes of "mission from the margins" and a mission spirituality modeled after the incarnation but connects these to the idea of power. What do you want to learn from African diaspora churches about vulnerability and power in mission? Do you, your church or organization need to undergo a process of self-emptying in order to tap into the power of the Holy Spirit?
4. In your opinion, are the host nation churches and denominations in your context willing to give diaspora churches a "place at the table" in the leading of mission strategies? What does/should this look like?

Bibliography

Bediako, K. (1993). John Mbiti's Contribution to African Theology. In J. K. Olupona, & S. S. Nyang, *Religious Plurality in Africa: Essays in Honor of John S. Mbiti* (367-396). Berlin: Mouton de Gruyter.

Bediako, K. (2000). *Jesus in Africa: The Christian Gospel in African History and Experience.* Akropong: Regnum Africa.

Carino, F. V. (2005). The Dynamics of Political Migrations as a Challenge to Religious Life. In J. d. Ana, *Religions Today: Their Challenge to the Ecumenical Movement* (86). Geneva: World Council of Churches.

Embassy of the Blessed Kingdom of God for All Nations. (2002). Embassy of the Blessed Kingdom of God for All Nations: 8th Anniversary. *Brochure*. Kiev, Ukraine.

Haar, G. t. (1998). *Halfway to Paradise: African Christian Presence in Europe.* Cardiff: Cardiff Academic Press.

Hanciles, J. H. (2003). Migration and Mission: Some Implications for the Twenty-First Century Church. *International Bulletin of Missionary Research*, 149-150.

Jenkins, P. (2011). *The Next Christendom: The Coming of Global Christianity.* Oxford: Oxford University Press.

Kim, S. H., & Ma, W. (2011). *Korean Diaspora and Christian Mission.* Oxford: Regnum Books International.

Kraemer, H. (1956). *Religion and the Christian Faith.* Cambridge: James Clarke.

Ma, W. (2011). A Millennial Shift of Global Christianity and Mission. In S. Hun Kim & Wonsuk Ma, *Korean Diaspora and Christian Mission* (11-24). Oxford: Regnum Books International.

Olupona, J., & Gemignani, R. (2007). *African Immigrant Religions in America.* Washington D.C.: New York University Press.

Ott, C., Strauss, S. J., & Tennent, T. C. (2010). *Encountering Theology of Mission: Biblical Foundations, Historical Developments, and Contemporary Issues.* Grand Rapids: Baker Academic.

Rodas, M. Daniel Carroll (2008). *Christians at the Border: Immigration, the Church and the Bible.* Grand Rapids: Baker Academic.

Wahrisch-Oblau, C. (2009). *The Missionary Self-Perception of Pentecostal/Charismatic Church Leaders from the Global South in Europe.* Leiden/Boston: E.J. Brill.

Walls, A. F. (2002). Mission and Migration: The Diaspora Factor in Christian History. *Journal of African Christian Thought*, 3-11.

Wanner, C. (2007). *Communities of the Converted: Ukrainians and Global Evangelism.* London: Cornell University Press.

22. Diaspora Family: Immigrant Church as a Family and Missional Families in Diaspora

Sam George

Introduction

Human dispersion is disruptive to family life and the challenges of diasporic living accentuate their sense of identity and belonging, forcing migrants to explore their spiritual moorings and new relationships. Understanding the relational dynamics amidst changing loyalties, fractured identities, cultural assimilation and many experiences of loss and loneliness are key to doing mission in the context of diaspora. And the reconceptualization of Christian Mission in terms of family is not only strategic to diaspora communities, but also to missions itself.

Generally, missiology has overlooked the lens of family. Most mention of family and mission are subsumed under the rubrics of missionary families (how to move your family to the mission field or raising missionary kids in another culture) or caring for overseas missionary families. However, in early Christian mission and thought we find the strategic importance of diaspora and *Oikos* (households), both of which advanced Christianity in surprising ways in the first century and continue to do so in the twenty-first century. Today, diaspora churches are emerging everywhere and they are built upon relational networks. Many have argued its vibrancy and critical influence on the host society where Christianity is declining, using concepts like reverse mission, immigrant Christianity and mission from everywhere to everywhere (Escobar 2003; Hanciles 2008; Nazir-Ali 1991). However, what makes the diaspora church so distinct and influential is its strong sense of family and community.

In this chapter, I explore the intersections of faith, family and diaspora. The long term, long distance migrations have affected traditional family sensibilities and yet they sustain migrants in the new world through reproduction and adaptations. On one hand, the family is crucial to faith formation, nurture and transmission; and on the other hand, faith is crucial to psychological well-being, relational health and stability. Diaspora contexts, marked by diversity, devotion and disruption, offer an enormous challenge to Christian Missions both in their adopted settlements as well as their ancestral homelands. This paper illustrates the critical nature of family ministry in immigrant congregations, how healthy families are key to genuine faith development and transmission, and the need to expand the missional concept to families. This chapter draws from my PhD research[1] on diaspora families, based upon ethnographic fieldwork among the first and second generation Indian immigrant pastors, counselors and families from different church backgrounds.

Diaspora families

Historically, long distance and long term migration were an exclusive prerogative of menfolk, as the arduous and risky journeys across lands and seas were thought too strenuous for women to undertake (Sowell 1996). The restriction of women during early colonial labor migration created enormous gender imbalances that led to breakdown in normal family life (Cohen 2008). However, over the last decade, there has been greater gender parity among global migrants. The World Migration Report 2013 (WMR) found that 49 percent of global migrants were women. (International Organization for Migration 2013)[2] But they do not belong to the same household, separating the breadwinners from the rest of their family and creating transnational families, who adopt a deliberate strategy of "living in two or more countries in order to maximize opportunities for education, employment and social advancement for their family members" (Levitt 2004).

The family reunion and family sponsorship provisions of immigration policies in many nations like the United States and Canada permit migrants to bring immediate family (spouse and minor children) to the places of settlement, leaving behind parents, siblings and other relatives. In some countries such as Australia and New Zealand, the family reunion was limited to around 40% of new residents (Ho and Bedford 2008). While other nations like Saudi Arabia and Japan, do not allow workers to bring even immediate family. Such restrictions have led to the development of new strategies amongst migrants for maintaining connections between spatially dispersed families. Subsequent to the abolition of miscegenation laws in many nations, there are increased incidences of interracial marriages and children. The nuclearization of family alters traditional marital and parental structure, norms and roles, breeding new dysfunctionalities into the family system and assimilation drives a wedge between generations.

Why look at diasporas through the lens of the family? In the past, migrants were treated as individuals who either departed (emigrant) or arrived (immigrant). Scholars have either under-theorized or fully neglected

---

1 See George, Sam. "Families in Diaspora: A Pastoral and Missiological Study of Asian Indian Christians in Greater Chicago (1965-2010)" (PhD dissertation, Andrew F. Walls Centre for the Study of Asian and African Christianity, Liverpool Hope University, Liverpool, UK 2013).

2 http://publications.iom.int/bookstore/free/WMR2013_EN.pdf (accessed Mar 10, 2014)

family migrations and only recently, they have begun to look closely at the family dimension of global human dispersion (Clark et al. 2009). Massey (1993) claimed that "families, households, or other culturally defined units of production, consumption and child-rearing" were the more "appropriate units of analysis for migration research" over against the "autonomous individual". Rabila (2009) proposed that migration research must "pay more attention to families than to individuals". By examining the impact of migration on individual well-being, the WMR 2013 goes beyond the conventional scrutiny, using emotional and relational well-being of the individual migrants, bringing out the key role family and relational networks play in diasporic life. Vertovec (2009) found that immigrants and refugees seem to adjust far more quickly when they live as an extended family and nations are more likely to integrate minorities if they respect communal networks. I concur with missiologist De Neui (2010) that "if Christian mission in Asia and most of the non-Western world is ever to advance, it must seriously consider the importance of family networks".

In his study of African diaspora, Arthur (2010) found that family relationships are critical to immigrants because kin relations serve as the agency within which migration decisions are made, implemented and sustained. Likewise, Goldin (2011) inferred that the family, not the individual, is the "primary unit of the migration decision making". About Afro-Caribbeans, Chamberlain (2006) claimed "families are micro-societies of their own, with their own histories and cultures, creating their own dynamics and ethos, continuities and ruptures, constantly evolving to accommodate growth and change". According to Foner (2001), recent immigrants maintain familial, economic, cultural, religious and political ties across national borders, thus making immigrant home and host societies a unitary social and cultural field. As a result, they never really leave home. They straddle multiple social space and cultural realities. With the possibility of home culture recreation in places far from home, they build bridges between the old country and the new. Modern transportation, communication technologies and the ubiquitous Internet make such access and interaction feasible and is now affordable. The relational bonds determine the extent of these interactions, ensuing in knowledge transfer, empowerment, cultural exchanges, and access to opportunity between dispersed people and their relatives in the ancestral homeland and elsewhere. Also, current migratory trends encourage frequent family visits, limited contractual relationships, intermittent stays abroad and sojourning, as opposed to permanent settlement and securing of citizenship of the destination country. The global networks are an increasingly dense web of social contacts between places of origin and destinations, spawned by spatial displacement, that are sustained on the basis of kin relationships (Portes 1997). Such unprecedented intermingling of people and cultures are rewiring relational networks and knitting together a new awareness of self and our global existence, resulting in an "intensification of consciousness" (Robertson 1992).

Most contemporary economists are quick to notice the nexus between remittances and human development, as money transfers from migrants have come to exceed international aid (Ratha, et al. 2015). Generally remittances are considered only as money sent by migrants to their family, but a more nuanced understanding points to a multidirectional flow that includes social, technological, political and cultural remittances (Levitt 1998). It builds and sustains long distance relationships across time zones and national boundaries as money becomes a medium of care and support to filial relationships and reciprocal obligations of care. Singh (2007) called remittance the "most visible and measurable form of transnational family ties" and it shapes and is shaped by relationships and cultural values. Remittances give senders a sense of continued belonging to family and eventual return to the homeland, as in cases of migrants to nations in the Middle East where permanent settlement is not an option. People seek economically-advantageous marriage alliances for family members from churches and friends in the diaspora. They procure ethnic products and services from relatives, keeping money within the community. They host nephews and nieces who seek college or vocational training and provide guidance for overseas prospects. They offer loans and credit for ethnic enterprises to fellow immigrants and relatives back home. Being part of a tightly knit diasporic community, family and kin-based economic transactions are made easier and safer. When business succeeds, it brings not just material rewards, but social approval and prestige within the minority group. If it fails, social sanctions provide a cheaper, more effective means of collecting bad debts than legal action. Thus, relationships are key to understanding dispersed people and their pursuits.

Family life in Diaspora

Migrants carry distinctive filial and religious traditions with them from their ancestral homelands, both of which are deeply intertwined and reciprocal, and try to transplant them in the host societies in order to produce a discrete identity and community life in an alien environment. For Asians, Africans and Latin Americans, the concept of family denotes broader meaning than the Western notion. Faith matters in diasporic settings remain a collective decision, rather than individualistic. They also face numerous hurdles in their domestic and religious life, many of which they fail to adequately comprehend and decisively deal with. Handlin (1990) described immigration to the United States, for example, "as the history of alienation and its consequence ... of the broken homes, interruptions of a familiar life, separation from known surroundings, becoming a foreigner, and ceasing to belong". Though migration helps some families, "to escape from the shackles of age-old family traditions and oppressive customary obligations," it also "exacerbates conflicts and has undermined conventional family sensibilities" (Bacon 1996).

Families undergo many essential transformations in diasporic settings. The most obvious ones include break up of family arrangement in the form of nuclearization, changes in gender roles, lack of a support system, reduction in family size, flattening of gender hierarchy, acculturation to host culture, conflicts arising out of differing values, need to communicate and negotiate new issues, alienation from extended family members, loss of community and collectivism, adjusting to dual career and different shifts, maintaining legal status and employment. As diaspora families pitch tent in the new world and adjust to new realities, it takes a toll on their psyche and marital strain, abuse, separation, divorce, and domestic violence become more common than in their motherlands. The nonexistence of culturally appropriate caregivers and delays in seeking help worsens the situation. The inability to deal with fresh dilemmas facing them, weakens the family well-being and the culture of shame and stigma against external intervention deteriorate the relational health of the whole community. The notion of living up to the expectation of the people they left behind, like old neighbors, friends, charities, religious bodies and others, is real as all who go abroad are perceived as wealthy and everyone feels entitled to share in the success of emigrants. Going away to faraway lands does not impede familial obligations or bonds, instead it strengthens them as migrants offer material and financial support to those who stay behind. Parents expect migrant children to send money home so they can construct a house, educate or marry off other children and meet communal obligations. In addition, they experience rivalry and economic pressure from fellow immigrants as financial success becomes the new currency of status in the new world causing enormous strain on relationships.

Families in diaspora suffer from many distinct stressors. Kulanjiyil (2010) noted that "adaptation to societal norms, cultural values and behaviors of host group constantly cause psychological distress." The racial discrimination, homesickness, culture shock, acculturation stress, fear and uncertainties of the future, perceived hate and loneliness are part of every immigrant journey. Contradictory values on dating, sexuality and mate selection, is a common struggle in many immigrant homes in the West. The belief of living and dying close to where you were born, curse of crossing seas, religious restrictions and emigrant having to undergo purification rituals to reenter the religious system kept people land locked for centuries and overcoming these age old tenets requires courage and results in consequences that may last for generations. The caste hierarchies, dietary customs, personal devotion and allegiance to local deities are compromised as a result of geographical displacement. Failure to carry out domestic duties, uphold household honor, discontinuation of multi-generational filial links, break in ancestral worship, pilgrimage to sacred places, abandonment of communal obligations, ceremonial visit to family graves, and fear of defilement by association with inferior others, results not only in an immediate drop in social status, but also soul pollution. Seeking marriage alliances, the prospects of children marrying outside of one's caste, language group and race, children's disregard for parents' tradition, loss of mother tongue proficiency, absence from family reunions, control of children's sexual and relational explorations and more, present complex family dilemmas.

Diaspora families also play a key role in socialization of the next generation as raising children abroad remains a daunting task. Having never been through the educational system in the host country, immigrant parents dread meeting school teachers who neither speak their language nor are conversant with their culture. The assault on long cherished values and the perceived anti-family attitude of the host society further isolates dispersed people. The roles reverse when wives become the lone breadwinners or children teach parents how to conduct themselves in the new environment. The prolonged absence of father or mother, have adverse consequences of anxiety, sadness, anger and insecurity in children, accumulated during the years of abandonment. The children of immigrants exhibit signs of neglect and abuse akin to absentee or single parent homes. As biculturals they struggle with identity confusion and social isolation. The pain of being misunderstood or having to clarify themselves to everyone in the host society affects the immigrant psyche permanently. No matter how well they try, there is a nagging sense that others will never really 'get it.' Family life in diaspora is also marked with guilt of having neglected their own parents who sacrificed much to get them where they are and not being around to care for them in their senior years. Many contemporary migrants to developed nations hall from societies where children are seen as the social security or retirement plan and the geographical displacement prevents emigrants from meeting filial, cultural and religious obligations toward their parents. Diasporic people also suffer from incomplete parenting, as in traditional societies where parenting extends until children become parents or even grandparents, which may adversely affect how they parent their foreign-born children, in addition to their ignorance of the host culture.

Missional family[3]

There exists a strong sense of family in immigrant churches. The commonality of place of origin, language, sociocultural and religious backgrounds, and struggles in the host society tend to bind them together in profound ways as one large family. Immigrants feel a kindred spirit and realize how their aspirations are so deeply intertwined with each other. The resurgence of ethnic identity when surrounded by people unlike themselves

---

3 For more on missional family and Theology of Trinitarian Missional Family, see my dissertation Families in Diaspora (2013).

lead them on a quest to find others like them, with whom they can recreate the missing pieces of community they left behind in their birthplaces. The sharing of religious rituals and spirituality serves as glue that holds the many disparate pieces of diasporic life together. Diaspora churches are characterized by a communitarian ethos and values of shared bonds, where social identities are forged, sustained and given specific cultural and normative contents. There is much altruism and a spirit of collective enterprise which nurtures ethno-specific culture and religiosity and is key to their survival in the new world. The religious assemblies in diaspora provide the social cohesiveness required for group identification and tend to maintain ecclesiastical and cultural linkages to ancestral homelands.

The fires of religious passion are fanned by long separation from familiar rituals that marked their spirituality and belonging and create a crisis of identity and community for diasporas. This is seamlessly addressed in transplanted faith expressions that bring together the resurgence of ethnicity and culturally shaped religiosity. Cohen (2008) claimed that religion provides a "cement to bind a diasporic consciousness," and Williams (1988) argued that immigrants experience a religious intensification by becoming "more religious than they were before they left home." Religious historian Marty (1972), described ethnicity as the "skeleton of religion in America because it provides the supporting framework" and in a substantial contemporary assessment of religion in the United States, sociologists Putnam and Campbell (2010) concluded "that ethnicity and religion are often mutually reinforcing and it is no coincidence that the US is both a nation of immigrants and a nation with high religiosity." Smith (1978) called migration a "theologizing experience" on account of the "intensification of the psychic basis of religious commitment." Many of the Asian and Hispanic immigrants to the United States who might not have been religious in their ancestral homelands, exhibit heightened spiritual awareness and many of them become Christians because of cultural affinity found within diaspora churches (Chen 2008; Crane 2003). Scholars have observed that immigrant religious institutions play an important role in immigrant adaptation, since they become the means to create community and transmit homeland culture and values to children. They provide economic benefits through information sharing and networking among members and act as a buffer against racism and discrimination (Ebaugh and Chafetz 2000; Warner and Wittner 1998).

Diaspora faith is a potent means of filial connection and social cohesion, while family life remains the foundation of the faith of the scattered. Single students and migrants find family in faith groups, while there is a noticeable rise in singlehood among children of diaspora. Though it can be stigmatizing, diaspora faith gatherings provide solace for broken families, single parents and struggling families. Inability to uphold the family culture that they had grown up in and continue to cherish and failing to associate with the families in the host society, forces them to establish ethnic-specific churches in the places of settlement, practicing a distinct faith and forming an elaborate support system for its members. The transplantation of culturalized Christianity from ancestral homelands provides much needed nostalgic comfort and sociality to scattered people and alternative forms of host land Christianity are no match for it. Putnam (2000) noted the declining social capital in the US and how it weakens moral character and ability to sustain family life. The missionary zeal in founding diaspora congregations has a family connection to it as it serves to recreate broken family ties, but is limited to ethnic particularities, failing to transcend cultural boundaries.

In their formation, diaspora churches exhibit high lay involvement and tend to have only a few families shouldering the major responsibilities and making much sacrifice, while its involvement with the host society remains minimal. Most immigrant congregations begin in the living rooms of one of the Christian families in their early years in a foreign land. The birth of immigrant churches is organic and often grows naturally out of these fellowships and informal gatherings which extend beyond spiritual matters and lead to the creation of social and economic support networks to facilitate survival in the new environment. They are marked with celebrations like children's birthdays, graduations and other festivities. Relationships within these groups get redrawn as a new extended family network, which is akin to the ones they left behind in ancestral homelands. All adults become "uncles" and "aunts" who feel responsible for the nurturance and the success of the next generation. Everyone feels hurt at a loss or tragedy a particular family may encounter, exhibiting communitarian propensities, fear of the possibility of facing similar crisis and the need for community support.

The church as a family[4] of families is truer in the context of diaspora than anywhere else. Diaspora churches become like a small village with a deep sense of obligation toward each other. They believe it takes a whole church to raise a child in a foreign land. When a biological family cannot be there for each other, live far away from home, or become abusive, emotionally restrained, or reclusive, immigrants develop substitute relationships that serve like a surrogate family. The diaspora pastors become surrogate fathers to the entire congregation, often times in the place of real fathers who are absent or preoccupied with survival struggles as foreigners. Women assume a disproportionate share of responsibility for continuing religious traditions and household duties. This alternate family of choice fulfills the roles for those who are deprived of natural family ties by recreating ancestral filial culture. The relational health and stability within families are key to effective ministry in diaspora churches.

---

4 For more on church as family, see (Hellerman 2009; Minear 1960; Christiano 1986; Osiek and Balch 1997; Stark 1996).

Furthermore, family plays a central role in religious reproduction and propagation in diaspora. The domestic space remains as a spatial configuration central to religious practice and faith transmission. As immigrants frequently react to alienation and confusion resulting from their uprootedness in religious terms, studies on diaspora faith experiences and of the processes of religious adaptation in new environments are extremely important. The household rituals and faith of the parents play a crucial role in the faith development of the foreign-born children, while immigrants tend to excessively depend on religious institutions to reinforce their desired cultural ideology. Pastors of immigrant churches spend a significant share of their time and effort in resolving relational conflicts and crises, and tend to uphold ethnic values to help families in their churches. They witness unspeakable heartaches, unresolvable tensions and unforeseen pain of immigrant families every day. Pastoral care for people who are separated from their spouses is a ministry that the church in the global south and north cannot ignore. Refugees, illegal migrants and asylum seekers experience strained family relationships and the psychological cost of migration may continue to haunt future generations. Even when a family lives in the same house, they are disjointed by different work shifts and schedules and thus are seldom together. The cultural dissonance alienates children of immigrants from their parents and many attempt to cope with diasporic struggles through substance abuse or violent behaviors.

Established diaspora churches exhibit an increased role of laity and higher participation from every family. Some exhibit heightened missionary zeal for fellow migrants, families back home and people in the host nations. Irrespective of financial success they have achieved, they also feel obligated to be generous toward the under-resourced. The community orientation and familial nature of the church is a primary motivating factor for some second generation people to continue in immigrant churches and to actively serve church youth or to want to raise their children in the church.

My research on Indian immigrant families confirmed that migration has been very disruptive to families and the transition to nuclear family has bred many problems. However, the sense of jointness has not entirely disappeared either. It is being recreated in new ways, through immigrant religious institutions and with the aid of modern technological gadgets, creating a new 'functional jointness.' I found that churches facilitate socialization by fostering surrogacy to compensate for the weakness of family fragmentation, disintegration, role transitions, absence of support systems, the lack of parental resources, and the challenges of the new world. When the church serves as an extended family, it enjoys certain benefits such as a greater sense of security and belonging due to sharing a wider pool of members to serve as resources during a crisis, as well as more role models to help perpetuate the desired behavior and cultural values in the next generation. With newly acquired prosperity and the ideals of the new world, they try to recreate the old values in new ways.

The families and pastors in the study confirmed that most families identify themselves by communal solidarities to which they belong rather than as individuals. But it also has some downsides, as the church gatherings become a stage to promote and reinforce certain negative cultural values, self-aggrandizement, and economic gains. It is also marked with ethnocentrism and superiority of one's own culture over what they see in the host nation, much of which stems from their protective instincts and fear of the unfamiliar. The extent of pain and brokenness in Indian immigrant households and churches are overwhelming, often hidden behind the façade of the "model minority" image. Many family problems remain unaddressed over protracted periods of time on account of shame or the inner compulsion to portray an image of perfection and success before fellow immigrants. They hide their misgiving and struggles before church members or leave diaspora churches to find the solace of anonymity in other churches.

One of the most pressing issues before the diaspora congregations is the drop out of the second generation from churches, popularly known as "the silent exodus" (Lee 1996). Many ethnic communities experience the challenge of keeping two generations together with differing assimilation, outlook and spirituality (Yep et al. 1998; George 2006; Rodriguez 2011). In many diaspora churches, the college and post-college age young adults are conspicuously absent as the second and third generations leave the ethnic-specific church for the very reasons their parents joined them. Scholars have argued that ethnic religion provides a locus of networking mechanisms by which they reproduce ethnic values in the next generation (Crane 2003; Kurien 1999), while Kim (2010) argued that the second generation of Korean Americans are creating a hybrid spirituality and new institutional structures. Min (2002) and I (2006) have argued that second generation peoples are neither denizens of their host nation, nor inhabitants of the land of forefathers, but are in the interstitial crevices of hybrid identities, and immigrant churches fail to adequately address their needs. What makes immigrant churches effective in reaching their own people also makes them ineffective in reaching others, including their own children. The intergenerational clashes abound in diaspora churches due to differences in cultural attitudes, linguistic competencies, and worship and leadership styles. The rotation of pastoral leaders from homelands continually keeps immigrant church fresh in ethnic flavors, estranging subsequent generations and others. In order to address generational discontinuity, diaspora churches must understand a life cycle approach to immigrant church and a generational transition plan for faithful Christian witness to the future generations.

Missional literatures in recent decades have reclaimed the missionary nature of the church[5] based on *Missio Dei* and Trinitarianism, and I hope to extend the concept of "missional" to families. Modern social sciences have long held family captive for its own sake through its many obsessions and therapies. Of course there is much to gain from scientific insights to help struggling families, but there exists an urgent need to align families to the eternal purposes of God. Central to this understanding of family is that Triune God is the model for family and all relationships, who calls and sends families through the Spirit into the world to participate fully in God's mission in the world. Abraham becomes an archetype of a missional family as his call included "in you all the families of the earth will be blessed" (Gen. 12:3 NASB).

For developing a theological basis for missional family, I turn to Trinitarian theology, particularly the social doctrine of God and the sending of God into the world, which provides an internal structural coherence as well as an external orientation. To be a human being is to be created in and for relationship with God (to become part of God's family) and with other human beings, starting with one's own family, then ecclesial family (church) and finally human family (world). Trinitarian conception provides the contemporary family the basis for unity, equality, mutuality, reciprocity, substantiality and relationality, while avoiding the problems of subordination, authoritarianism, exploitation and totalitarian ideas. If mission is understood as a movement from God to the world, then family and church are instruments of that mission to extend the reign of God in the world. Missional families make a church missional and give an individual a family of which to be part – something bigger than themselves. The divinely purposed family is the missing link between the purpose-driven individual and church. This also helps to hold together ideas such as church as a family, family as mission (mission to, through and beyond the family) and offers a framework for effective generational witness in diasporic communities. As Triune God is a community on mission, the church is to be a community on mission and hence, its constituent families should also be seen as a community on mission with God in the world.

Conclusion

With heightened filial and religious consciousness in the diaspora, it is critical to understand the role of family for the health and vitality of diaspora churches. While immigrant Christians reproduce rituals and practices with minor modifications in foreign lands by congregating as ethnic-specific churches, the relational subtleties within these bodies are analogous to the surrogate family system with its many benefits as well as

5 For more missional church, see (Guder 1998; Van Gelder and Zscheile 2011; Hastings 2012).

idiosyncrasies. Since religious identity and traditions are an inextricable part of ethnic identity and since the progressive assimilation of successive generations (rather than ethnic maintenance) is the most conspicuous pattern found in ethnic households and churches, they are most critical to navigating though generational transitions in diasporas. I have attempted to construct missional family as a framework to understand diaspora churches and to address the challenge of the future generations, which is key to establishing missional churches and communities everywhere.

For discussion

1. How does diaspora phenomenon, particularly as it is viewed through the lens of family, impact our ecclesiology and especially our understanding of the mission of the Church?
2. The author describes the strain of transnationalism, migration, and intergenerational transitions upon families. How are such challenges impacting diaspora families in your context? How can churches (diaspora and non-diaspora) bring good news in the face of familial struggle and brokenness?
3. If faith matters in diaspora tend to be collective rather than individualistic decisions, how can churches approach mission in a way that preserves the integrity of family relationships and which avoids creating unnecessary rifts between family members. Consider especially cases in which a single family member shows more interest in and openness to the gospel than do the others in her/his family.
4. The author argues that "what makes immigrant churches effective in reaching their own people also makes them ineffective in reaching others, including their own children". To what extent have you experienced this as true in your context? How can such churches begin to overcome these barriers and fulfill a broader vision of mission to all peoples?

Bibliography

Arthur, John A. *African Diaspora Identities: Negotiating Culture in Transnational Migration*. Lanham, Md.: Lexington Books, 2010.

Cao, Nanlai. "The Church as a Surrogate Family for Working Class Immigrant Chinese Youth: An Ethnography of Segmented Assimilation." *Sociology of Religion* 66, no. 2 (2005): 183.

Chamberlain, Mary. *Family Love in the Diaspora: Migration and the Anglo-Caribbean Experience*. New Brunswick, NJ: Transaction Publishers, 2006.

Chen, Carolyn. *Getting Saved in America: Taiwanese Immigration and Religious Experience*. Princeton, NJ: Princeton University Press, 2008.

Christiano, Kevin J. 1986. "Church as a Family Surrogate: Another Look at Family Ties, Anomie, and Church Involvement." *Journal for the Scientific Study of Religion* 25, no. 3 (1986): 339–54.

Chukwu, Donatus Oluwa. *The Church as the Extended Family of God: Toward a New Direction in African Ecclesiology*. Bloomington, IN: Xlibris Corp, 2011.

Clark, Rebecca, Glick Jennifer, and Bures Regina. "Immigrant Families over the Life Course: Research Directions and Needs." *Journal of Family Issues* 30, no. 6 (2009): 852–852–872.

Cohen, Robin. *Global Diasporas: An Introduction*. 2nd ed. London: New York : Routledge, 2008.

Crane, Ken R. *Latino Churches: Faith, Family, and Ethnicity in the Second Generation*. New York: LFB Scholarly Pub, 2003.

De Neui, Paul. *Family and Faith in Asia: The Missional Impact of Social Networks*. Pasadena, CA: William Carey Library, 2010.

Ebaugh, Helen Rose and Janet S. Chafetz. *Religion and the New Immigrants: Continuities and Adaptations in Immigrant Congregations*. Walnut Creek, CA: AltaMira Press, 2000.

Escobar, Samuel. *The New Global Mission: The Gospel from Everywhere to Everyone*. Christian Doctrine in Global Perspective. Downers Grove, IL: InterVarsity Press, 2003.

Foner, Nancy. *New Immigrants in New York*. New York: Columbia University Press, 2001.

George, Sam. "Families in Diaspora: A Pastoral and Missiological Study of Asian Indian Christians in Greater Chicago (1965-2010)" (PhD dissertation, Andrew F. Walls Centre for the Study of Asian and African Christianity, Liverpool Hope University, Liverpool, UK 2013).

George, Sam. *Understanding the Coconut Generation: Ministry to the Americanized Asian Indians*. Niles, IL.: Mall Publishing, 2006.

Goldin, Ian, Geoffrey Cameron, and Meera Balarajan. *Exceptional People : How Migration Shaped Our World and Will Define Our Future*. Princeton, NJ: Princeton University Press, 2011.

Guder, Darrell, editor. *Missional Church: A Vision for the Sending of the Church in North America.* Grand Rapids, MI: W. W. Eerdmans Publishing Co., 1998.

Hanciles, Jehu. *Beyond Christendom: Globalization, African Migration, and the Transformation of the West*. Maryknoll, NY: Orbis Books, 2008.

Handlin, Oscar. *The Uprooted: The Epic Story of the Great Migrations That Made the American People*. 2nd ed. Boston, MA: Little Brown, 1990.

Hastings, Ross. *Missional God, Missional Church: Hope for Re-Evangelizing the West*. Downers Grove, IL: IVP Academic, 2012.

Hellerman, Joseph. *When the Church Was a Family: Recapturing Jesus' Vision for Authentic Christian Community*. Nashville, TN: B & H Academic, 2009.

Ho, E. & Bedford, R. (2008). Asian transnational families in New Zealand: Dynamics and challenges. *International Migration*, 46(4), 41-62.

Kim, Sharon. *A Faith of Our Own: Second-Generation Spirituality in Korean American Churches*. New Brunswick, NJ: Rutgers University Press, 2010.

Kulanjiyil, Thomaskutty, and T. V Thomas. *Caring for the South Asian Soul: Counseling South Asians in the Western World*. Bangalore, India: Primalogue, 2010.

Kurien, Prema A. "Gendered Ethnicity: Creating a Hindu Indian Identity in the United States." *American Behavioral Scientist* 42, no. 4 (1999): 648–70.

Lee, Helen. "Silent Exodus." In *Asian American Christianity Reader,* edited by Timothy Tseng and Viji Nakka-Cammauf. Castro Valley, CA: Institute for the Study of Asian American Christianity, 2009.

Levitt, Peggy. "Social Remittances: Migration Driven, Local-Level Forms of Cultural Diffusion." *The International Migration Review: IMR.* 32, no. 4 (1998): 926.

Levitt, Peggy. "Transnational Migrants: When 'Home' Means More than One Country." *Migration Policy Institute* (October 1, 2004). http://www.migrationinformation.org/article/transnational-migrants-when-home-means-more-one-country.

Marty, Martin. "Ethnicity: The Skeleton of Religion in America." *Church History* 41, no. 1 (1972): 5.

Massey, Douglas, Joaquin Arango, Graeme Hugo, and Adela Pellegrino. 1993. "Theories of International Migration" *Population and Development Review* 19, no. 3 (1993): 431.

Min, Pyong Gap. *The Second Generation: Ethnic Identity among Asian Americans.* Walnut Creek, CA: AltaMira Press, 2002.

Min, Pyong, and Jung Ha Kim. *Religions in Asian America: Building Faith Communities.* Walnut Creek, CA: AltaMira Press, 2002.

Minear, Paul S. *Images of the Church in the New Testament.* Philadelphia, PA: Westminster Press, 1960.

Nazir-Ali, Michael. *From Everywhere to Everywhere: A World View of Christian Witness.* London, UK: Collins/Flame, 1991.

Osiek, Carolyn, and David L Balch. *Families in the New Testament World: Households and House Churches.* Louisville, KY: Westminster John Knox Press, 1997.

Portes, A. (1997). Immigration theory for a new century: Some problems and opportunities. *International Migration Review* 31: 799-825.

Putnam, Robert, and David Campbell. *American Grace: How Religion Divides and Unites Us.* New York: Simon & Schuster, 2010.

Putnam, Robert D. *Bowling Alone: The Collapse and Revival of American Community.* New York: Simon & Schuster, 2000.

Rabila, Mahiela. "Integrating a Family Perspective in International Migration Policy." In *Ninth Coordination Meeting on International* Migration. New York, NY: United Nations Population Division, 2009.

Ratha, D., Supriyo, D., Dervisevic, E., Plaza, S., Schuettler, K., Shaw, W., … Yousefi, S. Migration And Development Brief 24. *Migration And Remittances: Recent Developments And Outlook.* Washington, DC: World Bank, 2015. https://siteresources.worldbank.org/INTPROSPECTS/Resources/334934-1288990760745/MigrationandDevelopmentBrief24.pdf. Accessed 11 Feb. 2016.

Robertson, Roland. *Globalization: Social Theory and Global Culture.* London, UK: SAGE, 1992.

Rodriguez, Daniel A. *A Future for the Latino Church: Models for Multilingual, Multigenerational Hispanic Congregations.* Downers Grove, IL: IVP Academic, 2011.

Singh, Supriya. "Sending Money Home: Maintaining Family and Community." *International Journal of Asia Pacific Studies* 3, no. 2 (2007): 93–109.

Smith, Timothy. "Religion and Ethnicity in America." *The American Historical Review* 83, no. 5 (1978): 1155.

Sowell, Thomas. *Migrations and Cultures: A World View*. New York: BasicBooks, 1996.

Stark, Rodney. *The Rise of Christianity: A Sociologist Reconsiders History.* Princeton, NJ: Princeton University Press, 1996.

Sullivan, Kathleen. "Iglesia de Dios: An Extended Family." In *Religion and the New Immigrants,* edited by Helen Rose Ebaugh and Janet Saltzman Chafetz. Los Angeles: AltaMira, 2000.

Tanye, Gerald K. *The Church-As-Family and Ethnocentrism in Sub-Saharan Africa.* Münster: LIT Verlag, 2010.

Van Gelder, Craig, and Dwight J Zscheile. *The Missional Church in Perspective: Mapping Trends and Shaping the Conversation.* Grand Rapids: Baker Academic, 2011.

Vertovec, Steven. *Transnationalism*. London; New York: Routledge, 2009.

Warner, Stephen, and Judith G Wittner. *Gatherings in Diaspora: Religious Communities and the New Immigration*. Philadelphia, PA: Temple University Press, 1998.

Williams, Raymond. *Religions of Immigrants from India and Pakistan: New Threads in the American Tapestry*. Cambridge, UK; New York: Cambridge University Press, 1988.

World Migration Report 2013. Edited by Frank Laczko and Gervais Appave. Geneva: International Organization for Migration, 2013. http://publications.iom.int/bookstore/free/WMR2013_EN.pdf

Yep, Jeanette, Peter Cha, Paul Tokunaga, Greg Jao, and Susan Cho Van Riesen. *Following Jesus Without Dishonouring Your Parents.* Downers Grove, IL: InterVarsity Press, 1998.

23. The Mission of the Church through Understanding and Pursuing Intercultural Unity

Ken Baker, Chandler H. Im, and T.V. Thomas

Introduction[1]

In a world of staggering diversity and ever-accelerating flows of people from everywhere to everywhere, the deep-seated longing of the human heart for belonging and community has never been more pronounced. The Gospel of Jesus Christ is the only universal prescription, cure, and salvation that humans have to meet that need. In Jesus Christ, the believer receives the capacity of a new quality of human relationship and a unique possibility of bridging gulfs that separate fellow believers within a congregation. It is the supernatural presence of the Holy Spirit that enables believers to overcome differences and distinctions, and experience rich relational fulfilment across the breadth of the human family.

Biblically, it can be concluded that intercultural unity among God's people is an expected outcome of salvation. Each member of the Body of Christ is a new creation and thus given a new name and a new family. This Kingdom family consists of believers from every culture of the world and brings with it the expectation of unity while honoring diversity. In other words, understanding and embracing intercultural unity must be part of the mission of the Church to the world. (Please see the appendix to this chapter for a partial list of Christian networks around the globe, in evangelical circles, that highlight intercultural unity as a core value/goal.)

All of God's people and every gathering of His church must cross the boundaries of culture and make intentional efforts to move toward one another as we all move toward Christ. This is a lifestyle absolutely foreign to the unbeliever and largely unnatural even to the redeemed. We affirm, however, that it should be the goal of all believers to embrace and interact with one another in unity as an expression of Kingdom life.

In order to avoid confusion in our terminology, it is important to explain that we use the phrase "intercultural" to emphasize the reciprocal, two-way bridging (thus, inter-) between two or more cultural groups. Intercultural

---

1 See also Mary Pinkerton, "Understanding and Embracing Intercultural Unity," Ethnic America Network (EAN), released December 20, 2013, http://www.ethnicamerica.com/wpv1/wp-content/uploads/2015/11/Intercultural-Unity-EAN-paper-December-2013.pdf/.

unity is the supernatural and interdependent relationship between believers of different cultures, which is made possible only through the reconciling work of Christ on the cross. Unity does not mean "all the same" (that would be "uniformity"); rather it involves belonging together in spite of distinctions.

Theological framework for intercultural unity

1. If we belong to Jesus, then we belong to those who belong to Jesus.

Several biblical themes converge to support this rather simple but profound statement. The first is that we belong to each other because we were brought together by Christ when He redeemed us and made it possible to know peace with the Father. This act of reconciling makes each believer, and all believers, one in Christ with no distinction (Gal. 3:28).

The overwhelming wonder is that, at creation, humanity was brought into the inner circle of relationship with the Triune God. He desires the companionship of humanity. In the tragedy of the fall in the Garden of Eden, sin corrupted the relationship that man had enjoyed with the Creator. At that time, humanity lost intimate, daily fellowship with God. Consequently, sin disrupted harmonious relationships with fellow humans as well. It is amply clear that the complete intention or goal of God's entire salvation process is for: "His good pleasure that he set forth in Christ… to gather up all things in him, things in heaven and things on earth… who accomplishes all things according to his counsel and will" (Eph. 1:9-11 NRSV). God will restore all things together as they were originally intended to be and for the enthronement of Christ (Eph 1:20-21).

2. Our unity reflects the loving relationship of the Triune God.

Through the central act of atonement through the cross, God dealt with sin (Eph. 2:12), which removed *vertically* the wrath of God and *horizontally* the hostility of humans (Eph. 2:13-14). This created a new reconciled community, i.e., a new humanity with an inherent instinct for love!

With the door of reconciliation between humanity and God open and freely offered, we find that the same calling of Christ (i.e., the ministry of reconciliation) is now our calling as well (2 Cor. 5:18-20). In Christ, we are to imitate His example by personally and corporately reflecting in our human relationships the love which the Father, Son, and Spirit share. Therefore, division and separation between believers is a rejection of what Christ died to establish (1 Cor. 10:16-17). Refusal to embrace reconciled human relationships with all people regardless of culture is to reject the fullness of all that God intends to restore.

3. The Church embodies the new humanity.

The marvel of the incarnation of Christ signals two dimensions of our unity (Milne 2007). First, the incarnation established the possibility of transcending difference, and secondly, it authenticates the necessity to embrace one another in the new humanity. The incarnation bridged the widest gulf of differences conceivable when the eternal, infinite, uncreated, transcendent God became one with the temporal, finite, created, immanent human being (John 1:1-4, 14). The unifying possibilities increase with the intervention of this God of incarnation into our personal lives and congregations by the ministry of the Holy Spirit.

Ethnic and cultural differences are traits to embrace and enjoy because they aid in understanding God and bring glory to Him. The problem arises when these cultural characteristics become so much a part of how we see ourselves that we start to believe the characteristics are what truly define us as humans. But, our true identity rests in Christ. When we forget that Christ is our absolute identity and we make our ethnic distinctive the priority over the cause of Christ as the reason for our gathering, then we open ourselves to varieties of conflict.

We must never forget that Satan promotes and delights in division, separation, segregation, alienation, and enmity between people and cultures. These are a legacy of sin, the inheritance received from Adam. In contrast, love, redemption, forgiveness, reconciliation, community, and unity are the legacy of life, the inheritance we receive from Christ. Therefore, God has intentionally designed the Church, the Body of Christ, to display the restoration of human community as God intended (cf. Eph. 2:19-22). Unity in Christ *transcends* all other identities and affinities and their inevitable differences and divisions. The wonder of God's Kingdom is not just that there are believers from every culture. The true wonder is that when those from every culture come together as the Church, mutual love replaces the walls of division (2 Cor. 5:14).

4. Unity is a testimony of God's love to a divided society.

In John 17, with the cross before Him, Jesus turned His intercessory heart toward each follower then and now with the desire that all of us would be one with a unity of the same quality as existed between persons of the Trinity – just as He and the Father are one (John 17:11, 20-23). This visible oneness among believers is a testimony to the person and attributes of God and to the salvation He offers. The world is not necessarily surprised when people who are ethnically and culturally alike love each other. What is remarkable is when the Church chooses to live as a contrast community that looks and acts differently by embracing all Christ's followers as members of one united family (Acts 13:1). Is it not sobering to realize that the credibility of our witness of Christ rests on the beauty of mutual Christian love and togetherness?

5. Intercultural unity is a mandate to pursue.

Given the nature and extent of intercultural unity and its tie to the Triune God as the supreme example, we must be intentional about our obligation to work out this model in everyday life. Jesus effectively embodied and displayed this oneness on a daily basis, but when the Church does not display oneness, we demonstrate a false view of God.

Unfortunately, a common response to other cultural distinctions, whether in Christ or not, is indifference, which says, "I/we don't care about you." Those different from us then become the unconsidered masses, the generic "them." Indifference is sin, because it is a direct refusal to intentionally and actively love our brothers and sisters in Christ (or neighbors, or enemies). The joy and opportunity of intercultural unity envisions the day when our community in Christ so fully reflects God's love that there is no longer a "them," but only an "us."

Practical implications of intercultural unity

Given this goal of intercultural unity within the Kingdom of God, several statements are helpful in understanding this journey toward intentional belonging:

1. In diverse contexts, the actual demographics, as well as the history of a congregation, tends to communicate an unspoken message, to its own people, and the public, that either unity in diversity is important or separation is important.
2. Christian fellowships that are organized according to economic, cultural, linguistic, ethnic, generational, worship preference or lifestyle distinctions are incomplete expressions of Kingdom reality. While a homogeneous gathering (in whatever expression) has a place, timing, and trajectory, it is a *waypoint* on the Kingdom journey, not the destination. We *do not* mean to imply that there is only one viable, biblical model of church expression. Rather, we are stating and affirming that the character of interdependent belonging in the Body of Christ obligates us to move toward each other in intercultural relationship.
3. Cultural distinctions not only give texture and depth to the Body of Christ, but they also give texture and depth to the whole Christian experience. Language, culture, and customs are assets that enrich, not barriers to avoid.
4. We are incomplete without each other. The Church should not claim to be "the Body of Christ" without its essential character of intercultural unity. It is a great tragedy when congregations demonstrate through their networks that they think they are complete within their own linguistic, ethnic or affinity group.
5. Intercultural relationships and unity lead us into a new understanding of who God is, drawing us ever closer to Him. As our

brothers and sisters of other cultures reflect who God is in a way which is unique to their contexts, the Body of Christ grows stronger and is better able to proclaim Christ to the world.

6. We must seek to hear and embrace with empathy the stories of others including stories of their culture, history, perspective, and even their weaknesses.
7. As believers become aware of the need for intercultural unity and seek to actively pursue progress in becoming more unified, they are better equipped to defeat long-standing patterns of separation.
8. Every assembly should *anticipate* the blessing of sustained friendship across cultures while cultivating intercultural skills and celebrating the destruction of fear, threat, hostility, and enmity. The mere co-existence of ethnic congregations throughout the city does not adequately demonstrate the displayed unity of the Body of Christ envisioned in the Gospel. Celebrating Jesus together across cultures and fellowshipping with one another in personal relationship powerfully demonstrates unity in diversity.
9. Although language and tradition are often sources of the lack of intercultural unity in many long-standing congregations, it must be affirmed that unity is the goal which becomes realistic through inter-generational vision and faith.

It is not enough to say that "hope for change lies with the next generation" if the first generation does not proactively cultivate such hope among the next. Even if the first generation is unable to make significant progress in intercultural fellowship, they must communicate to their children about the values and contributions of fellow believers from other cultures. Failure to do so creates a legacy of fear rather than a faith-filled desire for reconciliation and unity. It is the responsibility of first generation immigrant congregations to encourage the next generation to move forward and outward. By faith, through their words and the testimony of God's Kingdom design for reconciliation in all relationships, the journey will continue toward expressions of oneness in Christ.

Conclusion

Separation, segregation, and division are the grievous stories of humanity attempting to compensate for the loss of meaning found only in God. These sad stories tell of humanity under the headship of Adam, not that of Christ. Intercultural unity, the journey of intentional belonging, however, is a picture of God's original and continuing intention for creation. It is the how-could-this-ever-be "mystery" which was "made known" through the revelation of Christ. Through the Gospel of the cross, all who believe become "members together of one body, and sharers together in the promise of Jesus Christ" (Eph. 3:2-6). It is a return to who we were created to be. It is a prophetic call of Christ that *we would be one*, and to invite everyone in Christ to journey together in order to understand and embrace the full implications of what this means.[2]

For discussion

1. How do diaspora phenomena create greater opportunities for the Church in your city and nation to fulfill its mission of intercultural unity? What are the greatest barriers to this in your context? What steps could be taken in the next six months to overcome these barriers?
2. How have sin and Satan sown disunity, division, and discrimination in your city? To what extent do local diaspora and host nation churches stand as a contrasting light in the face of this darkness? What are the best examples of intercultural unity you have witnessed in your context?
3. The authors state that "language, culture and customs are assets that enrich, not barriers to avoid". However, we very often treat them as barriers. How has your church, agency, or organization sought to enrich itself by embracing diverse languages, cultures, and customs? How can you personally lead by example?

Bibliography

Hofstede, Geert, Gert Jan Hofstede and Michael Minkov. *Cultures and Organizations: Software of the Mind*, 3rd Edition. New York: McGraw-Hill, 2010.

Law, Eric H. F. *The Wolf Shall Dwell With the Lamb*. St. Louis, MO: Chalice Press, 1993.

Lingenfelter, Sherwood G. *Leading Cross-Culturally: Covenant Relationships for Effective Christian Leadership*. Grand Rapids, MI: Baker Academic, 2008.

Livermore, David. *Leading with Cultural Intelligence: The New Secret to Success.* New York: AMACOM, 2010.

Milne, Bruce. *Dynamic Diversity: Bridging Class, Age, Race and Gender in the Church*. Downers Grove, IL: InterVarsity Press, 2007.

Peterson, Brooks. *Cultural Intelligence: A Guide to Working with People from Other Cultures*. London: Intercultural Press, 2004.

Pinkerton, Mary. "Understanding and Embracing Intercultural Unity," Ethnic America Network (EAN), released December 20, 2013, http://www.ethnicamerica.com/wpv1/wp-content/uploads/2015/11/Intercultural-Unity-EAN-paper-December-2013.pdf/.

Plueddemann, James. *Leading Across Cultures: Effective Ministry and Mission in the Global Church*. Downers Grove, IL: InterVarsity Press, 2009.

Sheffield, Dan. *The Multicultural Leader: Developing a Catholic Personality.* Toronto, ON: Clements Publishing, 2005.

---

2 See Appendix F.

Silzer, Sheryl Takagi. *Biblical Multicultural Teams: Applying Biblical Truth to Cultural Differences.* Pasadena, CA: William Carey International University Press, 2011.

Stevens, David, E. *God's New Humanity: A Biblical Theology of Multiethnicity for the Church.* Eugene, OR: Wipf & Stock, 2012.

24. The Church and the Soul of Singapore: An Escatological Vision for Mission in Global Cities

Lawrence Ko

Introduction: Singapore as a global city

The world of the twenty-first century will be urban. By 2050, experts project that 66% of the world will have become urban dwellers (United Nations 2014) and at present, as many as 3 million people are moving to cities every week (International Organziation for Migration 2015)! Increasingly, people are moving from everywhere to every city and the result is leading churches to ask a crucial question: Will the cities of the future have a soul or will they devolve into heartless masses of anonymous peoples packed away in cruel urban jungles?

Singapore is one such city. Today recognized as a major world city, a center for international trade and business and one of Asia's most important technology hubs, it is easy to forget its origins as a simple fishing village. Singapore's Prime Minister Lee Hsien Loong announced in November 2014: "Our vision is for Singapore to be a Smart Nation – a nation where people live meaningful and fulfilled lives, enabled seamlessly by technology, offering exciting opportunities for all." The vision for Singapore to be a "Smart Nation" within a decade is deemed possible because it has one of the world's highest levels of smart phone penetration and broadband connection in 90% of homes (Loong 2014). The availability of an educated populace and skilled workforce has enabled the development of highly specialized and networked services. But will this continued emphasis on technological convenience, wireless connectivity and round-the-clock productivity ultimately create a spiritual disconnect – a city without a soul?

Singapore is also a global city with a rich history as a diaspora hub and a current foreign-born population representing well over a hundred nations (Operation World 2015). Pluralism will characterize such a diverse urban population living in confined city spaces. Brenda Yeoh and Theodora Lam note, "This 'new pluralism' has become noticeable in the everyday landscape. It reflects the complexity of class, race, nationality, and national status that shape the conditions under which transnational migrants remain in and experience the city" (Yeoh and Lam 2015). Saskia Sassen adds to this the observation that "global cities around the world are the terrain where a multiplicity of globalization processes assume concrete, localized forms." She continues:

> These localized forms are, in large part, what globalization is all about ... The large city of today has emerged as a strategic site for a whole range of new types of operations – political, economic, "cultural", subjective. It is one of the nexi where the formation of new claims, by both the powerful and the disadvantaged, materializes and assumes concrete forms. (Sassen 2005)

What impact will these forces of pluralization, globalization, localization, and concretization have on the soul of the city and its increasingly diverse peoples? We may be earnest in our desire to welcome the stranger, celebrate diversity and recreate our unique identities in the context of multi-ethnic cities but in a soulless city, both locals and newcomers can find no center – identities drift aimlessly or harden around various particular ethnocentricities which hinder fruitful integration and foster alienation. Will resulting social tension and conflict be inevitable in a global city or can there be a greater sense of welcome, magnanimity and social acceptance? Diasporic trends tell us that the global city of the 21st century is where we will all eventually find ourselves. Can it also become the place where we all come together?

Urban culture and rooted cosmopolitanism

Conn and Ortiz note that cities seek to create a dynamic environment as an integrating center of influence and power, as the "symbolic centres that concentrate, intensify and orchestrate culture's re-creating forces" (Conn and Ortiz 2001). Singapore's cityscape with her architecture of global commerce and cultural diversity reflects the city-state's aspiration and claim as such a center. However, the importance of intentionally shaping the soul of the city and its peoples must not be neglected. Beyond concerns for technology, convenience, commerce, influence and power are the weightier matters of spirituality, family, love, hospitality, beauty, and friendship.

To grow as a city, a sense of spiritual transcendence is needed. Cities must grow their souls, connecting deeply with their humanity and their history, if they are to find the courage to fulfil their respective destinies in a global world. This will mean exploring the social dimensions of our city and probing deeper into our own shared consciousness. It will mean appreciating our cultural history and valuing our local places and stories. Cities should encourage and invest in home grown artists who can bring forth the beauty of the local contexts and offer it as their unique contribution to a wider global audience. Lily Kong notes that "no global city is worth its salt if it does not have a strong base of indigenous works that express local flavours and national identities" (Kong 2013).

Kwame Appiah's idea of "rooted cosmopolitanism" provides us with a possible way forward for cities seeking to learn how to effectively welcome new migrant peoples into their spaces (Appiah 1997). This seemingly contradictory concept can be applied in global cities like Singapore to illuminate the relationship between the pursuit of a stronger sense of the unique historic, cultural and ethnolinguistic identity of the city and the parallel pursuit of a sincere and wholehearted welcome to newcomers who are then free to make their own contributions to the evolving story of that city. As the roots of a tree dig deeper, the shoots can grow taller and eventually the tree can grow bigger. This affirms the Chinese adage that we need to know the past in order to appreciate the present, and indeed the future. Here is the soul of the city, rooted deeply and securely in its own urban identity and shooting forth with love and hospitality to welcome new people with new ideas and inputs. Here also is the mission of the Church – to help the global city stay connected to this soul.

The church and the soul of the city

At the turn of the century in 2001, Raymond Bakke noted that the world has come to the cities and the church needs to prepare for ministry in this new reality (Bakke 2002). Manuel Ortiz states that urban growth is more than a sociological reality; it is the fulfillment of God's intentions since the beginning of time (Ortiz 2002). The cultural mandate given to mankind to populate and steward the earth indicated that God has intended for human settlements to develop not only in the rural villages but also in the cities. As many have pointed out from their reading of Scripture, the history of mankind started in a garden but it will end in a city.

Urbanism, let us understand it as the distinctive culture of a given city and its peoples, is exciting and evolving and its creative innovators are constantly transforming and transmitting its forms, patterns and stories within and out from the city. The Church has a critical role to play in the ever-emerging urbanism of a city. As organic and organized communities with a clear mandate for mission in the urban centers, churches are well-suited to work to ensure that the particular urbanism of a city is the product of the kind of rooted cosmopolitanism we have already described. But churches must be strategically aligned and structured for transformational urban ministry with a broader vision and to re-invent herself for the opportunities which will call for innovative solutions and daring responses (Ko 2010). It will require mobilizing and equipping more believers to provide a whole range of services relevant to meet the needs of a global city – including both the needs for deep roots and broad branches. The churches in Singapore should be wary of simply replicating Western forms of worship and ministry and instead seek to be more culturally innovative and contextually relevant. We can and should contribute significantly to the envisioning of the global city's evolving identity in a way that bears positive fruit for the Kingdom of God, but this will require a commitment of churches to step out of comfort zones and encounter urban peoples and cultures and to engage in the local contexts.

Biblical examples of engagement in urban contexts

The Bible is replete with characters who were concerned with their cities and served in their urban contexts. Abraham prayed and interceded for the decadent cities of Sodom and Gomorrah. Joseph served ably as a premier in the Pharaoh's government and administered justice and famine relief in Egypt's capital city with regional impact. Nehemiah was the king's cupbearer in the Persian palace who rebuilt the city wall of Jerusalem and sought to revive the fortunes of the city, socioeconomically as well as spiritually. Jeremiah lamented over Jerusalem, prophetically calling for repentance. Indeed, the Lord Jesus himself wept over Jerusalem, loved its people and protested the corruption he found there among its political and religious leaders. Biblically speaking, caring for and shaping the soul of the city, is an important part of the mission of God's people – and all the more in an era marked by massive urban migration. We must combat dehumanization, alienation and oppression, ethnocentrism and hostility and celebrate creativity, history, diversity and positive transformation with a commitment to repentance and hope in redemption through Christ.

The Church has a great history of urban engagement, right from her inception in Jerusalem, born on the day of Pentecost as a Jewish, multilingual and inclusive church. There the rich and the slaves worshipped and served together in the new community of faith. The church in Antioch went a step further as not only multilingual but also multiethnic and multicultural. The acceptance of cultural diversity and the spirit of mutuality among the members prepared the Antioch church for a broad vision of urban ministry which ultimately extended to the other cities throughout the Roman Empire.

The turn has now come to the Church in Singapore which, just as its city leaders aspire to influence far beyond the Southeast Asian region, can become a modern day Antiochan church by serving cities throughout Asia and the world. Of course, this will require the growing of a larger vision for the churches of Singapore – to see ourselves as a global church with a global mission.

Vision of the church as an eschatological community

We can take a leaf from Manuel Ortiz who contends that the church has in her biblical ecclesiology the foundation needed for developing strategies for an extensive urban ministry (Ortiz 2002). Firstly the New Testament church was a new community and a new creation in Christ which transcended all earthly barriers of language, culture, socioeconomic status and nationality. It was a community which existed to care for one another and minister to the needy irrespective of traditional divisions. Secondly, the church is a priesthood both individually and corporately, where every member can engage in ministry, serve, pray, bless, and live simply and incarnationally. Thirdly, the church as a pilgrim community, is a migrant community, sojourners on their way to the celestial city, not made with human hands, whose architect and builder is God.

The image of the Church as a new creation in Christ, a pilgrim community, always going out and crossing boundaries, always giving of itself to reach out, to establish and to transform communities is a powerful one. However, this pilgrim vision is, by itself, incomplete. The Church must also recover the vision of the Future City of Revelation 7:9-10, where all national, ethnic, economic and cultural divides are finally bridged. In light of this more complete perspective, we realize that the Church is an eschatological community where intercultural unity is not only an ideal to be worked for now but a future reality – a promise. The complete picture of borderless pilgrims in a borderless world heading to an eternal city empowers churches to serve their present urban realities with hope because they have seen the future. The International Baptist Church in Singapore with over 120 ethnicities in her English-speaking congregation is a good example of what it can look like when this eschatological vision is embraced by city churches.

Bakke asserts that pastors need to be missiologists so that they can develop an integrative ministry for the city (Bakke 2002). It has often been said that missiology is theology on the road. The church must be therefore always missiological and innovative, transforming and being transformed along the journey of life. Pastors need to equip their churches to cross boundaries, cross cultures and actively engage the city – and this equipping must go beyond simply organizing occasional outreach gimmicks on special occasions. Bishop Emeritus Robert Solomon (2015) posited that the church can be the measure of the soul of the city, characterized by the qualities of conscience, community and compassion.

Many churches in Singapore have established social services in the city, from childcare centers to family service centers. Some have regular partnership programs with community clubs and resident committees in their vicinities to serve locals as part of community penetration and engagement efforts. Fairfield Methodist Church is one of the churches which has been active in serving the Chinatown community for years. Today they continue their outreach to hundreds of diaspora Chinese laborers from the mainland every Sunday. Asia Evangelistic Fellowship has subsidized medical health care work among the South Asian diaspora with a clinic set up in Little India. Inspired by friends at HealthServe working among migrant workers and addressing issues of social injustice, others have begun to serve South Asian construction workers living in the dormitories. Several local churches have also planted diaspora congregations with services in the languages of various new migrant groups. These outreach initiatives are encouraging steps towards shaping a Singapore with a soul rooted deeply in its unique urban identity and stretching out in loving welcome to its newest residents.

Individuals in the city: encountering the *other*

City life can enrich our soul and deepen our sense of humanity if we choose to reach out to and relate with those who are different from us – the "Other". The city bountifully provides us with opportunities to encounter the Other, but breaking through the barriers and entering into their worlds is far from easy. Martin Buber made a distinction between relating to the Other in an "I-Thou" relationship versus doing so in the "I-It" sense (Buber 1958). As individuals in a global city, we have a tendency to treat one another as mere objects or as a lesser creature to be despised or feared. We have witnessed shopkeepers denigrating customers who are foreigners, especially foreign workers. It has been said that foreign workers are needed but not wanted. We dehumanize the Other when we dismiss the person as a mere object. In a very real sense, ignoring, fearing and exploiting the Other dehumanizes ourselves. Such attitudes are infectious in the soulless city where fear and confusion reign.

The Church can lead in demonstrating the kinds of encounters and engagement needed to correct this dehumanization of foreign workers and other new diaspora groups in the city. We can encourage greater interaction within churches and then go beyond our comfort zone to encounter the Other in the community – to understand their needs and to provide practical acts of service as well as to learn to appreciate and embrace the value they bring to the global city. The urban churches in Singapore must do more than merely opening their doors to the public on Sundays in vain hope that outsiders will automatically come. The urban church must go out into the city and engage with the people and issues of the day. Churches on mission in the global city must know the city and be known in the city.

Singapore Centre for Global Missions (SCGM) has begun to partner with local churches to build communities of compassion and care in the city to reach across ethnic and cultural divides to touch lives with the faith, hope and love of Jesus Christ. Publications designed to stimulate missiological thinking among Singapore's church leaders, multicultural concerts and events that foster appreciation of and interaction with the Other, and training and conferences which focus on issues particularly relevant to Singapore today such as environmental stewardship and missional business are just some of the ways in which SCGM and local churches are seeking to shape their city with soul (Singapore Center for Global Missions 2014).

Much more can be done and must be done by churches in Singapore to ensure engagement happens at the street level, and that redemptive relationships are built so that newcomers become dear friends and strangers become loved neighbors (Ko 2015). As we serve one another, we affirm our humanity and grow the souls of our cities.

Conclusion

We are living today in a world that is increasingly dominated by the rise of global cities. The entire world has come to live in the close quarters of urban centers like Singapore, Manila, Paris, Kampala, Houston, Dubai and São Paulo. As Jim Wallis has put it, "We are all neighbors now" (Wallis 2013). The Church need not be reticent about the diasporic forces of urbanization and flee from its call to urban mission. The Church must be present at the street level and visibly engaged with both the rich as well as those marginalized by ethnicity, economics, and migration status. We have a mission to the global cities to help them dig deeper roots of identity and grow broader branches of hospitality. We are the eschatological community which hopes for an enduring city to come and feels its freedom as pilgrims now to serve and sacrifice to promote social cohesion and good neighbourliness – to reconnect the city to its soul. We pray that the Church's memory of Jerusalem and Antioch and hope for the city to come will inspire and inform present engagement in mission that transforms 21st century Singapore and all cities beyond.

For discussion

1. Consider your own city or a city that you know well. How can local churches help to root the city into its own unique urban identity in a way that promotes effective welcome to new migrant peoples? Are their churches that you believe are already doing this well?
2. As cities are transformed in face of globalizing forces fear of the "Other" is often the result. How are you seeing this fear manifest in your context? How have you seen churches respond in helpful and hurtful ways?
3. The authors speak of the Church embracing an eschatological vision of itself which holds both "pilgrim" and "Enduring city" identities in balance. How can the understanding of the Church as a pilgrim community help it to shape the soul of global cities? How can the understanding of the Church pursuing an enduring city help it to shape the soul of global cities?

Bibliography

Adeney, Miriam. "Colorful initiatives: North American diasporas in mission." *Missiology: An International Review*, 2011: 5-23.

Appiah, Kwame Anthony. "Cosmopolitan Patriots." *Critical Inquiry*, 1997: 617-639.

Baeq, Daniel Shinjong, Myunghee Lee, Sokpyo Hong, and Jonathan Ro. "Mission from migrant church to ethnic minorities: A brief assessment of the Korean American Church in mission." *Missiology: An International Review*, 2011: 25-37.

Bakke, Raymond. "Urbanization and Evangelism: A Global View." In *The Urban Face of Mission: Ministering the Gospel in a Diverse and Changing World*, edited by Manuel Ortiz and Susan Baker, 32. Phillipsburg, New Jersey: P&R Publishing, 2002.

Baxter, John. "The Local Church in Diaspora Missions." *Journal of Asian Mission* 11, no. 1-2 (2009): 113-119.

Bediako, Kwame. *Jesus in Africa: The Christian Gospel in African History and Experience*. Akropong: Regnum Africa, 2000.

Bediako, Kwame. "John Mbiti's Contribution to African Theology." In *Religious Plurality in Africa: Essays in Honor of John S. Mbiti*, by Jacob K. Olupona and Sulayman S. Nyang, 367-396. Berlin: Mouton de Gruyter, 1993.

Buber, Martin. *I and Thou*. New York: Charles Scribner & Sons, 1958.

Carino, Feliciano V. "The Dynamics of Political Migrations as a Challenge to Religious Life." In *Religions Today: Their Challenge to the Ecumenical Movement*, by Julio de Santa Ana, 86. Geneva: World Council of Churches, 2005.

Carmichael, Amy. "No Scar?" In *Toward Jerusalem*, by Amy Carmichael, 85. London: Holy Trinity Church, 1936.

Casiño, Tereso C. "Why people move: A prolegomenon to diaspora missiology." In *Korean Diaspora and Christian Mission*, edited by S. Hun Kim and Wonsuk Ma, 30-53. Oxford: Regnum Books, 2011.

Choi, Sungho. "Identity Crisis for Diaspora Community." In *Korean Diaspora and Christian Mission*, edited by S. Hun Kim and Wonsuk Ma, 20-29. Oxford: Regnum Books, 2011.

Chun, Do Myung. "Kingdom-centered identity: The case of bicultural Korea-Brazilians." In *Korean Diaspora and Christian Mission*, edited by S. Hun Kim and Wonsuk Ma, 115-132. Oxford: Regnum Books, 2010.

Commission on World Mission and Evangelism. "Mission spirituality and discipleship: Beyond and through contemporary boundaries." *International Review of Mission*, 2010: 106-124.

Conn, Harvey M., and Manuel Ortiz. *Urban Ministry: The Kingdom, the City, and the People of God*. Downers Grove, Illinois: IVP Academic, 2001.

Connor, Phillip. "A Biblical Missiology for North American People Groups." *North American Mission Board*. 2006. http://namb.net/WorkArea/DownloadAsset.aspx?id=8590117304/.

Cronin, Vincent. *A Pearl to India: The Life of Roberto de Nobili*. New York: E.P. Dutton & Co., 1959.

Embassy of the Blessed Kingdom of God for All Nations. "Embassy of the Blessed Kingdom of God for All Nations: 8th Anniversary." *Brochure*. Kiev, 2002.

Gamez, Ana. *Blessing OFWs to Bless the Nations*. Makati City: Church Strengthening Ministry, Inc., 2012.

George, Sam. "Diaspora: A hidden link to "From everywhere to everywhere" missiology." *Missiology: An International Review*, 2011: 45-56.

Haar, Gerrie ter. *Halfway to Paradise: African Christian Presence in Europe.* Cardiff: Cardiff Academic Press, 1998.

Hale, Chris. "Aradhna: From comfort to discomfort, from church to temple." *International Journal of Frontier Missions.* 2007. http://www.ijfm.org/PDFs_IJFM/24_3_PDFs/147-150Hale.pdf (accessed 2 18, 2011).

Hanciles, Jehu H. "Migration and Mission: Some Implications for the Twenty-First Century Church." *International Bulletin of Missionary Research*, 2003: 149-150.

Harvey, Thomas Alan. "Diaspora: A passage to mission." *Transformation: An International Journal of Holistic Mission Studies*, 2011: 42-50.

Howell, Brian M. "Multiculturalism, immigration and the North American Church: Rethinking contextualization." *Missiology: An International Review*, 2011: 79-85.

International Organization for Migration. *World Migration Report.* Geneva: International Organization for Migration, 2013.

International Organziation for Migration. *World Migration Report.* Geneva: Internatioanl Organization for Migration, 2015.

Jackson, Darrell. "Europe and the migrant experience: Transforming integration." *Transformation: An International Journal of Holistic Mission Studies*, 2011: 14-28.

Jenkins, Phillip. *The Next Christendom: The Coming of Global Christianity.* Oxford: Oxford University Press, 2011.

Jeong, Matthew. "Korean Evangelicals' response toward Muslim neighbours." In *Korean Diaspora and Christian Mission*, edited by S. Hun Kim and Wonsuk Ma, 157-173. Oxford: Regnum Books, 2010.

Jung, Min-young. "Diaspora and timely hit: Towards a diaspora missiology." In *Korean Diaspora and Christian Mission*, edited by S. Hun Kim and Wonsuk Ma, 54-63. Oxford: Regnum, 2010.

Kawthoolei Karen Baptist Bible School & College. "Brief history." *Kawthoolei Karen Baptist Bible School & College.* 2010. https://sites.google.com/site/kkbbsc/home/brief-history (accessed 2 15, 2011).

Kim, Hun. "Receiving mission: Reflection on reversed phenomena in mission by migrant workers from global churches to Western society." *Transformation: An International Journal of Holistic Mission Studies*, 2011: 62-67.

Kim, S. Hun. "Migrant workers and 'Reverse Mission' in the West." In *Korean Diaspora and Christian Mission*, edited by S. Hun Kim and Wonsuk Ma, 150-156. Oxford: Regnum Books, 2010.

Kim, S. Hun, and Wonsuk Ma. *Korean Diaspora and Christian Mission.* Oxford: Regnum Books International, 2011.

Ko, Lawrence. "Individuals in the City: Encountering the Other." In *Ethnic Rhythms: Life in the Global City*, edited by Lawrence Ko, 51-52. Singapore: Singapore Center for Global Missions, 2015.

Ko, Lawrence. "The Role of the Asian Church in Missions." In *Emerging Missions Movements: Voices of Asia*, 1-10. Compassion International and Asia Evangelical Alliance, 2010.

Kong, Lily. "Cultural Icons, Global City and National Identity." In *Engaging Society: The Christian in Tomorrow's Singapore*, edited by Michael Nai-Chiu Poon, 24-40. Singapore: Trinity Theological College, 2013.

Kraemer, Hendrik. *Religion and the Christian Faith.* Cambridge: James Clarke, 1956.

Lausanne Committee for World Evangelization. *Scattered to gather: Embracing the global trend of diaspora.* Manila, Philippines: LifeChange Publishing, Inc., 2010.

Lausanne Diaspora Educators Consultation. "The Seoul Declaration on Diaspora Missiology." *The Lausanne Movement.* 11 14, 2009. http://www.lausanne.org/content/statement/the-seoul-declaration-on-diaspora-missiology/.

LCWE. *Scattered to gather: Embracing the global trend of diaspora.* Manila, Philippines: LifeChange Publishing, Inc., 2010.

—. *Scattered to gather: Embracing the global trend of diaspora.* Manila, Philippines: LifeChange Publishing, Inc., 2010.

Lim, David S. "Seconnd Lausannne Philippine Congress (2012)." *http://www.lausanne.org/en/blog/1921-second-lausanne-philippine-congress-2012-report.html.* January 7, 2013. (accessed September 1, 2014).

Lisbe, Gerardo B. *Church-based OFW Family Care Ministry: An Ethnographic Study on the Structure and Activities that Filipino Create that Significantly Reduce OFW Family Dysfunction.* D. Min. Dissertation, Los Angeles, CA: International Theological Seminary, 2014.

Loong, Lee Hsien. "Smart Nation Initiative." November 24, 2014. https://www.youtube.com/watch?v=jGMbqpVRo9I.

Lorance, Cody "An Introduction to Contextualization Among Hindus." *Lausanne Global Conversation.* 6 6, 2010. http://conversation.lausanne.org/en/conversations/detail/10373 (accessed 2 14, 2011).

Ma, Wonsuk. "A Millenial Shift of Global Christianity and Mission. An Initial Reflection." In *Korean Diaspora and Christian Mission,* edited by S. Hun Kim and Wonsuk Ma, 11-24. Oxford: Regnum Books International, 2011

Oh, Doug K. "History of the Korean Diaspora Movement." In *Korean Diaspora and Christian Mission,* edited by S. Hun Kim and Wonsuk Ma, 2-16. Oxford: Regnum Books, 2011.

Olupona, Jacob, and Regina Gemignani. *African Immigrant Religions in America.* Washington D.C.: New York University Press, 2007.

Operation World. *Singapore.* 2015. http://www.operationworld.org/sing.

Ortiz, Manuel. "The Church and the City." In *The Urban Face of Mission: Ministering the Gospel in a Diverse and Changing World,* edited by Manuel Ortiz and Susan Baker, 43. Phillipsburg, New Jersey: P&R Publishing, 2002.

Ott, Craig, Stephen J. Strauss, and Timothy C. Tennent. *Encountering Theology of Mission: Biblical Foundations, Historical Developments, and Contemporary Issues.* Grand Rapids: Baker Academic, 2010.

Parreñas, Rachel S. *Servants of Globalization: Women, Migration, and Children.* Quezon City: Ateneo De manila University Press, 2003.

Photo Voice; Bhutanese Refugee Support Group. "Introduction." *Bhutanese Refugees: The Story of a Forgotten People.* March 12, 2010. http://www.photovoice.org/bhutan/ (accessed 2 17, 2011).

Pocock, Michael, Gailyn Van Rheenen, and Douglas McConnell. *The Changing Face of World Missions: Engaging Contemporary Issues and Trends.* Grand Rapids, MI: Baker Academic, 2005.

Programme, United Nations Development. *Human DevelopmentReport 2009 Overcoming Barriers: Human Mobility and Development.* New York: Macmillian, 2009.

Rajamanickam, S. "The Goa Conference of 1619 (A letter of Fr Robert de Nobili to Pope Paul V)." *Indian Church History Review*, 1968: 85.

Ratha, Dilip, et al. *Migration and Remittances: Recent Developments and Outlook.* Washington D.C.: The World Bank, 2015.

Richard, H.L. "Good news for Hindus in the neighborhood." *Rethinking Hindu Ministry II: Papers from the Rethinking Forum*, 2010: 32-35.

Rodas, M. Daniel Carroll. *Christians at the Border: Immigration, the Church and the Bible.* Grand Rapids: Baker Academic, 2008.

Santamaria, Francis. "Problems regarding Family Relations and Children of Migrant Workers." In *Filipino Women Overseas Contract Workers: At What Costs?*, by Mary Palma-Beltran and Aurora javate De Dios, 71. Quezon City: JMC Press, 1992.

Sassen, Saskia. "The Global City: Introducing a Concept." *Brown Journal of World Affairs*, 2005: 27-43.

Singapore Center for Global Missions. 2014. http://www.scgm.org.sg.

Solomon, Robert. "Soul of the Global City." *Speech at Singapore Centre for Global Missions.* Singapore, August 6, 2015.

Song, Minho. "The diaspora experience for the Korean Church and its implications for world missions." In *Korean Diaspora and Christian Mission*, edited by S. Hun Kim and Wonsuk Ma, 103-114. Oxford: Regnum Books, 2010.

Sydnor, Paul N. "Understanding the forced displacement of refugees in terms of the person." *Transformation: An International Journal of Holistic Mission Studies*, 2011: 51-61.

Tan, Kang-San. "In search of contextualized training models for Chinese Christian diaspora in Britain." *Transformation: An International Journal of Holistic Mission Studies*, 2011: 29-41.

The Lausanne Movement. "The Lausanne Covenant." *The Lausanne Movement.* 1974. http://www.lausanne.org/covenant (accessed 2 18, 2011).

Thomas, T.V. "Ministering to Scattered Peoples: Global Phenomenon of Diaspora." *Lausanne Global Conversation.* 11 12, 2010. http://conversation.lausanne.org/en/conversations/detail/11660 (accessed 2 17, 2011).

Trinity International Baptist Mission. *Our Story.* 2010. http://www.tibm.org/our-story.html (accessed 2 25, 2011).

United Nations. *World Urbanization Prospects.* New York: United Nations, 2014.

United Nations: Department of Economic and Social Affairs. *Trends in International Migrant Stock: 2013 Revision.* United Nations, 2013.

Vanier, Jean. *From Brokenness to Community.* Mahwah, NJ: Paulist Press, 1992.

Wahrisch-Oblau, Claudia. *The Missionary Self-Perception of Pentecostal/Charismatic Church Leaders from the Global South in Europe.* Leiden/Boston: E.J. Brill, 2009.

Wallis, Jim. *On God's Side: What Religion Forgets and Politics Hasn't Learned about Serving the Common Good.* Grand Rapids: Brazos Press, 2013.

Walls, Andrew F. "Mission and Migration: The Diaspora Factor in Christian History." *Journal of African Christian Thought*, 2002: 3-11.

Waltke, Bruce K. *Genesis: A Commentary.* Grand Rapids, MI: Zondervan, 2001.

Wan, Enoch. "Diaspora missiology." *Occasional Bulletin*, 2007: 3-7.

Wan, Enoch. "Diaspora mission strategy in the context of the United Kingdom in the 21st century." *Transformation: An International Journal of Holistic Mission Studies*, 2011: 3-13.

Wan, Enoch. "Korean diaspora: From hermit kingdom to Kingdom ministry." In *Korean Diaspora and Christian Mission*, edited by S. Hun Kim and Wonsuk Ma, 85-101. Oxford: Regnum, 2010.

—. "Ministering to Scattered Peoples – Moving to Reach the People on the Move." *Lausanne Global Conversation.* 10 22, 2010. http://conversation.lausanne.org/en/resources/detail/11438 (accessed 2 17, 2011).

Wan, Enoch, and Sadiri Joy Tira. "Diaspora Missiology." In *Missions in Action in the 21st Century*, edited by Joy Sadiri Tira and Enoch Wan, 55. Quezon City: LifeChange Publishing, Inc., 2012.

Wanner, Catherine. *Communities of the Converted: Ukrainians and Global Evangelism.* London: Cornell University Press, 2007.

Yeoh, Brenda, and Theodora Lam. "Divercity Singapore." In *Ethnic Rhythms: Life in the Global City*, edited by Lawrence Ko. Singapore: Singapore Centre for Global Missions, 2015.

SECTION 5: REGIONAL AND NATIONAL CASE STUDIES IN DIASPORA MISSIONS

Miriam Adeney and Tuvya Zaretsky, Section Editors

Regional and National Case Studies in Diaspora Missions: An Introduction

Section Editors: Miriam Adeney and Tuvya Zaretsky

Human diaspora flow from everywhere to everywhere. In this section we encounter eight regional case studies. These feature Jewish, Chinese, Korean, Indian, Latino, Brazilian, African, and Iranian peoples. Some overflow with comprehensive statistics, like the Chinese essay. Others explore specific congregations, like the essays on African and Iranian churches. The Brazilian essay emphasizes global mission, while the Latino focuses on local ministries. Taken together, these eight chapters abound in creative approaches to witness and service in challenging circumstances.

25. Jewish Diaspora Ministries

Tuvya Zaretsky

Diaspora has been the pattern of Jewish life for more than 2,500 years, according to Israeli historian H.H. Ben-Sasson (1976: 182). This chapter describes the Jewish diaspora, both historic and contemporary, and explores some of the ways that the gospel is blessing the global Jewish community today.

Definition of terms

The term *Jews* refers to the ethnic descendants of Abraham, Isaac and Jacob. It is the nation connected by blood lineage that indicates a distinct people. *Jewish* is the descriptive form for anything specifically identified with this population group, such as Jewish community, Jewish culture or Jewish values.

Jewry is a collective term for all Jewish people. It may be used globally – *world Jewry* – or locally – *Israeli Jewry*.

Judaism, as a religious descriptor, is one element of Jewish culture. This culture is diverse. Hence, while Judaism is the belief system affirmed by some Jewish people, it is not practiced or held by all Jewry. About one third of Jews in the US and Israel embrace Judaism and are considered "religious" at some level of practice (*dati* in Hebrew). Roughly two thirds of Jewish people in those two countries are secular (or *chiloni* in Hebrew). Overlapping those two categories are Jewish people who say that their religion is Judaism, but whose beliefs are more secular. They would refer to themselves as "traditional" (*masorti* in Hebrew). Therefore, Judaism is not a determining factor for defining an ethnic Jew. Religion is a cultural component, but not an ethnic distinction. The insider (emic) Jewish perspective is that a variety of beliefs are valid for ethnic Jews. However, by tradition that usually does not include faith in Jesus.

The term *Israel* is a source of confusion for many evangelical Christians. Since 1948, the *State of Israel* has been a sovereign republic in the Middle East. The Bible also speaks of a patriarch and his descendants as "Israel." Therefore, care is required when employing the term "Israel" to distinguish between a people, ancient and modern, the patriarch, a former kingdom or a current political state in the Middle East (Zaretsky 1998:36-39).

The term *diaspora* is defined elsewhere in this volume. However, as Ben-Sasson indicated, *diaspora* is a distinct feature of Jewish experience. The patriarch Avram, later Abraham, left his homeland and his extended family in Padan-Aram and the city-state of Ur to follow God. He and his children lived as aliens among Canaanites and later Egyptians. That remembrance is part of Jewish liturgy until today: "And you shall answer and say before the LORD your God: 'My father *was* a Aramaen, about to perish, and he went down to Egypt and dwelt there, few in number; and there he became a nation, great, mighty, and populous." (Deuteronomy 26:5 NKJV).

That nation grew as the descendants of Israel. It became the historical Kingdom of Israel under Saul, dividing about 930 BC into Samaria, the Northern Kingdom, and Judah, the Southern Kingdom. The Assyrian Empire invaded and displaced the population of the Northern Kingdom of Israel in 722 BC. The Babylonian army took captive the two remaining Jewish tribes in the South in 586 B.C. Diaspora has been fixed within Jewish history from that era until 1948. Establishment of the State of Israel changed the perspective of world Jewry. Today Israelis regard diaspora Jewry as people who have chosen to remain "in exile."

World Jewish population

The Jewish nation continues to grow even though it remains widely scattered, with ongoing sociological transitions, transnational migrations, and culture changes. In 2010, Israeli demographer Sergio DellaPergola estimated the world's Jewish population at 13,647,500 (Geltman 2012:26). The Jewish population in the State of Israel was 5.9 million, or just over 43% of world Jewry. For the first time in two millennia the ancestral homeland now hosts the single largest Jewish community worldwide.

The United States hosts 5,275,000 Jewish people. Thus, 82% of world Jewry resides in just two countries. The next twelve largest concentrations of Jewish people are in the following countries:

Canada – 375,000
United Kingdom – 292,000
Russian – 205,000
Argentina – 182,300
Germany – 119,000
Australia – 107,500
Brazil – 95,600
Ukraine – 71,500
South Africa – 70,800
Hungary – 48,600
Mexico – 39,400

Since the 1980s, the leading external influences in the demographic shifts of Jewish populations have been the disintegration of the Former Soviet Union (FSU) and Germany's reunification. Jewish immigration from the FSU yielded rapid population growth in Israel.

Significant internal trends also shaped Jewish population shifts. North American Jewish Population Surveys in 1990 and 2000/1 reported the

Jewish birthrate was 1.8 children per couple – under a replacement level – and disaffiliation from all Jewish institutions stood above 63%. "Selected Indicators of World Jewry" in 2012, say U.S. Jewish-Gentile intermarriage was 54%. Intermarriage rates for European Jewry averaged 45% while Russian and Ukrainian Jewish populations reported an out-marriage rate of 80% (Geltman 2012: 26-27, see note b).

Diaspora Jewry missiological trends

The early 1970s saw a dramatic spiritual movement within diaspora Jewry. Specifically, two unique developments occurred in the American Jewish community. As reported by Israeli scholar Yaakov Ariel, Assistant Professor for Religious Studies at the University of North Carolina Chapel Hill,

> Missions to the Jews were active in America from the early 19th century, but Jews for Jesus and the more dynamic and innovative evangelization campaigns of the early 1970s proved more successful than ever before. For the first time in American Jewish history, propagation of the Christian gospel among Jews proved successful and captured the souls of tens of thousands of young Jews (Ariel 2000: 211).

My own spiritual journey is a case study typical of ways in which the Lord moved among young American Jews. I came to faith in Jesus in 1970 (Zaretsky 2004). My parents were both children from Jewish families that immigrated from Belarus, Poland, and Hungary. My father was religiously observant in Toronto and my mother was raised in a traditional/culturally committed New York Jewish home. They married and settled in Northern California where we affiliated with Temple Emmanu-El in San Jose. There I received religious training and identification with the Jewish community. In that setting, Jesus and the gospel were irrelevant. A Hebrew School teacher told my class that Jesus was "Jewish until he converted to Christianity – and then he wasn't Jewish anymore." That set the cultural boundaries for us. Jesus was an outsider.

However, I had a love for God, Jewish history, our heritage and the Bible. I wanted to know God like Abraham, Moses and David had experienced Him. I called out to God during my Bar Mitzvah – the rite of passage when a young Jewish boy commits himself as part of the synagogue community. Along with the prophet Isaiah, I said, "Here am I God – send me" (Is.6:8). With those words, my focused search for God began in earnest.

Over the next ten years I waited, hoping that the God of my forefathers would show up. I had no suspicion that the answer would come amidst a spiritual movement that broke out in the North American Jewish community during the early 1970s when thousands of young adult post-Holocaust Jewish baby boomers came to faith in *Messiah Yeshua* (Jesus Christ). Experiencing both political and sociological upheaval, few of us expected that our activism would bring us to serve the gospel of Jesus. However, God was on the move within the American Jewish community, as historian Ariel observed.

Jesus' message came to many of us in the context of Messianic Bible prophecy. The State of Israel had recovered Jerusalem in 1967. While Christians were speculating on possible eschatological implications, our Jewish community pondered the significance for a settled Jewish homeland. If nothing else, such historic events raised questions about the existence of God. It was a time of spiritual awakening and renewed excitement in Jewish life. The Spirit of God was at work in our community.

Many of us did the unthinkable. We read the New Testament, and eventually turned to faith in Jesus. A modern movement of Messianic Jews emerged. One expression of that movement gathered in Northern California with encouragement from an insightful and unconventional Jewish mission leader named Moishe Rosen. I was privileged to become part of that team, discovering together that God had shown up in our lives and emboldened us to declare that we are "Jews for Jesus" (Tucker 1999).

Yaakov Ariel provides an insightful analysis of the movement from the perspective of a non-sympathetic Jewish observer.

> Jews for Jesus should be viewed as a revitalized form of the old evangelical quest to evangelize the Jews. Its novelty and uniqueness were not in its message, which missionaries had been preaching to American Jews for several generations, but in the fact that its leader was the first to realize that there was a new generation of American Jews with new interests and values, and he was willing to use new forms to approach them. Rosen's achievement was not in creating a new missionary agenda, but rather in using new strategies and means that made the mission more effective in achieving its goals (Ariel 2000: 219).

Below are four examples of effective contemporary ministries: the Messianic congregational movement; California Persian churches for believers of Muslim and Jewish background; global outreach to Israeli post-army travelers; and interfaith marriage counseling.

Messianic congregational ministry

Messianic followers of Jesus, sometimes called Messianic Jews or Jewish Christians, have affiliated with local churches of all varieties. In addition, some have nurtured indigenous Messianic Jewish congregations, both in Israel and across the world.

These distinctive congregations are not a new phenomenon. Joseph Rabinowitz, Zionist and Jewish community leader, founded a Messianic congregation in Kishinev in the late 19th Century (Kjær-Hansen 1995). Indeed, such fellowships emerged internationally within a year of Jesus' death. Diaspora Jews visiting Jerusalem who heard the gospel and confessed Jesus as Lord (Acts 2) returned to communities spread from

Persia to North Africa. Seedbeds of ideas, these diaspora Jewish communities hosted libraries, critical debate, and exegetical study of texts. They were ideal places for early believers in Jesus to sharpen doctrines of creation, grace, sin, atonement, and eschatology as well as skills in preaching, debating, and spiritual formation.

On contemporary Messianic congregations, Yaakov Ariel again offers a helpful perspective:

> Missionary societies such as The Chosen People Ministries, Jews for Jesus and Ariel Ministries, and denominational missionary bodies such as the Assemblies of God, Christian Missionary and Alliance, and lately (and famously) the Southern Baptist Convention, have decided to establish and support congregations of Messianic Jews. In the eyes of such missionary groups, these congregations proved to be effective in evangelizing Jews, as they demonstrated both the spiritual and communal merits of the Christian evangelical faith and were particularly compelling for those Jews who wished to retain their Jewish identity and continue to identify with Jewish causes (Ariel 2000: 243).

A 1999 survey documented more than 130 Messianic congregations in the State of Israel at the end of the 20th Century (Kjær-Hansen and Skjott 1999: 30-31). These congregations are diverse ethnically. Many worship in Hebrew, with translation into Russian and/or English. Other congregations are completely Russian-speaking or Amharic-speaking. Some include both Arab and Jewish believers in Jesus.

In the United States, hundreds of Messianic congregations are growing. They are found in every Jewish population center. Most are small and independent, and include a significant number of Gentiles. Messianic congregational ministry plays an important role in discipling Jewish followers of Jesus, providing communal identity, life cycle events, and culturally appropriate worship.

What Jewish ritual elements or cultural elements should be used in worship? What practices derived from Torah observance, but modeled in more rigorous forms of traditional Judaism, should be followed? Believers will hold different views. Messianic congregations may debate these. Critical thinking, thoughtful missiological analysis, and delicate balance emerge in such internal discussions. An introductory guide to some of those issues and to the Messianic congregational movement is available (Robinson 2005).

Case study: Persian congregations in California

Since the time of Daniel, Esther, and Nehemiah, Jewish people have lived in Persian/Iranian communities. When Christian witness has arrived, some Jews have responded to the gospel. Today in California the twenty-seven Persian Christian congregations listed on www.farsinet.com include both Muslim background believers (MBB) and Messianic Jewish believers as committed members. Almost all of these congregations are Farsi speaking, with translation into English or other languages. Many partner with local churches. Some have denominational connections. More than a few list their resources as "worship, Bible study and fellowship service open to all Farsi-speaking peoples, regardless of their religion."

Eighteen of these congregations are located in Southern California, from San Diego up into the San Fernando Valley. One is in the Central Valley city of Fresno. Eight more are in Northern California, from the Silicon Valley north to Sacramento, according to the worldwide directory of Iranian Christian churches (http://www.farsinet.com/icc/california.html).

Case study: outreach to Israeli post army trekkers

Eighteen-year old male and female Israelis are obligated to perform compulsory military service. Boys serve for three years and the girls for two. At the completion of their national service, these young adults often travel to various locations around the world to decompress and think about their next steps in life. Itineraries include Brazil for Carnival, U.S. cities, Southeast Asia, and the beaches of Goa, India, or the hiking trails in Northern India and Nepal.

In 1983, Bob and Joyce Wilhelmson of New Tribes Missions in Cochabamba, Bolivia, almost accidentally discovered an opportunity for ministry to these Israelis. Travelling through a remote area, young Jews regularly stumbled upon the Wilhelmson's New Tribes Mission outpost. Here the travelers received kindness, food and hospitality. The Wilhelmsons also explained to the Israelis the message that they gave to Bolivian tribes. These Jews were told about the Jewish Messiah, Jesus, and his "tribe" from the Bible. They also were offered Hebrew New Testaments. Before heading on down the trail, the young people would sign a guest registry and have a picture taken with their travel partners. Over time the mission documented direct ministry to over 11,000 Israelis who visited their station (Pex 2003: 64-66). The Wilhelmsons set a pattern for Jewish diaspora ministry two decades before others found Israelis on the mountain trails in Asia.

In 2001 and 2002, the Danish Israel Mission trained and deployed outreach teams of young Danish Christians to Thailand and India for the project "Jews in the East." They sought to engage Israeli post-army trekkers and present the gospel through conversations along the hiking trails. They offered literature and New Testaments in Hebrew (Renz 2002: 16).

Since 2007, the Jews for Jesus ministry has sent young American Messianic Jews to India on *Project Massah* (Hebrew for "Journey"). Each team consists of a dozen young believers. They undergo a five-week discipleship and outreach training program in Israel. Then they travel to cities in Northern India to meet Israeli post-army trekkers. For three to five weeks they live with Israelis in youth hostels, hike with them during the day, share meals with them, and every evening at chai shops engage in conversations about faith in Messiah Jesus. They offer New Testaments in Hebrew and exchange Facebook addresses. Over the years, they have developed a rapport with several hundred Israelis.

In 2012, for the first time a team of Israeli Hebrew speakers took part in a *Massah* project outreach. Their destination was Latin America. That outreach was successful on two levels. First, it provided discipleship training for Israelis who previously had been somewhat reluctant to do evangelism. Second, the participants discovered that being native Hebrew speakers with Israeli army experience increased their credibility among diaspora Jews.

So in 2013 a joint team of Israelis and Americans was trained in Israel and then deployed to India. As this is being written, the team is partnering with Indian Christians in Northern India. The Indians run youth hostels and restaurants that serve an Israeli menu intended for Israeli trekkers. Here four nations connect in a focused diaspora ministry that is intended to be a continuing partnership: American and Israeli Messianic Jews join together with Indian Christians to engage Israeli post-army trekkers.

Case study: Jewish-Gentile couples find spiritual harmony

Jewish-Gentile couples are a significant component of global Jewish life, and present one of the most exciting opportunities for ministry. While large number of Gentiles have entered Jewish communal life through intermarriage, they have not necessarily absorbed the culture or religion of Judaism. Unfortunately, many of these couples experience significant marital dissatisfaction. Because of unresolved cross-cultural challenges, marriages dissolve. Traditional Jewish institutions have responded with vigor but without effective means for care.

In 2004, an ethnographic missiological study explored the challenges confronting Jewish-Gentile couples. The most significant issue turned out to be the partners' inability to find a mutually satisfying spiritual harmony (Wan and Zaretsky 2004). Jewish spouses were reluctant to convert to a religious faith that appeared to be a foreign religion. At the same time, Gentile partners did not want to be pressed to embrace Judaism if it meant giving up Jesus (Zaretsky 2004 *LCJE BULLETIN*: 9-14).

To find a mutually satisfying resource for spiritual harmony, Messianic believers have counseled couples to seek together the God of Abraham, using Bible study, prayer and small group discussion. Taking the role of cross-cultural interpreters, these ministers have provided a service to increase understanding between Jewish-Gentile couple partners. Gentile partners are better able to understand Jewish cultural beliefs and sensitivities. Jewish partners acquire a new understanding about the Messiah Jesus from a Jewish perspective. They are able to realize a spiritual harmony in the one true God through mutual faith in His Messiah, Jesus (John 14:6 and Act 4:12).

Some Messianic congregations and missions have found it very effective to host small-group discussions for Jewish-Gentile couples. Beginning with texts that focus on truths about marriage and family life, discussions flow outward. Solutions to spiritual disharmony are found in the God of Abraham and his biblical revelation.

For discussion

1. What do you mean when you use the term Israel? How many ways can it be defined?
   Answers:
   a. Israel, or Jacob, the son of Isaac.
   b. The children of that patriarch, i.e., the sons of Israel
   c. All ethnic descendants of the patriarch as the people of Israel
   d. The land of Israel
   e. The kingdom of Israel under King Saul and unified under the ministry of King David
   f. The Northern Kingdom known as Samaria that was established by Jeroboam, 930 BC
   g. Israel, the sovereign political state created in May of 1948 in the Middle East
   h. The Israel of God mentioned in Galatians 6:15-16, a faithful Jewish remnant
2. Don't ethnic Jewish people already have a salvation relationship with the God of Abraham? What biblical reason could there be for pressing the message of Jesus on them?
   Answer: See John 14:6 and Acts 4:12 for text to stimulate this discussion.
3. How might you or your congregation be more welcoming to diaspora Jewish people who are already in your neighborhood? Are there ways that you could partner with others who are prepared to offer training in Jewish diaspora ministry?

26. The Chinese Diaspora Church and Cross-Cultural Mission

Paul Woods and Allen Yeh

Sixty million Chinese people live outside mainland China. Twenty million of these are in Taiwan, four million in Singapore and six million in Malaysia. Other large concentrations exist in North America, Australia, and New Zealand. To serve this diaspora, nine thousand Chinese churches are spread throughout the world. Eighty per cent of these churches are no more than twenty years old (Chang 2003).

To be an ethnic group dispersed in multiple locations is a defining characteristic of a diaspora population (Cohen 1997:26). People in a diaspora share a commitment to their original homeland, though the commitment may change from geography to culture over time (Safran 2004:17).

This essay asks what the Chinese diaspora is doing in cross-cultural mission. Statistics and statements by Chinese Christian leaders will guide our observations. Mission from mainland China will require separate treatment elsewhere. However, Hong Kong will be included here, as its churches share much with their peers in the diaspora.

Chinese churches across the globe

The Chinese churches in the west

Because diasporas settle in one society but retain a commitment to another, their members' identity is complex, formed in the presence of ethnic others (Kokot et al. 2004:7). Chinese Christians in America construct "adhesive identities" because conversion to evangelical Christianity in Chinese churches "preserve[s] certain aspects of Chinese culture with transformative reinterpretation" (Yang 1999:17, 133). The church's moral conservatism meshes well with Confucian ethics, protecting against a morally suspect American society and reinforcing Chinese identity, even among American-born Chinese (113). Yang's study of his own church in the United States is a particularly detailed source on Christian Chinese identity. I have encountered something similar in Chinese churches in the UK.

This ambivalence towards the mainstream – "wanting one's cake and eating it" (Cohen 1997:195) – is partly a resurgence of ethnic identity against homogenising forces, since reducing space between people increases ethnic solidarity (Cohen 1997:134). Yang mentions close relationships between American-born Chinese, who feel that they are different both from their parents and from their Caucasian peers. Again, I have come across similar behaviour in Britain.

Prejudice on both sides affects this identity. In the United States, Metzger (2012:6) mentions the sense of rejection caused by the 1882 Exclusion Act that targeted Chinese. In New Zealand, Bernau suggests that racism toward early Chinese immigrants inclined the community to turn inward (2005). For their part, Chinese themselves practice exclusivism, emphasizing physical differences and attitudes separating outsiders from insiders (Chan 2005:89; Bernau 2005).

Westernised children's attitudes contrast with those of their Asian-born parents. They may move gradually from the traditional culture and into the mainstream (Chan 2005:126). It is new immigrants that serve to maintain Chineseness in the churches (Yang 1999:107). Yet that renewing flow is slowing down as East Asia's wealth and openness increase. This raises questions for the future of the Chinese church in the West. Toronto's large Chinese and Korean churches are full today, for example. But where will they be in twenty years if they do not embrace multi-ethnic congregations?

On the other hand, it may be that second-generation Chinese in the West are now achieving a stable diasporic identity which will enable these younger people to take greater interest in mission. Loong (2012:1) believes that God's providential shaping of Chinese American Christians has removed "prejudice and pride" from younger people, who cross cultures easily. They are empowered, independent, and mature, and their parents should release them for missions, she asserts.

The Chinese churches in East Asia

In contrast with Chinese Christians in the West, the Chinese diasporas of East Asia do not look to the church for identity maintenance. This dominant ethnic group does not have a survival mentality, and intergenerational differences are smaller, helping them focus beyond culture and circumstances. In Singapore, Hong Kong, and Taiwan, there is no church-based reconstruction of Chinese identity or preservation of values within a non-Chinese mainstream. Yang's (1999:192) "willingly segregated ethnic ghetto" simply does not exist. In addition, because many East Asian societies are still relatively conservative and conformist, the difference between Christian values and those of the mainstream appears smaller than in the West. Although East Asia is changing fast, there is less of a siege mentality in the church.

Also, many churches in places like Singapore belong to large denominations with a history of multi-ethnic leadership and cross-cultural mission, in contrast to the smaller, independent Chinese churches in the West (Yang 1999, Lam 2008).

Hong Kong represents a stable diaspora with its own Cantonese cultural identity, although the change from British to Chinese sovereignty in 1997 may leave the territory's post-colonial identity unclear (Chen 2006).

Taiwan's complex identity has been shaped by post-colonialism (first Japanese rule and then Kuomintang control), as well as the island's *de facto* independence (Chen 2006). Like Hong Kong, Taiwan has developed its own hybrid identity, and its Christians do not struggle to negotiate culture and identity as do their cousins in North America (Chen 2006:53).

Singapore is the most ethnically diverse state. Here Chinese and others live side-by-side. A hybrid southern Chinese identity includes admixtures from the Malay Peninsula. Unlike Hong Kong or Taiwan, the government has crafted a local *Singaporean* identity, which sits above (or at least in tension with) Chinese, Indian, or Malay allegiances. Whereas Hong Kong and Taiwan preserve strong non-Mainland Chinese identities reinforced by Chinese language forms, the Singaporean Chinese identity and culture do not belong to Greater China (Chan 2005:105). That huge country three hours to the north is as foreign to many Singapore Chinese as Australia might be to an Englishman.

Statistics on the Chinese missionary force

Chinese church interest in cross-cultural mission began to gain momentum in the 1960s (Chang 2003). CCCOWE'S World Mission Seminar in the 1970s found that 110 out of 4000 Chinese churches were engaged in mission, with a total of 50 to 100 Chinese missionaries (Mok 1996:196). This rose to more than 300 by the end of the 1980s. A few years later, 10% of 7000 Chinese churches had some kind of mission programme. In 1996, the Hong Kong Association of Christian Missions (HKACM) put the global number of Chinese missionaries at 760 (Chang 2003). As of 2007, 9000 diaspora churches have sent 1600 missionaries, although it is unclear how many of these are cross-cultural (Lam 2007).

Reports published in different years in various countries provide snapshots of diaspora Chinese mission. These were summarized in an article in the Chinese magazine *Behold* in 2007 (Lam). Singapore's 400 churches sent out 450 missionaries as of 2002, the majority from English-speaking churches. Across the causeway, Malaysia's 1000 Chinese churches sent out 120 long-term missionaries, according to the National Evangelical Christian Fellowship. Moving north, Hong Kong's 1200 churches sent out 350 missionaries, 60% of whom serve in Asia. Taiwan's 3800 churches sent out 250 missionaries as of 2005.

In the West, 780 Chinese churches in the United States sent 200 people, and 350 Canadian Chinese churches sent 50. In Australia, 28 churches in Sydney supported missionaries, but very few sent people. Eight churches were actively engaged with non-Chinese people.

These global figures are summarised in Table 1.

Table 1. Numbers of Chinese missionaries from around the world in 2007

(Based on data from Lam 2007, Wan 2003, AWSJ 2010, PRB 2010)

Territory	*No. of missionaries*	*No. of churches*	*% Chinese population*	*% Chin. Christians*
Singapore	454	400	80	16.8
Hong Kong	356	1200	93.6	7.3
Taiwan	250	3800	97	1.1
US	200	780	1.1	5.6
Malaysia	100	1000	21.5	2.5
Australia	100	200	2.8	4.8
Canada	50	350	4.7	5.8
Total	1560			

Table 2 indicates percentages of Hong Kong missionaries reaching Chinese, non-Chinese, and multi-ethnic groups over the last decade. There is a steady increase in the number of missionaries, and a gradual trend towards non-Chinese work.

Table 2. Hong Kong missionaries serving Chinese and non-Chinese people worldwide.

(Source: Various Chinese-language files on the HKACM website)

Year	Reaching:						Total
	Chinese		Non-Chinese		Mixed groups		
	No.	%	No.	%	No.	%	
2012	194	40.2	178	36.9	98	20.3	470
2011	195	39.5	175	35.4	107	21.7	477
2008	214	48.3	145	32.7	79	17.8	438
2006	174	46.3	127	33.8	63	16.5	376
2004	143	46	99	31.8	60	19.3	311

The type of ministry undertaken by Chinese missionaries also is of interest. Table 3 shows the traditional evangelical emphases on evangelism and church planting in the efforts of Hong Kong missionaries. The gradual increase in community development, business as mission, and relief work meshes with Lausanne's and CCCOWE's broader understanding of mission. The slogan for CCOWE 2011 in Bali was *The holistic gospel of Christ to all peoples*.

Table 3. Ministries undertaken by Hong Kong missionaries (%).

Types of ministry/Year	2004	2007	2012
Evangelism	48	46	55
Leadership training	32	30	36
Church pastoring	30	28	36
Church planting	31	26	34
Community development	12	10	20
Student education	15	13	20
Administration and development	12	17	17
Relief work	5	5	8
Theological education	15	12	8
Business as mission	0	0	6
Medical mission	5	4	6
Literature work	8	7	4
Bible translation	4	5	3
Literacy work	3	2	3
Member care	0	0	2
Drug and gambling ministry	0	0	1
Broadcasting	1	1	0

The Hong Kong figures, describing actual placement of personnel, may be compared with data from Singapore in table 4, which represent the strategic priorities of churches. Note that the Singapore figures represent English-speaking churches and Hong Kong figures represent Chinese-speaking churches. Note also that there is a nine year gap.

Singapore and Hong Kong both value evangelism and church planting. Singapore also emphasises medical mission, discipleship, and Bible translation, while Hong Kong prefers church pastoring and leadership training.

Table 4. Types of ministry identified as strategic by Singapore churches in 1993 (%).

Type of ministry	%
Church planting	75
Evangelism	71
Discipling nationals	48
Christian education	38
Bible translation	30
Medical work	25
Relief & development	12
Literature work	11
Mass evangelism	10
Tentmaking	7

The final tables show where missionaries from Singapore and Hong Kong serve. Table 5 compares the two territories, while table 6 looks at trends for Hong Kong personnel over time. The distributions are similar, except that Singaporeans serve more in Asia, and Hong Kong workers more in Europe. This may be due to a developing ASEAN identity among Singaporeans and the regional focus of the denominations in the country, as well as Hong Kong's commitment to Cantonese-speaking people in Europe. The target locations of Hong Kong missionaries have remained fairly stable over the last decade.

Table 5. Locations of missionary personnel from Singapore and Hong Kong (%).

Destination	SG 1993	HK 2005
Asia	84	63
N America	4	2
Europe	5	17
Latin America	7	4
Singapore	9	
Africa	11	9
Oceania		4
No specific focus	19	

Table 6. Locations of missionary personnel from Hong Kong.

HK (year)	2005	2006	2009	2012
Asia	63	65	67	67
N America	2	1	<1	2
Europe	17	16	12	10
Latin America	4	3	9	2
Africa	9	9	9	9
Oceania	4	2	2	2

Strengths and challenges

Strengths of Chinese churches in mission

Chinese culture helps to shape good missionaries, according to the research department of the Hong Kong Association of Christian Missions (1996:120). Chinese people are hardworking, adaptable, and readily accepted. Also, it is argued, Chinese churches and mission agencies are financially stronger than their Western counterparts, with simpler organisational structures and greater flexibility. Younger generations, who have known neither difficulty nor poverty, have much to give (Loong 1996:127).

Culturally, Chinese people are familiar with demons and evil spirits (Loong 1996:131). In Ghana, for example, Lam Shiu-Yuen discovered cultural elements similar to Chinese ancestor worship and polytheism. This helped him understand local African converts' struggles (Lam 1991:49). Along with most non-Western peoples, Chinese emphasize the importance of family and respect for elders. Consequently, they are not as quick as Westerners to assume that personal salvation calls a believer to oppose his family (Hung 1996). Socially, Chinese are familiar with worship in small fellowship groups, as these were the birthplaces of many Chinese churches in the West. This model is suitable for mission in creative-access contexts (Loong 1996). Politically, increasing anti-Western sentiment worldwide does not apply to Chinese missionaries (Hung 1996:140).

Besides cultural strengths which equip Chinese for mission, some missiologists view the widespread diaspora of Chinese as divinely planned, indicating a special calling and providential empowering. In the framework of Acts 17:26, Hung (1996) asks why God has placed Chinese people and churches everywhere. She agrees with Lam (1985:15) that this is a preparation for the gospel, and with Chan (1993:3) that Chinese Christians' grasp of non-Chinese languages and cultures has equipped them for mission. Nevertheless, Chinese need to send more missionaries if they are to live up to their calling (Hung 1996:138).

Challenges for Chinese churches in mission

While gratefully recognizing these strengths, Chinese mission leaders also are frank about weaknesses.

INWARD FOCUS

Although Hong Kong and North American Chinese churches have many educated members, and quite a few attend seminary, the numbers of missionaries is not proportionate. Of 434,000 missionaries worldwide in 2003 (Barrett and Johnson 2003:25), there were only 1000 Chinese cross-cultural missionaries, compared to 3000 each from Myanmar and the Philippines. Of the 1000 Chinese, around 75% came from East Asia (mainly Singapore and Hong Kong), and less than one quarter from North America (Chang). Where are the Chinese missionaries?

Chinese churches focus too much on their own growth, programmes, and issues, and fail to cultivate a global mission vision, according to Chang (2003) and Wong (2009). Human and financial resources too often are trapped inside the church because leaders view the sending of missionaries as a drain on resources, and of little benefit to the local church (Lam 2007). This maintenance mode means that few members ask what their role is in

God's worldwide endeavours (Tsang 1989:306, Lin 2013). The "closed-door policy" of many churches results in only 10% being involved in cross-cultural mission (Wang 1989:31).

More broadly, Chinese Christians still may view themselves as recipients rather than givers and senders, because their churches originally were established by westerners (Lo 1996:184). Perhaps they are operating from a survival mentality. They have worked hard to make a decent life in a new country, but have yet to contribute to the kingdom. Yet if the church exists only to survive, Lo asks, what is it surviving for?

Several infrastructural elements may be weak as well. Seminaries may not require mission courses (Lo 1996). There is a dearth of Chinese language mission textbooks (Lam 2007). Annual mission conferences showcase genuine mission involvement and generate authentic enthusiasm, but this must be translated into action (Lo 1996, Lam 2007). Most of all, a pastor's vision is basic to the church's commitment to mission (Chang 2003).

CAREER, CULTURE, AND FAMILY

Many Chinese Christian professionals think that going into mission means putting aside their career for full time work in evangelism, church planting, and Christian training (Lam 2007). For some, such service is "not a live option" (Wong 2009). In light of this, tentmaking is an alternative that should be promoted (Mok 1996:205). As a secular professional, the worker can be a *crouching tiger, hidden dragon* (Lo 1996). Lam would like to see cultural, business, and computer professionals among Chinese missionaries. Lin (2013) urges medical specialists, lecturers, city planners, and even chefs, hairdressers, and beauticians to go to the field.

Yet this is not universally affirmed. I recently watched a gifted couple battle to persuade their church to support their "business as mission" project in a creative-access nation. They did not succeed. While their proposal was excellent, it failed to impress a missions committee who had never served in that nation. Theologically, too, there are differences of opinion. While some criticize an unhealthy "polarization between the 'spiritual' and the 'temporal'" (Wang 1989c:89), others fear that holistic mission could lead to nominalism and dilute the "purer gospel" that Chinese missionaries preach (Hung 1966).

Not only career expectations limit Chinese missionaries, but also family expectations. Traditional Chinese require children to obey their parents, making it hard for young people to go into mission (Lam 2007). Yang recalls the tension in his church when a pastor encouraged young people towards full-time service. Parents who had come to America seeking a decent future for their children were horrified at the prospect of them going overseas (1999).

Similarly, some older people may be unwilling to go while their children are still at school (Loong 1996). This demographic sandwich results in people being "trapped in the house" until parents have passed on and children have entered university (Lam 2007:18).

Once ready to go, missionaries face new hurdles. Learning a language is not easy. Appreciating a non-Chinese culture may involve struggles in areas such as hospitality, dealing with strangers, and personal space (Wu 2013). If reaching fellow Asians is difficult, working with Arabs may be too much to ask, Lam suggests (2007). Yet, even though cultural differences can be huge, Lin (2013) calls Chinese to minister among Muslims and Hindus. Historic Western missionaries managed to bridge cultural gaps between themselves and the Chinese. Migrants today overcome language and cultural obstacles in order to make their families' dreams come true. Surely we can do the same for the sake of the gospel.

Besides adapting to the field culture, missionaries also must learn how to work with new colleagues. Often these will come from other countries. While teams may be multicultural, in practice often they will tend to be Western-dominated. Differences in expectations, communication, and leadership styles may hurt feelings and team unity (Wu 2013).

Generally the *lingua franca* of such teams will be English (Lin 2013). It can be a challenge for Chinese missionaries to maintain their children's native language competency, yet that will be important for their identity and for their return home (Wu 2013). Wu also writes movingly of his preference for Chinese language in his spiritual practices, rather than English or the ministry language.

Gender presents one more issue. Many parts of the world are seeing Chinese missionaries for the first time. Unfortunately, female colleagues may be taken for servants or even prostitutes. This issue is outside the experience of non-Chinese team leaders. It must be handled by Chinese fellow missionaries (Wu 2013).

RACE AND STATUS

Chinese missionaries work mostly within their own culture or in cultures with close affinity (Lin 2013). Yang (1999:174, 193) describes his church's "Chinese first" policy, which focuses on South America and Africa, but only with the aim of reaching Chinese people there. For many Chinese missiologists, this is not satisfactory. Though enormous and diverse, China and Chinese people cannot be the total focus of mission, it is argued (Lam 2007). As early as 1989, Yap Un-han (1989:79) urged Chinese believers to "evangelize not only the Chinese, but also the non-Chinese", and Thomas Wang (1989:83) repudiated distinctions of "race or geography".

Yet this remains an issue. Reflecting on the diversity of God's people represented at the Lausanne III conference, Freda Cheung (2011) laments the Chinese' limited focus on Chinese. Only by committing to cross-cultural ministry – to Jerusalem/Judea, to Samaria, and even to the ends of the earth, in the words of Acts 1:8 – can the Chinese truly fulfil the Great Commission, it is asserted (Yau 2013). There are differences of interpretation, however. Some believe all the stages (Jerusalem, Samaria, ends of the earth) should occur simultaneously (Lo 1996), while others believe that our first responsibility is outreach to our own people, and that cross-cultural outreach should occur when our churches are mature (Tang 1989: 146).

A narrow ethnic focus is matched by a narrow social one (Cheung 2011:7). Chinese churches are reluctant to minister to addicts, delinquents, or the abused, perhaps because of a Confucian belief in sorting out our own problems, and not getting involved with other people's.

Nevertheless, there is progress. While Chinese churches always have sent missionaries to the Chinese in Southeast Asia (Lo 1996), today some are crossing cultural as well as national borders. Some North American Chinese congregations, like Houston Chinese Church, are planting local non-Chinese churches. Some Indonesian and Filipino Chinese churches have sent missionaries to other peoples within those nations (Lam 2007). While in the past most Hong Kong missionaries worked among overseas Chinese, now more than half serve other peoples (Lo 1996). A Chinese church in Manchester, UK, is reaching out among South Asian people there.

In light of global migrations today, Lin (2013) urges Chinese churches to undertake cross-cultural work in their localities among foreign domestic helpers, students, migrant workers, and even illegal immigrants. One Nigerian church in the UK already has planted 250 churches. "Chinese missionaries, where are you?" Lin asks.

Providential scattering

Instead of focusing on a reconstructed identity, Chinese churches in the West would benefit from a biblical and theological understanding of their diaspora identity. The Scripture contains many heroes of faith who have been migrants. There is no finer cross-cultural missionary than the Apostle Paul, a diaspora Christian with a complex cultural and religious identity. If diaspora Christians could move from a survival or closed-door church mentality to one which recognises the Lord's leading and provision in their migration experience, this might reduce the intergenerational tensions affecting cross-cultural mission and free up the next generation for full-time service.

The diversity of Chinese Christianity should be celebrated and different understandings of identity and ministry exchanged. One size does not fit all. Regional subgroupings, mainstream churches, mission agencies, and theological schools should share ideas. Chinese churches also could learn from the strengths and weaknesses of the Korean mission movement. As well, there is a need for historical perspective, since many diaspora Chinese Christians are people without a religious history. They would be inspired by stories about John Sung and R.A. Jaffray's Chinese Foreign Missionary Union, as well as more modern testimonies of faithful but not necessarily famous witnesses.

In the spirit of Acts 17, diaspora Chinese Christians can come to see their scattering around the world, and their resulting complex identities, as providential in the kingdom of God.

For discussion

1. List some important statistics about Chinese in mission.
2. How are Chinese churches in the West different from those in Southeast Asia?
3. Describe three challenges for Chinese in mission and discuss how to cope with these.

Bibliography

Barrett, David, and Johnson, Todd. "Annual Statistical Table on Global Mission: 2003," *International Bulletin of Missionary Research* 27, no.1 (2003): 24-25.

Bernau, Sharmila. "The Chinese and Indian Diasporas in New Zealand: An Oral History Project," *New Zealand Journal of Asian Studies* 7, no.1 (2005): 134-152.

Chan, Hay-him. "The Current State of Global Chinese Church Mission," *Go Unto All Nations* (Jun 1993) [in Chinese].

Chan, Kwok-bun. *Chinese Identities, Ethnicity and Cosmopolitanism* (London: Routledge, 2005).

Chang, John. "The 21st Chinese Mission Century," *Chinese Around the World* 184 (Nov 2003). http://www.cccowe.org/content_pub.php?id=catw200311-1.

Chen, Letty. *Writing Chinese: Reshaping Chinese Cultural Identity* (Basingstoke: Palgrave Macmillan, 2006).

Cheung, Freda. "Reflections on Lausanne III," *Great Commission News* (Winter 2011): 6-9.

Cohen, Robin. *Global diasporas: An Introduction* (London: Routledge, 1997).

Editorial Department. "Introduction to the Urbana Student Missions Conference," [in Chinese]. *Behold* 27 (2007): 19.

HKACM Research Department. "Maturing Chinese Mission Societies – Report on Questionnaires Given to Chinese Mission Societies," in *Chinese Missions – Towards the 21st century*, ed. Vanessa Hung (Hong Kong: Hong Kong Association of Christian Missions, 1996), 87-126 [in Chinese].

Hung, Vanessa. "The Characteristics and Advantages of Chinese Missionaries," in *Chinese Missions – Towards the 21st century*, ed. Vanessa Hung (Hong Kong: Hong Kong Association of Christian Missions, 1996), 137-142 [in Chinese].

Kokot, W., K. Tölölyan, and C. Alfonso. "Introduction," in *Diaspora, Identity and Religion*, ed. Waltraud Kokot, Khachig Tölölyan, and Carolin Alfonso (London: Routledge, 2004), 1-8.

Lam, Cyrus. *Chinese Churches: A Bridge to World Mission* (Hong Kong: China Alliance Press, 1985) [in Chinese].

Lam, Cyrus. "Current Status of Missions in Global Chinese Churches," *Behold* 25 (Mar 2007):16-19 [in Chinese].
Lam, Cyrus. "Mobilising Small Churches for Missions," in *Chinese Missions Can Become True*, ed. Lin, Ching-chu (Burlingame, CA: Gospel Operation International, 2008), 12-18 [in Chinese].
Lam, Shiu-yuen. *Introduction to People Group Ministry* (Hong Kong: CCCOWE, 1991) [in Chinese].
Lin, Ching-chu. "Looking at the Need for Cross-Cultural Mission from the Trends of Our Time," *Go Unto All Nations* (Apr 2013):4-7 [in Chinese].http://www.hkacm.org.hk/News/2550/p4_7.pdf.
Lo, Ka-man. "Overcoming Obstacles to Missions by Chinese Churches," in *Chinese Missions – Towards the 21st century*, ed. Vanessa Hung (Hong Kong: Hong Kong Association of Christian Missions, 1996), 143-151 [in Chinese].
Loong, Helen. "The Top Ten List for Preparing our Next Generation for Missions," *Great Commission News* (Winter 2012):1-3.
Loong, Titus. "Looking at Chinese Missionaries Through the Characteristics of Chinese People," in *Chinese Missions – Towards the 21st century*, ed. Vanessa Hung (Hong Kong: Hong Kong Association of Christian Missions, 1996), 127-136 [in Chinese].
Mok, Kit-ching. "Appendix 1: Beautiful footprints – A Short History of Chinese Missions," in *Chinese Missions – Towards the 21st century*, ed. Vanessa Hung (Hong Kong: Hong Kong Association of Christian Missions, 1996), 183-217 [in Chinese].
Population Reference Bureau 2010. Washington, DC: Population Reference Bureau. http://www.prb.org/pdf10/10wpds_eng.pdf.
Safran, William. "Deconstructing and Comparing Diasporas," in *Diaspora, Identity and Religion*, ed. Waltraud Kokot, Khachig Tölölyan, and Carolin Alfonso (London: Routledge, 2004), 9-29.

27. Transnational Ties of Indian Churches in the Arabian Gulf: Kerala Pentecostal Churches in Kuwait

Stanley John

Diaspora churches dot the landscape of every major city in the world. Virtually everywhere a migrant community exists, such churches can be found, even in regions that seem "unreachable." How do these churches begin? And what is the nature of their relationship to their members' home countries?

Since human groupings can be understood only in context, this paper will limit its focus to Pentecostal churches in Kuwait whose members come from the Indian state of Kerala. They represent no small body. Of the eighty-four churches from all nations that worship at the National Evangelical Church in Kuwait, twenty-five are Pentecostal churches planted by migrants from Kerala. Mission for Kerala Christians occurs both at the local level as well as the transnational context. In their diaspora location, they minister to their fellow Indian diaspora and migrants from other nations, as well as relationally with the native population. Transnational missions occur when they in engage in ministry to those in the homeland and other diaspora locations. This chapter will focus on the transnational ties of the Kerala Pentecostal churches to discern the pathways through which these churches engage in mission from Kuwait to India.

Following a brief introduction to Indian diaspora and its migration to the Arabian Gulf, the paper will identify four types of diaspora churches. Next, we will trace Kerala Pentecostal churches' transnational ecclesial affiliations, noting diverse expressions of Pentecostalism. Four types of ties will be identified: affiliated churches, independent/unaffiliated churches, charismatic fellowships, and apostolic networks. Finally, we will employ the four types to understand emerging neo-Pentecostal churches in Kuwait attended by migrants from Kerala.

As a member of the Indian diaspora in Kuwait, the author experienced the Kerala Pentecostal churches as the religious context for the development of his practice of faith. Fieldwork for this project appropriated an ethnographic model of participant observation in thirty-five worship services, as well as interviews with thirty-five leaders of Kerala Pentecostal churches in both homeland and diaspora contexts.

Migration to the Arabian Gulf

Long before the discovery of oil, Indians were moving to and from the Arabian Gulf. As well, merchants and seafarers from the Gulf came to South India to trade pearls for spices. The Indian rupee was the local currency in several Gulf countries until the middle of the twentieth century.

The discovery of oil changed migration significantly. First, the volume of people migrating to this region has been unparalleled. With low native populations, but needing laborers, Gulf countries have opened their doors to South and Southeast Asia and other Arab countries. Second, rapid economic and infrastructural development has transformed sparsely-populated desert regions into thriving metropolises. Revenue from the sale of oil, coupled with abundant cheap labor, has fueled this accelerated pace. Third, immigration from outside traditional Arab and Islamic areas has altered the region's ethnic and religious demography. Today the Arabian Gulf represents one of the most urban, economically developed, and ethnically diverse regions of the world. This growth has been possible only because of economic migration to the region since the discovery of oil.

Indian Diaspora in the Gulf

Out of the 20-25 million emigrants from India, 19% reside in the oil-rich Gulf countries (Khadria 2006: 5). Some accounts estimate that there are more than 3.5 million Indians in the Gulf. According to the *Report of the High Level Committee on the Indian Diaspora*, Saudi Arabia tops the list, with over 1.5 million Indian migrants (ICWA 2011). The United Arab Emirates has 900,000 Indians, accounting for 32% of the country's population, the highest percentage in the Gulf. In Oman, Kuwait, Bahrain, and Qatar, Indians account for 15-20% of their populations.

From Kerala to the Gulf

The state of Kerala is located on the southwestern tip of India, bordering the states of Tamil Nadu on its east, Karnataka to its north, and the Arabian Sea to the west. Dating back to 3000 BC, Kerala's spice trade built connections with the Middle East, Africa, and Europe. Local tradition holds that the Apostle Thomas followed the trails of the Jewish diaspora to arrive on the coast of Kerala in AD. 52. He planted seven churches in Kerala before being martyred in Tamil Nadu. The resulting small group of Christians grew significantly following the missionary efforts of the nineteenth century and the impassioned indigenous missions efforts of the twentieth.

In terms of economic and social development, Kerala has unusually high marks in the Indian human development index that measures education, healthcare, and income (Suryanarayana 2013). Such attainments, coupled with long- standing global trade relationships, have helped people from Kerala get jobs in the fast-developing economies of the Arabian Gulf.

Emigrants from Kerala to the Gulf outnumber emigrants from all the other states of India combined. As for their destination, nine out of every ten emigrants from Kerala travel to the countries of the Arabian Gulf. Out of 2,193,412 emigrants from Kerala in 2008, 1,941,422 went to this region. The United Arab Emirates (47.29%) and Saudi Arabia (25.93%) received nearly 75% of all emigrants from Kerala. The remaining migrants went to Oman (8.63%), Kuwait (6.66%), Qatar (6.26%), and Bahrain (5.22%) (Zachariah and Rajan 2010).

Kafala sponsorship system

The primary purpose of this migration is economic. In Kuwait, this is structured by a *Kafala* or sponsorship system, which links residency in the country directly to an employment contract with a particular employer who is the *kafeel,* or sponsor. The *Kafala* system is rooted in the tradition of bonded-labor relationships wherein "workers labored against a debt previously incurred instead of receiving wages" (HRW 2010: 36). The migrant's tenure in the country is limited to the duration of the employment contract. When it is finished, the worker must get the contract renewed, search for a new employer, or leave the country.

This system keeps migrants vulnerable, especially those who are low-skilled. Although abolishing the sponsorship system in favor of an alternate system has been proposed, infringement of migrants' rights continues undeterred, such as the confiscation of passports. So far, there exists no comprehensive pathway to naturalization for migrant workers in the Gulf States.[1] Arguably the most significant feature of migration to the Arabian Gulf is its impermanence. This feature of transience provides the interpretive key to understanding migrant life, specifically religious practice, in the diaspora.

Religious composition

The Pew Forum's Global Religious Landscape estimates that nearly 74.1% of the population of Kuwait is Muslim, although other reports claim as high as 85% (Pew Forum 2012). Among Kuwaiti citizens, apart from 200 Christian families and a few Baha'i, the population is overwhelmingly Muslim. Approximately two-thirds of these Kuwaiti Muslims are Sunni, including the royal family. One-third are Shia. Christians account for 14.3% of the total population, including temporary workers (Pew Forum 2012). These include adherents of the Roman Catholic Church (300,000),

---

1 The exceptions are the rare circumstances wherein migrants of Arab ethnicity who are Muslims are granted naturalization.

the Coptic Orthodox Church (70,000), the National Evangelical Church (40,000) and other Christian denominations (30,000). Hindus (300,000), Buddhists (100,000), Sikhs (10,000), and Baha'i (400) account for 11.6% of population (IRFR 2010).

Diaspora churches and migrant Christianity

When migrants move to a new locale, they carry their faith with them. Religious beliefs, symbols, and practices do not get left behind as excess luggage. Instead, faith and piety are practiced with increased fervor when people make their homes in a strange place. Either they gather with fellow migrants to worship and fellowship, giving birth to new churches, or they join existing churches in the foreign context.

Types of churches in the Diaspora

National churches, *international/multicultural churches*, and *diaspora ethnic/linguistic specific churches* are three ecclesial arrangements that serve the diaspora. In the first category, most of the church members are natives of the host country, and they worship in the national language. Such *national churches'* leaders are affiliated with denominational leadership that is usually within the country or region. These churches may or may not actively invite migrants into the congregation.[2]

International or multicultural churches are comprised of congregants from various nations or cultures. Even a single nation, like India, displays ethnic, cultural, and linguistic diversity. Thus multicultural worship may occur when people from only one nation join together. Multiple factors play a part in determining whether a church will be multicultural or predominantly national. These factors include diversity of congregants, diversity among the leadership, and intentionality to preserve and celebrate cultural identity.

Diaspora ethnic and/or linguistic-specific churches encompass migrants who share the same ethnic heritage. Typically they worship in their own native language. In the first two types of churches, migrants participate in a culture and language that is not their own, whether the host country or that of the predominant ethnic group in the congregation, or a globalized pattern that includes a language understood and spoken by the majority, such as English. However, in diaspora ethnic churches people worship in their

---

2 There are no national churches in several Arabian Gulf countries, since there are few Christians among the local people. Rev. Ammanuel B. Ghareeb is the only national clergyman in Kuwait. He serves as the minister of the Arabic Language Congregation at the National Evangelical Church Kuwait. The congregation is formed of economic migrants from various Arabic-speaking countries in the Middle East.

native language alongside believers of their own ethnicity and culture. This third type of church is the focus of our case study.

Kerala Christians in Kuwait

In 1953, Kerala Christian migrants gathered in the chapel of the Arabian Mission compound, called the National Evangelical Church in Kuwait (NECK), to form the Kuwait Town Malayalee Christian Congregation (KTMCC). All Christians from Kerala worshipped together in this ecumenical fellowship, irrespective of their prior ecclesial affiliations. This church continues to this day.

Faced with limited opportunities for social, cultural, and religious participation with citizens of the Arabian Gulf, migrants will gather together with one another to affirm their belonging in community. A central institution is the church. Nearly every day of the week, a church may offer worship services. Not only religious belonging is nurtured, but also social and cultural belonging. Church members become family, the support community for migrants away from home. Through church activities, migrants develop cultural, social, and religious knowledge and skills, practice leadership roles, and mitigate the marginalization they feel in the larger society.

As new migrants continued to arrive in Kuwait, new churches representing various denominations were created. Eventually Malayalees (people from the state of Kerala) gathered in the Mar Thoma Church, Church of South India (CSI), Malankara Orthodox Church, Brethren Fellowship, and Pentecostal church. All Pentecostals from Kerala worshipped together in one church called Pentecostal Church of Kuwait (PCK) during this period.

By the late 1980s – prior to the Gulf War, which sliced through Kuwait – various Pentecostal fellowships representing the diversity of Pentecostalism in Kerala could be found worshipping on the NECK compound. After the Gulf War, as migrants from Kerala continued to arrive in record numbers, they formed even more fellowships in keeping with their diverse ecclesial affiliations back home. Along with other independent churches, they gathered regularly for prayer, worship, fellowship, and ministry on the NECK compound in Kuwait City. In the first decade of the twenty-first century, the burgeoning of Pentecostal and neo-Pentecostal churches continued undiminished in response to the renewal and revitalization taking place in the traditional churches.

Transnational ecclesial ties

As migrants organize into worshipping communities in their new geographical context, all the while maintaining ties with their homeland, diaspora churches form organically. This follows a “process by which immigrants forge and sustain multi-stranded social relations that link together their societies of origin and settlement. We call these processes transnationalism to emphasize that many immigrants today build social fields that cross geographical, cultural, and political borders" (Basch et. al. 1994:7).

The ways in which migrant churches create and maintain ties with their respective churches and denominations in the homeland may be referred to as *transnational ecclesial ties*. Avenues and networks span national boundaries, traversed by numerous agents who move between the homeland, the diaspora, and other contexts. Religious representatives, for example, travel between the homeland and the diaspora to update the diaspora community on ministries at home and to provide opportunities for members of the diaspora to participate in these ministries.

Transnationalism often has been contrasted with assimilation, which shows migrants shedding their socio-cultural and linguistic identities for that of the dominant community in the host country. However, assimilation and transnational lifestyles need not be mutually exclusive. Rather, migrants can find ways to remain connected actively to the places from which they have originated even while they are incorporated into the countries where they reside (Levitt 2001: 4). Going beyond the confines of the boundaries of nation-states, they can establish social relations that transcend such limits.

Theorizing transnational religious organization

The Catholic Church may be viewed as an *extended* transnational religious organization, according to Levitt's classification (2001:11). Here migrant believers are members of a global religious system that is "legitimate, powerful and well organized," holding a "membership card that works everywhere." Protestant churches occupy a *negotiated* transnational religious organization in which they "extend and deepen ties already in place" (15). Unlike the Catholic Church that is highly hierarchical and centralized, these churches have "flexible ties that are not subject to pre-established rule, and must be constantly worked out" (15). Contrasting with historic Catholics and Protestants are new churches started by the migrants in the diaspora context, *recreated* transnational religious organizations (17).

Each of these types is found in the Arabian Gulf. The Catholic Church operates four parishes in various parts of the Kuwait. At the main cathedral in Kuwait City, thirty-four worship services or masses serve various migrant communities. Masses are offered in English, Italian, French, Arabic, Filipino, Sinhala, Bengali, Konkani, Tamil, and Malayalam. The parish of Kuwait falls under the oversight of the Bishop of Northern Arabia, H.L. Bishop Camillo Ballin, appointed by Pope Benedict XVI.

Protestant churches of interest to Indians here include the Church of South India (C.S.I.), the Brethren Assembly, and various Pentecostal fellowships. Each is affiliated to its respective denomination back home rather than connected through a global administrative body. Scores of other churches formed by migrants function independently, unconnected to any parent denomination. Yet at times these form organic networks that are transnational.

Three types of "religious organizational context" also may be identified, according to Levitt. In the first type, a migrant church has formal ties to a "sister congregation" in the home country. In the second type, a migrant church is a franchise of a sending-country group which supervises and even funds the diaspora chapter. In the third type, a migrant church is part of a worldwide denomination (Levitt 2003: 851). Levitt's three categories identify types of affiliations between the churches in the diaspora and a denomination in the homeland and/or affiliation with a worldwide institution. However, not all churches in the diaspora fit this typology, as many remain unaffiliated with any denomination. I have therefore created an alternate typology for Kuwait's Kerala Pentecostal churches. It includes *affiliated churches, independent churches, charismatic fellowships,* and *apostolic networks.*

Affiliated churches relate officially to their parent denomination back home and are dependent on the homeland for continued ecclesial identification and support. The homeland denominations provide ecclesial support and clergy for the churches in the diaspora, while receiving remittances from diaspora churches for various missions projects at home. This transnational affiliation facilitates mutual well-being and support for the ministries of the church.

The denominational headquarters in the homeland allows clergy to come to serve a diaspora church on a three-year labor contract. At the end of the contract, the pastor must depart the country, but another clergy person from the homeland may come to take their place. Other churches are served by bi-vocational pastors. They remain pastors for the duration of their secular employment contract, which can be renewed.

Independent churches are birthed in the diaspora and choose to remain unaffiliated with a denomination in the homeland or elsewhere.

Charismatic fellowships do not begin as churches. The participants are active members in various denominations. When ministry opportunities within their current churches appear limited, these fellowship groups open opportunities for lay people to lead. They also provide rich interdenominational fellowship. As well, they become a venue for outreach. In time, some of these groups do become churches.

Apostolic networks are started by economic migrants who remain independent and without formal affiliation but proactively plant churches cross-culturally and even internationally in various diaspora contexts as well as back in the homeland.

Pentecostal churches in Kuwait

Eighty-four churches worship at the NECK compound in Kuwait, serving various language groups and nationalities. Twenty-five of these churches are Pentecostal or neo-Pentecostal churches from Kerala. Kerala Pentecostal churches also meet at the St. Paul's Anglican Church compound in Ahmadi, as well as in various multipurpose facilities in residential areas where there is a significant concentration of migrants. These churches fit within the four types discussed above.

Distinguishing classical Pentecostal churches and Neo-Pentecostal churches in Kerala Pentecostalism

Pentecostal churches also may be divided between classical and neo-Pentecostal. In Kerela, the roots of classical Pentecostal groups such as the Assemblies of God (AG), the Indian Pentecostal Church (IPC), the Church of God (COG), and The Pentecostal Mission (TPM) can be traced to the early decades of the twentieth century. While Western missionaries led the AG and the COG in their early years, Indigenous leaders birthed the IPC and TPM. The second half of the twentieth century saw the rise of more indigenous Pentecostal ecclesial organizations such as Sharon Fellowship of Churches (SFC), New India Church of God (NICOG), and Pentecostal Maranatha Gospel Church (PMGC). All of these churches espouse the basic tenets of Indian Pentecostal theology and practice, particularly emphasizing the gifts of the Spirit, the importance of water baptism, abstinence from wearing jewelry, and self-identification squarely within the Pentecostal tradition.

Neo-Pentecostal churches do not share the classic Pentecostals' historical antecedents, the early missionaries or the early indigenous leaders. Churches such as Heavenly Feast, Devasia Mullakara, and others emerged in the last two decades as a response to revitalization in the Catholic Church, Orthodox Church, Jacobite Church, Mar Thoma Church, and other mainline churches in India, as well as conversions from other faiths. People join these churches when they experience physical healing or deliverance from evil spirits, attend revival meetings, or hear the gospel through various forms of media. Global media presenting charismatic televangelists further empower these movements. Sociologically, these churches stand in stark contrast to the classical Pentecostal churches' insistence on abstinence from jewelry, yet they espouse the importance of the gifts of the spirit, including speaking in tongues, healing, deliverance from evil spirits, and believer's baptism.

The key criterion to distinguishing between classical and neo-Pentecostals is their self-definition. Neo-Pentecostal groups do not wish to be connected to classical Pentecostals because of friction and schisms in the classical churches which the neo-Pentecostals deem hypocritical. Classical churches are too political and institutionalized, they lament. Furthermore, neo-Pentecostal churches are led by bi-vocational pastors who respond to a personal call to ministry, apart from any formal theological training. Established Pentecostals thus tend to deem the "new generation churches" as "shallow" and lacking in discipleship.

This paper will focus on neo-Pentecostal churches.

Neo-Pentecostal affiliated churches

The Heavenly Feast is led by Dr. Mathew Kuruvilla, affectionately known as Brother Thangu. After this businessman was healed miraculously, he became an evangelist. What started in 1998 as a prayer fellowship in his office has now become a global movement. More than 200 churches have been planted in various parts of India and among Indians in the Gulf, Europe, and North America. Such a revivalist movement finds its way to the diaspora primarily through the personal ties of economic migrants in the Gulf, but also through regular television programs that reach Indian homes worldwide. Churches under the oversight of the Heavenly Feast are born and flourish in the diaspora, fortified by regular visits from international leaders. Today there are Heavenly Feast congregations in five of the six Gulf countries.

Another "affiliated" group is the Church of the Eternity. The founder, Devasia Mullakara, served as a spiritual director at a Catholic retreat center before launching his ministry of healing and deliverance. In 2007, he was excommunicated from the Catholic Church for teachings against Mariology, veneration of the saints, prayers for the dead, and praying with the rosary. Through Christian broadcasting media networks such as PowerVision, Mullakara's teachings are broadcast to homes throughout the diaspora. Periodically certain believers will host special meetings. Migrants from various churches across ecclesial lines will attend, bringing their non-Christian friends to hear the gospel and receive prayer for the sick. After one series of meetings, migrants in Kuwait requested that a branch of the Church of the Eternity be started here. Today there are branch churches in Kuwait, Bahrain, UAE, and elsewhere in the Gulf. These churches are marked by significant oversight from the homeland as well as deference from the diaspora. Leaders visit them three or four times a year to encourage the churches and conduct weddings, water baptisms, and outreach services.

Neo-Pentecostal charismatic fellowships

Charismatic prayer fellowships emerge when the desire for spiritual vitality goes unmet within the traditional framework of the Eastern and mainline churches. If a charismatic group remains distinctly a fellowship without forming into a separate church, yet stays connected to its prior ecclesial roots, it may be termed a *charismatic fellowship*. On occasion, such an informal prayer fellowship will break off from its previous ecclesial affiliation to form a distinct church. Life Fellowship emerged as a prayer fellowship in 1983, with most of its leaders and participants coming from the Mar Thoma Church. In its early days, the group did not emphasize the need for water baptism or spirit baptism, but functioned simply as a place for spiritual vitality. In time, however, the fellowship offered water baptism. At that point, it found its prior ecclesial affiliation in question. Eventually it evolved into an independent interdenominational church.

Neo-Pentecostal independent unaffiliated churches

Independent churches are unaffiliated with any ecclesial denominations in the homeland or in the diaspora. They remain autonomous under the leadership of a charismatic lay leader who responded to a call to ministry after experiencing spiritual renewal. The Nations Outreach for Christ (NOFC) was started by a successful businessman who experienced spiritual awakening through various neo-Pentecostal prayer fellowships while he was a member of the Mar Thoma Church. Upon leaving that church, he started his own ministry and outreach to other migrant workers. This developed into a worshipping community. NOFC is connected to classical Pentecostal and neo-Pentecostal churches through its founders' personal network, but remains independent from any oversight from the homeland. The leader supports church planting, pastoral support, and orphanage ministries in various parts of India.

Neo-Pentecostal apostolic networks

Apostolic networks emerge out of the neo-Pentecostal churches in the diaspora and in apostolic fashion start churches in other countries where similar diaspora communities exist. This includes the homeland, but even there they plant churches cross-culturally, beyond ethnic boundaries. The Little Flock Fellowship started as a charismatic prayer fellowship, evolved into an independent church, and eventually became an apostolic network of churches. The vision and relationships of the leader and the financial gifts from the diaspora church support the network of pastors and ministries in other countries. In relatively unreached north India, Little Flock Fellowship supports forty-five missionaries in Andhra Pradesh, Chhattisgarh, and Orissa states.

Conclusion

Following the trails of the diasporas, churches are scattered throughout the globe. This paper highlights the journey of economic migrants from the southern Indian state of Kerala to Kuwait, and the churches that they have started. Kerala Pentecostal churches in Kuwait are a diaspora ethnic/linguistic specific type, among the diverse types of churches in the diaspora. Revitalization is taking place in the homeland and among the Kerala diaspora, and neo-Pentecostal churches are emerging as a response. Some are affiliated churches, others are independent or unaffiliated, others are charismatic fellowships, and others are part of apostolic networks.

Diaspora churches reflect the diversity and complexity embodied by migrants. Inductive case studies provide us with rich descriptive data from which we can begin to theorize on the practice of faith in this setting. Any research on diaspora churches must recognize diverse ethnic and linguistic-specific communities, varied types of churches, and transnational ecclesial ties between the churches at home and abroad. These transnational ties are the avenues which agents traverse between the homeland and the diasporas, and vice-versa, in order to inform, to disciple and to revitalize the people.

For discussion

1. What are the dangers of the kafeel sponsorship system?
2. What diverse functions does a diaspora congregation provide for migrants?
3. How do churches diversify when a diaspora population increases?
4. What criteria distinguish different kinds of Indian diaspora churches in Kuwait?
5. How do overseas Indian churches revitalize churches in India?

Bibliography

Basch, Linda G., Nina Glick Schiller, and Cristina Szanton Blanc. *Nations Unbound: Transnational Projects, Postcolonial Predicaments, and Deterritorialized Nation-States*. [S.l.]: Gordon and Breach, 1994.

Human Rights Watch. *Walls At Every Turn: Abuse of Migrant Domestic Workers Through Kuwait's Sponsorship System.* New York: Human Rights Watch, 2010.

ICWA. 2011. *Report of the High Level Committee on the Indian Diaspora*. Indian Council of World Affairs. Electronic Media. <http://indiandiaspora.nic.in/contents.htm> Accessed December 1, 2011.

Khadria, Binod. "India: Skilled Migration to Developed Countries, Labour Migration to the Gulf" in *Migracion Y Desarrollo.* Zacatecas, Mexico: International Network on Migration and Development, 2006.

Levitt, Peggy. "'You Know, Abraham Was Really the First Immigrant': Religion and Transnational Migration," *International Migration Review* 37, no. 3: 847-873, 2003.

Levitt, Peggy. "Between God, Ethnicity, and Country: An Approach to the Study of Transnational Religion." Oxford: University of Oxford. Transnational Communities Programme, 2001.

Pew Forum. *Global Religious Landscape*. 2012. http://features.pewforum.org/grl/population-percentage.php (accessed April 1, 2013).

Suryanarayana, M.H. 'Human Development in India: Costs of Inequality,' No. 198.

Brasília, International Policy Centre for Inclusive Growth, 2013.
U.S. Department of State. *International Religious Freedom Report for 2010.* Bureau of Democracy, Human Rights and Labor. http://www.state.gov/j/drl/rls/irf/2010/148828.htm (accessed April 1, 2013)
Zachariah, K.C. and Rajan, S Irudaya. "Migration Monitoring Study, 2008 Emigration and Remittance in the Context of Surge in Oil Prices" Working Paper 424. Thiruvananthapuram: Center for Development Studies, 2010.

28. Korean Diaspora Ministries

S. Hun Kim and Susie Hershberger

NB: Based on *Korean Diaspora and Christian Mission,* eds. S. Hun Kim and Wonsuk Ma

Beginnings of a movement

In Korea, the experience of diaspora is woven through the entire history of the church. The first Koreans who responded to Christ as Lord were emigrants living outside the country. Highly eager to share their faith, they returned home and preached in secret, since there was a tight government ban on foreign religion inside Korea at that time. Meanwhile, translation of the Bible into the Korean language began simultaneously in Japan and Manchuria. By 1887, the first Bible, the *Yesu-shungkyo-junsoe*, was published. One of the early translators, Sangyune Suh, re-entered Korea and distributed Scriptures widely. Thus when foreign witnesses were allowed into the country, they discovered many thousands of Christians who were conversant with the Bible. This indigenous Scripture-based heritage has provided a solid foundation for the Korean church.

Officially, emigration was prohibited until 1897 when King Gojong opened the country to modernization. Unofficially, however, natural disasters, famine, and political disorder in the mid-nineteenth century had impelled farmers to escape earlier into the country next door, China. This exodus had spiraled into a mass movement. When Russia began developing the Maritime Province of Siberia in 1858, and invited newcomers to create settlements and businesses there, even more Koreans left to seek their fortune. Korean families who took advantage of these opportunities prospered, both in Manchuria in China and in the Maritime Province ruled by Russia.

In 1901, after emigration became legal, the Emperor sent five Koreans to Hawaii to work on a sugar cane plantation. Soon ships were bringing many across the Pacific to the Americas. The first Korean church in Hawaii was planted six months after the first laborers arrived. This set a pattern. Wherever Korean immigrants went, they planted churches and created schools that employed the Korean language.

The years from 1910 to 1945 are known in Korea as the Japanese Occupation Period. To avoid the oppression and poverty intensified by Japanese colonization, many more Koreans left the country. Pastors were sent to shepherd the immigrant communities. Churches served as cultural as well as religious centers. Along with the Korean schools, these churches helped the immigrants maintain their national and Christian identities. Korean diaspora churches also were the main support for the independence the country sought from Japan.

After liberation in 1945, many Koreans returned home, but many more travelled abroad in search of prosperity and new opportunities. Today Koreans can be found in 180 countries. As of this writing, both the head of the United Nations, Ban Ki-Moon, and the head of the World Bank, Jim Yong Kim, are of Korean descent. Unquestionably, Koreans are global. Amid this vast diaspora, Christians are prominent. Outside the homeland there are over 5,000 Korean churches.

Korean Christianity worldwide

Inside Korea, Christianity has grown remarkably. Twenty per cent of the population identify as Christian. Although the church suffered severe persecution under the Japanese occupation, the faith was not squelched but was fanned into flame. Several of the largest churches in the world are located in this nation. These include Yoido Full Gospel Church, Myungsung Church – known as the largest Presbyterian Church in the world – and Kwanglim Church, known as the largest Methodist church in the world. In prayer, hard work, missions, and the presence of Christian citizens in the marketplace and in politics, the Korean church has been outstanding.

Yet growth has plateaued in the face of public critique about nominalism, ethical lapses, and indifference to social needs. Renewal movements led by pastors have arisen, calling Christians back to their "first love." These movements are large and span many denominations (Min 2009).

Meanwhile, Korea sends out the second-largest contingent of foreign missionaries of any nation in the world. There are approximately 20,000 Koreans engaged in full time mission work outside the country. Half are men and half are women. Most focus on evangelism, discipling, church-planting, Bible translation, and theological education. Mission finance channeled through mission agencies is estimated to be the equivalent of US $363,005,083.00 in 2012 (Moon 2013: 96).

Beyond this dedicated missionary force is the worldwide Christian Korean diaspora with its 5,000 churches. Many have viewed this dispersal as part of the plan of God. In spite of disturbingly cruel happenings in the homeland's history, God in his sovereignty "allowed the tragic event(s)…to be part of his plan to bring the good news" (Song 2011:118). The displacement and migration of Koreans around the world led to the simultaneous dispersing of the gospel. Just as Abraham, Daniel, and Esther were lights to the nations, so Koreans have scattered seeds of witness in 180 countries, expecting a great harvest.

Unfortunately, however, with the passing of the decades, quite a few Korean diaspora churches have turned inward. From the beginning, the church overseas had been a place where new migrants could find community, practical help, and a familiar language and culture. While this remains important, this cannot be the primary call of the church. Instead, diaspora churches must live apostolically and incarnationally in their communities. They must be missional, seeking to serve the needs of those around them in the cities where they are situated rather than just enjoying fellowship behind the safe walls of the church. Recovery of such an apostolic nature is essential to the health of the church. Raising up developmental leaders who will bridge the gap between cultures and become "transcultural mediators" is essential. If walls rise between the church people and the people outside, and eliminate opportunities to minister, they must be torn down (Song 2011:126-127).

An outward orientation, offering action opportunities and creative challenges, might catch the imagination of younger members as well. At present, many second generation immigrants suffer from an identity crisis. In the United States their "silent exodus" from the church has been enormous (H. Lee 1996). Alternatively, rather than leaving the church altogether, some second-generation Koreans have helped start "pan-Asian" diaspora churches that incorporate Koreans, Chinese, and Japanese descendants in a larger but still Asiancommunity.

Four diaspora churches which provide exemplary models have been described by Steve Sang-cheol Moon (2011:84-100). They were selected because of the remarkable instrumental work they do out in the community as well as inside the church. These congregations are the Yohan Tokyo Christian Church, the Korean Presbyterian Church of Thailand, the Shanghai Korean Community Church, and the Beijing Twenty-First Century Korean Church.

While these four churches vary in their emphasis on hierarchy, all demonstrate flexibility. Decisions often are de-centralized, rather than simply being made by the top leadership. Various groups of members take ownership of activities. Horizontal teamwork accomplishes much of what needs to be done. Stable structures and systems provide room for innovative situational responses. Thus in the Tokyo church, "many people are faithfully engaged in church activities in one way or another." In the Thailand church, which is somewhat more loosely structured, there is an overall enthusiasm for volunteering and availability of church members.

A concern for harmony and an emphasis on community are also keys to the success of these churches, a collectivist rather than an individualistic orientation to mission and ministry. The churches also aim to be "incarnational rather than attractional," which is thought to be a key characteristic of a missional church. They plan programs that take them out into the community, and encourage their members to interact personally with people outside the church. Gospel concerts are one example of such programs.

Further recommendations for these churches, according to Moon, would include more organizational learning based on core values, protecting leadership teams for a healthy approach to mission and outreach, and an emphasis on passing on spiritual truths and heritage to the next generations.

One more example of diaspora churches' outreach involves Mongolians. In 2010, eleven of the thirteen Mongolian immigrant churches in the U.S. had help from Korean American churches, including (1) establishing the church itself and ministering there, (2) providing a place for the church to meet, (3) paying the rent for them to meet elsewhere, (4) providing financial support in the training of Mongolian ministers, either in their homeland or in the U.S., or (5) financially supporting the relocation of a Mongolian minister from Mongolia to the U.S. to serve the Mongolian believers (M. Lee 2011:29).

Special populations

When laborers from other countries come to work in Korea, they do not have an easy time. Historically a monocultural society, Koreans have not developed the habit of embracing foreigners, particularly ordinary workers. "The biggest obstacle for foreign workers to adjust to in Korean society is our prejudice toward them" (Jun 2011: 211).

Churches and mission organizations must step forward to support human rights, ease tensions, express "golden rule" love, meet needs, share the gospel, and train these believers to be missionaries when they return home. "They are God's gift to Korean Christians," Jun asserts, particularly as they become equipped to spread the good news to their own countries. Friends of All Nations is one Korean Christian organization that serves these people.

Multicultural Christian schools serve another population. When children are born to a multicultural marriage with only one Korean parent, they may suffer discrimination. Alternative Christian schools can help. For example, Sae Nal School embraces multiculturalism, instills the fear of God, and encourages sharing and serving. The school was established to teach children from a Christian perspective how to live as good citizens in Korea while preparing to be leaders in the world at large. Their international background becomes an asset in these schools. The students learn to view this from a missional perspective.

Strong mission training programs abound in connection with seminaries, institutes, mission organizations, or independently. Since more than a quarter of Korea's missionaries work in majority-Islamic countries, Islamic peoples constitute a special population deserving attention during training. North Koreans constitute another.

Of course training for cross-cultural service must begin with an understanding of Korean cultural values. Many have been shaped by the Confucian heritage. Enoch Wan lists some of these values: education, family, community cooperation, honor and saving face, loyalty, filial piety, authoritarian social structure, and reciprocity of obligations. Customarily, "organizational arrangement is highly centralized, with authority and decision-making concentrated in senior levels. Personal ties often take precedence over job seniority, rank or other factors (e.g., performance and productivity)" (Wan 2011:102-103).

Offering excellent specific suggestions for an "incarnational lifestyle" for missionaries, Julie Ma laments "the Crusades model of mission...from the 'haves' to the 'have-nots,'" and asks: "Does Korean missionary engagement smell of *kimchi*? Do (we) approach the nationals with a Big Brother attitude? ... A patronizing or even a hierarchical relationship... is not 'partnership'" (Ma 2011:143).

University students constitute one more "special population." The University Bible Fellowship propels students into world mission as self-supporting professionals who are simultaneously lay missionaries. These doctors, businessmen and businesswomen, IT specialists, diplomats, and musicians have evangelized and discipled from Russia to India to Germany to Indonesia and many other parts of the world.

For example, Dr. Yoo "met Jesus in the first semester of his medical studies, and received discipleship training" (Chang 2011: 234). Later, after serving as a medical doctor and professor, he became a missionary to Africa. Here he battled AIDS and malaria amid limited supplies and patchy security. He also "dedicated himself to campus mission and disciple-making," seeing students as the hope of the nation. His mission hospital became a base camp for short term medical teams from Korea.

Mr. Lee is CEO of a highly successful company that manufactures socks in Mexico. He has 200 employees. One hundred have become committed disciples of Jesus. He also has opened a Christian conference center in Mexico.

The Shin and Lim families worked for the Korean ambassador in Mongolia. In their spare time, they studied Mongolian language at the university, and eventually helped establish a multi-agency translation team to complete the whole Bible in Mongolian. They have helped a group of 200 Mongolian students study the Bible and hold Sunday worship services in their own language.

Another Mr. Lee immigrated to Paraguay, learned the language, and eventually developed a farm and an electronics business. All throughout, he has been witnessing to students and discipling them.

Mr. Ahn went to Sri Lanka as an engineer. He too holds Bible studies for students and nurtures them toward Christian maturity.

All these diaspora witnesses were trained by the University Bible Fellowship in Korea.

What does such training involve? Deep Bible studies are foundational, along with early morning prayer meetings. Each student in training writes a weekly meditation based on their Bible study and shares it with peers and mentors, either in a group or one on one. Bible memorization also is basic. Practicing common life together, students learn self-denial as well as mutual support. Specific mission preparation is offered as well.

Multidirectional ministry

"Since the beginning of Christianity in Korea, mission activity also has existed. The Korean church did not waver during the brutal regime of the Japanese colonization (1910-1945) or the devastation of the Korean War (1950-1953). Moreover, the church flourished during the unsettling times of social turmoil during the periods of industrialization and democratization between the 60s and 70s. Then, with the synergistic effect of greater awareness of missions and the freedom to travel after the Seoul Olympics (1988), Korean mission…began to awaken. Since then, the Korean church has experienced explosive growth in missions" (Baeq *et.al.* 2011:26).

In the context of such a remarkable dispersal of professional and lay witnesses, the Korean Diaspora Forum has been formed. It aims to foster healthy church ministries that will contribute to world mission over generations, believing that "the multi-directional partnership among the privileged Korean churches in Korea, the diaspora Korean churches, and the local churches in the mission field can be an effective strategy for mission" (S. Lee 2011: 203).

For discussion

1. How did Korean history contribute to the development of diaspora churches?
2. Name some Korean organizations and networks involved in diaspora missions.
3. Describe four outstanding Korean diaspora congregations.
4. How has university ministry nurtured diaspora outreach?

Bibliography

Baeq, Daniel Shinjong; Myunghee Lee; Sokpyo Hong; and Jonathan Ro. "Mission from Migrant Church to Ethnic Minorities: A Brief Assessment of the Korean American Church in Mission." *Missiology*, Vol. 39, No. 1, January 2011, 25-37.

Chang, Peter. "International Evangelical Student Mission Movement: UBF Case Study," *Korean Diaspora and Christian Mission* eds. S. Hun Kim and Wonsuk Ma. Eugene, OR: Wipf and Stock Publishers, 2011, 223-241.

Jun, Chul Han David. "A South Korean Case Study of Migrant Ministries," *Korean Diaspora and Christian Mission,* 207-222.

Lee, Helen. "Silent Exodus," *Christianity Today.* Vol. 60, No.12, August 12, 1996.

Lee, Myunghee in Baeq *et.al.*
Lee, Soon Keun. "The Founding and Development of the Korean Diaspora Forum," *Korean Diaspora and Christian Mission,* 197-206.
Ma, Julie, "A Critical Appraisal of Korean Missionary Work." *Korean Diaspora and Christian Mission* eds. S. Hun Kim and Wonsuk Ma. Oxford: Regnum, 2011. 131-145.
Min, Pil Won. "The Contemporary Church Renewal Movement in Korea," paper presented at the American Society of Missiology annual meeting, 2009.
Moon, Steve Sang-cheol. "The Korean Diaspora Models of a Missional Church," *Korean Diaspora and Christian Mission,* 84-101.
Moon, Steve San-cheol. "Missions from Korea 2013: Microtrends and Finance," *International Bulletin of Mission Research,* Vol. 37, No. 2, April 2013.
Song, Minho. "The Diaspora Experience of the Korean Church and is Implications for World Missions," *Korean Diaspora and Christian Mission,* 117-13.
Wan, Enoch. "Korean diaspora: From hermit kingdom to Kingdom ministry." In *Korean Diaspora and Christian Mission*, eds. S. Hun Kim and Wonsuk Ma.. Oxford: Regnum, 2011. 101-116.

29. From Sao Paulo to Al-Alam Arab (The Arab World): The Brazilian Evangelical Missions Movement

Ed Smither

When American Bible Society representatives set foot in Brazil in 1816 to distribute Portuguese Bibles, they saw Brazil – along with the rest of Latin America – as a mission field. Throughout the nineteenth century, North American Methodist, Presbyterian, and Baptist missionaries agreed with that view. So did Pentecostal, parachurch, and other workers who arrived in the twentieth century (Smither 2012:22-35).

That has changed. Through the faithful witness of foreign and Brazilian Christians, the nation's evangelical population has grown from 143,000 in 1890 to about thirty million (Prado 2000; Prado 2005:54). Beyond providing a model for growth, Brazilians also have birthed a new missionary movement. At the COMIBAM (Ibero-American Missionary) Conference in São Paulo in 1987, missiologist Luis Bush noted this change: "From a mission field, Latin America has become a mission force" (Prado 2005:52). Supporting the oldest and largest evangelical missionary movement from Ibero-America, the Brazilian church superbly illustrates this vigorous propulsion.

This essay will tell part of that story, focusing on Brazilians serving among Arabs and other Muslims in nearby regions. Data comes from the analysis of interviews with forty-five past and present Brazilians who have ministered among Arabs, as well as ten Brazilian mission leaders. The interviews were conducted in 2009-2010. These reflections have been developed more fully in *Brazilian Evangelical Missions in the Arab World: History, Culture, Practice, and Theology* (Smither 2012).

A brief narrative of Brazilian missions

Although a visible Brazilian evangelical missions movement did not appear until the 1970s, there were a few Brazilian missionaries sent out in the early twentieth century (Smither 2012:54-55). By the second half of that century, international missions organizations present in Brazil were encouraging Brazilians to take their place in global mission (Ekström 1998:8-10). At the 1974 Lausanne Congress, Shedd and Landry reported that Brazilians were serving in twenty-one countries. Nine of those were in South America. Another four were Portuguese-speaking countries (Douglass 1974:1344).

From the mid-1970s, Brazilian engagement in missions accelerated. In 1975, the first Brazilian indigenous mission was founded, *Missao Antioquia* (Antioch Mission), following a revival in a Bible institute in the southern state of Parana (Burns 2000:515-17; Smither 2012:55-56). Momentum continued the following year when 500 Latin American student delegates gathered at the University of Paraná in Curutiba for a missions conference organized by IFES (International Fellowship of Evangelical Students). This included 450 Brazilian students. The conference's concluding declaration affirmed that "the church is a missionary church or it is no church at all" (Salinas 2008:147; Escobar 2002:157). A decade later, in 1987, the continental mission network COMIBAM met for its first conference in São Paulo. Here 3100 Latin American participants called on "all of our brothers and sisters in Ibero-America to get involved with us in the faithful completion of the mission that He has given us" (Ruiz 2007:9).

Besides international mission organizations in Brazil that mobilized Brazilians (e.g. Operation Mobilization) and national denominations that sent Brazilians out (e.g. Brazilian Baptist Convention), new missions organizations sprang up in the 1980s and 1990s. PMI (Muslim People's International) was founded in 1984. This was the first Latin American mission focused on the Muslim world. Its Brazilian office opened in 1998. In 1992, Brazilian pastor David Bothelo partnered with the Wales-based mission World Horizons to birth *Missao Horizontes*. This mission aimed to send Brazilians to the "10/40 window," the band between latitudes 10 and 40. Most of those who never have heard the gospel live in this swathe around the globe. In two cycles, in 1998 and 1999, *Missao Horizontes* mobilized more than 100 Brazilians – mostly from historical Pentecostal churches – to serve in the Sahel region of Africa (Decker and Keating 2003). In 1996, Crossover Communication International, at the invitation of Brazilian partners, established a Brazilian base (CCI-Brasil) with the aim of sending Brazilians to plant churches among "least reached peoples," especially Muslims (Smither 2012:186-88).

As these organizations developed, the number of Brazilian missionaries increased. Ekstrom has tracked the growth:

Year and Number of Brazilian Missionaries

Year	Number
1972	595
1980	791
1988	2040
1992	2755
2000	4754

"Today, Brazilian missionaries are working on every continent," Ekström observes (2009a:372).

Over 5000 Brazilian evangelicals now serve in cross-cultural ministry, working through at least 115 missions organizations (Ekström 2009b:369). While nearly 2000 of these people minister cross-culturally within Latin America, a growing percentage also work in Africa, Asia, and the Middle East. There is great interest in reaching the Muslim world (Limpic 2005).

Supporting networks include COMIBAM, the continental association which encourages missions sending from all Latin American countries. Nationally, the *Assaciacao de Missoes Transculturais Brasileiras* (Association of Transcultural Missions Agencies) connects and serves about forty Brazilian missions organizations. AMTB aims to mobilize Brazilian evangelical churches to greater mission involvement, promote dialogue and cooperation between mission organizations, develop materials to educate Brazilian churches in global mission, and encourage and offer training for Brazilian missionaries. Since 1990, AMTB has convened a strategic conference every few years (Ekstrom 1998:55-112; Smither 2012:60-61).

Brazilian mission practice

Within the broad field of Brazilian evangelical missions, how are Brazilians ministering in the Arab-Muslim world? During interviews with forty-five Brazilian missionaries in this region, more than two-thirds stated that a primary part of their ministry was personal evangelism. This is facilitated by Brazilians' strengths in building relationships. Brazilians prioritize friendships, and enter enthusiastically into everyday life in the local context. This creates opportunities for evangelism (Smither 2012:123-34).

"During the past years, I've learned to look at my friends here as people created according to the image of God, people with human value and dignity," one missionary shared. "To love my friends who are part of the major [Muslim] religion is the basis for sharing the gospel" (Smither 2012:167). Building on this relational foundation, Brazilians witness to the gospel while showing hospitality, visit those who have corresponded with media mission outlets, lead evangelistic Bible studies, and story the gospel with oral learners (Smither 2012:167-68).

About two-thirds of those surveyed also indicated that discipleship was a key part of their work, while one-third emphasized church planting. Once Arabs have embraced the gospel, evangelistic relationships became discipleship relationships. Some discipleship strategies include Bible studies and even more formal training classes. Some disciplers launch house church fellowships.

> My husband, along with other workers, helped to pastor a small group of national believers," one missionary reported. "From this small group has come a crop of dynamic young leaders who have gone on to lead and multiply the church. They have their own vision for reaching their people and

are developing a national structure. Through them, the church is taking root in this land. (Smither 2012:171)

As well as prioritizing relationships, Brazilians and Arabs also share an emphasis on the family. This cultural similarity has helped in planting churches, since church plants often are centered in homes and involve Arab families and their social networks.

Besides evangelism and discipleship, one remarkable aspect of Brazilian missions among Arabs is a commitment to humanitarian work. Around half of the Brazilians surveyed noted that humanitarian work is a part of their ministry. Largely working through or partnering with NGOs, some missionaries serve in centers for women or for the handicapped, while others care for refugees. Nurses participate in a development strategy known as community health evangelism (CHE). Other Brazilians create businesses and jobs through microfinance programs. Others teach English, which is a useful competency everywhere.

Although some Arab/Muslim countries are rich, there are also large populations that remain destitute. Here crises will erupt. These require Christians to respond in the form of humanitarian aid. Brazilians seem especially sensitive to such needs. Due to their own economic history, many Brazilians can empathize with those who are experiencing physical suffering and material lack. Furthermore, Brazilians, along with other Latin Americans, have cultivated a theology that intuitively integrates evangelism and compassion ministries, spurred by the conviction that we must minister to the whole person (cf. Smither 2012:211-30). Operating out of this context, as one Brazilian worker related, "God has opened doors to work with refugees and we have seen people healed and desiring to follow God" (Smither 2012:173).

A final important part of Brazilian missions is sports ministry. Some missionaries work as personal trainers and fitness instructors, and share the gospel in the context of relationships with their clients. Not surprisingly, many Brazilians also are incorporating soccer into their ministries. Although it is Brazil's national sport, soccer is also popular in most of the Arab world. While a number of missionaries build relationships with Arabs through informal pick-up matches, others have been hired as coaches for schools and clubs. Others have organized soccer camps for children.

For example, in a highly restricted region in the Middle East, two Brazilian soccer coaches have been able to connect with a displaced people group through their sport. With the blessing of community leaders, the coaches have organized a soccer school for the children who have little to do to occupy themselves on a daily basis, and little to hope for in the future. Though the coaches are not free to evangelize openly, they convey life skills based on biblical principles in their coaching curriculum. In short, "with a soccer ball and jersey, they have accessed places where [Western] doctors and teachers never have been allowed to enter," and to minister in an area that is otherwise packed with tension (Smither 2012:177). Some organizations such as the Brazilian Baptist Convention have packaged a soccer and evangelism strategy, and are training personnel around the world to implement it. For many Brazilian missionaries, however, soccer remains simply a natural way to exercise, build relationships, and share the gospel. "I love using sports – something I really enjoy – for ministry," one worker said. He speaks for many (Smither 2012:178).

Strengths and weaknesses

What are the strengths of Brazilians who are engaged in mission with Arabs/Muslims? What are their weak points? Among their strengths, Brazilians have demonstrated skill in building relationships as a context for sharing the gospel in Arab contexts. This is summarized by Marcos Amado, a veteran Brazilian missionary to North Africa and former director of PMI:

> My definition of success [in ministry] is being able to have Muslims trust you for what you are, for your life and faith, and through words and deeds be able to communicate the love of God. Because of that, you see people coming to the Lord, you are discipling them, and eventually they become part of the local church. In light of this goal, most Brazilians have been very successful at building friendship with Muslims and earning their trust (Smither 2012:189-90).

Beyond creating strong relationships, a second and related strength is that Brazilians seem skilled at adapting to cultures in the Arab world. Daniel Calze, director of PMI Brazil put forward this view: "I believe that this success [in ministry] comes as a result of the [Brazilian's] natural gifts to adapt himself to a context and particularly to Muslim culture" (Smither 2012:190). This may be facilitated by the fact that Brazilian and Arab cultures share some values. However, Brazilian cultural adaptability seems to entail something more. Overall, Brazilians seem to be particularly resilient and able to find a way to negotiate difficult circumstances and hardships, including those encountered during cross-cultural ministry (cf. Smither 2012:161-63).

A third strength is that Brazilians place a high value on ministry both in word (proclamation) and in deed (service). Brazilians have shown sustained commitment to proclamation while also caring for the poor, marginalized, and displaced through winsome humanitarian work.

Finally, Brazilians seem to be equipped for the realities of spiritual warfare that are encountered in "folk Islam" contexts. Because Spiritism is so prevalent in Brazil, workers from across the evangelical spectrum do not seem to be shocked by spiritual conflict. Many already have participated in deliverance ministries before they go to the Arab world. In this sense, they are probably more prepared for a "folk Muslim" context than their Western colleagues (cf. Smither 2011).

If those are Brazilian missionaries' strengths, what are the areas where growth is needed in the Brazilian missions movement in the Arab world? The first weakness is that Brazilian churches in general could do a better job of supporting their missionaries. This is not unique to missions to Arabs. Like many churches around the world, Brazilian congregations often are consumed with ministries in their own communities. They often lack a global focus.

Even if churches happily send missionaries out into the world, most lack a plan for communicating with their workers and offering member care to them (Smither 2012:193-97). Perhaps it is not surprising that most Brazilian missionaries appear to be under-supported financially. Evangelical churches must rethink their missions giving. At the same time, tentmaking and business-as-mission paradigms are being explored by a number of groups such as CCI-Brasil and Interserve (Smither 2012:203-206).

Though Brazilians adapt well in Arab contexts, there are two cultural areas where improvement is needed. First, a high number of Brazilians report struggles with learning Arabic. Some lack the funds to stay enrolled in language classes. Others seem impatient with the rigorous and time-consuming process of language acquisition. As a result, some end up pursuing ministries in which they speak only English or Portuguese (Smither 2012: 197-201).

Secondly, many Brazilian women say that is it hard to adapt to Arab culture and thrive there. Because the culture is male-dominated, they feel that their personal freedom is limited greatly. Some women, paralyzed by fear, withdraw from building relationships, while others demand the rights that they would normally enjoy in Brazil. For both groups of women, it appears that their effectiveness in ministry has been diminished as a result (cf. Smither 2012:206-210).

What is Evangelical?

As Brazilian evangelicals move forward today in the Arab world after just one generation of visible missions-sending from their country, the global church has much to learn from them.

And there is more. In this paper we have described only part of the Brazilian evangelical missions story, specifically those sent by churches and through organizations. However, there are many more Brazilian laborers going into the world. Some are independent missionaries. Others are expatriate workers whose jobs are taking them to different points around the globe. While this diaspora of Brazilian Christians ought to be celebrated, it also raises questions. How can these secular workers be trained in Bible, theology, missiology, and the basics of cross-cultural living? How will these laborers benefit from what has been learned in the first forty years? What specific strategy networks (regional, professional/vocational, issue-oriented) need to be formed to serve them?

There is one more cluster of questions facing Brazilian evangelical missions: What does it mean to be evangelical? What is the *evangel*? The word *evangel* means "gospel." What is the gospel? Surely this is a fundamental question.

With the explosion of independent, neo-Pentecostal churches – some of which appear to mix Pentecostalism, Catholicism, and even Brazilian Spiritism – it is becoming increasingly difficult to establish the parameters of Brazilian evangelical orthodoxy (cf. Lopes 2012). Some Brazilian pastors and mission leaders are distancing themselves from the term "evangelical." As a result, it is difficult to gain an accurate count of Brazilian evangelical Christians today and, for our purposes, how many Brazilian evangelical missionaries are serving around the world. More important than the challenge to research, however, is the challenge to the gospel. It appears that one of the biggest issues facing Brazilian evangelical missions in the immediate future and in the years to come will be primarily theological in nature.

For discussion

1. How many evangelicals were in Brazil in 1890? In 2010?
2. How many Brazilian missionaries were there in 1972? In 2010?
3. How do Brazilian cultural values strengthen mission outreach in the Arab world?
4. What particular challenges face Brazilian missionaries?

Bibliography

Associação de Missões Transculturais Brasileiras (web site) http://www.amtb.org.br/ (accessed June 28, 2013).

Burns, Barbara, "Brazilian Antioch, Community, Spirituality, and Mission." In *Global Missiology for the 21st Century: The Iguassu Dialogue,* edited by William D. Taylor, 515-17, Grand Rapids: Baker, 2000.

Decker, Murray and Keating, Ryan, "The Radical Project: A Revolutionary Latin American Model for Mission Mobilization." *Evangelical Missions Quarterly* 39:3 (2003) Online: www.emqonline.com.

Douglass, JD. "Brazil National Strategy Group Report," in *Let the Earth Hear His Voice: International Congress on World Evangelization Lausanne Switzerland.* Minneapolis: World Wide Publications. (1974): 1344.

Ekström, Bertil, "Brazilian Sending." In *Perspectives on the World Christian Movement: A Reader.* 4th ed., edited by Ralph Winter and Steve Hawthorne, 371-72, Pasadena, CA: William Carey Library, 2009.

Ekström, Bertil, "Missões a Partir do Brasil." In *Perspectivas No Movimento Cristao Mundial,* edited by Kevin D. Bradford et al., 367-69, São Paulo: Vida Nova, 2009.

Ekström, Bertil, "Uma Análise Histórica dos Objetivos da Associação de Missões Transculturais Brasilerias e o seu Cumprimento," MTh thesis, Faculdade Teológica Batista de São Paulo, June 1998.

Escobar, Samuel. *Changing Tides: Latin America & World Mission Today.* Maryknoll, NY: Orbis, 2002.

Limpic, Ted, "O Movimento Missionário Brasilerio (2005)." No pages. Online: http://www.comibam.org/transpar/_menus/por/09jogo-mb.htm

Lopes, Augustus Nicodemus Gomes, "The Growing Crisis Behind Brazil's Evangelical Success Story," *The Gospel Coalition* (blog) August 1, 2012, Online: http://thegospelcoalition.org/blogs/tgc/2012/08/01/the-growing-crisis-behind-brazils-evangelical-success-story/

Prado, Oswaldo, "A New Way of Sending Missionaries: Lessons from Brazil," *Missiology: An International Review* 33:1 (2005): 48-60.

Prado, Oswaldo, "The Brazil Model," *AD 2000* (web site) http://www.ad2000.org/gcowe95/prado.html.

Ruiz, David, "COMIBAM as a process leading to a Congress," *Connections* (April-May 2007), 8-10.

Salinas, J. Daniel, "The Great Commission in Latin America." In *The Great Commission: Evangelicals and the History of World Missions,* edited by Martin I. Klauber et al., 134-48, Nashville, TN: B & H Academic, 2008.

Smither, Edward L. *Brazilian Evangelical Missions in the Arab World: History, Culture, Practice, Theology.* Eugene, OR: Pickwick, 2012.

30. LATINO DIASPORA MINISTRIES IN THE USA

Miriam Adeney

"You want to leave? The only way you can leave is in your coffin."

This is the creed of gangs like M-13 and M-18, some of the most violent gangs in the Western Hemisphere. Both began in Los Angeles. In the early 1990s, the U.S. deported many Latino young men, with a special focus on gang members. Once back in Central America and southern Mexico, the gangs reorganized, and immediately extended their tentacles transnationally along the pulsating routes of migration reaching to the north.

Yet the quote above is not quite accurate. There is one other way to get out of a violent Latin American gang. If a member exhibits true Christian conversion, often he – or she – can leave. The gang watches the convert. Strict Christian behavior is expected: no cursing, no carousing, no extramarital sex, no fighting back, constant attendance at church meetings and testimony of transforming supernatural encounters. If this continues, the gang may shrug and walk away. They don't want to interfere with God (Brenneman 2012:3).

Latinos, also called Hispanics, comprise almost fifty million people in the United States today. God is at work dramatically in many sectors of this population. Gangs are only a small part. Major groupings include descendants of the original Spanish-speaking settlers that made their homes here before the United States existed, as well as later Mexican and Central American, Puerto Rican, Cuban, and other migrants.

Ten generations

Some Latinos have lived in this land for more than ten generations. From Texas to California, Spanish-speaking people were farming and conducting business when the U.S. acquired the territory after a war with Mexico in 1848. Establishing residency here so long ago, these people are less "foreign" than are the heirs of the Puritans.

Since then several waves of Mexicans have pulsed across the border. During Mexico's revolution in the early 1900s, one million Mexicans fled north. Many were deported back during the Depression, including legal residents of the U.S. During World War II, the U.S. invited Mexican farm laborers to fill in for Americans who had enlisted in the armed forces. This "bracero program" continued into the 1960s.

Vegetable and fruit farms still require labor, and Mexicans still stream across the border to provide it. There are also jobs in meat-packing plants, fishing, construction, race courses, and service industries that attract unskilled migrants. In time, many move to better jobs, learn English, marry and have children, and buy houses and land. A few abandon wives and children left behind in the old country. Others return home with enough money to start small businesses, build homes, and make life better for their families and communities.

Puerto Ricans' history is different. Their island was absorbed by the U.S. as a result of the Spanish-American war of 1898. When New York City expanded after World War II, many Puerto Ricans migrated to jobs in the northeastern U.S. Legal residence papers were easy to get since their island was not a separate nation but a commonwealth of the United States. Today significant theological seminaries in Puerto Rico serve Spanish speakers from both continents.

Cuban Americans' history is also distinctive. The Cuban revolution of 1959 ushered in a Marxist state. Some Christians were persecuted and even imprisoned, along with other non-Marxist thinkers. A wave of refugees whooshed out of Cuba and washed up in Florida, which today boasts large Cuban American churches. Many of these Cubans were educated people, and have continued to provide teachers and writers within the Hispanic community.

Central Americans – particularly people from Guatemala, El Salvador, and Honduras – suffered devastating civil wars in the 1970s and 1980s. To escape violence or simply to find a way to make living, many fled north. They sneaked across Mexico and into the U.S. Some U.S. churches provided "sanctuaries" for them, defending them from the government when they lacked legal residence documents. Nicaraguans also constitute a significant presence.

Spanish is not only a mother tongue for millions of people in the United States but also the language of business, media, and the neighborhood. Moving back and forth between the U.S. and Latin America, and staying in touch through the internet, these Latinos are more transglobal than ever. Yet in their home neighborhoods in the U.S., many struggle with substandard conditions. In his book *The Future of the Latino Church,* Daniel Rodriguez lists "modern Goliaths in the urban barrio": poverty, poor health care, poor schools, high drop-out rate from schools, unemployment, teen pregnancies, gangs and crime, unsafe neighborhoods and uncomprehending police, broken families, and hopelessness. Many second generation Latinos have few prospects to escape lower class status. They are among the Americans most likely to live in poverty.

Facing Goliaths

To face these Goliaths, God sends Davids armed with his Spirit. Even the humblest Hispanic church is likely to set out loaves of bread that anyone can take home for their own use or for a needy neighbor. Megachurches multiply this exponentially. Consider New Life Covenant Ministries, pastored by Wilfredo De Jesus in Chicago. Formerly named Templo Cristiano Palestina, New Life serves over 5,000 worshippers each weekend. They want to be "A Church for the Hurting," according to the logo mounted on their walls. Their ministries include (Rodriguez 2011:120-121):

- Manna 4 Life is a food pantry that gives groceries to people in the community.
- Foundation Family Ministry helps families learn how to make wise financial decisions, communicate, and set priorities.
- Kingdom Economic$ helps members further with financial planning within the framework of a biblical worldview.
- Dream Center for Women serves women from the streets whose lives have been wrecked by gangs and addictions. It offers "a fifteen month faith-based program providing hope and residential care for women suffering from drug addiction, alcoholism and any other life-controlling issues. It provides a protective and nurturing environment where women are exposed to the life-transforming power of Christ revealed in the Bible and through the power of the Holy Spirit."
- Battle gives shelter, legal aid, and hope in Christ to women who are in dangerous abusive relationships.
- Gangs to Grace reorients gang members in Christ.

Victory Outreach is another ministry that serves social outcasts – addicts, gang members, prostitutes, and ex-convicts. For VO's founder, Sonny Arguinzoni, heroin and gang life led to jail. Teen Challenge brought him to Christ. Recognizing that most gang members don't fit into typical Hispanic churches, VO establishes churches as well as rehab homes and Bible training centers. These extend to twenty four countries, though most ministry is Latino. VO's Urban Training Centers develop young adults into leaders, with 6-12 months intense immersion in Bible study and hands-on ministry guided by local pastors and their wives.

Of all the social "giants" facing Hispanics, legal residency is the biggest. Eleven million people live in the U.S. illegally. Most are Latinos. As this is an issue that deserves in-depth attention, it will be the focus of the last section.

In spite of these local burdens, Latinos also reach out in foreign missions, not only through church-based outreaches, but also through networks like Pueblos Musulmanes (Muslim Peoples) and COMHINA (Cooperacion Misionera de los Hispanos de Norteamerica). Across Africa, Asia, and the Middle East, these networks' projects range from English or Spanish classes to microfinance and handicapped-assistance programs, all undergirding witness, discipling and church planting.

Latino theologies

There are more than 40,000 Protestant congregations in the National Hispanic Christian Leadership Coalition, which is allied with the National Association of Evangelicals. The largest Latino denominations are Assemblies of God, Baptists, Seventh Day Adventists, Church of God (Cleveland), Apostolic Assembly of the Faith in Christ Jesus, and United Methodists.

In spite of the pain in many communties, these Latinos exude resurrection joy, particularly Pentecostals. Definite conversion experiences, the sweet presence of the Holy Spirit, miraculous deliverances, and the authority of the Scripture are the norm, propelling minimally- trained witnesses out into the community to testify. When they gather in fellowship groups, everybody is ready to talk about what God has done this week. Church historian Juan Martinez (2011) emphasizes *teologia en conjunto* (theology in community) and *teologia en cotidiana* (theology in everyday life). Community, spirituality, *mestizaje*, and exile/marginality are themes cited often by Hispanic theologians. (*Mestizaje* refers to the racial mixing of aboriginal, European, and African strains, praised by a secular writer as *la raza cosmica,* the "cosmic race.")

Theologian Eldin Villafane (1993) has titled his book on Hispanic Christians *The Liberating Spirit*. Church historian Justo Gonzalez (1990) has titled his book on Latino Theology *Manana* (*Tomorrow*), emphasizing new possibilities for the future. The venerable pioneering theologian Orlando Costas (1982: 185) gave voice to the struggle in which Latinos live out their faith when he wrote, "Evangelization in the US means bearing witness in the power of the Spirit to the new world that God has promised in Christ…And this is happening in the OTHER American church – the church of the disenfranchised racial minorities, which have been living and witnessing from the underside of American history". Echoing this, Daniel Rodriguez (2011: 130) asserts that Latino theology "requires visceral understanding of *la lucha* (the fight) of our people, of life in the hyphen". (The "hyphen" connects the general word "American" to a specific ethnicity, such as Spanish-American.)

In relation to public issues, Latinos "reconcile both the vertical and the horizontal arms of the cross," emphasizing not only "covenant, faith, and righteousness" like white evangelicals but also "community, public policy, and social justice," like many black evangelicals, according to NHCLC president Samuel Rodriguez. For example, *evangelicos* are 100 per cent pro-life and also 100 per cent committed to the alleviation of poverty (S. Rodriguez 2009).

What is appropriate theological education for such Latinos? Clearly it must be done in context. Denominations sponsor a number of good Spanish-language Bible schools and seminaries. Yet many potential students stay away because they lack money and educational credentials and time, due to full-time work and active ministries. Congregation-based training provides a popular alternative. Combining classes with apprenticeships, these programs plant many churches in a short period of time and successfully pass on leadership to second and third generations.

English language is gaining in popularity in large Hispanic churches. Increasingly these churches offer separate worship services in each language. (Bilingual services move too slowly for the English speakers!) By encompassing both sets of speakers, the church keeps the whole multigenerational family, even though the members may attend different services. Could such a church cease to be Latino? As long as it has (1) Latino pastors (2) some services available in Spanish and (3) most of the worshippers of Hispanic descent, then the church will remain Latino (Martinez 2011:14). Martinez raises a deeper question: As Hispanics get richer, will they still stand with Christ, the suffering servant who cares for the poor?

Immigration and the law

The issue that strikes at the heart, and therefore the faith, of many Latinos is immigration. As of this writing, eleven million people reside illegally in the U.S. The great majority are Spanish speaking. Most are Mexican. Acquiring legal documents has been arduous. Regular deportations have split families. Latino Christians strongly support immigration reform that balances respect for the law with compassion. Providentially, new legislation is promising.

Meanwhile,

> Most Latino Protestant pastors regularly serve undocumented immigrants…There are also many undocumented Latino Protestant pastors. Some arrive with ministry credentials from their countries of origin, credentials that normally would be accepted by sister denominations across national boundaries. Should denominations recognize the credentials of undocumented pastors who want to serve in a church in the United States? Should denominations ordain pastors who are undocumented, particularly if they cannot qualify for a religious visa? Should Bible institutes and seminaries train the undocumented for pastoral ministry, particularly those who have been in the United States for many years? (Martinez 2011:44)

Christians at the Border by Daniel Carroll-Rodas traces biblical teaching on migration. In the beginning, all people were created in the image of God. This has implications for human rights, as well as for migrants' self-respect. Within the context of Middle Eastern hospitality, Carroll-Rodas explores Jewish law's special emphasis on mercy to the poor and limits on human governments. Both apply in the command to "love the alien" (Lev. 19:34; Deut: 10:19).

Many biblical characters moved from their home countries. In the Old Testament period we know of Abraham, Jacob and his sons, Moses, Ruth, David among the Philistines, and Daniel and all the displaced Jews in the

Babylonian and Persian periods, including Jeremiah, Esther, and Nehemiah.

> A fascinating point to ponder is the wealth of biblical books of assorted genres that were produced by those living outside the promised land. Being away from the familiar proved to be a creative space for thinking about God, life, the direction of history, and the nature of hope (Carroll-Rodas 2008: 87).

In the New Testament period, Philip and other Christians were scattered. Paul and his missionary companions, from Barnabas to Luke to Priscilla and Aquilla, were called to travel. John was exiled to the island of Patmos. Peter directed his epistles to uprooted believers. These "aliens and strangers" (1:1, 17; 2:11) were not citizens of the places where they resided. Undoubtedly they understood what it was like to be hassled regarding their residency documents. Sometimes they were falsely accused. Yet rejection was not the last word. These aliens were empowered to be "living stones" in God's building (1 Pet. 2:2-4). What might Peter's message mean for Christians in the poor *mestizo* underclass, Daniel Rodriguez (2003) ponders – a high school dropout, an undocumented laborer, a single mother on welfare, a believer who has been a drug addict or a prostitute?

Even Jesus and his family fled as refugees to Egypt. Later Jesus gave special attention to outsiders like Samaritans. Noting Jesus' story of the sheep and goats in Matthew 25, Carroll-Rodas says:

> Many Hispanic believers who come as immigrants are needy. Does the Christian church of the host culture not have some responsibility to help 'the least of these brothers' in the name of Christ? Does not Christ dwell among and in them too? Would this revelation that the judgment on the nations is based in part on the treatment of disciples have any application to the United States? Will the Son of Man and the Father in any way demand an accounting of this country's actions toward Christian Hispanics? ...Do we have as comprehensive an ethic as Christ had? ...Along with... honesty in the workplace, fidelity in marriage, and good stewardship of money must also stand compassion toward the outsider. (2008: 124, 126)

Law must be honored. Yet immigration law is confused, contradictory, and at times clearly unfair to various parties. The U.S. government recognizes the need for changed law in this area. Furthermore, ordinary residents have a right to express opinions and press for change.

> If one begins with a biblical orientation that includes the centrality of the importance of the immigrant as made in the image of God, if one can appreciate how pervasive migration experiences are to the history and faith of the people of God, if Old Testament law projects an ethics of compassion, if the thrust of Jesus' ministry and the New Testament as a whole is to love the outsider, then the inclination is to be gracious to the immigrant" (Carroll-Rodas 2008: 131).

This is where faith meets action for many Latino Christians.

Revitalizing America

The gang member who receives his life back because of his faith in Jesus knows what it means to be born again. Among the poor, and also among the comfortable, witness to this new life is spreading through the neighborhoods of U.S. cities at the grassroots because of Latinos. Some believe that is why they were led to the U.S.: to revitalize the faith of this nation.

For discussion

1. How are Hispanic churches serving the needy in their own communities? What are they doing in mission internationally?
2. What are some key themes in Hispanic ethnotheology?
3. What are basic biblical teachings on immigration? Who are some examples of biblical people who migrated?

Bibliography

Brenneman, Robert. *Homies and Hermanos: God and Gangs in Central America.* Oxford: Oxford University Press, 2012.

Carroll-Rodas, Daniel. *Christians at the Border.* Grand Rapids, MI: Baker, 2008.

Costas, Orlando. *Christ Outside the Gate: Mission Beyond Christendom.* Maryknoll, NY: Orbis, 1982.

Gonzalez, Justo. *Manana: Christian Theology from Hispanic Perspective.* Nashville, TN: Abingdon, 1990.

Martinez, Juan. *Los Protestantes: An Introduction to Latino Protestantism in the US.* Santa Barbara, CA: Praeger, 2011.

Rodriguez, Daniel. "No Longer Foreigners and Aliens: Toward a Missional Christology for Hispanics in the United States," *Missiology,* Vol. 31, No. 1, (2003), 51-69.

Rodriguez, Daniel. *A Future for the Latino Church.* Downers Grove, IL: InterVarsity Press, 2011.

Rodriguez, Samuel. Quoted in "Separated Brothers: Latinos are Changing the Nature of American Religion," *Economist* online, July 16, 2009.

Villafane, Eldin. *The Liberating Spirit: Toward an Hispanic American Pentecostal Social Ethic.* Grand Rapids, MI: Eerdmans, 1993

31. African Diaspora Christianity: Mother Cooper and New York City

Mark R. Gornik and Allison Norton

When Marie Cooper flew from Monrovia, Liberia to New York City's John F. Kennedy Airport in 1984, she brought with her two very full suitcases. Among her possessions were a white clerical robe, a small wooden cross, and her Bible. With these items, "Mother Cooper" transported across the Atlantic not merely things of personal significance, but also religious beliefs, practices and experiences shaped by the representative of the Church of the Lord (Aladura), an African Independent Church.

At first Mother Cooper attended an African-American church in New York. Yet she felt something missing spiritually. Taking the initiative, this daughter of the Church of the Lord (Aladura) began a prayer group. Within a decade, the prayer group had grown into an official congregation recognized by the African denomination and under its authority. The congregation in the Bronx is a branch of the Church of the Lord (Aladura) Worldwide, which is headquartered in Ogere, Nigeria.

"Aladura" refers to "prayer churches." While the term is specific to the Church of the Lord, in a more general sense it can apply to a family of Yoruba independent churches. The Yoruba word *aladura* is translated "people of prayer" or "praying people." In 2007, the Church of the Lord (Aladura) identified 2,124 branches worldwide, including 1,000 in Nigeria and 500 in Liberia. The congregation started by Mother Cooper in New York City is the first North American branch.

Mother Cooper's story provides a window into African Christianity as it crosses borders. In this age of movement, church takes place along the way. While mission can be global, it is lived out in local stories, grassroots realities and concrete Christian communities. Mother Cooper's transatlantic journey recalls an observation from Irenaeus in the second century: the Christian tradition is most ably transmitted not through words composed on paper but embodied in human flesh. The diffusion of faith occurs not through free-floating ideas but through inspirited bodies that carry histories, practices, motives, and movements along global pathways. Faith *expressed* in human and ecclesial bodies relocates into new spiritual-social spaces like New York City. The authors have been immersed in these communities. Mark Gornik's knowledge of Mother Cooper and her church results from participant observation, interviews, and correspondence with a variety of congregations, church leaders, and ordinary members over seven years of research. This is more fully reported in *Word Made Global: Stories of*

African Christianity in New York City[1]. Allison Norton's knowledge comes from seven years of ministry and research with the Ghanaian-led Church of Pentecost, USA.

Beyond Mother Cooper's story, this chapter will provide a glimpse into other sub-Saharan African Christian diaspora congregations in the United States. Heterogeneity will be evident within the institutions, forms, and theologies of African diaspora Christians. Shared themes will conclude the chapter.

A house of prayer in New York City

Marie Cooper was born on June 15, 1938 in Monrovia, Liberia. In 1953, she met Odulowe, a Nigerian missionary who had been sent to establish the Church in Liberia. Marie's mother was Pentecostal. When she died in 1955, Odulowe's wife, known as Mother Delitia, comforted and cared for Marie. This drew Marie closer to the Church of the Lord (Aladura). In 1955 she joined the Church. As her involvement in its activities and programs grew, she "started to develop in the Spirit." The "Spirit started to use me" and the "love of God filled my heart," she says. But, she emphasizes, "Aladura did not draw me to God, I was just meant to serve God."

One night she had a dream that would prove to be important for her calling. "I saw one eye, a single eye, just in the sky, looking down. I saw someone like the Lord in the sky, and moving toward the east. I said in my dream, 'That's Jesus! That's Jesus!'" After she woke up, she felt that it was "incredible that the Lord would speak to me."

On hearing about the dream, Odulowe said, "The eye of the Lord is upon you. He wants to use you." This dream would help to guide Marie Cooper into a lifetime of ministry in the Church of the Lord (Aladura).

Church offices and titles are highly structured and regulated in this body, with an emphasis on promotion of ministers based not on seniority but on ministerial development. Mother Cooper explains the criteria as "commitment to the church, the way you serve, and way you carry yourself…[being] Christ-like." A person is promoted "when people see that in you…see the Spirit of the Lord in you."

The novice office of the Church of the Lord (Aladura) is Cross-Bearer, which Mother Cooper entered in 1965. A Cross-Bearer carried a small wooden cross, and the training process involved praying over seven people a day during the course of ordinary routines. "You had to do that to develop spiritually," Mother Cooper says. When you were really formed, that

1 Following recent literature, I understand diaspora not simply as dispersal, but also as an identity formed by people who have moved yet maintain ties between homeland and host country. The term African Christianity emphasizes a shared identity across traditions and developments, while the phrase African Christianities recognizes a plurality of visions, practices, and theological expressions of faith. Both terms are useful.

number increased to twenty-one. In 1989 Marie became a deaconess, and in 1993 a Senior Prophetess. All of these ordinations took place under the authority of the Liberian See, although she had migrated to New York in 1984. In 2000, she was named an Archdeaconess, and this time the ordination took place in the Bronx, administered by the visiting Primate, who was global head of the Church of the Lord (Aladura).

When Mother Cooper first came to New York City, she attended two largely African-American churches, Epworth United Methodist and then St. Matthew's A.M.E. But she felt that the beliefs and spirituality of the Church of the Lord (Aladura) were missing. So within a year she began a prayer group in River Park Towers in the Bronx. They met on Wednesday and Friday evenings, and moved around between different apartments.

Mother Cooper's prayer group received official recognition as the first branch of the Church of the Lord (Aladura) in North America. In time she was able to purchase the house on Monroe Street. It became known officially as a "house of prayer," an important space in the Aladura tradition. The church receives no financial assistance from the Church of the Lord (Aladura) headquarters or the Liberian See, and as a consequence, Mother Cooper has had to build the church by her own grit and initiative. For example, she could redo the bathroom only when funds were gathered.

The house of prayer is located in the Bronx, a community where Spanish is the language heard in the streets and the Yankees are the team that plays in the stadium. Down these sidewalks come the members of the Church of the Lord (Aladura), wearing white robes with colorful sashes. They pray and fast for days and weeks at a time. They help one another through the ordinary crises of daily life. They faithfully continue broader Church of the Lord (Aladura) patterns of worship, leadership, and spiritual life. Week after week, a complex of twenty-two worship components are performed in the basement sanctuary. But this fixed liturgical range is combined with spontaneity of testimony, healing, prayer, prophecy and sermon, all ultimately conducted, it is stated, under the direction of the Holy Spirit. The organizational structure in New York follows established Church of the Lord (Aladura) patterns, reflecting its hierarchical approach to formal leadership and importance of titles.

In the past few years, the small church also has begun to hold services across the Hudson River in New Jersey, as well as nurturing a smaller fellowship in Brooklyn.

Pilgrimages: a mountain and a mission

Every August the Church of the Lord (Aladura) celebrates Taborrar. This is a distinctive season of spiritual focus and renewal. It began in 1937, when the Church's founder received a command in a vision to go to a certain site and pray. There he experienced revelations, which he later circulated. Mount Tabborrar, the name of the site, echoes the biblical Mount Tabor.

Since then, the Church's leader has retreated to Mount Tabborrar annually. His new revelations are sent to all the churches. During this month, members fast and pray for thirteen days, followed by a grand service with thirteen blessings – actually thirteen liturgies flowing one into another. Power, healings, material benefits and spiritual transformations are expected. These are celebrated with hand bells, calabashes swirling, drums pounding, ecstatic shouts, and loud calls, "Thank you, Jesus!" The thirteen liturgies are preceded by Scripture reading, hymns, and a homily. Not only does this happen in Nigeria. In the sacred month and sacred space of the house of prayer in the Bronx, the mountain comes to New York.

Mother Cooper also goes to Liberia periodically. The year that she purchased the building in the Bronx, her husband died. She accompanied James Cooper's body back to Liberia, where services were held in both Episcopal and Church of the Lord (Aladura) sanctuaries before he was buried. Then she returned to New York to continue her ministry.

Meanwhile, she opened a school and an orphanage in Liberia, which she continues to support. Towering to the ceiling in the Bronx church are taped-up boxes filled with donations for the Liberian children, as well as blue barrels and well-traveled suitcases. Mother Cooper returns to Liberia regularly to oversee the work. She lives, as she put it in 2013, "between here," that is between the United States and Liberia.

African immigrants and African-Americans

Possibly one out of every ten people in New York City is Pentecostal, according to the *New York Times*. At least 2000 churches have been planted here by international immigrants since the 1980s, according to City Seminary's research. Among these are more than 200 African Churches – both historic Catholic and Protestant churches as well as independently-formed bodies like the Church of the Lord (Aladura) and newer Pentecostal and charismatic "ministries." In fact, African churches can be found from Dallas, Texas to Phnom Penh, Cambodia to Dublin, Ireland. They constitute a global phenomenon.

The African diaspora originally referred to the African-American communities created by the descendants of people who had been transported forcibly across the Atlantic and sold into slavery. This chapter, by contrast, focuses on the "new" African diaspora in America: sub-Saharan Africans who migrated to the United States beginning in the 1960s and then in larger numbers starting in the 1990s. The *African* churches they have developed in America contrast with *African-American* churches. The latter serve people whose ancestors were brought to this land roughly two hundred years ago. Such African-Americans can count back eight generations on American soil. During that time, they have developed distinctive cultural orientations. Some of these they share with other Americans.

Though varied, these lifestyle patterns contrast with some of the patterns brought by new immigrants from Africa. In *Beyond Christendom,* Sierra Leonean-American professor Jehu J. Hanciles suggests that new immigrants are surprised by some established African-Americans' language, clothing, sexual expressions, work patterns, and self-identifications. For their part, African-Americans may distance themselves from new immigrants if they view Africa as the face of poverty, disease, calamity, degradation, and backwardness – not a "cool" place. Yet the two communities have much in common: shared ancestry, strong spirituality, legacy of migration, the importance of community, the value of elders, the centrality of music in worship, the need for healing and deliverance, the awareness of suffering, the respect for the Bible read aloud, and pervasive religiosity. There are few atheists in either group (Hanciles 2006:319-321).

African Christianity: a global phenomenon

The explosive growth of Christianity in Africa since the 1970s has had a dramatic effect on world Christianity. As Africans have migrated internationally, they have inserted African Christianity into the global religious landscape: African Christians now are active on every continent. Migration has been the prime catalyst for African missionary initiatives over the last several decades. In the West, African-led churches which demonstrate a deeply rooted commitment to evangelism and mission have been planted. Remarkably, the two largest churches in Europe are led by African pastors (Church of the Blessed Embassy of the Kingdom of God for all Nations in Kiev and Kingsway International Christian Centre in London).

For many African Christians, a sense of divine call and mission is part of the journey of migration. While economic factors are present, that does not negate a divine sense of purpose: Though envisioning hope for a better economic future, such migrants also see themselves as agents of hope in their new contexts. They embody what Bongmba (2007:102) calls the "portability" of the Christian faith and a "global mission project of the Christian tradition". Gerloff (2009:16) further points to the missional role of African immigrant Christians in deconstructing a "colonial mission" model, and leading to a potential "renewal of contemporary Christianity, the 'rebirth' of African theology, and the lived-out diasporic conviction that our universal humanity counts more than any nation state".

African immigrant Christianity encompasses a range of expressions, including African Instituted Churches (AICS), Orthodox Christianity, Roman Catholics, Protestants, and Charismatics and Pentecostals. Their ecclesial structures also are diverse. Hanciles has contributed a typology of African immigrant church formations that demonstrates this diversity: 1) the Abrahamic type, independent churches founded by an individual African migrant, 2) the Macedonian type, congregations started through the planned, missionary-sending initiatives of African-led or based organizations, 3) the Jerusalem type, African-led churches associated with Western mainline denominations with significant African membership, and 4) the Samuel-Eli type, churches that have attracted a large number of African migrants (Hanciles 2008:326-328).

This section will provide a brief overview of two Pentecostal "Macedonian type" churches, the Church of Pentecost and the Redeemed Christian Church of God.

Church of Pentecost

The Ghanaian-led Church of Pentecost (CoP) has congregations located throughout the United States. At the close of 2014, there were 152 congregations in the U.S., with a membership of nearly 18,000 (2015). CoP churches in the United States usually are initiated by small communities of Ghanaian immigrants who meet for prayer. In time the members may petition the CoP for pastoral help. This usually results in the ordination of local leaders and the sending of a pastor.

The CoP "appears to be the African church with the highest number of congregations outside its national boundaries" (Omenyo 2013, 50). Originally the church's international spread was not an organized endeavor. It grew through the migration and transnational networks of its members. After many people left Ghana in the 1980s in search of better economic opportunities, the CoP established an official missionary network under the office of the International Mission Director. This office oversees the work of all church branches outside of Ghana. In line with this centralized structure, the term "missionary" is used to describe the work of all pastors who either work outside of Ghana or outside of their countries of origin. Such a centralized structure, organized along clear hierarchical lines of authority, fits Ghanaian culture and promotes a sense of security, accountability, and discipline (Onyinah 2004, 223). Paired with strong emphases on lay leadership and creative initiatives, this structure has facilitated the spread and growth of the CoP globally. Today the CoP has branches in over eighty-three countries, with a worldwide membership numbering over 1,900,000 (The Church of Pentecost 2011).

In vision and mission, the CoP "exists to bring all people everywhere to the saving knowledge of our Lord Jesus Christ through the proclamation of the gospel, the planting of churches and the equipping of believers for every God-glorifying service." The fulfillment of this vision and the interpretation of the church's mission is rooted in prophetic utterances, starting in the 1940s, which proclaimed that God would raise up a nation out of Africa to be a light to the world, an international church that would send missionaries everywhere (Johnson 2000, 149). Echoed in these prophecies is the belief that the CoP has something unique to contribute to the world. In particular, CoP furthers world evangelization through mission to the Ghanaian diaspora (Onyinah 2004, 235).

Along with the International Missions Office, there are several other institutional structures supporting the church's evangelistic emphasis. These include Evangelism Week, Internal Missions Week, and McKeown's Missions Week, which are annual events when the CoP raises money, prays, and preaches on mission. Throughout the year there are monthly missionary offerings. Ongoing witness ministry expresses evangelism at local, regional, national, and international levels. Every regular churchgoer is considered a member of the witness team. In the United States, this includes outreaches like passing out tracts or working with local food kitchens or other social services. However, formal institutional activities are not the primary expression of mission in the Church of Pentecost, particularly in urban contexts shaped by migration. Rather, the core theology of the priesthood of all believers encourages each member to view mission as a part of everyday life. Everyone is encouraged to spread the gospel message, whether at work or at school or wherever they may be.

Redeemed Christian Church of God

The Redeemed Christian Church of God (RCCG), headquartered in Nigeria, provides another glimpse into the vast global initiatives and missionary networks of African-led movements. Few African diaspora churches are as organized as the RCCG, which has implemented an impressive church-planting movement with the goal of creating parishes within five minutes' walking or driving distance in every city and town in the world.

Members of the RCCG are taught that they should take initiative in planting church parishes if none exist in the areas to which they migrate. The stated mission and vision of the church is "to make heaven," taking as many people with them as possible, desiring to "have a member of the RCCG in every family of all nations" (RCCG, 2013).

Started in 1952, the RCCG now has churches in over 147 countries and an estimated worldwide membership of over 5 million. As in the Church of Pentecost, early doctrines and prophecies indicated a global goal, that the church eventually would reach to "the ends of the earth" (Rice 2009). There are currently over 750 congregations in North America, and the Church hopes to add at least 100 new churches each year (Burnett 2014).

The Dallas-Fort Worth area houses the largest concentration of adherents in the United States. In 2013, the church dedicated a $15.5 million Pavilion Center in Texas. This seats over 10,000 and is part of a center known as Redemption Camp. It marks the fruition of a 25-year-old dream cherished by the church's worldwide leader, General Overseer Pastor E.A. Adeboye. Before even one RCCG congregation was planted in the United States, the Holy Spirit revealed to Pastor Adeboye that the

Dallas-Fort Worth area would become the North American headquarters. Now the RCCG has over 50 congregations in North Texas alone (Blair 2013). Pastor Adeboye sums up the church's expansion history in these words: "Made in heaven, assembled in Nigeria, exported to the world" (Rice 2009).

Africans and the Ephesian moment

Mother Cooper's story and the brief insights into the Church of Pentecost and the Redeemed Christian Church of God illustrate several facets of African diaspora and Christian mission in the West.

First, as people move, it is not just their faith that travels, but faith as part of ecclesial histories and commitments. This is a movement of community, of caring for one another in Christ. We must see the church in order to understand mission.

Second, movement across borders often means the expansion of mission. As Thomas Oduro says, few AICs "conform to mainstream missionary categories and dynamics" (Oduro 2014, 86). They may not organize "mission weeks" or mission conferences, yet there are AIC congregations on every continent, where members minister cross-culturally, following a framework of missionary outreach rooted in Acts 1:8. Mother Cooper's community prays vigorously not only for the healing of persons but also for many parts of the world. They depend not on denominational budgets and involvement, but on the Holy Spirit and the leadership of people in the local context. They minister within the web of everyday relationships, both in New York and Liberia. The Church of Pentecost and Redeemed Christian Church of God have more organized missionary initiatives, but in all examples in this chapter it is the movement of migrants that has provided the primary catalyst for expansion.

Third, Mother Cooper's story indicates the important role that women play in African churches, both in Africa and in the diaspora. Although their role is under-reported and under-recognized, women are prominent in leadership and dedicated in church and mission work. As Dana L. Robert indicates, world Christianity is significantly a women's movement, with women constituting the majority of active participants (Robert 2006).

Fourth, size is not as important as presence. We may be "a little place, but we have gifts here," Mother Cooper often comments. These gifts are for the healing of the world in the name of Jesus and the power of the Spirit. We are not yet able to see the full fruit resulting from our efforts, nor the end of the story. But because of our theological convictions, we can trust that our work will be part of the fullness of God's kingdom, she asserts. One of the most important characteristics of African Christianity in the West is its generally charismatic nature, with a theology that believes God can equip any believer for missionary work.

In summary, the African diaspora churches that are highlighted here fulfill a historic vision of mission expansion. At the same time, they attend to people's immediate spiritual needs at the grassroots level. When they gather, they follow routines that have been established in their African Christian movements. Here they find guidance and strength to continue their journeys of life and faith. This blossoms into witness, and the faith spreads.

Christian history traces movement through the thought and idioms of Judaism to Hellenistic culture and on through a succession of border crossings, translations, and reinvigorations. Today, in this moment of global interconnections, cities like New York and Dallas-Fort Worth are points of convergence. They are sites for the spread of Christianity born in Africa, and equally places of new encounter. They provide what missiologist Andrew Walls has described as an "Ephesian moment – the social coming together of people of (different) cultures to experience Christ." The Word made flesh is still flowing, moving, and travelling, the body impressed as a letter, the Spirit incarnate in physicality.

What do we know without ambiguity after our years of worshiping with African Christians? They pray. They pray standing up, they pray moving around, they pray kneeling down, they pray in loud voices, they pray all night. African Christians believe in the efficacy of prayer, join in with regular and intense fasting, and offer their lives to a God who hears and acts. For them, prayer is theology lived.

For discussion

1. Where is the international headquarters of the African immigrant congregation described here?
2. How is leadership developed in this denomination?
3. What happens during worship in this congregation?
4. Describe Taborrar celebrations.
5. Contrast African Americans and African immigrants.

Bibliography

2015 National Council Meeting Report. Elizabeth, New Jersey: The Church of Pentecost USA, Inc, 2015.

Baduh, Johnson Agyemang editor, "God's first covenant promises with the Church of Pentecost," *The Church of Pentecost Songs,* 149-151. Accra: Pentecost Press, 2000.

Bateye, Bolaj Olukemi. "Forging Identities: Women as Participants and Leaders in the Church among the Yoruba," *Studies in World Christianity*, Vol. 13, No.1, 2007, 1-12.

Blair, Leonardo. "Nigeria's Redeemed Christian Church of God Dedicates $15.5m Pavilion Center in Texas." *Christian Post* June 20 2013.

Bongmba, Elias K. "Portable Faith: The Global Mission of African Initiated

Churches (AICS)." *African Immigrant Religions in America*. Eds. Olupona, Jacob K. and Regina Gemignani. New York and London: New York University Press, 2007.

Burnett, John. "Nigerian Church Spreads African-Style Zeal across North America." NPR 2014. Web. August 4 2015.

Connor, Phillip, D'Vera Cohn, and Ana Gonzalez-Barrerra. Changing Patterns of Global Migration and Remittances: More Migrants in U.S. And Other Welathy Countries; More Money to Middle-Income Countries: Pew Research Center, 2013.

D'Alisera, JoAnn. 2009. "Images of a Wounded Homeland: Sierra Leonean Children and the New Heart of Darkness." In *Across Generations: Immigrant Families in America*, edited by Nancy Foner. New York and London: New York University Press.

Gerloff, Roswith. "The African Diaspora and the Shaping of Christianity in Africa: Perspectives on Religion, Migration, Identity and Collaboration." *Ecumenical Theological Education (ETE) and Partners in Africa*. World Council of Churches, 2009.

Gornik, Mark. *Word Made Global: Stories of African Christianity in New York City*. Grand Rapids, MI: Eerdmans Publishing Co., 2011.

Hanciles, Jehu. *Beyond Christendom: Globalization, African Migration, and the Transformation of the West*. Maryknoll, NY: Orbis Books, 2006.

Handbook of Liturgy of the Church of the Lord (Aladura). Lagos: The Publication Committee, n.d.

Horton, Robin, "African Conversion," *Africa*, Vol.41, No.2, 1971.

Knott, Kim and Sean McLoughlin, eds. *Diasporas. Concepts, Intersections, Identities*. London: Zed Books, 2010.

Kwiyani, Harvey C. Sent Forth: African Missionary Work in the West. Maryknoll, NY: Orbis Books, 2014.

Larbi, Emmanuel Kingsley. *Pentecostalism: The Eddies of Ghanaian Christianity*. Sapc. Eds. Gifford, Paul, Ogbu U. Kalu and E. Kingsley Larbi. Accra: Centre for Pentecostal and Charismatic Studies, 2001.

Mackendrick, Karmen. *Word Made Skin: Figuring Language at the Surface of Flesh*. New York: Fordham University Press, 2004.

Miles, Margaret. *The Word Made Flesh: A History of Christian Thought*. Malden, MA: Blackwell, 2005.

Mwaura, Philomena. "Unsung Bearers of Good News: AIC Women and the Transformation of Society in Africa," *Journal of African Christian Thought*, Vol. 7, No.1, 2004, 38-44.

Oduro, Thomas A. 2014. "'Arise, walk through the length and breadth of the land': Missionary concepts and strategies of African independent churches." *International Bulletin of Missionary Research* 38 (2):86-89.

Omenyo, Cephas N. "Agenda for a Discussion of African Initiatives in Christianity: The West African/Ghanaian Case." Missiology: An International Review 39.3 (2011): 373-90.

Omenyo, Cephas N. "Trans-National Protestant Missions: The Ghanaian Story." Swedish Missiological Themes 101.1 (2013): 41-66.

Onyinah, Opoku. "Pentecostalism and the African Diaspora: An Examination of the Missions Activities of the Church of Pentecost." *Pneuma* 26.2 (2004): 216-41.

Ositelu, Rufus. *African Instituted Churches: Diversities, Growth, Gifts, Spirituality and Ecumenical Understanding*. Munster: LIT Verlag, 2002.

Quayson, Ato and Girish Daswani, eds. *A Companion to Diaspora and Transnationalism.* Wiley-Blackwell, 2013.

Rice, Andrew. "Mission from Africa." New York Times 2009. Web. August 4 2015.

Robert, Dana L. 2006. "World Christianity as a women's movement." *International Bulletin of Missionary Research* 30 (4):180-182.

Sanneh, Lamin. *Disciples of All Nations: Pillars of World Christianity.* New York: Oxford University Press, 2008.

Sundkler, Bengt. *The Christian Ministry in Africa.* Uppsala: Swedish Institute of Missionary Research, 1960.

Taylor, Charles. *A Secular Age.* Cambridge, MA: The Belknap Press of Harvard University, 2007.

Ukah, Asonzeh. "Reverse Mission or Asylum Christianity?" *Africans and the Politics of Popular Culture*. Eds. Falola, Toyin and Augustine Agwuele. Rochester: University of Rochester Press, 2009. 104-26.

Walls, Andrew. *The Cross-Cultural Process in Christian history: Studies in the Transmission and Appropriation of Faith.* Maryknoll, NY: Orbis Books, 2002

Williams, Ritva. *Stewards, Prophets, Keepers of the Word: Leadership in the Early Church.* Peabody, MA: Hendrickson, 2006.

32. Iranian Diaspora Ministry

Peter von Kaehne

For the past twelve years, my family has participated in an Iranian church in Glasgow, Scotland. Currently, thirty to forty members meet on Sunday afternoons on the premises of a Scottish church for shared worship, Bible study and fellowship in the Persian language. On other days we conduct courses, prayer meetings and house group gatherings. The service on Sunday is somewhat informal, a period of worship and shared prayer and a sermon of variable length, followed by more prayer and worship. Often the intercession focuses specifically on the needs of several members. For example, the concerns may involve preparation for an asylum court hearing, a sick relative in Iran, or family problems, particularly problems back home.

Although quite a few Christians in Iran are in jail for their faith, the gospel is flowing actively among Iranians both outside and inside the country. In 1979, on the brink of Iran's fundamentalist Islamic revolution, it was estimated that there were about 500 Iranian Christians from an Islamic background. This estimate included those within Iran as well as everywhere else in the world. (In addition, there were Armenian, Assyrian, Messianic, and other Christians who were Iranian citizens but not from Muslim heritages.)

Today the picture has changed. There are many tens of thousands, maybe hundreds of thousands, of Iranians from Muslim background who confess Jesus Christ as Lord. Several thoughtful scholars hold that there are over a million Iranian believers. These spread across national boundaries. There are strong Persian (Muslim background) churches inside Iran. There are also many outside. The congregation that will be described in this essay is one of them.

Iranian awakening

Iran is the center of Shi'ah Islam. Since its Islamic Revolution in 1979, Iran has become known as one of the main powers behind worldwide Islamic resurgence. Iran also has an ancient Christian tradition. Probably the first non-Jewish witnesses to Jesus' birth were Persians, when the wise men from the East came to visit the Christ child. Later, when the Holy Spirit came upon the disciples in power at the feast of Pentecost and the gospel was preached in many languages, as recorded in Acts 2, there were Iranians in the crowd who heard and responded – Persians and Medes who came to faith. They were descendants of Jews who had been brought to the Persian region by the Babylonians, and developed settled communities there. Daniel, Esther, and Nehemiah were part of that story, as was Cyrus, the humane Persian ruler who gave the exiles the option of returning to their homeland.

After celebrating Pentecost with the apostles in Jerusalem, the Iranian believers went back home and founded churches. They studied and published extensively. They created networks of Christian fellowships, complete with bishops in cities like Herat and Meshed. One of the greatest missionary movements in all history went right through Iran, the Nestorian passage along the Silk Road to China. It was powered by Persian Christians.

Even at the best of times, however, Christians were a minority religion here, persecuted by both worldly and religious authorities, never entirely accepted or left in peace. For the past 1000 years, Iranian Christians have belonged mostly to two ethnic minorities, Armenians and Assyrians. While the fundamentalist revolution of 1979 unleashed fresh persecution, the three and a half decades since also have seen the gospel break through to the Islamic Persian-speaking majority population. Today the number of those believers has skyrocketed. For the first time in hundreds of years, there are again strong churches of Persian background both inside and outside the country.

A lot of this growth has happened in the diaspora. Every year approximately 200,000 Iranians emigrate. Approximately 40,000 are students, with Malaysia, USA, Canada, Germany, and the UK as the top five receiving countries. Many Iranian emigrants are highly educated. Frequently they seek asylum in Western countries. Britain currently has a population of about 75,000 residents from an Iranian background. Hundreds, probably thousands, of these have become Christians during this journey.

Today there are Iranian churches and fellowships in most major UK cities, and in many smaller ones. Most of these churches and some of the smaller fellowships are members of the Council of Iranian Churches in Western Europe. Some Iranian churches in the UK are independent. Others are Persian-language fellowships linked with British churches. Only a few of the ministers are trained theologically and ordained. These tend to be based in larger churches, and are expected to supervise several smaller churches and groups. Leaders usually are not paid, although some senior leaders may receive funding from a variety of sources, such as mainstream churches or Iranian publication ministries. Church memberships can fluctuate rapidly. Mobility is high, as people relocate to other parts of the country. They may or may not reconnect with an Iranian church. Crises and breakdowns are not uncommon.

This essay focuses on one congregation in Glasgow. While missiological literature has focused some coverage on Iranian ministry in North America, less has been documented regarding similar work in Europe. This report will help to balance the record.

Leaders and members

The Iranian congregation in Glasgow, Scotland, is led by a pastor and a team of elders. Our pastor lives in London and travels to Glasgow for weekends. During the church's first ten years, the pastor made this trip every week. Now he comes once or twice a month, and stays for a longer period. While this arrangement often has been difficult, it is unavoidable for a variety of reasons.

Most of the elders focus on trustee responsibilities, and involve themselves less in pastoral work. However, their prayers are sought and valued during worship services. Among the elders, I am one who preaches frequently. Although not Iranian, I learned Persian and developed fluency after I became a believing Christian in 1987. The group of elders has been extremely important, and has kept the church together at points of crisis. Much of the communication among the elders is informal. Twice we have experienced a major breakdown of unity among the elders. Both times, the church suffered badly.

Apart from the team of elders, there is a group of mature members who are the pillars of the church. Many of these now have been in the faith for eight years or more, and most of them have come to faith in our own church. Much of our work as elders is concentrated on these members. In turn, this group runs most of the evangelistic outreach and the informal discipling of our newer members. Membership in this subgroup fluctuates, defined more by actual ministry responsibilities than by titles, and dependent on current level of commitment. Many who participated at this level in our church but later migrated to other cities, now serve in leadership positions in other Iranian or British churches.

Our members are a mixture of mature and new believers. Practically all are from an asylum- seeking background, with all the difficulties this entails. Many are unemployed, and some older members are unemployable due to lack of language skills. Subsequently, many of our members are quite poor, though they try to hide this. While most are healthy in a physical sense, many struggle with feelings of depression, a sense of worthlessness, anxiety, etc. Marriages often are under severe strain. Trying to raise and guide teeenage children in a poorly-understood culture causes various difficulties. Amid these pressures, the experience of *aramesh* peace or quietnessfrequently is offered as the reason that people continue to come to church after an initial visit. Such life struggles require pastoral intervention and prayer.

Our membership is also highly mobile. Initially these Iranian refugees are forced to live in Glasgow because this is the location to which they have been assigned by the asylum system. However, once they have been granted asylum, many will move within a few months to a sunnier place, commonly to London or to the southeast of England. Mobility means that our membership fluctuates. Sometimes it is as high as 100, and at other times it is as low as thirty. Increases mostly are caused by new baptisms and decreases mostly are due to mobility.

Worship and prayer

The Sunday worship service is led by a team. A number of older members take turns guiding the time of worship and prayer. The pastor, one of the elders, or an invited guest will preach. Other participants greet people, run the projector and sound system, and cook tea. Sermons are usually in Persian. If not, they are translated into Persian.

When there is communion or a particularly enthusiastic preacher, a service may last up to three hours. However, usually the formal part of the service will finish in two hours. Then the informal fellowship will begin. While this may start with casual chat, it may shift back into prayer or counseling at any time. People show a stunning trust in the power of prayer, expecting specific and clear responses to their petitions. And they do indeed receive answers. Seeking such answers to prayer is most often quoted as the reason for initially coming to church. People come because they see the power, and stay because they see the truth.

While prayer vitalizes the Sunday service, the heart of the prayer life of the church is a meeting on Saturday night. Here prayer becomes intensely personal, expressed in an atmosphere of great trust.

Baptism and asylum claims

In Britain, a documented conversion can be used to build an asylum claim. Naturally this opens the door to false claims. Former Muslims who claim Christian conversion often are regarded dubiously by government gatekeepers. Meanwhile, many Western pastors enthusiastically support even the most unconvincing claims of past persecution and maltreatment, in the hope – usually vain – that they are being instrumental in a major move of the Spirit. On the other hand, many older Iranian believers and some pastors view asylum seekers almost cynically. When these people ask for help in their claims, these pastors declare such requests to document conversions unspiritual and deceitful. We have experienced some of this tension in our own church and with our British host churches. On some occasions we have needed to rebuke older members who dismissed new attenders as “fakes.” In other cases we found our British hosts promoting people who were attractive more because of their ability to impress than because of their character.

We have found that our initial policy decisions in this matter have stood the test of time. We will baptise those who ask for it, once they have concluded an initial course and have shown signs of a changed life. The course loosely corresponds to Alpha and Beta courses as promoted by Holy Trinity Brompton, London. This takes a few months, but not the years people often have to wait in Iran or in other Iranian churches.

We will then support these new Christians in their asylum applications, once they are baptised. Our support will include testimony to court as to what we have actually seen, but we never explore or comment on anything referring to the past. We routinely do not allow anyone new to make public claims in our church regarding any previous persecution or involvement in churches within Iran. This has worked well. Our testimony in courts is considered reliable (and subsequently helpful). And we maintain an open door for confession and forgiveness of sin regarding fraudulent claims. We also ensure that people will not lose face in the church due to having made public vacuous claims of persecution and martyrdom in Iran.

Islam is not the focus

We do not teach on Islam, other than responding very occasionally to direct questions. It appears to me that Islam does not seem to play a great role as a personal faith in the lives of most Iranians. I can count on single digits the number of convinced Iranian Muslims I have met personally both inside and outside of Iran. However, we do engage directly with patterns of behavior and thinking which draw in part on Islamic thinking – works versus grace, understanding of church versus mosque, leadership, relationships including marriage and courtship, truth and honesty, and pride and anger.

Pride and reconciliation

I have found it impossible to predict with any reliability who will develop into a committed worker of the church, after showing some level of interest, and who will not. At times it has felt frustrating and disappointing when someone who seemed to do well suddenly vanished after having "consumed" a lot of input. Initially I thought our pastor had a better way of predicting, but now I think he simply became more inured to disappointment earlier in his life. Maybe the only useful generalization is that overt and explosive anger issues seem to matter less in the long term than hidden anger camouflaged as sensitivity. Also, pride is pernicious and can take a long time to truly give way.

Internal church crises have impelled people to leave the church at times. During one severe crisis last year, we had fewer than ten attendees for a while. Generally the church crises have started within the group of mature and committed members. Problems around arrogance, pride, and uncontrolled anger tend to come out here and have led on occasion to relationship breakdown. Reconciliation within this group, often preceded by genuine apology and humility, tends to be lasting. The love shown here is a very powerful witness.

For discussion

1. What occurs during worship in the Iranian congregation described?
2. What is the first reason that people are attracted to this church?
3. How does the church support people in asylum claims? What limits does the church draw?
4. How is the church governed?
5. Describe mobility of this population, and its impact on the congregation.

Bibliography

Mandryk, Jason. *Operation World: The Definitive Prayer Guide to Every Nation.* Biblica, 2010.

Moffat, Samuel. *A History of Christianity in Asia: Beginnings to 1500.* Maryknoll, NY: Orbis Books, 1998.

Stewart, Emma. "UK Dispersal Policy and Onward Migration: Mapping the Current State of Knowledge," *Journal of Refugee Studies,* Vol. 25, No. 1, 2012, 25-49.

SECTION 6: ISSUES IN GLOBAL DIASPORA MISSIOLOGY

Paul Sydnor and Larry Caldwell, Section Editors

ISSUES IN GLOBAL DIASPORA MISSIOLOGY: AN INTRODUCTION

Section Editors: Paul Sydnor and Larry Caldwell

The global diasporas of the present time are unique in human history. These movements of peoples are thoroughly embedded in the economic, political, and social realities of twenty-first century globalization. What has changed is not only the volume of migration but also the economic and political conditions that create the context for migration, as well as advances in travel and communication technologies that generate new identity options for peoples on the move. The following case studies illustrate the necessity for diaspora missions strategy to factor in these global realities.

The economic, social, and psychological forces that affect the millions of people moving about the globe are too numerous to consider in one short chapter. What these case studies ably do is illustrate how ministries have grappled with particular issues. The result is not a set of definitive answers but rather suggested approaches that may apply to other problems as well. An observation common to all the studies is that old ministry paradigms – appropriate for people groups relatively static in their geography and rate of cultural change – have decreasing applicability to diaspora missions.

The global diaspora is largely a Majority World story, and that fact alone should attune our ears to the voices of the actual participants in this great global drama. When we attend to the diaspora actors we most often find refugees, the displaced and migrating workers from poorer lands. We see them collide with the entrenched economic, political, and social systems of more wealthy societies. This context of relative weakness and the suffering it generates cannot be ignored if we are to work effectively among diasporic peoples.

In the follow pages you encounter real stories of refugees fleeing horrific dangers, legal and illegal immigrants looking for better economic opportunities, and churches which are battling old prejudices and struggling to absorb these recent arrivals. You are invited into the personal lives of immigrants struggling to preserve families, as well as their own sense of personal identity in the tension between their old and new cultures. You are asked to experience the powerlessness of immigrants as they often face hostile legal systems, the trauma of individuals trafficked for sex or labor, and the despondency of the empty years of refugee internment.

In these stories both churches and mission agencies are grappling with how to respond, especially when the negative effects of migration demand holistic involvement. For the unevangelized arrivals, the gospel becomes the good news of welcome and care. For Christians on the move, continuing pastoral care, social advocacy, and practical help is essential if they themselves are to become bearers of the gospel. These stories ask us to step into the lives of those who are attempting to forge a new trans-national identity, or who face the surprising sense of cultural distance upon returning home after years away, or who learn to work in ministry organizations whose culture and structure are alien.

Our hope as editors is that in reading these case studies you will both see the importance of the global context of economic, political, and social forces that shape the flows of migration, and also, for at least a moment, enter into the personal world of those on the move.

33. WELCOMING THE STRANGER: A CASE STUDY OF AN INTERNATIONAL CHURCH IN MALTA

Paul N. Sydnor

The case of a migrant church

With a population of approximately 500,000 people on a small island in the Mediterranean Sea, Malta is one of the most densely populated countries in the world. Today, over 20,000 foreign nationals live in Malta. Sixty percent of these are from other EU countries and the remainder come from outside the EU as migrants, asylum seekers and refugees (UNHCR Malta 2014).[1] Malta has one of the highest rates of asylum seekers per capita in all of Europe (UNHCR 2014, 15).[2] Particularly with the increase of forcibly displaced persons from the surrounding regions, Malta faces the issue of migration at a magnified level and its protection of human rights has sometimes been questioned (DeBono 2012, 269; Pisani 2012, 219). The issues are complex along Europe's southern border because all kinds of migrants are mixed together (Swing 2012).[3] In the midst of these diverse groups of migrants, a small English-speaking international church near the capital city of Malta has responded to the mandate to love and welcome the stranger.[4]

---

1 There is no single definition for a migrant. I use the term to mean those who move to another country in regular ways such as foreign workers and through immigration. Whereas, asylum seekers and refugees are those who are forced to move and most of these come to Malta in irregular ways –without documentation and by boats. Approximately 80 percent of the asylum seekers will receive a right to remain and work in Malta. Less than five percent of the asylum seekers are refugees. See the UNHCR Malta website for more information. http://www.unhcr.org.mt/statistics.

2 The Asylum Trends (UNHCR 2014, 15) reports there were about 20 applicants for Malta per 1000 inhabitants in 2013, while the EU average is 2.9. Since 2014, many of the refugees crossing the Mediterranean Sea have been rescued and taken directly to mainland Europe. With the large influx of refugees into Europe these statistics have changed, however, the high level of asylum in Europe is now similar to the situation that Malta has also experienced.

3 The director of IOM (International Organization for Migration) notes that more violence causes an upsurge in people fleeing as well as ones who are trapped, making it difficult to uphold human rights. He calls on those with a mandate to respond to work together.

4 I have based the following case study on interviews made in 2011 among those in this church. All names have been changed.

Daniel and Martha pastor this international church. Daniel is an African immigrant with Maltese citizenship and Martha, his wife, is Maltese. Daniel attended seminary in Europe and has been trained as a pastor and a lawyer. Coming from an evangelical Pentecostal tradition, today the church is made of predominantly West African migrants from multiple countries. In addition there are Filipino workers, some EU nationals and a few Maltese. Forty to sixty people meet regularly on Sundays for worship, and some take part in several activities throughout the week like prayer meetings, bible studies, and music rehearsals.

Originally the church was almost strictly Maltese. When it went through a difficult transition, the church asked Daniel to be their pastor, just after he had finished seminary. Daniel and Martha have since built a ministry that welcomes strangers and offers support and fellowship to all those in the church. As Julie, a Filipino worker, recalled: "I have lived half of my life as a migrant worker and the hardest part is being separated from my family. The church helped me as a family." Daniel and Martha's ministry loved these foreigners. The church filled a great need in the migrants' lives; it has been a natural development in Daniel and Martha's respective identities as foreigners and as ones called to mission.

Around this time, large numbers of irregular migrants began arriving in Malta by boat.[5] The Maltese authorities responded with a policy of mandatory detention for anyone who entered the country as an irregular migrant.[6] Daniel visited these newly arrived migrants in detention, bringing food and supplies and offering opportunities for worship and bible study. Other ministries soon developed from these visits. Detention for many of the migrants is yet another trial that is equal to some of the difficulties they have already faced (Pace 2012, 250).[7]

Franklin was one of those who were placed in detention upon arrival. While being isolated in detention, he was greatly encouraged when ones

---

5 "Irregular" migrants are those who enter or remain in a c"ountry without valid authorization. In Malta's case, most of the irregular migrants arrive by boat, after they have been intercepted or rescued at sea (Suban 2012, 163). Since 2002, Malta has received increasing numbers of irregular migrants. For example, in January 2012 the violence then in Libya forced 700,000 people to flee with 50,000 attempting to cross the sea in rickety boats. However, as noted previously, with the EU rescue operations at sea since 2014, most of the current migrants are taken directly to mainland Europe.

6 According to Debono (2012, 264-265), there have been many criticisms of this policy, noting things such as: overcrowding; lack of privacy; sexual abuse; unhygienic conditions; lack of health care; mental health concerns; and withholding information.

7 The compulsory detention of all migrants who enter Malta without documentation can trigger mental health disorders, especially since a majority of these detainees have experienced some degree of trauma. MSF (2009), for example, reports that the detention in Malta has increased the risk of post-traumatic stress disorder among the migrants.

from the church came to visit him. "I felt welcomed, and this was so different from being put into detention. Their visit reminded me to focus on God and that God would help me to pass through the difficult time. Now, I remind the others that we are the church and we need to visit those in hard times and help each other to persevere." The effort to welcome and visit those in detention, characterizes a holistic concern for fellow human beings who need help, spiritual fellowship and fair treatment.

It never occurred to Daniel or Martha that the church would be either international or only Maltese; rather it would simply be a welcoming church that would not reject strangers. However, this was a new approach for this Maltese church, most of whom wanted to emphasize their Maltese identity. It was important for the Maltese congregation to define who others are as people, to tell them what they can do, and how they should fit in. Unfortunately, this attitude set groups apart and gave importance to some at the expense of others.

In contrast, Daniel and Martha decided not to yoke those coming in with additional expectations. They wanted to focus on those aspects that were common for all Christians and to emphasize discipleship, preaching, and teaching. They saw the need to identify as Christ's church rather than as a national church. In their minds, welcoming the strangers shifted the church away from a specific ethnic focus to a more global one. This welcoming attitude greatly strengthened the migrants, but it led to resentment among many of the Maltese who eventually left the church.[8]

The migrants, however, readily attest to the importance of being welcomed. George says as a migrant, his faith will sometimes suffer. "My faith will go down, so church is a place to pick up a word of encouragement from others." Baldwin says, "I feel happy in church, because I know my faith is being strengthened. I can remember again that God rescued me when I crossed the sea. So, I pray now for a strong faith, because I know this is what we need to pass through this temporary world." Esther doesn't feel good about much in her life. The church, however, is where she can come and feel at home. It gives her a family that she has lost. Another migrant in the church felt unwanted in Malta. He was held against his will because of the restrictions on his status. Despite these difficulties his faith has increased and he says, "I have seen that God brought me here. God will provide for me and God will take me home one day."

Today in welcoming others, the international church in Malta aims to build a strong community of support and fellowship in several ways. First, they offer activities around shared values such as family, prayer, and relationship. This approach not only builds community, it also helps migrants to break their isolation in the larger society. Their involvement in

---

8 Debono (2012) describes the lack of cosmopolitanism in Malta – where the world stops at its shores – as a significant factor in its struggle to respect the rights and dignity of the migrants coming in.

the church community gives the support they need to live and work as migrants.

Second, the church addresses issues that are relevant to those being welcomed. For example, migrant women make an unusually large sacrifice by moving away from their children and families for the sake of earning an income. The church has encouraged these women as they face the guilt and cost of this sacrifice.

Third, the church recognizes the strengths of those coming in and the need for them to contribute and take responsibility in the community. This is not always easy to do. As Martha noted, the same development and education problems in their countries back home are creeping into the church, where the women are asked to serve the coffee, wash the floor and prepare food, yet they are not asked to share in other leadership and ministry responsibilities. To overcome this creeping tendency, the church has formed a leadership team that includes women to help share the responsibilities and to give full voice to those in the church.

Yet, despite the community emphasis and the international flavor of the church, even the fellow leaders themselves need reminding of what it means to welcome others. For example, sometimes the African leaders will insist on forms and styles of worship that exclude others. Daniel will remind them: "This is not an African church; this is God's church. If God could accommodate all of us, then we too need to show the same attitude toward others different from us." The concern is not for individual recognition or gain, but rather for the life of the community.

From the perspective of the stranger, being welcomed happens through a ministry approach that involves the community. It touches the whole of life and it lasts from the first welcome to the last goodbye. It reaches out to others in the name of Christ and encourages them to live in faith wherever God takes them.

Global implications

The case of this small international church in Malta illustrates several global implications. These implications are both for local churches welcoming diaspora peoples as well as for the migrants themselves.

First, the care and concern shown by the local church is the start that many migrants need to find the stability and strength to rebuild their lives and establish themselves in a new land. Many of the migrants are in the country because they need a job, or for the protection of a safe place. They may not see how they are in Malta because of God. As the local church welcomes these migrants, it also needs to remind them that God is in control of their lives and that they are there to also influence the local church.

Second, the migrants are often looking for bigger and better opportunities, and most plan one day to return home. This reality means that for every welcome in the local church there is also a goodbye; it is not unusual for the small church to see four to five people move on every year. This reality challenges the church: to find continuity in a ministry among transient people; to address the question of how to develop leadership among ones who may not stay; and to prepare migrants to re-engage in local church life in their new situations.

Third, welcoming strangers challenges the status quo. This is often a good thing as it causes reliance on God. But if not handled well it may lead to alienation on the part of the long-term local church members. Looking at her own ministry Martha said: "We have adapted well to the different groups of migrants, but we also need to minister to the local Maltese. The church not only needs to be welcoming, but it needs to do this in a relative way for the local context." The challenge is to welcome newcomers without pushing out others who also have an important role to play in the life of the church.

The reality of welcoming strangers is that it faces challenges at every level. However, this reflects the nature of faith in this world; the potential gain, in terms of trust in God for all those involved, outweighs the loss. The remainder of this case study discusses three implications of welcoming the stranger that are important for everyone to consider.

The focus of *Missio Dei*

First, there is a focus on the *missio Dei.*[9] In redemptive terms, this focus sees God at work throughout the ages who has always welcomed the nations (Bevans 2013, 160). In practical terms, a focus on *missio Dei* makes Christ the center of church life. The aim of a welcoming church is to follow Christ's example, which was to do the work of his father.[10] When the church welcomes others, it acknowledges the popular phrase, "God is good all the time."

Daniel and Martha's ministry paradigm for welcoming strangers consciously rejected the ethnocentricity of focusing on either the Maltese nationality or any other ethnic group, and they readily remind the migrants from different ethnicities of this approach. The need has been to focus on the goodness of God in Christ who joins the church together, and not to focus on some preferred style or context. This is difficult in many cultural contexts, and no less so in Malta.

Missio Dei is important for welcoming others because it reminds us that God's entire story from beginning to end has been about salvation, not just

---

9 Missio Dei is a Latin term translated as "mission of God." The term reminds us that God's work in this world has extended across the ages and that it is greater than any one expression or approach might give it. Likewise the obedience of Christ is the sum of this mission, in which God in Christ became like humanity so that we might be like Christ (Placher, 2009, 27).

10 Cf. John 5:17; 10:37-38.

for a people, but for the world. This is significant for the unwanted migrant because they often see themselves in God's story (Groody 2013, 150). They identify with Jesus who himself entered our story and said again at the end of his ministry: "…I was a stranger and you visited me… I was in prison and you came to me" (Matt. 25:35-36). Welcoming the stranger as God has done facilitates integration, and this has historically been difficult.[11] It is easy to have a siege mentality, where the enemy is outside threatening the culture and nation. However, when the church welcomes outsiders, it consciously signals to the world that salvation comes from God alone.

Missio Dei is God's work for God's people. Crossing all borders, *missio Dei* reflects the transformation of heart that happens in both foreigners and nationals, and it manifests itself in the giving (up) of ourselves and our own ideas of how things should be.

The attitude of kenosis

Second, welcoming others happens in an attitude of kenosis. Philippians 2:5-8 summarizes what this means; it is the practice of selflessness:

> "Have this mind among yourselves, which is yours in Christ Jesus, who though he was in the form of God, did not count equality with God a thing to be grasped, but emptied himself, by taking the form of a servant, being born in the likeness of men and being found in human form, he humbled himself by becoming obedient to the point of death, even death on a cross."

Whether as the church that welcomes or the stranger who receives, to engage as Christians on issues of migration requires self-sacrifice and letting go like Christ has shown us. Groody describes the spiritual journey of migrants as one that is rooted in Christ, because like Christ they have relinquished everything they own, knowing that God has entered into their vulnerability with them (Groody 2013, 152). The journey of the migrants in this case study also requires a Christ-like kenosis in the face of rejection, vulnerability, and suffering that accompanies their journey. The "welcoming" aligns us with an attitude of self-denial and self-emptying that is important for every Christian.

As much as the journey requires self-sacrifice though, it also requires a determination for self-preservation. In matters of faith, this self-protection needs to be tempered with humility. The migrant leaders themselves challenge their fellow immigrants' ideas and opinions, not only in their faith, but also about their host society. Just as the local society needs to

---

11 Such integration is especially difficult in island countries (Ragonesi 2012, 204). For example, Malta has a history of siege. The islanders defended against the Great Siege in 1565 and turned away the Ottoman Turks in their invasion of Europe. They endured the incessant bombing and blockade of WWII. And now the influx of migration especially by irregular migrants is like another siege in the minds of many Maltese.

temper their own monocultural concerns, so, too, the migrants need to lower their own judgments. The migrant needs a community around him or her for feedback and to help make the important adjustments and decisions related to faith and life. The church needs to guard against not only the ethnocentric ways of culture, but also the equal force of egocentric tendencies. In this age of migration, the pride of a nation and the pride of a person are like oil and water that will not mix. Both sides need humility.

The attitude of kenosis reminds us of the cost that goes along with the migrant journey. The cost requires humility, and embracing this path brings challenges for all those involved. The path is often unmarked and those along the way need more than simply permits, jobs, and money to support themselves and their families, but rather they need mentoring and nurturing in their faith.

The practice of reciprocity

Third, those involved in welcoming others are both givers and receivers. As much as some migrants might be objects of assistance, in the church these migrants are also subjects who initiate mission. Hanciles reminds us that Christianity itself is not only migratory in nature, but every Christian migrant is also a potential missionary (Hanciles 2004, 99). The relationship between different cultures and people is a two way street. As Daniel said, "The church is not a social charity. We are willing to share, but we want you to share with us."

Such reciprocity offers the basis for sharing and learning from one another that can address the issues in a balanced way. It establishes the needed common ground between different groups and people. The impact of poverty and the concern for family are areas that many in the church have in common. The integrity of faith and life in these areas does not end only with prayer and teaching, but it continues in the day to day living and reciprocal interaction with one another.

As much as these migrants find themselves in Christ's story, they also need to see Christ in their own story. This does not happen magically or instantly, but rather through reciprocity. It happens where there is give and take in relationship with the community and with God, where self-sacrifice and humility are prioritized and where integrity is built up through healthy challenge and critique. This is discipleship.

Conclusions

Welcoming the stranger is the first step to help migrants, asylum seekers, and refugees to establish and rebuild their lives in a new land. Daniel, Martha and the example of their international church in Malta, reminds us of the importance of this ministry. However, welcoming others also has its challenges that remind us of our dependence on God, calling us to consider the aspects of *missio Dei*, kenosis, and reciprocity. These aspects give us the following profile of a welcoming church.

- The church welcomes others in the name of Christ and not with an emphasis on one specific group over another.
- While welcoming strangers, shows attention and concern for those outside, it needs to be relevant at the same time to the local context.
- A welcoming church seeks the welfare of the other through self-sacrifice and humility.
- Welcoming others builds an environment for reciprocity through mutual learning, shared leadership, and appreciation for the different voices and contributions of the community.
- The issues in this list are not only relevant to international churches. They are relevant for every church context where God's people are, first and foremost, a part of a complex global community and citizens of the kingdom of God.

For discussion

1. The long-term need for many strangers in our communities is to establish and rebuild their lives. What obstacles do they face in the task of rebuilding their lives?
2. What are the challenges that your church faces as it considers or engages in welcoming the stranger?
3. What aspect of welcoming strangers is difficult for you personally, and what are you doing to improve in that area?

Bibliography

Bevans, Stephen B. 2013. "Migration and Mission: Pastoral Challenges, Theological Insights." In *Contemporary Issues of Migration and Theology*, edited by Elaine Padilla and Peter C. Phan, 157-177. New York: Palgrave Macmillan.

DeBono, Daniela. 2012. "Human Rights for the Maltese First: Irregular Migration and Human Rights in Malta." In *Migration and Asylum in Malta and the European Union: Rights and Realities 2002 to 2011*, edited by Peter G. Xuereb. Msida: Malta University Press.

Groody, Daniel G. 2013. "The Spirituality of Migrants." In *Contemporary Issues of Migration and Theology*, edited by Elaine Padilla and Peter C. Phan, 143-156. New York: Palgrave Macmillan.

Hanciles, Jehu. 2004. "Beyond Christendom: African Migration and Transformations in Global Christianity." *Studies in World Christianity* 10(1):93-113.

Médecins sans Frontières (MSF). 2009. *Not Criminals.* http://www.medicisenzafrontiere.it/sites/italy/files/allegati/Immagini/file/pubblicazioni/Report_Malta_04_2009.pdf

Pace, Paul. 2012. "Health Care for Migrants in Malta." In *Migration and Asylum in Malta and the European Union: Rights and Realities 2002 to 2011*, edited by Peter G. Xuereb, 237-256. Msida: Malta University Press.

Pisani, Maria. 2012. "The Elephant in the Room: A look at How Policies Impact the Lives of Female Sub-Saharan Afrian Rejcted Asylum Seekers Living in Malta." In *Migration and Asylum in Malta and the European Union: Rights and Realities 2002 to 2011*, edited by Peter G. Xuereb, 217-236. Msida: Malta University Press.

Placher, William C. 2009. "How Does Jesus Save?" *The Christian Century* 2009 (June 2):23-27.

Ragonesi, Isabelle Calleja. 2012. "The Politics of Integration in a Small Island Peripheral State: The Case of Malta." In *Migration and Asylum in Malta and the European Union: Rights and Realities 2002 to 2011*, edited by Peter G. Xuereb, 191-212. Msida: Malta University Press.

Suban, Robert. 2012. "Irregular Immigrants in the Maltese Labour Market: Current Situation and Problems." In *Migration and Asylum in Malta and the European Union: Rights and Realities 2002 to 2011*, edited by Peter G. Xuereb, 163-189. Msida: Malta University Press.

Swing, William Lacy. 2012. "Broadening our perspective." *Forced Migration Review* 39:3.

United Nations High Commissioner for Refugees (UNHCR). 2014. *Asylum Trends 2013: Levels and Trends in Industrialized Countries*. UNHCR. http://www.unhcr.org/5329b15a9.html

United Nations High Commissioner for Refugees (UNHCR) Malta. 2014. *Know the Facts: A Toolkit on Asylum and Migraton for Maltese MEP Candidates*. UNHCR. Accessed September 9, 2014. http://www.unhcr.org.mt/statistics

34. (Sub)Mission: A Case Study on the Complexities of Political and Prophetic Action in Migrant Detention

Maria-Jose Soerens

The scriptural mandate to both care for the least of these[1] and for the strangers in our land, call for urgent missional engagement. But what is the role of the Church in this murky place of policy, advocacy, and social justice? What is a distinctively Christian response that honours the need for political action while making space for the work of the Spirit in the world, without reducing mission to either liberal policy or to religious practices alone? How do we move beyond the false, yet commonly enacted dichotomy between a dualistic spirituality that ignores the need for advocacy on the one hand, and a charge for liberation that reduces mission to political means on the other?

In what follows, I argue that the right response to migrant detention engages two dimensions of experienceprophetic and politicalcoming together under the Christian principle of kenosis. Kenosis is defined here, following Coakley (2002), as the 'voluntary self-emptying on the part of the second person of the Trinity' (3); inviting followers of Jesus to practice 'losing one's life in order to save it.' This is what Coakley has called the 'power-in-vulnerability paradox.' Coakley identifies two aspects of kenosis: Christological what Jesus did and spiritual the invitation for Christians to adopt a non-grasping attitude,[2] or an attitude of self-emptying to God.[3] Taking this definition as my point of departure, I argue that kenosis is the thread that weaves together in mission both religious conviction and political engagement, keeping them from being reduced to one or the other. Furthermore, I will demonstrate how for those living under oppressive conditions, a divestment of their own power in favour of submission to God becomes the very means to assert their personal agency. Such submission has both prophetic and political implications. My argument is made from the perspective of migrant detainees held at the

---

1 Matthew 25:39-40.

2 2 Corinthians 12:9

3 Kēnosis is an equivocal term. Coakley identifies six different understandings of kēnosis in the Christian tradition. She chooses the third – choosing to never have false and worldly power that is wrongly construed as divine (2002, 31). This definition is based, at least partly, on a Paulinian interpretation of Jesus as a second Adam, whose sin was to seek becoming like God.

Northwest Detention Center (NWDC) in Tacoma, Washington, USA, who embody such kenotic attitude, opening space for the Spirit to act. This self-emptying brings about a paradoxical new reality of political action and self-empowerment.

Detainees in this facility are notorious for their religious engagement. Within the overwhelming isolation of daily life in detention and the constant threat of abusive retaliation, detainees have organized spontaneous bible studies and prayer groups that meet three times daily. These groups have mushroomed throughout the different pods or units. For the past seven years, religious organizations like World Relief have offered weekly services in languages ranging from Russian to Spanish. Yet, the strength of this movement lies in its ground-up approach and organic development, yielding a strong community of faith that enacts prophetic resistance through mutual support and political engagement through informal networks.

To advance my argument, I will first provide a brief overview of the context of detention,[4] to then lay out my proposal to see prophetic and political action united under the principle of kenosis. Three stories of migrants in detention will work as our connecting threads highlighting the irreducible nature of prophetic action neither as solely political, nor as exclusively religious.

Context: the problematic nature of migrant detention

Flynn (2012) defines immigration detention as 'The deprivation of liberty of non-citizens because of their statuses' (42). This definition highlights the problematic nature of migrant detention in a number of counts. Firstly, detention does not respond to a crime[5] nor is mandated by a court. Instead, migrant detention is administrative; migrants are detained indefinitely while they wait for the outcome of their case, usually asylum requests. It is solely based on a person's lack of status as citizen and does not serve any other purpose than administrative convenience. An immigrant can be detained for two months to over four years waiting on a decision, without right to representation.

Secondly, it highlights that migrants are detained in facilities that closely resemble prisons, despite their names as 'shelters' (Flynn 2012). These facilities are privately run and are characterized by an impressive lack of

---

4 For reasons of space I am unable to give a comprehensive account of migrant detention. The issue is particularly complex because it involves the immigration laws of different countries as well as international law (Wilsher, 2012). The reader is encouraged to seek information from specialized websites such as at the Global Detention Project, or the International Detention Coalition and from the work of the following authors: Michael Flynn (2012) and Daniel Wilsher (2004, 2012).

5 In most countries illegal entry is considered a civil, not a criminal, offense. See Flynn (2012)

accountability and oversight (Wilsher 2012). Reports indicate that they operate below international standards and several cases of human rights violations have been reported.[6] The Global Detention Project (GDP) estimates that there are over 100,000 individuals detained around the globe on any given day (Flynn 2010).

In the US The Geo Group (GEO) holds the largest contract with Immigration and Custom Enforcement (ICE), running over 100 facilities. GEO receives over US$150 per day per detainee, rounding to more than US$1,5 billion in revenue in 2013. While the private profiting from an excessive and unnecessary service funded with federal dollars is clearly problematic, the practice was legalized by congress in 2009 under 'the bed quota,' which states that the Department of Homeland Security (DHS) 'shall maintain a level of not less than 34,000 detention beds through September 30, 2014.'[7] The bed quota was introduced in the 2009

---

6 These include, but are not limited to, sexual abuse; denial of medical care often leading to detainees' deaths; administrative detention of pregnant women, which is specifically against the law in the U.S.; lack of information to family members regarding the location of detainees; unlawful retaliation such as solitary confinement as a punishment for detainees' reasonable requests for standard conditions; etc. See NILC and the ACLU of Southern California for the United Nations Special Rapporteur on the Human Rights of Migrants, U.S. Immigration Detention System: Substandard Conditions of Confinement and Ineffective Oversight, May 2007 http://www.nilc.org/immlawpolicy/arrestdetUNspecial rapporteur_presentation_2007-05-03.pdf; The Women's Commission for Refugee Women and Children and The Lutheran Immigration and Refugee Service, Locking Up Family Values: The Detention of Immigrant Families, February 2007 http://www.womenscommission.org/pdf/famdeten.pdf; Amnesty International USA, Unaccompanied Children in Immigration Detention, June 2003 http://www.amnestyusa.org/refugee/pdfs/children_detention.pdf; Shadow Report to the U.N. Committee on the Elimination of Racial Discrimination by the Rights Working Group, Equal Treatment Denied: United States Immigration Enforcement Policies, 2008 http://65.36.162.162/files/RWG_ICERDShadowReport_2008.pdf; CERD Shadow Report to the US Human Rights Network by the Immigration Working Group, Right of Immigrants and Migrants to the United States: A Critical Look at the United States and its Compliance Under the Convention, 2007. http://huachen.org/english/bodies/cerd/docs/ngos/usa/USHRN3.doc; ACLU, Conditions of Confinement in Immigrant Detention Facilities, June 2007 www.aclu.org/pdfs/prisonunsr_briefing_materials.pdf; Additional Briefing Materials Submitted to the UN Special Rapporteur on the Human Rights of Migrants, Promotion and Protection of All Human Rights, Civil, Political, Economic, Social and Cultural Rights, Including the Right to Development, March 2008 http://huachen.org/english/issues/migration/rapporteur/docs/A-HRC-7-CRP-3.doc; International Federation for Human Rights, United States – Mexico Walls, Abuses, and Deaths at the Borders, March 2008 http://www.fidh.org/IMG/pdf/USAMexiquemigran488ang.pdf

7 "Consolidated and Further Continuing Appropriations Act, 2013." H.R.933 http://www.gpo.gov/fdsys/pkg/BILLS-113hr933eas/pdf/BILLS-113hr933eas.pdf

appropriations bill by Senator Byrd with no public comment (Figueroa 2014), and has failed to be removed despite efforts from members of congress, immigration agencies, and the administration. The bed quota results in the unnecessary imprisonment of thousands of migrants who do not pose a threat to public safety, separating families, and putting a price tag on migrant lives.

The NWDC is one of the biggest facilities in the country with capacity for up to 1500 detainees. Migrants are held in overcrowded pods and subject to dehumanizing conditions.[8] A hallmark of the NWDC is its power to keep detainees under social isolation. Calls to family members can cost up to US$2 per minute; detainees are subject to 'no-contact' visits, making crying toddlers a common sight in the visitation room on the other side of the window. No civil group is allowed to provide enriching activities for the detainees. Religious organizations may conduct services but must leave immediately after, yielding no time for *koinonia*. The officers on each pod establish their own sets of arbitrary rules, such as no noise before noon, leading to excessive use of disciplinary actions. Such was the case of Ramón Mendoza, placed in solitary confinement for greeting a Russian fellow detainee with a fist bump and accused of 'incitation' through an internal proceeding in which his lawyer was not allowed to participate. Detainees are generally threatened with retaliation by means of losing their bed, being transferred to a different pod, or to an undisclosed location.

Religious expression as kenotic posture

It is in this context of social isolation, lack of representation, and complete uncertainty, that a large number of detainees have chosen to engage in religious activities such as bible studies and prayer groups.[9] These engagements are characterized by a self-emptying posture. 2 Corinthians

---

8 Reports from detainees included: lack of basic sanitary services for treatment of infected wounds; tardiness to respond to requests for medical intervention resulting in ER visits; disproportionate amounts of bathrooms per individuals (80 to 4).

9 While it is understandable that people will congregate to fight isolation, this alone does not explain the religious character of such coming together. Research on religious activity in prisons indicate that religion serves the purpose of maintaining one's identity and helps inmates cope with detention while also promoting pro-social behaviors (See Kerley, Matthews, and Blanchard 2005, Kerley and Copes 2009, Thomas and Zaitzow 2006). Most research, however, has been conducted with populations of individuals with criminal charges who have been given a specific sentence, which presents a whole set of different dynamics than the ones found in migrant detention. While some parallels have been drawn between what has been called 'The New Jim Crow' (Alexander 2012), and 'The Juan Crow' (Pavey 2013), the subjective experience of indefinite detention without representation nor bail, and for no other reason than lack of status, is qualitatively different than the subjective experience in federal prison, despite their common ground as expressions of systemic injustice in the U.S.

12:9 is constantly mentioned in casual conversation by detainees, 'My grace is sufficient for you, for my power is made perfect in weakness.' In this way, disempowering events take a liturgical significance. The intake, a procedure in which the newly detained are dispossessed from all their belongings by ICE, is reworked as a re-birth; the opportunity of a new beginning in which God will have space to work in one's life.

Part of this new beginning is a self-understanding of detainees as missionaries to the detention centre and to any other place where they are sent if they are to be deported.[10] Such is the case of Cecilia Huayamares,[11] a paralegal from Peru who had been in the US since age 14. Cecilia was detained for three months before being deported. During that time she helped hundreds of women fill out their asylum forms. She explained,

> "Before I came here I prayed that God would use me to help a lot of people, "a mí no me importa el cambio aunque sea un cambio brusco," I didn't care if it was a rough change... a week later I was here... [laughs]."

While in detention Cecilia helped women who did not speak English and had no representation. She reported being told, 'We've been praying for someone like you to help us with our papers.'

Another woman, Lorena, an asylum seeker from Honduras and pastor in NC, reported after eight months in detention, 'All my life I have wanted to disciple women and I get to do that here.'

Gloria, a migrant woman from Mexico who has led a bible study for over two years in detention, described the experience of many women at the NWDC, while difficult, as *tiempos de refrigerio*[12] (Acts 3:19); as a time to be set apart for God. She observed,

Some women say, "I told the Lord that I wanted to live my own life, [...] away from my family, and here I am, they have no idea where I am at. But I am learning about God, I am being prepared [...], reading the Bible and trusting God more." They describe this as being set apart, because they believe this is the best way God could have spoken into their life, to be restored, "*tiempos de refrigerio*."

Luis described how upon his arrival to the NWDC, *los hermanos* told him, 'Brother, this is not a jail; this is a training camp in God's word.'

Far from merely reframing a terrible situation into a meaningful way to cope, the detainees' response reflects a commitment to mission as opening space for the Spirit. Gloria, for example, was not originally planning on teaching bible studies. It was another detainee who told her, 'God has a plan for you but you are ignoring it.' Gloria explained that she prayed for direction and 'the Lord worked in [her] life.' She said, 'He gave me an immense hunger and desire to preach.' She gathered a group of 37 women

---

10 Staff at World Relief often share stories of detainees who have converted at the NWDC and planted churches in their country of origin after deportation.

11 The detainees allowed the author to use their real names.

12 Trans. 'Times of refreshing.'

and began 'teaching them art so that they would clear their minds,' and helping in any other way she could.

Political action: agency in the subversion of every day encounters

Gloria's bible studies not only provide discipleship, they are also spaces to mobilize material, spiritual, and psychological resources for fellow detainees. When new women arrive at detention, Gloria and *las hermanas* introduce themselves and offer them resources. If anyone has cutlery, plates, or feminine products, which can only be bought from the commissary at exuberant fees, they let the new ones borrow them. Cecilia's work as a paralegal is also an example of such mobilizing.

In order to appreciate the political dimension of these actions, one must move beyond conventional definitions of the political as formal participation in institutions or voting (cf. Ellul 1977), towards a focus on power relations operating in the context of engagement (Zontini 2008). As Zontini (2008) argues, a narrow view of political action misses the ways in which migrants, particularly women, organize in everyday life and challenge power structures through participation in informal networks. Focusing on power dynamics in the everyday setting, says Zontini, shifts the common view of migrants as passive and excluded, drawing our attention to the assertive use of their agency.

Yet Gloria's and Cecilia's activism, while political, cannot be understood outside of their identity as Christ's servants.[13] Herein lies the paradox: for those living under oppressive conditions, a divestment of their own power in favour of submission to God becomes the very means to assert their personal agency. Such submission has both prophetic and political implications. Although political power is not the end of such submission – in other words, this submission to God is not a utilitarian means to political power; the very act of religious submission embodies a statement of prophetic action that has a transformative power in the world, which has the potential to be political.

Prophetic action is understood here, following Brueggemann (2001) as the act 'to nurture, nourish, and evoke a consciousness and perception alternative to the dominant culture around us' (3). It means to bring about a 'language of newness'' often as a response to dehumanizing totalitarian conditions (Brueggemann 2001, xxiii). Prophetic action tends to emerge most notably under oppressive circumstances that are sustained by the capacity of the totalitarian system to define reality (Herman 1997). In such contexts, to resist is to enact newness, and in conditions of high constraints,

13 Gloria said it as plainly as, 'The greatest desire in my life is to continue serving the Lord. The Bible says that he came to serve, and we as his heirs come to serve Him and his people; to look for the lost souls, the thirsty... sometimes I say to myself, "I feel discouraged," but I respond, "Yes, but I came to serve." I exist to serve; and that is what keeps me going each day.'

this enactment is done by way of submitting oneself to the narrative of the gospel through religious performance (cf. Cavanaugh 1998). Thus the line dividing prayer meetings from organizing, or hunger strikes from fasting, and even missionary from mission field, becomes blurry.

Prophetic action: dehumanizing totalitarianism and humanizing dissent

At times prophetic action takes the form of a conventional political act. One such opportunity was the hunger strike that took place at the NWDC during spring of 2014. While the strikers' political demands is what made the news, a closer look at their actions revealed that for many of them the strike, or fasting as some called it, was a prophetic attempt to embody newness in the midst of a totalitarian system that robbed them from their humanity. For them the strike was simultaneously an act of submission to God; a prophetic statement of an alternative reality in which their humanity is maintained; and a call for political action from the wider society.

Ramón Mendoza, one of the leaders of the strike, spent over 30 days in solitary confinement while fasting (Soerens 2014). During this time Ramón read the Bible in its entirety. He said that Scripture not only gave him encouragement but it also resonated with his daily experience in incarceration. Each night Ramón prayed for discernment for the next day. One Friday the medic falsely informed Ramón – as they often do to the detainees – suggesting his kidneys were failing due to the hunger strike. Ramón felt unease with the news and considered quitting. However, he reported feeling a divine inspiration to keep going. By Monday, lawyers from ACLU had been able to discover GEO's attempts to dissuade strikers by means of false information and Ramón decided to continue.

At the core of Ramón's actions we do not find political activism alone, although the strike brought about hope for political change. Instead we find a prophetic attitude of 'the affirmation of a spiritual truth against the error of the moment' (Ellul 1989, 29): the truth that migrant detainees are not human abjection, but created in God's image and made free by Jesus' restorative power. This is the good news, that no matter who wants to profit from their vulnerability, their humanity is defined by God's love. 'I refused to be an object,' Ramón declared.

There is an impulse to be suspicious of these religious expressions, and for many in the church, the power-in-vulnerability paradox rings as a controversial idea. For those with a concern for justice, it is difficult to adopt vulnerability as a practice of resistance because it does not necessarily lead to social liberation. At the 2012 American Academy of Religion (AAR), for example, Serene Jones responded to Sarah Coakley's proposal of vulnerability, making it akin to invite people 'already drowning in the sea of social injustice to go even deeper.'

It seems outrageous to highlight submission as desirable for the oppressed, and the idea begs for clarification. For the oppressed, a kenotic attitude emerges as a statement of freedom; no one can be forced into it, and this submission is not to any other human but to God as the one who visits the oppressed in their darkest hour. A reaction against the idea of spiritual vulnerability from part of the materially vulnerable is understandable because vulnerability goes against what Ellul (1977, 197), has called 'the obsession of our age:' a preoccupation with means, goals, and results; an obsession particularly visible in the relatively recent 'justice' trend among privileged evangelical circles.

Suspicious of anything involving technique, Ellul (1989) calls Christians to engage in social change by opening space for the action of the Spirit, giving up prescriptions and grand goals while keeping our engagement. All we have, says Ellul (1977), is a point of departure – God's love and grace, and our works should not seek a specific objective, but be open-ended. It is in the seeming futility of prophetic action, says Ellul, where we truly find freedom,

To want to attain results is necessarily not to be witness to the free gift of God. If we are ready to be unworthy and unprofitable servants, although busy and active at the same time, then our works can truly redound to the glory of him who freely loved us first (197-8).

Thus the apparent futility of fasting, or of responding to a call to be a missionary within detention, are acts of freedom insofar as they are open-ended and done for the sake of making space for the Spirit to act. It is in these very 'futile' religious acts that the prophetic and the political emerge as a response to the totalitarian context of administrative detention. Yet the relationship between these two can be properly understood only by paying attention to the paradoxical nature of the power dynamics operating in migrants' religious engagement with the Christian tradition, which promotes an attitude of kenosisa divestment of our own power in order to open space for the divine.

For discussion

1. What makes a social issue like migrant detention problematic for the Church at large?
2. What are some other examples of prophetic and political action, and how are these together important for mission work?
3. How do we relate our identity as Christ's followers to the political and social issues around us, and what tensions do we face as we try to respond to these issues in mission?

Bibliography

Alexander, Michelle. 2012. The new Jim Crow: mass incarceration in the age of colorblindness. Rev. ed., Mass incarceration in the age of colorblindness. New York: New Press. Jackson, TN: Distributed by Perseus Distribution.

Brueggemann, Walter. 2001. The prophetic imagination. 2nd ed. Minneapolis, MN: Fortress Press.

Cavanaugh, William T. 1998. Torture and Eucharist: theology, politics, and the body of Christ. Oxford: Blackwell.

Coakley, Sarah. 2002. "Kenōsis and subversion: On the repression of 'vulnerability' in Christian feminist writing." In Powers and submissions: spirituality, philosophy and gender, 3-39 Oxford: Blackwell.

Ellul, Jacques. 1989. The presence of the Kingdom. Colorado Springs: Helmers & Howard.

Ellul, Jacques, and Bromiley, Geoffrey (trans). 1977. The politics of God and the politics of man. Grand Rapids, Mich.: Eerdmans.

Flynn, Michael. 2010. Immigration Detention and the Aesthetics of Incarceration. In The Theory and Practice of Immigration Detention Workshop. Oxford: University of Oxford Podcasts – Audio and Video Lectures.

Flynn, Michael. 2012. "Who must be Detained? Proportionality as a Tool for Critiquing Immigration Detention Policy." *Refugee Survey Quarterly* 31 (3):40-68.

Hamilton, Kimberly R. 2011. "Immigrant detention centers in the United States and international human rights law." *Berkeley La Raza Law Journal* 21:93-132.

Herman, Judith, M.D. 1997. Trauma and Recovery: The Aftermath of Violence – from Domestic Abuse to Political Terror. 14th ed. New York: Basic Books.

Human Rights Watch. 2010. Costly and unfair: flaws in US immigration detention policy. New York, NY: Human Rights Watch.

Itamar, Mann. 2011. The EU's dirty hands: Frontex involvement in ill-treatment of migrant detainees in Greece. New York, NY: Human Rights Watch.

Kerley, Kent R., and Copes, H. 2009. "'Keepin' my mind right': identity maintenance and religious social support in the prison context." *International journal of offender therapy and comparative criminology* 53 (2):228-44.

Kerley, Kent R., Matthews, Todd L., and Blanchard, Troy C. 2005. "Religiosity, Religious Participation, and Negative Prison Behaviors." *Journal for the Scientific Study of Religion* 44 (4):443-457.

Pavey, Steve. 2013. "America, you must be born again! Does the US have an immigrant rights problem or a freedom and justice problem?" *Prism*, Mar/Apr 2013, 9.

Seattle University School of Law, and One America. 2008. Voices from detention: a report on human rights violations at the Northwest Detention Center in Tacoma, Washington. Seattle: Seattle University School of Law.

Silverman, Stephanie J. 2012. "'Regrettable but Necessary?' A Historical and Theoretical Study of the Rise of the U.K. Immigration Detention Estate and Its Opposition." *Politics & Policy* 40 (6):1131-1157.

Soerens, Maria-Jose. 2014. "What is good news: a hunger strike, detention, and the bread of life" Missio Alliance, June 11, 2014. http://www.missioalliance.org/what-is-the-good-news-a-hunger-strike-detention-the-bread-of-life/.

The GEO Group, Inc. 2014. 2013 Annual Report. Boca Raton, Florida: Geo Group.

Thomas, Jim, and Zaitzow, Barbara. 2006. "Conning or Conversion? The Role of Religion in Prison Coping." *The Prison Journal* 86 (2):242-259.

Wilsher, Daniel. 2004. "The Administrative Detention of Non-Nationals Pursuant to Immigration Control: International and Constitutional Law Perspectives." *International and Comparative Law Quarterly* 53 (4):897-934.

Wilsher, Daniel. 2012. Immigration detention: law, history, politics. New York: Cambridge University Press.

Zontini, Elisabetta. 2008. "Resisting Fortress Europe: The everyday politics of female transnational migrants." *Focaal* 2008 (51):13-27.

35. Trauma as Mission: A Case Study Response to the Scourge of Sex Trafficking

Diane Langberg and Philip G. Monroe

Introduction

Nineteen year old Sarah lived in a Lagos, Nigeria slum. She ran into a distant relative who told her of a job opportunity in Europe. Desiring to break out of grinding poverty, she followed her relative to a small shop to meet her new boss. Unbeknownst to Sarah at the time, she had just been sold into forced prostitution to be trafficked to Europe. Stripped of her clothes, phone, and identification, Sarah was put through harsh training, beaten, forced to learn how to pick pocket, and provide sexual services. She was raped, repeatedly. Just before her illegal immigration to Austria, Sarah was forced to make an oath to a witch doctor promising she will never reveal the identities of her traffickers. If she does, she believes her parents will become cursed and die. Ending up on the streets of Vienna, Sarah felt alone, unable to flee, unable to live, hoping to die.[1]

Sarah is not alone. It is a dangerous world and uniquely so if human traffickers deem you defenseless and a commodity able to support a growing 32 billion dollar industry. The United Nations reports some 2.4 million individuals are enslaved and trafficked at any single moment (as cited in USA Today, 2012). Of those, as many as eighty percent are victims of sexual slavery. During the course of an entire year, UNICEF estimates some 700,000 to four million women are subjected to forced prostitution (Vlachovd & Biason, 2005). The same report estimates between 120,000 and 500,000 women are sold each year to brothels and pimps in Europe. Such trafficking is one of the more lucrative forms of slavery as victims constitute a reusable commodity, sold as many as 10 and 30 times each day, until they succumb to HIV and are tossed aside.[2] Despite perceptions that sex trafficking only targets women, boys and men account for as much as 25 percent of victims (UNODC, 2012, 28). And yet few of the suspected millions of trafficking victims are identified by law enforcement (Department of State, 2013, 46).[3]

---

1 Journalist Tobore Ovuorie experienced some of these situations in an undercover assignment. Read her harrowing story: https://www.premiumtimesng.com/news/153844-investigation-inside-nigerias-ruthless-human-trafficking-mafia.html#sthash.GXv8uO1d.dpbs

2 See Siddarth Kara's 2009 book detailing the business of sex trafficking.

3 Given the hiddenness of trafficking, identifying numbers of victims will always be difficult. Whether there are 2.4 or 27 million victims each year, adequate care for

While we may not know the names of these faceless victims, we do know their traumatic experiences rarely start with being trafficked. Poverty, domestic violence, and incest place individuals at risk to be trafficked. In those nations where domestic violence, "is simply part of the culture," as we were once told, high incidences of trafficked women follow.

If we survey the world and really see the great suffering around the globe, we will realize that trauma is one of the primary mission fields of this century. How are we to equip the church around the world to respond to the evil of trauma and trafficking in an effective and healing way?

Summary of the case

Sarah's degrading experiences of sexual slavery are incomprehensible to most. The damage done to her sense of self, place in the world, and hope for a future is unimaginable. Such traumatic experiences usually result in deeply traumatized human beings. Trauma means living with the recurrent, tormenting memories of atrocities witnessed or borne. Memories infect victims' sleep with horrific nightmares, destroy relationships, inhibit capacity to work or study, torment their emotions, shatter their faith, and mutilate hope. Trauma is extraordinary you see, not because it rarely happens, but because it swallows up and destroys all normal human ways of thinking and living.

There is a growing field of local and international Christian laborers eager to bring change and healing to traumatized people. However, local helpers frequently lack support from church leaders and have had little to no training in bringing together faith and the world of trauma. In addition, these lay helpers often report lack of training in the most basic helping skills, and desire to understand how better to help those traumatized after sexual violence. Some are tempted to attribute signs of posttraumatic stress disorder to evidence of demonic activity. Unfortunately, training and interventions provided by well-meaning international mental health professionals often fail to help due to lack of understanding of the local cultural context, existing power structures, and relationship systems. These two problems (absent local expertise, absent cultural competency within mental health professionals) place victims at risk of harm, either by dangerous interventions or by loss of hope when trauma symptoms remain.

What is needed is a model to provide bi-directional training, bringing together local caregivers and missionally-minded mental health professionals from around the world to learn how best to enter in and serve international victims of sex trafficking.

---

these individuals remains a significant challenge. Indeed, as the Scriptures say, "the dark places of the earth are full of the habitations of cruelty" (Psalm 74:20).

Training needs for local and international helpers

It isn't hard to sell most Christians on the need to serve trafficked persons with excellence. What can be hard is to help good-hearted helpers *understand what they need to know in order to provide that excellent care*. International helpers may have the financial means and some of the knowledge to help a woman like Sarah, however, they often lack deep understanding of culture (e.g., the meaning of relationships, faith, religious practices, gender, marriage, birth, death, grief, emotions, work, adulthood, family, suffering, healing, etc.) of the people they most want to help. For example, mental health professionals bringing a well-respected trauma counseling intervention to Kurdish Iraqis, discovered that existing local values did not support talk therapy, cross-gender discussions, or enable easy follow-up assessment (Kaysen, 2013). In addition, many humanitarians do not consider sustainability and exit plans until after already beginning interventions. Failures such as these may dis-enfranchise victims and provide local helpers with promises of skills, but without adequate support.

To rectify this problem, a new model of trauma recovery training is being developed at Biblical Theological Seminary (Greater Philadelphia, PA, USA, www.biblical.edu) to respond to the two identified problems: deficits in local and international helpers.[4] This model is based on several foundational assumptions. One, the need is global and requires many believers trained in trauma recovery to work across borders. Two, God has called his church to bring light and life to the suffering and oppressed in this world. Three, the church needs to be grounded in a theology of evil and suffering, and a theology of justice, along with knowledge of cross-cultural work. Four, a deeper grasp of the nature of trauma, its profound impact on human lives, and best practices is needed to care for traumatized individuals or communities. Five, the most effective international trauma recovery efforts utilize local ministries, qualified and gifted nationals, and support the work they are already doing so as to effectively come alongside and strengthen what is already occurring. It is far more effective to invest in training/mentoring people around the world who live in the same culture, speak the same language, and understand trafficking in their specific environment. Six, professional mental health practitioners and teachers need to learn from these gifted local caregivers in order to provide useful training in return.

The Global Trauma Recovery Institute (GTRI, www.globaltraumarecovery.org) at the seminary was established to train

4 See www.globaltraumarecovery.org/what-is-gtri-all-about/. GTRI is directed and led by the co-authors and supported by an initial grant from The American Bible Society. For more information about Dr. Monroe's work, see www.wisecounsel.wordpress.com. Information about Dr. Langberg's work and publications can be found at www.dianelangberg.com.

mental health professionals, pastors, lay caregivers, and NGO workers in the United States. The purpose is to (a) invest in local and international leaders who work with trauma and trafficking victims, and (b) encourage local/international learning and dialog. Training content includes the biological, psychological, spiritual, and relational impact of psychosocial trauma, theology of suffering and justice, ethics of helping, cultural competency skills, introductory and advanced listening skills, faith engagement, community-oriented mental health trauma interventions, and adult dialogue education practices. Pedagogical methods include lecture, discussions, readings, dialogue practice across cultures, and cross-cultural experiences. For example, participants discuss personal knowledge of trauma and intervention strategies within their respective communities so as to increase each other's knowledge base. In the most recent cohort, participants in Austria, Greece, Uganda, and the United States described the problem of trafficking in their community, current interventions, and ongoing care needs present.

In order to ensure adequate learning, mental health participants may choose to join in an international field experience led by GTRI staff and national trauma counselors where the focus is both to train local caregivers and to improve listening skills as they explore trauma impact and recovery efforts within a particular community and cultural context. These immersion experiences include intensive listening and study of the culture, as well as interacting with those at various ministries and agencies who are working with victims. The reader may note that immersion trips, as described above, focus more on the training of Western counselors than the training of local caregivers. It is our experience that more damage is done by well-intended outsiders than under-trained local caregivers. For example, Andrew Solomon (2008) noted the serious damage done by some mental health practitioners in Rwanda after the genocide. Local caregivers told him,

> We had a lot of trouble with western mental health workers who came here immediately after the genocide and we had to ask some of them to leave.... They came and their practice did not involve being outside in the sun where you begin to feel better. There was no music or drumming to get your blood flowing again. There was no sense that everyone had taken the day off so that the entire community could come together to try to lift you up and bring you back to joy. There was no acknowledgement of the depression as something invasive and external that could actually be cast out of you again. Instead they would take people one at a time into these dingy little rooms and have them sit around for an hour or so and talk about bad things that had happened to them. We had to get them to leave the country.

The listening done during immersion trips extends beyond personal stories to the study of local culture, norms, rituals, and traditions. Cultural competency includes grasping the geo-political and historical context, as well as the role outsiders have played in the region. For example, in situations like Rwanda, such listening is vital if the complexities of the current society and the lingering effects of genocide, as well as the failed response of the International community, are to be understood. Student engagement with these issues builds understanding for the context of suffering and the role of the church in the midst of it.

Response to training, ongoing needs

Thus far GTRI participants living outside the United States include those committed to caring for trafficked and abused people and who are eager for further education and skill acquisition. They understand how trafficking takes place in their own countries, where existing effective ministries are, and the current needs. At the end of the training, most report, "We are better equipped to do the work as nationals but we still want ways to bring deeper theological training and much more extensive trauma training to our colleagues and leaders." In one such illustration, a locally run Christian counselor association started this year in Rwanda after five years of joint trainings. The association intends to provide its own ongoing training, as well as offer training to incoming international helpers. While the goal of locally derived training remains, free resources, such as conference videos produced by The World Reformed Fellowship, exist as adjunct supports (see www.wrfnet.org/resources/media).[5]

Those participants from the United States include humanitarians and mental health professionals seeking advanced training in trauma recovery and in cross-cultural competency. They report that the program helps them expand cultural listening skills, practice bi-directional learning, and re-imagine their role as collaborative capacity-builders.[6] These participants also note the need for even more detailed trauma-informed interventions that can be used by local church leaders, as well as ongoing engagement with local bridge builders who can translate and explain local culture.

Conclusion

Returning to Sarah, we find her still on the street, but connected to Austrian believers encouraging her to accept their help to free her from bondage.

---

5 World Reformed Fellowship has adopted Human Trafficking and Gender Violence as one of its key initiatives.

6 Participant Heather Evans described her training this way, "Cross-cultural experience requires one who will humbly engage, listen and bear witness.... While I took this [training] because of my interest in trafficking worldwide, it has greatly impacted my work with trafficking survivors in my own backyard. Among many concepts, we learned the value of understanding the nature of trauma and what it looks like in various cultural contexts. We learned the importance of listening in trauma healing work. We learned the necessity of harnessing an individual or a group's capacities and resilience, rather than dwelling on weakness, problems and pathology" (personal communication, August 27, 2104).

While she values the listening ear and tangible gifts, she refuses to name her traffickers for fear of bringing curses upon her family. In addition, she has stolen items from those who sought to provide counsel. Those who listen to her story find improved patience with Sarah's ambivalence as they grow in awareness of the social and cultural complexities of Sarah's life. While maintaining the goal of rescue, her helpers recognize their work entails ongoing mercy ministry as well as educating fellow Austrians about the heart of God for the hurting, and about the demand for women like Sarah that keeps the steady flow of victims coming to their community.

There are many lessons learned from engaging in global trauma recovery especially in the arena of sex trafficking:

1. There is incomprehensible evil being relentlessly committed against vulnerable populations. In much of the Western world, our current levels of comfort and safety allow us to engage in complicity born of ignorance.
2. Because of demand and economic value, trafficking will never be voluntarily stopped. If it is to stop, it must *be* stopped, and those who follow Christ should be crying out against the evils perpetrated on those created in the image of their God.
3. The recovery from brutal violence, humiliation, and degradation cannot simply consist of rescue and education or job skills training. The wounds of trafficking are in the mind, heart, and soul, and they require understanding and specialized training.
4. There are many committed Christians around the globe involved in rescuing and caring for the victims of trafficking. They are asking for greater understanding of the Scriptures in the face of incredible evil and suffering, and ongoing training in trauma recovery interventions as they sacrificially care for these victims.
5. Working in partnership with these ministries and training others to do this as well, requires an understanding of the strengths in existing ministries so they can be nurtured, and a listening attitude so responses fit their true needs and they can be better equipped. The mentoring of workers and ministries globally must be done by not only by those trained in cross-cultural work, the knowledge of the psycho-social aspects of trauma, and the components of healing, but who also come with a spirit of humility and an eagerness to learn from others.
6. If the church fails to enter into ministry to those trafficked, the loss to humanity will be unspeakable. Girls, boys, and women will die or be so brutally treated that recovery becomes almost impossible. Precious people, designed by our God and meant to grow and gift the world with what he has given them, will be thrown to the trash heaps and we will be the poorer for it.
7. Work among the suffering is both incarnational and redemptive – certainly for the victims of sexual violence, but also for the church

herself. As she enters into the lives of ruined creatures, and with humility bows to the work of loving, strengthening, and calling others to light and life, she will find herself growing more and more into the likeness of the one who did exactly that for her.

8. *Trauma is indeed one of the primary mission fields of the 21st century*. Suffering makes people vulnerable and hungry for help. If the church will truly live out the goodness of our God in the dark places of the earth, she will find hearts open to his grace and mercy, and kindness in those who have never tasted such things. The glory of our God will begin to overshadow the habitations of cruelty.

For discussion

1. What social, political, historical or other factors have led to sex trafficking and trauma in your region?
2. How is suffering understood? How are psychological issues dealt with? How are emotions understood and experienced? And, what does healing look like in these areas?
3. What is the role of the church regarding life and health in your region?

Bibliography

Amnesty International. 2005. *Facts and Figures: Women and Violence*. http://www.amnesty.org.au/svaw/comments/2370/ (Accessed September 1, 2014)

Department of State. 2013. *Trafficking In Persons Report, June 2013*. http://www.state.gov/documents/organization/210737.pdf (Accessed September 1, 2014)

Kara, Siddarth. 2009. *Sex Trafficking: Inside the Business of Modern Day Slavery*. New York: Columbia University Press.

Kaysen, Debra, Kristen Lindgren, Goran A. Zangana, Laura Murray Sabir, Judy Bass & Paul Bolten. 2013. "Adapation of Cognitive Processing Therapy for Treatment of Torture Victims: Experience in Kurdistan, Iraq." *Psychological Trauma: Theory, Research, Practice, and Policy* 5: 184-192.

Solomon, Andrew. 2008. "Notes on an Exorcism." *The Moth: True Stories Told Live*. http://themoth.org/posts/stories/notes-on-an-exorcism (Accessed September 1, 2014)

The Economist. 2010. "Gendercide: The Worldwide War on Baby Girls". March 4. http://www.economist.com/world/international/displaystory.cfm?story_id=15636231 (Accessed September 1, 2014)

USA Today. 2012. "U.N.: 2.4 Million Human Trafficking Victims." April 4. http://usatoday30.usatoday.com/news/world/story/2012-04-03/human-trafficking-sex-UN/53982026/1 (Accessed September 1, 2014)

United Nations Office on Drugs and Crime (UNODC). 2012. *Global Report on Trafficking in Persons*. United Nations. http://www.unodc.org/documents/data-and-analysis/glotip/Trafficking_in_Persons_2012_web.pdf (Accessed September 1, 2014)

Vlachovd, Marie & Lea Biason, Eds. 2005. *Women in an Insecure World: Violence against Women Facts, Figures, and Analysis*. Geneva: Geneva Centre for the Democratic Control of Armed Forces. http://www.unicef.org/emerg/files/women_insecure_world.pdf (Accessed September 1, 2014).

36. MIGRATION, MATERIALISM AND BRAIN DRAIN: A CASE STUDY OF THE CHURCH IN GHANA AND MIGRATION

J. Kwabena Asamoah-Gyadu

Migration and world Christianity

Recently, Wesley Granberg-Michaelson noted that the world today is witnessing "a post-Western awakening of Christianity" with postcolonial societies of the non-Western Hemisphere "fashioning expressions of faith that can appropriately be called 'post-Western'" (2013, 3). Granberg-Michaelson's book is an important addition to a number of scholarly works that recognize that Christianity has virtually developed into a non-Western religion with a majority of those professing the faith now living in the Southern continents.[1] Christianity is not simply flourishing in numbers in the global South, but also non-Western Christians are keeping the faith alive in the former heartlands of the faith. Churches made up of African, Asian, and Latin American immigrants have been revitalizing the faith in the global North. In an early publication on this issue, Gerrie Ter Haar wrote that African church leaders in Europe today are convinced of Africa's mission to bring the gospel back to those who originally provided it. These immigrant church leaders consider that God has mandated them "to spread the good news among those who have gone astray" (Ter Haar 1998, 1-2).

Claudia Währisch-Oblau arrives at a similar conclusion as ter Haar's work, noting how migrant churches have caused a fundamental change in the make-up of North Atlantic Christianity (2009, 4). There are African churches in the diaspora made up of migrants with their roots in the historic mission denominations. However, the religious terrain in Africa has changed with the formation of contemporary Pentecostal/charismatic churches with their international aspirations and dominion theology.[2] Their other key features include an emphasis on spiritual gifts, dynamic and expressive contemporary worship forms, extensive use of modern media and preaching a message of prosperity that sees material things as important indices of God's favor. A number of these new initiatives have taken place in the diaspora where African immigrants, looking for places of spiritual empowerment and communal bonding, come to together in worship in which the African religious experience remains a cherished one.

---

1 See, for example, Adogame (2013).

2 See Asamoah-Gyadu (2013).

As a result, most of the African migrant churches are of the Pentecostal/charismatic stock with its emphasis on revivalist forms of worship, extensive and intensive prayer culture, and a certain interventionist and prosperity theology. Pentecostal/charismatic migrant churches insist on being seen as new mission churches. This is instructive, for as Währisch-Oblau explains, the designation underscores a certain theological self-definition that stresses an identity not related to the foreign nature of these Christian communities, but rather to the reason for their emergence. A number of these African migrant Christian communities – whether Pentecostal or not – claim a missionary calling to reverse Western secularism (Währisch-Oblau 2009, 35).

Migration, materialism and brain drain

African churches in the diaspora may be contributing to the revival of Christianity globally. However, there is also a relationship between migration as a means of prosperity and brain drain. It is not uncommon for African professionals who are Christians to migrate to Europe and other developed countries, believing the process to be a means of divine breakthrough in material terms. Given the levels of poverty, African immigrants contribute immensely to the upkeep of families in their home countries. Immigrants remit money for the payment of school and hospital fees and for keeping domestic economies running. Nevertheless, the massive African Christian presence in the West, leading to the sort of transformation of World Christianity that Granberg-Michaelson and others write about, has implications for the overall economic development of the continent. The brain drain is only one of several issues that arise from mission, migration, and materialism.

A number of the initial immigrant churches – from whichever tradition they come – were set up inadvertently. The migration of African citizens to other countries in search of work, to study, or simply to explore alternative contexts of settlement, is a perennial phenomenon. The military interventions in post-independence African politics led to persecution of political opponents. A number of wealthy individuals and their businesses and enterprises came under attack leading to economic collapse. People, particularly professionals, left their countries in frustration. In democratic Africa, what has taken people abroad include higher education and the search for better economic opportunities. Regardless of their reason for leaving the continent, the search for better economic fortunes, in particular, led to massive migrations of African intellectuals to the West, between 1970 and 1990. Statistics are difficult to come by, but it is generally known that against the backdrop of the economic difficulties of the country from the 1970s, a good number of those who left for further studies did not return. This has also been the period in which Pentecostal/charismatic Christianity with its dynamic spirituality has exploded in the African religious landscape. The rich and dynamic Christian traditions of the non-Western world means that African Christians who had migrated ,felt the spiritual hunger that had engulfed their host societies abroad due to the recession of Christian presence in those contexts.

The prosperity gospel, in particular, resonates very much with the economic reasons why people migrate. If historically evangelicalism warned against the dangers of material wealth and encouraged believers to store up their treasures in heaven, contemporary Pentecostals take a different attitude towards money and earthly goods. African Pentecostal/charismatic Christian culture shares the prosperity mindset of its North American word-of-faith versions. Nigerian pastor Frederick C. Price expresses the fundamental belief of this movement when he notes:

> Name it and claim it?! You better believe it! I am the name it and claim it man! Everything I have truly desired over the last 20 years (prior to the writing of this book) that I have truly desired, I have named it, claimed it, and I got it. So maybe it just works for me. May be I am God's special child! (Price 1992, 27).

Prosperity preachers like Price have had great influence in shaping contemporary Pentecostalism in Africa. The prosperity gospel, which is based on the name-and-claim-it religious philosophy described by Price above, promotes a theological worldview that resonates with African traditional ideas of salvation. Religion in Africa is very much a survival strategy that is supposed to be the source of power, protection, progress, success, and spiritual and material wellbeing. The power to bless and curse may be considered biblical, but are is very much a part of the African worldview.

According to Price people must experience what God says in his word by operating in the power of positive confession. He supports the prosperity gospel with Philippians 4:19 "And my God will fully satisfy every need of yours according to his riches in glory in Christ Jesus" (NRSV). There is a way in which we can put our needs and desires together, he comments:

> You cannot find where it specifically says that God will give you a Cadillac, Mercedes Benz, Rolls Royce or a Volkswagen. But it does say He will supply your need…The Rolls Royce was the best in my opinion. So, I believed God for a Rolls Royce and He gave me one…He gave it to me because I asked for it. CONFESSION WORKS! (Price 1992, 35).

This is what contemporary Pentecostals may refer to as divine breakthrough. It has implications for good health and physical vitality but also measured in terms of material acquisitions in life. When people are seeking better economic fortunes, this Christianity of positives and possibilities makes much sense in their aspirations. The emphasis on the relationship between material wealth and faith extends from positive confession to the faithful fulfillment of tithing obligations. Once a person believes God and fulfills his or her economic obligations to the church, success according to the prosperity gospel would be virtually guaranteed.

The relevance of this discussion to migration and brain drain lies in the fact, in most of Africa, international travel offers opportunities for material success and economic breakthroughs. The prayers for visas in charismatic churches today rank next only to healing. The churches are filled with professionals and unemployed graduates and other young people with great material aspirations in life and relocating to a Western country is one that is coveted in prayer. I have sat through prophetic meetings in which the charismatic leader has received visions of people breaking through by traveling to London, Hamburg, New York or some such location abroad. The prophecies were received with great enthusiasm as people responded: "I receive it; I receive it; I receive it." This is simply because within the contemporary Pentecostal mindset of divine prosperity, international travel as noted, is an important matter for prayer. If we consider the fact that the churches concerned are filled with young professionals and graduates, one can see why a number of African countries are losing their healthcare personnel, especially doctors and nurses, to Western countries.

The example of Lighthouse Chapel International

A number of charismatic churches in Ghana and other African contexts even hold annual "home-coming" summits that bring together members living abroad. The home coming seminars and revival meetings are indicative of how proud the churches are of these developments. A useful example of this is the Lighthouse Chapel International (LCI) led by Bishop Dr. Dag Heward-Mills. It is one of the most prominent charismatic churches in Ghana, with branches in many African countries, Europe, and also in the Americas. Heward-Mills is a trained medical doctor who, after his training in Ghana's University of Ghana Medical School, opted to start a Christian fellowship of medical professionals in the late 1980s that he then transformed into a charismatic church in 1991. LCI has attracted professionals – particularly doctors, architects, and lawyers – as pastors and that has helped the church recruit many such people into the church. The leaders of the international branches are made up almost exclusively of Ghanaian immigrants with professional backgrounds in those locations. The LCI branches in London, Geneva, Basel, Amsterdam, and Hamburg remain some of the largest and most vibrant African immigrant churches in Europe. The story is the same for several North American states in which they are present. In almost every case LCI branches are led by Ghanaian professionals who either trained abroad or left the shores of Ghana to study or look for better economic breakthroughs in the last two decades or less.

There are other reasons why charismatic churches like the LCI possess a special attraction for upwardly mobile young people. Living abroad can be a very precarious enterprise due to the constant tightening of immigration rules by Western governments. The creation of "Fortress Europe," as ter Haar likes to call it, through the tightening of immigration rules, has led to high rates of unemployment among Ghanaian immigrants and, as a result, for many of these immigrants "religion is an outstanding way of coping with their surroundings" (Ter Haar 1998, iv). Yet as the media constantly informs us, the ardent desire to migrate and the perilous journeys it occasions have not ceased. Hundreds of potential migrants risk their lives either by boat or through the Sahara in desperate attempts to reach Europe in search of a better life. Most of those involved in these risky endeavors belong to the lower social strata of African societies. Nevertheless their desperate attempts to travel say much about perceptions of the developed world as havens of divine breakthroughs and prosperity.

Missiological implications

There are several missiological implications, both for the churches in the non-West who are sending out diaspora peoples as well as for the diaspora peoples who are establishing new churches in the West. I will mention two key ones here.

1. Migration ethics and prosperity

Those who succeed to migrate, whether legally or illegally, quickly discover that finding jobs, proper resident papers or even reuniting with family are hurdles that may never be cleared. Churches of charismatic orientation possess an interventionist theology that provides the ritual contexts for dealing with existential problems. Thus in the African diaspora churches under study here, immigrants turn to these spiritual communities where they can find the religious contexts that provide the appropriate prayer and prophetic rituals to deal with their problems. Charismatic prophets, as discussed by Adam Mohr (2013) are invited from Ghana to Europe and North America to organize prayer services and revival meetings in immigrant churches. The focus of these religious activities tends to be the search for *edwuma* ("work"), *nkrataa* ("papers"), and *ebusua* ("family"). The situation of some immigrants can be difficult and heart breaking as many can live in the diaspora for up to two decades and more without the proper resident papers.

In many cases, Christian ethics and morality are compromised as people use false identities to secure jobs and engage in arranged marriages to those with the requisite papers to enable them regularize their own status. I have participated in immigrant churches in which notices have been given in Ghanaian languages to the effect that "a member of the congregation has papers for securing work" and members in need of such documents are invited to see a particular church elder for discussion. Even more disturbing is the situation of those who have high-end professional backgrounds in medicine, nursing, pharmacy, architecture, and law and who for lack of resident papers, have had to contend with undertaking menial jobs to survive. For many of the people in these sorts of situations, returning home is not an option as they may have been away so long without achieving the material success they desired. In most African contexts, returning home from sojourning abroad when you have not been able to secure landed property in particular, is considered a failure in life and to avoid the shame associated with it, many people simply refuse to return.

As a result, church leadership in Africa needs to prepare and educate its current and future diaspora people for more than divine breakthrough and prosperity. The African church needs to prepare them for possible hardships and difficulties, as well as help them develop a Christian ethic that does not allow for compromise. Furthermore, the African diaspora particularly must be made aware of their strategic importance in furthering the good news of the Kingdom of God among their own people, other diaspora peoples, as well as those peoples of their adopted countries. This strategic missional significance of their diasporic deployment must be given increased emphasis.

2. Immigrant Christianity and pastoral care

The main elements of immigrant Christianity, as described by Ter Haar (1998, 7), include a belief in the power of the Spirit, the concept of a church as constituted by the community of believers, the importance of worship as a form of celebration, the central role of the Bible, the emphasis on the concept of love, and the meaning which they ascribe to healing. The reference to "community of believers," "love," and "healing" are important ingredients of what I described earlier as the interventionist role that religion plays in the lives of African immigrants. Thus an important role played by Black immigrant churches in the lives of members and patrons is the spiritual and emotional support that is provided within the spiritually and physically precarious environment in which people find themselves. The environment is spiritually precarious first, because of secularization, but more importantly because of the worldview that evil powers are usually the cause of life's misfortunes. It is physically precarious because of the immigration problems that come with living abroad as undocumented migrants.

General Overseers, like Heward-Mills, and their representatives frequent their branches abroad to provide various forms of pastoral care for Ghanaian immigrants. The relationship is reciprocal because of the teaching that a person's success in life partly hinges on observing the rules of prosperity by "seed-sowing" in the life and ministry of the anointed of God. In my estimation, there is usually little or no attempt by the leadership of the churches to engage constructively with the socio-economic implications of migration, either for the migrants or the countries from which they have migrated. Living abroad has become such a prestigious endeavor that as we have noted, many professionals have preferred to work in fields that do not require their expertise rather than return home to help build their countries of origin.

As a result, the church in Africa needs to develop a theology of migration that demystifies living abroad as some sort of divine destiny, and yet ensures that Christians living abroad legitimately receive needed pastoral care so that they can put their gifts and graces at God's disposal for ministry. The hope of material prosperity may have worked for some immigrants. However for many others, their aspirations remain just that, hope, for which they continue to look up to God for some supernatural intervention so that his Kingdom, understood here in existential terms, might come upon his people.

For discussion

1. For churches that know or send workers into foreign lands, what can your church do to help develop a sound theology that will undergird the situations these workers will actually face in their new lands?
2. For churches that know or send workers into foreign lands, what can your church do to lower the financial expectations that church members might have in relationship to those overseas workers?
3. How might pastors help the members of their congregations become more missionally strategic?

Bibliography

Adogame, Afe. 2013. *The African Christian Diaspora: New Currents and Emerging Trends in World Christianity.* London: Bloomsbury.

Asamoah-Gyadu, J. Kwabena. 2013. Contemporary Pentecostal Christianity: Interpretations from an African Context. Oxford: Regnum.

Granberg-Michaelson, Wesley. 2013. *From Time Square to Timbuktu: The Post-Christian West Meets the Non-Western Church.* Grand Rapids: Wm. B. Eerdmans.

Mohr, Adam. 2013. *Enchanted Calvinism: Labor Migration, Afflicting Spirits, and Christian Therapy in the Presbyterian*

Church of Ghana. Rochester: University of Rochester Press.

Price, Frederick K.C. 1992. Name and Claim It! The Power of Positive Confession. Benin City, Nigeria: Marvelous Publications.

Ter Haar, Gerrie. 1998. *Halfway to Paradise: African Christians in Europe.* Cardiff: Cardiff Academic Press.

Währisch-Oblau, Claudia. 2009. *The Missionary Self-Perception of Pentecostal Charismatic Church Leaders from the Global South in Europe: Bringing Back the Gospel.* Leiden/Boston: E.J. Brill.

37. Transnationalism, Identity and Virtual Space: A Case Study of One Woman's Attempt to Negotiate Two Worlds

Trevor Castor

The story of Miriam

Miriam was born in a small mud house in Waziristan, in northwest Pakistan, April 10, 1990 – at least that's what her birth certificate says. In reality, she has no idea when her birthday is, or even what year she was born. Her birth certificate was forged in 2008 when she and her family came to the United States on asylum.

Prior to that historic moment, Miriam lived with her mother and three siblings in her Uncle's home while her father worked in the United States. Miriam's father was the sole provider (including extended family) in Waziristan as more than twenty people relied on his remittances for survival. He was not present for the births of his four children, recalls Miriam: "He was always working and never really spent that much time with us. Every year or two he would come and live with us. The longest he would stay would be for six months."

Life was difficult. Although her father was likely the wealthiest man in the village, his wife and children struggled. He frequently sent money, but they rarely saw the full amount, and Miriam remembers being frustrated with the process: "My father would send money to my mother, but there is no way a woman can go and get the money by herself. He would send 10,000 rupees and my mother would get like 2,000. For days we had nothing to eat." Miriam was ashamed of male relatives and therefore refused to tell her father how much they were siphoning off.

Then, after several years of living abroad, Miriam's father took an American wife. "It didn't really bother us that much because we were there and he was here and we wanted him to be happy because he didn't know anyone." Miriam's father and his new wife soon began preparations to bring his immediate family to the States. He would keep reminding the children he was doing the paperwork but they didn't take it seriously. She used to think, "Oh, he is saying that but we are never going to go there!" He wanted his children, particularly his daughters, to get a college education, something he knew would be impossible back home. The children recall numerous asylum interviews in Islamabad and returning home with little hope of joining their father. Then, in 2007 after what seemed like another pointless interview, Miriam heard these astonishing words: "Congratulations, you are going to the United States of America!"

According to Miriam, extended family members were quick to criticize, particularly her Uncle, with whom they lived:

> When these girls go to America they will change. The minute you go to America you forget about Islam and your culture. They will be doing things they shouldn't. They will change their clothes, and they will marry whoever they want. Now they are supposed to marry their cousins, after a few years they will be like 'no we don't want to marry them.' You won't pray anymore. You won't fast anymore. When you go there you will become right away like them, completely changed.

Despite her Uncle's opposition and warnings, four days after the final interview, Miriam and her family boarded a plane for New York. She recalled what should have been a celebration as a time of mixed emotions:

> You can't imagine living your whole life in a village, never being outside, never being around any man that you don't know, and then the next day we arrived. For the most part, I was scared. I was leaving my friends and my family. Coming out from the airplane, when I saw my father and his wife, I couldn't open my eyes, my tears were just running.

In less than a month, all of the children were enrolled in public school. In Waziristan, Miriam was in an all-girls' Islamic school and in her final semester with one month before graduation, when granted asylum. Since she didn't speak English, she was placed in the ninth grade in America, and as the only eighteen-year-old freshman, remembers feeling uncomfortable. Cultural differences, however, were far more overwhelming. "It was completely shocking for me! I've never seen people dress that way. Where I grew up, I wore a *burqa* and I was coming here with no *burqa*, sitting close to boys, seeing girls in shorts, and I thought 'that's not going to work for me' so for two years never talked to anyone."

Despite language barriers and cultural differences, Miriam graduated with honors. As a result she won a state scholarship and admittance into a state school. Yet, the slow green card process meant she had to pay out-of-state tuition and could not use the earned scholarship, making even Community College unaffordable. Additionally, the burden of caring for the entire extended family back in Pakistan was simply too much for Miriam's father to bear alone, and his dream of educated daughters was quickly fading.

Miriam, however, was determined to attend college and pursued part-time work in order to save for tuition. Her first job was at a *halal* grocery store, but soon her father advised her to quit. He feared someone from the local mosque might recognize her, and send word back to their village that she had a job. Eventually, she too realized that the dream of college would remain a dream: "One day my hope just died … I will always have this thing in my mind that I wish I went to school. I will regret that for all my life."

When college was no longer an option, Miriam did the unthinkable. She told her father she no longer wanted to marry her first cousin, the one promised to since birth. She had always been willing to marry him in order to preserve peace in the family, but since leaving home, discord with extended family escalated. Miriam feared they would use this as a way to control her family but was pleasantly surprised when her father said: "If you don't want to marry him, that's your life, you don't have to." After nullifying the engagement, her father was soon taken to court by his brother, ordered to pay money and distribute properties equally. Subsequently, he attempted to make an arrangement for his daughter with another Pashtun American immigrant. The terms of the engagement were quickly agreed upon and the wedding was set. Then, three days later, everything was abruptly called off. Through a mutual friend, Miriam's future father in-law heard about her nullified engagement back in Pakistan and was advised not to pursue the marriage because her former fiancé would likely seek revenge.

Miriam and her siblings have taken turns visiting throughout the year so she always has someone with her. Tomorrow, she leaves to join her mother and assist in arrangements for her brother's upcoming wedding. Her brother did not receive permission to travel so he will not even be present at the ceremony. In fact, there is little chance he will even meet his wife in the foreseeable future. For now, their relationship will be limited to the computer and telephone. This marriage is more about families [than, not then] two individuals. The brother's marriage ensures engagements for his sisters, and perhaps in six months Miriam too will return either engaged or married.

Missiological implications of Miriam's story

The story of Miriam has several missiological implications for those who are working with diaspora peoples. These three are the most significant:

Transnationalism

Miriam's story demonstrates how the perception of an immigrant uprooting herself from her homeland, family, culture, and learning a new language in order to make a new life in her country of settlement is no longer adequate (Basch, Schiller, Blanc-Szanton 1994). Transnationalism, or transnational migration "is the process by which immigrants forge and sustain simultaneous multi-stranded social relations that link together their societies of origin and settlement" (Schiller, Basch, and Blanc-Szanton 1995, 48). Immigrants today should be viewed in light of the fact that their "daily lives depend on multiple and constant interconnections across international borders and whose public identities are configured in relationship to more than one nation-state" (1995, 48). They often maintain extensive social networks in societies of origin and settlement, creating a "fluid continuum rather than a radical divide compartmentalizing life into two separated worlds" (Lima 2001, 910).

Miriam's transnational identity is indeed fluid – simultaneously grounded both in her society of settlement and her society of origin (Schiller, Basch, and Blanc-Szanton 1992). Regular interactions in both social fields produce "a bicultural or integrated identity: feeling that one is both part of an ethnic group and part of the larger society" (Phinney et al. 2001, 505). The context of Miriam's daily interactions with an extended Pakistani family is primarily online. Her transnational identity and the digital contexts in which it is maintained have significant missiological implications.

Identity formation

The concept of identity most often used in social anthropology is in reference to ethnic identity (Sokefield 1999). Certainly, Fredrik Barth's (1969) seminal work *Ethnic Groups and Boundaries* is largely responsible for this focus. Barth challenged "the simplistic view that geographical and social isolation have been the critical factors in sustaining cultural diversity" (1998, 9). He argued that "ethnic distinctions do not depend on an absence of social interaction and acceptance, but are quite to the contrary often the very foundations on which embracing social systems are built" (Barth 1998, 10). In other words, the interaction of ethnic groups will make distinct cultural forms or boundary markers more prominent. This perspective allows the individual or group to renegotiate and define the aspects of culture most significant in defining and maintaining ethnic identity. The primary difference between Barth's ethnic boundaries and the emergence of transnationalism is the latter focuses on the continued social interaction between societies of origin and settlement. Barth's primary point is on the distinct cultural features that display an ethnic boundary and thereby affirm a self-ascribed identity amidst diversity. In contrast, transnational practices of the 21st century demand that ethnic boundaries affirm a self-ascribed identity in both her society of settlement and origin simultaneously.

Miriam's transnational identity formation began as a child in Pakistan. Frequent phone interaction with her father in the United States was the impetus for renegotiating cultural practices in her village. For example, prior to attending an all-girls' Islamic school, she was one of a handful of girls to temporarily attend a boys' school. This was certainly not the cultural norm for a Pashtun girl; rather, it was the result of her father's transnational influence. Much like her father, she now maintains daily contact with extended family back in Pakistan and has influence in their daily lives and vice versa. In fact, her entire family has unofficially nominated her as a bridge builder between two often competing and conflicting cultures. Miriam is the one who best understands both languages and cultures and can skillfully navigate in both settings. She is responsible to integrate her family, ensuring they are capable of navigating in both worlds. Pointedly, she must demonstrate how to maintain ethnic and religious identity to skeptical Pakistani members.

Identity in virtual space

For Miriam, the Internet recently surpassed the telephone as the most effective tool in linking her worlds. International phone calls are expensive and the Internet is increasingly accessible for her Pakistani family. It is the "quintessential diasporic medium, ideally suited to allowing migrants in diverse locations to connect, share information, and analyses, and coordinate their activities" (Bernal 2006, 175). For much of the world, technology is quickly becoming the primary medium of communication in everyday life (Murthy 2012). This is especially true of immigrants, who like Miriam, often use virtual space to renegotiate identity (Brinkerhoff 2009, Alonso and Oiarzabal 2010). Miriam constantly uses social media, ethnic forums, and YouTube to reinforce her Pashtun identity. Digital transnational social space allows her to create a sense of belonging through daily virtual returns to her homeland. While the Internet is essentially de-territorialized and often disembodied, this is not the case for Miriam. Her virtual space is "anchored in offline contexts rather than as a self-contained, disembodied universe" (Van den Boss and Nell 2006, 216). In other words, Miriam uses this virtual space to re-territorialize her community by blending her two social fields (Bustamante 2010).

Miriam arrived in the United States knowing some Pakistani family members anticipated she would abandon her religion and culture. At times it seems she is trying to prove them wrong. Miriam spends a significant amount of time and energy reinforcing a Pashtun identity by watching YouTube videos of Pashtun weddings, parties, funerals, and music videos. She often reads literature posted in Pashtun websites and has found a new interest in Pashtun proverbs and folklore. In some ways, she is more Pashtun than ever and her Muslim faith is rooted back home. In fact, she has become more connected to the Imam and mosque life back in Pakistan since moving to America.

She uses social media (especially Facebook) to strengthen offline relationships back home, and assure them she and family members remain committed Pashtun Muslims. Since it is culturally taboo for her to have an online profile, Miriam uses her younger brother's account. All but four of her brother's eighty-eight Facebook friends are extended Pakistani family members. She often makes posts on his wall affirming his Pashtun identity and Islamic commitment. The truth is, her younger brother is more interested in basketball than being Pashtun or Muslim, for that matter. Miriam's Facebook posts are more of a socially-desirable identity than an actual one (Zhao et al. 2008). Hence, the greatest challenge of Miriam responding to the gospel is her desire to remain fully Pashtun and staunchly Muslim. Conversion to Christianity would mean a complete abandonment of family back home.

Concluding thoughts

It is not surprising that Miriam seems haunted by her Uncle's words before leaving Pakistan: "The minute you go to America you forget about Islam and your culture." She knows that her family back home is watching and waiting to see how America changes her. As Miriam anticipates leaving tomorrow for a six-month visit to Pakistan, she imagines what her extended family will ask her, "do you pray five times a day, do you guys fast, are they letting you guys [practice] Islam?"

Although transnationalism, in some ways, makes coming to faith more difficult for Miriam, there are certainly benefits. For example, she is unlikely to assimilate into an American-style Christianity, but rather a contextual one that allows her to retain Pashtun identity. Moreover, the life of transnationals is filled with constant challenges and stresses. They often feel as though they have their feet in two societies but do not fit in either. Yet this tension creates an openness to the Gospel. The other good news is that experience in renegotiating culture in building a bicultural identity for two conflicting societies has uniquely prepared her as an effective evangelist in transnational networks. Miriam's deepest desire is a place of belonging. How much sweeter is the hope of heavenly citizenship where Jesus has prepared a place for her, a place where she belongs (Phil. 3:20; John 14:2) and is "accepted in the beloved" (Eph. 1:6).

For discussion

1. How does the gospel become good news for Miriam in the midst of her transnational identity and the tension between holding on to her old culture while adapting to her new culture?
2. What role do generational differences play in the formation of transnational identities? How will Miriam's children address issues of their own religious and cultural identity?
3. Do missionaries need to reflect on their own transnational identities and how these might affect their cross-cultural ministry effectiveness?

Bibliography

Alonso, Andoni, and Pedro J. Oiarzabal, eds. 2010. *Diasporas in the New Media Age: Identity, Politics, and Community*. Nevada: University of Nevada Press.

Barth, Fredrik, ed. 1998. "Ethnic Groups and Boundaries: The Social Organization of Cultural Difference." Long Grove, IL: Waveland Press.

Basch, Linda, Nina Glick Schiller, and Christina Blanc-Szanton, eds. 1994. *Nations Unbound: Transnational Projects, Postcolonial Predicaments, and Deterritorialized Nation-States*. New York: Routledge.
Bernal, Victoria. 2006. "Diaspora, Cyberspace and Political Imagination: the Eritrean Diaspora Online." *Global Networks* 6(2):161-179.
Brinkerhoff, Jennifer. 2009. *Digital Diasporas: Identity and Transnational Engagement*. Cambridge: Cambridge University Press.
Bustamante, Javier. 2010. "Tidelike Diasporas in Brazil: From Slavery to Orkut." In *Diasporas in the New Media Age: Identity, Politics, and Community*, edited by Adoni Alonso and Pedro J. Oiarzabal, 170-189. Nevada: University of Nevada Press.
Lima, Fernando. 2001. "Transnational Families: Institutions of Transnational Social Space." In *New Transnational Social Spaces: International Migration and Transnational Companies in the Early Twenty-First Century*, edited by Ludger Pries, 77-93. New York: Routledge.
Murthy, Dhiraj. 2008. "Digital Ethnography: An Examination of the Use of New Technologies for Social Research." *Sociology* 42(5):837-855.
Phinney, Jean S., Gabriel Horenczyk, Karmela Liebkind, and Paul Vedder. 2001. "Ethnic Identity, Immigration, and Well-being: An Interactional Perspective." *Journal of Social Issues* 57(3):493-510.
Schiller, Nina, Linda Basch, and Cristina Blanc-Szanton. 1992. "Towards a Definition of Transnationalism." *Annals of the New York Academy of Sciences* 645(1):ix-xiv.
Schiller, Nina, Linda Basch, and Cristina Blanc-Szanton. 1995. "From Immigrant to Transmigrant: Theorizing Transnational Migration." *Anthropological Quarterly* 68(1):48-63.
Sökefeld, Martin.1999. "Debating Self, Identity, and Culture in Anthropology." *Current Anthropology* 40(4):417-448.
Van den Bos, Matthijs, and Liza Nell. 2006. "Territorial Bounds to Virtual Space: Transnational Online and Offline Networks of Iranian and Turkish–Kurdish Immigrants in the Netherlands." *Global Networks* 6(2):201-220.
Zhao, Shanyang, Sherri Grasmuck, and Jason Martin. 2008. "Identity Construction on Facebook: Digital Empowerment in Anchored Relationships." *Computers in Human Behavior* 24(5):1816-1836.

38. Holistic Care: A Case Study of Heart for Lebanon's Unique Role in the Syrian Refugee Crisis

Katie E. Horn and Camille E. Melki

Introduction

There are more refugees today in the world than ever before. They form a diaspora that needs more than a crisis response. Holistic ministries offer the broad base of support that uprooted people need in order to find stability for rebuilding their lives. The influx of Syrian refugees into Lebanon, has challenged evangelical communities to respond in a holistic way that gives attention to the whole being, including the spiritual, physical, intellectual, and psychological needs of the person. Led by the example of faith-based organizations like Heart for Lebanon, church communities who have responded holistically have not only faced their own prejudices, but also discovered a renewed sense of mission. This has brought healing for their own wounds, and it has served both the Syrian refugee and Lebanese communities.

Background of the Syrian conflict and Syrian refugee community in Lebanon

The Syrian Civil War began in March 2011 in Damascus and the southern city of Deraa. The unrest rapidly escalated into chaos, and Syria soon saw its first internally displaced persons.[1] By the end of 2012, there were more than 497,965 people who had fled Syria as refugees, and this number has rapidly grown. The UNHCR estimates as of September, 2014 the number of Syrian refugees has climbed to 3,010,835, which translates into 17% of the Syrian population who are living as refugees (UN Refugee Agency 2014). The refugees have fled into countries throughout the region including: Egypt (139,430), Iraq (215,303), Jordan (615,546), Turkey (840,217), and Lebanon (1,176,971).

With over a million refugees in Lebanon, one out of every four people in Lebanon today is a Syrian refugee[2]. The Lebanese population, including

1 By definition, an internally displaced person (IDP) is someone who flees within their own country, while a refugee is someone who crosses an international border in order to flee.

2 In August 2014, the UNHCR reported 1,176,971 Syrian refugees are now residing in Lebanon, representing 39% of the total Syrian refugee population.

evangelicals, has generally shown a negative attitude towards these Syrian refugees. Even the news has reported on the mistreatment and misconception of the Lebanese towards their new neighbors. In November 2013, the BBC interviewed one local Lebanese man who reported:

> Somehow I feel scared – because I have to watch for my phone, I have to watch for my wallet, I have to watch for my car. Until recently I started to lock my car from inside because you hear stuff, you hear people doing many bad things.

This view is far from the exception, and reports like these have shown the deeply rooted distrust of the Syrian refugee population by the Lebanese. The ongoing economic struggles in Lebanon, along with the long and tumultuous history of the recent Syrian occupation of Lebanon have led to these prejudices.[3] The Syrian army first entered Lebanese territory in 1975 following the eruption of Lebanese-Palestinian warfare that April, coupled with intense fighting between the Christian Maronites and the leftist National Movement coalition (Nisan 2000). Under the pretense of a feared Christian-Muslim partition of Lebanon, then-president Hafez al-Assad sent troops into northern Lebanon in late 1975; by the following year, the Syrians numbered 25,000. With the entrance of these soldiers, the idea of a separate and free Lebanon was threatened, and the start of a thirty-one year occupation established (Nisan 2000).

Part of this occupation was the immediate disarming of a number of Lebanese militias and the disintegration of the Lebanese army to a size of 3,000 troops–12% of the size of the occupying Syrian army.[4] This culminated in the bombardment of Christian East Beirut, resulting in the flight of 300,000 people as well as the execution of many Lebanese civilians. Car theft and arson were also widespread in the Christian areas of Lebanon and churches were bombed.

Some suggest that the occupation by Syria was responsible for the deaths of approximately 100,000 Lebanese and the emigration of around half a million individuals (Sakr 1999). The practice of kidnapping and arresting Lebanese citizens and the use of torture also played a role in the Syrian occupation; through the establishment of detention facilities in Tripoli, Beirut, and the Bekaa Valley, Syrian officials imprisoned any Lebanese citizen accused of political activities against Syria (Nisan 2000)[5].

Now, seven years since the end of the occupation, the Syrian Civil War stretches on and the number of refugees residing in Lebanon has grown. The Lebanese still feel their own pain and anger, which in turn breeds

---

3 The specific Syrian occupation of Lebanon in mind took place during the late 20th and early 21st centuries.

4 A large part of this reduction by the Syrian forces was targeting the Christian Lebanese Forces in particular.

5 It is important to note, also, that the Christian population had shrunken from around 50% to 30-40% as a result of forced emigration and death.

further discrimination and violence toward the current Syrian refugees. One example is the restriction of movement of Syrians, who commonly settle in the low-income areas such as the eastern Beirut suburb of Bourj Hammoud (al-Saadi 2014, 2). Surveys show that more than 90% of the Lebanese were supportive of night curfews and other restrictions of Syrian refugees (al-Saadi 2014, 3).

The prejudices have also developed into violence. In December 2013, Lebanese residents in the Bekaa Valley threatened a group of 400 refugees living nearby in tents. They burned down 100 tents, forcing the Syrians to flee again and to find new shelter (Al-Ahkbar English 2013). This is a small example of the tensions–mental, social, and physical–that exist between the local Lebanese and Syrian refugee communities.

Escaping the tension and diverting conflict, is often impossible due to the general lack of resources available, both financial and physical. The refugees are dispersed across the country, often according to their economic and social status. Families considered upper or middle class in Syria are residing in Beirut in average to above average housing and are able to take care of their basic needs. Lower class families are residing in dilapidated housing in Beirut, among the minority groups in the South and the central cities of Anjar and Zahle in the Bekaa Valley, or among the tent communities on the outskirts of Lebanon's boarder with Syria in the Bekaa Valley[6]. Those affected by the conflict with the means to seek asylum have already done so, while countless others lack this option (*Aid & Asylum Map*, Migration Policy Centre).

Summary of the holistic care among refugees

The holistic approach to ministry highlighted here was born out of a troubled background and it was initially implemented by a number of faith-based NGOs in Lebanon. While these organizations were on the front lines from the start of the conflict, the local churches at first removed themselves entirely from the equation. Like much of the Lebanese population at the time, the evangelical community was rife with discrimination towards the Syrian refugee population. This prejudice between the two communities, made outreach from the church out of the question, and the role of the church as a helping hand of Christ's love, impossible.

In holding onto these prejudices, churches initially missed a vital opportunity to answer one of God's major callings; "Learn to do good, seek justice, correct oppression, bring justice to the fatherless, plead the widow's

6 In general, the Muslim Syrian refugees are residing in the tent communities as they occupied the rural class in Syria, while the Christian Syrian refugees of these classes are residing among the minority groups and in poor housing in Beirut. It is important to note that many of these rural farmers also resided in tent-like settlements in Syria, but the conditions they now face in Lebanon are much worse and exacerbated by general struggle to support themselves financially.

case" (Isaiah 1:17). Similarly, Jesus' work was primarily done on the outskirts of society with those least regarded by society. For the evangelical community, this certainly described the Syrian refugee population.

Slowly the evangelical community in Lebanon began to confront their long-held prejudice and anger. The holistic care brought by Heart for Lebanon (H4L) facilitated this process. Its holistic ministry brought hope by creating a basis for healing wounds and building relationships. The ministry approach has been driven by the compassionate heart of Jesus Christ, to reach the lost and broken, advance peace, justice and equality, and to empower the marginalized and rejected. The vision is to see lives changed and communities transformed by the power and grace of God. The concern was not only for the physical needs brought on by the refugee crisis, but also for the intellectual, psychological, and spiritual issues as well. Slowly this approach began to incorporate and affect local churches as well as the Lebanese community as a whole.

The holistic ministry among the Syrian refugees has addressed the recovery needs in four ways. Physically, the care brings important food and hygiene items. Spiritually, it has offered bible programs geared for men, women, and children. Intellectually, there are informal opportunities for basic education in Arabic, Math, English, and character development. Finally, psychologically and socially, local church members and staff build relationships with the refugees through visits and prayers. This approach ministers along the entire continuum of recovery. It works closely with a bouquet of organizations and service providers to bring stability and it takes steps toward recovery, effecting not only refugees, but also local churches and communities.

Missiological effects of holistic ministry among the Diaspora

There have been two important results of holistic ministry among the Syrian refugees. First, church involvement in caring for the refugees has helped to reduce and even dismantle discrimination within the evangelical churches and the surrounding Lebanese community. In joining the work already underway, the local church became fully engaged with each individual, from delivering monthly food portions to inviting them to spiritual programs geared toward the entire family.

One local church that partners with H4L to reach Syrian refugees in their community has been an outstanding example of this.[7] As the refugee crisis exploded in Lebanon and it became clear that there was no visible end in sight, many people in Lebanon lost their desire to help and the clash between the two cultures became devastatingly apparent. For many of the church members, it was an overwhelming struggle to live beside a

7 To protect the identity of any congregation members (including Syrian refugee members) the name of this church is withheld from this case study.

predominately Sunni Muslim community with the stark contrast in hygiene, appearance, and behavior. The historical tension seemed too much to overcome.

The occupation of Syrian troops was a painful memory for those with firsthand experience. The Syrian soilders robbed shops and homes, and they restricted the Lebanese in their own country. There were countless embarrassing, hurtful, and physically traumatizing events that sowed mistrust and prejudice, ultimately creating a blockade of unforgiving bitterness and discrimination. The Lebanese easily associated the incoming Syrian refugees with the Syrian soldiers of their memories. There were countless reasons for churches not to get involved, claiming they first needed to help the Lebanese at-risk in their own community. These excuses became a façade to avoid facing the true feelings of anger, resentment, and bitterness.

The fear and rejection changed, however, when the church began working alongside others in holistic ministry. The food deliveries and regular visits between leaders and families began to break through the walls. Relationships grew between church members and refugees. Many of the refugees have even come to know Christ as their savior and a number have been baptized and are now leaders themselves, teaching and leading their own group within the church community (Malky, Interview).

Jesus calls his disciples, to engage as an extension of the church in God's mission plan for the *whole* world (Coleman 1999, 122-125). Through holistic engagement, the groundwork for reconciliation was laid as God transformed former enemies and the hearts of all those involved. The local church experienced closure and forgiveness for those who had wronged them, seeing them not as oppressors but as fellow humans and victims of the conflict.

The second result to note is the increased recognition of God's missional commands. The success of holistic ministry inspired the evangelical community to continue reaching out to others. "You are the light of the world. A city set on a hill cannot be hidden. Nor do people light a lamp and put it under a basket, but on a stand, and it gives light to all in the house. In the same way, let your light shine before others, so that they may see our good works and give glory to your Father who is in heaven" (Matt. 5:14). The local church experienced the truth of Jesus' words. Likewise, the broader Lebanese community recognized the change of heart and the wider service.

The Lebanese community watched with curiosity and a number of local Lebanese started coming to church. The love of God began to take root in their hearts as well, causing some of these also to turn away from discrimination and to turn their minds and hearts instead towards the salvation of Jesus Christ. Forsaking their pride and following Jesus to serve the community and people that they previously condemned, the evangelical church began serving the marginalized and broken.

Conclusion

Through holistic ministry, some local churches in Lebanon have seen themselves as the hands and feet of Jesus among the Syrian diaspora. Just as Jesus walked among strangers and prisoners and even saw himself as one of them, so too have these local churches seen themselves in God's missional plan. Seeing ourselves in Christ and Christ in us is the key to ministry that transforms and rebuilds.

For discussion

1. Why is the social, political, and historical background important for holistic ministry among diaspora groups?
2. Is there a community around you that you have intentionally or unintentionally not reached out to? What steps could you take to develop a holistic ministry?
3. What barriers do you or your church face as you try to develop a holistic approach to ministry?

Bibliography

Al-Saadi, Yazan. "The Diversion Strategy: Lebanese racism, classism, and the refugees". *Al-Akhbar English*, 10 June 2014.

Coleman, Robert. 1999. "The Master's Plan". *Perspectives: On the World of Christian Movement* 3:122-125.

39. Overcoming Destitution in Diaspora Ministry: A Case Study of *There is Hope*

David Aeilts

There is Hope – Malawi

There is Hope – Malawi has been serving individuals and communities in and around the Dzaleka Refugee Camp in Malawi, Africa since 2006. This locally based, Christian NGO complements the United Nations' mandate to shelter and provide for displaced people. The NGO offers hope beyond subsistence to many of the 19,000 refugees and asylum seekers from Rwanda, Burundi, and the Democratic Republic of Congo who reside in this camp operated under the United Nations High Commissioner for Refugees (UNHCR).[1] (UNHCR in Malawi, 2014, 1-2) In addition to working with individual refugees, **There is Hope** seeks to partner with some 50 refugee churches within Dzaleka, to improve the lives and prospects of people inside and outside the camp's walls. (Magambi Interviews, 2013)

Since its formation in 1950, the UNHCR and its partners have stood in the gap, providing for the protection and the daily needs[2] of people in danger of perishing – first in Europe (following World War II) and today worldwide. (UNHCR Website – About Us) There are important things, however, that an institution like the UNHCR does not claim to provide and for which local, faith-based organizations, like the local church and **There is Hope – Malawi,** are eminently qualified and resourced to provide refugees. These things include appealing to the refugee's faith as a source of spiritual sustenance, and helping the refugee confidently chart a personal future beyond the camp's walls.

António Guterres, the U.N. High Commissioner for Refugees, contends that faith-based organizations are an integral component to refugees' surviving long-term as well as thriving. "For the vast majority of uprooted people, there are few things as powerful as their faith in helping them cope

1 A handful of Somali and Ethiopian refugees and asylum seekers also reside in Dzaleka Refugee Camp located about 45 minutes north and west of Malawi's capital city, Lilongwe. Some Dzaleka residents include children and grandchildren of people who fled conflicts dating back to the 1970s and who lived in other refugee camps before moving to Malawi in search of better opportunities.

2 Daily needs of displaced people include providing physical protection, food and housing, medical care, legal aid, and basic education. These things the UNHCR and its partners do well.

with fear, loss, separation and destitution," says Guterres, adding. "Faith is also central to hope and resilience."[3] (Guterres, 2012)

Hope and resilience are crucial since the durable solutions the world offers refugees are not a quick fix by any stretch of the imagination and millions languish for years in temporary havens like Dzaleka. [4] (Magambi Interviews, 2013)

Rather than give physical shelter and food to refugees and asylum seekers, a role the UNHCR and its partners already fulfill, **There is Hope – Malawi** works with refugees and churches within the Dzaleka Refugee Camp, as well as vulnerable people outside the camp, to help them rise above difficult circumstances by fully utilizing their potential. The goal of **There is Hope** is that these individuals would become self-sufficient and make a positive contribution to society, whether they leave camp or remain.

Beyond what the UNHCR contends is the integral role faith-based organizations must play in the long-term success of displaced persons. **There is Hope** possesses another unique qualification for its mission. The organization was founded in 2006 by a refugee who continues to lead it to this day. A displaced person for 27 of his 34 years, Innocent Magambi knows the cycle of poverty, corruption, and oppression that keep East African refugees down rather than elevating these resilient, resourceful people. While he is no longer considered a refugee, Innocent has a vantage point from which to understand a displaced person's long-term challenges – one that few leaders of NGOs can claim. (Magambi Interviews, 2013)

In this case study, we will explore how a refugee who was destitute and without the apparent support network available to a recognized citizen of any country, would or could begin a refugee ministry in his host country. We'll also consider the unique position of this ministry to promote the long-term welfare of displaced people.

The beginning

Innocent Magambi was a refugee at birth. Born to Burundian parents who fled their nation's 1972 tribal killings and settled in Zaire (now D.R.

---

3 Forty-nine percent of migrants (those who have lived outside of their home country for more than a year) identify as Christians and 27% identify as Muslim, hence the value of faith based organizations to the world's refugee crisis. (Heneghan, 2012)

4 The UNHCR offers three durable solutions for displaced people – voluntary repatriation, local integration and resettlement. (UNHCR Framework, 2003, 5-6) In many countries from which people have fled, conflict continues so repatriation is not an option. 86% of the world's refugees are hosted in developing nations, so local integration is not practical because of the economic burden it would impose. Furthermore, less than 1% of the world's refugees were resettled to developed nations in the most recent year. (IAFR Website, 2014, Ministry-Resources/Handouts)

Congo), this child-without-a-country acquired his name early in life as the "innocent" victim of war, of his parents' eventual divorce, and of maltreatment toward refugees. Over his first 27 years, Innocent lived in five refugee camps or settlements in four countries – Zaire, Zambia, Tanzania, and Malawi. He faced abandonment by his mother and later by his father, fled for his life twice, and was frequently robbed, swindled, and marginalized by his fellow refugees and by citizens of his host countries.[5] (Magambi Interviews, 2013) Nevertheless, because other people cared for him and because of a personal determination to learn and improve his personal value, Innocent not only survived these insults – he thrived.

Fleeing civil war in Zaire where he spent his childhood, 16-year–old Innocent journeyed first to Tanzania and then to the Meheba Refugee Settlement in Zambia where he spent a lonely year not knowing if his family or anyone else that he knew had survived the fighting. Still he drew comfort, even in his darkest days, from the faith instilled in him as a boy and from the fellowship of believers. (Magambi, 2014, *There is Hope,* chap 4)

In 1997, a local radio station broadcast to the refugees in Meheba the disheartening news that Zaire's capital city, Kinshasa, had been captured by the rebels. Innocent, along with other Congolese/Burundian refugees, experienced an overwhelming sense of loss and despair. Would he ever again return to the country of his birth or even to his family's beloved Burundi? The following Sunday, Innocent's church sang songs of surrender to God, with lyrics such as "God knows all my fears, all my tears. He sees everywhere. He is omnipotent." Innocent called that service "vital" because it presented another view of the refugee's situation: that God is aware of it and is still able to bring a hope and a way out. "It was an injection of hope and comfort in a very distressing time," Innocent commented later. "If the church had not been there, there would have been total hopelessness and complete misbehavior that affects those who feel like life does not matter." (Magambi Interviews, 2013)

The son of an entrepreneur, Innocent also took the opportunity, while living in Meheba, to hone his business skills and learn English. Both would serve him well in the future. At 17, he moved to a refugee camp in Tanzania and reunited with family and friends. Their encouragement and the mentoring he received as a result of his affiliation with the Free Methodist Church prepared Innocent for life. Still, Innocent would not have achieved the level of growth he did without personally taking the initiative to lead his fellow students at a crucial juncture in their final studies in secondary school. (Magambi, 2015, *Refugee for Life,* chaps 4-5)

---

5 The following facts about the early life of Innocent Magambi, including quotations, were gathered in a series of interviews conducted by this author, beginning in November 2013. I conducted these interviews in preparation for the co-writing of Innocent Magambi's memoir, Refugee for Life.

This duet between outside help and encouragement, and personal initiative repeats itself throughout Innocent's story. He talks freely of these two factors as critical to his forward momentum growing up as a refugee.

"As my brother Hari enfolded me in his strong arms, I reflected on the struggle I endured alone in Zambia," said Innocent of his arrival in Tanzania and his reunion with his family. "At last I felt secure." **That's outside help and encouragement.** (Magambi, 2015, *Refugee for Life*, chap 5)

Of his decision to resume his quest for his secondary certificate, he declares a few pages later:

> All of my dreams and future prospects depended on the level of education I could attain. I was determined to spend as much time and attention as possible on school matters, so that the goals I had for my life would have a chance of becoming reality." **That's personal initiative.** (Magambi, 2015, *Refugee for Life,* chap 5)

Having earned his secondary school certificate, Innocent fled discord and violence once again, this time within the Burundian refugee community. He traveled to Malawi to live in the Dzaleka refugee camp. Again, through a combination of compassion and initiative, he flourished. From an unlikely source, Innocent received funding for a college education, but he had to earn his degree. A call came for him to help people who shared his experiences as a refugee, and he had to answer it. (Magambi, 2015, *Refugee for Life,* chaps 7-8)

Finally, Innocent took the initiative to return to Burundi, at his own expense and without invitation from the government, to apply for a passport. On July 13, 2007 at the age of 27, Innocent held in his hand his first passport which declared to the world his Burundian citizenship. He was no longer a refugee. *(Magambi Interviews, Nov. 2013-present)*

The call

Growing up, Innocent at various times dreamed of becoming a musician[6], a journalist, a lawyer or a legislator with the goal of changing the politics of his beloved Burundi for the better. He even dreamed of one day standing for election to the Presidency of Burundi. It is fair, then, to ask what compelled Innocent to found and lead an NGO dedicated to reaching back into the last refugee camp in which he resided to give hope and a hand-up to those he left behind.

Priorities changed, according to Innocent, during his first semester in college. "While attending a class," he states, "God put a very clear and strong sense in my heart that I was here to acquire the tools that would eventually help people living in refugee camps." A refugee from his birth and still living outside his beloved Burundi, Innocent believes God was

---

6 Innocent Magambi is an accomplished singer/songwriter.

preparing him to deliver a message of hope to refugees from many people groups. (Magambi Interviews, 2013)

The message

Clearly expressed in the name of the organization Innocent founded, this message is a combination of compassion and encouragement to take personal initiative. The two-part message is "you are not alone" and "you are the solution."

It's a message reinforced time and again in the life of this native Burundian as he experienced both the comfort of those who loved him and the positive results of taking the initiative to grow and improve his circumstances. Even at his lowest point emotionally, separated from family in the Zambian refugee camp and failing in business, God provided Innocent assurance through His Word (in song) that the young man was not alone. God also assured Innocent, through his deliverance from embezzlement and outright thievery that He (God) would bless Innocent as Innocent followed Him. (Magambi, 2015, *Refugee for Life,* chaps 4-5)

The unique mission

There is Hope is uniquely equipped to deliver this message of hope because its founder has walked in the shoes of the men, women, and children to whom the local NGO directs its services – the displaced people of Eastern Africa. It is also perfectly positioned to deliver this message because its emphasis is not on providing for the daily needs of the refugees (that is the purview of the UNHCR and its partner agencies) but rather to walk alongside all who will to envision a future beyond their present circumstances.

Refugees play the most important part in fulfilling their own desires and hopes for the future, according to Innocent. "Those who sit on their hands, waiting to go back to their old life are the unhappiest," he observes. "Those who take risks like furthering their education or starting a new career while in the U.N. camp are the ones who will make it on the inside and on the outside." (Magambi Interviews, 2013)

There is Hope lives out its unique mission in the five key areas of focus discussed below (TIH Staff, 2013):

1. **Partnering with refugee congregations within and outside Dzaleka. There is Hope** walks alongside the church in exile to help it engage in sound teaching of God's Word, to support small-scale projects which benefit members and their communities, and to train future Christian leaders. Twenty-five young men and women (all refugees) recently graduated from a one-year post-secondary Bible education course sponsored by a refugee congregation. **There is**

Hope supported part of the course-work and the NGO's staff served as adjunct professors.

2. **Offering refugee scholarships for University education.** Studies beyond the secondary school certificate Dzaleka offers can give refugees access to better employment opportunities, allow them to provide for their extended families, and be a positive role model for generations to come. Since beginning its scholarship program five years ago, **There is Hope** has sponsored 18 students for higher education in Malawi. Many of these students have completed studies and have achieved diplomas and/or degrees in Nursing, IT, Business Management, Community Development and other areas.
3. **Helping develop and establish income-generating activities.** This initiative focuses on, but is not limited to, vulnerable women. The vast majority of people residing in Dzaleka have skills required to be financially independent, but lack starting capital and a little encouragement. **There is Hope** supports small groups setting up and building their individual businesses. Success stories include greeting card sales, chicken rearing, tailoring shops and marketing vegetables or clothes. Another example: an out-of-work Congolese doctor who is also a refugee recently received a loan from **There is Hope** to sustain him and his family while he finished a six-month unpaid orientation in Malawi's health system. He's found a job as a doctor in a rural hospital and has paid back his loan in full.
4. **Connecting with refugee prisoners.** Refugees held in Malawi prisons either awaiting trial or convicted for crimes lack the support network of family and friends available to citizens. **There is Hope's** objectives in this area have been to break their isolation and to meet some of their basic needs by monthly distributions of food and toiletries, spiritual and emotional guidance, assistance with re-integration to the refugee community when released, and small business loans to released refugee prisoners.
5. **Fostering the artistic and creative talents of the refugees. There is Hope** aims to provide refugees with the media and opportunities they need to express their artistic skills in music, dance, poetry, drawing, painting and other creative forms. Case in point, a refugee group called the Amahoro Burundian Drummers recently performed for the British Counsel, the Goethe Institute in Lilongwe, and at a national event before the president of Malawi. The Amahoro Burundian Drummers were sponsored by **There is Hope.**

Future initiatives of **There is Hope** include partnering with the government of Malawi to invest in Early Childhood Development Centers in the communities outside Dzaleka's walls.[7] (TIH Staff, 2013, 13)

---

7 An overlooked reality of the worldwide refugee crisis is the impact refugee camps have on the local population because of land usage, environmental destruction and

In all five areas of its focus and in everything it does, **There is Hope – Malawi** delivers the truth stated boldly in the organization's name, along with its two-part message:

1. **You are not alone.** We are standing with you. While **There is Hope** serves refugees regardless of their religious affiliation, this is especially meaningful to the Christian believer whose God has said, "Never will I leave you; never will I forsake you." (Hebrews 13:5 NIV)
2. **You are the solution.** Your personal initiative, as you apply to it to your present circumstances and to the circumstances of those around you, can result in positive change. For the many refugees who profess belief in Christ, this message carries special significance, because the Apostle Paul stated, "I can do all things through Christ who strengthens me." (Phil. 4:13 NKJV)

The take-away

The brief history of **There is Hope – Malawi** suggests that perhaps the person best positioned to start an organization dedicated to helping refugees, asylum seekers, and vulnerable people rise above their difficult circumstances is someone who has experienced those circumstances – a refugee himself. Support of **There is Hope** by hundreds of individuals and organizations across Europe and the U.S. also suggests this idea has traction.

Drawing from his failures and successes over 27 years in East Africa's refugee camps, Innocent Magambe founded an organization in 2006 that embodies the truth that there is hope – a truth desperately needed by every displaced person once their daily needs are met.

This hope stems from two important principles learned by Innocent and communicated by **There is Hope** to every refugee, asylum seeker or impoverished Malawian with whom it works: 1) You are not alone, and 2) you are the solution.

The rise of this local NGO comes at a time when the UNHCR, which provides support to most East African camps, has recognized the importance of organizations like **There is Hope** to the long-term success of displaced persons. "I see faith-based organizations, and in particular local religious communities, as having great potential to more effectively contribute to the achievement of durable solutions," said António Guterres. "The search for lasting solutions for refugees remains one of the greatest protection challenges we are faced with…" (Guterres, 2012)

---

various social interactions. In Malawi, residents of the area surrounding the Dzaleka Refugee Camp are underserved in terms of aid and development, education, skills training, access to water and other important technology for sustainable farming practices.

Though eight years young, **There is Hope – Malawi** has accumulated a proven track record of success in walking alongside refugees and providing them with the wherewithal to rise above their challenges.

For discussion

1. How does an organization, like **There is Hope,** address the long-term recovery challenges of displaced people and what are some of the barriers to overcome?
2. Why is the two part message, "You are not alone" and "You are the solution" important for refugees and local communities alike?
3. How do we nurture a healthy relationship between entitlement and individual initiative among forcibly displaced people?

Bibliography

Guterres, Antonio. "Opening remarks to the High Commissioners Dialogue on Protection Challenges – Theme: Faith and Protection" (Dec. 12, 2012). http://www.unhcr.org/pages/501a39ce6.html (accessed Aug. 25, 2014).

Heneghan.Tom. "Far more Christian than Muslim migrants worldwide" (March 8, 2012). http://www.reuters.com/article/2012/03/08/us-religion-migration-idUSBRE82716420120308 (accessed August 25, 2014).

International Association for Refugees (IAFR) Website. http://www.iafr.org.

Magambi, Innocent; Aeilts, David. *Refugee for Life* (Minneapolis, MN: International Association for Refugees, 2015).

Magambi, Innocent. Various interviews conducted in person and by e-mail in preparation for writing *Refugee for Lie*, starting Nov. 2013 and continuing to the present.

There is Hope – Malawi Web site. http://www.thereishopemalawi.com.

"UNHCR Operation in Malawi: Fact Sheet" (May 31. 2014). http://www.unhcr.org/pages/49e4856b6.html (accessed Aug. 23, 2014).

TIH Staff. *There is Hope: The First Seven Years*. Lilongwe, Malawi: (unpublished magazine, August 2013).

"UNHCR Framework for Durable Solutions for Refugees and Persons of Concern" (2013). http://www.unhcr.org/3f1408764.html (accessed Aug. 25, 2014).

UNHCR Web site –About Us. http://www.unhcr.org/pages/49c3646c2.html (accessed Aug. 25, 2015).

40. Taking Care of the Flock: A Case Study of the Role of the Local Church in Sending and Caring for Overseas Filipino Workers

Gerardo B. Lisbe, Jr.

Angel's husband Ryan[1] was already an Overseas Filipino Worker (OFW) before they were married. She sought to convince him to find work in their city in the Philippines to be close to her, but Ryan complained that he had difficulty finding a job locally. As a former OFW used to a fixed monthly income, within a few months of their wedding Ryan felt the angst of being jobless. After twenty months of searching for employment, Ryan applied for work abroad and found a position as a hospital maintenance employee in Jeddah, Saudi Arabia. At the same time Angel continued to pray and hope her husband would find a good-paying job in the Philippines.

Ryan did not consult any of their church leaders nor ask others for advice before making the decision to work abroad. He made the decision and Angel reluctantly submitted. The family benefited financially, and they were able to invest in parcels of land in their home town and other nearby places. Since they did not yet have children, they were also able to save some money and help other family members.

However when Angel reflected on the negative effects of Ryan's overseas job, she often felt incomplete as a wife. She missed him dearly, especially his companionship. She longed for her husband to be physically present – a husband to lean on in times of difficulties and great struggles. She never wanted this long separation. Increasing her emotional pain was the absence of other family members and close friends who could understand and help bear her frustrations and sorrows.

To help strengthen their relationship despite the distance, they communicated daily through the internet using the SKYPE program. Both of them found this regular communication helpful in avoiding sexual temptation, especially Ryan. Ryan revealed to Angel that his life in Jeddah was generally boring. His day usually revolved around home and work, and most of the time he was alone in his apartment because his companions had a different work schedule. His normal graveyard shift often contributed to the tiredness and boredom he felt which served to increase his vulnerability to sexual temptations. Even though Angel was glad for her husband's willingness to confide his struggles, it increased her fear that Ryan might

1 Their real names are withheld due to a confidentiality agreement. The author of this article did an in-depth interview with Angel on January 6, 2014.

give in to sexual temptations, especially after he communicated that some of his married OFW companions were in adulterous relationships.

Angel's response was to be even more faithful in prayer for him and to stay in constant communication with him. Even when she felt exhausted after a whole day's work, every night she forced herself to stay awake from 11:00 p.m. until 3:00 a.m. in order to talk with him and encourage him over the internet. Many times though she fell asleep while chatting with her husband.

In spite of their efforts to stay connected there came a day when Ryan suspected Angel was having an affair with another man. In his loneliness, he reasoned that her employment as a church worker required her to be with people – both male and female – while doing ministry, which gave her opportunity to be unfaithful. His suspicions grew when he saw pictures of Angel on Facebook with men that he did not recognize. For Angel, Ryan's show of distrust was the most painful aspect of their separation. She knew in her heart how very much she had remained committed and loyal to him despite the difficult loneliness of her situation. She felt that nothing could be worse than the emotional pain of being suspected and accused of having an affair.

Angel also worried about the negative effects of Ryan's overseas deployment on his spiritual life. She could sense that her husband was not growing in the Lord. For a while Ryan attended a Filipino church in Jeddah but stopped going after the adulterous relationship of the pastor's wife was discovered. His disappointment with the church led him to suspect the church was mostly interested in his financial support.

Important characteristics of Ryan and Angel's experience

It is important to note that Ryan and Angel's experience is not exceptional. They represent thousands, if not millions, of couples (Christian and non-Christian alike) in the Philippines who go through similar challenges and experiences on a daily basis due to their unique position as OFW couples and families. Putting children into the picture makes matters even more complex.

Studies on the OFW phenomenon reveal that a high percentage of OFW couples experience some form of dysfunction in their relationships (Human Development 2009, 72; Santamaria 1992, 71). In the case of Ryan and Angel, both husband and wife experienced the pain of prolonged separation. Angel felt incomplete as a wife since her husband was not with her most of the time. Angel's fear that Ryan might be tempted sexually was reasonable considering his circumstances. Ryan acknowledged the reality of sexual temptations while away from his wife and his feeling of distrust towards Angel may have resulted from a psychological projection in attributing to his wife his own emotional state. These experiences created an environment of distrust and feelings of betrayal which greatly increased the emotional pain of separation.

Implications of Ryan and Angel's story for Diaspora missions

There are important implications of Ryan and Angel's story for diaspora missions. The potential of tent-making missions of Christian OFWs throughout the world is immense and should be promoted by the evangelical churches of the Philippines. This potential was recognized at a Lausanne Philippines Congress held in Makati City in 2012. At this meeting, seventy-one churches and missions organizations in the Philippines pledged themselves to train thousands of OFWs to become effective cross-cultural witnesses and disciple-makers among the least-reached peoples of the world (Lim 2013). If this goal is reached, it will significantly contribute to world evangelization. The hope is to see thousands of people like Ryan who will be trained and commissioned as effective witnesses for Christ in Jeddah and beyond.

But as the Philippine church embraces this goal, it must take into account the weaknesses inherent in its present mobilization and training strategies. Fifty percent of OFWs, like Ryan and Angel, are married; most have children. It is easy to imagine the myriad family-related issues and dysfunctions these families will face. The essential proposition of this study is that these OFW-family dysfunctions, if not acknowledged and cared for, will sufficiently degrade the missions potential of these diasporic workers and erode their efforts for world evangelization.

Diaspora missiologists Enoch Wan and Sadiri Joy Tira recommend that further studies must be done to determine how local churches can effectively "provide pastoral care for the families of diaspora individuals left behind in the homeland" (Wan and Tira 2012, 55). In addition to the left-behind family members, churches should also provide pastoral care for those who are presently working abroad. The local church plays an integral part in helping minimize the effects of the OFW family dysfunctions. As John Baxter rightly contends, "the local church has the relational resources to adequately care for OFWs and their families" (Baxter 2009, 118). Baxter explains further the tension at the heart of Filipino diaspora missions saying:

Unlike traditional missions, OFW missions contains a deep-seated ambiguity. Simply put, the Filipino labor migration has caused harm to the social fabric of the nation in that it has seriously damaged family life. This inherent harm does not exclude OFW missions from the plan of God to fulfill the Great Commission. However, it does call for sensitivity on the part of sending and training agencies so as to avoid harm to families while seeking to promote missions. Any training that adequately prepares Filipinos for overseas work and ministry must take this essential negativity into account. This reality requires that training must go beyond seminars and become part of the long-term ministry strategy of the church (118).

Model churches in the Philippines

The good news is that some evangelical churches in the Philippines have already adapted an intentional OFW family ministry as part of their long-term missions strategy. These churches provide services that address the pre-departure, post-departure, and re-entry issues of the OFW phenomenon. Listed below are several of the OFW ministries, services, and resources that evangelical churches are creating as they respond to OFW family needs.[2]

Pre-departure ministries

Counseling and prayer are the most common pre-field services offered to current and prospective OFWs and their families. Most Filipino evangelicals do not seek advice from their church when making the decision to work overseas; however, some churches have been able to offer such counseling. When leaving poses a substantial risk for family health, these churches have encouraged their members to seek alternatives to overseas employment. Unfortunately there are times when overseas employment is sought as a means to escape from family problems (Parreñas 2003, 68). Pre-departure counseling from the church can address the actual motives for seeking overseas employment, and help church members find better solutions for family problems than running away to an overseas job.

A growing number of churches offer a Pre-employment Orientation Seminar (PEOA 2014) in order to help prospective OFWs weigh carefully their options before making a commitment to spend years away from the family. The PEOS deals with overseas job application procedures, documentary requirements and fees, and important information to safeguard against illegal recruitment.

Other churches have what Ana Gamez calls the "OFW Ministry Desk" or OMD. Gamez explains:

> Since most churches are not aware of the tentmaker missions strategy Filipino style and do not have any tentmaker missionary program in place, the OFW Ministry Desk (OMD) is an effective avenue to get this started. *First*, an OFW ministry helps the local church develop a vision for global missions. *Second*, it expands the role of church members from spectators to member care providers. *Third*, it provides a valuable opportunity for the church to pray for the countries where their OFW members are and for the people groups they work with (Gamez 2012, 50).

A few evangelical churches in the Luzon area have adopted the OMD because they see the need of intentionally reaching out to the OFW families

2 A more detailed description is found in the author's research (Lisbe 2014).

as part of their diaspora missions strategy. When a decision has been made to work overseas, churches may offer family enhancement seminars. Some of the larger churches invite marriage counselors to present workshops on parenting and other marital issues. Often these family seminars include financial experts who conduct financial literacy workshops as a way of helping OFW families to be able to spend, save, and invest their hard-earned income wisely. A common source of conflict between overseas workers and the families they leave behind is finances. Many workers have returned home to find themselves in the same financial status as when they left because the remittances sent home through the years were not used wisely. The inability to save and invest monies earned overseas can lead to a cycle of extended tours of overseas separations.

Pre-field training in churches usually includes workshops on evangelism and discipleship. To help churches equip OFWs in cross-cultural ministry the Philippine Missions Association (PMA 2014) – a partnership of evangelical mission agencies, churches, and denominations – offers written training materials and a series of four workshops to aid churches in preparing their members for cross-cultural ministry overseas.

Post-departure ministries

A growing number of churches seek to continue training, encouragement, and care for their OFW members even after they have left the Philippines and are established in the new employment setting. A common approach is to provide online counseling with OFW members abroad via cell phone, Facebook, or Skype. Online OFW church members have an avenue to share their concerns and problems with their church leaders in the Philippines and to receive regular encouragement, prayer, and advice. A few churches are able to periodically send leaders abroad to meet personally with their overseas members.

A large church in Manila has established "Skypleship" or doing discipleship online via Skype. It is their way of ministering to the OFWs who want to become part of a group that meets regularly online for the purpose of studying God's word, fellowship, prayer, mutual support, and accountability. Participants in the online groups include church members living both in the Philippines and in other work destinations around the globe.

Continuing care for families of OFWs

For the family members left behind, local churches can provide visitation, counseling, and prayer services. These are tangible ways of showing concern for the families separated from either the husband or wife who is working in foreign lands. By doing this, church leaders are able to listen to

OFW family members' problems, give them wise counsel, and pray with the families.

To help strengthen the relationships among OFW family members churches offer family enhancement seminars on how to sustain long-distance relationships for spouses and children. Families of OFWs are encouraged to join cell groups or circles of care (COC) which meet regularly and are oriented to the struggles of OFW families. Other churches concentrate on bringing together the young people of OFW families and addressing their issues created by parental absence. Through these events, OFW young people are able to share their blessings, heartaches, and concerns, and find support from adult church leaders and other teens that live in OFW families.

Re-entry ministries

OFWs return to a changed family. In their absence other family members have taken on the absent parent's roles and responsibilities, or these family functions have ceased or been reduced to the detriment of the family. The fears, suspicions, hurts, and frustrations that have been building during the long separation are waiting to be addressed. At present, little is offered to help families through this adjustment time. Some churches do offer informal debriefing. Through the counseling of the church leaders, OFW members are able to share their experiences abroad, whether good or bad, and the ministry team is able to assess whether the OFW has been a faithful witness for Christ overseas, and also address family problems. Family problems left unresolved can become a reason for escape in the form of another multi-year overseas contract, which furthers family dysfunction.

Missiological implications

The social and economic forces that help to propel millions of OFWs into the global work force often create hardship, suffering, and family dysfunctions among these workers. Yet these are the very people that God is choosing to use as missionaries to the unreached peoples of the world. Their effectiveness in missions is connected to their emotional, spiritual, and relational health. Diaspora missions strategy must include an understanding of the causes and solutions for these difficulties that so often accompany people on the move. One of the most important roadblocks to effective ministry by those working overseas is family problems occasioned by long periods of separation.

The best setting to address these problems is the local sending church. Through pre-departure, post-departure, and re-entry ministries, churches can greatly aid their overseas workers to make healthy decisions about overseas employment, prepare those who are leaving with basic discipleship skills, create on-going systems of encouragement and accountability when they are overseas, care for the families that are left behind, provide counseling and practical help in the midst of common family problems that arise during the separation, and prepare them to deal with the problems of re-entry.

It is simply common sense that overseas workers dealing with severe family dysfunctions will be ineffective in missions. Sending agencies, denominations, and churches around the world can greatly help the cause of diaspora missions through understanding the important role of local churches in sending and caring for the millions of Christian overseas workers.

For discussion

1. For churches that are sending workers into foreign lands, what can your church do to help support their life in Christ and their witness to others?
2. For churches in lands who are receiving workers from other nations, what can your church do to help support their life in Christ and their witness to others?
3. How might mission sending agencies help resource churches in the Global South to train and care for their overseas workers?

Bibliography

Adeney, Miriam. "Colorful initiatives: North American diasporas in mission." *Missiology: An International Review*, 2011: 5-23.

Appiah, Kwame Anthony. "Cosmopolitan Patriots." *Critical Inquiry*, 1997: 617-639.

Baeq, Daniel Shinjong, Myunghee Lee, Sokpyo Hong, and Jonathan Ro. "Mission from migrant church to ethnic minorities: A brief assessment of the Korean American Church in mission." *Missiology: An International Review*, 2011: 25-37.

Bakke, Raymond. "Urbanization and Evangelism: A Global View." In *The Urban Face of Mission: Ministering the Gospel in a Diverse and Changing World*, edited by Manuel Ortiz and Susan Baker, 32. Phillipsburg, New Jersey: P&R Publishing, 2002.

Baxter, John. "The Local Church in Diaspora Missions." *Journal of Asian Mission* 11, no. 1-2 (2009): 113-119.

Bediako, Kwame. *Jesus in Africa: The Christian Gospel in African History and Experience.* Akropong: Regnum Africa, 2000.

Bediako, Kwame. "John Mbiti's Contribution to African Theology." In *Religious Plurality in Africa: Essays in Honor of John S. Mbiti*, by Jacob K. Olupona and Sulayman S. Nyang, 367-396. Berlin: Mouton de Gruyter, 1993.

Buber, Martin. *I and Thou.* New York: Charles Scribner & Sons, 1958.

Carino, Feliciano V. "The Dynamics of Political Migrations as a Challenge to Religious Life." In *Religions Today: Their Challenge to the Ecumenical*

Movement, by Julio de Santa Ana, 86. Geneva: World Council of Churches, 2005.

Carmichael, Amy. "No Scar?" In *Toward Jerusalem*, by Amy Carmichael, 85. London: Holy Trinity Church, 1936.

Casiño, Tereso C. "Why people move: A prolegomenon to diaspora missiology." In *Korean Diaspora and Christian Mission*, edited by S. Hun Kim and Wonsuk Ma, 30-53. Oxford: Regnum Books, 2011.

Choi, Sungho. "Identity Crisis for Diaspora Community." In *Korean Diaspora and Christian Mission*, edited by S. Hun Kim and Wonsuk Ma, 20-29. Oxford: Regnum Books, 2011.

Chun, Do Myung. "Kingdom-centered identity: The case of bicultural Korea-Brazilians." In *Korean Diaspora and Christian Mission*, edited by S. Hun Kim and Wonsuk Ma, 115-132. Oxford: Regnum Books, 2010.

Commission on World Mission and Evangelism. "Mission spirituality and discipleship: Beyond and through contemporary boundaries." *International Review of Mission*, 2010: 106-124.

Conn, Harvey M., and Manuel Ortiz. *Urban Ministry: The Kingdom, the City, and the People of God.* Downers Grove, Illinois: IVP Academic, 2001.

Connor, Phillip. "A Biblical missiology for North American people groups." *North American Mission Board.* 2006. http://staging.namb.net/nambpb.aspx?pageid=8589967111 (accessed 2 16, 2011).

Cronin, Vincent. *A Pearl to India: The Life of Roberto de Nobili.* New York: E.P. Dutton & Co., 1959.

Embassy of the Blessed Kingdom of God for All Nations. "Embassy of the Blessed Kingdom of God for All Nations: 8th Anniversary." *Brochure.* Kiev, 2002.

Gamez, Ana. *Blessing OFWs to Bless the Nations.* Makati City: Church Strengthening Ministry, Inc., 2012.

George, Sam. "Diaspora: A hidden link to "From everywhere to everywhere" missiology." *Missiology: An International Review*, 2011: 45-56.

Haar, Gerrie ter. *Halfway to Paradise: African Christian Presence in Europe.* Cardiff: Cardiff Academic Press, 1998.

Hale, Chris. "Aradhna: From comfort to discomfort, from church to temple." *International Journal of Frontier Missions.* 2007. http://www.ijfm.org/PDFs_IJFM/24_3_PDFs/147-150Hale.pdf (accessed 2 18, 2011).

Hanciles, Jehu H. "Migration and Mission: Some Implications for the Twenty-First Century Church." *International Bulletin of Missionary Research*, 2003: 149-150.

Harvey, Thomas Alan. "Diaspora: A passage to mission." *Transformation: An International Journal of Holistic Mission Studies*, 2011: 42-50.

Howell, Brian M. "Multiculturalism, immigration and the North American Church: Rethinking contextualization." *Missiology: An International Review*, 2011: 79-85.

International Organization for Migration. *World Migration Report.* Geneva: International Organization for Migration, 2013.

International Organziation for Migration. *World Migration Report.* Geneva: Internatioanl Organization for Migration, 2015.

Jackson, Darrell. "Europe and the migrant experience: Transforming integration." *Transformation: An International Journal of Holistic Mission Studies*, 2011: 14-28.

Jenkins, Phillip. *The Next Christendom: The Coming of Global Christianity.* Oxford: Oxford University Press, 2011.

Jeong, Matthew. "Korean Evangelicals' response toward Muslim neighbours." In *Korean Diaspora and Christian Mission*, edited by S. Hun Kim and Wonsuk Ma, 157-173. Oxford: Regnum Books, 2010.

Jung, Min-young. "Diaspora and timely hit: Towards a diaspora missiology." In *Korean Diaspora and Christian Mission*, edited by S. Hun Kim and Wonsuk Ma, 54-63. Oxford: Regnum, 2010.

Kawthoolei Karen Baptist Bible School & College. "Brief history." *Kawthoolei Karen Baptist Bible School & College.* 2010. https://sites.google.com/site/kkbbsc/home/brief-history (accessed 2 15, 2011).

Kim, Hun. "Receiving mission: Reflection on reversed phenomena in mission by migrant workers from global churches to Western society." *Transformation: An International Journal of Holistic Mission Studies*, 2011: 62-67.

Kim, S. Hun. "Migrant workers and 'Reverse Mission' in the West." In *Korean Diaspora and Christian Mission*, edited by S. Hun Kim and Wonsuk Ma, 150-156. Oxford: Regnum Books, 2010.

Kim, S. Hun, and Wonsuk Ma. *Korean Diaspora and Christian Mission.* Oxford: Regnum Books International, 2011.

Ko, Lawrence. "Individuals in the City: Encountering the Other." In *Ethnic Rhythms: Life in the Global City*, edited by Lawrence Ko, 51-52. Singapore: Singapore Center for Global Missions, 2015.

Ko, Lawrence. "The Role of the Asian Church in Missions." In *Emerging Missions Movements: Voices of Asia*, 1-10. Compassion International and Asia Evangelical Alliance, 2010.

Kong, Lily. "Cultural Icons, Global City and National Identity." In *Engaging Society: The Christian in Tomorrow's Singapore*, edited by Michael Nai-Chiu Poon, 24-40. Singapore: Trinity Theological College, 2013.

Kraemer, Hendrik. *Religion and the Christian Faith.* Cambridge: James Clarke, 1956.

Lausanne Committee for World Evangelization. *Scattered to gather: Embracing the global trend of diaspora.* Manila, Philippines: LifeChange Publishing, Inc., 2010.

Lausanne Diaspora Educators Consultation. "The Seoul Declaration on Diaspora Missiology." *The Lausanne Movement.* 11 14, 2009. http://www.lausanne.org/documents/seoul-declaration-on-diaspora-missiology.html (accessed 2 18, 2011).

LCWE. *Scattered to gather: Embracing the global trend of diaspora.* Manila, Philippines: LifeChange Publishing, Inc., 2010.

—. *Scattered to gather: Embracing the global trend of diaspora.* Manila, Philippines: LifeChange Publishing, Inc., 2010.

Lim, David S. "Seconnd lausannne Philippine Congress (2012)." *http://www.lausanne.org/en/blog/1921-second-lausanne-philippine-congress-2012-report.html.* January 7, 2013. (accessed September 1, 2014).

Lisbe, Gerardo B. *Church-based OFW Family Care Ministry: An Ethnographic Study on the Structure and Activities that Filipino Create that Significantly Reduce OFW Family Dysfunction.* D. Min. Dissertation, Los Angeles, CA: International Theological Seminary, 2014.

Loong, Lee Hsien. "Smart Nation Initiative." November 24, 2014. https://www.youtube.com/watch?v=jGMbqpVRo9I.

Lorance, Cody "An Introduction to Contextualization Among Hindus." *Lausanne Global Conversation.* 6 6, 2010. http://conversation.lausanne.org/en/conversations/detail/10373 (accessed 2 14, 2011).

Ma, Wonsuk. "A Millenial Shift of Global Christianity and Mission: An Initial Reflection." In *Korean Diaspora and Christian Mission,* edited by S. Hun Kim and Wonsuk Ma, 11-24. Oxford: Regnum Books International, 2011.

Oh, Doug K. "History of the Korean Diaspora Movement." In *Korean Diaspora and Christian Mission,* edited by S. Hun Kim and Wonsuk Ma, 2-16. Oxford: Regnum Books, 2011.

Olupona, Jacob, and Regina Gemignani. *African Immigrant Religions in America.* Washington D.C.: New York University Press, 2007.

Operation World. *Singapore.* 2015. http://www.operationworld.org/sing.

Ortiz, Manuel. "The Church and the City." In *The Urban Face of Mission: Ministering the Gospel in a Diverse and Changing World*, edited by Manuel Ortiz and Susan Baker, 43. Phillipsburg, New Jersey: P&R Publishing, 2002.

Ott, Craig, Stephen J. Strauss, and Timothy C. Tennent. *Encountering Theology of Mission: Biblical Foundations, Historical Developments, and Contemporary Issues.* Grand Rapids: Baker Academic, 2010.

Parreñas, Rachel S. *Servants of Globalization: Women, Migration, and Children.* Quezon City: Ateneo De manila University Press, 2003.

Photo Voice; Bhutanese Refugee Support Group. "Introduction." *Bhutanese Refugees: The Story of a Forgotten People.* March 12, 2010. http://www.photovoice.org/bhutan/ (accessed 2 17, 2011).

Pocock, Michael, Gailyn Van Rheenen, and Douglas McConnell. *The Changing Face of World Missions: Engaging Contemporary Issues and Trends.* Grand Rapids, MI: Baker Academic, 2005.

Programme, United Nations Development. *Human Development Report 2009 Overcoming Barriers: Human Mobility and Development.* New York: Macmillan, 2009.

Rajamanickam, S. "The Goa Conference of 1619 (A letter of Fr Robert de Nobili to Pope Paul V)." *Indian Church History Review*, 1968: 85.

Ratha, Dilip, et al. *Migration and Remittances: Recent Developments and Outlook.* Washington D.C.: The World Bank, 2015.

Richard, H.L. "Good news for Hindus in the neighborhood." *Rethinking Hindu Ministry II: Papers from the Rethinking Forum*, 2010: 32-35.

Rodas, M. Daniel Carroll. *Christians at the Border: Immigration, the Church and the Bible.* Grand Rapids: Baker Academic, 2008.

Santamaria, Francis. "Problems regarding Family Relationns and Children of Migrant Workers." In *Filipino Women Overseas Contract Workers: At What Costs?*, by Mary Palma-Beltran and Aurora javate De Dios, 71. Quezon City: JMC Press, 1992.

Sassen, Saskia. "The Global City: Introducing a Concept." *Brown Journal of World Affairs*, 2005: 27-43.

Singapore Center for Global Missions. 2014. http://www.scgm.org.sg.

Solomon, Robert. "Soul of the Global City." *Speech at Singapore Centre for Global Missions.* Singapore, August 6, 2015.

Song, Minho. "The diaspora experience for the Korean Church and its implications for world missions." In *Korean Diaspora and Christian Mission,* edited by S. Hun Kim and Wonsuk Ma, 103-114. Oxford: Regnum Books, 2010.

Sydnor, Paul N. "Understanding the forced displacement of refugees in terms of the person." *Transformation: An International Journal of Holistic Mission Studies*, 2011: 51-61.

Tan, Kang-San. "In search of contextualized training models for Chinese Christian diaspora in Britain." *Transformation: An International Journal of Holistic Mission Studies*, 2011: 29-41.

The Lausanne Movement. "The Lausanne Covenant." *The Lausanne Movement.* 1974. http://www.lausanne.org/covenant (accessed 2 18, 2011).

Thomas, T.V. "Ministering to Scattered Peoples: Global Phenomenon of Diaspora." *Lausanne Global Conversation.* 11 12, 2010. http://conversation.lausanne.org/en/conversations/detail/11660 (accessed 2 17, 2011).

Trinity International Baptist Mission. *Our Story.* 2010. http://www.tibm.org/our-story.html (accessed 2 25, 2011).

United Nations. *World Urbanization Prospects.* New York: United Nations, 2014.

United Nations. *World Urbanization Prospects.* New York: United Nations, 2014.

United Nations: Department of Economic and Social Affairs. *Trends in International Migrant Stock: 2013 Revision.* United Nations, 2013.

Vanier, Jean. *From Brokenness to Community.* Mahwah, NJ: Paulist Press, 1992.

Wahrisch-Oblau, Claudia. *The Missionary Self-Perception of Pentecostal/Charismatic Church Leaders from the Global South in Europe.* Leiden/Boston: E.J. Brill, 2009.

Wallis, Jim. *On God's Side: What Religion Forgets and Politics Hasn't Learned about Serving the Common Good.* Grand Rapids: Brazos Press, 2013.

Walls, Andrew F. "Mission and Migration: The Diaspora Factor in Christian History." *Journal of African Christian Thought*, 2002: 3-11.

Waltke, Bruce K. *Genesis: A Commentary.* Grand Rapids, MI: Zondervan, 2001.

Wan, Enoch. "Diaspora missiology." *Occasional Bulletin*, 2007: 3-7.

Wan, Enoch. "Diaspora mission strategy in the context of the United Kingdom in the 21st century." *Transformation: An International Journal of Holistic Mission Studies*, 2011: 3-13.

Wan, Enoch. "Korean diaspora: From hermit kingdom to Kingdom ministry." In *Korean Diaspora and Christian Mission*, edited by S. Hun Kim and Wonsuk Ma, 85-101. Oxford: Regnum, 2010.

—. "Ministering to Scattered Peoples – Moving to Reach the People on the Move." *Lausanne Global Conversation.* 10 22, 2010. http://conversation.lausanne.org/en/resources/detail/11438 (accessed 2 17, 2011).

Wan, Enoch, and Sadiri Joy Tira. "Diaspora Missiology." In *Missions in Action in the 21st Century*, edited by Joy Sadiri Tira and Enoch Wan, 55. Quezon City: LifeChange Publishing, Inc., 2012.

Wanner, Catherine. *Communities of the Converted: Ukrainians and Global Evangelism.* London: Cornell University Press, 2007.

Yeoh, Brenda, and Theodora Lam. "Divercity Singapore." In *Ethnic Rhythms: Life in the Global City*, edited by Lawrence Ko. Singapore: Singapore Centre for Global Missions, 2015.

41. When the New Believers Return Home: A Case Study of Christian Returnees to China

Carolyn Kemp

Introduction

Christians, working with transient diaspora communities living outside their home countries – whether students, business people, the mobile workforce, and so on – may one day see those who come to Christ return to their home countries. As a result, two critical questions must be asked: 1) Are these new converts standing firm in their faith once they return to their home context? and 2) What does it mean to give culturally appropriate discipleship to a new believer who will eventually return to their home country? The following case study looks at answers to these questions specifically from the mainland Chinese diaspora context, offering insights that apply to all who work with diaspora peoples who will one day return home.

The story of John and Lucy

John[1] became a Christian while studying in the United Kingdom. He and his wife both were, and are, accomplished academics and university professors in China. John's upbringing context was as the son of a farming father who was violent and aggressive to John, his sister, and his mother. He managed to get to a good university in China when his climb up the academic ladder started. Eventually he won a scholarship to come to the UK. It was here, in November 2008, while accompanying his wife at "English Corner,"[2] that John came into contact with Christians. He wrote:

> Since the first time I went there, I began to love the place because every teacher there is very kind and nice. After that, my wife and I went to English Corner nearly every time. Thanks to sermons on every Thursday from

1 John is not his real name; all names have been changed to protect the individuals concerned. Likewise, the organization that is primarily referred to in this case study has been renamed Love China Ministries (LCM). Many of the Christian leaders referred to in this case study are LCM diaspora workers.

2 "English Corner" is the place where English is taught informally through one-to-one or one-to-two conversations with mother tongue English speakers using "everyday" English. It is a way to build friendships and serve the Chinese when they come to study in a non-intrusive way of coming alongside to share Christ naturally through relationships.

> Douglas and Peter, hymns, globe café activities organized by Sabine and Graham, Christianity Explore sessions held by ... [the] Church, and the preaching of Keith, I got to know more about Christianity. And some of my biases against Christians changed.

This was all part of John's journey with the Lord. In April 2009, at a Christian conference which explored discipleship issues in John's "heart language"[3] of Mandarin and thinking through what it would mean for him to return as a Christian to China, that John gave his life to Christ. John explains his conversion: "I immediately felt peace and joy in my heart as I became a child of God, and Jesus Christ became my best and close friend."

The realities facing John and Lucy

As we all know from experience, but very rarely seem to acknowledge, in our discipling of people, the decision to follow Christ is not the end but just the beginning. LCM internal research has shown the following stark reality concerning Christian Chinese who return to China following their conversion experience:

> Students returning to China after completing studies overseas in 2012 was 272,000, up by 46.6 percent over 2011. The Chinese church in the USA estimates that 10 to 15 percent of the returning 272,000 expressed faith in Christ, so roughly 27,200 using the minimal percentage. Therefore, the question of why or why not Christian returnees are thriving in their home contexts is critical for assessing the impact of diaspora ministry in general.

So how are these 27,200 doing in their faith journey upon their return to China?

> After visiting 180 returnees in China, multiple times, and maintaining communication with 60 more, one ... worker [with international students] said, "only a handful show any signs at all of being Christians! This includes several who made strong professions of faith and were baptized [in the overseas country where they studied] no longer walking with the Lord at all!

This experience is shared by other workers in China who suggest that only 15 to 25 percent of those who professed faith in Christ overseas are now meeting regularly with other Christians. That is a loss of between 20,400 and 23,120 returning Chinese Christians, using the above minimal figure of 27,200. These losses occurred in just one year; every year the number of returnees goes up, along with it the number of losses. Thus, the question of the pre-return discipleship of these diaspora Chinese Christians urgently needs to be addressed.[4]

---

3 Discipling in one's "heart" or first language is critical for a clear understanding of the subject(s) and to being able to see this new worldview as contextualised to one's own culture.

4 For further information contact the author.

John and his wife, Lucy, came to Christ in the United Kingdom. They knew from the beginning that they would one-day return to China. Would they be one of the 85 percent who returned professing faith in Christ only to fall away?

The context to which John and Lucy would return

The vast majority of international students, business people, and the mobile workforce return to their home countries after their education, contract, or job is finished. John and Lucy were no exception. Again, LCM internal research gives the following picture of the China to which John and Lucy would return:

> Although this is changing and sometimes we find there can be Christians back home, more often than not every relationship – whether with a family member, friend, or co-worker – is with a non-Christian. While overseas, the need for community attracted the Chinese student into Christian groups. Now it works in the opposite direction: they are flung back into a network of relationships which may now clash with changed values. Stress and isolation increases. The cross-cultural friendships that they enjoyed in Christian groups overseas are all gone. All of the available social activities are now hosted by non-Christians, and choices have to be made in those contexts. Adjustments need to be made at every turn: living with parents and other family members again, loss of privacy and independence, discovering how much everything changed while they were away, and experiencing deep feelings of not belonging and not fitting in.
>
> It is within this backdrop that many major, life-changing decisions have to be made in the first year after returning. These range from finding a job, which is no longer easy as your relational networks in China have diminished, to getting married and the pressure is on to marry a non-Christian. Then there is the decision to identify yourself as a Christian … or not! Was that all just part of the overseas experience? And the question arises of where is there a church anyway? If you do find a church and seek to grow as a Christian, then your new job probably demands brutally long hours, not to mention a long commute. Opposition from other belief and value systems is encountered in the workplace as well as the family. Your values have been reshaped. You have been forged into something different now. You can no longer agree with the things you used to in the past.[5]

What happened when John and Lucy returned?

From the time they professed faith in Christ to the time they returned to China, John and Lucy had 18-24 months. For those 18-24 months they had input into their lives from many different dimensions.

John and Lucy attended a local British church, which had good nurturing biblical teaching. The church allowed them to slowly explore their giftings,

---

5 For further information contact the author.

without pressure, and they learned what it meant to serve people in the church. Very soon after conversion they were at the church door on a Sunday morning giving out the songbooks and chatting to people on their way in. It was a safe place for them, with nurturing relationships and people who were excited to see their growth in the Lord. The church also gave them time to engage with other ministries outside of church, to learn what it means to be a servant. They also had contact with at least two para-church organizations as part of their initial contact, both of which had input into their lives.

John and Lucy had developed a close relationship with two [LCM diaspora] workers who ran English Corner, Peter and Jane, the place where they first heard about Christianity. This is the same couple that took them to the Christian conference where they gave their lives to Christ. Peter and Jane met with John and Lucy frequently both before they became Christians and afterwards; this role was one of mentoring and life coaching. Peter and Jane (Jane less fluently) can speak Mandarin which enabled them to talk freely and deeply with John and Lucy about all sorts of subjects. When they became Christians their relationship was one that allowed for a much deeper discipling dialogue. Peter and Jane's focus was to prepare them to live as trusting and obedient followers of Jesus on their return to China. It was here that much contextualised (culturally sensitive to China) discipleship took place. They also got involved in helping at English Corner, sometime sharing and speaking, at other times serving the tea and coffee. They attended and took part in a missions conference with Peter and Jane, exposing them to what it means to engage in mission. They also took them to different kinds of churches, exposing them to various ways and modes of worship and helping them to see different expressions of the Christian faith. Today Peter and Jane still connect with, talk with, share with, and mentor John and Lucy.

Through someone at English Corner (who had covered the cost), John also had the chance to attend a Preachers Training Course. John and Lucy went on to run a seeker's bible study at their own home for fellow students. Lucy also worked with another church in their toddlers group, learning to serve and work with children. They also had good relationships with other local Christian diaspora workers. This brought them to the Globe Café (an evening café run by volunteers for International students). Here they gathered with others, like themselves, who had recently arrived in the country, who wanted to develop friendships, and who had many questions about life and choices. Here they also learned about service. John eventually became more formerly involved in befriending and sharing the gospel with international students for a year.

As can be seen, both John and Lucy had an incredible amount of input from several people and churches in the 18-24 months they had before they went back to China. It really was a multi-dimensional, relational, and contextual discipling of them both.

Key factors in the discipleship of John and Lucy

What are some of the key factors in the way that John and Lucy were discipled in the U.K. that prepared them for life and service once they return back to China? There are several observations:

1. Firstly, and significantly, the discipleship of John and Lucy was not based on a discipleship "program" but rather it was about journeying together. It was not a one-size-fits-all discipleship but very much customised to suit what God was doing in John and Lucy's life day-by-day: responding to what God was doing and addressing issues bit by bit on the journey of discipleship.
2. John and Lucy had input from several people, which gave them a richer and broader experience of living for Jesus than they would have had if they had only one couple or one person working with them.
3. John and Lucy were exposed to various ways to serve, both in the local church and with para-church organizations. This gave them a chance to explore different people, expressions of faith, their own giftings, and to encounter and learn to deal with different challenges that are inevitable in the daily life and fabric of faith communities.
4. John and Lucy were trusted to serve and were given responsibilities. They were not kept dependent on others, under constant observation and supervision. Rather they were rather nurtured and encouraged to engage in mission, both within the context of the local church and in the bigger context outside of the church: Globe Café, reaching students, and leading bible studies. Furthermore, they were given the platform to serve and the freedom to make mistakes and learn from them.
5. John and Lucy had people who were aware of the context to which they would eventually return. As a result, they mentored them to think, process, and evaluate what it would mean to return to China as followers of Jesus. What these people knew of China – the workplace, family life, society, church, relationships, and so on – intentionally informed the way they discipled John and Lucy.
6. The relationships that John and Lucy had with Peter and Jane and others, was about friendships and relationships. It was done in such a way that life was shared: hours spent having relaxing meals, walking in the park, sitting talking over coffee, and from day one sharing the day-to-day life together from the very beginning. The focus was not on giving answers to life's questions but rather on journeying together and being intentional about learning the lessons. It was modeling what it means to be a follower of Jesus and discovering together about what it means to have Christ as Lord, and to trust Him. The focus of the discipleship was about sharing the character and nature of God, letting what we know of God – based on scripture and nurtured in relationship with Him – inform

the lessons He has for us. It was about building on who God had already made them, "I was searching for the truth and now I've found it." John's desire was to know the truth, and in finding the Lord he found someone he could grow to trust.

These several factors, and more, resulted in a more "fully orbed" discipleship of John and Lucy. As a result, they were well prepared for their return to China.

How are John and Lucy doing now?

John and Lucy returned to China and had very tough time. Ironically, at first the source of their greatest difficulties was with other Christians, and they struggled to find a good sound Bible teaching group for fellowship. But that did not stop them from sharing Christ.

They soon started having groups of students in their home. One day, while John was away, Lucy had a group in their home when they were raided by the police. There were consequences for the students: they were told they would not be given scholarships that semester (we do not know if that was ever carried out). John was told he would not be eligible for promotion and Lucy was demoted in her work at the university. This was a very challenging time for them, but they knew from lessons learned in the past that God would work His plans out. Interestingly, this event has indeed worked out for the best, as John is actually content to stay as part of a research team rather than be promoted and have much more administration to do. Lucy's demotion was to a job that actually suited her better. They are now living in a new home but have some security concerns, as their neighbors are known informers.

Despite of all this, John and Lucy are very eager to take every opportunity to share the Good News. They now host a Bible study during the week and groups from two different universities meet in their home on alternate weeks. These two groups get together once a month for worship. John and Lucy also attend a new house church where they seem to be settled. This group is (wonderfully) growing too big so they need to decide on a new meeting place. John has also been involved in baptizing others.

John and Lucy are taking difficult stands for Christ in the work place, working diligently so that He is honored, shining a light in a dark place, blessing their local fellowship, running Bible studies for students and sharing Christ with them. This young couple is being used by the Lord to impact their local context in China!

Lessons to learn

So what lessons can be learned from the experiences of John and Lucy that have significance for all who are discipling diaspora Christians who will one day return to their homeland? These four are the most significant:

1. Discipling is not about numbers. Discipleship involves a high investment in people, in relationships, and in nurturing. It's about going deep. If we want to see those returning sparking a discipleship movement on their return home we must invest in their lives while they are away from home and model to them deeply what it means to obey and trust Christ.
2. Disciples are God's, not ours. Everyone involved in the discipling of John and Lucy were not possessive about them being "their convert" or "their contact," but rather willingly gave of themselves to come alongside this couple who had just fallen in love with Jesus. They were more concerned for the disciple than their own perceived success or "their ministry."
3. Discipleship is God's agenda. The agenda is not "what can I tell them?" or "what gem do I have to share?" but rather "what is God doing now and how can I help in that process?" We need to listen to the Lord, watch what He is doing in the lives of new believers and come alongside to facilitate that. We need to journey with them as they explore their new life in Christ. Any "teaching" needs to be done through mentoring and modeling.
4. A missional DNA is crucial to discipleship. The 18-24 months that John and Lucy had before they returned to China was rich in Christian experience: varied, full, challenging, nurturing, exciting and molding. They were intentionally given opportunities to serve. These opportunities are critical if we want to see people being able to serve when they return to China (or their home country, wherever that might be). This missional DNA must come into play in the very fabric of what it means to disciple. If it is caught it will be taught. We must bring this missional dimension into discipleship, for if there is no missional emphasis (integral mission) has discipleship really taken place?

Although the statistics and research show that only 15 to 25 percent of those who return to China professing faith in Christ are still walking with Him six months to a year afterwards, this can change. We can see disciples return to their home country with a passion for and trust in Christ. We can see disciples return and honor God in all that they do, living faithfully, living missionally, and transforming the arena that God has placed them in. To see this happen, however, will require a paradigm shift in the way we disciple.

For discussion

1. When immigrants become Christians what can churches and ministries in the foreign setting do to help the new believers continue in their faith upon returning to their cultural homeland?

2. What can churches and mission agencies – working in the cultural homeland of new believers converted in foreign countries – do to prepare for those Christians who return home?
3. In some cultures returning Christians from foreign lands find great difficulty in re-assimilation back in their home country. What role should these returning Christians play in the evangelization of their own people?

42. Crossing the Divide: A Case Study of a Western Mission Agency's Encounter with Diaspora Missions

John F. Baxter

Introduction

Missions work among diaspora peoples is changing how mission agencies – especially Western agencies – are doing ministry. As agencies recognize the new global realities of the diaspora they are being forced to reevaluate how they engage migrating peoples, especially in regards to the growing importance of informal missionaries, the realities of persecution, poverty, and suffering, and a willingness to explore their own institutional prejudices. This case study examines how one Western mission agency has changed and consequently developed better ways to utilize mission opportunities among people on the move.

In 2012, an Arab Egyptian Christian family residing in the United States applied to become missionaries with HBC, a mid-size US based Baptist denomination of over one thousand churches and 150 foreign missionaries.[1] Their story captures many of the key realities and issues that affect church and mission agency engagement with diaspora missions.

Samir and Miriam were born into Christian families in Egypt. After college they joined the staff of a large US-based mission organization that worked throughout the Middle East. For thirteen years they served in several different ministry positions in Egypt. In 2003, Samir was granted the opportunity for further theological education in the United States. Over the next decade he received a master's degree in theological studies from a well-known evangelical graduate school and secured a teaching position in a small mid-western evangelical college. The entire family, especially their three young children, adapted well to the American evangelical sub-culture.

During their years in America, Samir and Miriam had opportunities to regularly return to Egypt and other Middle Eastern locations for ministry opportunities. Their involvement in evangelistic campaigns within both Christian and Muslim communities, theological training seminars, and compassion ministries increased during these years and accelerated with the dawning of the "Arab Spring" conflicts and the growing persecution of the Egyptian churches under the rule of the Muslim Brotherhood.

---

1 All persons and ministries described in the study are real, but with altered names.

Samir and Miriam desired to return to fulltime ministry among Egyptians, but their experience as immigrants shifted their ministry focus to the Egyptian diaspora, both throughout the Middle East and North America. Through the influence of Egyptian friends they approached HBC, applied, and were accepted as missionary appointees for Egypt and the Egyptian diaspora.

They chose to continue their primary residence in the United States. Their former public role in Egyptian ministry and the rising tide of persecution in Egypt, as well as the inclusion of the North American Egyptian diaspora in their ministry plan, prompted this decision. The choice also included considerations of family welfare – both economic and emotional – especially since their children were acculturated to life in the US and not Egypt.

Their ministry plan includes working with HBC districts and churches in America to promote outreach to immigrant Muslim populations, as well as numerous trips to network and train Egyptian Christians who are living and working throughout the Middle East. Their goal is to prepare Egyptians in the diaspora to evangelize Egyptians and other unreached immigrant peoples among whom they live and work.

At this stage their story is illustrative of many well-known diaspora realities. Samir and Miriam fit the largest demographic of the global diaspora: those migrating to locations of increased opportunity (Goldin et al 2011, chp. 4) which in their case was from Egypt to the United States for education and employment. They also portray the fact that the largest percentage of those on the move are Christians (Pew 2012, 11). They are also an example of those who are encouraged to migrate, either initially or to remain abroad, because of religious persecution. A final reality is their experience of transnationalism and its effect upon family and ministry.

The need for deep change

As an immigrant family Samir and Miriam's personal and ministry profile is very different from the typical American HBC missionary. The agency's desire to engage in diaspora missions has occasioned a critical examination of the agency's ministry philosophy, values, and organizational structure. There is a growing recognition among agency leadership that effective engagement with the global diaspora requires deep change throughout the organization.

To address the need for deep change, the position of Director of Diaspora Ministries was created within the International Ministries department of HBC. The director was given responsibility to determine the conceptual, methodological, and organizational challenges within HBC International Ministries that hinder engagement with people on the move, and to make recommendations for change.

Affinity focus

The first recommendation for change was organizational. As other sending agencies have learned, reliance on a geographic field structure is counter-productive for diaspora missions. In a traditional mission field the organizational structure for ministry, resources, and accountability is coterminous with the geographical boundaries of the target people's cultural homeland. But this structure becomes a hindrance when the target people group is enlarged to include those who have emigrated from their homeland to other areas.[2]

HBC has begun to experiment with an affinity focus structure for some of its target Unreached People Groups (UPG). Intentionally vague in definition, an affinity group for HBC denotes a cluster of target peoples who share relevant characteristics, such as Arab Muslims. An affinity focus allows HCB to network all missionaries working with the same larger affinity group, even though they target distinct UPGs and are in different countries. Even HCB missionaries working with people groups completely outside of the affinity block are brought into the network if applicable. For example, missionaries in the Philippines may have some connections to the Arab Muslim affinity group because of the large number of Christian Filipino overseas workers in the Middle East and Europe. Planning, oversight, and resourcing is beginning to move away from distinct geographic fields to larger regional structures. More than one affinity block may fall under the supervision of a regional director. An affinity focus eliminates the distinction between US-based and foreign-based missionaries who are working with the same unreached people group.

This newer structure is reflected in Samir and Miriam's ministry plan in which they work with Egyptians in three distinct areas: the United States, throughout the Middle East, and Egypt. At present they are accountable to Diaspora Ministries, and not a geographic field.

Majority world focus

Two of the diaspora realities described above – the predominance of Majority World peoples in the global diaspora, and the significant presence of Majority World Christians on the move – impinge directly upon conceptual and methodological challenges that HBC faces.

---

2 The International Mission Board of the Southern Baptist Convention is an example of a mission agency that has moved away from a traditional field structure to an affinity focus. The IMB affinity structure and the reasons for its adoption are discussed in two reports published in 2009, available from imb.org. The reports are To the Ends of the Earth (http://media1.imbresources.org/files/103/10333/10333-55180.pdf), and Affinity Group Overview (http://www.imb.org/globalresearch/maps/AffinityGroupOverview.pdf).

Western mission agencies are accustomed to being in the driver's seat. In the past agencies typically initiated mission strategies following Western planning models, staffed these strategies with Western personnel, and created funding streams from Western sources. This model breaks down in the global diaspora.

Like Samir and Miriam, the vast majority of people on the move are not from Western countries. Diaspora missions has not arisen from the strategic planning of Western agencies. The rise of diaspora missions coincides with the seismic shifts that have occurred throughout world missions. The Majority World church is emerging as the dominant player in evangelizing the unreached peoples of the world. More than ever before the fulfillment of the Great Commission is powered by movements of Christian lay persons seeking secular work throughout the globe. These informal, Majority World missionaries are the emerging face of world missions.

The greatest potential for diaspora missions is not within the ranks of career missionaries, but in the millions of Majority World lay Christians on the move. The ministry priority of HBC missionaries involved with diaspora missions, such as Samir and Miriam, is to mobilize and equip Christians in the diaspora.

As HBC attempts to focus on the mission potential of Majority World lay Christians scattered among the nations, it encounters challenges concerning past methods. HBC has a long history of involvement in leadership development. But the target audience for training has remained centered on full-time, vocational ministry, whether as pastor or missionary. The preponderance of this training has occurred in formal education programs at Bible colleges and seminaries around the world. Since the vast majority of Christians in the global diaspora will not attend these schools, local churches must become the focus of mobilization and training. This church-based missions program includes mobilization, training, and on-going accountability and care of overseas workers. It occurs first in the sending church in the worker's homeland, and continues in the new church in the diaspora.

Whether the goal for current HBC missionaries is to train Filipinos living in Hong Kong or West Africans residing in France or Brazilians finding work in North Africa, all of these diasporic groups have in common the need for discipleship and training in cross-cultural evangelism. But they also share the inability to access most of the present training venues offered by the agency. Most of these overseas laborers do not have the inclination or time to pursue the types of career-oriented theological and ministry training now offered by HBC schools. Often they are pushed into these global labor flows by poverty, natural disaster, or oppression in the home country and lack funding for extensive theological training. The bottom line is that they rarely see themselves as potential missionaries and therefore have little desire or ability to seek formal training. While mission agencies and schools can provide materials, seminars, and online resources, mobilization and training must be centered in the local churches of the Majority World.

HBC missionaries can help to create new training resources and church-based delivery systems that are adjusted to the learning level and interest of Majority World lay persons. These things must be done in cooperation with Majority World local churches and denominations. As HBC missionaries, Samir and Miriam are tasked with developing this type of training structure for the Egyptian diaspora. Being part of the Egyptian diaspora is a definite asset.

Partnership focus

Beyond changing particular ministry methods, however, is the question: Is HBC, and other Western mission agencies, willing to embrace the type of deep change required for diaspora missions effectiveness? Samir and Miriam's presence in the mission force of HBC raises this yet unanswered question. While the concept of partnership between Western and Majority World missions is quite familiar, the realities of diaspora missions calls for increased levels of genuine cooperation. Since the global diaspora is primarily a Majority World experience, the Western mission agency enters as learner into this new realm.

HBC's desire for greater cooperation with Majority World mission forces is expressed primarily at two levels. First is the desire to see more Samirs and Miriams become part of the International Ministry staff. The second level is to seek a servant's role in working with Majority World churches and denominations as they deploy their diaspora missions forces.

The realization of the first goal, to increase the number of HBC career missionaries recruited from the diaspora, has uncovered difficulties inherent in mission partnerships. The experience of Samir and Miriam has revealed HBC organizational values and structures that hinder missionaries from non-Western cultures. HBC has not been successful in funding missionary appointees from the global diaspora. Many International Mission staff and US-based church planters recruited from immigrant groups have been unable to raise sufficient funds to meet the agency requirements.

This failure has led to an examination of agency values and organizational structures. HBC places a high value on individual initiative and entrepreneurship. The Ministry Partner Development (MPD) process is seen as an indicator of later success on the mission field. It is believed that the same traits of individual initiative and perseverance needed for support-raising are also needed for future ministry success on the field. But these agency values are at times in conflict with the more collaborative and communal cultural norms of the non-Western missionaries that are being recruited.

Perhaps at its deepest level, HBC's experience of bringing on non-Western staff reveals a hidden cultural prejudice – the belief that the Western planning and management patterns used by HBC and most other agencies in North America are the "correct" way to do missions. Genuine partnership for HBC in diaspora missions will only occur when the agency is willing to experience the difficulties of negotiating a new operating paradigm with non-Western staff and its Majority World church partners that creates space for other cultural values and methods.

In the funding area, HBC has recognized two possible solutions. One is to continue the present system and expect mission personnel recruited from within the global diaspora to adapt to Western values and methods. The second option is for the agency to expand the number and types of Ministry Partner Development paradigms that it uses, and to allow differing compensation packages to be more inclusive of other cultures. The agency's temptation is to pick the first option because the status quo is easier than change. Fortunately, HBC International Ministries has resisted taking the easy option and instead has established an MPD study group to identify alternative funding pathways.

The second level of seeking genuine partnership with Majority World churches in diaspora missions is the acceptance of a servant's role. The local churches and denominations in the Global South and East are the directors of this new mission drama. The players are the informal missionaries who have been scattered among the unreached peoples of the earth. The HBC missionary force, like the stage crew in a theater, must find the places where it can enable the primary actors and add value to the performance. God, of course, has written the script and set the transnational flows of people into motion.

As discussed above, a tangible expression of this service role is the reconfiguration of the content and delivery of HBC training resources to fit the church-based and lay person orientation of diaspora missions. Training resources need to be developed in partnership with those in the diaspora because there are important characteristics common to migrating peoples that renders diaspora missions different from missions to sedentary people. For example, migrating people often develop a transnational identity, especially children in the diaspora. Those who have experienced the blending of cultural viewpoints, such as Samir and Miriam, have an advantage in creating relevant resources for discipleship and evangelism.

Focus on suffering

Another important feature of global migration is the high degree of suffering that often accompanies those on the move. Similar to the persecution Samir and Miriam encountered, there are negative forces that propel and keep people in the diaspora. Unemployment and underemployment, natural disaster, political conflict, prejudice, or various types of oppression drive others out of their homelands. Upon arriving in their new country, workers from the Majority World often find themselves near the bottom of the social and economic ladder, vulnerable and many times abused. Some, like Samir and Miriam, are able to keep the family together in their journeys, but millions of overseas workers are separated from family for years.

A profound sense of dislocation is a constant companion for many. Others experience loneliness and guilt for leaving spouses and children. Unresolved conflicts such as these can prompt destructive behaviors that negatively affect the discipleship process (Baxter 2009, 117). If HBC had any misgivings concerning the appropriateness of holistic missions, these doubts fall away in the face of diaspora realities. HBC has recognized the necessity of holistic care for people on the move. The social and emotional dysfunctions inherent in the present patterns of global migration must be addressed in order for Christians in the diaspora to be effective ambassadors for Christ, first to their fellow countrymen on the move, and then to the unreached peoples among whom they live and work. The challenge for HBC is to learn from those in the diaspora, such as Samir and Miriam, how to be wise partners with the Majority World churches in providing care to people on the move.

Summary

In its mission endeavors that are relevant to the global diaspora, HBC is experiencing change. As the agency recognizes relevant issues and realities concerning the global diaspora, and as it grows through the experience of working alongside of people from the diaspora, such as Samir and Miriam, HBC International Missions is changing in the following ways to better take advantage of mission opportunities among people on the move:

1. Reorienting organizational structures away from geography and toward an affinity focus. Missions from everywhere to everywhere.
2. Affirming the primacy of the Majority World church in the completion of the Great Commission.
3. Increasing commitment to genuine partnerships with Majority World churches, denominations, and mission agencies.
4. Evaluating sources of cultural prejudice in HBC mission values, methods and structures.
5. Prioritizing the Diaspora Reaching the Diaspora.
6. Creating pathways to recruit and fund HBC missionaries from within the global diaspora.
7. Shifting the focus of theological and ministry education away from formal programs for professional clergy towards church-based training programs for overseas, secular workers.
8. Providing holistic care as an essential component of diaspora missions.

For discussion

1. Can your church or mission agency locate possible areas of cultural prejudice in majority world partnerships or in mobilizing missionary staff from other ethnicities?
2. How can your church or mission agency help churches in the Global South mobilize, train and care for their overseas workers?
3. Discuss ways that your church or mission agency can better understand the contexts of weakness and suffering that is characteristic of the global diaspora.

Bibliography

Baxter, John F. 2009. "The Importance of the Local Church in Diaspora Missions." *Journal of Asian Mission* 11(1-2) (March-September):113-119.

Goldin, Ian, Geoffrey Cameron, and Meera Balarajan. 2011. *Exceptional People: How Migration Shaped Our World and Will Define Our Future.* Princeton: Princeton University Press. Kindle edition.

The Pew Forum on Religion and Public Life. 2012. *Faith on the Move: the Religious Affiliation of International Migrants.* Washington: Pew Research Center. Accessed at http://www.pewforum.org/2012/03/08/religious-migration-exec/, September 12, 2014.

SECTION 7:
GLOSSARY, APPENDICES AND MINISTRY RESOURCES

Tereso Casiño and Charles Cook, Section Editors

GLOSSARY

A

Absorption: A social reality that takes place when a nation that took more people in (i.e., non-natives) as compared to a nation from which people moved out or away. (Ernest George Ravenstein)

Activists for Diaspora: Social workers, politicians, the NGOs, and other diaspora advocates and allies who are caring for the scattered and arguing for their basic human rights. (Grant McClung)

Adopted Land: The land where migrants and displaced people settle, to make for themselves new homes. (Chase Robinson)

Afro-Caribbean Diaspora: A cross reference to the elements of the Jewish diaspora with the movements of the African-American community associated with the diaspora of Moses and Abraham. (Robert Cohen)

Age of Migration: A description of the increasing scale and scope of migration throughout the world. (J. D. Payne)

Alien: Any individual who is not a national of the state in which he or she is present. (Paul Sydnor)

Ashkenazim: Jews who settled in "Northern Europe" during the reign of Charlemagne. (Robin Cohen)

Assimilation: A social process of adapting one's (the diasporas) lifestyle to the social class to which they aspire to belong. (Darrell Jackson)

Asylum: The grant, by a State, of protection on its territory to persons from another State who are fleeing persecution or serious danger. Asylum encompasses a variety of elements, including non-refoulement, permission to remain on the territory of the asylum country, and humane standards of treatment. (UNHCR)

Asylum Seeker: An individual who is "seeking international protection. In countries with individualized procedures, an asylum seeker is someone whose claim has not yet been finally decided on by the country in which he or she has submitted it. Not every asylum seeker will ultimately be recognized as a refugee, but every refugee is initially an asylum seeker." (UNHCR)

Attractive Force: Symbolizes the OT where Temple and Tabernacle served as places where people became attracted to meet with God. The Bible records where several other foreigners were also attracted to Israel because of the evidence of God's blessing. (Janak BC)

B

Babel Complex: A desire to be centripetal, but never centrifugal. (LDLT)

Battlefield Diasporas/Military Diaspora: Soldiers stationed overseas away from their homeland. (Sadiri Joy Tira)

Benefactor Mentality: A false assumption that migrants are to be viewed only as objects of clarity. (Cody Lorance)

Borderless:[1] Originally used by economists to describe the state of political economy in which institutions operate globally and are not fixed to a specific place. (Sadiri Joy Tira)

Borderless:[2] The lack of separation between countries. (Thomas Hieber)

Borderless World:[1] People no longer remain in their own countries due to transnationalism, decentralization, and deterritorialization. (Sadiri Joy Tira)

Borderless World:[2] The state of political economy in which institutions operate globally and are not fixed to a specific place, given that people all around the world are connected twenty-four hour, seven-days-a-week, in 'real time,' and travel technologies enable people to cross time zones in hours. (Sadiri Joy Tira)

Bridge Peoples:[1] Bi-cultural people who, because of their dual ethnic identities, fit in both their home countries and their new locations. (J. D. Payne)

Bridge Peoples:[2] Bicultural people who, because of their dual ethnic identities, fit in both their home countries and their new locations. (Winston Smith)

C

Center-margin: When Christian faith withers in the center, it begins anew at the margins. (Sam George)

Chain Migration: The arrival city sends cash and provides basic lines of credit to the village; it arranges jobs and marriages across international boundaries and sets up schemes to circumvent immigration restrictions. (Doug Saunders)

CHASTE: Churches against Sexual Trafficking in Europe.

Christian Hosts: People who intentionally engage with immigrants and share the gospel of Jesus Christ with them; hosts are needed even in countries where Christianity is readily accepted. (Sadiri Joy Tira)

Conservation Migration: The mover changes residence to maintain his present standard of living, and innovative migration where the move is made in order to improve living standards. (Kenneth C. W. Kammeyer)

Contrapuntal Perspective: As exiles and migrants cross borders and break barriers of thought and experience, they become aware of simultaneous dimensions that make possible an originality of vision. (Edward W. Said)

Cultural/Hybrid/Postmodern Diaspora: Diaspora created through physical migration and airwaves (e.g., the migration of ideas or music). (Robin Cohen)

D

Decentralization: The dispersal of peoples from centralized areas. (Bob Roberts)

Demanding Assimilation: The desire for everyone else to conform to the host's cultural preferences. (Cody Lorance)

Deterritorialization: The dispersal of territories from central areas. (Bob Roberts)

De-territorialized: The loss of social and cultural boundaries in missions strategy. (Enoch Wan and Sadiri Joy Tira)

Diaspora:[1] A biblical word and a vital biblical theme in redemptive history; from the Greek word, διασπορά (in the New Testament): Translated as 'dispersion,' 'dispersed,' 'scattered.' (LDLT)

Diaspora:[2] A missional means decreed and blessed by God (Gen. 1:28; 9:1; 12:3; 28:14) under His sovereign rule to promote the expansion of His Kingdom and the fulfillment of the Great Commission (Matt. 24:14; 28:17-20). (LDLT)

Diaspora:[3] A reference to a collective trauma, a banishment, where one dreamed of home but lived in exile. (Robin Cohen)

Diaspora:[4] A positive and ongoing relationship between migrants' homeland and their places of work and settlement. (Robin Cohen)

Diaspora:[5] Refers primarily to 'a scattering,' describing the large-scale movement of people from their homeland to settle permanently or temporarily in other countries. It was first used of the Jewish people scattered in exile from the 6th century BC onwards. The word is also used in the New Testament of God's new people, the followers of Christ scattered in 'exile' (1 Pet. 1:1; James 1:1). There have been many Diasporas over the centuries. However, the 20th and the 21st centuries have seen unprecedented movements of peoples, mostly because of war, famine, economic needs, and opportunities. The effects of these migrations are deep and wide-ranging for the Diaspora communities themselves, for their host countries, and for their country of origin. (LOP #55: *The New People Next Door*)

Diaspora:[6] Communities with shared identities such as "language, religion, custom of folklore" that have settled outside their natal (or imagined natal) territories" and that maintain some sort of loyalty and emotional links with "the old country." (Robin Cohen)

Diaspora:[7] The dispersion of persons and people within God's redemptive plan in human history." (LDLT)

Diaspora:[8] The dispersion of individuals or any ethnic group.

Diaspora:[9] "Historically the word was used to refer to the population of Jews exiled from Israel in 607 BC under the Babylonians and from Judea in 70 AD under the Roman Empire." (Enoch Wan)

Diaspora:[10] Refers to people on the move who cross national borders, specifically, the scattered peoples of the world. (T. V. Thomas, Sadiri Joy Tira, and Enoch Wan)

Diaspora:[11] For the Greeks, from whose language the word originated, diaspora meant the dispersal of population through colonization. (Robin Cohen)

Diaspora:[12] Originally referring to the Jewish exilic dispersion, but has since included the endless categories of people who are currently on the move, displaced by socio-economic factors, hostile government actions, religious intolerance or cultural shifts. A description of the postmodern human beings who have experienced collapse in life experiences and a sense of loss of future hope. (Aniedi Abasiekong)

Diaspora:[13] Originally a Greek word referring to the Jewish dispersion, i.e. to the scattering of Jews outside Palestine (Lev. 26:33; Deut. 28:64; Ezek. 36:19) and also refers to the scattering of Christians of the early Church in the New Testament (Acts 8:1, 4; 11:19). Over the centuries, the term diaspora has been added to contemporary vocabulary in reference to the People on the Move who will cross national borders, i.e. the scattered peoples. Other terms such as migration, emigration and immigration have been used in reference to People on the Move. (T.V. Thomas, Sadiri Joy Tira, and Enoch Wan)

Diaspora:[14] People who have relocated from their lands of birth for whatever reason. (Sadiri Joy Tira)

Diaspora:[15] People who take up residence away from their places of origin. (Enoch Wan)

Diaspora:[16] When used in the singular form, diaspora refers to the fact of leaving one's homeland and being on the move (voluntary or involuntary migration/immigration) of an individual or a people-group, i.e., Filipino diaspora, the Brazilian diaspora. (LDLT)

Diaspora:[17] The mass migrations and displacements of the second-half of the twentieth century, particularly in reference to independence movements in formerly colonized areas, waves of refugees fleeing from war-torn states, and fluxes of economic migration in the post-World War II era. (Jana Evans Braziel and Anita Mannur)

Diaspora:[18] The word 'diaspora' is derived from the Greek verb *speiro* (to sow) and the preposition *dia* (over). When applied to humans, the ancient Greeks thought of diaspora as migration and colonization. By contrast, from Jews, Africans, Palestinians and Armenians the expression acquired a more sinister and brutal meaning. Diaspora signified a collective trauma, a banishment, where one dreamed of home but lived in exile. Other peoples abroad who have also maintained strong collective identities have, in recent years, defined themselves as diasporas, though they were neither active agents of colonization nor passive victims of persecution. (Robin Cohen)

Diaspora:[19] "People who are temporarily residing abroad and pilgrims on the earth." (LDLT)

Diasporas: When used in the plural form, the term diasporas refers to a group of people or groups as a whole leaving their homeland (voluntary or involuntary migration/immigration), being on the move. (LDLT)

Diaspora Academies: Educational institutions actively moving the new, emerging missiological discipline of "diaspora missiology" forward with educators' consultations, training seminars, and publications. (Grant McClung)

Diaspora Activists: Diaspora missions leaders who are the social workers, politicians, and other diaspora advocates and allies. (Grant McClung)

Diaspora Agencies: The parachurch missions who are leading international diaspora initiatives with resources and assigned staff leaders. (Grant McClung)

Diaspora Agenda: Informed by the priorities and vision of the Lausanne Movement, the agenda refers to the commitment and intentional effort to evangelize, disciple, and mobilize people on the move. It is reaching out to the scattered peoples in the world. (Sadiri Joy Tira)

Diaspora by Design: The strategic movement and placement of people groups on their own accord for the purpose of benefiting and pushing forward their influence on the global scene. (J. Kottin)

Diaspora Champion: Kingdom workers who *champion* the cause of Diaspora Missiology. (Sadiri Joy Tira)

Diaspora Church Planting: The process of starting church plants, specifically targeting diaspora populations. (Cody Lorance)

Diaspora Community: This includes permanent immigrants, naturalized citizens, and second generation immigrants. (Christopher Lawrence)

Diaspora Conditions: This includes economic migrants seeking work; internally-displaced peoples because of war or natural disaster; refugees and asylum seekers; victims of ethnic cleansing; people fleeing religious violence and persecution; famine sufferers – whether caused by drought, floods, or war; victims of rural poverty moving to cities. (Sadiri Joy Tira)

Diaspora Dependencies: This refers to recipients who eventually become dependent on "diaspora donations" given by diaspora congregations. (Sadiri Joy Tira)

Diaspora Dollar:[1] This refers to money that migrant workers spend and invest in their home countries including the support of families, education, investing in real estate, assisting in developing the agriculture in their communities, buying vehicles and building houses for their loved ones, and supporting local schools and healthcare initiatives. Remittances are sent home for relief work and emergency assistance. Migrant worker dollars are received in their home countries and are used for needs as well as leisure. (Sadiri Joy Tira)

Diaspora Dollar:[2] Monies earned by immigrants, naturalized citizens, and even second generation immigrants, invested in the local economies of their host nations, and support the homeland through remittances, which makes the diaspora people major contributors to their homelands and to their host nations abroad. (Sadiri Joy Tira)

Diaspora Dollar:[3] Money that is introduced to an economy by people in diaspora, whether it goes back to their home country or stays in the country of their residence. (Sadiri Joy Tira)

Diaspora Dollar:[4] This refers to funding used for diaspora people groups/missions. (Sadiri Joy Tira)

Diaspora Factor: A paradigm shift that has had increasing numbers of missionaries from the "non-Western" world, involving people on the move. (Sam George)

Diaspora in Missions: A reference to the dispersed ethnic groups who are actively engaged or actively involved in fulfilling the Great Commission regardless of vocations and denominational affiliations of individuals involved. (Sadiri Joy Tira)

Diasporic: A term used to describe a range of different activities and conditions, from the trauma of exile to political mobilization to cultural creativity. (Kevin Kenny)

Diaspora Ministries Field: Global borderless mission field, which is one of five major strategic focuses for OMF International as a mission. It crosses borders and brings strategic direction to something that has not been strategic in the past. (Carolyn Kemp)

Diaspora Ministry:[1] A ministry amongst diaspora populations and returnees. (Carolyn Kemp)

Diaspora Ministry:[2] Serving the diaspora in the name of Jesus Christ and for His sake in these two ways: (1) ministering to the diaspora, i.e., serving the diaspora, and (2) ministering through the diaspora, i.e., mobilizing the diaspora to serve others." (Enoch Wan)

Diaspora Ministry Facilitator: A Christian who does research and documents the different locations of a people group, researching who is reaching out to members of the people group, networking with those who could network with another people group, seeking to interest other churches and individuals in reaching out to the group, visiting some of the points in the diaspora to network and get firsthand information and seeking funding for projects that could benefit the whole people group. (Al Lee)

Diaspora Missiology:[1] A missiological framework for understanding and participating in God's redemptive mission among people living outside their place of origin. (LDLT)

Diaspora Missiology:[2] A missiological framework for understanding and participating in God's redemptive mission among diaspora groups; an interdisciplinary study of integrating Missiology with human geography, cultural anthropology, political demography, urban/ethnic studies, communication sciences, etc. (Enoch Wan)

Diaspora Missiology:[3] A Christian response to the diaspora phenomena in the twenty-first century. (Enoch Wan)

Diaspora Missiology:[4] An approach to thinking about the missionary work of the church from an integrated perspective, including the sending of cross-cultural missionaries to work with the migrants who return. (J. D. Payne)

Diaspora Missiology:[5] A new strategy for missions. Diaspora missions is a providential and strategic way to minister to 'the nations' by the diaspora and through the diaspora. (Sadiri Joy Tira and Enoch Wan)

Diaspora Missiology:[6] An integrated discipline, bringing migration research to bear on the study of missions. (J. D. Payne)

Diaspora Missiology:[7] A specialized study of missiology and migration theory. As previously suggested, this data is to be analyzed resulting in missiological implications for missions planning and strategy. (Sadiri Joy Tira)

Diaspora Missiology:[8] God is orchestrating both the movement of Israel and the church to bring his people and His blessing to the people of the world. (Michael Pocock)

Diaspora Missiology:[9] An interdisciplinary study of academic fields related to who, what, when, where, and how populations are moving, e.g., anthropology, demography, economics, geography, history, law, political science, sociology, and classic missiological study, e.g., theology, missiology, biblical studies, evangelism. (Sadiri Joy Tira)

Diaspora Missiology:[10] A study of social groups that are identified by ethnicity, migration patterns, or pop culture. They are either outside of their place of origin or are in the midst of transition. (Tuvya Zaretsky)

Diaspora Missiology:[11] An emerging missiological discipline that studies the various aspects of missional thinking and strategies for reaching the diaspora people groups around the world. It includes a combination of educators, consultants, seminars, missionaries, para-church agencies, publications, statisticians, among others. (Grant McClung)

Diaspora missions: The practical application of diaspora missiology that includes ministering to (in evangelism and service), ministering through (motivate and mobilize) the diasporic groups, and ministering beyond them (to other groups) in the fulfillment of the Great Commission. (Sadiri Joy Tira)

Diaspora missions:[1] A strategy in response to the reality of the demographic trend of diaspora in the 21st century. Diaspora missions includes 'missions to the diaspora,' 'missions through the diaspora,' and 'missions by and beyond the diaspora.' (LDLT)

Diaspora Missions:[2] Christians' participation in God's redemptive mission to evangelize their kinsmen on the move, and through them to reach out to natives in their homelands and beyond. (Enoch Wan)

Diaspora Missions:[3] The practical application of diaspora missiology that includes ministering *to* (in evangelism and service), ministering *through* (motivate and mobilize) the diasporic groups and ministering *beyond* them (to other groups in the fulfillment of the Great Commission). (T.V. Thomas, Sadiri Joy Tira, and Enoch Wan)

Diaspora Missions:[4] A missionary effort based on the premise that missions is economically sustainable, benefits from travel accessibility to the target audience, has less political and legal restrictions, partnership among like-minded people and organizations committed to the Great Commission, and missions are done not only by few experts or international workers. (Enoch Wan)

Diaspora Missions:[5] The Christian's participation in God's redemptive mission to evangelize their kinsmen on the move and through them, to natives in their homeland and beyond. (T. V. Thomas, Enoch Wan, and Sadiri Joy Tira)

Diaspora Missions:[6] The ways and means of fulfilling the Great Commissions by ministering to and through the diaspora groups. (LDLT)

Diaspora Movement: A global trend that has marked the 20th and 21st centuries that touches most countries of the world. More than 200 million people now live and work outside their homeland. (T.V. Thomas, Sadiri Joy Tira, Enoch Wan)

Diaspora Networks: An archipelago of nodes linked together by shared cultural space and aided by technology and modern transportation. (Sam George)

Diaspora People: People belonging to more than one culture who have to learn to adapt. (LOP #55: *The New People Next Door*)

Diaspora People Group: A people group that has been scattered and crossed country borders. (Christopher Lorance)

Diaspora Returnee: Peoples returning to their country of origin after being previously dispersed. (Carolyn Kemp)

Diasporas of the Battle Field: People who are relocated to other countries because of their military services. (Sadiri Joy Tira)

Dichotomized Approach to Missions: This term is used to describe the split, in common mission's approach thinking within churches and denominations, that there is a difference between "foreign vs. home missions." This sort of mindset is singularly focused on getting missionaries from here to there instead of from everywhere to everywhere. The dichotomy puts the international mission's responsibility on those who are international workers instead of motivating, mentoring and mobilizing the ordinary migrant "Kingdom Workers." (Sadiri Joy Tira)

Displaced People: Refugees or asylum seekers who may be either temporary or permanent residents. (LOP #55: *The New People Next Door*)

Displacement: This describes the condition of being uprooted. Whereas, forced displacement refers to specific groups such as refugees, exiles, and trafficked persons, displacement refers to the situation faced by many mixed migrant groups and therefore, it summarizes the defining condition common to many diaspora people. (Paul Sydnor)

Durable Solutions: This refers to three options for responding to forcibly displaced persons defined by the UNHCR as (1) Return to their homeland; (2) Resettlement in a new country; and (3) Integration in the country where they have fled to. (Paul Sydnor)

E

Economic Migrant: Someone who leaves their country of origin in order to improve their quality of life. "Persons who leave their countries of origin purely for economic reasons not in any way related to the refugee definition, or in order to seek material improvements in their livelihood. Economic migrants do not fall within the criteria for refugee status and are therefore not entitled to benefit from international protection as refugees." (UNHCR)

Emigration: The departure from one's country to settle elsewhere. (J. D. Payne)

Expatriate: A person temporarily or permanently residing in a country and culture other than that of the person's upbringing. (Sadiri Joy Tira)

Floating Communities: All sorts of groups people who move, and traverse, the globe by ships. (Sadiri Joy Tira)

Floating Population: In China, these "are people living in the city but holding village registration papers" and "are not entitled to urban housing, welfare, medical care, or access to schooling for their children in the city." (Doug Saunders)

Flying Communities: The flying communities are diaspora people (all sorts of people) who get in airplanes and move from one geographic/social/economic/cultural location to another. (Sadiri Joy Tira)

Forced Migration: A general term used to describe a migratory movement in which an element of coercion exists, including threats to life and livelihood, whether arising from natural or man-made causes (e.g. movements of refugees and internally displaced persons as well as people displaced by natural or environmental disasters, chemical or nuclear disasters, famine, or development projects). (International Organization of Migration)

Foreign Born: Persons who have become naturalized, that is, who have taken on the nationality (or citizenship) of the receiving country. (J. D. Payne)

Foreign Nationals: Excludes those who have taken on the nationality of the receiving country, but includes children born to immigrants who retain their parents' nationality. (Stephen Castles and Mark J. Miller)

G

Gateway City: A broadly successful arrival city: its poor neighborhoods send out successful middle-class and upper-working-class migrants to wealthier neighborhoods at rates similar to their intake of poor villagers. (Doug Saunders)

Globalization: A process of international integration arising from the interchange of world views, products, ideas, and other aspects of culture due to advances in telecommunications, faster and safer forms of transportation, as well as new political structures; helped facilitate the movement of large numbers of people on a global scale. (J. D. Payne)

Global Cities: The global shifts in the location of financial services, industrial plant and other constituents of the world economy impose a defining spatial grid on the patterns of global power. (Robin Cohen)

Global Diaspora Network (GDN): Organized in Cape Town, South Africa, during Lausanne III in order to broaden the Diaspora network and take on the diasporas beyond the congress event. GDN *is a catalytic movement that motivates and mobilizes diaspora Christians to partner for global missions.* (Sadiri Joy Tira)

Global Human Diaspora: God's activity of purposefully scattering his image-bearers around the world in order to gather disciples to himself from every people, nation, tribe, and tongue (Cody Lorance)

Global Nomads: These are migrants or scattered people. (Sadiri Joy Tira)

Glocal: The engagement in "global missions at home" and often in homes and other settings of hospitality by local citizens of a host-nation with people from other nations. (Leiton Chinn)

H

Habiru: This term is not an ethnic group but a marginal social stratum or class who tended to live in bands or clans on the edges of society, and were generally to be found in a broad swath of societies and nations across the ancient near east. (Enoch Wan)

Hidden Generation: Children of immigrants whose struggles have to do with the notion of their identity, belonging, and vocational commitment. They suffer from double marginalization – first because of their ethnicity, and secondly due to generational differences. They become a minority within a minority in the multiethnic, multicultural world of the West and this acute marginality eats them up from the inside. (Sam George)

Hollow Village: Rural enclaves of children and grandparents where the aging grandparents have become responsible for raising the children of their children because the parents are away in the arrival city. (Doug Saunders)

Host Culture: The national culture of the country a person in diaspora is residing in, not the culture of their home. (Paul Haenze)

Human Trafficking: The U.N. defines human trafficking as "…the recruitment, transportation, transfer, harbouring or receipt of persons, by means of the threat or use of force or other forms of coercion, of abduction, of fraud, of deception, of the abuse of power or of a position of vulnerability or of the giving or receiving of payments or benefits to achieve the consent of a person having control over another person, for the purpose of exploitation." This exploitation can take different forms, including but not limited to prostitution or other kinds of sexual exploitation, forced labor or services, slavery or practices similar to slavery, and the removal of organs. Victims of trafficking have either never consented to the trafficking or their initial consent has been rendered meaningless by the coercive, deceptive or abusive actions of the traffickers. (Paul Sydnor)

Hybridized Identities: This refers to fragmented, postcolonial identities in the choppy seas of postmodernism. (Robin Cohen)

I

I.F.E.S.: This stands for the International Fellowship of Evangelical Students which started in 1947 and has indigenous student ministries, mostly college and university level with some high-school and vocational school outreaches in more than 150 nations. (Leiton Chinn)

Illegal Immigrant (or Illegal Alien): A term widely used in both public and official discourse in many countries to denote those people who have entered a country "illegally" – without proper visas or identity papers. The United States defines an "illegal alien" as a "comprehensive term intended to include those foreign-born individuals who enter, reside, or work in the United States without complying with U.S. immigration law" (Department of Homeland Security Office 2006). Considered a disparaging term by many rights advocates, "illegal immigrant" is also a legally misleading term because most countries who detain people on migration grounds do so for administrative purposes and do not charge them with having committed a crime. (Paul Sydnor)

Immigrant: An all-encompassing term usually referring to someone who leaves their native land and goes to another country as a permanent resident (e.g., as distinct from a holidaymaker). (Paul Sydnor)

Immigration: The movement of people into another country to settle. (J. D. Payne)

Immovability: When a Christian or group of Christians resist large or small scale geographic movement in favor of the comfort, security, predictability, and/or familiarity of home. (Enoch Wan)

Imperial/Colonial Diaspora: Migrants who go to another land that has been conquered by their own nation and enjoy higher status on account of their ethnic ties to the ruling power. Do not adapt to local customs, locals adapt to their customs. (Robin Cohen)

Institute of Diaspora Studies: A joint effort of researchers and practitioners seeking to understand and minister to the people of diaspora – people dispersed from their original homeland. (Global Diaspora Network)

Integration: A long-term and multi-dimensional process, requiring a commitment on the part of both migrants and non-migrant members of society to respect and adapt to each other, thereby enabling them to interact in a positive and peaceful manner. (Darrell Jackson)

Intentional Diaspora Training: A concerted effort made to teach diaspora missiology both at the formal and non-formal level, training future pastors, international workers (missionaries), and lay leaders. Intentional diaspora training would prepare workers for ministry in the borderless world. (Enoch Wan)

Interculturalism: This assumes the need for encounter, mutual understanding, integration, respect, co-existence, and exchange. It is apparent, however, that what constitutes the practice of intercultural dialogue is still far from clear. (Darrell Jackson)

Internal Migration: Moving to a different location in one's country. (J. D. Payne)

Internally Displaced People (IDPs): People who have been forced to flee their homes, but not their country. IDPs and refugees are often uprooted by similar causes (e.g. war, persecution, violations of human rights, etc.). Some IDPs are displaced by natural disasters (e.g. tsunamis, earthquakes, volcanoes, cyclones, etc.). IDPs are the largest group of forcibly displaced people in the world. (Paul Sydnor)

International or All Nations Churches: Congregations that openly and purposely welcome people of all languages and nations. (Chase Robinson)

International Church: A church that primarily serves people of various nationalities (expatriates) and church backgrounds living outside their passport (home) countries, and a "missional" church as one that is "shaped by and oriented around the mission to which Christ has commissioned His followers. (Sadiri Joy Tira)

International Church Planting: Churches made up of members from multiple nations. (LOP #55: *The New People Next Door*)

International Migrant: "Someone who has been living one year or longer in a country other than the one in which he or she was born." (Pew Forum's Faith on the Move)

International Migrants: People who are on the move from their homeland; people whose migration challenges our ideas about home missions vs. foreign missions. (Sadiri Joy Tira)

International Student Ministries (ISM): A ministry among international students, which is a highly strategic component of "world evangelization in reverse," where relationships and interaction with students of the world occur in one's own country's campuses, communities, and churches, rather than in another nation. Historically, ISM has focused primarily among college and university undergraduate and graduate students, but is expanding to embrace the increasing number of international pre-college high-school and middle-school students, language students, and non-degree students at vocational and technical institutions, and may include university post-graduate scholars, researchers, faculty and administrators. ISM is a variation of the broader context of diaspora ministry of serving and loving the foreign-born God brings to our neighborhoods. (Leiton Chinn)

Intra-Ethnic Group Church Planting: A collaborative effort among established diaspora churches to work together by sharing resources for planting new churches for the new immigrants. (LOP #55: *The New People Next Door*)

Irregular Migrant:[1] This refers to someone who lacks legal status in a transit or host country. These have often entered a country without legal documentation, and in many cases they have been forced to take extreme measures to cross borders because of circumstance outside of their control. (Paul Sydnor)

Irregular Migrant:[2] The term applies to migrants who infringe a country's admission rules and any other person not authorized to remain in the host country (also called clandestine/ illegal/undocumented migrant or migrant in an irregular situation). (International Organization of Migration)

Irregular Migrants:[1] "People who have fled their homes for reasons similar to refugees, but who remain within their own national territory and are subject to the laws of that state." (Jojo Manzano)

Irregular or Illegal Immigrants:[2] People who do not come the 'normal way' with a proper visa stamped in their passport. (Thomas Hieber)

ISM in Reverse: A strategy by those involved in International Student Ministry in their country to intentionally enroll as international students in order to minister to both the nationals of another country as well as among international students in the host nation. This is analogous to being an "academic tent-maker." This equally applies to a faculty who proactively seeks teaching opportunities abroad. (Leiton Chinn)

L

Labor Diaspora: Those who move across international borders to work in one country while remaining citizens in another. (M. Weiner)

Labor/Service Diaspora: Individuals or groups of people who move as indentured servants or move for jobs and work. (Robin Cohen)

Language of Convenience: Verbiage that seems to suggest that the reason to engage in diaspora missions is that doing so is cheaper, sager, less time-consuming or otherwise more convenient. (Cody Lorance)

M

Macro-Migration: A theory that was developed to explain labor migration in the process of economic development. (Douglas S. Massey et al.)

Micro-Migration: When the moving of people on an international scale is directly tied to personal choices based global labor trends. (Andrew S. Rawls)

Migrant:[1] A person whose decision to migrate is taken freely due to reasons of "personal convenience" and without intervention of an external compelling factor. (International Organization of Migration)

Migrant:[2] A person in transition that is experiencing the loss of roots and may be open to new commitments. (Samuel Escobar)

Migrants: Those who would be categorized as long-term workers or short-term workers, students, refugees, stateless people, asylum seekers, and people in the process of immigrating as well as those who have immigrated to another country. (J. D. Payne)

Migrant Worker:[1] A person admitted by a state for a specific economic activity which is remunerated from within the receiving country. The length of stay and type of employment are usually restricted. (Paul Sydnor)

Migrant Worker:[2] A person who is to be engaged, is engaged or has been engaged in a remunerated activity in a State of which he or she is not a national (Art. 2, International Convention on the Protection of the Rights of All Migrant Workers and Members of Their Families, 1990).

Migration:[1] This is defined broadly as a permanent or semi-permanent change of residence. No restriction is placed upon the distance of the move or upon the voluntary or involuntary nature of the act, and no distinction is made between external and internal migration. (Everett Lee)

Migration:[2] "The movement of a people from one location of residence to another location of residence." (J. D. Payne, *Strangers Next Door*, 27.)

Migration Industry: The rising trend that involves private lawyers, travel agents, recruiters organizers, fixers and brokers who sustain links with origin and destination countries. Such intermediaries are driven by the cash nexus and make no distinctions, except in terms of price, between refugee and migrant, professional or unskilled, illegal or legal migration. (Robin Cohen)

Migration Theories: Refers to approaches that examine the initiation of migration and those that look at how migration processes develop their own momentum once started. (International Migration Institute)

Missiology:[1] The study of mission – including biblical, theological, historical, contemporary, and practical reflection and research. (Christopher J. H. Wright)

Missiology:[2] The systematic and academic study of missions in the fulfillment of God's mission. (Enoch Wan)

Missional Church: A church shaped by and oriented around the mission to which Christ has commissioned His followers (Missional International Church Network)

Missional Transnationals: Those migrants whose missions initiatives regularly transcend borders with an ongoing cross-border missions involvement. (Sadiri Joy Tira)

Mission Hospitality: The whole church working toward rekindling a love of hospitality, and, in doing so, to reach out to their religious (and nonreligious) neighbors. (Gina A. Bellofatto for the Lausanne Movement)

Mission in Reverse or Reverse Mission: Initiated by spontaneous Christians in non-Western world, like Africa, Asia, and Latin America, non-Western churches return with the gospel to the societies to which they have been greatly indebted for the purpose of building capacity for the world mission together. (Hun Kim)

Missions Mathematics: A term used to describe the use of mathematic-like problem solving templates to strategies for reaching the diaspora and the unreached people groups of the world. (Sadiri Joy Tira)

Missions *beyond* the Diasporas:[1] Missions done by the diasporas cross-culturally, evangelizing members of the host society and other ethnic groups in their immediate context. (LDLT)

Missions *beyond* the Diasporas[2]: A reference to diasporic believers who are not only called to reach their own peoples but also to be involved in cross-cultural missionary labors. (J. D. Payne)

Missions *by* and beyond the Diaspora: A reference to the motivation and mobilization of diaspora Christians for cross-cultural missions to other ethnic groups in their host counties, homelands, and abroad. (Enoch Wan)

Missions *through* the Diasporas:[1] A reference to the diasporas who are evangelizing their kinsmen in their homeland or elsewhere. (LDLT)

Missions *through* the Diaspora:[2] A reference to diaspora Christians reaching out to their kinsmen through networks of friendship and kinship in host countries, their homelands, and abroad. (Enoch Wan)

Missions *through* the Diasporas:[3] A reference to the diasporic believers who return to their countries to share the good news and plant churches among their peoples. (J. D. Payne)

Missions *to* the Diaspora:[1] A reference to the fact that when God is moving the diasporas geographically making them accessible, the Church should not miss any opportunity to reach them with the gospel." (LDLT)

Missions *to* the Diaspora:[2] A reference to reaching the diaspora groups in forms of evangelism or pre-evangelistic social services, then disciple them to become worshipping communities and congregations. (Enoch Wan)

Mixed Migration: Complex groups of people including: refugees, asylum seekers, economic migrants, and others who are living outside of their place of origin due to multiple reasons. (Paul Sydnor)

Monoculturalism: The assumption that all other people are like us, resulting in the tendency to judge other peoples' actions and attitudes on the basis of our own. (Van Rheenen)

Multiculturalism:[1] The assumption that several different cultures (rather than one national culture) can coexist peacefully and equitably in a single country. (Darrell Jackson)

Multiculturalism:[2] A reference to the policies and rules that govern an area that is demographically diverse in an attempt to promote such diversity. (Sadiri Joy Tira)

N

National/Immigrant Churches: Churches that serve a particular nationality that is different from the nation it is within. Oftentimes these churches are conducted in the language of the immigrants. (Peter Brierley)

Nation-Peoples: A reference to groups evincing a "peoplehood" through the retention or expression of separate languages, customs, folkways, and religions. (Robin Cohen)

Non-Refoulement: A core principle of international refugee law that prohibits States from returning refugees in any manner whatsoever to countries or territories in which their lives or freedom may be threatened. The principle of non-refoulement is a part of customary international law and is therefore binding on all States, whether or not they are parties to the 1951 Convention. (UNHCR)

Non-spatial: In reference to diaspora missiology, non-spatial means not geographically divided or confined to dichotomized categories like home/foreign, regional/global, and urban/rural. Diaspora missions is borderless. (Enoch Wan)

O

Overseas Foreign Workers: A term that generally refers to Filipinos working overseas who, along with their families, are often subject to harsh conditions and abuse. (Sadiri Joy Tira)

Overstayer (also, **Overstay**): A term used in many countries to designate non-citizens who have remained in a country after their visas have expired. (Paul Sydnor)

P

Parallel Expansion: The term refers to multiple centers of Christianity. (Sam George)

Paternalistic: In reference to the practice of diaspora missions, the term highlights the lack of relational touch and partnership. (T. V. Thomas, Sadiri Joy Tira, and Enoch Wan)

People Blindness: A blindness to the existence of distinct people groups within countries (Cody Lorance)

People Group: A significantly large sociological grouping of individuals who perceive themselves to have a common affinity with one another. (Christopher Lorance)

People Movements: A phenomenon of a significant number of the people of one tribe, class, or caste converting to Christ together (David Hesselgrave)

Permanent Migrants: Immigrants or legal permanent residents abroad whose stay does not depend on work contracts. (Jojo Manzano)

Prophetic Migrant: A reference to how God uses cultural outsiders to prophetically challenge locals in their comfort, affluence, and cultural insulation. (Craig Greenfield)

Protracted Refugee: A reference to a situation in which 25,000 or more refugees of the same nationality have been exiled for five years or longer in any given asylum country. (UNHCR)

Psychological Alienation: As a result of alienation through political, religious, militaristic, trade moving. This can occur when the relocation through migration or immigration has caused the mover to fail to connect with the new surrounding, thus, leaving the mover alienated. It is different from other forms of alienation in that it combines other forms of alienation and internalizes them into the psyche of the mover. (Andrew S. Rawls)

Psychological Alienation: A reference to lack of "bonding in the new setting." (Robin Cohen)

Push and Pull Factors: It is the human movement precipitated by a complicated combination of factors that "push" a people out of their place of origin and "pull" them into a particular host country. (Enoch Wan)

Q

Quasi-Diaspora: Those people who move temporarily from their places of origin within a country (e.g., students for academic pursuit, migrant workers from rural urban centers for employment, travelers or tourists, airline crew members, internally displaced persons) and people who go abroad temporarily (e.g., students diplomats, embassy staff, military servicemen). (Enoch Wan)

R

Recreational Migrants: A reference to long-term tourists. (Sadiri Joy Tira)

Reentry Shock: Cultural disorientation experienced when people return to their own country. It is based upon the fact that both they and their home culture have significantly changed during their time on the mission fields. (Gailyn Van Rheenen)

Refugees:[1] Refugees are people who have been uprooted from their homes and forced to seek refuge in a foreign country. Often, the word is used in a general way to refer to many kinds of forcibly displaced people. Technically, the word also describes a narrowly defined legal status that is given to some forcibly displaced people based on the UNHCR definition: "A refugee is someone who owing to a well-founded fear of being persecuted for reasons of race, religion, nationality, membership of a particular social group or political opinion, is outside the country of his nationality, and is unable to, or owing to such fear, is unwilling to avail himself of the protection of that country." (UNHCR)

Refugees:[2] People who flee their homeland. This fleeing can take place for a number of reasons including political, religious, ethnic, among others. (J. D. Payne)

Refugees:[3] People who are looking for a place where they can find a place of refuge, protection, and provision. (Peter Vimalasekaran)

Relational Paradigm: A paradigm of missions that measures success via qualitative values regarding relationships with unreached people groups. (Enoch Wan)

Religious Diasporas: Peoples who practice a particular religion but are displaced from the their original countries or homeland. (Chase Robinson)

Relocation: A reference to movement of individuals or peoples that may not involve permanent resettlement. It does not include the international sending of missionaries to the nations, but rather the movement of peoples, usually in larger numbers, at times involuntary, and unintentional. (Enoch Wan)

R.E.P.S. Strategy: A missions strategy for reaching the strangers next door, and stands for Reach, Equip, Partner, and Send. (J. D. Payne)

Resource Mobilization: The systematic and planned process by which organisations solicit funds from donors and partners. (Josias Conradie)

Returnees: People who have been part of diaspora but are now returning to their home country. In the context of diaspora missiology, returnees are seen as key people in spreading the gospel. They can be linked with missionaries in their field and help establish churches. (Carolyn Kemp)

Return Migration: A reference to the movement of people who return to their countries of origin or habitual place of residence after spending at least one year in another country. Return migration can be voluntary or the result of an expulsion order. (Paul Sydnor)

Reverse Mission: Non-Western churches return with the gospel to the societies to which they have been greatly indebted for the purpose of building capacity for the world mission together. (Hun Kim)

Reverse Missions: In the context of diaspora missiology, reverse mission refers to the carrying out of mission work in the post-Christian West by diaspora Christians or Christians of the global south. It is also the sending of members of diaspora groups to their homelands or to other countries for mission work. (Enoch Wan)

S

Seasonal Migrants: People who serve as temporary contract workers. (Sadiri Joy Tira)

Secondary Migration: Refugees who move from state-to-state because of family reunification and/or economic factors. (Cody Lorance)

Settler Migration: A reference to people who stay for longer than a season and return home at a favorable time. (Janak BC)

Skype Discipleship: The utilization of skyping and other video-conferencing means to disciple international students who have returned home or moved to another country or location. (Leiton Chinn)

Smuggling of Migrants: "The procurement in order to obtain, directly or indirectly, a financial or other material benefit, of the illegal entry of a person into a state of which the person is not a national or permanent resident." It differs from human trafficking in that it involves the consent of the migrants involved and ends with the arrival of the migrants at their destination. (United Nations)

Sojourning: The cyclical pattern of emigration and return. (Robin Cohen)

Solidarity Co-ethnic Members: In the context of living in countries other than their own, solidarity refers to the sense of unease of difference that diaspora peoples feel in their countries of residence and is paralleled by a tendency to identity instead with follow members of their diaspora in other countries. (Robin Cohen)

Stranded Minority: A reference to groups that often occupy little enclaves that arise through boundary changes. (Robin Cohen)

T

Temporary Migrants: Persons whose stay overseas is employment related, and who are expected to return at the end of their work contracts. (Jojo Manzano)

Terminal Churches: Churches which may have spiritual vitality but can reproduce only arithmetically (2, 4, 6, 8, 10, 12, etc.). Missionaries are teaching others but not training their converts to become reproductive; they are initiating churches but not preparing leaders of these churches to plant other churches. (Gailyn Van Rheenen)

The Old Country: The conception of a linkage, actual or perceived, to a natal land that lays some claim on the community's loyalty and emotions. (Ted Rubesh)

Trade Diaspora: Merchants from one community would live as aliens in another town, learn the language, customs and commercial practices of their hosts, then start the exchange of goods. (Robin Cohen)

Trade Diasporas: An expression used to describe networks of proactive merchants who transport, buy and sell their good over long distances – a phenomenon that has been documented for a number of the world's regions. (Robin Cohen)

Transmigrants: Persons who, having migrated from one nation-state to another, live their lives across borders, participating simultaneously in social relations that embed them in more than one nation-state. (Nina Glick-Schiller)

Trans-migration: The act of moving from the natal land, and translocation into an alien one, together with all of the uncertainties, risk and adjustments inherent in such a move, are recognizable diaspora themes. (Eugene Merrill)

Transnational Migration: A reference to the concept that in the 21st century, more people will belong to two or more societies at the same time. People who fit this category are known as transnational migrants because they work, pray, and express their political interests in several contexts rather than in a single nation-state. Some will put down roots in a host country, maintain strong homeland ties, and belong to religious and political movements that span the globe. (Peggy Levitt)

Transnational Missions: A reference to an integrated approach to missionary strategy. It is the recognition of the reality of international migration, the importance of social networks, and the use of travel and telecommunications to make disciples of all nations without geographical constraints. (J. D. Payne)

Transnational Perspective: A view that describes international migrants not as anomalies, but rather as representative of an increasingly globalized world who found it possible to have multiple localities and arguably also multiple identities. (Nadje Al-Ali and Khalid Koser)

Transnational Missions: An integrated approach to missionary strategy. It is the recognition of the reality of international migration, the importance of social networks and the use of travel and telecommunications to make disciples of all nations without geographical constraints. (J. D. Payne)

Transnationalism: Definitions vary, but generally centre[s] on exchanges, connections and practices across borders, thus transcending the national space as the primary reference point for activities and identities. With respect to migration [transnationalism is] being connected to several places at once – or 'being neither here nor there.' [It] has long been a defining feature of the experience of being a migrant." IOM International Organization for Migration, "International Dialogue on Migration Intersessional Workshop on Migration and Transnationalism: Opportunities and Challenges." March 9-10, 2010. Available at https://www.iom.int/jahia/webdav/shared/shared/mainsite/microsites/IDM/workshops/migration_and_transnationalism_030910/background_paper_en.pdf. Accessed January 3, 2016.

Traveling Cultures: A reference to cultures that have lost their territorial moorings. (Robin Cohen)

U

Undocumented Asylum Seekers: These are people who have entered a country but not yet registered for asylum. They are undeclared asylum seekers and they do not have the appropriate documentation. This includes, among others: "ones (a) who have no legal documentation to enter a country but who manage to enter clandestinely, (b) who enter using fraudulent documentation, (c) who, after entering with legal documentation, have stayed beyond the time authorized or otherwise violated the terms of entry and remained without authorization." (IOM)

V

Victim Diaspora: A class of people who have been banished from their place of origin and sent to another land usually through expulsion, conquest, persecution, enslavement, genocide deportation, genocide, and "ethnic cleansing." (Robin Cohen)

Appendix A
The Baguio Challenge

Filipino Theological Educators Consultation, Filipino International Network, Philippine Baptist Theological Seminary, Baguio City, Philippines, January 4-6, 2006

1. That the Filipino church will continue to excel in equipping all Christians for growth and witness, and training leaders for effective ministry globally.
2. That theological institutions, especially those in the Philippines, will embrace the reality of Filipino diaspora missions and will include missiological training for all pastors and Christian workers.
3. That region-specific curricula be developed to prepare the Filipino diaspora Christians to engage in effective and contextualized ministry.
4. That a sustainable multi-delivery system of formal and non-formal theological education be sensitively coordinated and implemented for diaspora Filipino believers in creative access nations.
5. That networking and partnership be sought with other Diaspora groups and networks to enhance and expand the availability of theological education for all Christians.

APPENDIX B
THE SEOUL DECLARATION ON DIASPORA MISSIOLOGY

LCWE Diaspora Educators Consultation 2009
Torch Trinity Graduate School of Theology, Seoul, South Korea
November 11-14, 2009

Convening as missions leaders, mobilizers, educators, trainers, and kingdom workers in the diaspora at the Lausanne Diaspora Educators Consultation on November 11-14, 2009 in Seoul, Korea, in partnership with and an extension of the Lausanne Diaspora Strategy Consultation held in Manila, Philippines on May 4-8, 2009.

We Acknowledge

1. That the sovereign work of the Father, Son, and Holy Spirit in the gathering and scattering of peoples across the earth is a central part of God's mission and redemptive purposes for the world.
2. That the church, which is the body of Christ, is the principal means through which God is at work in different ways around the globe. We honor the uniqueness, dignity, and beauty in each person and culture, celebrating the collaboration of the church with the broader society.
3. That "diaspora missiology" has emerged as a biblical and strategic field of missiology and is defined as: *a missiological framework for understanding and participating in God's redemptive mission among people living outside their place of origin.*

We Affirm

1. That our missional focus and ministry integrates and cooperates with the mission and vision of the Lausanne movement for world evangelization as published in The Lausanne Covenant and The Manila Manifesto.
2. That although we draw from various disciplines, our understanding and practice of the mission of God must be informed by, integrated with, and conformed to biblical and theological foundations.

We Appeal

1. To the whole people of God in local churches and church movements, mission agencies, the academy, and the marketplace to mobilize, train, deploy, support, work together with, and empower "diaspora kingdom workers" for the diaspora fields ripe for harvest.
2. To church and mission leaders to recognize and respond to opportunities in world evangelization presented by the realities of the global diaspora.
3. To missions leaders and educators to give strategic priority in the funding and training of personnel and to provide space for the development of "diaspora missiology" in training systems and curricula.
4. To the Lord of the harvest to send forth laborers into the harvest and raise up worldwide intercession for an unprecedented move of the Holy Spirit so that *the Whole Church takes the Whole Gospel to the Whole World.*

LCWE Diaspora Educators Consultation 2009, Torch Trinity Graduate School of Theology, Seoul, South Korea. November 11-14, 2009.

Appendix C
Far East Asia Diaspora Educators' Resolutions

Far East Asia Diaspora Educators Consultation
Manila, Philippines, August 12-13, 2011

Resolutions:

We derive the ethos for diaspora missions and ministry from the Holy Scriptures.

- We believe that all people are created in the image of God regardless of their ethnicity, status, and gender.
- We believe that movements of peoples around the world reflect God's creative and redemptive purpose for the Kingdom. The acceleration and intensification of the movement in this generation require a new response from the church.
- We believe that God's mission unfolds from Genesis to Revelation and that mission and ministry to, through, and beyond diaspora peoples is integral to this.

Therefore, we believe that theological educators have a prophetic call to read the signs of the times in the light of the Scripture, advancing the cause of diaspora missions and ministry.

We commit to:

- Developing interdisciplinary curriculum, courses, programs, research projects and publications, resource books, and textbooks for mission and ministry education at the tertiary level.
- Networking with fellow academics, mission agencies, NGOs, and local churches as deemed appropriate.
- Equipping local churches by developing programs and media for awareness and training, models, manuals, workbooks, and case study books.

Developed in the spirit of the Lausanne Movement 2010 Cape Town Commitment, these resolutions will serve to envision, empower, and equip the whole church to bring the whole gospel to the whole world, particularly to people on the move.

APPENDIX D
NORTH AMERICA DIASPORA EDUCATORS' RESOLUTION

Chicago, Illinois, September 20, 2012

Cognizant of the multicultural society that North America has become, the continuing gathering of multinational people groups as a result of diaspora movements to and from all corners of the world, and the proliferation of multifaith communities across the continent,

- We affirm that God has a redemptive plan for all people.
- We recognize that God sovereignly incorporates the movements of peoples around the world within the redemptive purpose for His Kingdom.
- We acknowledge the coherent narrative in Scripture of God's mission *to*, *through*, and *beyond* diaspora peoples.

Therefore, we theological educators of North America are committed to promote the ethos of diaspora missiology and practice by:

- Mobilizing educators, practitioners, institutional and denominational executives, pastors, church leaders, and strategists.
- Developing multidisciplinary curriculum, programs, and materials for theological schools and institutions.
- Providing consulting services to educational institutions, missions organizations, and congregations for the advancement of diaspora missiology.

Embracing the Lausanne Movement's Cape Town Commitment, these resolutions call upon the whole church to engage peoples on the move as *recipients* of grace, *participants* in mission, and *catalysts* to bring the whole gospel to both North American communities and the whole world.

APPENDIX E
THE CAPE TOWN COMMITMENT

Part II – For the World We Serve: The Cape Town Call to Action

C. Living the love of Christ among people of other faiths
5. Love reaches out to scattered peoples
https://www.lausanne.org/content/ctc/ctcommitment

People are on the move as never before. Migration is one of the great global realities of our era. It is estimated that 200 million people are living outside their countries of origin, voluntarily or involuntarily. The term 'diaspora' is used here to mean people who have relocated from their lands of birth for whatever reason. Vast numbers of people from many religious backgrounds, including Christians, live in diaspora conditions: economic migrants seeking work; internally-displaced peoples because of war or natural disaster; refugees and asylum seekers; victims of ethnic cleansing; people fleeing religious violence and persecution; famine sufferers – whether caused by drought, floods, or war; victims of rural poverty moving to cities. We are convinced that contemporary migrations are within the sovereign missional purpose of God, without ignoring the evil and suffering that can be involved. [Genesis 50:20]

- We encourage church and mission leaders to recognize and respond to the missional opportunities presented by global migration and diaspora communities, in strategic planning, and in focused training and resourcing of those called to work among them.
- We encourage Christians in host nations which have immigrant communities of other religious backgrounds to bear counter-cultural witness to the love of Christ in deed and word, by obeying the extensive biblical commands to love the stranger, defend the cause of the foreigner, visit the prisoner, practise hospitality, build friendships, invite into our homes, and provide help and services. [Leviticus 19:33-34; Deuteronomy 24:17; Ruth 2; Job 29:16; Matthew 25:35-36; Luke 10:25-37; 14:12-14; Romans 12:13; Hebrews 13:2-3; 1 Peter 4:9]

We encourage Christians who are themselves part of diaspora communities to discern the hand of God, even in circumstances they may not have chosen, and to seek whatever opportunities God provides for bearing witness to Christ in their host community and seeking its welfare. [Jeremiah 29:7] Where that host country includes Christian churches, we urge immigrant and indigenous churches together to listen and learn from one another, and to initiate co-operative efforts to reach all sections of their nation with the gospel.

Appendix F
Global Mission Networks and Intercultural Unity

Below is a partial list of worldwide Christian networks, especially in evangelical circles, that places an emphasis on intercultural unity as a core value/goal.

Asia Evangelical Alliance (www.asiaevangelicals.org)

Founded in 1983, the Asia Evangelical Alliance is a collaboration of 16 national evangelical fellowships throughout Asia that envisions the transformation of Asia through united evangelical cooperation and action. Several departments within the AEA focus upon a range of initiatives in "mission, church planting, theology, church renewal, religious liberty, social concern, women's ministry, youth ministry and leadership development."

Association of Evangelicals in Africa (www.aeafrica.org)

The Association of Evangelicals in Africa is a collaboration of 36 national evangelical fellowships throughout Africa, representing over 100 million Christians across the continent, who aspire to be "a symbol of African evangelical unity." Sponsoring a vast network of schools, institutions, and ministry agencies, the AEA seeks to "mobilize and empower evangelical churches and mission agencies for total transformation of Africa through evangelization and effective discipleship."

COMIBAM (www.comibam.org)

COMIBAM is an evangelical collaboration between Iberian and Latin American churches and denominations seeking to cultivate mission vision, training and mobilization toward unreached peoples in the world through recognizing that each Iberian and Latin American culture has a unique contribution in this mission endeavor. COMHINA is the North American expression of COMIBAM and it aspires toward equipping, mobilizing and unifying Hispanic churches throughout North America.

Ethnic America Network (www.ethnicamerica.com)

As a coalition of 80-plus mission organizations and evangelical denominations in the USA and Canada, Ethnic America Network places a high emphasis on intercultural unity. Promoting intercultural unity among churches and diverse members of the Body of Christ in North America is an essential value and one of the key reasons for EAN to exist as a network.

European Evangelical Alliance (www.europeanea.org)

Affiliated with the WEA, the European Evangelical Alliance seeks to "connect, equip and represent" evangelical Christians in Europe through unity and common identity. With the vision of Christ-centered transformation within European societies and worldwide proclamation of the Gospel, the EEA seeks to "think globally and act locally, nationally and regionally."

The Lausanne Movement (www.lausanne.org)

Driven by a passion for worldwide evangelization and Christian unity, Billy Graham, in 1974, convened a global congress in Lausanne, Switzerland. Evangelical Christians who gathered in the second Lausanne Congress in Manila, Philippines in 1989 envisioned "the whole church taking the whole gospel to the whole world." These gatherings have led to subsequent global events and fostered an entire movement of worldwide evangelical collaboration toward mission mobilization, compassion, and justice.

Mosaix Global Network (www.mosaix.info)

Fueled by a biblical conviction toward racial and ethnic reconciliation, Mosaix Global Network is a network of pastors, educators, researchers, church planters, and ministry leaders committed to cultivating healthy intentionally multi-ethnic and economically diverse churches throughout the world. MGN promotes this vision through "casting vision, connecting leaders, conferencing and coaching."

World Evangelical Alliance (www.worldea.org)

The World Evangelical Alliance is a global collaboration of evangelical denominations and churches representing some 600 million Christians. The purpose of the WEA is to foster a worldwide evangelical identity and speak with a common voice toward extending the presence and impact of the

Kingdom of God through the proclamation of the gospel and the witness of Christian unity.

Additional Resources

Discipleship Essentials; http://www.discipleshipessentials.org/
Diaspora Research; http://diasporaresearch.com/
Diaspora Research Initiatives; http://www.nextmove.net/
Gospel of John Film; http://www.thegospelofjohn.org
Global Diaspora Network, http://www.global-diaspora.com/
Global Diaspora Links; http://www.linkingglobalvoices.com/diasporas
Institute of Diaspora Studies; http://www.westernseminary.edu/centers/institute-of-diaspora-studies
Jesus Film; http://www.jesusfilm.org/
People Groups; https://www.peoplegroups.info/
The Lausanne Global Conversation – Diasporas; http://conversation.lausanne.org/en/home/home/914/featured

LIST OF CONTRIBUTORS

Adeney, Miriam (PhD-Anthropology, Washington State University) is Associate Professor of World Christian Studies at Seattle Pacific University and Chair of the Faculty Advisory Committee of the Asian American Ministry Program. She serves on the board of Christianity Today International, is a Mission Associate of the World Evangelical Alliance Mission Commission, is a member of the diaspora task force of the Lausanne Movement, is past President of the American Society of Missiology, and is an author of books on global Christianity including *Kingdom Without Borders.*

Adhikari, Lachi is a genocide survivor from Bhutan who grew up in UN-sponsored refugee camps in Nepal before resettling as a refugee with her family in the United States. She has experience in cross-cultural missions and diaspora church planting in the United States as well as in leading holistic community development efforts in the refugee camp where she lived.

Aeilts, David (BS, Northern State University) has been a business writer for 40 years. Currently, serving with IAFR as a freelance writer, David partnered with IAFR to document the 27 year journey of a Burundian man along the Refugee Highway, in the book, "Refugee for Life".

Asamoah-Gyadu, J. Kwabena (PhD, University of Birmingham) is Baeta-Grau Professor of African Christianity and Pentecostal/Charismatic Theology at the Trinity Theological Seminary, Accra, Ghana, where he also directs Graduate Studies and chairs the Center for the Study of Christianity in Africa. Prof. Asamoah-Gyadu's research interests include African Pentecostalism, African immigrant Christianity and Religion and Media use in Africa.

Baker, Ken (DMiss-Intercultural Communication, Trinity International University) spent 24 years in church planting in multiethnic contexts in West Africa, both urban and rural. For nine years Ken directed Culture ConneXions, a ministry helping churches engage cross-culturally in their communities. He is currently International Ministry Training Facilitator for SIM International and an adjunct lecturer in missiology at the Institut Missiologique du Sahel in Burkina Faso.

Baxter, John (DMin-Intercultural Studies, Reformed Theological Seminary) is the Director of Diaspora Ministries for Converge Worldwide. John is an International Catalyst for the Global Diaspora Network of the Lausanne Movement, and the Director of NextMove Diaspora Ministries, a

Converge Worldwide and US Center for World Mission partnership that helps mission-sending agencies effectively engage with diaspora missions.

Butcher, Andrew (PhD, Massey University) is an Adjunct Researcher in the Office of the Pro Vice Chancellor, College of Humanities and Social Sciences, Massey University. He has published extensively on international education and migration. Dr. Butcher is Chairman of International Student Ministries of New Zealand.

Caldwell, Larry W. (PhD-Intercultural Studies, Fuller Theological Seminary) was Professor of Missions and Hermeneutics at Asian Theological Seminary for 20 years, five of those years serving as Academic Dean; he also edited the Journal of Asian Mission. Currently, Larry is Director of Training and Strategy for Converge Worldwide, as well as Professor of Intercultural Studies at Sioux Falls Seminary.

Carroll (Rodas), M. Daniel (PhD, University of Sheffield) is the Distinguished Professor of Old Testament at Denver Seminary. He is affiliated with the Evangelical Theological Society, Institute of Biblical Research, Society of Biblical Literature, Society for Old Testament Study (Great Britain), the Fraternidad Teológica Latinoamericana, and Evangelicals for Social Action.

Casiño, Cecilia J. (ThD) has served as professor at the Philippine Baptist Theological Seminary and Asia Baptist Theological Seminary in Baguio City, Philippines, and will serve as adjunct professor in Pastoral Care and Counseling and Christian Education at the School of Divinity, Gardner-Webb University. She has also taught at South Korea with Yongsan International School of Seoul (formerly, International Christian School, Seoul), a K-12 institution attended by students from approximately fifty nations. She is actively involved in ministering among people on the move in North Carolina and beyond.

Casiño, Tereso (ThD, Asia-Baptist Graduate Theological Seminary; PhD, Asian Center for Theological Studies and Mission) is Professor of Missiology at Gardner-Webb University. His areas of research interest include the global diaspora, the history of mission movements in Asia, and world religions. Prior to joining the faculty of the School of Divinity, he served as Professor of Systematic Theology and Intercultural Studies/Missions at Torch Trinity Graduate School of Theology in Seoul, South Korea.

Castor, Trevor (PhD Cand., Australian College of Theology) serves as the Managing Director of the Zwemer Center for Muslim Studies at Columbia International University (CIU). He is also a professor of inter-cultural and

Muslim studies. He has a Masters Degree in Muslim Studies and is a PhD candidate at The Australian College of Theology.

Chang, Steven S. H. (PhD, University of Aberdeen) is Professor of New Testament at Torch Trinity Graduate University. He has taught Greek at Trinity Evangelical Divinity School as a Teaching Fellow and pastored in Illinois, Maryland, and now, Korea.

Chinn, Leiton Edward (MA-Cross Cultural Studies, Fuller Theological Seminary) is the Lausanne Senior Associate for International Student Ministries and serves on the World Evangelical Alliance Mission Commission, as well as the national teams of the Mission America Coalition and Ethnic America Network.

Chinn, Lisa Espineli (MA-Communication, Wheaton College Graduate School) served 14 years as the National Director of International Student Ministry of InterVarsity (IVCF)/USA. Lisa also worked as campus staff with IVCF Philippines, IVCF/USA and International Students, Inc. (ISI) for over 3 decades.

Chung, Miyon (PhD, Southwestern Baptist Theological Seminary) is Lecturer in Theology at Morling College in Australia. She works with Baptist World Alliance and Asia Pacific Baptist Federation.

Cook, Charles (PhD, Trinity International University) is presently Professor of Global Studies and Mission at Ambrose University. When he is not teaching, he can be found involved in collaborative kingdom ministries in various corners of the world including ReGen Community Development Foundation, the Onesimus Global Foundation, Church Partnership Evangelism, the onSite Study Abroad program, Canadian Missiological Resources and the Jaffray Centre for Global Initiatives at Ambrose University.

George, Sam (PhD, Liverpool Hope University) is the Executive Director of Parivar International, a Christian family ministry to the South Asian communities in North America. Parivar means family in many Indian languages. Sam holds degrees in engineering, management, and theology.

Gornik, Mark R. (PhD, University of Edinburgh) is the Director of City Seminary of New York. Mark helped launch New Song Community Church in Harlem, and researches African Christianity in New York City.

Harvey, Thomas (PhD, Duke University) is the Academic Dean of the Oxford Centre for Mission Studies in Oxford, England. He has served in theological education and ministerial formation in Singapore and China. He is an Advisory Board member of the Global Diaspora Network.

Hershberger, Susie (BA, Seattle Pacific University) was research assistant to Miriam Adeney.

*Horn, Katie E. (*BA-Global Affairs, George Mason University) grew up outside of Washington, D.C. in the shadow of a very culturally, religiously, and ethnically diverse area. Katie volunteers with “Heart for Lebanon” currently serving on the administrative staff with an emphasis on reporting, grant-writing, photography, and documenting the stories of the refugee families.

Im, Chandler H. (PhD, Fuller Seminary) is Director of Ethnic America Network and Director of Ethnic Ministries at the Billy Graham Center at Wheaton College Graduate School (USA). He also serves as the U.S. Lausanne Movement's National Coordinator for Ethnic/Diaspora/ International Students Ministries.

Jackson, Darrell (ThD, University of Birmingham) is Senior Lecturer in Missiology at Morling College in New South Wales, Australia. He is a Mission Commission Associate of the World Evangelical Alliance and was founding Director of the Nova Research Centre at Redcliffe College in England.

John, Stanley (PhD, Asbury Theological Seminary) is a member of the Indian diaspora having been born and raised in Kuwait. He is the Director of the Alliance Graduate School of Missions and Intercultural Studies at Alliance Theological Seminary (Nyack) and is passionate about forming servant leaders for missions in a context of world Christianity, global migration and post-Christendom.

Kemp, Carolyn (BSc-International Studies) has worked for OMF International since 1993; spending several years in Manila’s slums as a church planter, involved in 3 church plants. She has been with OMF’s Diaspora Ministries Field since 2003. Carolyn was instrumental in OMF developing Diaspora Ministries into a Field ministry and is currently in the role of Field Director.

Kim, S. Hun (PhD Cand) is a reflective practitioner and researcher on mission and diaspora/migration with OCMS, UK. After completing Bible translation in Azeri language with Wycliffe, he was engaged with the Global Diaspora Network. He is serving as Diaspora Consultant with Wycliffe, and Director of Korean Research Institute for Diaspora in Oxford.

Ko, Lawrence (MDiv, Trinity Theological College) is the National Director of Singapore Center for Global Missions and Founder- Director of Asian Journeys Ltd. He also serves as the Chairman of Asia Evangelical Alliance mission commission and as a member of the executive committee of the Asia Lausanne Committee for World Evangelization.

Langberg, Diane (PhD-Counseling Psychology, Temple University) is a psychologist whose clinical expertise includes 40 years of working with trauma survivors and clergy. Dr. Langberg is clinical faculty of Biblical Theological Seminary and core faculty with the seminary's Global Trauma Recovery Institute.

Lisbe, Jr., Gerardo Bacos (DMin, International Theological Seminary) currently serves as full-time faculty and Vice-President at Baptist Theological College (BTC) and Dean at Cebu Graduate School of Theology (CGST) both in Mandaue City, Philippines. He researches on the structure and activities that Filipino churches create that significantly reduce OFW family dysfunctions.

Lorance, Cody (MA-Intercultural Studies, Wheaton College Graduate School) is President and CEO of Borderless, a family of businesses, organizations and churches dedicated to breaking barriers in a borderless world for the sake of Kingdom transformation

Mack-Lacey, Carol (DMin, Midwestern Baptist Theological Seminary) has worked with diaspora people groups for over 15 years. She conducted a one-year study of undocumented foreign workers in South Korea through a U.S. Fulbright Student award in 2003. Her research interests continue to include: global people movements, psychology of prejudice, cross-cultural competency, and corporate social responsibility.

McClung, Grant (DMiss, Fuller Theological Seminary) is President of Missions Resource Group and Missiological Advisor to the World Missions Commission of the Pentecostal World Fellowship. He is a member of a number of missions related boards and advisory groups including the Global Diaspora Network Advisory Board (Lausanne Committee for World Evangelization), the U.S. Lausanne Committee, and the Advisory Committee for the Evangelical Missions Quarterly (EMQ). A veteran field missionary and missions leader, McClung is currently serving in an at-large capacity for global missionary education through Church of God World Missions.

McGrath, Terry (MPhil-Development Studies, Massey University), is former National Director now serving as Senior Consultant for

International Student Ministries (ISM) of New Zealand. Terry also serves as a University Chaplain to post graduate international students at Massey University in Palmerson North and with the Lausanne Movement as Asia Pacific Regional facilitator for ISMs as part of the Global Leadership Network for ISMs team. His current research focus is in International Student pastoral care; post academic transition; intercultural discipleship and disciple-making.

Medeiros, Elias (PhD, Reformed Theological Seminary) is Professor of Missiology at Reformed Theological Seminary in Jackson, Mississippi. He is a member of the Advisory Board of the Global Diaspora Network and a member of the Brazilian Evangelical Diaspora movement, where he was a pioneer church planter and theological educator.

*Melki, Camille E. (*Hon DTh, Warner Pacific College) was born and raised in Lebanon, and passing through 18 years of civil war, Camille's focus in ministry is for building a new generation of leaders for Lebanon and the region. In 2006 he began the relief and compassion ministry called Heart for Lebanon (H4L). Currently, H4L is ministering to nearly 3000 Iraqi and Syrian refugee families.

Monroe, Philip G. (PsyD-Clinical Psychology, Wheaton College Graduate School) is Professor of Counseling and Psychology at Biblical Seminary, Hatfield, Pennsylvania/USA where he directs the MA in Counseling program along with the Global Trauma Recovery Institute. In addition to teaching, training, and consulting, he maintains a private practice with Diane Langberg & Associates.

Mordomo, João (PhD, Vision International University) is the co-founder of Crossover Communications International (CCI) and serves as President of CCI-Brasil. João is actively involved in BAM (business as mission) as well as serves as Senior Associate for BAM at the Lausanne Movement, where he also serves on the Educators Task Force of the Global Diaspora Network.

Norton, Allison (PhD studies, Fuller Theological Seminary) has worked at the Pan African Christian University College in Ghana, and is a deaconess in the Church of Pentecost. Her professional interests include migration, transnationalism, mission, and the children of slave immigrants.

Oh, John Jungho immigrated to the States in 1976 when he was ten years old with his parents. After working as an engineer and completing his seminary education in southern California, John worked as a mobilizer at a mission agency then joined Wycliffe Bible Translators in 1998, serving as a Bible translator in Southeast Asia. He currently serves as the Director of

Korean Church Engagement in the States and provides missions education and training to assist the Korean diaspora churches to participate in the mission of God.

Otto, Martin (ThM, Whitfield Theological Seminary) started an evangelical ministry to seafarers in 1987 in Hamburg, Germany. Martin is the Director of the Church on the Oceans Seminary in Manila, Philippines which was founded in 2008.

Rajendran, P. is an Indian musician and filmmaker with extensive experience in cross-cultural training and social justice advocacy.

Reeve, Warren (DMin-Leadership and Evangelism, Gordon Conwell Theological Seminary) founded the Missional International Church Network in 2000. He has served as the Senior Pastor of the Lighthouse Church in Kuwait and the Vice President of the National Evangelical Church of Kuwait representing the Arab, Indian and English congregations.

Remigio, Jr., Amador (PhD, Imperial College of Science and Technology at Wye, University of London) has served as a resource consultant in the fields of geography, environmental studies, and sustainable development. Currently, he is the Community Pastor of New Life Alliance Church in Vancouver, British Columbia, Canada.

Robertson, Brian (MDiv, Gardner-Webb University School of Divinity) resides in Shelby, NC and currently serves as the Youth Pastor at Eastside Baptist Church.

Sibley-Bentley, Victoria (MATheol (Hons), MA-Religion and Public Life, Leeds University) is a University Chaplain at Massey University Palmerston North and a Vocational Deacon with the Anglican church. Rev. Sibley's current research is in International Student focused on pastoral care and intercultural discipleship and disciple-making.

Smither, Ed (PhD-Historical Theology, University of Wales; PhD-Intercultural Studies, University of Pretoria, South Africa) is Dean of the College of Intercultural Studies at Columbia International University. Ed previously served for fourteen years in intercultural ministry working primarily among Muslims in France, North Africa, and the USA.

Soerens, Maria-Jose (MPhil, PhD-Theology, Oxford Centre for Mission Studies, Middlesex University, London) is a graduate student at the Oxford Centre for Mission Studies, UK, where she conducts research on the religious narratives of suffering of undocumented women. She is a licensed mental health counselor and the founding Director of Puentes: Advocacy,

Counseling & Education, a Seattle based organization providing mental health services and advocacy to undocumented migrants and their families in WA State.

Sydnor, Paul N. (PhD studies, Oxford Centre for Mission Studies, Middlesex University) is the Director for the EU and Asylum Seeker Ministries in the International Association for Refugees (www.iafr.org). Paul has helped to build church-based ministries among refugees and asylum seekers throughout Europe since 1985.

Thomas, T.V. (DMin) is a Malaysian Canadian evangelist with The Christian and Missionary Alliance in Canada and the founding Director of the Centre for Evangelism and World Mission in Regina, Saskatchewan, Canada. He is Chairperson and a member of the Advisory Board of the Global Diaspora Network and Co-Chair of the International Network of South Asian Diaspora Leaders (INSADL) as well as Chair of the Ethnic America Network (EAN).

Tira, Sadiri Joy (DMiss,Western Seminary; DMin, Reformed Theological Seminary) is the Lausanne Movement's Senior Associate for Diasporas. Sadiri serves as Vice President for Diaspora Missions for Advancing Indigenous Missions (AIM) as well as Diaspora Missiology Specialist at the Jaffray Centre for Global Initiatives at Ambrose University and Seminary (AUS), Calgary, AB, Canada.

Vijayam, Joseph (MBA-Information Systems, Georgia State University) is the Managing Director of Olive Technology. He serves as the Senior Associate of Technology for the Lausanne Movement and on the Boards of Global Disciples, Partners International, TENT India, and on the Advisory Board of BAM Global and the Editorial Board of BusinessasMission.com.

Vimalasekaran, Peter (DMin-Intercultural Studies, Reformed Theological Seminary) has lived and worked among refugees in Germany since 1998. He also holds a Bachelor of Divinity from Queen's University of Belfast, and pursued a Master of Philosophy, also from Queen's University of Belfast.

von Kaehne, Peter (DCH MRCGP) works as a family physician near Glasgow. He is also a postgraduate theology student in the University of Aberdeen. In his spare time, Dr. von Kaehne helps lead an Iranian church in Glasgow.

Wieland, George (PhD, University of Aberdeen), is Director of Mission Research and Training, Carey Baptist College, Auckland, NZ. George served in mission and pastoral ministry in Brazil and the UK before joining the faculty of Carey Baptist College, NZ, where he taught New Testament for a number of years before moving to his present mission role. He has published books and articles both on the New Testament and on migration and mission.

Woods, Paul (PhD) is a research tutor specialising in Southeast Asia at the Oxford Centre for Mission Studies, UK. His first PhD concerned the cognitive linguistics of Chinese noun classifiers and his second developed a theological response to migration in East Asia. He taught and trained in Singapore for seven years, and previously taught English in China, the US, and the UK.

Wright, Christopher (PhD, University of Cambridge) is an Old Testament scholar. He was Chair of the Lausanne Theology Working Group from 2005-2011, and the chief architect of The Cape Town Commitment, from the Third Lausanne Congress, 2010. Currently, he is the International Ministries Director of Langham Partnership International.

Yamamori, Tetsunao (PhD-Sociology of Religion, Duke University) is Senior Fellow of the Center for Religion and Civic Culture of the University of Southern California. He is also President Emeritus of Food for the Hungry International, and was International Director of the Lausanne Committee for World Evangelization, 2004-2006, remaining active as its Senior Advisor. He has written and edited two-dozen books.

Yeh, Allen (DPhil, Oxford University) is Associate Professor of Intercultural Studies and Missiology at Biola University's Cook School of Intercultural Studies. He is a missiologist and historian who specializes in Latin America and China. Allen also serves on the Board of Trustees for the Foundation for Theological Education in Southeast Asia.

Zaretsky, Tuvya (DMiss-Intercultural Studies, Western Seminary) is one of the founders of the Jews for Jesus ministry and was the first field missionary beginning his service in February 1974. Tuvya currently serves with Jews for Jesus as Director of Staff Development internationally and with the Lausanne Movement as Senior Associate for Jewish Evangelism.

Zurlo, Gina A. (PhD Cand, Boston University) is a Research Associate at Boston University's Institute of Culture, Religion and World Affairs and Assistant Director of the Center for the Study of Global Christianity at Gordon-Conwell Theological Seminary. She is co-editor of the World Christian Database (Brill) and also contributes to the World Religion Database (Brill).

Regnum Studies in Global Christianity

In the latter part of the twentieth century the world witnessed significant changes in global Christian dynamics. The Regnum Studies in Global Christianity series explores the issues with which the global church struggles, focusing in particular on ministry rooted in Africa, Asia, Latin America and Eastern Europe.

Not only does the series make available studies that will help the global church learn from past and present, it provides a platform for provocative and prophetic voices to speak to the future of Christianity. The editors and the publisher pray particularly that the series will grow as a public space, where the voices of church leaders from the majority world will contribute out of wisdom drawn from experience and reflection, thus shaping a healthy future for the global church. To this end, the editors invite theological seminaries and universities from around the world to submit relevant scholarly dissertations for possible publication in the series. Through this, it is hoped that the series will provide a forum for South-to-South as well as South-to-North dialogues.

Volumes in this series are printed in paperback, unless otherwise stated.

Jesus and the Resurrection
David Emmanuel Singh (Ed)
2014 / 978-1-870345-58-4 / 205pp
Our aim here is to build a bridge between Muslims and Christians with Jesus in the centre of the discourse. As an idea, 'resurrection' is shared by and is central to the eschatologies of Christianity, Islam and Judaism. In Islam, the belief in life after death, resurrection and the day of judgement are so central that they are considered to be one of its 'Five Pillars'. Life has meaning because in resurrection, humanity will meet its maker on the Day of Judgement.

Seeing New Facets of the Diamond
Gillian Mary Bediako, Benhardt Y Quarshie, Kwabena Asamoah-Gyadu (Eds)
2014 / 978-1-908355-59-1/ 378pp
In the five years since Kwame Bediako passed away there has been a growing desire among colleagues and friends to put together a book that would honour his memory. The title has been chosen to reflect the range of interests and concerns that motivated Bediako's scholarly work, including his founding and nurturing of ACI.

Bernhard Reitsma

The God of My Enemy:
The Middle East and the Nature of God

2014 / 978-1-908355-50-8 / 206pp

Bernhard Reitsma lived and worked among Christians in the Middle East for several years. He has shared their struggles and was challenged to reconsider different kinds of Israel theology. In this the core questions is whether the God of my enemy can also be my God. How can the God of the present State of Israel also be the God of the Palestinians?

Following Jesus: Journeys in Radical Discipleship – Essays in Honor of Ronald J Sider

Paul Alexander and Al Tizon (Eds)

2013 / 978-1-908355-27-0 / 235pp

Ronald J. Sider and the organization that he founded, Evangelicals for Social Action, are most respected for their pioneering work in evangelical social concern. However, Sider's great contribution to social justice is part of a larger vision – biblical discipleship. This book brings together a group of scholar-activists, old and young, to reflect upon theradical implications for the 21st century.

Relectuant or Radical Revolutionaries?

Cawley Bolt

2013 / 978-1-908355-18-8 / 287pp

This study is based on extensive research that challenges traditional ways of understanding some evangelical missionaries of nineteenth century Jamaica and calls for revision of those views. It highlights the strength and character of persons facing various challenges of life in their effort to be faithful to the guiding principles of their existence.

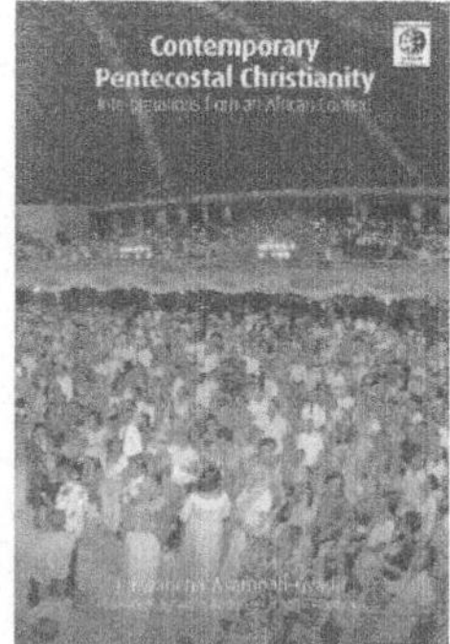

Contemporary Pentecostal Christianity:
Interpretations from an African Context

2013 / 978-1-908355-07-2 / 194pp

J Kwabena Asamoah-Gyada

Pentecostalism is the fastest growing stream of Christianity in the world. The real evidence for the significance of Pentecostalism lies in the actual churches they have built and the numbers they attract. This work interprets key theological and missiological themes in African Pentecostalism by using material from the live experiences of the movement itself.

For the full listing, visit www.ocms.ac.uk/regnum